Object Database Development
CONCEPTS AND PRINCIPLES

David W. Embley

 ADDISON-WESLEY

**Addison-Wesley is an imprint
of Addison Wesley Longman, Inc.**

Reading, Massachusetts • Harlow, England • Menlo Park, California
Berkeley, California • Don Mills, Ontario • Sydney
Bonn • Amsterdam • Tokyo • Mexico City

To my wife, Ann, and our children: Jeanine, Jennifer, Kristin, Angela, Jason,
Matthew, Melinda, Sonya, Janelle, Mark, Michael, Ryan, Jared, and Eric.

Sponsoring Editors: Lynne Doran Cote / Katherine Harutunian
Production Editor: Amy Willcutt
Compositor: Chiron, Inc.
Copyeditor: Stephanie Kaylin
Proofreader: Lorraine Ferrier
Cover Designer: Diana Coe

Library of Congress Cataloging-in-Publication Data

Embley, David W.
    Object database development: concepts and principles / David W. Embley.
        p.   cm.
    Includes bibliographical references and index.
    ISBN 0-201-25829-3
    1. Object-oriented databases. 2. Database design.   I. Title.
QA76.9.D3E591998
005.75'7—dc21   97-36123
                                                            CIP

Access the latest information about Addison-Wesley titles from our World Wide
Web site: http://www.awl.com/cseng

The programs and applications presented in this book have been included for their
instructional value. They have been tested with care but are not guaranteed for
any purpose. The publisher does not offer any warranties or representations, nor
does it accept any liabilities with respect to the programs or applications.

Many of the designations used by manufacturers and sellers to distinguish their
products are claimed as trademarks. Where those designations appear in this
book, and Addison-Wesley was aware of a trademark claim, the designations have
been printed in initial caps or all caps.

Cover image © Carlos Alejandro Photography, 1997

1 2 3 4 5 6 7 8 9 10-MA-0100999897

Preface

Object database development is becoming one of the best ways to build software for many advanced applications. To succeed in creating these advanced applications, we need a disciplined approach to development that is based on sound principles. This book presents the fundamental principles and concepts needed for developing advanced database applications, showing how to apply these principles successfully.

The development approach presented in this book is object oriented, but the approach allows for a broad range of target database systems. The range includes standard relational database systems, object-relational database systems, object-oriented database systems, and active database systems.

Besides being object-oriented, the approach in this book is also model driven. The underlying model, which is computationally complete, has a formal foundation rooted in mathematical model and proof theory. The model also supports multiple views, including both a graphical and textual views. Furthermore, the model is applicable over the full range of development activities, from analysis through specification, design, and implementation. This capability allows for seamless and reversible software development.

The book is aimed at both university students and sophisticated practicing professionals. University instructors can use the book to teach database application development to undergraduate students or object-oriented database theory and its application to development environments to graduate students. (See the section "Teaching from this Book" for some specific suggestions on how to organize courses with various objectives.) Practicing professionals can read the book for a wide range of reasons, including (1) to learn a rigorous, object-oriented approach to application development, (2) to learn object-oriented design and development theory, (3) to learn about the formal foundations of database systems and languages, and (4) to use the underlying theory as a guide for developing support tools.

The book is not written for systems programmers who are implementing transaction-processing and concurrency-control systems, query optimizers, indexing and hashing schemes, or crash-recovery systems. It does not, however, ignore these underlying system components on which database applications are built. Although the main focus is on application development, the book covers each of the system components just listed in enough depth to provide sufficient understanding for platform-independent application development.

Organization and Underlying Philosophy

Prerequisites for the book include a solid introduction to programming and discrete mathematics. Ideally, the practice of programming and the theory of discrete structures would have been taught in a unified course of study. We also take this approach here, unifying theory and practice throughout the book.

The book consists of an introductory chapter and three parts: preliminaries, preparation, and production. Chapter 1, the introduction, discusses database application development in general and motivates both the book's concepts-and-principles approach to development and its development model—a conceptual model that makes it easy to describe the world as it is.

The preliminaries part of the book includes five chapters. Chapter 2 is about conceptual database fundamentals, including database abstractions and data models and languages. Chapter 3 presents system and physical database fundamentals, covering much of the underlying system-level implementation information, which is used later to motivate design decisions based on cost analyses and assumptions about the services provided by the underlying system. Chapter 4 gives a detailed description of the model used throughout the book for database application development. Chapter 5 discusses predicate calculus and other theoretical foundations of database theory. Based on this foundation, Chapter 6 shows how to formalize applications in terms of the model described in Chapter 4. Chapter 6 also uses the same formalization to give a formal definition of the model in terms of itself.

The preparation part of the book comprises five chapters, which cover analysis, specification, and design. Chapter 7 explores analysis methods, model integration, and analysis validation. It includes some new results on object-set congruency, which provide a way to measure the cohesiveness of an object-set definition and to find missing object sets of potential interest. Chapter 8 covers system boundary and interface specification and introduces a specification language for both declarative and procedural specification. The specification language is a newly developed, model-equivalent, textual language that allows specification size to scale up while remaining faithful to the underlying model.

Chapters 9 and 10 discuss data design. Although relational database textbooks base their design discussions almost exclusively on normal forms, this book takes a different approach. It does not directly introduce normal forms at all, except in the exercises. Instead, it develops a design theory systematically based on information- and constraint-preserving hypergraph transformations. This solves several of the problems that have recently caused normalization theory to fall into some disfavor.

The data-design approach taken in this book does the following:

- Provides a smooth connection to analysis and specification because the model we use (unlike standard Entity-Relationship models) already *is* a hypergraph over object sets (that is, attributes).

- Provides an easy and systematic way to extract functional, multi-valued, and join dependencies automatically from analysis/specification models. Too often, proponents of normalization theory have assumed that these constraints are given or are easy to obtain, but obtaining them is hard work and should not be ignored.

- Does not make the universal-relation assumption. This assumption is another often-ignored trap in applying normalization theory; in the real world, the assumption often fails. The book attacks the problem directly, showing how to resolve the issues involved.

- Develops a unified approach to dependency theory, integrating design methods based both on functional and on join dependencies as a single unified whole. Often the treatment of dependencies, although appearing unified, is almost totally disjoint.

- Introduces the notion of a trade-off between object identity and lexical identity and provides for transformations between these two representations. Usually relational discussions ignore object identity and object-oriented discussions ignore lexical identity, but there is a place for both.

- Treats the design of nested relations and complex object schemes as a natural extension of flat scheme design. It also includes a discussion of the properties of nested normal form, a new theoretical result that has not appeared in other texts. (Again, only the theory and properties are discussed as they apply to making design decisions—the normal form itself is in the exercises.)

- The design objectives for the approach are driven by time and space efficiency concerns, rather than by a desire for higher normal forms.

Chapter 11 discusses the design of object modules and shows how to integrate data design with behavior design. Continuing the design-transformation approach in Chapters 9 and 10, this chapter shows how to transform application-model hypergraphs into object modules. An object module is a generalization of the concept of an object class, as found in object-oriented languages, and it is the link to implementation. The discussion about object modules includes an exploration of the concepts of class, type, encapsulation, inheritance, and polymorphism, all of which are important for object-oriented database systems. The transformational approach then continues by showing how behavior patterns can be transformed into object modules either for single-processor database systems or for multiprocessor, distributed database systems.

The production part of the book has six chapters. Chapter 12 discusses ODMG implementation as a generic example. Chapters 13 through 17 follow with five case studies. Each of the case studies takes a problem all the way from application description to working code, using a particular database system. The case studies are small, about one thousand lines of code on average, and are representative of what might be expected of a student for a semester's project. As a group, the case studies also show an application of all the topics covered in the text, thus also serving both as a review of the material and as an illustration of the theory in practice. The chosen systems represent the range of applications for which this book has been developed, including Oracle, which represents standard relational database systems; UniSQL, which represents object-relational database systems; O_2 and ObjectStore's persistent storage engine for Java, both of which represent object-oriented database systems; and Ode4.1, which represents active database systems.

We use an on-line shopping example throughout the book to illustrate system development. Chapter 4 introduces the example. The example then passes through analysis (Chapter 7), specification (Chapter 8), design (Chapters 9–11), and finally into code (Chapter 12). The example is more realistic than typical textbook development scenarios, where the thought process behind the development is mostly hidden. Usually an author has done all the work and has made all the simplifying assumptions beforehand. As presented here, the running example takes several twists and turns and has some false starts and later corrections. This is intentional. With such an approach, readers receive a more realistic view of the actual development process. The example is not fully realistic, however, because it makes many simplifications to control the possible explosion in the number of concerns that should be fully resolved. Nevertheless, a reader should get the impression that there is much to do in order to analyze, specify, and design, as well as implement, a large project.

Teaching from this Book

This book strikes a balance between being too theoretical, on the one hand, and largely ignoring theory and its role in practice, on the other hand. In general, the main body of the text presents a rigorous and disciplined approach to application development, but largely omits theorems, except for some of the most important claims, and omits proofs. To allow for a more theoretical approach, however, the text includes numerous exercises, not only to help students understand the basic concepts presented, but also to review technical background material and to expand on theoretical ideas only claimed or briefly presented in the main body of the text. Some of the exercises are a series of learning experiences, where new concepts are introduced piecemeal and then checked in exercises. Other exercises define some of the standard concepts that have been omitted from the main body of text, such as the well-known normal forms. One of the appendices contains answers for some of the exercises, particularly for those requesting proofs of central theorems and for those that introduce new material. The exercises, especially those with answers in the book, make it possible for instructors to extend the text into areas of their particular interest and to present a more theoretical course.

This book can serve as a text for several different types of courses:

1. An upper-division course on application development for object-oriented databases.

   The focus of this course would be on application development for an object-relational or object-oriented database system such as UniSQL or O_2. No previous introduction to database systems should be necessary. Suggested coverage includes all of Chapters 1–4, a brief overview of Chapters 5 and 6, all of Chapters 7 and 8, a "cookbook" approach to Chapters 9 and 10, all of Chapters 11 and 12, and the case studies in Chapters 14–16. A similar course could be taught under the assumption that the students had already taken a standard introductory database course as a prerequisite. When taught as a second course, Chapters 2 and 3 should not be necessary, although they can serve as an excellent review. The additional time gained by not needing to cover Chapters 2 and 3 and by being able to assume that the students have already been introduced to normalization theory would make it possible to cover Chapters 9 and 10 in detail rather than by using a "cookbook" approach.

2. An upper-division course on application development for relational databases.

   The book is well suited for an introductory course on relational database systems in which application development is emphasized. Suggested coverage includes all of Chapters 1–3; Chapter 4, with an emphasis on data modeling in Section 4.1; Chapter 5 and Section 6.1, which provide the theoretical foundation for relational database systems; a brief overview of Chapters 7 and 8 on analysis and specification; a thorough study of Chapters 9 and Sections 10.1–10.7 on data design, including the supplementary exercises on relational normalization theory; and the relational database case study in Chapter 13. For a more theoretically inclined relational-database course, an instructor could spend extra time on relational calculus and Datalog in Chapter 5 and delve deeper into the properties of schemes produced from canonical hypergraphs while omitting Chapter 8 and all but Section 4.1 of Chapter 4 and Section 7.4.2 of Chapter 7. For a course more inclined toward practical application development, an instructor could cover all of Chapter 4, omit or provide only a brief overview of Chapters 5 and 6, and spend extra time on Chapter 7 and on interface forms in Chapter 8.

3. A senior or graduate-level course on application development for active databases.

   Because two-thirds of the underlying model described in the text is on active object behavior, this is an excellent text for studying the general principles of active objects, particularly active objects in database systems. Suggested coverage includes Chapters 1–3; Chapter 4, with an emphasis on behavior and interaction modeling; a brief overview of Chapter 5 for foundational material; Chapter 6, with an emphasis on dynamic and temporal formalization; Chapters 7 and 8, with an emphasis on functional specification; an overview of Chapters 9 and 10; a thorough study of Chapters 11 and 12; and the active database case study in Chapter 17.

4. A senior or graduate-level course on tools for database application development.

   The book can nicely support a course on the development of CASE tools and environments for developing database applications. The text itself suggests some tools and gives several basic algorithms that could form the basis for additional tools. Furthermore, the rigorous approach and underlying formalism provide the basis for many more tools. The course could consist of identifying and giving high-level designs for tools across the entire development spectrum, plus doing an implementation of one, or part of one, of the identified tools. The entire book can serve as background reading, but the meat of the course should emphasize Chapter 6; the congruency exercises in Chapter 7; the language in Chapter 8; the transformations in Chapters 9–11; and code generation in Chapter 12.

5. A graduate-level object-oriented database theory course.

   The formalism of the text can nicely support a graduate-level theory course. The main body of the text provides the context for the theory, including the motivation, the main flow of thought, the basic formalism, and theorems for some of the central ideas. The exercises, structured to be instructional as well as aids to learning, provide the remaining material needed for a theory course. Suggested coverage includes an in-depth study of Chapters 5, 6, 9, and 10 and the theorem-and-proof exercises in Chapter 11, and a careful reading of the proofs in the appendix containing answers for selected exercises.

Teaching material for the text is available both in the book and outside the book. Each chapter begins with a list of topics to which the reader should pay particular attention and a series of thought questions the reader should keep in mind while reading the chapter. A summary at the end of each chapter follows up on these topics and answers these questions. Included in most chapters are boxed comments that add ancillary insight and commentary. Sometimes these boxed comments are motivational, sometimes they help tie theory and practice together, and sometimes they merely add interesting comments as side notes. Instructors may choose from among the many exercises both to aid students in learning and to emphasize particular topics of interest. An appendix provides answers to selected exercises. An instructor manual contains answers to additional exercises. The manual also contains teaching suggestions and transparency masters for Chapters 1 through 12. A World Wide Web site has an implementation for the case studies. The instructor's manual includes one additional case study on deductive databases similar to the five case studies included in the book. There are also some tools available. These include a drawing tool to create diagrams for application models and a syntax checker for the model-equivalent language. Some tools developed as suggested for Course 4 above have also been implemented, but these tools are only available on an "as-is" basis with no assurance that they will even work. Links to all the supplements can be found on the book's official web site at http://www.awl.com/cseng/titles/0-201-25829-3/.

Acknowledgements

I appreciate the feedback and encouragement of the Object-oriented Systems Modeling (OSM) research group at Brigham Young University. This book is fundamentally tied to the research efforts of this group. During the book's development, the OSM research group included Eric Carter, John DuBois, Terry Haas, Kimball Hewett, Robert Jackson, Stephen Liddle, Wai Yin Mok, Gordon Roylance, Scott Woodfield, Patrick Williams, and Mingkang Xu. I am especially grateful to Wai Yin Mok for the many enjoyable hours we spent discussing the underlying theory. I am also especially grateful to Stephen Liddle and Scott Woodfield for their work on the OSM-L language and grammar and for their help in working out and checking the ODMG C++. Special thanks is also due to Eric Carter, who extended the OSM drawing tool, which allowed me to do the figures for the text without having to use a different tool.

I appreciate the feedback and the patience of the members of my CS 552 course, winter semester 1996, who were the first to experience this text. The members of the class were Bilal Ahmed, Conan Albrecht, Brian Bouck, Eric Carter, Todd Curzon, John DuBois, Terry Haas, Bruce Hansen, Kimball Hewett, Matthew Lundgreen, and Michael Martin. Including the one in the instructor's manual, these students worked on the initial versions of four of the six case studies:

UniSQL — Bilal Ahmed, Eric Carter, and Bruce Hansen
O_2 — Conan Albrecht, Todd Curzon, and Kimball Hewett
Ode — Brian Bouck, Matthew Lundgreen, and Michael Martin
Datalog/Prolog — John DuBois and Terry Haas

A deep debt of gratitude is also due to Eric Carter, who revised and polished code for the case studies, including the code for ObjectStore's persistent storage engine for Java, which he wrote from scratch.

The members of my CS 353 undergraduate database course, spring term 1996, were the second to experience the text and the first to whom I taught the upper-division relational database course. The members of this class were John Beatty, Alex Bradley, Derrick Brundage, Gordon Chamberlin, Brian Chandler, Wai Kei Fung, Rana Matared, Kostadinka Sharp, Randy Smith, John Sorensen, Joanne Spencer, Luis Takada, Eric Wadsworth, and Ryan Winkler. Minglei Xu was the teaching assistant for this course. His careful study of the text and his feedback were invaluable in improving the text. Other students in subsequent courses added their comments and corrections. Those deserving specific mention include Kenyon Porter, Spencer Proffit, and Gopalakrishnan Thevar.

The members of my CS 551 course, winter semester 1997, were the first to whom I taught the graduate-level theory course. The members of this class were Eric Carter, Jin Lim, Dong Lin, Song Peng, Randy Smith, Joanne Spencer, Zhangqiong Tang, and Andre Turgeon. These students challenged me on several issues, resulting in some refinements to the text. They were also the first to tackle the theoretical exercises, which helped solidify the claims in the text.

Willie Favero, Bill Grosky (Wayne State University), Junping Sun (Nova Southeastern University), Mei-Ling Liu (Cal Poly, San Luis Obispo), Cyrus Shahabi (University of Southern California), and Henry A. Etlinger (Rochester Institute of Technology) read initial copies of the book. Their numerous suggestions led to additional motivational material, to introductory overviews and thought questions for each chapter, to summary material for each chapter, to more specific ties between the theory and practice, and to the boxed comments that provide additional insight to the material being presented. Their efforts are deeply appreciated.

Others, on their own initiative, read parts of the book and offered feedback and encouragement. These include Lynn Brough (Novell, Inc.) and Bogdan Czejdo (Loyola University, New Orleans). Several others also deserve my appreciation. Yiu-Kai Ng carefully reviewed Chapters 2 and 3, making several corrections and worthwhile suggestions. Kelly Flanagan helped me understand disk drives. Katherine Harutunian (Addison-Wesley Publishing Co.) coordinated and summarized reviews of the book and made working with the publisher unusually pleasant. Kim Greenburg, a staff member of the manuscript-editing service in the English Department at Brigham Young University, carefully edited the initial versions of the book's chapters. Her corrections improved the writing and presentation of the material in this book considerably.

Table of Contents

8 Specification 337

9 Data Design—Reduction 421

Part III Production

12 Implementation 683

13 Relational DBMS Case Study   733

14 Object-Relational DBMS Case Study   751

15 Object-Oriented DBMS Case Study I   769

Chapter 1

Introduction

This introductory chapter explains what a database is, what a database system is, what a database application is, and what database application development is. The focus of this book is on database development and database application development. The approach is object oriented, providing a practical real-world perspective, as well as rigorous and systematic, providing a firm foundation of concepts and principles.

The chapter also explains how all the succeeding chapters fit together. Some provide foundational material that is needed either to capture and represent a database and its applications or to explain the underlying formalism and related theoretical concepts. Other chapters describe the systematic approach to application development and give the many details necessary to successfully bring a database and its applications to fruition. Additional chapters present specific examples that illustrate database application development by taking a sample application from an initial description to a full implementation in one of several commercial or prototype systems.[†]

The following topics in this chapter are particularly important:

- Database and database-system characteristics.

- Requirements of emerging database applications.

- The development methodology espoused in this book.

- Stated model requirements: formal, seamless, language-equivalent, practical, and ontological.

The following questions should also be kept in mind:

- Why are traditional database systems inadequate for some advanced applications?

[†] Code for these implementations is available on the World Wide Web; the URL is http://www.awl.com/cseng/titles/0-201-25829-3/.

- How does object technology help meet these requirements?

- What are the advantages of taking a systematic, rigorous, model-driven, concepts-and-principles approach to database application development? Are there disadvantages?

- How do the chapters of this book fit together to present this approach to database application development?

1.1 Databases and Database Systems

A *database* is a large, persistent, integrated collection of dynamic data that provides some operations to describe, establish, manipulate, and access this data.

Although some small main-memory databases exist, "large" in this description of a database usually means that a single computer's primary storage is insufficient to hold the data. Secondary storage such as hard disks, often connected to multiple computers in a distributed system, holds the data of a database. The speed differential between primary and secondary storage and among various network connections has vast implications for the storage and retrieval of data in a database. As an example of "large," consider the census data for a country.

"Persistent" means that the data outlasts application programs that operate on it. Often these application programs are short retrieval or update programs that run as a single transaction against a database. They may also be longer programs that do extensive searches or that interact with users or with something else in the environment. Even so, the data typically persists beyond these long-running programs, often outlasting even the hardware on which it is stored and processed. Persistent data must also survive hardware and software crashes. As an example of "persistent," consider the student records for all current and past students at a university; these records must last longer than any program that prints one of them, checks them to see which students deserve scholarships, or performs any of a number of other operations.

"Integrated" means that a database is of interest to several different users or user groups, although some small databases may be of interest to only one person. Multiple groups of users all vying for access to the same data can cause problems, such as the inability to store the data optimally to service all user requests or to service update requests for the same data simultaneously. As an example of "integrated," consider a worldwide enterprise with various offices across the globe and with various divisions and departments. All the information from these offices, divisions, and departments can be brought together into one logical database, and any information common to more than one office, division, or department can be consolidated instead of being stored redundantly.

"Dynamic" means that the data changes over time. Users invoke operations that initialize, update, and retrieve the data. Some data changes rapidly and some slowly. It is possible to have a totally static database, although this is not common. The typically dynamic nature of the data makes it difficult to store and maintain in an optimal organization. This dynamism also causes problems for maintaining data integrity, both because incorrect information may creep into a database and because constraints that should hold may be violated. As an example of a "dynamic" database, consider the financial records of a bank. Money is constantly being deposited, withdrawn, and transferred from one account to another.

The "data" consists of values of interest, as would be expected, as well as relationships among the values of interest. The relationships among the data form larger meaningful structures over atomic values. Besides individual values and relationships among these values, a database also stores data about the data, which we call *metadata*. Metadata describes the data and includes information such as data types for individual values and a description of the meaning of relationship information for larger aggregates of data. As an example, consider vehicle ownership. We can represent people and cars as values, relate these values together to represent ownership, and describe the ownership abstractly as an instance of a set of relationships we might call "Person owns Car," which is an example of metadata because it describes the person/car relationships.

A *database system* supports a database by providing languages and services that make it possible for database administrators and users to build, maintain, and efficiently query and update the database. The languages include data-definition languages that let administrators define the data and metadata for a database and data-manipulation languages that let users establish, maintain, and access the data. The services provide support for overcoming the problems caused by the large, persistent, integrated, and dynamic nature of the database. Services include storage structures and optimizers that provide efficient access to large amounts of data, crash recovery features to protect the data when the hardware or software fails, concurrency control mechanisms that let multiple users access and update the database simultaneously, and constraint checking to maintain integrity.

1.2 Database Applications

A *database application* is a database along with an application program or a coordinated collection of application programs that runs on a database system. A database application stores its data in a database and uses the services of a database system to retrieve and update the data and to protect and maintain its integrity. A database application also provides application-specific services to end users. As an example, for a banking application, the services include opening an account, transferring funds, and closing an account. The ultimate purpose of a database application is to help satisfy end-user business needs. Throughout this book we use the term "database application development" to refer to the development of a database for an application, to refer to the development of application programs that run on the database, or to both.

Since the book is about developing database applications, it is therefore about deciding what data to store in a database and how the data should be organized logically, as well as about creating algorithms to query and update a database and to do the processing required to satisfy end-user needs. The book is not about developing database systems and therefore is not about designing and developing storage structures, optimizers, concurrency-control protocols, constraint checkers, and crash-recovery mechanisms. Because the applications they develop must work with these database-system services, however, database developers must have a basic understanding of these services. In an ideal world, a database system would take any application and service it efficiently, but in the real world, the application developer must meet the database system halfway by providing a design that can be run efficiently by the services of the system. Therefore, although its main focus is on database application development, this book also provides a basic introduction to these database-system topics.

What database applications are currently of interest to us? For a long time, the community of database users has been interested in traditional applications that support standard business processing; we still are, but we are also interested in making these systems better serve user needs. For example, we may wish to extend database applications by involving them in decision making, market forecasting, and planning, and by having them control and report on some aspects of day-to-day operations, alerting us to problem areas that need attention. We may also wish to store more exotic data in databases, including representations of complex objects with active behavior and multimedia data such as images, video, and sound.

Database technology is also extending into other areas of interest besides business applications, including the following:

- Design applications—the design of physical objects such as buildings and bridges and the design of nonphysical objects such as computer software;

- Knowledge-based applications—intelligent agents for decision making, such as stock market analysis, and for scientific endeavors, such as the human genome project;

- Multimedia applications—visual presentations of cartographic and demographic information and of products and services for on-line shopping;

- World Wide Web applications—search engines for tidbits of useful information, data-mining applications, and mediators to filter and make sense of acquired information; and

- Evolving applications—business reengineering and change management for evolving rule bases, such as tax documents and regulations for government agencies.

1.3   Object Technology

Traditional programming languages and database systems are inadequate in many ways for satisfying the needs of emerging applications of interest. Traditional programming languages (e.g., C and C++) lack persistence in particular and the services of database systems in general. Adding persistence and database services from scratch is usually too much work for an application programmer. Traditional database systems (i.e., standard hierarchical, network, and relational databases) are also inadequate because they are tuned for business processing with simple records, large numbers of users, and short-duration transactions. They need some of the features of programming languages for handling information with highly complex structures, and they need additional features that support triggers, rules, long-running transactions, histories, version control, multimedia, and views.

In attempting to bring all these features together into a single system, object technology has emerged as a unifying paradigm. Object technology is intriguing because of its direct correspondence to the world being modeled. The technology lets us represent physical or conceptual real-world objects by simulating them in a computer. Using this basic theme, we can imagine and build simulations for all kinds of objects:

- Simple passive objects that merely hold a value;
- Complex passive objects that represent complex structures;
- Multimedia objects that represent images, videos, or sound;
- Service objects that respond to requests;
- Active objects that perform some task independently;
- Reactive objects that respond to events in their environment;
- Intelligent objects that exhibit reasoning powers; and
- Evolving objects that can change their behavior.

Object technology also provides other practical features for system implementation such as inheritance, which can reduce the amount of work required to specify related objects, and encapsulation, which helps control interfaces among objects.

These last two features will be discussed later. As we begin, however, our interest in object technology is in the direct correspondence between simulated objects and real-world objects. This direct correspondence gives us a good way to begin to model objects, their relationships to other objects, their behavior, and their joint, interactive behavior with other objects. If we can accurately model a complex system of objects and all their relationships and behavior, we can go a long way toward developing interesting database applications. Indeed, we can succeed in developing interesting database applications if we can transform such a model into an efficient, robust, maintainable implementation.

This is the objective of this book. It presents a way to model objects— their relationships, behavior, and interactions—and a way to transform what is modeled into an implementation.

1.4　Database Application Development

To achieve our objective, we take a systematic, rigorous, model-driven, concepts-and-principles approach to database application development. This approach has the advantage of being able to specify in great detail what must be done and how to do it. Because of its rigor, this approach also has the advantage of being able to support sophisticated tools that can do some (perhaps even much) of the work and tools that can synergistically help a developer complete the task. Because the tools cannot always properly make every decision for every application, this approach also requires a knowledgeable developer who understands the goals and objectives of the development task and the means by which these are achieved.

To make this approach to database application development work, we need a model that is

- Formal,

- Seamless,

- Language-equivalent, and

- Ontological.

The model around which we build our approach to database application development is the Object-oriented Systems Model (OSM). OSM has a formal syntax and semantics based on a temporal, first-order logic. At the same time, OSM allows for a multitude of expressive, high-level views. The model is also object-oriented. This combination provides the basis for OSM's being both expressive and rigorous—both practically and theoretically sound. Using OSM's object-oriented features, we can model a database application directly. Based on the underlying formalism, we can then transform the application model systematically into an implementation model. Because of the formalism, we can show that the various transformations are information and constraint preserving, providing confidence that the implementation model represents the specified application model faithfully.

To make this transformational approach work, our development environment must be seamless. *Seamless* means that there are no artificial gaps or mismatches between successive development activities and that there is one underlying model for all development stages. OSM provides the basis for seamless development because

- OSM is a single conceptual model that serves for analysis, specification, design, and implementation;

- OSM allows for multiple views appropriate for various needs in the same or different stages of development; and

- OSM is defined formally and thus can be executed both in a prototype mode for analysis, specification, and design, and in a production mode for implementation.

A model that successfully spans and supports all development activities must have both graphical and textual representations. The graphical representation of OSM appears in Appendix A; such notation is necessary for analytical work and for client presentations and discussions. Graphical representations, however, do not scale up. They become awkward and bulky as systems become large, and although we can layer presentations through high-level views, there must eventually be a more compact representation for detailed specification and design and for implementation. Thus a model that spans and supports all the development activities must have, in addition to a graphical representation, a model-equivalent language that provides a textual representation. A *model-equivalent language* is a linear, textual representation of a model whose constructs match one-to-one in every respect with the model. OSM has a model-equivalent language, called OSM-L (OSM Language). Every construct of the model has an equivalent OSM-L representation. The converse also holds; thus, we can take any cohesive OSM-L code segment and reengineer it to provide an equivalent graphical representation. Appendix B contains the grammar of OSM-L.

In trying to ensure that a model successfully spans and supports all development activities, a model can sometimes be too close to the design and implementation side and thus be more of a preliminary design model than a model that reflects real-world objects and their behavior. This makes it easier to span all development activities but harder to work with clients because it effectively requires that clients become knowledgeable designers, or at least knowledgeable high-level designers. OSM avoids this pitfall by taking an ontological approach to modeling. An *ontology* describes and explains the nature of being; thus an *ontology* describes the world as it is. OSM allows objects and object behavior to be described independent of computers and computer software, and indeed could have been used to describe objects and object behavior long before the advent of computers in the middle of the twentieth century. This ontological approach contrasts sharply with the typical approach to creating models for computer-software development, which usually consists of extending design and implementation representations to higher levels of abstraction. OSM holds strictly to an ontological perspective. Real-world objects always correspond one-to-one with OSM objects, and real-world object behavior always corresponds precisely with OSM object behavior.

Based on OSM, the methodology we espouse in this book is model-driven. Rather than presenting a step-by-step procedure, a *model-driven* methodology provides a model that serves as a framework for development. Using this framework and knowing the end objective, a developer arrives at the end objective by whatever means are best. Although a step-

---

Differences between the Usual Object-Oriented View and OSM's Object-Oriented View

Readers acquainted with object technology as typified by C++ and related object-oriented languages and paradigms should note that OSM takes a different view of object orientation. OSM objects are not based on Abstract-Data Types (ADTs). States of OSM objects are not based on instance variables. OSM object behavior is not defined in terms of methods. And OSM object interaction is not based on messages that invoke methods. We can, however, map OSM into ADTs whose operations are methods. But this is exactly the point of taking an ontological view as the starting point. Instead of converting real-world objects, object relationships, object behavior, and object interactions into ADTs with methods before representing them, OSM developers first model the world as it is and then transform these real-world representations into a design and eventually into an implementation.

---

by-step methodology often seems appealing, when the task becomes long and hard, this approach often fails because it is easy to become lost and not know how to get back on track. With a model-driven approach, however, developers do not get lost; they know where they are and where they are going and thus can use the framework provided by the model to devise a way to get there. A model-driven methodology does not preclude suggesting possible steps; indeed this book gives many suggestions and examples that show the way. A model-driven methodology, however, does not rely solely on being able to make and complete development activities according to a predefined step-by-step methodology.

1.5   Overview of the Book

The book consists of three main parts: Preliminaries (Part I), Preparation (Part II), and Production (Part III). Part I provides the preliminary concepts and principles needed to understand object database application development. It also introduces the on-line shopping example used throughout the book to illustrate application development. Part II describes analysis, specification, and design—the preparatory steps to implementation. All these activities are independent of the target system on which the application is to be implemented. Part III shows how to produce the implementation. This third section is target-system dependent and explains how to transform a design into the implementation language of various systems. These target systems include a generic object database system as defined by the Object Database Management Group (ODMG),[†] a relational database system, an object-relational database system, two object-oriented database systems, and an active database system. As should be clear from this list, we can target a design to many different kinds of database systems. As should also be clear, the target system is not always an object-oriented system. The development process, however, is object-oriented in the sense that it is based on an object-oriented model, and the result is an object-based implementation, in that it is based on objects even when its representation in the target system may not be a classical object-oriented one.

Textbook Software Development

In textbooks, it is usual to see only finished products; everything works smoothly, and there are no false starts, wrong turns, or tasks to repeat. In practice, though, software development is not so smooth and direct. Many problems arise and need to be solved, and many times we take a wrong path, only to discover later that we should have taken a different path, and even later that we have taken another wrong path. We illustrate a few of these problems—false starts, wrong turns, and some of the consequent rework—by the way we present our running example and our case studies. We allow ourselves to find some problems, take some wrong turns, and later discover different alternatives and thus take a different path.

Chapters 2 through 6, the preliminary chapters, may be skipped by readers who are already familiar with standard database systems, conceptual modeling, and the formalization of conceptual modeling. Skipping these chapters, however, is not recommended unless the reader's practical and theoretical database background is strong and his or her conceptual modeling background is not only strong but also based on OSM.

Chapter 2 provides a basic conceptual understanding of a database system. It explains how to describe and manipulate a database both abstractly and concretely.

[†] ODMG is a consortium of companies whose purpose is to define a standard for object database management systems.

Chapter 3 explains how database systems physically store and support databases.

Chapter 4 defines and illustrates OSM, the ontological conceptual model on which our development methodology rests. Appendix A is a succinct summary of OSM's graphical notation.

Chapter 5 provides the formal basis for our approach to application development. Predicate calculus serves as a basis for defining both database integrity constraints and high-level nonprocedural database languages. Model theory provides the underlying formal definition of a database in its cleanest and most pristine form. Proof theory provides the theoretical basis for logic programming, a way to view and access databases. Although proof theory is the essential component of deductive databases, this part of Chapter 5 can be skipped without loss of continuity if deductive databases are not of interest to the reader.

For readers particularly interested in deductive databases, supplementary material for the book can be found on the web (http://www.awl.com/cseng/titles/0-201-25829-3/) that explains how to use the concepts and principles presented here to develop deductive databases. The supplementary material on deductive databases includes a case study about the implementation of an optically scanned table-recognition problem in Prolog. This case study emphasizes views of objects and relationships and shows an interesting application of some of the underlying model and proof theory. It also illustrates how to use the algorithms, concepts, and principles discussed in this book to automate the design of fact schemes for deductive databases.

Chapter 6 shows how to automatically transform an OSM application model into a model-theoretic view of a database, as defined in Chapter 5, and thus how to automatically transform an OSM application model into a database in its cleanest and most pristine form. This transformation formalizes an application model and thus prepares it to undergo information- and constraint-preserving transformations during design. Since we can formalize application models, and since we can treat OSM itself as an application we wish to model, we can use OSM to represent itself. We can thus formalize OSM in terms of itself and provide a formal syntactic and semantic definition for OSM. The second part of Chapter 6, which explains this formalization, can be skipped without loss of continuity. It is useful, however, to have a formal definition for OSM because then there can be no argument about what is meant by an OSM application model or any of the constructs of an OSM application model.

Chapters 7 through 11, the preparation chapters, present the application development methodology espoused by this book. The presentation assumes that the reader is well-grounded in the concepts in Part I (except those sections specifically mentioned as being unnecessary for continuity).

Chapter 7 presents analysis. The purpose of analysis is to study, understand, and document a system. The chapter provides ways to do analysis and ways to validate the results.

Chapter 8 presents specification. The purpose of specification is to develop a detailed and precise proposal for a system. Although a specification need be only as detailed and precise as necessary for the task at hand, it must be possible to specify every detail fully and formally. To provide for the possibility of a fully formal specification, we need a more compact representation of OSM than the graphical representation as presented in Chapter 2. Chapter 8 thus introduces and explains OSM-L, the model-equivalent language for OSM. The full grammar of OSM-L appears in Appendix B. Chapter 8 also introduces an alternative, more intuitive notation for specifying interactions that cross the system boundary to or from the system's environment.

Chapters 9 through 11 present design. The purpose of design is to organize a system to help achieve particular goals. Although goals such as maintainability, extensibility, and portability are possible, we focus mostly on efficiency, showing how to organize a system to reduce time and space requirements. Chapter 9 explains how to transform the data component of an OSM application model into a form from which we can synthesize a good database description. Chapter 10 explains how to carry out this synthesis transformation, as well as what properties a synthesized database description has and how a database description can be adjusted to account for time and space characteristics of an application. Chapter 11 addresses the problem of designing object modules in preparation for implementation. An object module encapsulates data and operations and provides services for other object modules. In designing object modules, we must define types for variables and functions and procedures for services, and we must specify inheritance, concurrency, and visibility requirements.

The concepts presented in Part II rely on the concepts and principles presented in Part I as follows. Chapters 7 and 8 build directly on OSM, as presented in Chapter 4. The transformations from the data component of OSM to a database description as presented in Chapters 9 and 10 rely directly on the application-model formalization in Section 1 of Chapter 6, which builds on the model-theoretic view of a database presented in Section 2 of Chapter 5, which in turn builds on predicate calculus as presented in Section 1 of Chapter 5. The cost-analysis part of Chapter 10 is an application of Sections 1, 2, and 3 of Chapter 3. The idea of an object module builds directly on the notion of abstraction as presented in Section 1 of Chapter 2. Our concurrency-control discussion in Chapter 11 depends on an understanding of transaction processing as presented in Section 4 of Chapter 3. The end result of design provides a database that can be described and manipulated in ways similar to those described in Sections 2 and 3 of Chapter 2.

Chapters 12 through 17, the production chapters, present several case studies that illustrate object database application development. Together, the case studies illustrate all major concepts in the OSM development process, but no one case study makes use of every concept discussed in the book.

Chapter 12 gives a generic implementation for the on-line shopping example developed in preceding chapters. This case study considers the C++ binding for ODMG as its target system. The case study introduces the idea of a derived view of an application that is particularly tuned to a target system and also illustrates the use of a formal specification (as described in Section 8.2) to bridge the gap directly to implementation.

Chapter 13 presents an implementation of a university parking application in Oracle, a relational database system. This case study emphasizes some aspects of validation (Section 7.4), interface specification (Section 8.4), design reductions (Chapter 9), and relation-scheme generation and relation-scheme properties (Sections 10.1–10.6).

Chapter 14 describes an implementation of a travel-agent application in UniSQL, an object-relational database system. This case study emphasizes application model integration (Section 7.3), system-boundary specification (Section 8.1), nested-scheme generation (Section 10.8), generalization/specialization transformations (Section 11.3), and behavioral design transformations (Section 11.5).

Chapter 15 discusses an implementation of a satellite tracking system in O_2, an object-oriented database system. This case study emphasizes complex computational methods (Section 11.2), cost analysis, and exceptions to standard nested scheme-generation algorithms (Sections 10.7–10.9), and concurrency among multiple objects (Section 11.5).

Chapter 16 presents an implementation of a geographic database application in ObjectStore, another object repository. This case study emphasizes ontological analysis (Section 7.2), inheritance, late binding, overriding, and polymorphic implementations (Sections 11.1 and 11.7), conversion of computable relationships to code (Section 11.2), and data structures (Section 11.4).

Chapter 17 describes an implementation of a home security system in Ode, an active database system. This case study emphasizes OSM-L local declarations and control structures (Section 8.2), OSM-L functional specification (Section 8.3), interface forms (Section 8.4), object modules (Section 11.1), behavioral design transformations (Section 11.5), and information hiding (Section 11.6).

In closing this overview, we point out four special aids to learning included in this book:

1. Introductory pointers and questions. At the beginning of each chapter we list topics to which readers should pay particular attention and questions that readers should keep in mind while reading the chapter. These topics and questions should help readers concentrate on the most important ideas in the chapter.

2. Boxed comments. Interesting insights that pertain to the material being discussed sometimes fall outside the main flow of presentation. We present these insights as boxed comments. These boxed comments typically provide helpful commentary to motivate readers or to provide contextual information to help them better understand an idea or why a particular approach is taken.

3. Exercises. As usual, the primary purpose for the exercises at the end of each chapter is to check a reader's understanding. In addition, however, some of the exercises provide definitions and illustrate concepts from discrete mathematics, and some are designed to enrich understanding and challenge readers. Appendix C contains answers to selected exercises.

   Like most database books, this one assumes a course in discrete mathematics as a prerequisite to their subject. Unlike other books, however, this one includes exercises that provide, explain, and illustrate with examples all the important concepts needed from discrete mathematics. In addition, these exercises show how the concepts apply to the ideas being presented. Readers with a thorough understanding of discrete mathematics can skip these exercises, while those who need a review should read the definitions and do the exercises.

The book gives several theorems but omits their proofs in the main flow of presentation. The exercises ask the reader to do these proofs, and appendix C provides proofs for several of the central theorems presented in the book. Additional proofs in the exercises are there to challenge theoretically inclined readers. Exercises marked with an asterisk are moderately challenging, and those marked with a double asterisk are challenging. Most proofs, for example, have an asterisk or double asterisk.

4. Summaries. At the end of each chapter we restate the main concepts and principles discussed and answer the questions posed at the beginning of the chapter.

1.6   Chapter Summary

Topic Summary

- A database stores data and lets users update and retrieve it. A database system provides services that let users define and efficiently access a database and that protect the data from integrity-constraint violations, from inappropriate simultaneous access, and from system and hardware crashes.

- Emerging database applications require all the features of traditional database systems plus support for complex objects, triggers, rules, long-running transactions, temporal semantics, multimedia, and views. Object technology helps meet these needs by providing a paradigm of encapsulated objects that range from simple, passive objects to complex, intelligent, active objects.

- This book presents a systematic and rigorous way to model application objects and a practical way to transform an application model into an implementation. The approach is model-driven and is based on an ontological model that has a formal definition and seamlessly spans and supports all development activities. The book presents concepts and principles—both underlying

theory and ordinary practicalities—that a developer needs to
understand this approach and to implement object database applications successfully.

Question Summary

- Why are traditional database systems inadequate for some
  advanced applications?

  Traditional databases are designed for alphanumeric data and
  transactions of short duration. These features do not support
  advanced applications whose needs include multimedia objects,
  active agents, long-duration interactive sessions, and knowledge-
  based decision support.

- How does object technology help meet these requirements?

  Object technology supports complex objects with active behavior.
  System support for such objects makes it easier—and in some
  cases now feasible—to model these applications and develop software for more sophisticated advanced applications.

- What are the advantages of taking a systematic, rigorous, model-
  driven, concepts-and-principles approach to database application
  development? Are there disadvantages?

  Taking this approach places database application development on
  a strong foundation, one that helps developers firmly grasp the
  fundamental ideas and issues in designing and building a
  database application. This foundation also provides tool builders
  with the necessary theory for developing environments that can
  assist developers in more ways than mere bookkeeping. Theory
  also tends to withstand change, so prevalent in the computer business. Theory for its own sake can be a disadvantage when it does
  not promote greater understanding and result in better tools and
  production methodologies.

- How do the chapters of this book fit together to present this
  approach to database application development?

  The chapters in part I put the foundational material in place. The
  chapters in part II show the developer how to begin with analysis
  and proceed through specification and design, and the chapters in
  part III show the developer how to turn a design into an implementation.

1.7   Bibliographic Notes

Textbooks related to this book include books on database-system fundamentals [Date95, Elmasri94, Hansen92, Helman94, Korth97, O'Neil94, Ullman82], books on database theory [Abiteboul95, Atzeni93, Maier83], books on conceptual modeling [Batini92, Booch94, Coad91, Firesmith93, Jacobson92, Reenskaug96, Rumbaugh91, Shlaer88, Shlaer92], paper collections about object-oriented database systems [Bancilhon92, Bukhres96, Gupta91, Nahouraii91, Zdonik90], and other books about object-oriented database systems [Bertino93, Cattell91, Chorafas93, Kemper94, Kim90]. In general, this book differs from other books on database systems, including those on object-oriented database systems, because it focuses directly on application development. It differs from books on database theory because it focuses on the integration of theory and practice. And it differs from books on conceptual modeling because it presents a fundamentally different conceptual model.

For a good article that evaluates object technology, see [Pancake95]. For a good article on mixing theory and practice in database design that espouses the same principles discussed in this book, see [Reiner94].

OSM is an extension of OSA (Object-oriented Systems Analysis) [Embley92]. [Liddle94b] presents some initial ideas on extending OSA to OSM and making it seamless. The ontological approach of OSA and OSM has many similarities to the ontology presented by [Bunge77] and [Bunge79]. The argument we make about taking an ontological approach to modeling using OSM is similar to the argument made by [Wand89].

In [Hoydalsvik93] the authors assert that most so-called analysis models are more like preliminary-design models than analysis models. They mention OSA as a possible exception. [Embley95] follows up on this idea by comparing some of the prominent analysis models and showing the differences between them and OSA.

1.8   Exercises

1.1*   Discuss the pros and cons of object technology.

1.2*   Discuss the proper balance between theory and practice in application development.

1.3*   Discuss the pros and cons of using ontological models for development rather than computer-related object-oriented models.

1.4* Discuss the pros and cons of model-driven versus step-by-step development methodologies.

1.5* Discuss the pros and cons of using a single conceptual model with a model-equivalent language and different views for each major development activity versus using different conceptual models and representations for each major development activity.

Chapter 2

Conceptual Fundamentals

This chapter explains how to describe and manipulate a database. As explained in this chapter, we describe and manipulate a database as an abstract data type. This both lets us think of a database and lets application programs use a database independent of its internal representation.

We can describe a database in several ways, each with its own purpose. Various models with graphical representations, such as the Entity-Relationship Model or the Object-Role Model, presented in this chapter, provide a high-level view that is particularly suited for working with end-user clients to discuss an application. A crisp, concise description of the metadata, such as a set of relation schemes as described in this chapter, provides a clean representation for theoretical work and serves as a basis for internal implementation. Data administrators define a database for commercial use with a language, such as the SQL language described in this chapter.

We can also manipulate a database in various ways, each with its own purpose. Theoretically clean manipulation languages, such as the relational algebra discussed in this chapter, provide a solid foundation for internal implementation and optimization. Commercial query languages, such as the SQL language described in this chapter, provide end users and application programmers with ways to access and manipulate commercial databases.

The entire chapter builds on one example—a simple database that describes customer orders. We view this database variously as an Entity-Relationship Model, as an Object-Role Model, as a set of relation schemes, and as an SQL description. As the chapter unfolds, we build from abstract high-level descriptions to concrete implementable descriptions. We then turn to data access and explain how to access this customer-order database using both relational algebra and SQL statements.

The following topics in this chapter are particularly important:

- Abstraction and the three-level database architecture.

- An abstract-data-type view of a database.

- Conceptual modeling as illustrated by the Entity-Relationship Model and the Object-Role Model.

- The definition of a database in terms of relation schemes.

- The relational algebra operators project (π), select (σ), and join ($\bowtie$), which are central and peculiar to databases.

- SQL, a commercial data-definition and data-manipulation language.

The following questions should also be kept in mind:

- How can we make database application programs independent of the internal representation of a database?

- What are the roles of the various database models, schemes, and languages?

2.1   Abstraction

"Abstract" can mean many things. Our interest is in making specifications concrete so that they can execute on computers. We therefore say that a specification is *concrete* if it is directly executable on a computer, and that otherwise it is *abstract*. Some abstract specifications, such as computer programs, can be made concrete automatically by compiling them, some could be made concrete if translators existed to make them concrete, and some could never be made concrete because they are incomplete or informal.

We are interested in all three of these kinds of abstraction. When we develop a database application, we begin with an incomplete and informal specification. Then, using languages, tools, and translators with enough formalism that they either are or could be made concrete, we wish to complete and formalize the specification, and eventually turn it into an abstraction that can be compiled automatically into an executable database application. In one sense, this entire book is about abstractions that are useful in database application development. Although we discuss abstractions in this book all the time and in various ways, we rarely worry about specifically referring to them as abstractions.

To begin with, we are interested in a particular abstraction of a database called the "three-level architecture," which we give in Fig. 2.1. The bottom level of the three-level architecture is the physical database, an abstraction that describes the data files and data-manipulation mechanisms of the

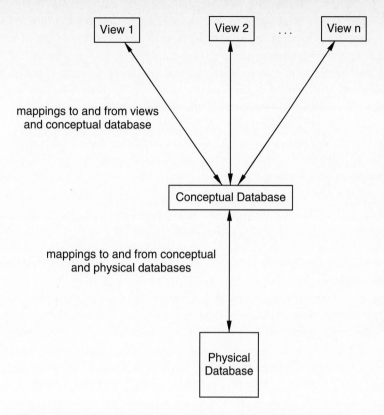

Figure 2.1 The three-level architecture of database systems.

database. It includes information about file organization, about how the data is stored within the file organization, and about how to optimize and service requests to manipulate the data.

The middle level of the three-level architecture is the conceptual database. This abstraction conceptually describes the entire database in a way that makes it usable for application programs and ad hoc retrieval and update requests. It mainly includes descriptions of the information to be stored in the database. Each description is called a *scheme* or a *schema*. Although it is common to refer to one of these descriptions as a "schema," we prefer the less common "scheme;" schema refers to diagrammatic representations whereas scheme refers to any systematic representation. Since we use both diagrammatic and nondiagrammatic representations, we should call them schemes, not schemas.

We may think of a scheme as a record descriptor for the records in a database file. We may, for example, wish to describe a record that contains an employee's identification number, name, address, phone number, and email address. The descriptor would specify a field for each of these attributes and could include additional details about each attribute, such as the number of digits or the specific form of the identification number and the maximum number of characters for each of the other record components. In this way schemes describe the actual data instances stored in or yet to be stored in the database. A scheme may also specify some constraints among the records in a file, such as a uniqueness constraint on the employee identification number that guarantees that an identification number identifies one employee record at most. More complex schemes may also describe other relationships among potential data values or operations that apply to individual records or groups of records.

The top level of the three-level architecture in Fig. 2.1 consists of one or more views. Each view describes a part of the conceptual database tailored to a particular subapplication. Examples of subapplications for a business database include payroll, inventory, sales history, and personnel. Often a database is so large and complex that it makes sense to create views of just one small part so that developers doing application programming or users doing query specification need not be concerned about irrelevant parts of the database. Views are also useful as a mechanism for security, as a focus for increasing performance, and as a subunit for backup and recovery.

Our main interest in this book is in developing the middle level of the three-level architecture. In developing the middle level, we may integrate several top-level views together, or we may derive the top-level views after creating the middle level, but we do not focus specifically on creating a view. For the bottom level, tools and compilers exist that can generate the physical-database description automatically and can turn it into executable code. Ideally, application developers should not need to be concerned about this bottom level. Tools and translators, however, are not yet sophisticated enough to yield satisfactory results in all cases. Developers must therefore provide some help by producing a high-level design that can be implemented efficiently. Designers who understand the bottom level well are in a better position to produce good high-level designs.

In addition to the three levels, Fig. 2.1 also shows mappings between them. Between the top two levels, the mappings in one direction tell us how to derive views, while the mappings in the other direction tell us how to manipulate the conceptual database according to operations applied to views. View derivation is usually straightforward, often consisting only of a specification of which parts of the database are of concern for the subapplication. In this straightforward case, operators applied to a view apply directly to the underlying conceptual database. When the derivation is more complex, the mappings may also become more complex, and developers may have to specify the mapping details.

The mappings between the bottom two levels tell us how to translate data specifications and applicable operations for a conceptual database into a physical database, as well as how to translate results retrieved from a physical database back into a conceptual database. Mapping from a physical into a conceptual database is usually straightforward because it is basically about presenting the data retrieved to an application program in the way the program expects it. Mappings to the physical database, on the other hand, can have a wide range of complexity. In their simplest form, a conceptual database and a physical database can be the same—a conceptual file of records is a physical file of records, and each conceptual operation has a direct implementation. More commonly, however, efficiency concerns call for us to add indexes of various kinds or to introduce hash tables, and to optimize operations using various established techniques. These techniques include reorganizing sequences of operations, aggregating atomic operations into higher level operations, and making appropriate use of underlying file organization such as continuous record layout and internal pointers, as well as auxiliary structures such as indexes.

Because we specify applications with respect to a conceptual database, it is possible to change the corresponding physical database without affecting applications. When we change the physical database, the mapping between the conceptual and physical levels must change, of course, but application programs need not change. This principle, which makes applications immune to changes in the physical database, is variously called *information hiding*, *data independence*, or *implementation independence*. When we think of this principle as information hiding, we are saying that the structure and operations of the physical database are hidden from application programs. Since they are hidden, application programs cannot use them directly. Therefore, if there are changes to the physical database and if the mapping changes to reflect these changes such that the interface to the underlying physical database remains the same, no change is necessary in an application program. When we think of this principle as data or implementation independence, we are saying that the way the data in the database is stored or the way the underlying implementation works is independent of the interface presented to application programs. The interface remains the same, but the mapping to the underlying data or implementation changes to accommodate changes in underlying file organizations or optimization techniques.

2.2 ADT View of a Database

Conceptually, a database is an abstract data type. An *Abstract Data Type* (*ADT*) is a pair (S_v, S_o) where S_v is a set of values and S_o is a set of operations applicable to the values in S_v. Figure 2.2 shows three ADTs, the last of which begins to hint at the kind of ADT that can represent a database conceptually.

In the first ADT in Fig. 2.2, the set of values consists of all the integers and the set of operations consists of addition, subtraction, and multiplication. In the second ADT, the given set of ordered pairs constitutes the set of values, and the operations are ordinary relation composition (∘) and *swap*, which interchanges the values in an ordered pair. In the third, the values in the set are themselves sets, consisting of ordered pairs of letters, and *select* is the only operation. When applied to a set of ordered pairs of letters for a given letter x and column number n, *select* yields the subset of ordered pairs that have x in their nth column. For example, $select_{(c, 2)}$ yields {<a, c>, <b, c>} when applied to the first set in the ADT, and it yields {<c, c>} when applied to the second set in the ADT.

Implicit in the ADTs in Fig. 2.2 are some constraints and properties. One implicit constraint is that the operations should make sense for the values. We would not want, for example, to put the *swap* operator of the second ADT in Fig. 2.2 into the operator set of the first ADT. Implicit also are the semantics of the operations and whether an operator is unary, binary, or, in general n-ary, where n is the number of values an operator takes as input.

An implicit property of interest is whether the set of operators is closed. An ADT operator implicitly yields one value, but the value may or may not be an element of the ADT's set of values. An n-ary operator p for an ADT (S_v, S_o) is *closed* if p always yields a value in S_v. If every operator in S_o is closed, the set of operators is *closed*. The set of operators in the first ADT in Fig. 2.2 is closed, but neither of the other operator sets is closed.

Also implicit is the representation for both S_v and S_o. When we implement an ADT, we can implement it any way we wish. We are thus free to choose a computer representation for the values in S_v that lets us code the operations in S_o efficiently. In an ADT, we hide the implementation so that

$$({0, ±1, ±2, ... }, {+, -, *})$$

$$({<1, 2>, <2, 3>, <3, 2>, <1, 1>}, {∘, swap})$$

$$({{<a, c>, <b, c>, <c, b>}, {<c, c>, <b, e>}}, {select})$$

Figure 2.2 Sample ADTs.

a client program of the ADT can use it only by invoking its operations. Client programs cannot (or in cases where it might be possible, they should not) go around the operations and directly use the implementation. Because the representation is hidden, we have implementation independence. The implementor may thus alter the implementation of the ADT as desired, perhaps to represent the values more efficiently or to code one or more of the operations more efficiently.

When ADTs become more complex, as they do when they represent databases, we need more powerful ways to specify them. We need, for example, a way to make implicit assumptions explicit. Said another way, we need to be able to turn abstract (incomplete and informal) specifications into concrete (complete, formal, and executable) specifications. The data and the relationships among the data elements in a database can be highly complex. We therefore need a way to characterize the data and express the relationships more easily, without getting bogged down in the many details that must be provided. The operations are also complex, so sophisticated languages are needed to express them. We discuss these issues in the following two subsections, where we explain how to make ADTs for databases more expressive by using data models and data languages.

2.3   Data Models

With respect to our ADT point of view, a *data model* provides a convenient way to specify the value set (S_v in our ADT definition). Value sets for databases can be highly complex and very large. Complexity comes because we may wish to aggregate atomic values into associations with other values to form complex objects of various kinds, or to constrain the relationships among these (complex) objects, or both. Size comes not only because databases may be large, containing gigabytes and sometimes even terabytes of data, but also because conceptually there may be even more data of interest beyond what is actually stored. This additional data is either derivable from what is stored in the database or may be added to the database later as it changes dynamically.

2.3.1 Entity-Relationship Model

The Entity-Relationship Model (ER Model) is a popular data model that has been used extensively to specify the data for a database. Figure 2.3 is a diagrammatic representation of an ER application model for a simple database.

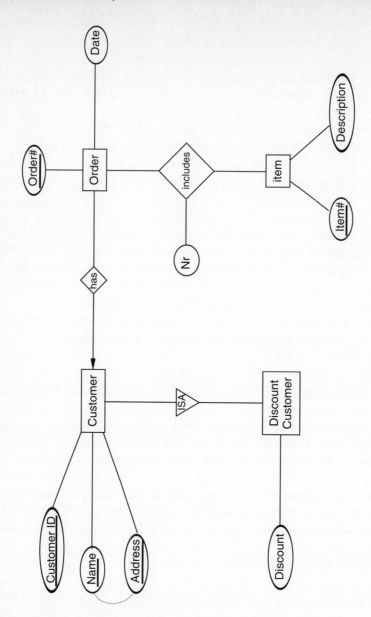

Figure 2.3 ER application model.

Models, Application Models, and Model Instances

In the conceptual modeling world, there has been long-standing confusion about the word "model." In this book, the phrase *X model* refers to an *X* model (e.g., the ER model or the OSM model) and denotes the available modeling constructs supported by model *X*. The phrase *X application model* or just *application model*, when the context is clear, refers to a particular model instance created using the constructs of the *X* model. An application model is an instance of an *X* model describing a particular application.

The basic ER modeling constructs are entity sets, relationship sets, and attribute sets, also sometimes (loosely) called entities, relationships, and attributes. In an ER diagram for an ER application model, rectangles denote entity sets, diamonds represent relationship sets, and ovals represent attribute sets. In Fig. 2.3, for example, *Item* and *Order* are entity sets, *includes* and *has* are relationship sets, and *Item#*, *Description*, and *Nr* are attribute sets.

An entity set represents a set of entities, which may be concrete objects such as people and equipment or conceptual objects such as departments and jobs. Figure 2.4 shows a specific data instance for our ER application model in Fig. 2.3. The *Item* objects in Fig. 2.4, for example, are *I1*, *I2*, *I3*, *I4*, and *I5*. A relationship set represents a set of relationships; relationships are connections among objects. The *has* relationship set in Fig. 2.4 relates *C1* to *O1*, *C2* to *O2*, and *C2* to *O3*. Attributes are properties for either entities or relationships. Properties for customer *C1*, for example, are customer ID *a11*, name *John*, and address *12 Maple*. The relationship between order *O3* and item *I5* has the number attribute *2*, meaning that order *O3* includes a request for two *I5* items.

Besides representing entities, relationships, and attributes, an ER diagram can also represent several kinds of constraints, some explicitly and some implicitly. One of the explicit constraints in Fig. 2.3 is the *ISA* constraint, depicted as a triangle. An *ISA* constraint specifies that the entity set connected to the lower vertex of the upside-down triangle is a subset of the entity set connected to the upper base of the triangle. In Fig. 2.4, we can see that the set of discount customers is a subset of the set of customers.

Another explicit constraint in Fig. 2.3 is the arrowhead on the *Customer* side of the *has* relationship set. It specifies that the relationship set is one-many from *Customer* to *Order*. This allows one customer to have many

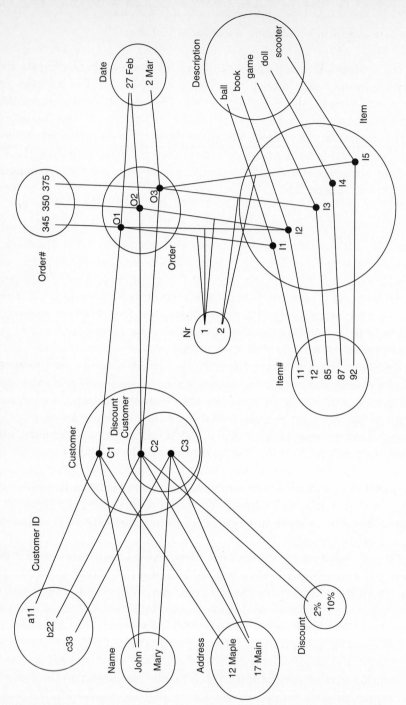

Figure 2.4 A data instance for the ER application model in Fig. 2.3.

Objects and Representations for Objects

Real-world objects, both physical objects and conceptual objects, are things. In conceptual modeling, we use object identifiers to represent real-world objects, such as people and buildings, and conceptual objects, such as organizations and travel arrangements; we use strings to represent writable objects, such as names and part numbers and descriptions; and we use digitized images and sound to represent seeable and hearable objects. It is common to refer to these representations as the objects themselves. We do not concern ourselves with being particular about the difference because we know that in both conceptual and computer modeling there are only representations for objects.

---

potential orders, but restricts orders to be for only one customer. As Fig. 2.4 shows, there is only one customer for each order, but customer *C2* has two orders. A one-many relationship does not require more than one, but rather allows more than one. A customer may have many orders, but zero orders and one order are also possible, as Fig. 2.4 shows. Seen from the many side, the one-many *has* relationship set says that an order determines (points to) one customer. In general, this means "at most one," although we would want it to be exactly one for the application we are discussing.

The absence of arrowheads makes a relationship set many-many, like the *includes* relationship set in Fig. 2.3. As Fig. 2.4 shows, an order may include many items, and an item may be included in many orders. Arrowheads on both ends make a relationship set one-one so that there is a one-to-one correspondence between the objects in the two entity sets. There is a one-to-one correspondence between *Order#* and *Order* in Fig. 2.4, but this is *not* a one-one relationship set because *Order#* is an attribute of *Order*, not another entity set related to *Order*.

This one-to-one correspondence between *Order* and *Order#* is nevertheless significant. Indeed, if the one-to-one correspondence always holds (as it does for our example), it makes *Order#* a key for *Order*. A *key* is an attribute (or a set of attributes) whose value (or composite value) uniquely identifies an object. In ER diagrams, we make key constraints for entity sets explicit by underlining them. *Customer ID*, *Item#*, and *Order#* are examples of single-attribute keys in Fig. 2.3. *Name* and *Address* together form a *composite-attribute key* or *composite key*. To denote composite keys for entity sets in ER diagrams, we not only underline the components of a composite key, but we also connect the ovals with an arc, as in Fig. 2.3.

Key properties are invariant even when the database changes. In Fig. 2.4, it looks as though *Discount* could be a key for *Discount Customer* because the discount customers are in a one-to-one correspondence with the discounts, but this is just a chance happening. We could add another customer *C4* who also has a 10% discount. We could not, however, add another customer with customer ID *a11*.

There are various kinds of keys of interest. A *minimal key* is a key that does not have any superfluous attributes. Clearly, *Customer ID* together with *Name* uniquely identify a customer because *Customer ID* alone is enough. *Name* is superfluous, and thus the composite key {*Customer ID, Name*} is not a minimal key. The composite key {*Name, Address*}, however, is minimal. Both are necessary—in Fig. 2.4, for example, the name *John* relates to two customers, as does the address *17 Main*, so neither *Name* alone nor *Address* alone is sufficient to identify a customer. We are usually interested only in minimal keys. Keys that may not be minimal are called *superkeys*. A *superkey* designates any set of attributes, minimal or not, that uniquely identifies an object.

Several minimal keys may exist for an entity set. *Customer*, for example, has two minimal keys—*Customer ID* and {*Name, Address*}. When there are several minimal keys, we choose one as a *primary key*. If there is only one, we also call it a *primary key*. Moreover, when there are several, or even only one, we refer to each as a *candidate key* because each is a candidate for being the primary key. As we shall see, the set of candidate keys for an entity set (i.e., the set of minimal keys for the entity set, from which one may be chosen as a primary key) is quite important in database design.

Keys identify relationships as well as objects. For one-many or many-one relationship sets, the primary key on the many side uniquely identifies a relationship. Any key on the many side would do, but this is the reason for designating a primary key—so that we know which one to use. In Fig. 2.3, *Order* is on the many side of the one-many *has* relationship set. Since there is only one customer for any order, knowing the order indeed designates exactly one relationship. Since *Order#* is the primary key for *Order*, an order number designates exactly one order and thus designates exactly one relationship in the *has* relationship set.

For one-one relationship sets, the primary key of either entity set is a key for the relationship set. We should not use both together as a composite key, for then the key would not be minimal. Thus, if *A* and *B* are primary keys for two entity sets connected by a one-one relationship set *R*, *A* is a candidate key for *R* and *B* is a candidate key for *R*, but {*A, B*} is not a candidate key for *R* because it is not minimal. We can choose either *A* or *B* as the primary key for *R*.

For many-many relationship sets, the composition of the primary keys of the connected entity sets is usually a key, but sometimes additional attributes are needed. For our example in Fig. 2.3, {*Order#, Item#*} is a key for the *includes* relationship set. It is also a minimal key—*Order#* by itself is not enough because an order may include several items, and *Item#* by itself is not enough because an item may be included in several different orders. To see that the composition of primary keys may not be enough, consider the ER diagram in Fig. 2.5. If students are allowed to repeat courses, then {*Student ID, Course#*} is not enough to identify a *has taken* relationship because a student may have taken the same course more than once. Since students may not take a course more than once in the *same* semester, however, {*Student ID, Course#, Semester*} is enough to uniquely identify a particular course offering a student has taken.

As these examples of finding keys for relationship sets show, we make use of primary keys from entity sets to form keys for relationship sets. When we use a primary key of an entity set in a relationship set, we call the attribute (or set of attributes) in the relationship set a *foreign key*. *Item#*, for example, is a foreign key when we use it in the *includes* relationship set because *Item#* is a primary key for the *Item* entity set. The set of objects referenced by a foreign key in a relationship set must be a subset of the set of objects referenced by the same primary key in an entity set. In Fig. 2.4, for example, the set of items referenced in the *includes* relationship set is {*I1, I2, I3, I5*}, which is a subset of {*I1, I2, I3, I4, I5*}, the items referenced in the *Item* entity set.

This idea of relationships referencing only objects that exist in connected object sets is called *referential integrity*. Referential integrity is an implicit constraint in an ER application model. In Fig. 2.5, for example, courses referenced in the *has taken* relationship set must be a subset of the courses in the *Course* entity set. We could not, for example, delete a course that is no longer being taught from the *Course* entity set, unless we also delete any

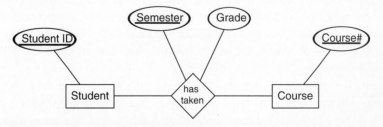

Figure 2.5 An ER application model that needs a relationship attribute as a key component.

relationships in the *includes* relationship set that reference the old course. For if we were to delete an old course from *Course* without deleting relationships that connect to it, there would be relationships in the *has taken* relationship set that reference a course that no longer exists in the *Course* entity set. Note that it is impossible to draw a diagram like the one in Fig. 2.4 that violates referential integrity. It is not impossible to violate referential integrity, however, when we store a relationship set and its attributes in a different file from an entity set and its attributes, as we often do when implementing a database.

Another kind of implicit constraint in an ER diagram concerns domains. Names should really be names, and addresses should really be addresses. We would not want an address to be an item number or a customer ID, for example. Typical ER diagrams do not include domain specifications. Even when we do write them down, they are usually rather loose. We may write, for example, *Discount: integer(1, 100)* in place of *Discount* in Fig. 2.3 to mean that a discount is an integer between 1 and 100 inclusively. We probably intend, however, to have only relatively small discounts in the range. Names and addresses are also problematic. We can let them be varying length strings with some maximum number of characters, but we usually have no way to verify whether they are really names or addresses or even if the maximum number of characters is large enough to accommodate all real-world names or addresses.

2.3.2 Object-Role Model

ER models are not the only kind of data models we use to represent the data of a database; there are many others. We briefly describe another data model here, both to show that there are alternatives and to introduce another family of data models that differ significantly from ER models. The alternative we present is the Object-Role Model (OR Model).

Figure 2.6 shows an OR diagram that represents the same information as the ER diagram in Fig. 2.3. In an OR diagram, circles represent entity sets and divided rectangles represent relationship sets. There are no attributes—indeed, this is the main feature that distinguishes ER models from OR models.

Seen another way, we could also say that OR models have no entity sets, but only attribute sets and relationship sets. Each circle represents a set of values. The name in a circle names the values, and the parenthetically enclosed name specifies the domain of permissible values. *Discount* in Fig. 2.6, for example, names the discount values, which are integers in the range

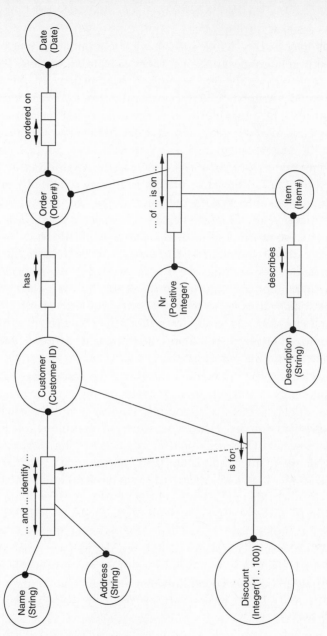

Figure 2.6 OR application model.

1 to 100. The so-called entity sets are thus value sets, which can be thought of just as easily as attribute sets.

Relationship-set rectangles each have two or more compartments, called *roles*. Each role connects to one entity set and designates the role that objects from that entity set play in the relationship set. Relationship-set names provide the intended meaning for the roles. We read binary relationships left to right, plugging in the connected entity-set names before and after the label. For example, we have *Description describes Item* as the full name of the *describes* relationship set and *Discount is for Customer* as the full name of the *is for* relationship set. For *n*-ary relationship sets, $n > 2$, labels with ellipses (...) tell how to read the full name. The ellipses correspond left-to-right, one-for-one with the roles. Thus, for example, we read the ternary relationship set labeled *... of ... is on ...* as *Nr of Item is on Order*, meaning that so much of some item is part of some order.

The horizontal double-headed arrows above the roles in the relationship sets denote key constraints. The double-headed arrow spans the roles that must be unique for the relationship set. Thus, for example, in the *Customer has Order* relationship set, order values are unique, and hence *Order* is a key for the relationship set. In the *Nr of Item is on Order* relationship set, *Order* and *Item* together uniquely identify a relationship. Thus {*Order, Item*} is a composite key for the relationship set.

We can use these uniqueness constraints to derive one-one, one-many, and many-many characterizations for relationship sets. If a relationship set is binary (has two roles) and one role is unique and the other is not, we have a one-many binary relationship from the nonunique role to the unique one. *Customer has Order*, *Discount is for Customer*, and *Description describes Item* are all one-many relationships, and *Order ordered on Date* is a many-one relationship set. If a binary relationship set has a uniqueness constraint that spans both roles, the relationship set is many-many. If *Nr* were not a role of *Nr of Item is on Order*, the relationship between *Item* and *Order* would be many-many. Even with *Nr*, we can view the relationship as being many-many. If a binary relationship set has two uniqueness constraints, one for each role, it is a one-one relationship set. If we extend this idea of two non-overlapping uniqueness constraints that together span all the roles, we also have a one-one relationship set between the (composite) values in the entity sets represented by the two uniqueness constraints. For example, in Fig. 2.6 we have a one-one relationship between *Customer* and *Name-Address* pairs.

Dots on connections in an OR diagram represent mandatory participation constraints. The dot for the connection of *Customer* to the *Name and Address identify Customer* relationship set means that every customer participates in the relationship set and thus that every customer must have a name and address. On the other hand, the absence of a dot for *Customer* in the *Discount is for Customer* relationship set means that the participation is optional—every customer need not have a discount.

The dashed arrow from the *Customer* role in the *is for* relationship set to the *Customer* role in the *... and ... identify ...* relationship set denotes a subset constraint. The customers who have discounts must be a subset of the customers who have names and addresses. Because of the mandatory and optional participation constraints, this subset constraint is already implied. If, however, the participation of customers in the *... and ... identifies ...* relationship set were not mandatory, then the subset constraint would indeed add a constraint not already implied. Although the constraint is not necessary here, we show it to illustrate the explicit notation that corresponds to the *ISA* constraint in the ER diagram in Fig. 2.3.

OSM

The data-description component of the OSM model, which we use in most of this book, is more closely aligned with the OR family of models than with the ER family. For our purpose in this book, ER models are both not expressive enough and too expressive. They do not have enough constructs to support some features of interest, and they have one construct, namely attributes, that imposes an unnecessary and often unwanted point of view on application developers. Additional constructs can be added easily, and many extensions to the ER model do include most, if not all, of the expressive power we need. It is difficult, however, to remove the notion of attributes. We also mention that neither the OR model nor the ER model accounts for behavior. For much of what we want to do, we need a strong conceptual model for behavior.

2.3.3 Relation Schemes

In addition to data models, we also have relation-scheme data descriptions that describe the data of a database. When moving from analysis to implementation, we often map both ER and OR models to relation-scheme data descriptions. Figure 2.7 shows a relation-scheme application model for both the ER and the OR application models we have been discussing.

A *relation scheme* is a named template for a set of *n*-tuples with the following features: (1) It has a name—*Customer*, for example, in Fig. 2.7. (2) It

Customer(Customer ID, Name, Address)
   primary key: Customer ID
   key: Name, Address

Discount Customer(Customer ID, Discount)
   primary key: Customer ID
   foreign key: Customer ID references Customer ID in Customer

Order(Order#, Customer ID, Date)
   primary key: Order#
   foreign key: Customer ID references Customer ID in Customer

Item(Item#, Description)
   primary key: Item#

OrderInfo(Order#, Item#, Nr)
   primary key Order#, Item#
   foreign key: Order# references Order# in Order
   foreign key: Item# references Item# in Item

Figure 2.7   Scheme-level data description.

has n attribute names, one for each component of the n-tuples being represented. The attribute names are usually just called attributes. The n
attributes must all be different so that they form a set. In Fig. 2.7, the *Customer* relation scheme includes three attributes. (3) Optionally, we can add
key constraints explicitly. We designate an attribute (or a set of attributes)
whose value (or values) uniquely determine at most one tuple as keys, and
we designate one of these keys as the primary key. Often there is just one
key, which therefore is the primary key. In the *Customer* scheme, *Customer
ID* is the primary key, and {*Name, Address*} is another key. (4) Optionally, we
can also designate referential integrity constraints, which we designate by
specifying foreign keys. When an attribute is a foreign key, the values for
the attribute in the n-tuples for the scheme must be a subset of the values
for the attribute in the m-tuples of the referenced scheme. This prevents us
from referencing objects that do not exist. Thus, for example, the customer
IDs in the *Order* tuples must be a subset of the customer IDs in the *Customer*
tuples, and the item numbers in the *OrderInfo* tuples must be a subset of
the item numbers in the *Item* tuples. (5) Optionally, we may also add additional information about each scheme. Later in the book we comment on
examples that include other constraints we wish to express.

A *relational database scheme* is a set of relation schemes. Figure 2.7 is an
example, and we shall explain how to obtain the relational database scheme
in Fig. 2.7 from both the ER diagram in Fig. 2.3 and the OR diagram in

Fig. 2.6. Detailed explanations of these kinds of transformations are an important part of our later discussions.

For ER diagrams like the one in Fig. 2.3, we generate one relation scheme for each entity set, and we generate one relation scheme for each many-many relationship set. For an entity set, the name of the relation scheme is the name of the entity set. The schemes *Customer*, *Discount Customer*, *Order*, and *Item* in Fig. 2.7 come from entity sets. The attributes of the schemes are the attributes of the entity set plus the primary key of any entity set on the one-side of a connected many-one relationship set. We obtain the attributes for *Order* scheme in Fig. 2.7, for example, by taking *Order#* and *Date*, which are directly connected attributes, plus *Customer ID*, the primary key of *Customer*, which is on the one-side of a connected many-one relationship set. The attributes for *Customer*, on the other hand, are only the directly connected attributes. We do not include the primary key of *Order* because it is on the many-side of the one-many relationship set, rather than on the one-side of a many-one relationship set. For many-many relationship sets, the name for the relation scheme usually must be supplied by the developer, although we can sometimes use the relationship-set name or some variation. We have chosen *OrderInfo* to represent the many-many relationship in Fig. 2.7. The attributes are the primary key attributes of the connected entity sets, plus any attributes directly connected to the many-many relationship set. Thus the attributes for *OrderInfo* are *Order#* and *Item#*, which are the primary key attributes of the connected entity sets, and *Nr*, which is an attribute directly connected to the many-many relationship set. One-one relationship sets are a special case of one-many relationship sets. For one-one relationship sets, the name is the name of either entity set or a chosen name and the attributes are the attributes of both entity sets. For all schemes keys and referential-integrity constraints come directly from the ER diagram.

For OR diagrams like the one in Fig. 2.6, we generate one relation scheme for each relationship set, except that we may combine schemes if they have the same role in a uniqueness constraint and the role is mandatory. In generating a scheme for a relationship set, each role becomes an attribute. We can choose our own names for both scheme names and attribute names, but we are usually able to take names directly from OR diagrams for both scheme and attribute names. In Fig. 2.7, we have one relation scheme for each relationship set, except that we have combined the *has* and *ordered on* relationship sets, as allowed. As an example, for the *describes* relationship set the attributes come from the roles, and we name them *Item#* and *Description*, and the scheme name comes from the connected *Item* entity set. When there is a single-role uniqueness constraint, the name of the entity set for the role is often an appropriate name for the relation scheme, and the name of the domain of permissible values is often an appropriate name for the attribute for the role. We have made this choice in Fig. 2.7 for *Customer* and *Customer ID*, *Order* and *Order#*, and *Item* and *Item#*. As for an ER application model, keys and referential-integrity constraints come directly from the OR diagram.

2.3.4 Implementation Schemes

Once we have a set of relation schemes, we can translate them into implementation schemes. We call the language we use to express implementation schemes a *Data-Definition Language (DDL)*. Figure 2.8 shows an example for the application we have been discussing. The DDL in Fig. 2.8 is written in SQL, a standardized commercial database language for specifying, updating, and querying a database.

We can basically obtain the DDL straight from the relation schemes, but some additions and changes are necessary. Usually, we must add type information. For each attribute, we have chosen a type provided by SQL, such as **integer** or **char**(20) and have combined the *Customer* and *Discount Customer* schemes. This design choice is based on the specifics of the application. We can reason, for example, that we could give everyone a discount and just make it 0% for everyone who has no discount; in this way we need not store the customers who have discounts separately. Except for these additions and changes, relation schemes map directly into DDL.

Syntactically, note that the schemes in Fig. 2.8 are introduced by *create table* commands. In SQL, and elsewhere in the commercial world, relations are called *tables* and relation schemes are called *table headers*. Note also that primary keys have the same label in both descriptions, but that other keys for a DDL table are labeled as being *unique* for a table rather than as being keys for a relation. Thus we have **unique** (*Name*, *Address*), which makes a

---

SQL

SQL is an acronym for Structured Query Language. Although the name seems to indicate that it is a language only for querying a database, SQL also has commands for data definition and data update. SQL is a standard database language developed by the American National Standards Institute. Vendors usually comply with these standards, which promotes interoperability and portability among them.

```
create table Customer(
    CustomerID char(10) primary key,
    Name char(20),
    Address char(25),
    Discount integer,
    unique (Name, Address)
    );

create table Order(
    OrderNr integer primary key,
    CustomerID char(10) references Customer,
    Date date,
    );

create table Item(
    ItemNr integer primary key,
    Description char(50)
    );

create table OrderInfo(
    OrderNr integer references Order,
    ItemNr integer references Item,
    Nr integer,
    primary key (OrderNr, ItemNr),
    );
```

Figure 2.8 SQL DDL for an application.

name-address pair unique for the *Customer* table description and hence unique within any actual *Customer* table. The SQL DDL uses *references* to designate foreign keys.

To conclude this section, let us return to our initial reason for having data models and data-definition languages and discuss the instances for the data component S_v of our database ADT. The schemes tell us which tuples can be stored in the database. The *Order* scheme in Fig. 2.8 states that we can store any tuple of three components—an integer for an order number, a string of up to 10 characters for a customer ID, and a date—so long as it satisfies certain key and referential-integrity constraints. There are many such tuples; indeed there would be an infinite number except that in computer implementations the set of integers is finite, as is the set of dates and the set of characters from which strings may be formed. From this extremely large set of possible tuples, we form sets of tuples, called *relations*. Each member of the power set of the set of all possible tuples for each scheme is a relation and thus a possible element of S_v. We restrict S_v somewhat, however, because we accept only relations that satisfy the key constraints and the referential-integrity constraints. As if this enormous set were not enough, we also include in S_v all the relations we can form by applying the operators in S_o of our database ADT. As shown in the next section, these operators can generate an immense number of relations, all in S_v, from a few given relations.

We consider these ideas more rigorously in the exercises, where we formally define a relation scheme and a relation. It should be clear, however, that the elements in S_v are all relations (sets of tuples) and that the number of elements in S_v is typically so large as to be almost unfathomable. Indeed, S_v would be unfathomable without the aid of data models and data-definition languages.

2.4   Data Languages

With respect to our ADT point of view, a *Data-Manipulation Language* (*DML*) provides a convenient way to specify a set of operations (S_o in our ADT definition). A DML has two kinds of operations—update operations and retrieval operations. Update operations insert tuples into relations, delete tuples from relations, and modify tuples in relations. Retrieval operations obtain tuples from relations that satisfy certain conditions and combine these tuples in various ways to produce result relations. A DML is often referred to as a *query language*. Although technically we should only call the set of retrieval operations a query language, we commonly refer to all the operations, including the update operations, as being operators of a query language.

After a short section in which we discuss updates, we describe two different kinds of query languages, relational algebra and SQL. Relational algebra is a generic query language and is used mainly as a succinct way to describe derived relations for theoretical work and as an intermediate language for query optimization. SQL is a standard commercial query language.

2.4.1 Updates

DML update operations are usually straightforward. Figure 2.9 shows some sample insertion, deletion, and modification operations, written in

insertion operations

> **insert into** *Customer* **values** (*'a*11*', 'John', '*12 *Maple',* 0)
> **insert into** *Customer* **values** (*'b*22*', 'John', '*17 *Main',* 2)
> **insert into** *Customer* **values** (*'c*33*', 'Mary', '*17 *Main',* 10)

modification operations

> **update** *Customer* **set** *Discount* = 5 **where** *CustomerID* = *'c*33*'*
> **update** *Customer* **set** *Address* = *'*15 *Oak'* **where** *Address* = *'*17 *Main'*

deletion operations

> **delete from** *Customer* **where** *Discount* > 0
> **delete from** *Customer* **where** *CustomerID* = *'a*11*'*

Figure 2.9   Sample SQL update operations.

SQL, for the *Customer* scheme in Fig. 2.8. The insertion operations insert tuples that represent the data for customers in Fig. 2.4 (where 0 is the default discount for customers without a discount). The first modification operation changes the discount for *Mary* from 10 to 5. The second changes each customer's address whose current address is *17 Main* to *15 Oak*. The first deletion operation removes all customers whose discount is greater than 0, and the second removes the customer whose ID is *'a11'*.

2.4.2 Relational Algebra

DML retrieval operations are unary and binary operations that apply to relations and produce relations as results. Although there are common alternative sets of operations, the set of query operations we discuss here is $\{\sigma, \pi, \cup, -, \cap, \rho, \times, \bowtie\}$. This set of operators is closed—the result of every operation is a relation. We can thus build complex expressions by recursively applying any of these operations to any result.

To discuss these operations, we use the set of relations in Fig. 2.10, which shows the data in Fig. 2.4 as relations (i.e., as elements of S_v). A set of relations, one for each relation scheme in a relational database scheme, represents the *current state* or the *base relations* of a relational database. All relations in S_v other than those in the current state are implicit. The operations we will discuss allow us to derive many, but not all, of these implicit relations. In principle, we can obtain all the implicit

---

Syntactic Markings

Query languages use different conventions for marking strings and other literals. When we are specifically discussing a commercial query language, we will be faithful to the conventions of that query language. Otherwise we will simplify by just using the data values directly, without special markings to distinguish among various types of representations. This convention is common, especially in analysis where we are not interested in forcing our end-user clients into seeing representations in a different form. Perhaps someday this practice will become more common in the syntax of computer models and languages.

Customer	(CustomerID	Name	Address	Discount)
	a11	John	12 Maple	0
	b22	John	17 Main	2
	c33	Mary	17 Main	10

Order	(OrderNr	CustomerID	Date)
	345	a11	27 Feb
	350	b22	27 Feb
	375	b22	2 Mar

Item	(ItemNr	Description)
	11	ball
	12	book
	85	game
	87	doll
	92	scooter

OrderInfo	(OrderNr	ItemNr	Nr)
	345	11	1
	345	12	1
	350	12	1
	375	85	2
	375	92	2

Figure 2.10 Sample database.

relations if in addition to the retrieval operations we also have the update operations.

The operator σ, called *selection*, selects tuples from a relation that satisfy a given condition. The operator

$$\sigma_{Discount > 0}Customer$$

selects the customer tuples whose discount is greater than 0. The result for the data in Fig. 2.10 is the following relation:

CustomerID	Name	Address	Discount
b22	John	17 Main	2
c33	Mary	17 Main	10

Only the second and third tuple of the *Customer* relation are included in the result because they are the only ones whose discount is greater than 0. Note that the resulting relation does not have a name. Base relations have names, but derived relations do not.

The condition of a σ operator may be a Boolean expression. The expression $\sigma_{Name = John \wedge Discount > 0}Customer$ yields the following relation:

CustomerID	Name	Address	Discount
b22	John	17 Main	2

The operator π is called projection. The projection operator "projects" on the columns in a list of attributes, which means that it keeps only the columns whose attributes are in the list. For example,

$$\pi_{Name, Address}Customer$$

yields the following relation:

Name	Address
John	12 Maple
John	17 Main
Mary	17 Main

The listed attributes must be a set—there can be no duplicates in the list. We usually give a set by listing the attributes separated by commas, but we may omit the commas if we wish. When we use single-letter attribute names, we may also omit the blanks.

Since relations are sets, π eliminates any duplicates that may arise when we project out the values in one or more columns. For example, we can get the dates for orders by executing $\pi_{Date}Order$, which yields the following relation:

Date
27 Feb
2 Mar

Note that even though there are two *27 Feb* dates in the *Order* relation in Fig. 2.10, there is only one *27 Feb* date in the result.

Since our set of operations is closed, we can form expressions from the basic operators by applying operators to the results of other operators. For example, we can get the names and addresses of customers who have discounts greater than 0 by executing the query $\pi_{Name, Address}(\sigma_{Discount > 0}Customer)$, which yields the following relation:

Name	Address
John	17 Main
Mary	17 Main

Without parentheses, a sequence of unary operators executes from right to left. Thus we may omit the parentheses in this expression and write the query as $\pi_{Name, Address}\,\sigma_{Discount > 0}Customer$.

Since relations are sets, we would expect the operators *union* ($\cup$), *intersection* ($\cap$), and *set difference* ($-$) to apply, and they do. We can, for example, take the difference between the customer IDs in the *Customer* relation and the customer IDs in the *Order* relation to find out which customers do not have orders. The expression $(\pi_{CustomerID}Customer) - (\pi_{CustomerID}Order)$ yields the following relation:

CustomerID
c33

If we wish, we can omit the parentheses in the expression because unary operators have precedence over binary operators. We could also put either $\cup$ or $\cap$ in place of $-$ in this expression to obtain the union or the intersection, respectively.

When we apply a set operator, the schemes of the two relations must be identical. For example, the query $\pi_{OrderNr}Order \cap \pi_{ItemNr}Item$, is not valid. The scheme of $\pi_{OrderNr} Order$ is *OrderNr*, whereas the scheme of $\pi_{ItemNr} Item$ is *ItemNr*. Thus the schemes to which the intersection applies are not identical and the expression is not valid.

If we really wish to find the intersection of order numbers and item numbers, we can do so by renaming one or both of the attributes in the intermediate results. The operator ρ *renames* an attribute. For example, $\rho_{OrderNr \leftarrow DesignatingNr} \pi_{OrderNr} Order$ and $\rho_{ItemNr \leftarrow DesignatingNr} \pi_{ItemNr} Item$ yield the following relations.

DesignatingNr	DesignatingNr
345	11
350	12
375	85
	87
	92

We can now take the intersection of these two relations, which for this example is the empty relation whose scheme is the single attribute *DesignatingNr*. The expression

$$\rho_{OrderNr \leftarrow DesignatingNr} \pi_{OrderNr} Order \cap \rho_{ItemNr \leftarrow DesignatingNr} \pi_{ItemNr} Item$$

yields this empty result.

The back arrow ($\leftarrow$) in the ρ operator can be read as "is replaced by." Observe that to be valid, we may not rename an attribute in a relation scheme to have the same name as some other attribute in the scheme. The expression $\rho_{Name \leftarrow Address} Customer$, for example, is not valid because if we change *Name* to *Address*, we would have two columns named *Address* in the resulting relation. The attribute to be renamed, of course, must be in the scheme of the relation. Thus, for the ρ operator to be valid, the attribute on the left of the back arrow must be in the scheme of the relation to which the operator is applied, and the attribute on the right of the back arrow must not be in the scheme.

The $\times$ operator is called *cross product*. It is like an ordinary cross product of sets, which yields a set of ordered pairs, except that the pairs are not ordered. Instead of using order to keep track of which value came from which set, we keep track by using attribute names. Indeed,

A	B	=	B	A	=	A	B	=	B	A
1	2		2	1		3	4		4	3
3	4		4	3		1	2		2	1

and neither the order of the columns nor the order of the rows matters. Also, the × operator is actually applied to sets of tuples, not sets of atomic values. It is like an ordinary cross product of a set of *n*-tuples with a set of *m*-tuples, which yields a set of pairs of *n*- and *m*-tuples, except that we combine the pairs to form $m + n$-tuples.

As an example of the × operator, if we execute the query *Order* × *Item*, we obtain the following relation. Observe that *Order* tuples are 3-tuples and that *Item* tuples are 2-tuples. Thus the *Order* × *Item* tuples are 5-tuples. Altogether *Order* × *Item* has 15 5-tuples because *Order* has 3 tuples and *Item* has 5 tuples and thus there are 3*5 = 15 pairs.

OrderNr	CustomerID	Date	ItemNr	Description
345	*a*11	27 Feb	11	*ball*
345	*a*11	27 Feb	12	*book*
345	*a*11	27 Feb	85	*game*
345	*a*11	27 Feb	87	*doll*
345	*a*11	27 Feb	92	*scooter*
350	*b*22	27 Feb	11	*ball*
350	*b*22	27 Feb	12	*book*
350	*b*22	27 Feb	85	*game*
350	*b*22	27 Feb	87	*doll*
350	*b*22	27 Feb	92	*scooter*
375	*b*22	2 Mar	11	*ball*
375	*b*22	2 Mar	12	*book*
375	*b*22	2 Mar	85	*game*
375	*b*22	2 Mar	87	*doll*
375	*b*22	2 Mar	92	*scooter*

In order to make the schemes work out right for the × operator, we require that the intersection of the attributes in the schemes of the two relations be empty. For *Order* × *Item* the intersection of {*OrderNr, CustomerID, Date*} and {*ItemNr, Description*} is empty.

We can use our ρ operator to rename attributes when we wish to apply × to relations whose schemes have a nonempty intersection. For example, the query *Customer* × $\rho_{CustomerID \leftarrow CustomerID'}$*Order* yields the following relation:

$$Customer \bowtie Order$$

yields the same result as does the expression

$$\pi_{CustomerID, Name, Address, Discount, OrderNr, Date}\sigma_{CustomerID = CustomerID'}$$
$$(Customer \times \rho_{CustomerID \leftarrow CustomerID'}Order)$$

In general, if we let r be a relation whose set of attributes is R and let s be a relation whose set of attributes is S, and if $R \cap S = A_1 ... A_n$, then

$$r \bowtie s = \pi_{R \cup S}\sigma_{A_1 = A_1' \wedge \cdots \wedge A_n = A_n'}(r \times \rho_{A_1 \leftarrow A_1'} \cdots \rho_{A_n \leftarrow A_n'}s)$$

where $\wedge$ denotes the Boolean **and** operator.

The join operator, since it is derivable from the other operations, is not necessary. It is certainly convenient, however, and we definitely want it as part of our set of operators. If we want a more efficient set, we can eliminate the $\times$ operator and keep $\bowtie$ along with the other operators we have discussed because if $R \cap S = 0$, then $r \bowtie s = r \times s$.

To illustrate many of the operators we have been discussing in a single example, suppose we wish to obtain item descriptions of the intersection of the items ordered by John who lives at 12 Maple and the items ordered by John who lives at 17 Main. The expression

$$\pi_{Description}\sigma_{Name = John \wedge Address = 12 \, Maple}$$
$$(Customer \bowtie Order \bowtie OrderInfo \bowtie Item)$$
$$\cap$$
$$\pi_{Description}\sigma_{Name = John \wedge Address = 17 \, Main}$$
$$(Customer \bowtie Order \bowtie OrderInfo \bowtie Item)$$

computes this result and yields the following relation:

Description
book

This expression would be much longer if we were to use $\times$ and ρ rather than $\bowtie$.

2.4.3 SQL

SQL, a standard commercial query language, can be used to pose ad hoc queries against a database. Basic queries in SQL can be thought of as being

CustomerID	Name	Address	Discount	OrderNr	CustomerID′	Date
a11	John	12 Maple	0	345	a11	27 Fe
a11	John	12 Maple	0	350	b22	27 Fel
a11	John	12 Maple	0	375	b22	2 Mar
b22	John	17 Main	2	345	a11	27 Feb
b22	John	17 Main	2	350	b22	27 Feb
b22	John	17 Main	2	375	b22	2 Mar
c33	Mary	17 Main	10	345	a11	27 Feb
c33	Mary	17 Main	10	350	b22	27 Feb
c33	Mary	17 Main	10	375	b22	2 Mar

Building on this result, suppose we now wish to obtain the custome information, the order number, and the date of each order for each cus tomer. We can proceed by selecting only rows where $CustomerID = Cus$ $tomerID′$ and then project on the attributes we want in the result, all but the duplicate $CustomerID′$. The expression

$$\pi_{CustomerID, Name, Address, Discount, OrderNr, Date} \sigma_{CustomerID = CustomerID′}$$
$$(Customer \times \rho_{CustomerID \leftarrow CustomerID′} Order)$$

computes this result, which is the following relation.

CustomerID	Name	Address	Discount	OrderNr	Date
a11	John	12 Maple	0	345	27 Feb
b22	John	17 Main	2	350	27 Feb
b22	John	17 Main	2	375	2 Mar

The particular sequence of operations in this expression is very com mon. It consists of

1. Renaming the common attributes in one of two relations,

2. Taking the cross product of the two relations,

3. Selecting only the tuples in the cross product for which corre sponding values for attributes that were identical in the original two schemes are equal, and

4. Projecting on all the attributes except those that were renamed.

This sequence is so common, in fact, that we have a special operator fo The operator, called the *join* (also called the *natural join*),[†], is denoted by symbol ⋈. The operation

---

[†] Later we will encounter other kinds of joins. In this book, "join" always means "r join" unless otherwise designated. We sometimes use "natural join" when we wish emphasis.

relational algebra with some syntactic sugar. SQL also includes additional features for computations and for sorting query results.

The query statement in SQL is called a **select** statement, which has the basic form

> **select** $A_1, \ldots, A_n$
> **from** r
> **where** c

where the A_i's are attributes, r is a relation, and c is a condition. This **select** statement has the same meaning as the relational-algebra expression

$$\pi_{A_1 \cdots A_n} \sigma_c r$$

SQL results retain duplicate tuples, however, unless we explicitly request that they be discarded by adding the keyword **distinct** after the **select** keyword.

We now consider several sample SQL queries, which we use to explain the meaning of the constructs in the SQL syntax. For the examples we assume the sample database instance in Fig. 2.10. Each example includes a query statement in English, an SQL query, and the result. We comment on the query to provide additional insight into SQL.

Query 1.   List all information about items.

> **select** *
> **from** *Item*

ItemNr	Description
11	ball
12	book
85	game
87	doll
92	scooter

The **select** clause specifies which columns are wanted and what their names should be. The * is a shorthand way of specifying that all the columns are wanted and that their given column names are to be used as the names for the columns in the result. The **from** clause specifies which relations are to be used in the query. For Query 1, the result is simply the specified relation.

Query 2.   List the names of customers.

select *Name*
from *Customer*

Name
John
John
Mary

Here, only the *Name* column appears. Notice that the resulting relation includes duplicates. If we wished to list only distinct names, we would insert the keyword **distinct** between **select** and *Name*, writing the query

select distinct *Name*
from *Customer*

to obtain the result

Name
John
Mary

Query 3.   What is the average discount rate?

select **avg**(*Discount*)
from *Customer*

avg(*Discount*)
4

Query 3 shows an example of an aggregate operation, which we use to compute the average discount rate. Other aggregate operations provided by SQL include **min**, **max**, **sum**, and **count**. We note that SQL's duplicates are exactly what is usually wanted to make averages and sums come out right and that duplicates are of no consequence for minimums and maximums. To provide the flexibility needed for counting distinct elements, SQL includes an optional **distinct** keyword for the **count** operator. The operation **count**(**distinct** *Discount*) in place of **avg**(*Discount*) in Query 3 counts the number of distinct discount rates, whereas **count**(*Discount*) counts all the discount rates, which is the same as counting all the tuples in the *Customer* relation.

SQL also includes standard arithmetic operations. If we wish to know what twice the average discount rate is, for example, we can replace **avg**(*Discount*) in Query 3 by 2∗**avg**(*Discount*). The result would be 8 instead of 4. Rather than use the expression as the resulting column name, we could provide a descriptive name such as *Twice the Avg* by adding "*Twice the Avg*" after 2 ∗**avg**(*Discount*) in the **select** clause. A quoted name provides an alternative name for a column.

Query 4.   List names and addresses of customers who have a discount rate greater than 5%.

> **select** *Name*, *Address*
> **from** *Customer*
> **where** *Discount* > 5

Name	Address
Mary	*17 Main*

Query 4 shows how to select a subset of the tuples by adding a condition with the **where** clause. Only those tuples that satisfy the condition remain in the result. Thus only *Mary*, whose discount rate exceeds 5%, is in the result.

Query 5.   Compute the cross product of the *Customer* and *Order* relations.

> **select** *Customer.CustomerID* "*Customer CID*", *Name*, *Address*,
> *Discount*, *OrderNr*, *Order.CustomerID* "*Order CID*", *Date*
> **from** *Customer*, *Order*

Customer CID	Name	Address	Discount	OrderNr	Order CID	Date
a11	*John*	*12 Maple*	*0*	*345*	*a11*	*27 Feb*
a11	*John*	*12 Maple*	*0*	*350*	*b22*	*27 Feb*
a11	*John*	*12 Maple*	*0*	*375*	*b22*	*2 Mar*
b22	*John*	*17 Main*	*2*	*345*	*a11*	*27 Feb*
b22	*John*	*17 Main*	*2*	*350*	*b22*	*27 Feb*
b22	*John*	*17 Main*	*2*	*375*	*b22*	*2 Mar*
c33	*Mary*	*17 Main*	*10*	*345*	*a11*	*27 Feb*
c33	*Mary*	*17 Main*	*10*	*350*	*b22*	*27 Feb*
c33	*Mary*	*17 Main*	*10*	*375*	*b22*	*2 Mar*

Query 5 is unusual, but it illustrates some interesting points. First, Query 5 shows that listing multiple relations in the **from** clause logically designates their cross product. Although we rarely want this cross product, understanding that the data in the listed relations can be thought of as being matched in all possible ways gives us a basis to write the conditions we need to get what we want. Second, the query shows what happens when column names are ambiguous. If we had written only *CustomerID* in the **select** clause, SQL would not have known whether we were referring to the *CustomerID* in the *Customer* relation or the *CustomerID* in the *Order* relation. SQL forbids this ambiguity and would have rejected the query as being syntactically incorrect. The solution is to prefix ambiguous attribute names with relation names. Since these names are often long, SQL provides a way to use aliases for names. Our next example shows both the use of aliases and how the cross product, with an appropriate condition, can be useful to obtain the results we want.

Query 6. List the names and addresses of customers who have placed orders and the dates on which they placed these orders.

> **select** *Name, Address, Date*
> **from** *Customer C, Order O*
> **where** *C.CustomerID* = *O.CustomerID*

Name	Address	Date
John	12 Maple	27 Feb
John	17 Main	27 Feb
John	17 Main	2 Mar

Observe how the aliases *C* and *O* disambiguate *CustomerID* in the condition by designating which *CustomerID* is meant—the *CustomerID* in *O* (the alias for *Order*) or the *CustomerID* in *C* (the alias for *Customer*). Observe also that the condition *C.CustomerID* = *O.CustomerID* selects just three tuples out of the cross product, namely the first, fifth, and sixth, because these are the only tuples in which *C.CustomerID* = *O.CustomerID*. The result here is equivalent to the relational algebra expression $\pi_{Name, Address, Date}(Customer \bowtie Order)$. There is no natural join in SQL. The query writer must construct the natural join from the cross product by selecting only those tuples whose values are equal on the intersecting attributes.

Query 7. List Customers who have the same name. For each pair, give the name and the two customer ID numbers, but list a pair only once (i.e., do not list a customer c_1 as matching with a customer c_2 and then also list c_2 as matching c_1) and do not list the same customer ID as a pair (i.e., do not list a customer as matching with herself or himself).

```
select Name, C1.CustomerID, C2.CustomerID
from Customer C1, Customer C2
where C1.Name = C2.Name and C1.CustomerID < C2.CustomerID
```

Name	CustomerID	CustomerID
John	a11	b22

This query computes the cross product of *Customer* with itself. It then selects rows in which the names are the same, but only if the customer ID of the first customer is less than the second customer ID. This ensures that we do not list customers as having the same name as their own and that we do not list the same pair twice. Thus we do not also have *<John, b22, a11>* in the result. Note that SQL allows duplicate attributes in the result.

Query 8. List the following order information as specified: the order number in descending order and the description of an item for an order in ascending order.

```
select OrderNr, Description
from OrderInfo O, Item I
where O.ItemNr = I.ItemNr
order by OrderNr desc, Description asc
```

OrderNr	Description
375	game
375	scooter
350	book
345	book
345	game

Query 8 shows how to sort the tuples in the results. We can sort the results in ascending or descending order by specifying the keywords **asc** and **desc** respectively, and we can specify the order of sort keys by listing them in order of highest precedence first in the **order by** clause. Since **asc** is the default, we need not specify it unless we want to add it for emphasis, as in Query 8.

Query 9. Find the total number of items ordered for each order. Sort the results in descending order on the total.

```
select sum(Nr) "Total", OrderNr
from OrderInfo
group by OrderNr
order by Total
```

Total	OrderNr
4	375
2	345
1	350

As Query 9 shows, we can use the **group by** clause to group tuples before applying an aggregate operator. Here, we find the total number of items for an order by first grouping the numbers by order and then summing. If we wish to restrict this list to just those orders whose total is greater than one, we can add a **having** clause, so that the query is

```
select sum(Nr) "Total", OrderNr
from OrderInfo
group by OrderNr
having Total > 1
order by Total
```

The result for this query is

Total	OrderNr
4	375
2	345

In general, the **having** clause restricts the results computed by an aggregate operation to only those satisfying the **having** condition.

Query 10. List the name and address of those customers who do not have a current order.

```
select Name, Address
from Customer
minus
select C.Name, C.Address
from Customer C, Order O
where C.CustomerID = O.CustomerID
```

Name	Address
Mary	17 Main

Query 10 takes the set difference of the *Name* and *Address* tuples in the customer relation and the *Name* and *Address* tuples in the join of the *Customer* and *Order* relations. We could also take the union (**union**) or the intersection (**intersect**). When the column names do not match, the column names for the output are the names in the first **select** statement.

Query 11.   List the discount rates of customers who do not currently have an order.

```
select distinct Discount
from Customer
where CustomerID in
        (select CustomerID
        from Customer
        minus
        select O. CustomerID
        from Customer C, Order O
        where C. CustomerID = O. CustomerID)
```

$$\frac{Discount}{10}$$

Query 11 shows one query nested inside another. The nested query is similar to Query 10, differing in that we obtain the *CustomerID* rather than the *Name* and *Address*. The **in** clause in the query restricts the tuples selected from the *Customer* relation to those whose *CustomerID* is included in the result of the nested subquery. Thus only customers who do not currently have orders are selected. We obtain the list of (distinct) discount rates for these customers. In place of **in** we could have **not in**, which would then list the discount rates of customers who do have current orders.

2.5   Chapter Summary

Topic Summary

- The three-level architecture of a database system lets us see the database as (1) a collection of views, (2) a conceptual whole, and (3) a physical implementation. Views limit the scope of usability for subapplications. The conceptual whole lets us design the database as an integrated unit, while the physical layer provides an actual implementation.

- Abstractly, a database is an ADT. We can describe its values using an ER model, an OR model, a set of relation schemes, or SQL DDL, and we can describe its set of operations using relational algebra or SQL DML.

- The ER model describes a database as entities, attributes, and relationships, whereas the OR model describes a database only as entities and relationships. Relation schemes describe a database in terms of scheme names and attributes along with various key constraints. SQL DDL provides a **create table** statement that lets us syntactically describe relation schemes for a commercial database system.

- Relational algebra provides a way to manipulate relations by the operators select (σ), project (π), union ($\cup$), set difference ($-$), intersection ($\cap$), renaming (ρ), relational cross product ($\times$), and join ($\bowtie$). SQL DML uses a **select** statement to implement these same operations. The **select** statement also includes some facilities beyond relational algebra, including sorting, aggregate functions, grouping, and conditions on aggregate operations over groups.

Question Summary

- How can we make database application programs independent of the internal representation of a database?

  We can write database application programs with respect either to a view or to the conceptual database of the three-level architecture. Then if the underlying physical database changes, only the mapping to the physical database need change; application programs need not be altered.

- What are the roles of the various database models, schemes, and languages?

  ER and OR model descriptions support high-level, client-oriented discussions. Relation schemes and relational algebra give us a theoretically clean way to describe and manipulate a relational database. SQL DDL and SQL DML provide for implementation on a commercial database system.

2.6 Bibliographic Notes

Many textbooks are devoted to the topics in this and the next chapter [Date95, Elmasri94, Hansen92, Helman94, Korth97, O'Neil94, Ullman97]. These books provide an expanded coverage of the topics covered here.

The three-level architecture has been standard for some time [CODA-SYL71]. The idea of an abstract data type (ADT), which we can use as an abstract way to think about the three-level architecture, originated in [Liskov74], although its roots go back to the programming language Simula [Birtwistle79]. Thinking about a database as an ADT is more recent; [Helman94], for example, takes this approach.

Codd wrote the seminal paper for the relational model [Codd70], which not only included the original definition of a relational database but also the original definition for relational algebra. SQL, which was an outgrowth of some of this early work on Sequel [Chamberlin74] and Square [Boyce75], eventually became the IBM product Database/2 or DB2 and finally an ANSI standard [ANSI86, Date89].

Data models became popular ways to describe databases with the advent of the Entity-Relationship Model [Chen76]. Since its beginnings, the ER Model has been extended and used extensively to describe and develop database systems [Teorey86]. Object-role (OR) modeling is a common alternative to ER modeling. Originating with the NIAM Model [Verheijen82], various OR models have been developed and used for database design and development [Halpin95a].

2.7 Exercises

2.1 Consider an $m \times n$ array as it might appear in the three-level database architecture.

   a. Explain how the array could be organized in physical storage.

   b. Explain how the array appears in the conceptual level.

   c.* What are some of the possible views? How many different views are possible? Explain.

2.2 Consider the attribute Date, which we can implement as an integer of the form *yyyynnn* (e.g., 1999049 is February 18, 1999).

Suppose that we wish to view Date in terms of the attributes Year, Month, and Day. (Note that the *only* value that will be actually stored in the physical database for a date is the single integer.)

a. Explain what we would have to do to display the answer to a database query that requests the Day, Month, and Year.

b. Explain what we would have to do to answer a query that depends on a Month value, for example, finding all cars sold in January.

c. Explain what we would have to do to update a Date, for example, to change the year value.

d. How do answers to these questions illustrate mappings in the three-level database architecture?

2.3   Consider each of the following ADTs and answer the questions. Also, summarize by stating what should be learned about database systems from this exercise.

a. *Real* (the pure mathematical real numbers). Describe the value set S_v for the ADT. Is the set of operators $S_o = \{+, *\}$ closed? Is the set of operators $S_o = \{+, -, *, /\}$ closed?

b. *Float* (the real numbers as implemented on a computer). Describe the value set S_v for the ADT. What two problems arise because the set of operators $\{+, *\}$ is not closed for the *Float* ADT? How do we deal with these problems?

c. *List*. Suppose we wish to create a list of integers of arbitrary length. Describe the value set S_v for the ADT. Give a reasonable set of operators S_o for the ADT. Describe two different ways to store a *List*. Think about the efficiency and also the ease and/or difficulty of programming the operators in S_o for these two different storage schemes.

d. *Polygon*. Suppose that the value set S_v is a set of polygons with n sides, $n \geq 3$, and that the operator set S_o is {*area, perimeter*}. Explain why the operators in S_o should be implemented differently for the regular polygons such as squares, triangles, and trapezoids than for the irregular polygons whose edges vary in length and whose shapes may be concave or convex.

2.4   A *function f from a set A to a set B*, denoted $f: A \rightarrow B$, is a set of ordered pairs $(a, b) \in f$ such that for every element $a \in A$ there is one and only one element $b \in B$. The set A is the *domain*; the set B is the *codomain*; and the projection of f on B (i.e., the set of second elements in f) is the *range*.

State whether each of the following sets of ordered pairs is a function. For each set that is a function, give the set of elements in $C - R$ where C is the codomain and R is the range. For those that are not functions, note for each whether it is the "one" or the "only one" part of the definition that is violated. Also, state how this problem relates to ER diagrams.

a. *has_name* : {*Person*1, *Person*2, *Person*3} → {*Alice, John, Mary, Zed*} = {(*Person*1, *John*), (*Person*3, *Alice*), (*Person*2, *John*)}

b. *is_taking* : {*Person*1, *Person*2, *Person*3} → {*CS*100, *Math*100, *Chem*100} = {(*Person*1, *CS*100), (*Person*1, *Math*100), (*Person*1, *Chem*100), (*Person*2, *Chem*100), (*Person*3, *CS*100), (*Person*3, *Math*100)}

c. *has_phone_nr* : {*Person*1, *Person*2, *Person*3} → {378-1111, 378-2222} = {(*Person*1, 378-2222), (*Person*3, 378-1111)}

d. *is_married_to* : {*Person*1, *Person*2, *Person*3, *Person*4} → {*Person*1, *Person*2, *Person*3, *Person*4} = {(*Person*1, *Person*3), (*Person*2, *Person*4), (*Person*3, *Person*1), (*Person*4, *Person*2)}

2.5 A *binary relation r from a set A to a set B* is a set of ordered pairs $(a, b) \in r$ such that $a \in A$ and $b \in B$.

a. Which of the sets of ordered pairs given in Exercise 2.4 are binary relations?

b.* Prove or disprove: Every binary relation is a function.

c.* Prove or disprove: Every function is a binary relation.

d. Explain how (b) and (c) let us say that we can model every attribute in an ER diagram using a relationship, but not vice versa.

2.6 Let r be a binary relation from A to B. The relation r is *1-1* ("one-to-one" or "one-one") if for each element in the projection of r on A there is one and only one element in B, and for each element in the projection of r on B there is one and only one element in A. The relation r is *1-n* ("one-to-many" or "one-many") if it is not 1-1 and if for each element in the projection of r on B there is one and only one element in A. A relation r is *n-1* ("many-to-one" or "many-one") if it is not 1-1 and if for each element in the projection of r on A there is one and only one element in B. The relation r is m-n ("many-to-many" or "many-many") if it is not 1-1, 1-n, or n-1.

   a. Classify the sets of ordered pairs in exercise 2.4 as 1-1, 1-n, n-1, or m-n.

   b.* Prove or disprove: Every n-1 binary relation r from A to B is a function from the projection of r on A to B.

   c. Prove or disprove: Every 1-n binary relation r from A to B is a function from the projection of r on A to B.

   d. Let r be a binary relation from A to B. If A is the only minimal key for r, is r 1-1, 1-n, n-1, or m-n? Also answer this question when B is the only minimal key, when AB is the only minimal key, and when both A and B are minimal keys.

2.7   Students are identified by their student ID# and have a name and address. Faculty members are identified by their faculty ID# and have a name and an office#. Courses are identified by their course# and section# together. A faculty member may teach one or more courses, but a course is taught by only one faculty member. A student may enroll in one or more courses and a course may have several students enrolled in it. A student has a single faculty advisor, and a faculty advisor may advise many students.

   a. Create an ER diagram for this description.

   b. Mark the candidate keys.

   c. Produce relation schemes from the ER diagram. (Choose good names for scheme names.)

   d. Give the minimal keys and foreign keys for each relation scheme.

   e. Write SQL DDL for the relation schemes. Include designations for all keys, including primary keys, unique keys, and foreign keys.

2.8   Repeat Exercise 2.7 for the following description.

A customer has an identifying customer# and a name and address, which together also identify a customer. A customer insures one or more vehicles with an insurance company as of some date (a vehicle is insured by only one customer). A vehicle# identifies a vehicle, and a vehicle also has a make and model. A customer may have filed zero or more claims. A claim# identifies a claim, and a claim is filed for a certain amount. A claim is for one of the customer's vehicles, and there may be several claims for a single vehicle.

2.9 Consider the ER diagram in Fig. 2.11.

  a. Produce relation schemes for this diagram.

  b. Give the minimal keys and foreign keys for each relation scheme.

2.10 An orchard has a name, which identifies it, and an owner and a location, which together identify it. Every orchard has one or more trees. A tree within an orchard is identified by a row and column number together. (Be careful here—a row and column number do not uniquely identify a tree, only a tree within some orchard.) Each tree has a variety name (e.g., Red Delicious, Elberta, Bartlett, ...) and a generic fruit type (e.g., apple, pear, peach, ...). Each year each tree produces a certain yield, which is a quantity measured in bushels.

  a. Create an OR diagram for this description.

  b. Produce relation schemes from the OR diagram.

  c. Give all minimal keys for each relation scheme.

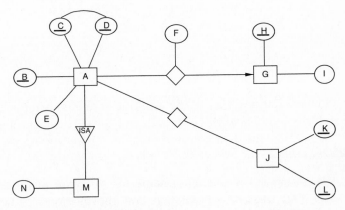

Figure 2.11 An ER application model.

d. Write SQL DDL for the relation schemes. Include designations for all keys, including primary keys, unique keys, and foreign keys.

e.* Consider creating an ER diagram for this description. If only the ER modeling constructs discussed in this book are used, what difficulty is encountered? Why is this difficulty not encountered for OR diagrams?

2.11* We often wish to simplify the definition for a relation scheme to its essence. As a basic essential definition, we say that a *relation scheme R* is a nonempty set of attribute names $R = \{A_1, A_2, ..., A_n\}$. To avoid having to continuously say "names," we say "attributes" to mean "attribute names." Further, because we use relation schemes so much, when we have single-letter attributes we reduce the set notation by dropping the braces, commas, and spaces. Thus, we write the preceding set R as $A_1 A_2 ... A_n$. Each attribute A has a domain, denoted $dom(A)$, which is a set of values.

A relation is always defined with respect to a relation scheme. To denote that a relation r is defined with respect to a relation scheme R, we write $r(R)$, read "r is a relation on scheme R" or just "r is a relation on R" or even just "r on R" if we know that r is a relation. A *relation* is a set of n-tuples, $\{t_1, ..., t_k\}$, where n is $|R|$, the cardinality of R. Let scheme R be $A_1 A_2 ... A_n$. Then, an $n - tuple$ t for a relation $r(R)$ is a function, from R to the union of domains $D = dom(A_1) \cup dom(A_2) \cup ... \cup dom(A_n)$, with the restriction that $t(A_i) \in dom(A_i), 1 \le i \le n$.

We usually write a relation as a table, for example,

$r =$	A	B
	a	1
	b	1
	b	2

where the domains of the attributes are either implied or given. Here, we let $dom(A)$ be $\{a, b, c\}$, and $dom(B)$ be $\{0, ..., 9\}$. Show that r satisfies the definition for a relation by answering the following questions:

a. What is the relation scheme for r? Write this scheme using both regular set notation and the relation-scheme notation. (Note that this is the domain for the tuple functions.)

b. Give the union of domains D for A and B. (Note that this is the codomain for the tuple functions.)

c. Let the three tuples in the table be t_1 for the first, t_2 for the second, and t_3 for the third. Write the three functions, t_1, t_2, and t_3, as sets of ordered pairs. Then form a set from these three sets of ordered pairs. (Observe that the set that contains the sets of ordered pairs satisfies the definition of a relation. Observe also that the transformation of a relation from a table form to a function form is straightforward.)

d. Give a tuple t_4 for r that satisfies all the required properties except the restriction $t(A) \in dom(A)$. (Observe that for the tuples t_1, t_2, and t_3, this range restriction holds.)

e. Let $s = \{u_1, u_2\}$, where $u_1 = \{(Name, Nancy), (Address, 12\ Oak), (Age, 21)\}$ and $u_2 = \{(Name, Zak), (Address, 12\ Oak), (Age, 15)\}$. Write relation s as a table. (Observe that the transformation of a relation from a function form to a table form is straightforward.)

f. How many different equivalent layouts are there for the table for s, where different means a different ordering of attributes or a different ordering of tuples? (Observe that there is really only one definition for s because rearranging the order of the elements of a set means nothing.)

g. Evaluate: $t_1(A)$ and $t_2(B)$ for r and $u_1(Name)$ and $u_2(Age)$ for s. (Observe that these are standard function evaluations.)

h. As a shorthand, when we have a scheme, we often use the order of the attributes and write $t_1 = <a, 1>$ for $t_1 = \{(A, a), (B, 1)\}$. We also extend this idea and write $t_1(AB)$ as $<a, 1>$. Using this simplified tuple form, write $t_2(AB)$ for r and $t_3(X)$ for r, where $X = AB$, and $u_1(Y)$ for s, where $Y = Name\ Age$. When there is only one value in this tuple form, we drop the angle brackets. Thus, $t_3(A) = <a> = a$, which is the same result obtained by simply evaluating the function t_3 in the standard way.

2.12** Given a relation scheme $R(A_1 \cdots A_n)$, what is the maximum number of candidate keys R can have? (Hint: Solve the problem for $n = 2$, $n = 3$, and $n = 4$ and observe the pattern.)

2.13* Let r and s be relations on scheme R. Assume that both r and s have a minimal key $K \leq R$ and $K \neq \emptyset$. Which of the following relations must necessarily have K as a minimal key?

a. $r \cup s$

b. $r \cap s$

c. $r - s$

d. $\pi_K r$

e. $\sigma_{A=a} r$ for attribute $A \in R$

2.14 Let $r(ABC)$ and $s(BCD)$ be relations with a in $dom(A)$ and b in $dom(B)$. Which of the following expressions are properly formed?

a. $r \cup s$

b. $\pi_B r - \pi_B s$

c. $\sigma_{B=b} r$

d. $\sigma_{A=a \wedge B=b} s$

e. $r \bowtie s$

f. $\pi_A r \bowtie \pi_D s$

2.15 Let r and s be relations as follows:

$$r \quad = \quad \begin{array}{cc} A & B \\ \hline 1 & 1 \\ 2 & 1 \\ 4 & 5 \end{array} \qquad s \quad = \quad \begin{array}{cc} B & C \\ \hline 1 & 1 \\ 1 & 3 \\ 6 & 7 \end{array}$$

Compute the relation for each of the following:

a. $\pi_B r$

b. $\sigma_{A>2} r$

c. $r \bowtie s$

d. $r \bowtie \rho_{B \leftarrow D} s$

e. $(\pi_B r) - (\pi_B s)$

2.16 Consider the following database scheme:

> *student(ID, Sname, Major, GPA) key: ID*
> *faculty(SSN, Fname, Dept, Salary) key: SSN, key: {Fname, Dept}*
> *is_teaching(SSN, CourseNum) key: CourseNum*
> *is_taking(ID, CourseNum) key: {ID, CourseNum}*

Using this scheme, write relational-algebra expressions for the following queries:

a. Find the names of faculty members in the math department.

b. Find the name and major for all students who are taking CS1.

c. Find the names of faculty members who are teaching some course and earn less than $50,000 a year.

d. Find the names of students who are taking a course being taught by Johnson in the CS department.

e. Find the names and ID#-SSN pairs for students and faculty members who have the same name.

f. Find the ID# and Course# for each student who is taking a course from a faculty member whose name is the same as the student's name.

g.* Find the names of students taking all the courses being taught by Johnson in the CS department.

2.17 Consider the following database scheme:

supplier(*Sname, Saddress*) *key*: *Sname*
item(*ItemNumber, ItemName, Color, Weight*) *key*: *ItemNumber*
shipment(*Sname, ItemNumber, Quantity, ShipDate*) *key*: {*Sname, ItemNumber*}

Using this scheme, write relational-algebra expressions for the following queries:

a. Find the names and numbers of all blue items.

b. Find the names and addresses of suppliers who have shipments in quantities greater than 500.

c. Find the names of suppliers who have shipments of items that weigh more than 50 kilograms.

d. Find the name and item number of shipments that have a quantity less than 200 or a weight greater than 20 kilograms.

e. List pairs of item numbers of items that have the same color. Do not list an item number with itself, and do not list a pair of item numbers in both orders.

f.* Find names of suppliers who supply all items.

g.* Find names of suppliers who supply all green items that weigh less than 50 kilograms.

2.18** *Relational division* ($\div$) can simplify some relational-algebra expressions. Let $r(R)$ and $s(S)$ be relations where S is a proper subset of R. Let R' be $R - S$. The expression $r \div s$ divides r into groups of tuples such that the $\pi_{R'}r$ values are all the same. Then, for each group, the $\pi_{R'}r$ value is in the result if the $\pi_{S}r$ values in each $\pi_{R'}r$ group include all the values in s. For example, let

$r =$	A	B		$s =$	B
	1	1			1
	1	2			2
	1	3			
	2	1			
	3	1			
	3	2			

Then

$r \div s =$	A
	1
	3

The groups of r are the first three tuples where $A = 1$, the fourth tuple where $A = 2$, and the last two tuples where $A = 3$. The 1 is in the result because the B values for $A = 1$, which are $\{1, 2, 3\}$, include all the values in s, which are $\{1, 2\}$. The 2 is not in the result because the B values for $A = 2$, which are $\{1\}$, do not include all the values in s. The 3 is in the result because the B values for $A = 3$, which are $\{1, 2\}$, include all the values in s.

a. Use relational division to answer (g) in Exercise 2.16.

b. Use relational division to answer (f) in Exercise 2.17.

c. Use relational division to answer (g) in Exercise 2.17.

2.19** Let A be an attribute in a relation scheme R, let $R' = R - A$, let r be a relation on R, and let $A \neq R$. What relationships exist between the number of tuples in the relations r, $\sigma_{A=a}r$, $\pi_{A}r$, $\pi_{R'}r$, and $\sigma_{A=a}\pi_{A}r$? Give your results in a partial ordering diagram.

2.20 Write SQL queries for (a) through (f) in Exercise 2.16.

2.21** Write an SQL query for (g) in Exercise 2.16. (We show in chapter 5 how relational calculus leads to a nice SQL solution for this query.)

2.22 Write SQL queries for (a) through (e) in Exercise 2.17.

2.23 Using the database scheme in Exercise 2.16, write SQL queries for the following:

    a. List all student information for the CS majors. The list should be in descending order by GPA, and in ascending order by name for those with the same GPA.

    b. Find the number of courses each faculty member is teaching. List the number along with the faculty member's name and SSN.

    c. Find the highest faculty salary in every department. Sort the department-name/max-salary pairs in descending order on this maximum salary.

    d. Find the departments in which the average salary is less than $40,000. Sort these departments in ascending order on average salary.

2.24 Using the database scheme in Exercise 2.17, write SQL queries for the following:

    a. List item number, item name, and weight of blue items. The list should be in ascending order on name and in descending order on weight for items with the same name.

    b. Find the average weight for each color of item.

    c. For each supplier, find the number of shipments. List the name and address of each supplier along with the number of shipments.

    d. Find the suppliers whose maximum shipment quantity is greater than 100 kilograms. Sort these suppliers in descending order on these maximum quantities.

Chapter 3

Physical and System Fundamentals

In this chapter, we provide implementation details for the database ADT, which we developed in the last chapter. We discuss storage structures—how the data is stored—as well as operational and support features—how the data is managed.

The purposes of this chapter are (1) to explain the basic idea of how a database management system works and (2) to provide the reader with the background necessary to estimate costs and specify concurrency for design. Sections 10.7 and 10.9 in Chapter 10 depend on a basic understanding of cost estimation, and Section 11.5 in Chapter 11 depends on a basic understanding of concurrency control. The necessary background for cost estimation is in Sections 3.1, 3.2, and 3.3, and for concurrency specification is in Section 3.4.

The following topics in this chapter are particularly important:

- The time cost of disk head movement, rotational latency, and block transfer.

- Indexing and hashing for secondary storage.

- The basic global strategy for query optimization.

- Transactions and their role in protecting a database.

The following questions should also be kept in mind:

- How do the speed differences among access to data in memory, in a disk-drive cache, under a current read head, or elsewhere on disk influence our strategies for implementing a database efficiently?

- Which applications are best suited to sequential and indexed-sequential files, to hashing techniques, and to B^+-tree indexes?

- Why do we need both query rewriting and choice of low-cost access methods to optimize queries?

- How can we protect a database from software and hardware failures and from misuse, both intentional and unintentional?

- How can we maximize concurrent use of a database and at the same time prevent concurrent processes from interfering with each other?

3.1   Secondary Storage

Secondary storage is necessary because a database usually is so large that we cannot store all the data in main memory. Even if we could, because main memory is volatile, we would still need nonvolatile secondary storage for the sake of persistence and crash recovery. For database systems, our primary interest is in the kind of secondary storage that consists of one or more hard disks. Other kinds, such as tapes or jukeboxes, do not provide us with the random access we need, do not match the performance speeds of hard disks, or are not widely available.

Because a disk is an electromechanical device, its access time is slow compared with main-memory access and with processor instruction-execution speeds. A hard-disk access takes about 12 milliseconds. A processor can execute 100 million instructions per second. Thus in the time it takes to access a disk we can execute 100,000,000*0.012 = 1,200,000 instructions! Successfully managing this speed difference is crucial to implementing a database system efficiently.

Figure 3.1 shows a schematic of a hard disk drive. Figure 3.1a shows a top view; Fig. 3.1b, a side view. A hard drive consists of several platters mounted on a central spindle. These platters rotate constantly at a high rate

---

Time Estimates for Disk Operations

We take time estimates for disk operations from the manufacturer's specification for a particular disk drive (Seagate's Barracuda 4LP Family, ST32171N). These representative times are intended to give readers a feel for the general characteristics of disk drives. Be aware that disk-drive characteristics can vary widely, however, and that they change over time. See current manufacturer specifications, available on the WorldWideWeb(e.g.,http://www.mm.mtu.edu:80/drives/seagate/scsi), for alternative characterizations.

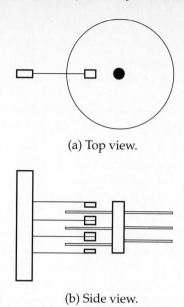

(a) Top view.

(b) Side view.

Figure 3.1   Schematic view of a hard disk drive.

of speed (e.g., 7200 rpm—revolutions per minute). Each platter has many concentric tracks (e.g., 5288). A track contains magnetically encoded data, organized into smaller units called blocks (e.g., 132 blocks of 512-bytes per track). As a reading head moves along a track, the head reads one or more blocks of data (often the entire track) and transfers the data to a buffer, normally on the disk drive itself. The transfer rate is about 12 megabytes per second (i.e., between 9 and 15 megabytes per second, depending on whether an inner track or outer track is being read). From a buffer on a disk drive, the information is then transferred into main-memory buffer areas over a high-speed link at about 20 megabytes per second.

As Fig. 3.1b shows, there are several reading heads. These heads move together as a unit; they all align over the same track on different platter surfaces. The tracks above and below one another form a conceptual cylinder. Together, these cylinders—one for each track—store all the information on the drive. A typical 5¼-inch hard drive can store up to about 8 or 9 gigabytes, and a 3½-inch hard drive can store up to about 4 gigabytes. For example, our sample disk drive has three 3½-inch platters, six heads, and 5288 cylinders that each hold 406,578 bytes of data, for a total capacity of 2.15 gigabytes.

A random access of a block of data on a disk requires a *seek* to move the reading heads to the right cylinder, a *rotational latency* to allow the beginning of the block to spin to the location of the head, and a *block transfer* to read the data in the block and store it into a main-memory buffer. Seek times require physical movement from one cylinder to another and thus vary depending on how far the head has to move (from about 0.8 milliseconds for a track-to-track seek to about 19 milliseconds for a seek across the entire surface of a disk). For making estimates, we often use the average seek time (e.g., about 8 milliseconds). Rotational latencies can vary; we may be lucky and be ready to read a block just as it comes under the head, or we may be unlucky and just miss the beginning of the block and have to wait for it to come around again. An average rotational latency is about half the time for one revolution (e.g., about 4 milliseconds for a disk spinning at 7200 rpm). The transfer rate for a block depends on the speed of rotation and on how densely the data is packed on a track. For our sample disk drive, at 12 megabytes per second for a disk drive-buffer transfer and at 20 megabytes per second for a main memory-buffer transfer, it takes (512 bytes / 12 megabytes/sec) + (512 bytes / 20 megabytes/sec) = 68.1 microseconds to transfer a block to main memory (assuming no delay for synchronizing with the operating system). Altogether, when we add the times for seek, rotational latency, and block transfer, it takes an average of about 12 milliseconds (8 milliseconds + 4 milliseconds + 68 negligible microseconds) to retrieve a block of data.

If the data is already in a buffer in main memory or on a disk drive, we say that the data is *cached*. When we request a block of data that is cached, it is not necessary to go all the way to the disk platter to retrieve it. If the block is cached in main memory, we can obtain it faster than if it is cached on a disk drive; if it is cached on a disk drive, we can obtain it faster (usually much faster) than if we must retrieve it from the platter of a disk. There are also processor caches, which are faster than main-memory caches, but we are not normally concerned with these caches. We must also realize that we cannot just build huge main-memory caches and discard disk storage— the cost per unit of storage of a main-memory device far exceeds the cost for the same unit of storage for a disk drive.

Knowing the characteristics of a disk drive and understanding how a disk drive works provide us with some guidelines for designing efficient data storage schemes. In summary, a database developer should be aware of the following places where data can be located, listed from the most quickly to the least quickly obtainable:

1. Data in main memory (nanosecond speeds);
2. Data in a disk-drive cache or under a current read head (microsecond speeds); and
3. Data elsewhere on a disk (millisecond speeds).

3.2 File Organization

We can organize records on disk in many ways. The best organization for a file strongly depends on how we wish to use it. Do we want to access the entire file, or only one record in the file, or several selected records? If data is in multiple files, must we join the records together to obtain the desired relationships? How often do we join the files compared with how often we access them without joining? Answering these questions for a single application is complex, and even more so when we must balance the requirements of several applications simultaneously. Because it is usually impossible to find a single organization that is best for all applications, we must settle for a reasonable balance among the competing demands—a balance that is itself difficult to find. We simply do the best we can and make adjustments as necessary.

3.2.1 Sequential Files

One straightforward way to organize a file on disk is sequentially. In a sequential file, we place records in a block one after another until there is no room for another complete record in that block. We then fill the next available block—often the one that comes physically next on the disk, but sometimes one in another location, with a physical pointer linking the sequential blocks. We then fill the next available block, and so on until all the records have been placed in logically consecutive blocks. If we wish to access all the records, one after another, this is a highly efficient file organization.

Suppose, however, that we wish to find only one record. We may have to search the entire file, reading one block at a time to find the record. On the average, we would have to read in half the blocks of the file. If we are searching for a record with a given primary key value and if the sequential file is physically sequential with no pointers and is sorted on the primary key, we can reduce the time by using a binary search on the blocks of a file. If we have an index on the primary key, we can do the search even faster. Furthermore, indexes can also speed up the search for a record based on values other than the primary key.

An *index* is an auxiliary structure for a file that consists of an ordered sequence of value-pointer pairs, or, more generally, an ordered sequence of value-tuple/pointer-list pairs. A value-pointer pair, for example, might be a customer-ID value and a disk-address pointer that points to the block that includes the customer-ID value. A sequence of these pairs ordered by customer ID would be an index. More generally, the value can be a value-tuple because we may be searching on a composite key such as {*Name*, *Address*} or on several attribute values such as *Customer ID* and *Date* to find an order. Since a value-tuple is also a value, we need not and do not distinguish these two cases in our discussion. The pointer part is more generally a pointer list because there may be more than one record in more than one block that contains the value of interest. As a specific example, we could have an index on *Customer ID* for our *Order* relation, which we illustrated in Fig. 2.8 in the last chapter. This would help us quickly find all orders placed by a customer even though these orders may be in several different blocks.

The general idea of an index is simple, but there are a number of factors to consider. One is whether the index itself is stored on disk or in main memory. If the index is on disk, we must consider the number of disk accesses required to read it into main memory. The number of disk accesses depends on the size of the index. If it is especially large, we may organize it as a two- or three-level, or in general as an *n*-level, index tree so that we need not read all the blocks of the index to find the index value we are seeking. Pointers in the upper-level blocks of an index tree point to index blocks; pointers in the leaf-level blocks, to file blocks.

When the values in the index pairs are primary keys, we call an index a *primary-key index* or sometimes just a *primary index*. When the values are not primary keys, we call an index a *secondary-key index* or often just a *secondary index*. (Secondary keys are not keys in the sense that they uniquely identify a tuple, but instead are merely keys used to access records.) If the file is sorted, it is almost always sorted on its primary key. Indeed, if it is sorted on any other key, for all intents and purposes we may as well consider it to be the primary key. Files sorted on a nonkey value are rare. If a file is sorted on a key, the index can be *sparse*, which means that it has a value-pointer pair for only one record in each block of the file. An index that has pointers for every record is called a *dense index*.

A sequential file sorted on its primary key, along with a sparse index on the primary key, is called an *indexed sequential file*. Figure 3.2 provides an example of an indexed sequential file organization for our *Customer* relation. The index holds the *CustomerID* value of the first record in each block. We can use the index to find a record with a given customer-ID—say *b12*—as follows. First, we do a binary search on the index to find that *b12* lies between *a92* and *b22*. The record, if it exists, must therefore be in the second block. Hence, we make one access to the disk to retrieve the second block and then do a binary search on the records of the second block to retrieve the record. If we fail to find the record, we need not look elsewhere, and we can report that it does not exist.

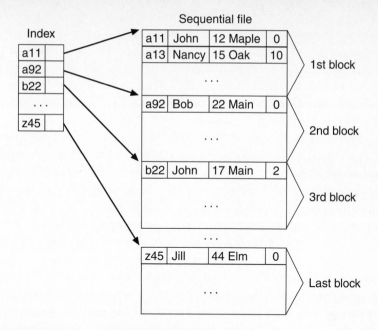

Figure 3.2   An indexed sequential file.

Having an index on a file does not preclude us from having another index on the same file. We could, for example, also have an index on discount values for the file in Fig. 3.2. This index would be a secondary index and necessarily would be dense. A value/pointer-list pair in this index would consist of one of the discount values v and a list of pointers to blocks containing any record with a v discount value. It is possible that every pointer list in this index could point to every block in the file. In this case, the index is not very useful. A secondary index on *Address* is also possible, and, unlike the index for discount values, would likely have a small number of pointers in its pointer list. In general, we can index every attribute and every combination of attributes, but it is not always wise to do so.

If we only wish to retrieve records, sequential files with indexes serve quite well. Updates, however, lead to several problems and potential pitfalls, which are often severe enough to cause us to use different file organizations.

Suppose we wish to delete a record. Although we are generally interested in reclaiming unused space, we should not reclaim it by going through all blocks of a file and moving each record up by one. This procedure is slow not only because it accesses all blocks beyond the deletion, but also because it requires changing some (possibly all) pointers in all indexes on the file. A record is said to be *pinned* to a block if there is a pointer to the block for the record. Moving a pinned record out of a block requires updating all pointers that reference the record. Thus, instead of reclaiming space in this way, we mark the record deleted, usually by setting a delete bit specifically put aside for this purpose.

Insertions are even more problematic than deletions. Suppose we wish to insert a record into an indexed sequential file. We can use the index to find the block in which we should place the record. If we are lucky, there will be enough space for the record, either because at least one record has its delete bit set, or because we initially underfilled the blocks anticipating that we would later need the space. Even if the space is not in exactly the right place, we can reorder the records in a block so that the sort order is retained.

Sometimes, however, we will not be lucky, and there will be no space. In this case, we can use an *overflow bucket*, which consists of one or more blocks that contain all the overflow records of the indexed sequential file. Since we obtain these blocks for the overflow bucket as needed, we have no guarantee that they will be physically next to each other, and it is best to assume that they are scattered on disk. We can keep the records within the regular blocks of an indexed sequential file sorted by always bumping the last record in a block to the overflow bucket. Records in the overflow bucket, however, are not sorted. Attempting to keep them sorted could be time consuming because the overflow bucket may be several blocks long and randomly scattered on disk. When there is an overflow bucket, we might not find a record in the regular block in which it should be found. In this case, we search the overflow bucket sequentially, perhaps causing as many disk accesses as blocks in the bucket.

An overflow bucket can become long with respect to the size of an indexed sequential file. The longer an overflow bucket becomes, the more an indexed sequential file degenerates into an unordered file. Periodic reorganization, which rebuilds the indexed sequential file from scratch, may be necessary to keep the file efficient. This can be expensive because it requires not only that all the data be reorganized, but also that the primary index and any secondary indexes also be reorganized. For some applications, there may be times when the database is not in use; file reorganization can occur then. For other applications, however, it may be difficult, if not impossible, to find convenient times to reorganize the data.

Before discussing some ways to alleviate the problems with indexed sequential files, we present one more idea. Record modification at first glance might not seem like much of a problem. Indeed, it is not a problem if the records are fixed in length, because then we can obtain the block that contains the record, change the field value, and rewrite the block. Since no space is added or deleted for fixed-length records, this procedure always works.

Variable-length records can be useful in an application in which similar objects relate to a nonuniform set of data. For example, a representation of persons in an application may have many attributes in common such as name, address, and identification number, but the representation may also have attributes such as college degrees, kinds of job skills, and hobbies that apply variously to different persons. An even more common use of variable-length records is for objects that each have an unspecified number of repeating groups of attribute values. In the application discussed in Chapter 2, for example, we might make a single record that would include all the information for an order. Instead of storing the information for *Order*, *Item*, and *OrderInfo* in Fig. 2.8 in three separate files, we might have one file, as Fig. 3.3 shows.

In Fig. 3.3, each order includes a set of nested tuples that represent the items ordered. For this organization, if we are interested in looking up a particular order, all the information resides together on disk. If we want the same information but store it in three different files, we would have to look up the information in each file and join it. If, on the other hand, we want to update an order by adding another item, we would likely be unable to add the information easily for either organization.

In general, we store variable-length records by reserving enough space to accommodate the variable part of any variable-length record of interest, by chaining a variable number of fixed-length components together, or by

Order	(*OrderNr*	*CustomerID*	*Date*	(*Nr*	*ItemNr*	*Description*)*)
	345	*a*11	27 *Feb*	1	11	*ball*
				1	12	*book*
	350	*b*22	27 *Feb*	1	12	*book*
	375	*b*22	2 *Mar*	2	85	*game*
				2	92	*scooter*

Figure 3.3 A nested relation with variable-length records.

combining of these two techniques. In a combination technique, for our *Order* example in Fig. 3.3, we could reserve space for n items, where n is reasonably small but is large enough to hold the number of items expected for most orders. The rest of the items could be placed sequentially at the end of an overflow bucket, with a pointer from the initial record to the record in the overflow bucket where the list begins. We would thus be able to retrieve most orders with one disk access, but for some we would need a second disk access, and possibly more if the list were to span more than one overflow block.

3.2.2 Hashing

If we wish to find a single record given its primary key value, a good hashing technique provides the fastest way to retrieve it. Usually, only one disk access is necessary. Moreover, there is no auxiliary structure such as an index, and thus no need to worry about whether the auxiliary structure is in memory or on disk and how much time it takes to access the structure. Hashing also solves the problem of record insertion and deletion.

Closed static hashing, which we discuss here, is a standard hashing technique that can be used for database systems. (Open hashing and dynamic hashing are more common, but beyond the scope of the introductory material here.) For closed static hashing we reserve a fixed amount of space sufficient to hold at least as many records as we anticipate being in the file at any one time. We require that the file consists of fixed-length records, with a designated primary key. For simplicity, we ignore blocks and block boundaries, but it is not difficult to convert record offsets within the fixed space to block addresses.

Let N be the maximum number of records that fit in the reserved space. Let K be the set of possible key values. A hash function h maps K to $\{0 \ldots N-1\}$ (usually, $|K| \gg N$). If the fixed-length records each have b bytes, then to insert a record r whose primary key value is k, we compute $h(k)$ and try to place r at location $bh(k)$ in the file. If no other record is already at location $bh(k)$, we place r at this location. Otherwise, we search forward through the file, wrapping around to the beginning if necessary, until we find the next available record location, where we insert r. To retrieve a record r, which is known to be in the file and whose primary key value is k, we look first in location $bh(k)$. If r is not there, we search forward through the file (wrapping around, if necessary) until we find it. To delete a record r, which is known to be in the file, we locate it and then mark it deleted.

In a hash file, every record location either is occupied by a record or is available because it contains a deleted record or has never held a record. We insert records in any available location, as just described. If we wish to locate a record for a given primary key value k, however, and if we are not sure whether a record for k is in the file, we distinguish between locations with deleted records and locations that have never held a record. If in our forward search we encounter a location that has never held a record, we can stop, certain that the record is not in the file.

Several factors determine how well closed static hashing works. Our chosen hash function h should distribute the records uniformly over the space. If the hash function is perfect, so that there are never any collisions, we can always store and retrieve a record with at most one disk access. It is highly unlikely, however, that we can find a perfect hashing function. Usually the number of key values far exceeds the maximum number of records N, and many key values map to each value between 0 and $N - 1$. Nevertheless, if we choose a good hash function that randomly and uniformly distributes the set of possible key values over $\{0 \ldots N - 1\}$, we can minimize the number of collisions.

Closed static hashing also depends on whether we can find enough contiguous available space initially and on how full we fill the space. If we cannot find enough contiguous space, we should use open hashing, which lets us use disk blocks that are not necessarily contiguous. If we completely fill the space, closed static hashing breaks down. Although we could provide an overflow bucket, this would cause a major degradation in performance. If we are likely to run into this problem because we cannot estimate the expected maximum number of resident records accurately, we should use dynamic hashing, which allows us to change dynamically how much space we use.

The simple forward search described here is not always the best way to resolve collisions. It works well, however, for database systems whose files are in secondary storage. This is because we always read a block of data, not just a single record. If the hash function is good and the fill factor is not too high, there is an excellent chance that the record will be in the block accessed even when there is a collision. When this happens, there is still only one disk access. Furthermore, if the record is beyond the end of the block, it is most likely in the physically next block on disk. Empirical studies have shown that if a hash function is well chosen and the fill factor is reasonable (around 75%), we can expect to retrieve a randomly chosen record with one disk access.

It is hard to beat hashing if we want to store and retrieve single records based only on their primary key. Unfortunately, application requirements are not usually so simple. Queries that require accessing a file by nonkey attribute values or by a range of values are not well suited to hashing. If we try to hash on a nonkey attribute, every record with the same value for the attribute hashes to the same location, which can cause the collision rate to skyrocket. For range queries, such as a query that requires us to find all the orders between January 1 and March 31, we would have to hash on every value in the range, even if there is no record with the date. This could drive us through nearly every block in the file multiple times. It would be far better just to search the entire hash file directly from beginning to end.

In addition to individual queries that are not well suited to hashing, we often need to pose several different queries on the same file. This may cause us to access a file in many different ways, by many different attribute values, or by many different combinations of attribute values. Here again, hashing is not helpful, because we can only hash a file in one way.

For all these situations, indexing is a better choice. We can use secondary indexes for nonkey attributes. We can use a subtree in an index tree, rather than just a path in an index tree, to handle range queries, and we can have multiple indexes on a file to satisfy different access needs. As discussed earlier, however, indexed sequential files are problematic, especially for highly dynamic files. We therefore need a better way to index; a possible approach is discussed next.

3.2.3 B⁺-tree Indexes

B-trees are n-way, balanced trees whose nonroot nodes are always at least half full. Unlike indexed sequential files, B-trees maintain good retrieval, insertion, and deletion times indefinitely and therefore never require reorganization. For files with frequent insertions and deletions, these advantages easily compensate for the overhead incurred by insertion and deletion operations plus the overhead of added space.

A number of B-tree variations exist; here we present only the most common variation, a B⁺-tree index for single-attribute keys over a file of unordered data records.

Figure 3.4 provides an example of a B⁺-tree index on *ItemNr* for our sample *Item* file. To keep the example small, we let n, the number of pointers per node in the index, be 4 and the number of data records in a block of the data file be 5. (Since B⁺-tree nodes are usually disk blocks, a more typical value for n would be 20 to 100 or so, and more than 5 item records would likely fit in a typical block.) Observe that in Fig. 3.4 the tree is balanced—every path from root to leaf has length 2. Observe also that each

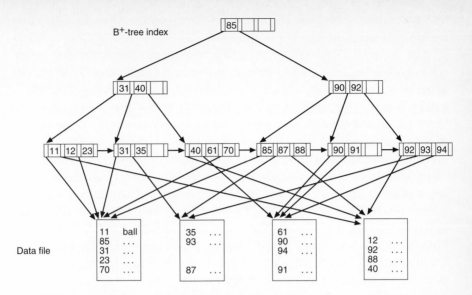

Figure 3.4 A B+-tree index and data file.

node in the tree has $n = 4$ pointers and $n - 1 = 3$ key values. For leaf nodes, we define "half full" in terms of values and require that each leaf node have at least $\lceil (n - 1)/2 \rceil$ values—every leaf node in Fig. 3.4 has two or three values. For nonleaf nodes we define "half full" in terms of pointers and require that each nonleaf node have at least $\lceil n/2 \rceil$ pointers—every nonleaf node in Fig. 3.4 has two or more pointers. The root node can be an exception and have fewer than $\lceil n/2 \rceil$ pointers. When $n = 4$, of course, this is not possible, but if n were 5, we could still have only one key value and 2 ($< \lceil 5/2 \rceil$) pointers in the root.

Although the leaf nodes and nonleaf nodes in a B+-tree index look similar, they are not the same. The leaf nodes are a dense index for the data file, while the nonleaf nodes are a sparse index for the key values in the leaf nodes. The leaf nodes contain all the key values, sorted in ascending order. The pointer preceding a key value k in a leaf node points to the block where the record whose key is k resides. The last pointer in each node points to the next leaf node. Even though the records in the data file are unordered, this organization lets us access the entire file in ascending order on the key by traversing the leaf nodes in order and following the record pointers to the blocks where each record resides. Using a slight variation, we could speed up the sequential search within a block by maintaining the records in sorted order within the block or by maintaining a block-pointer and offset rather than just a block pointer in the dense index. The trade-offs here are minimal; whether they are worthwhile depends on the kinds of access that are typical for a particular application.

The nonleaf nodes also contain key values sorted in ascending order, but not all key values. A key value k in a nonleaf node is the smallest key value in the subtree whose root is pointed to by the pointer succeeding k. In Fig. 3.4, for example, 85 is the key value in the root. Its succeeding pointer points to the subtree with 90 and 92 as its key values. Lower down in this subtree, we see the key value 85, which is the smallest key value in the entire subtree rooted at the node with 90 and 92 as its key values. The succeeding pointer of 90 points to the node (degenerate subtree) whose smallest key value is 90, and the succeeding pointer of 92 points to the node whose smallest key value is 92. The initial pointer of each nonleaf node points to the subtree whose values are all less than the first key value. Thus, for every key value k in a nonleaf node, we can find all the key values less than k by looking in the left subtree of k and all the key values greater than or equal to k by looking in the right subtree of k.

We search for a record using a B^+-tree index in a straightforward way. Suppose, for example, that we wish to find the record whose *ItemNr* value is 91. Starting at the root, we see that $91 \geq 85$. We thus follow the right pointer to the right subtree, whose key values are 90 and 92. Since 91 falls between 90 and 92, we follow the pointer between 90 and 92 to find the leaf node containing 91. We then follow the left pointer of 91 to the block containing the record for which we are searching, read the block from disk, and search it sequentially until we find the record whose key value is 91. Note that if we are searching for a record that does not exist, such as for the record whose item number is 7, we can know for sure that it does not exist when we arrive at the leaf node that should contain 7.

If the index is itself on disk, each node is (usually) in a separate disk block. Since to locate a record, we have to search at most only one path in the B^+-tree, we have to access at most only $\log_{\lceil n/2 \rceil} N$ n-way B^+-tree disk blocks, where N is the number of key values in the file. If we have $n = 100$, for example, we could index at least 5000 records and up to 1,000,000 records with a 3-level B^+. Often we keep the root or the upper two levels of a B^+-tree in main memory. This, of course, can further reduce the time to search a B^+-tree index and can make access times for B^+-tree comparable to access times for hashing.

Insertion and deletion algorithms for B^+-tree indexes are interesting because we must maintain the balance in the B^+-tree. Some insertions and deletions are straightforward. If a leaf node includes space for the key value of a record to be inserted, basically we just drop the value in place in the node and put the record anywhere there is space in the data file or, if necessary, in a new block of the data file. For example, if we insert a record for a new item whose item number is 37 in the B^+-tree organization in Fig. 3.4, we see that the 37 and a pointer can go in the open space in the 31-35 node, and that the record could go in the second block of the data file. If the key value is 33, we do almost the same, except that we move the 35 and its pointer to the open space and insert the 33 between the 31 and 35. If the key value must be the first value in a leaf node, we insert it after moving all the others down one, and recursively propagate its value up the tree as far as is necessary. Inserting 29, for example, in the 31-35 node changes the 31 in the 31-40 node to 29 also.

Deletion is much the same, so long as there are sufficient key values left in the leaf node to maintain the requirement that the node be at least half full. Suppose we delete the record with key value 61, for example. We first locate the record in the data file and mark it deleted. (By the way, we also update our space-management information to reflect the fact that there is now more space in the data block from which the 61 record was deleted.) We then move the 70 and its pointer left one slot to the space previously occupied by 61. (It should also be clear that we need to maintain some information in each node that states how many key values are actually stored there. Here, for example, we would reduce the count from 3 to 2, so that we know that any values in spaces beyond the count are garbage.)

Insertion and deletion are far more complex when we need to insert into an already full node or delete from a node that is just half full. Since a complete discussion of these ideas is beyond our purpose here, we provide only a basic explanation and some examples. One important note about both insertion and deletion is that the worst-case time complexity for these operations is proportional to $\log_{\lceil n/2 \rceil} N$, where N is the number of key values in the file, and n is the number of pointers in a node. This is because we travel down at most once to the one leaf where the insertion or deletion is to take place, and we travel up along the same path at most once, making adjustments along the way.

The basic idea for insertion into a full node is to split it into two nodes, each half full, and to add a new key value into the parent. Of course, if the parent is also full, we need to split it and add a new key into its parent, and so on. If we need to insert into a full root, we split it and create a new root. In this special case, we also increase the height of the B^+-tree. Figure 3.5 shows what happens to the B^+-tree in Fig. 3.4 when we insert 15 (Fig. 3.5a) and then 47 (Fig. 3.5b). Promoting key values from leaf nodes and from nonleaf nodes is different. When we promote a value from a leaf node, we leave a copy in the leaf, but when we promote a value from a nonleaf node, we do not leave a copy in the nonleaf node. In Fig. 3.5a, we see that

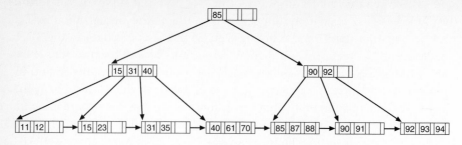

(a) Insertion of 15 into the B$^+$-tree in Fig. 3.4.

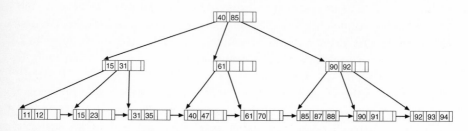

(b) Insertion of 47 into the B$^+$-tree in Fig. 3.5a.

Figure 3.5 B$^+$-tree insertions.

the 15, which was promoted from a leaf node, was copied into the proper nonleaf node, whereas the 40, which was promoted from a nonleaf node in Fig. 3.5b, was moved to the root. Note, by the way, that the nonleaf node containing only 61 is half full, as required, because it has $\lceil n/2 \rceil$ pointers (= 2 for our example where $n = 4$).

The basic idea for deletion from a node that would become less than half full by a simple deletion is to combine siblings and, if necessary, redistribute values. Figure 3.6 shows what happens to the B$^+$-tree in Fig. 3.5b when we delete 23 (Fig. 3.6a) and then 47 (Fig. 3.6b). A simple deletion of 23 leaves the 15-23 leaf node with only one value, too few for a leaf node. Since either sibling has sufficient space, we choose one, the left sibling here, and move the 15 to the 11-12 node and discard the old 15-23 node. This, of course, requires adjusting the parent of the discarded node. Since there no longer is a node with 15 as its first element, we discard the 15 and its pointer and shift everything else in the node one place to the left. The result is Fig. 3.6a. Continuing, we now delete 47, causing the 40-47 node to have too few values. Since we can combine with the sibling on the

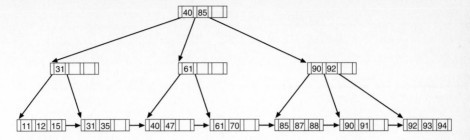

(a) Deletion of 23 from the B⁺-tree in Fig. 3.5b.

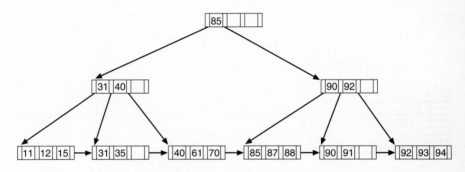

(b) Deletion of 47 from the B⁺-tree in Fig. 3.6a.

Figure 3.6   B⁺-tree deletions.

right, we do. Now, however, the 61 is no longer the first value of any node. We therefore delete the 61 in the parent node, causing this node to have too few values. We therefore try to combine the parent node with too few values with a sibling, both of which have sufficient space. Combining with the left sibling causes the 40 to be deleted from the root and placed in the combined node. After making the necessary adjustments to the root, we end up with the B⁺-tree in Fig. 3.6b.

To show that redistribution of values is sometimes necessary, consider deleting 90 from the B⁺-tree in Fig. 3.6b. Since neither node to the left or right of the 90-91 node has space for the remaining 91 value, we cannot combine nodes. Instead, we move some of the values from either sibling into the empty space in the 90-91 node. In particular, we move the 88 into the node and make the necessary adjustments to the parent. Figure 3.7 shows the result.

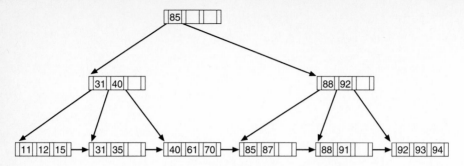

Figure 3.7 Deletion of 90 from the B⁺-tree in Fig. 3.6b, causing redistribution.

3.3 Query Optimization

Ideally, every access we make to the database should be optimized fully. Because it is difficult to check whether we have fully optimized any access, however, we use optimization heuristics and proceed as best we can. Although our "optimization" is guided only heuristically and thus not always really optimized, and although we "optimize" updates as well as queries, nevertheless historically the process has been called "query optimization," and probably always will be.

Query optimization involves two basic ideas: query rewriting and cost estimation. As its name suggests, query rewriting involves rewriting a query as an equivalent, but more efficient, query. Cost estimation, on the other hand, involves comparing the cost—usually the estimated number of disk accesses—of two or more ways to do the query. The least costly way is chosen and executed. Usually both query rewriting and cost estimation are performed.

To guide our discussion, let us consider a motivating example. Suppose we have a simple database with two relations, r with attributes A and B, and s with attributes C and D. For our example, we assume that all data values are integers. We further assume that there are no keys for either r or s, or equivalently that AB is the key for r and CD is the key for s. Now, suppose we wish to execute the query

$$\pi_A \sigma_{B=C \,\wedge\, D=2}(r \bowtie s)$$

As we shall see, we can rewrite this query equivalently as

$$\pi_A \sigma_{B=C}(r \bowtie \pi_C \sigma_{D=2} s)$$

Let us compare the cost of executing these two queries under the following assumptions. We assume that both r and s have 10,000 tuples and that for both r and s we can place 100 tuples in a block. For both r and s, we also assume that blocks constituting the files are stored randomly on disk, linked together by pointers, and that the records in neither file are sorted. We further assume that there is some working space in main memory equivalent to 10 blocks, enough to hold 1000 tuples or 2000 integer values.

For both queries, we use the same basic algorithm. We read in one block of r and then as much of what we need from s as possible to fill the remaining working space. We then find the tuples in r whose B value is equal to some C in memory, but only for C values whose associated D value is 2. We then output the A values of these tuples in r. Continuing, we obtain more of s and do the same until we have exhausted it. We then read the next block of r and begin again, continuing until we have processed every block of r.

Under the assumptions we have made, this basic algorithm turns out quite different in its specific application to our two queries. For

$$\pi_A \sigma_{B=C \,\wedge\, D=2}(r \bowtie s)$$

the algorithm becomes

> For each block of r -- this r block occupies 1 of the 10 available
> > For each 9-block segment of s
> > > Output the A value of each r-tuple whose
> > > > B value is equal to a C value of some s-tuple
> > > > whose D value is 2.

Whereas, for

$$\pi_A \sigma_{B=C}(r \bowtie \pi_C \sigma_{D=2} s)$$

the algorithm becomes

> For each block of r -- this takes 200 of the 2000 available integer slots
> > For each 1800 distinct C values in s in a tuple
> > > whose D value is 2
> > Output the A value of each r-tuple whose B value is
> > > equal to one of these C values.

We can now calculate the number of disk accesses for these two specific algorithms and compare the results. Under our assumptions both r and s have $10,000/100 = 100$ blocks. Our first algorithm reads each block of r once and each block of s once for each block of r or 100 times. This yields $100 + 100*100 = 10,100$ disk accesses. To compute the number of disk accesses for the second algorithm, we need some information about the number of distinct C values in s. If there are fewer than 1800, then we read each block of r once and each block of s once, for a total of $100 + 100 = 200$ disk accesses. There cannot, of course, be more than 10,000 distinct C values since there are only 10,000 tuples in s. Thus in the worst case, we must read each block of $s \lceil 10,000/1,800 \rceil = 6$ times, which yields $100 + 6*100 = 700$ disk accesses. When compared with 10,100 disk accesses, even 700 disk accesses is very few, only about 7% of the cost.

3.3.1 Query Rewriting

Doing query rewriting well requires a strategy. Our motivating example indicates that a good strategy is to make intermediate results as small as possible. This allows us to maximize the use of main-memory space and minimize the number of disk blocks required when we must store intermediate results on disk. Other strategies of interest include removing unnecessary operations and reusing intermediate results of common subexpressions, but here we consider only size reduction of intermediate results.

The queries we rewrite are relational-algebra queries, the natural choice because even though relational algebra is not a commercial query language, the first step in executing any query is to convert it into an intermediate form equivalent to relational algebra. It is this intermediate form that we optimize by rewriting. Our interest therefore is in rewriting relational-algebra expressions.

To carry out our strategy of making intermediate results small, we apply projections and selections as early as possible. Projections reduce the number of columns in a relation, and selections reduce the number of rows. Other strategies, such as reordering join sequences to reduce join size, are also possible, but here we restrict our discussion to an early application of projections and selections.

Table 3.1 shows several equivalences. In the rules, e, e_1, and e_2 stand for any valid relational-algebra expression, and f, f_1, f_2, and f_3 stand for any valid Boolean function.

Before applying these rules, we should first be sure that they are correct. Here we explain briefly why each rule holds, but we leave the proofs for the exercises.

		Table 3.1	
Rule	Expression	Equivalent Expression	Condition or Comment
1.	$\pi_X(e)$	e	$scheme(e) = X$
2.	$\pi_X(\sigma_f(e))$	$\pi_X(\sigma_f(\pi_{XY}(e)))$	f mentions the attributes in Y
3.	$\sigma_f((e_1) \bowtie (e_2))$	$\sigma_{f_1}(\sigma_{f_2}(e_1) \bowtie \sigma_{f_3}(e_2))$	$f = f_1 \wedge f_2 \wedge f_3$ f_1 pertains to both e_1 and e_2 f_2 pertains only to e_1 f_3 pertains only to e_2
4.	$\pi_X((e_1) \bowtie (e_2))$	$\pi_X(\pi_{X_1Y}(e_1) \bowtie \pi_{X_2Y}(e_2))$	$X_1 = X \cap scheme(e_1)$ $X_2 = X \cap scheme(e_2)$ $Y = (scheme(e_1) \cap$ $\qquad scheme(e_2)) - X$
5.	$\pi_X(\pi_Y(e))$	$\pi_X(e)$	
6.	$\sigma_{f_1}(\sigma_{f_2}(e))$	$\sigma_{f_1 \wedge f_2}(e)$	
7.	$r_1 \bowtie r_2$	$r_2 \bowtie r_1$	
8.	$(r_1 \bowtie r_2) \bowtie r_3$	$r_1 \bowtie (r_2 \bowtie r_3)$	
9.	$r \bowtie r$	r	

Rule 1. When the set of attributes X in a projection is the same as the set of attributes in the resulting scheme of e, which we denote by $scheme(e)$, there is no need to do the projection.

Rule 2. We can discard (project out) columns of e before selecting and projecting so long as we keep the attributes we need for the selection and projection.

Rule 3. We can distribute selections of a conjunctive Boolean function over a join so long as we make sure that the conjuncts we distribute pertain only to one or the other of the two expressions being joined. A Boolean conjunct pertains to an expression e if its attributes are all included in e. Note that any of the conjuncts f_1, f_2, or f_3 can be absent. Thus, for example, $\sigma_f((e_1) \bowtie (e_2)) = (\sigma_{f_2}(e_1)) \bowtie (\sigma_{f_3}(e_2)))$ and $\sigma_f((e_1) \bowtie (e_2)) = \sigma_{f_1}((e_1) \bowtie (\sigma_{f_3}(e_2)))$, among others, are also possible variations of this rule.

Rule 4. We can distribute projections over a join so long as we make sure that the union of the projection attributes is equal to the original set of attributes, that the intersection of the projection attributes is the same as the intersection of the schemes for the two expressions being joined, and that the projection attributes are in the schemes of their respective expressions.

Rule 5. Selecting tuples by the condition f_1 and then by the condition f_2 is the same as selecting tuples by the conjunction of the conditions f_1 and f_2.

Rule 6. Projecting the result of an expression e onto a set of attributes Y and then onto a set of attributes X is the same as projecting the result of e onto X. Since we assume that the expressions are syntactically correct, we know that $Y \subseteq scheme(e)$ and $X \subseteq Y$.

Rule 7. Join is commutative.

Rule 8. Join is associative.

Rule 9. Join is idempotent.

Rules 3 and 4 are the main rules of interest for our rewriting strategy because they distribute selections and projections over joins, which means that we make relations small before we do joins. The other rules help set up these distributions or make needed simplifications. We illustrate the application of our heuristic strategy for query rewriting by showing that this strategy together with the rules in Table 3.1, transforms the first query in the preceding motivating example into the second query. Recall that $r(AB)$ and $s(CD)$ and that our given query is

$$\pi_A \sigma_{B=C \,\wedge\, D=2}(r \bowtie s)$$

We rewrite this as an efficient query:

$\pi_A(\sigma_{B=C \,\wedge\, D=2}(r \bowtie s))$	given—parentheses added
$\pi_A(\sigma_{B=C}(r \bowtie \sigma_{D=2}s))$	Rule 3
$\pi_A(\sigma_{B=C}(\pi_{ABC}(r \bowtie \sigma_{D=2}s)))$	Rule 2
$\pi_A(\sigma_{B=C}(\pi_{AB}r \bowtie \pi_C\sigma_{D=2}s))$	Rule 4
$\pi_A(\sigma_{B=C}(\pi_{AB}r \bowtie \pi_C\sigma_{D=2}\pi_{CD}s))$	Rule 2
$\pi_A(\sigma_{B=C}(r \bowtie \pi_C\sigma_{D=2}s))$	Rule 1 (twice)
$\pi_A\sigma_{B=C}(r \bowtie \pi_C\sigma_{D=2}s)$	superfluous parentheses removed

3.3.2 Cost Estimation

Our motivating example showed some calculations for estimating the number of disk accesses required to execute a query according to some particular algorithms and assumptions. There are often many ways to execute a query; among these alternatives, we would like to choose the best.

Since an exact time measurement for executing a query with a particular algorithm is usually impossible to obtain, we use heuristics to estimate the execution time. Disk access almost always dominates the time, usually by an order of magnitude or more. Hence we estimate the time by estimating the number of disk accesses. Obtaining the exact number of disk accesses is difficult because queries do not run in isolation and because the system often tries to be helpful by caching disk blocks for us in case we need them again. Moreover, we seldom know the exact statistical characteristics of a file, such as the distribution of its nonkey attributes and the layout of its records in underfilled and overflow blocks.

Considering all these factors, we might seem to have little chance of obtaining good estimates. Indeed, probably we should not try to use our calculations to choose between two methods whose estimated number of disk accesses is nearly the same. An arbitrary choice in this case may be as good as any. When the estimated number of accesses differs by an order of magnitude, however, we can definitely make a good choice. We therefore proceed to obtain the best estimates we can and use them to choose the "best" alternative.

To see some of the possibilities, let us consider several alternatives for our motivating example, $\pi_A \sigma_{B=C}(r \bowtie \pi_C \sigma_{D=2} s)$. Suppose that we have B$^+$-tree indexes in memory on B in r and on C and D in s. Suppose further that the pointers in these indexes are record pointers (block/offset pointers). We can proceed as follows.

```
Use the index on D to get a list L₁ of s records with D = 2.
Traverse the leaf nodes of the B and C indexes (which are sorted)
      for each pair of identical record pointers (one from the
            B index and the other from the C index)
          if this record pointer p is also in the list L₁
              place the record pointer p on a list L₂
Sort the block/offset pointers in L₂ by block yielding a
            list L₃ of blocks
For each block in list L₃
      retrieve the block
      for each record offset for the block
          retrieve the A value of the record and print it
```

In this algorithm, observe that we access the disk only to obtain blocks that appear on list L_3. This list may be empty, in which case we have no disk access. If every block of r appears on the list L_3, we have 100 disk accesses since r has (10,000 records)/(100 records per block) = 100 blocks. If we can estimate the average—say we know that about 10% of the records of r are likely to join with the records of s that have a D value of 2, and that these records are likely to appear randomly in about 10% of the blocks of r, so that about 10 blocks of r would be accessed—then we can estimate that there will be 10 disk accesses. We can see that the 0–100, with an expected average of 10 here, beats the estimated 200–700 disk accesses for the best preceding algorithm.

As we noted, however, we are assuming that the B$^+$-tree indexes are in memory. They take space. Would we be better off to discard the indexes and use the space? The answer is no, because the best preceding algorithm requires a minimum of at least 200 accesses, which is still worse than 100, the worst case for using the indexes, and because we are likely to be able to read the indexes into memory with far less than 200–100 disk accesses.

Next suppose that we do not have the indexes, but that we do have the space for them. Should we create them on the fly, just to execute this query? It is easy to estimate the number of disk accesses required to build the indexes, because we simply have to read in every block of both files. Since we are assuming that the blocks are scattered randomly on disk, 100 disk accesses are required to create the index on B for r, and 100 disk accesses are required to create both the index on C and the index on D for s. Thus the total number of disk accesses for executing the query in this way is between 200 and 300, with 210 being the expected number when we assume that about 10% of the records of r are likely to join with the records of s that have a D value of 2. Since with this extra space we are likely to be able to run the initial algorithm for the optimized expression in about 200 (possibly 300) disk accesses, the trade-off is essentially a toss-up.

3.4   Transaction Processing

A *transaction* is a program unit that accesses the database; it retrieves and may update data. A database system has the responsibility of executing a transaction so that it is both atomic and correct. To be atomic, a transaction must either execute to completion or must not execute at all. To be correct, a transaction must transform the database from one consistent state to another. A database is in a consistent state if it satisfies all its integrity constraints. During a transaction, the database may be inconsistent, but if at the end of a transaction the integrity constraints do not hold, then the database system must abort the transaction and leave the database in a state as if the transaction had not executed.

Some examples of what can cause a transaction to abort include the following. Suppose that while a transaction is executing, the database system crashes because of some hardware or software error. Changes made by the transaction may be partial, and we cannot allow them to stand. Under these circumstances, the database system must recover to a consistent state as if the transaction had not executed. We explain how a database system can handle this problem in Section 3.4.1, on crash recovery.

Suppose, as a second example, that several transactions are running at the same time and that two of them update the same data item simultaneously. The results may not accurately reflect the application being modeled. As a specific example of the potential problems, suppose that one deposit transaction reads a bank customer's account balance, but that before it is updated, another deposit transaction also reads the same customer's account balance. Since both transactions are adding to the same account-balance value, the last transaction to write its value will overwrite the first, and the new balance will be incorrect. We explain how a database system can resolve this problem in Section 3.4.2, on concurrency control.

As a third example, suppose that a transaction inserts a new tuple in a relation, but that the tuple's primary-key value is the same as the primary-key value of a tuple that is already stored in the relation. Such an insertion would violate a key constraint and must not be allowed. Before making such a change, the database system should check this key constraint. If the key constraint would be violated by completing a transaction, the transaction should not be allowed to complete, but should be aborted. As we shall see in Section 3.4.1, the way that a database system handles its data updates for crash recovery can also be used to resolve this problem.

3.4.1 Crash Recovery

A transaction executes according to the state diagram in Fig. 3.8. When a transaction starts, it enters the *Active* state. Once a transaction executes all of its statements, including any integrity checking that must be done, it becomes *Partially Committed*. While in the *Active* state, a transaction may fail for a variety of reasons and enter the *Failed* state. These reasons include system crashes, failure to satisfy integrity constraints, and the need for the database system to abort the transaction, for example because of deadlock. When a transaction is in the *Partially Committed* state, it may still fail

Disk Crashes, Natural Disasters, and Sabotage

Safely storing information on disk provides no certain guarantee that information will not be lost because the disk itself may crash. Duplicate storage on multiple disks and other schemes can ameliorate this problem. These protection schemes may still be insufficient, however, because major power surges and natural disasters such as fires, floods, and earthquakes may destroy duplicate storage devices simultaneously. We can, of course, use surge protectors and build buildings that are resistant to natural disasters, but these measures may be expensive and may still not provide absolute protection. Even when protection from a natural disaster is in place, sabotage—both destruction of physical devices and intentional corruption of stored data—is still a possibility. These problems are all real but are beyond the scope of this book.

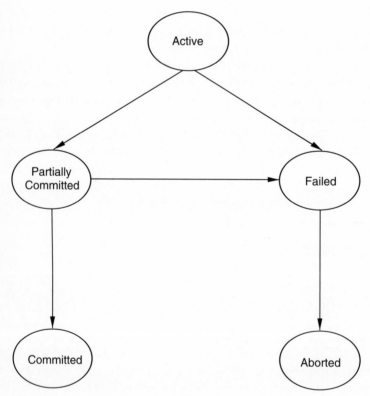

Figure 3.8   Transaction state diagram.

because its results have not yet been safely stored on disk. Once a transaction fails, it eventually moves into the *Aborted* state. Before moving into the *Aborted* state, the database system may need to make some adjustments, such as rolling the database back to a consistent state. While in the *Partially Committed* state, if we can guarantee successful completion, a transaction moves into the *Committed* state. There are several ways to guarantee successful completion. The fundamental requirement is to place enough information for recovery safely on disk before committing the transaction. One way to guarantee successful completion is to record all changes to the database in a log on disk, recording both the old and the new value of every data item changed. If the system crashes or the transaction aborts, we can use this log to undo any changes. If, on the other hand, the transaction has committed but the system crashes before we can write all the new data to disk, we can use the log to do or redo any updates we are not certain have been completed.

Specifically, we process a transaction T as follows:

```
When T starts:
    Record <T, starts> in the log.
```

```
For each update of a field F in a record of a file f
        whose primary key is K:
    Record <T, f, F, K, old value, new value> in the log.
```

```
The log, or part of the log, may be written to disk
    at any time.
```

```
After a log entry is written to disk, make the actual
        change for the entry.
    These updates can be immediate or deferred, being
        accumulated in a buffer until it is efficient to
    do the actual write.
```

```
When T completes its processing (including all integrity checks):
    Record <T, commits> in the log.
    Write the log, or remainder of the log, to disk.
    Do any remaining updates at a time that is efficient for
        the system.
```

This procedure lets us recover from all possible states for a single transaction and lets us recover from all possible states for multiple transactions if we order the recovery properly. For a single transaction T, if $<T, starts>$ is in the log on disk, but not $<T, commits>$, then for each of T's log records on disk, we overwrite the F value in the record of file f whose key value is K with the *old value*. We proceed in reverse order on the log entries for T in case a field is updated more than once in transaction T. This *undo* operation for transaction T resets the database in a consistent state as if T had not been executed. If $<T, starts>$ and $<T, commits>$ are both in the log on disk, then for each of T's log records, we overwrite the F value in the database with the *new value*. We proceed forward through the log entries in T in case a field has been updated more than once. We never know how many actual updates may have already been done, but this does not matter because the correct new value will be in place. Since some values (possibly all values) may have already been written to the database, we refer to this action as a *redo* operation for transaction T.

For example, suppose we have a transaction that adds one percentage point to every customer's discount, but only if the discount rate is nonzero. For the data in Fig. 2.10, the complete log would be as follows:

$<T, starts>$
$<T, Customer, Discount, b22, 2, 3>$
$<T, Customer, Discount, c33, 10, 11>$
$<T, commits>$

If the system crashes after this transaction has committed, since all the log entries are on disk, we can redo the transaction by setting the values to 3 and 11, the values that should be in the customer records after successfully completing the transaction. If the system crashes or the transaction aborts before $<T, commits>$ is written to disk, we can undo any updates that may have already taken place. If, for example, the first change entry that changes 2 to 3 is there, but the second change entry is not, we would write 2 as the discount for the customer record whose key is $b22$. Whether the 2 has been changed to a 3 or not does not matter—overwriting either 2 or 3 with a 2 gives it the proper value. No other changes are necessary. Our procedure guarantees that the 10 has not yet been changed to 11 because we must write the log entry to disk before actually changing the database.

For multiple transactions we follow the same procedure, except that we order the transactions serially, as explained in the next section. During recovery, we first redo the committed transactions according to this serial order, and then undo the started-but-not-committed transactions in reverse serial order. With multiple transactions, the log transaction identifier is used to determine which log record belongs to which transactions. We can thus maintain only one log and write log records to disk from several different transactions without concern for any intermixing.

After recovery from a crash, we can also automatically restart each transaction that did not commit. If an individual transaction fails, we can use the transaction identifier to extract the entries for that particular transaction from the log. Transactions that fail individually should be restarted only if the transaction itself did not cause the failure.

To prevent having to do a recovery based on the entire, potentially very long log, the database system should periodically do a "checkpoint." Unless a checkpoint operation is performed, we do not know how far back through the log we must go to ensure that we have undone or redone all the transactions that must be processed to bring the database into a consistent state. A checkpoint operation stops initiating new transactions, completes any running transactions, and makes sure that all actual database updates are written to disk. It then enters *<checkpoint>* in the log. Then, when recovering after a crash, we need only go backward through the log until we encounter the first *<checkpoint>* entry. Processing all log entries from the last *<checkpoint>* entry forward is sufficient to bring the database into a consistent state.

3.4.2 Concurrency Control

Transactions can interfere with each other when they read and write the same data values. If we are lucky and the transactions access different data values, we can process them concurrently without concern for interference. There is almost always a potential for accessing the same data values, however, and hence we must provide a way to prevent this interference from causing the database to be updated improperly.

There are several ways to ensure that concurrently executing transactions do not interfere with each other. One way, of course, is to execute transactions serially, one at a time. This does not make efficient use of resources, however, because of the wasted idle time, most of it the result of waiting for disk accesses. Also, strict serial execution of transactions prevents us from using several different processors to execute queries simultaneously. To maximize the throughput, a database system should control the possible conflicts among transactions so as to maximize the use of system resources.

Since serial execution works (although not efficiently), one way to control concurrency is to allow concurrent execution, but to ensure that transactions execute as if they were all executed serially, in some order.

Concurrency-control techniques that are based on this idea are said to ensure serializability.

Serializability can be ensured in many ways. The most popular, which we present here, is to use the *two-phase locking protocol (2PLP)*. As the name tells us, 2PLP has two phases. Phase one is the locking phase; phase two, the unlocking phase. During the locking phase, a transaction may lock data values, but it may never unlock data values. During the unlocking phase, a transaction may unlock data values, but it may never lock data values. The following paragraphs present several examples that show the features of 2PLP and how it works.

We first show that 2PLP solves our problem of updating the same bank account concurrently. Figure 3.9 shows a schedule that gives the parallel execution of two transactions T_1 and T_2. This schedule is possible if we have no concurrency control. A *schedule* shows the order of execution of the operations in one or more transactions. In a schedule, there is one operation per line, and the order of execution is line by line from top to bottom. Thus for the schedule in Fig. 3.9, the sequence of operations is:

> T_1 reads A (from the database)
> T_2 reads A (from the database)
> T_2 adds 50 to (its local copy of) A
> T_1 adds 75 to (its local copy of) A
> T_1 writes A (back to the database)
> T_2 writes A (back to the database)

This schedule, of course, does not give us the proper result. If the account balance A is initially $100, the result is $150, not the expected $225.

Locking prevents this schedule from being executed. An exclusive lock on a database value V held by one transaction prevents any other transaction from reading or writing V. We denote an exclusive lock on a database value V by $LX(V)$ and an unlock by $UN(V)$. A database system may grant

T_1	T_2
Read(A)	
	Read(A)
	$A \leftarrow A + 50$
$A \leftarrow A + 75$	
Write(A)	
	Write(A)

Figure 3.9 A schedule with concurrent execution of two transactions.

Notational Simplicity and Locking Granularity

For simplicity, we can think of V in $LX(V)$ as a simple variable that denotes a particular database value. There must be enough information, however, to identify the file, record, and field for the variable. Furthermore, we often lock larger units such as records, blocks, or files, not just variables. These larger locking granularities, however, are not discussed here.

---

an exclusive lock for a particular database value to only one transaction at a time. A transaction, on the other hand, may not read or write a value without a lock. Thus, in the schedule in Fig. 3.9, an $LX(A)$ would necessarily have to precede the $Read(A)$ for both T_1 and T_2, and a $UN(A)$ would follow $Write(A)$ for both T_1 and T_2. This, however, would create an overlapping time period during which both T_1 and T_2 hold an exclusive lock on A, which is not allowed. Thus the schedule is not possible and would be disallowed.

The locking protocol, however, does allow the schedule in either Fig. 3.10a or Fig. 3.10b. Both of these schedules produce the correct result—$225 when A is initially $100. Observe that we have dropped the *Read* and *Write*. These operations are implied, being allowed by the exclusive lock, and we omit them for simplicity. In schedules, we sometimes also drop the operations, implying that any valid operation on exclusively locked values is possible.

The schedules in Fig. 3.10 are two-phase, but only trivially two-phase. Indeed, for this example, a simple locking protocol, without the need for being two-phase, is sufficient to ensure serializability. Figure 3.11 shows that we need more than a simple locking protocol for some cases. Figure 3.11 shows a schedule that executes under a simple locking protocol; however, it is not serializable. When executed with $A = 3$ and $B = 3$, for example, the schedule in Fig. 3.11 yields $A = 24$ and $B = 30$, which is not the same result we obtain either by executing first T_1 and then T_2, which yields $A = 56$ and $B = 14$, or by executing first T_2 and then T_1, which yields $A = 19$ and $B = 25$.

The schedule in Fig. 3.11 does not satisfy 2PLP, however, because it unlocks A before locking B. If we satisfy 2PLP for this example, we obtain only the same results we would obtain by executing first T_1 and then T_2 or by executing first T_2 and then T_1. Observe that the results obtained by serializing in different ways can be different. This is not a problem. It is a problem, however, when multiple transactions read and write to the same field independently and clobber each other's work.

T_1	T_2
$LX(A)$	
$A \leftarrow A + 75$	
$UN(A)$	
	$LX(A)$
	$A \leftarrow A + 50$
	$UN(A)$

(a) Serial schedule with T_1 first, then T_2.

T_1	T_2
	$LX(A)$
	$A \leftarrow A + 50$
	$UN(A)$
$LX(A)$	
$A \leftarrow A + 75$	
$UN(A)$	

(b) Serial schedule with T_2 first, then T_1.

Figure 3.10 Serial schedules producing correct results.

T_1	T_2
$LX(A)$	
$A \leftarrow A + 1$	
$UN(A)$	
	$LX(B)$
	$B \leftarrow B * 2$
	$UN(B)$
	$LX(A)$
	$A \leftarrow A * B$
	$UN(A)$
$LX(B)$	
$B \leftarrow B + A$	
$UN(B)$	

Figure 3.11 A schedule with a simple locking protocol that is not two-phase.

Another problem we can encounter in locking schemes is deadlock. As an example, consider the schedules in Fig. 3.12. In Fig. 3.12a, two transactions run serially without deadlock. If we start as we do in Fig. 3.12b, however, we have deadlock because T_1 is waiting for an exclusive lock on B, which T_2 holds, and T_2 is waiting for an exclusive lock on A, which T_1 holds. In this case the database system should detect the deadlock and abort one of the transactions.

The examples given thus far do not include much concurrency, which of course we would like to maximize. Under locking protocols, we tend to

T_1	T_2
$LX(A)$	
$LX(B)$	
$Read(A)$	
$Read(B)$	
...	
$Write(A)$	
$Write(B)$	
$UN(A)$	
$UN(B)$	
	$LX(B)$
	$LX(A)$
	$Read(B)$
	$Read(A)$
	...
	$Write(B)$
	$Write(A)$
	$UN(B)$
	$UN(A)$

(a) Two transactions that can but do not deadlock.

T_1	T_2
$LX(A)$	
	$LX(B)$
...	

(b) The same two transactions in deadlock.

Figure 3.12   Deadlock.

maximize concurrency by locking for as little time as possible and by locking exclusively only when there will be a write operation. Transactions can
share locks if they are only reading values. We denote a shared lock on a
database value V by $LS(V)$. The database system may not grant an exclusive lock on a database value V while any other transaction holds either a
shared or an exclusive lock on V. A database system may also not grant a
shared lock on V if another transaction holds an exclusive lock on V. If
only shared locks are held on V, however, a database system may grant
additional shared locks on V.

Figure 3.13 depicts an example of three transactions running under
2PLP. Each transaction has both a locking and an unlocking phase, and
there is no overlap in these phases. Since 2PLP guarantees serializability,
these three transactions are serializable. Executing this schedule yields the
same results as executing T_2, T_1, and then T_3 or as executing T_2, T_3, and
then T_1. Different transaction-execution orders may not yield the same
results, but this does not matter—2PLP does guarantee that there is at least
one serial order that works, and this is all we need to know. Observe that
for the schedule in Fig. 3.13, the execution of the transactions does overlap
and that shared locks allow more overlap than would otherwise be possible. Although 2PLP does not always allow for maximum concurrency, it
does represent a reasonable trade-off between being able to guarantee serializability and providing a reasonable degree of concurrency.

T_1	T_2	T_3
$LS(A)$		
	$LX(B)$	
		$LS(A)$
	$LS(A)$	
	$UN(B)$	
$LS(B)$		
	$UN(A)$	
		$LS(B)$
		$UN(A)$
$UN(B)$		
$UN(A)$		
		$UN(B)$

Figure 3.13 A 2PLP schedule showing shared locks and overlap.

3.5 Chapter Summary

Topic Summary

- Access to data in primary storage is an order of magnitude faster than access to data in a disk-drive cache or under a current read head, which is in turn an order of magnitude faster than access to data elsewhere on a disk. To manage these speed differences effectively, database systems try to organize data within and move it through this memory hierarchy as efficiently as possible.

- Various types of indexes such as indexes for indexed-sequential files and B^+-tree indexes, as well as various types of hashing techniques, can speed up data access significantly.

- Query optimization consists of both rewriting queries and choosing access methods that reduce cost. An important strategy for query rewriting is to make intermediate results small by applying projection and selection as early as possible, which generally reduces the cost of expensive operations such as a relational join. Cost estimates depend on data placement and organization. With a knowledge of how the data is organized physically within the memory hierarchy and of the time costs of various hardware devices in the memory hierarchy, it is possible to obtain time costs for various data-access algorithms. Choosing among the algorithms, the database system executes the lowest-cost access method.

- To protect data, a database system enforces integrity constraints, provides a crash-recovery mechanism, and manages concurrent processes that may corrupt the data by simultaneous or nearly simultaneous access. Logging is a common way to recover when transactions cannot complete successfully either because they would violate integrity constraints or because of system crashes. Locking, especially using the two-phase locking protocol, is a common way to control concurrent database access.

Question Summary

- How do the speed differences among access to data in memory, in a disk-drive cache, under a current read head, or elsewhere on disk influence our strategies for implementing a database efficiently?

Although we would like to have data where we need it, when we need it, this is not always possible. Based on the speed differences, we develop strategies to make data available. They recognize that random access to data in memory is two orders of magnitude faster than random access to data on disk. They also recognize that we both read and write data and that our access to data is not always predictable.

- Which applications are best suited to sequential and indexed-sequential files, to hashing techniques, and to B^+-tree indexes?

The following rules of thumb apply. If we need to add records only to the end of our data file and if we access data only one record after another in the order they were inserted, we should use a sequential file. If our data is relatively static once we initialize it and if either we access individual records by the primary key or we access ranges of data in order sorted on the primary key, we should use an indexed-sequential file. If our data is dynamic and if we access individual data records only by a primary key, we should use hashing. If our data is dynamic and if we access it in several different ways or if we access ranges of data, we should use B^+-tree indexes.

- Why do we need both query rewriting and low-cost access methods to optimize queries?

These techniques attack different aspects of the optimization problem. Query rewriting is independent of an implementation and tries to make individual queries more efficient by reducing the size of intermediate results. The choice of a low-cost access method depends on the implementation and tries to take maximum advantage of available or constructible storage-organization techniques. Since we can obtain speedups both by reducing the size of intermediate results and by taking maximum advantage of storage-organization techniques, we need both techniques.

- How can we protect a database from software and hardware failures and from misuse, both intentional and unintentional?

To protect a database from software errors, main-memory and CPU failures, and attempts to violate integrity constraints, we can use standard techniques such as logging. To protect against disk failures, we either can keep multiple disks in tandem or can make backups. In general, it is difficult to protect a database from every kind of natural disaster and from all kinds of intentional and unintentional misuse.

- How can we maximize concurrent use of a database and at the same time prevent concurrent processes from interfering with each other?

This is a hard question. Although we want to maximize concurrency, preventing concurrent processes from interfering with each other depends on the application. General protocols, such as the 2PLP, while preventing concurrent processes from interfering with one another and giving us some concurrency, do not guarantee maximum concurrency.

3.6 Bibliographic Notes

As stated in Chapter 2, many textbooks are devoted to the topics in this chapter and that one [Date95, Elmasri94, Hansen92, Helman94, Korth97, O'Neil94]. These books provide an expanded coverage of the topics covered here. Other books focus exclusively on file structures [Salzberg88, Livadas90, Folk92], and on transaction processing [Bernstein87].

3.7 Exercises

3.1 Suppose that we have two tracks worth of data that we wish to access together. Is it better to place the data on two tracks next to each other on the same platter, or to place the data on two tracks on different platters but on the same cylinder? Explain.

3.2 Suppose that on the average it takes 12 milliseconds to read a random block of data into memory from the disk and that it takes 68 microseconds to read a block into memory from the disk once a read head is positioned at the beginning of the block.

   a. Estimate the number of milliseconds to read 10 blocks of data that are scattered randomly on the disk.

   b. Estimate the number of microseconds to read 10 blocks of data that are physically sequential on disk. Assume that physically sequential means that when a disk has finished reading one block, it is ready to read the physically next block. Do not assume that the disk is ready to read the first block.

c. Give the difference between (a) and (b) in microseconds.

3.3 Let F be an unordered sequential file that occupies 25 randomly scattered blocks on disk. Suppose that we wish to delete a record R, which is in the first block of F. For time estimates, assume that it takes about 12 milliseconds to read or write a disk block.

a. Explain why the blocks of F are likely to be scattered rather than all together. In your explanation, note what conditions would cause them to be scattered and what conditions would be required to ensure that they could all be together physically.

b. Explain how the system could keep track of which 25 blocks belong to F and in what order the blocks appear in F.

c. Estimate the time required to delete record R by moving every record of the sequential file up one.

d. What disk reads/writes are required to mark R as being deleted?

e. Estimate how long it would take to delete R by marking it deleted.

f. Estimate the time required to find the location vacated by R if we insert a new record after R is deleted.

g. Suppose R were in the fifteenth block of F instead of in the first. How much time would it take to scan F sequentially to find the location vacated by R?

h. What could we do to speed up the insertion process for F? Assume that we insert first into vacated record locations and insert at the end of the file only if there are no vacant record locations.

3.4 Indexes are all around us—for example, guide words at the top of the pages in dictionaries and in phone books and standard indexes at the back of textbooks. Consider some of the characteristics of these indexes by answering the following questions.

    a. Is the index for guide words in a dictionary a primary index or a secondary index? For indexes in a textbook?

    b. Is the index for guide words in a dictionary a dense or sparse index? For indexes in a textbook?

    c. What characteristics of dictionaries and textbooks cause them have the kind of indexes usually included?

3.5   To see how an indexed-sequential file works, suppose that we build and modify a simplified indexed-sequential file whose characteristics are as follows. The records are single-field records that store positive integers. Each block holds at most three records. Overflow blocks, also holding at most three records, are chained together by pointers. Deletions are done by marking a record deleted. Draw a schematic view of the indexed sequential file, including the index and any overflow buckets, after each of the following operations.

    a. Initialize the file and index by loading 10 records, 10, 20, and 30 in the first block, 40, 50, and 60 in the second block, 70, 80, and 90 in the third block, and 100 in the fourth block. Let the index pointers point to the first entry in a block.

    b. Add 105 to the file.

    c. Add 45.

    d. Add 95.

    e. Delete 20.

    f. Add 102.

    g. Add 35.

    h. Add 37.

    i. Add 11.

    j. Delete 95.

    k. Delete 40.

3.6*   Consider the creation of a genealogical database of family records. Each family record has basic information on parents and on each child born to the parents. Suppose we choose to implement a family record using variable-length records having a fixed-length entry for parent information and a variable number of fixed-length entries, one for each child. Give the time and space advantages and disadvantages of representing these variable-length records in the following ways.

a. By reserving enough space to accommodate the variable part of any variable-length record.

b. By chaining a variable number of individual fixed-length components together.

c. By using a combination of these two techniques in which groups of n $(n > 1)$ fixed-length components are chained together.

Which alternative is best for this application? Would your choice be different for an application involving employee records with a variable number of punch-in/punch-out times for two-week pay periods? Why?

3.7 To use the hashing technique discussed in this chapter in a database system, we assumed that all parts of the file could be stored contiguously on disk and that we could hash directly to record locations. Several adjustments are needed, however, because files are stored in blocks on disk and because we are not likely to be able to store large files contiguously on disk.

a. Suppose that we can indeed find the contiguous space we need to store the file. Then, if we can convert the record addresses to block addresses plus record offsets, we can use the technique directly. Assume that the addresses for individual records are 0, ..., $N-1$ and that we can store n records per block. Give a formula that converts record addresses to block addresses and record offsets.

b. Suppose that we cannot find enough continuous space to store the file. Then, instead of hashing directly to records or to blocks with record offsets, we can create a much smaller hash table with locations 0, ..., $B-1$, called buckets. Each bucket consists of a single pointer to a chain of disk blocks that contain dense-index entries for the records of the file. Thus, to find a record R, we hash a key K into a location L, $0 \le L < B$, follow the pointer to the chain of disk blocks, which we search until we find K and then follow the pointer associated with K to the block containing R. For this scheme to work well, the chains of disk blocks should average only one block per chain. Then, if the hash table is in main memory, with a single-block access to the dense index we can retrieve the pointer to the block containing the record for which we are looking, and with a second access we can obtain the record. If the hash table is on disk, we need one more disk access to retrieve the initial pointer. For this scheme, give a formula to calculate the value for B so that the chains should have an expected length of 1. Assume that the file has N records, that a block can hold 100 dense-index entries, and that we have a hash function that distributes the keys uniformly into the B buckets.

c. To get an idea about the difference in how many contiguous blocks are needed for hashing schemes (a) and (b), let the number of records N in the file be 1,000,000. Assume that 10 records fit in a block. How many contiguous blocks are needed for scheme (a)? Use your formula for computing B to compute the number of initial pointers needed. Assuming that we can store 200 pointers per block, how many contiguous blocks are required to store the pointers?

3.8 Consider an n-way B$^+$-tree b used as an index for a file F. Let $n = 10$.

a. What is the minimum number of pointers the root of b can have?

b. What is the minimum number of pointers in a nonroot, nonleaf node of b?

c. What is the minimum number of record pointers in a leaf node of b?

d.* If b has three levels, what is the maximum number of records F can have?

e.* If b has three levels, what is the minimum number of records F can have?

f.* If F has 10,000,000 records, what is the maximum number of levels b can have?

g.* If F has 10,000,000 records, what is the minimum number of levels b can have?

3.9 Consider the B$^+$-tree in Fig. 3.14. Do each of the following sequences of additions or deletions, starting over each time with the B$^+$-tree in Fig. 3.14. Give as a result the new B$^+$-tree.

a. Add 75; add 72.

b. Add 49; add 51.

c. Add 99; add 82.

d. Delete 81; delete 93.

e. Delete 91; delete 97.

f.* Delete 12; delete 23; delete 35.

3.10 Let R be a relation scheme and let r be a relation on R. Let $X \subseteq R$, and let t be a tuple in r. The *restriction* of t to X, written $t[X]$, is the projection of the tuple t onto X.

Consider the following relation.

	A	B	C	D
$t_1 =$	1	2	3	4
$t_2 =$	5	6	7	8

a. What is $t_1[A]$? $t_2[A]$?

b. What is $t_1[ABCD]$? $t_2[ABCD]$?

c. What is $t_1[BC]$? $t_2[BC]$?

d. What is $t_1[AD]$? $t_2[AB]$?

3.11* Let t be a tuple in $r(R)$ and let X, Y, and Z be subsets of R. What condition is needed to make the expression $t[X][Y][Z]$ valid? Simplify this expression.

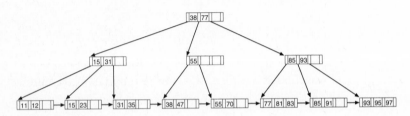

Figure 3.14 B$^+$-tree.

3.12*   Let r be a relation on R. Let $X \subseteq R$; then, $\pi_X r = \{t[X] \mid t \in r\}$.

   a.   Prove that Rule 1 in Table 3.1 is sound.

   b.   Prove that Rule 5 in Table 3.1 is sound.

3.13*   Let r be a relation on R. Let f be a Boolean function on the tuples in r. Then, $\sigma_f r = \{t \mid t \in r \text{ and } f(t)\}$.

   a.   Prove that Rule 2 in Table 3.1 is sound.

   b.   Prove that Rule 6 in Table 3.1 is sound.

3.14*   Let r be a relation on R, and let s be a relation on S. Then, $r \bowtie s = \{t[RS] \mid t[R] \in r \text{ and } t[S] \in s\}$.

   a.   Prove that Rule 9 in Table 3.1 is sound.

   b.   Prove that Rule 8 in Table 3.1 is sound.

   c.   Prove that Rule 7 in Table 3.1 is sound.

   d.   Prove that Rule 3 in Table 3.1 is sound.

   e.   Prove that Rule 4 in Table 3.1 is sound.

3.15*   Give a formal definition for $r \times s$, where r and s are relations on R and S, respectively. Be certain that the rule requires R and S not to have any attributes in common. Use the rule to prove that if $R \cap S = \varnothing$, then $r \times s = r \bowtie s$.

3.16*   Let r and s be relation schemes, both on relation scheme R. Then, $r \cup s = \{t \mid t \in r \text{ or } t \in s\}$, $r \cap s = \{t \mid t \in r \text{ and } t \in s\}$, and $r - s = \{t \mid t \in r \text{ and } t \notin s\}$. Consider the following query rewriting rules

$$\pi_X((e_1)\ \theta\ (e_2)) = \pi_X(e_1)\ \theta\ \pi_X(e_2)$$
$$\sigma_f((e_1)\ \theta\ (e_2)) = \sigma_f(e_1)\ \theta\ \sigma_f(e_2)$$

where θ can be union ($\cup$), intersection ($\cap$), or set difference (-). There are six rules here, two of which do not hold. Find which two do not hold and give examples to show that they do not hold.

3.17*   Let $r_1(ABC)$, $r_2(CDE)$, and $r_3(ACF)$, and assume that the domain for all attributes is the set of integers. Rewrite the following queries so that they are optimal in the sense that all π and σ operations are done as early as possible. Resolve any conflicts between doing π or σ earlier, by doing π earlier. Show your work and justify each step with one of the equivalence laws in Table 3.1 or in Exercise 3.16. Label all the valid laws in Exercise 3.16 as Rule 10.

a. $\sigma_{B=4 \wedge C=6 \wedge F \geq 7}(r_1 \bowtie r_2 \bowtie r_3)$

b. $\pi_A \sigma_{C \leq 9}(\pi_{AC} r_1 - \pi_{AC} r_3)$

c. $\sigma_{A \leq B} \pi_{ABD}(\pi_{AB} r_1 \bowtie \pi_{DE} r_2)$

d. $\pi_{AE}(r_1 \bowtie r_2)$

e. $\sigma_{A=1 \wedge F<5} \pi_{AF}((r_1 \bowtie r_3) - \pi_{ABCF}(r_1 \bowtie r_2 \bowtie r_3))$

3.18*   Prove or disprove each of the following. For any that do not hold, determine whether a subset holds one way or the other and if so, then prove the weaker rule.

a. If r is a relation on R, then $\sigma_{\neg F} r = r - \sigma_F r$.

b. If X is a subset of R and r and s are relations on R, then $\pi_X(r \cap s) = \pi_X r \cap \pi_X s$.

c. If r and s are relations on R, then $r \cap s = r \bowtie s$.

d. If r and s are relations on R and X is a subset of R, then $\pi_X(r \cup s) = \pi_X r \cup \pi_X s$.

e. If r and s are relations on R and X is a subset of R, then $\pi_X(r - s) = \pi_X r - \pi_X s$.

f. If r is a relation on R and s is a relation on S, then $\pi_R(r \bowtie s) = r$.

3.19   Consider relations $r(ABC)$ and $s(CDE)$ and suppose that r has 10,000 tuples, stored 20 per block and that s has 30,000 tuples, stored 30 per block. (Here, as usual in this context, "access" means that the disk head moves.)

a. Estimate the number of block accesses required to execute $\sigma_{A=1} r$ assuming that r is stored as a sequential file that is not contiguous and not sorted.

b. Estimate the number of block accesses required to execute $\sigma_{A=1} r$ assuming that r is stored as an indexed-sequential file, in memory and indexed on A, which is the primary key.

c. Estimate the number of block accesses required to execute $r \bowtie s$ assuming that both r and s are stored as sequential files that are not contiguous and not sorted. Assume that the algorithm reads one block of r and then all of s in groups of 9-block increments, repeating this pattern until all blocks of r have been processed.

d. Estimate the number of block accesses required to execute $r \bowtie s$, assuming that both r and s are stored as sequential files that are not contiguous and not sorted. Assume that the algorithm reads one block of s and then all of r in groups of 9-block increments, repeating this pattern until all blocks of s have been processed.

e. Why are your answers for (c) and (d) different? Can you state a general rule for using this block-oriented join algorithm for doing a join with different-size files?

f. Devise an algorithm to execute $r \bowtie s$ that minimizes the number of block accesses for the following assumptions. Both r and s are sorted sequentially on C. Assume that the blocks are not contiguous, but are linked together by pointers. Also, estimate the number of block accesses your algorithm requires to execute $r \bowtie s$.

3.20 As an alternative to the crash-recovery scheme discussed in the text, consider the following scheme. In this log-with-deferred-modifications crash-recovery scheme, we record *starts* and *commits* entries in the log as before, but do not record old values in log entries for updates. Thus the format for an update log entry is

$$<T, f, F, K, \textit{new value}>$$

where T is the transaction identifier, f is the file identifier, F is the field identifier, and K is the primary-key value that identifies the updated record. The *new value* is the new value recorded when T executes. In this we defer all write operations until the transaction commits and the log has been stored on disk.

a. Explain how we recover for a transaction T if there is a crash after $<T, starts>$ has been logged on disk along with several update entries but before $<T, commits>$ has been logged on disk.

b. Explain how we recover for a transaction T if there is a crash after $<T, commits>$ has been logged on disk. (Assume that there are no $<checkpoint>$ entries.)

c. Give an example to show how an inconsistent database state could be the result of this recovery scheme if writes are not deferred, that is, if we write an updated block to disk before committing the transaction.

3.21 Consider the following transactions:

$$T_0: \quad Read(A) \qquad T_1: \quad Read(A)$$
$$A := A + 200 \qquad \qquad A := A - 100$$
$$Write(A) \qquad \qquad Write(A)$$
$$Read(B)$$
$$B := B + 100$$
$$Write(B)$$

Let A initially be 750, and let B initially be 30. Assume that T_0 executes, then T_1 executes. If the recovery scheme is using a log with deferred modifications, show the state of the log if the system crashes just after "$B := B + 100$." Assume that all possible log entries have been written to disk. Explain how the system recovers.

3.22 Consider transactions T_0 and T_1 in Exercise 3.21.

a. Add LX and UN instructions to transactions T_0 and T_1 so that they observe 2PLP.

b. Add LX and UN instructions to transactions T_1 so that they are valid, but violate 2PLP.

c. For this example, does it matter whether the locking protocol is two-phase? Explain.

3.23** A *schedule* for a set of transactions is a recording of the order in which the elementary statements of the transactions are executed. (As shown in this chapter, we record a schedule as a table.) A schedule is *serial* if all the statements for each transaction occur consecutively (not interleaved). A schedule is *serializable* if its effect is equivalent to some serial schedule. Prove that 2PLP ensures serializability.

Chapter 4

Conceptual Modeling

Conceptual modeling is about organizing abstract ideas into concrete descriptions. In software and data engineering, a conceptual model of an application describes a system that will be built. Its description consists of information represented in some modeling language.

To be practical in object database application development, a conceptual model should provide information representations that capture knowledge about

1. Objects and their relationship to other objects,

2. Object behavior, and

3. Interactions among objects.

For each of these three aspects of knowledge capture, the model should

1. Include a rich set of abstraction features,

2. Support various types of views,

3. Allow a high degree of flexibility in model construction,

4. Possess an underlying formal foundation, and

5. Be easy to understand and use.

To have a sufficiently rich set of abstraction features, a conceptual model should use notation that denotes real-world semantics directly and that has the requisite power to describe complex problems. In particular, the model should allow developers to represent objects, classify them into meaningful object sets, describe relationships among objects and sets of objects, and group relationships into common relationship sets. For object behavior, the model should allow developers to represent states in which objects may find themselves, conditions that cause transitions among states, and potential actions that occur in various states and transitions. For object interaction, the model should allow developers to specify how objects communicate and share information with one another.

To support various types of views, a conceptual model should provide high-level views for every major modeling construct. Thus the model should have facilities for high-level object abstractions, high-level relationship abstractions, high-level behavior specifications, and high-level interaction descriptions. Views should allow complexities to be hidden easily and to be exposed gradually as more detail is wanted. They should also allow the detail itself to be informal or formal or to have any mixture of informality or formality, and they should allow for various perspectives ranging from analysis through specification and design.

To allow a high degree of flexibility in model construction, a model should permit developers to begin anywhere and be able to pursue paths of investigation serially or in parallel, discovering and describing objects, relationships, behaviors, and interactions in any order. A developer should be able to build model instances as desired, using any combination of top-down or bottom-up investigation techniques. A model should support a consistent paradigm that allows separate investigation paths, distinct views, and different levels of abstraction to be integrated into a single coherent description of the real world.

To have an underlying formal foundation, the syntax and semantics of all modeling constructs must be expressible mathematically. Formalism provides uniformity of interpretation so that different people can understand a model instance in the same way. Formalism also provides the basis for tool development and enables sound engineering practices. Tools can verify syntax, ensure internal consistency, carry out transformations, and help developers be more complete, precise, and concise. Imposing formalism on developers, however, can be counterproductive because of its very nature. It is therefore imperative that the formalism be "tunable" in the sense that it allow for various degrees of mathematical rigor ranging from completely informal to completely formal. Underlying formalism must exist but should not inhibit a developer.

To be easy to understand and use, the model must allow mapping from a real-world description to an application-model description to be simple and direct. The simpler and more direct the mapping, the easier it is for developers to use and for clients to understand. An ontological, real-world object viewpoint is useful here because it provides for a convenient point of correspondence. Various visual representations are also useful. Unfortunately, just as beauty is in the eye of the beholder, so is elegance of a chosen representation in the eye of the beholder. There is no universally agreed-upon notation. We can see, however, whether the notation provides a

---

OSM and Ontology

In that OSM takes an ontological approach to modeling, it is different from many other conceptual models used for software and data engineering. The ontological approach makes the correspondence to the real world more direct. When trying to decide how to model some object, users should ask what its relationships really are, how it really behaves, and how it really interacts with other objects. OSM should allow answers to these questions to be represented directly in terms of its modeling constructs. Observe that this is different from asking how the real world fits into the computer-based notion of an object, which requires instance variables to represent its state and methods to represent its behavior.

---

simple and direct mapping to the real world and use this correspondence as a rough measure of understandability.

The conceptual model used in this text, called the Object-oriented Systems Model (OSM), embodies the characteristics required for a practical conceptual model for object database application development. OSM includes three integrated submodels: an Object-Relationship Model (ORM) for representing objects and their relationships to other objects, an Object-Behavior Model (OBM) for representing individual object behavior, and an Object-Interaction Model (OIM) for representing interactions among objects.

Each of the integrated submodels has a rich set of features, which we describe in this chapter. Appendix A concisely summarizes the graphical notation that we present here. We also describe in this chapter some of the view capabilities, including high-level object and relationship sets, high-level states and transitions, and high-level and abstract interactions. We present analysis, specification, design, and implementation views in Chapters 7 through 12. The formal definition of OSM appears in Chapter 6.

To drive our discussion, we use a simplified on-line shopping example. Customers can access an on-line database and order items from a store; they can also come into the store and purchase items. The system keeps track of inventory and employees, routes delivery instructions, and places backorders for customers when stock is insufficient. We use this running example throughout the text, eventually ending up with an implementation description in Chapter 12. We introduce parts of the example here without concern for where we are going. Beginning in Chapter 7, we use the

---

Graphical Representation for a Conceptual Model

There is no universally accepted graphical notation for conceptual modeling. OSM has a notation that is convenient and consistent, and we recommend that it be followed. We point out, however, that the graphical notation is not the model—indeed, as mentioned in Chapter 1, there is a completely equivalent textual representation. Alternative representations are also possible, but they are not recommended because their use makes communication difficult.

---

example for presenting analysis concepts; we continue using it in Chapters 8 through 12 to present specification, design, and implementation concepts.

The following topics in this chapter are particularly important:

- Objects, object relationships, object behavior, and inter-object interaction.
- Participation constraints and co-occurrence constraints.
- Inter-object and intra-object concurrency.
- One-way and two-way interactions.
- High-level abstractions.
- Templates.

The following questions should also be kept in mind:

- How do constraints help determine the semantics of an application model?
- How do real-world concepts of objects and relationships among objects correspond to OSM representations of objects and relationships?
- How does real-world object behavior correspond to OSM representations of object behavior?
- How do real-world object interactions correspond to OSM representations of object interactions?
- How do high-level constructs help reduce the information overload for large application models?

- Why is it helpful for high-level constructs to have the same semantics as their atomic counterparts?

4.1 Object-Relationship Modeling

In OSM we model objects and relationships among objects using ORM (Object-Relationship Model) components. A basic ORM component is an object. An object may be atomic or molecular, having component parts whose aggregate constitutes the object. Although an ORM allows us to model objects and relationships directly, we usually group them into sets and model sets of relationships among sets of objects. ORM components also allow us to model special subsets of a set of objects in generalization/specialization hierarchies. To control complexity and provide for views, ORMs also provide high-level object and relationship sets, which group lower level object and relationship sets together into a higher level abstraction. We now present the details of ORM components.

4.1.1 Objects and Relationships

An *OSM object* is a person, place, or thing. It may be physical or conceptual. We denote objects graphically by a solid dot. Figure 4.1 shows several objects that might be part of our on-line shopping example.

Every OSM object is either lexical or nonlexical. An object whose representation is considered indistinguishable from the object itself is *lexical*. Identifiers such as *"Nancy"* and *"North America"* and times such as 1:00 am represent themselves and are lexical objects. Images and videos are also lexical objects.[†] An object whose representation differs from the object is *nonlexical*. We represent nonlexical objects by object identifiers, which are system-provided surrogate values. For convenience, we may provide readable/writable denotations of these object identifiers such as *Person1* or *Customer97*.

In OSM we represent lexical objects by well-established conventions—strings within quotation marks, integers and reals as such, and other commonly used lexical objects like dates, times, and money in a standard notation. In Fig. 4.1, for example, *"Deluxe 2-Person Tent"*, *$100*, and *"XLC96"* are lexical objects. We represent nonlexical objects by a category

---

[†] In OSM we stretch the meaning of lexical to cover not just the words of a language but any basic representation for communication.

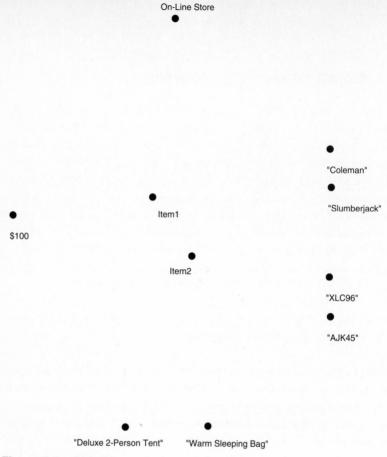

Figure 4.1 Objects.

name or designator and a number (if there is more than one from a category). For example, in Fig. 4.1, *Item1* and *Item2* are nonlexical objects whose category is *Item*.

An *OSM relationship* relates two or more objects and has a name that describes the relationship. We denote a relationship among n objects by n connected lines, each attached to one of the n objects. We name a relationship by a descriptive phrase that includes the names of each of the objects connected by the relationship. For binary relationships, we usually simplify the notation to contain only a line that connects the two objects, plus a phrase and reading-direction arrow. The phrase and reading-direction arrow tell us how to construct the relationship name and how to include the object names in the relationship name.

Figure 4.2 shows some sample relationships. The relationship among *Item1*, *"Coleman"*, and *"XLC96"* is a 3-ary or ternary relationship. Its name is *Item1 is "Coleman" "XLC96"*. The name of the binary relationship between *Item1* and *$100* is *Item1 sells for $100*. The phrase *sells for* and the reading-direction arrow pointing from *Item1* toward *$100* tell us how to construct the relationship name.

4.1.2 Object and Relationship Sets

In OSM, we usually group objects into a set, called an *object set*; we also group relationships into a set, called a *relationship set*. We denote an object set by a rectangle that encloses an object-set name. The name identifies an

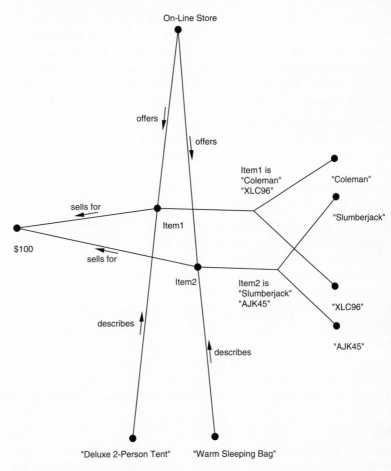

Figure 4.2   Relationships.

Attributes

One common modeling feature that OSM does not have is attributes. Thus OSM developers do not, and need not, distinguish between attributes and objects. Developers simply identify all "things" as objects and all relationships among "things" as relationships. As we shall see in this text, once objects and their relationships are established, the process of deciding which objects should map to implementation objects and which should map to implementation attributes largely can be automated.

---

object set uniquely. Thus we can place multiple occurrences of an object set with the same name in a diagram, but this is only for convenience, such as making it easy to connect object sets to relationship sets. By convention, we make an object-set name singular so that it names a single item within the set. We may also place any objects that belong to the set within the rectangle, but we usually do this only for instructional purposes.[†] The objects in an object set are usually either all lexical or all nonlexical. If the objects are all lexical, the enclosing rectangle is dashed, and we refer to the object set as a *lexical object set*. If the objects are all nonlexical or mixed lexical and nonlexical, the enclosing rectangle's edges are solid lines, and we refer to the object set as a *nonlexical object set*.

Figure 4.3 shows object sets that enclose the objects we have been discussing. *Item* is a nonlexical object set, and *Price*, *Make*, *Model Nr*, and *Description* are lexical object sets.

We denote a relationship set by a diamond with lines connected to object sets or individual objects. The name of a relationship set includes the names of the connected object sets and any individual objects. A relationship-set name uniquely identifies a relationship set. As for binary relationships, we usually simplify binary relationship-set names by omitting the diamond and providing a phrase and reading-direction arrow.

Figure 4.4 shows relationship sets for the relationships we have been discussing. We give the diagram in Fig. 4.4 in its usual form, without showing the individual objects that are within the object sets. The diagram is thus intensional, representing the scheme for the objects but not the objects themselves. For example, the relationship set *Item sells for Price* indicates

---

[†] Normally, there are far too many objects to place within a set; when there are only a few, OSM provides better representations, which we give later.

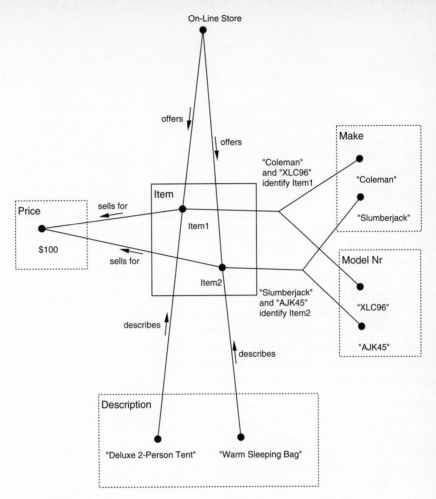

Figure 4.3 Object sets.

that items may relate to prices. Figure 4.3 gives an explicit extension for the intensional diagram in Fig. 4.4, which says that *Item(Item1) sells for Price($100)*, and *Item(Item2) sells for Price($100)*.

Objects, object sets, relationships, and relationship sets all may have multiple names. Figure 4.5 shows some examples. A bar separates the names of objects and object sets. Both *On-Line Store* and *The Store* are names for the object in Fig. 4.5, and both *Spouse* and *Significant Other* name the object set related to the *Employee* object set. The relationship set between the two object sets has six names:

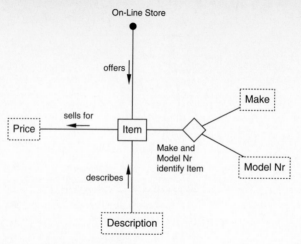

Figure 4.4 Relationship sets.

> *Employee has Spouse*
> *Employee has Significant Other*
> *Employee is married to Spouse*
> *Employee is married to Significant Other*
> *Spouse is married to Employee*
> *Significant Other is married to Employee*

A reading-direction arrow in both directions indicates that we can read a relationship-set in either direction. The relationship set between *The Store* and *Employee* has four names:

> *Employee works for On-Line Store*
> *Employee works for The Store*
> *On-Line Store employs Employee*
> *The Store employs Employee*

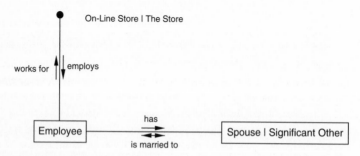

Figure 4.5 Multiple names.

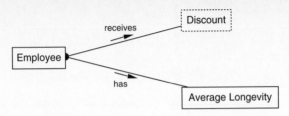

Figure 4.6   Object-set object.

Sometimes we wish to consider a set of objects as an object. OSM provides *object-set objects* for this purpose. Figure 4.6 shows an example. Here the half-dot on the object set *Employee* represents the object-set object. Like ordinary objects, it may relate to other objects or object sets. Figure 4.6 shows that the employees all receive the same discount and as a group have some average longevity with the store. Object-set objects may have names, but they usually do not have a name other than the implied name *<object-set name> Set*. Here the object-set object has the name *Employee Set*. The relationship set names in Fig. 4.6 are thus *Employee Set receives Discount* and *Employee Set has Average Longevity*.

4.1.3 Constraints

OSM supports several kinds of constraints: implicit OSM constraints, explicit OSM constraints, and general constraints. The implicit constraints that apply to the OSM features we have introduced so far include set constraints and referential-integrity constraints. Explicit constraints that apply to the features already introduced include cardinality constraints for object and relationship sets. General constraints are generally applicable, as the name implies. We discuss these constraints here and discuss others that apply to other OSM features as we introduce them.

Set constraints mean that OSM object sets and relationship sets are sets in the mathematical sense. There are no duplicates, and there is no order among the elements of a set. For uniformity, and to make all ORM constructs conform to sets, we consider an individual object to be a set with exactly one object in it and an individual relationship to be a set with exactly one relationship in it. We therefore also refer to objects as *singleton object sets* and to relationships as *singleton relationship sets*. This greatly simplifies the mathematical formalization of OSM (see Chapter 6) and also simplifies our discussion because we need not distinguish among the various combinations when talking about relationship and relationship-set connections among objects and object sets.

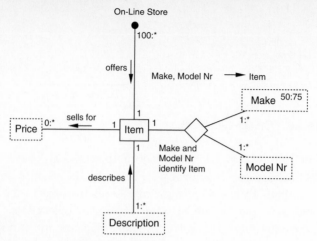

Figure 4.7 Cardinality constraints.

A *referential-integrity constraint* means that a relationship in a relationship set connected to an object set S may not reference an object x for that connection unless $x \in S$. Thus, for example, we may not record a relationship for the diagram in Fig. 4.4, which states that an item *Item3* sells for a price of *$50* unless *Item3* is an object in the *Item* object set and *$50* is an object in the *Price* object set. Put another way, we may not assert *Item(Item3) sells for Price($50)* unless we also assert *Item(Item3)* and *Price($50)*.

A *participation constraint* specifies how many times an object may participate in a relationship set. A *co-occurrence constraint* specifies how many times an object (or an *n*-tuple of objects) may co-occur in a relationship with another object (or *m*-tuple of objects). An *object-set cardinality constraint* specifies how many objects may be in an object set. Figure 4.7 shows the diagram in Fig. 4.4 with some participation, co-occurrence, and object-set cardinality constraints.

The *1* participation constraints next to the *Item* object set say that an item participates once and only once in each of the connected relationship sets. That is to say, an item has one price, one description, one make, and one model, and is an item for the on-line store. The *100:** participation constraint for *On-Line Store* specifies that the store participates in the relationship set at least 100 times and thus offers a minimum of 100 items. The maximum is *, which designates an unspecified number larger than the minimum. The *0:** participation constraint on *Price* specifies that a price need not participate in the *sells for* relationship with any item and that there is no limit to the number of times a price may participate. Here we are saying that there may be a price of interest but that no item has that price. (The price may be of interest, for example, because it is the proposed sale price for some item.)

The *1:** participation constraints on *Make* and *Model Nr* in Fig. 4.7 specify that a make and a model number each participate one or more times in the *Make and Model Nr identify Item* relationship set. That is, a make may associate with several items, and the same model number may associate with several items. Thus neither a make nor a model number identify an item uniquely. A make and model number together, however, uniquely identify an item. The co-occurrence constraint

$$Make, Model\ Nr \rightarrow Item$$

captures this concept. It specifies that for any make/model-nr pair in the *Make and Model Nr identify Item* relationship set, there is exactly one item. Thus this co-occurrence constraint guarantees that make and model number together identify an item uniquely.

There is one object-set cardinality constraint in Fig. 4.7, namely *50:75* in the *Make* object set, which specifies that there are between 50 and 75 different makes of interest in the application. This may be a bit unrealistic, but it shows that we can limit the number of objects in an object set. For a more realistic example, we may wish to say that there are exactly two genders or exactly 50 states in the United States.

In OSM, cardinality constraints have the general form

$$min_1: max_1, \cdots min_n: max_n$$

which specifies a set of ranges. For example, instead of the cardinality constraint *100:** for items offered by the store, we could have written

$$100:200,\ 500:1000,\ 2000:*$$

which would say that the store has between 100 and 200 items or between 500 and 1000 items or more than 2000 items. We may wish to specify the constraints in this way to capture the idea that the store is a small store, a medium-sized store, or a large store, and that the notion of size is captured by these range constraints.

Usually, however, OSM cardinality constraints have only one range, and most often that range is *0:**, *1:**, *0:1* or *1:1*. As a shorthand for *1:1*, we use *1*, and we extend this idea to any integer, so that for *n:n*, we use *n*. For co-occurrence constraints, when no cardinality constraint is given, as with the co-occurrence constraint in Fig. 4.7, the default is *1*. Although inconsistent with our story, we could specify that a make and model number may associate with between 3 and 17 or exactly 20 items by writing

$$\textit{Make, Model Nr} \xrightarrow{\textit{3:17, 20}} \textit{Item.}$$

General constraints in OSM let us specify anything we wish. We may specify, for example, that items whose make is "Slumberjack" must always have a price greater than $50. In this case, we would add the general constraint

A "Slumberjack" item must sell for more than $50

We often write general constraints informally, but eventually they must be written formally if we wish to enforce them in a software system. In Chapter 6 we explain how to write these constraints formally.

In OSM we can use a combination of general constraints and cardinality constraints with variables to express a wide range of interesting constraints. Figure 4.8 provides a simple example. Here we have participation constraints a and b for *Hourly Rate* and the general constraint $a + b > 0$. This specifies that each hourly rate must participate at least once with a manager or worker. Thus every hourly rate applies to either a manager or a worker or both. At the same time, the cardinality is not overly constrained. For example, the constraints in Fig. 4.8 allow 3 managers and 10 workers to earn $35 per hour, since 3+10 > 0; 5 other managers and 0 workers to earn $50 per hour, since 5+0 > 0; and 0 managers and 40 other workers to earn $10 per hour, since 0+40 > 0.

General constraints, even informal ones, should not be confused with notes, which are also part of OSM. Constraints constrain one or more object or relationship sets, whereas notes merely provide additional information. We may wish, for example, to explain the *1:** participation constraint on *Description* in Fig. 4.7 by adding a note. We could say, for example,

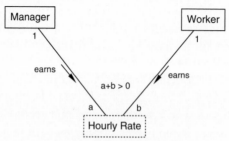

Figure 4.8 Cardinality constraints with variables.

Cardinality Constraints

OSM has many cardinality constraints but does not provide a way to represent a one-many binary relationship set directly. One-many relationship sets are directly derivable, however, from participation constraints. If relationship set R relates object sets A and B and if A has a $0:*$ participation constraint and B has a 1 participation constraint, then R is one-many from A to B. In general, if A has a maximum that allows many Bs and B has a maximum that allows at most one A, then R is one-many from A to B. The advantage of not providing a direct notation for one-many relationship sets is that a modeler need only ask the question, "How many times can an object participate in a relationship?" This question is simpler to answer than the question, "Is this relationship set one-many, and if so which is the one-side and which is the many-side?" Furthermore, the question of participation applies to n-ary relationship sets in the same way as it applies to binary relationship sets. The only possible disadvantage is that when we need one-many relationship sets, we must derive them—the derivation, however, is straightforward.

A Description may describe several different items—e.g., there may be several "Deluxe Tents".

4.1.4 Generalization/Specialization

OSM supports generalization and specialization by an *isa* feature. We may, for example, declare that an employee is a person, as Fig. 4.9 shows. Here *Person* is the generalization object set and *Employee* is the specialization object set. A clear triangle denotes a generalization/specialization and connects to a generalization at an apex of the triangle and to a specialization at the opposite base.

As a constraint, a generalization/specialization specifies that the set of objects in a specialization object set is a subset of the set of objects in a generalization object set. In Fig. 4.9, the set of employees is a subset of the set of persons. A generalization may also be a specialization. Thus we may capture an entire partial ordering among sets using generalization and specialization. When we wish to refer to the entire partial ordering, we call it a *generalization/specialization hierarchy* or, more often, an *isa hierarchy* since *isa* is shorter than *generalization/specialization*. As a degenerate case, we sometimes refer to a single generalization/specialization as an *isa* hierarchy.

Figure 4.9   Generalization/specialization.

A generalization may have several direct specializations; when it does, we may express constraints among them. A union symbol (∪) in an *isa* triangle specifies that the set of objects in the generalization is a union of the specialization object sets. A plus (+) specifies that the specialization sets are mutually exclusive. The two symbols together (⊎) specify that the generalization is a partition of the specializations since there is both a union and a mutual-exclusion constraint. Figure 4.10 presents an example. Here we see that every person is either an employee or a customer or both, that every employee is a manager or a worker but not both, and that *Customer1* and *Customer2* are two different customers, but that there may be other customers.

The *Customer* example in Fig. 4.10 also shows how we can say that an object is in an object set. As explained previously, we can think of an object

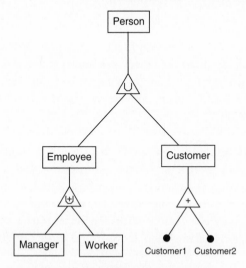

Figure 4.10   Generalization/specialization constraints.

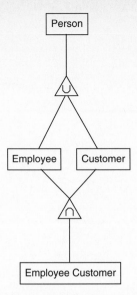

Figure 4.11   Generalization/specialization intersection constraint.

as a singleton object set. It then makes sense to think about singleton object sets as subsets of another object set and as having a disjoint intersection. We can thus use specialization as a way to say that an object is in an object set. We can also use *isa* constraints to say that objects are mutually exclusive, as we do in Fig. 4.10, or that they are both mutually exclusive and constitute all of the objects in the set, as we could with a partition constraint. For small sets it is common to use a partition constraint and enumerate every object in the object set as a specialization, allowing us to show the entire contents of an object set conveniently.

A specialization may have several direct generalizations. When it does, we can impose an intersection constraint by placing an intersection symbol (∩) in the triangle to say that the set of objects in the specialization is exactly the intersection of the generalization object sets. If we omit the intersection constraint, the specialization may be a proper subset of the intersection of the generalizations. Figure 4.11 shows how we can single out the set of customer employees using an intersection constraint.

Like any object set, object sets in an *isa* hierarchy may have associated relationship sets. When they do, the specialization object sets are said to *inherit* the relationship sets of their generalizations. They also transitively inherit the relationship sets of their generalization's generalizations. In Fig. 4.12, for example, employees, managers, and workers all have a name and

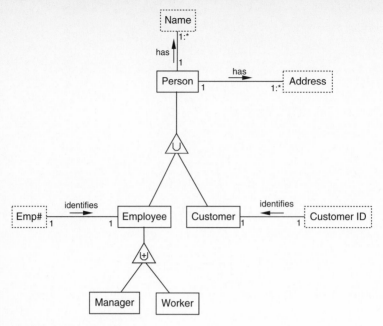

Figure 4.12 Inheritance.

address. Persons, however, need not have an employee number or a customer ID.

Roles are a special kind of specialization. Consider the ORM diagram in Fig. 4.13. Here *Boss* is the role of a manager who manages managers, that is, *Boss* designates those managers who participate on the managing side of the *manages* relationship set. The role *Boss* implicitly denotes an object set that is a specialization of *Manager* and that consists of those managers who are bosses. Because of the role *Boss*, the *manages* relationship set has the name *Boss manages Manager* and the participation constraint for *Boss* in this relationship set is *1:** rather than *0:**. Note that this *1:** participation constraint does not appear in the diagram. The constraint is implied by the role *Boss*, however, because all roles imply at least a *1*-minimum participation constraint for the implied connection to the role itself. Alternatively, we could depict the role explicitly as the object set *Boss*, add an *isa* triangle between *Boss* and *Manager*, connect the *manages* relationship set to *Boss*, and change the participation constraint to *1:**. For either alternative, the meaning is the same. Consider the object set *Spouse* in Fig. 4.13. We could write the *Spouse* object set as a role by connecting the *is married to* relationship set to *Person*, changing the *1* participation constraint to *0:1*, adding *Spouse* as a role name on the relationship set, and deleting the *Spouse* object set and the

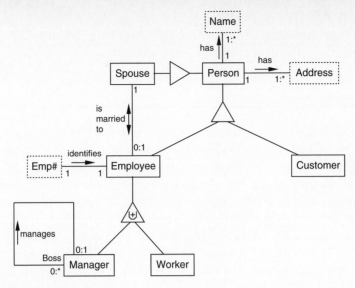

Figure 4.13   Roles.

connecting generalization/specialization. Here again, the meaning would be exactly the same.

Recursive relationship sets—those with at least two connections to the same object set—usually require roles for readability. Although we can sometimes determine what the role must be by inferring it from the name of the relationship set, it is often best to have an explicit role. Also, for our formalism, we often wish to be able to ignore recursive relationship sets. Adding roles is a simple way to turn a recursive relationship set into a nonrecursive relationship set because, as explained previously, a role techni-

---

OSM Templates

OSM templates are a shorthand notation for patterns that occur commonly in OSM diagrams. Roles are an example. Instead of explicitly requiring the *isa* triangle and an object set for the objects that participate in a relationship set, we can provide a role name. Another example is aggregation, where we express coordinated *is subpart of* relationship sets as a single concept. We consider two other templates in the exercises—one for sets of sets, which we call association, and one for object sets whose objects represent relationships, which we call relational object sets. In Chapter 11 we explore templates for common bulk-data types such as arrays and lists.

cally moves a connection from an object set to the role object set. Thus the *manages* relationship set is not technically a recursive relationship set. It would be, however, if the *Boss* role were not present.

4.1.5 Aggregation

Aggregation is a part/subpart relationship, as shown in the examples of Fig. 4.14. In the figure, *Address* is an aggregation, as are *Street Nr, Name,* and *Store.* A black triangle represents an aggregation. The aggregate object set connects to the apex of the black triangle, and the subpart object sets connect to the opposite base. An aggregation stands for one or more *is subpart of* binary relationship sets. For the *Name* aggregation we implicitly have the binary relationship sets *Given Name is subpart of Name* and *Family Name is subpart of Name.* We place participation constraints for these binary relationship sets on the connections between a black triangle base and the subpart object sets. For the *Family Name is subpart of Name* relationship set, for example, the participation constraints are *1* for *Name* and *1:** for *Family Name.*

The aggregation for *Address* illustrates some additional features. In addition to the two implied binary relationships for *Street Nr* and the four binary relationship sets for *Address,* there are also two implied transitive

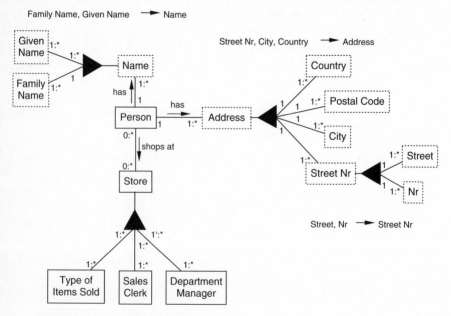

Figure 4.14   Aggregation.

binary relationships. These implied transitive binary relationships are *Street is subpart of Address* and *Nr is subpart of Address*. Aggregation is a transitive relationship. Subparts of subparts are subparts of the whole. These transitive relationships all have *0:** participation constraints; we do not try to compute a tighter bound although we could for some cases.

One additional feature of the aggregations *Address*, *Street Nr*, and *Name* is their co-occurrence constraints. The co-occurrence constraint for the *Name* aggregation, as well as the *Street Nr* aggregation, say that all the subparts together identify the aggregation uniquely. Sometimes not all the subparts are needed to identify the aggregation uniquely. The co-occurrence constraint for the *Address* aggregate shows that we assume that *Postal Code* is only an aid to routing and is not really needed to make an address unique. Sometimes one of the subparts alone is enough to identify an aggregate. For example, we could have included a *Store ID* as a subpart of *Store* in Fig. 4.14. In this case, no co-occurrence constraint would be needed because we could use a *1* participation constraint on *Store ID* to declare this uniqueness. Finally, we sometimes have no unique identification of the aggregate among the subparts. Neither *Type of Items Sold*, *Sales Clerk*, nor *Department Manager* uniquely identifies a *Store* in Fig. 4.14. Normally several stores sell the same types of items, and clerks and managers could work for more than one store. When we do have a co-occurrence constraint, we have an implicit *n*-ary relationship set connecting the object sets named in the co-occurrence constraint. The co-occurrence constraint has its usual meaning for this implied relationship set. The participation constraints for the implied relationship set for the co-occurrence constraint are *1:**.

4.1.6 High-Level Object and Relationship Sets

High-level constructs provide abstract views of information. For high-level relationship sets, there is also a provision for view derivation. A high-level object set (high-level relationship set) groups object sets and relationship sets into a single object set (relationship set). Figure 4.15 shows both a high-level object set and a high-level relationship set. In Fig. 4.15a we show the exploded form, with all details exposed; in Fig. 4.15b, we show the imploded form, with the details hidden inside the high-level constructs.

As Fig. 4.15 shows, we shade high-level constructs. When they are imploded, the shading shows that we can explode them to reveal more information. When they are exploded, the shading helps show the extent of the high-level construct. Although not required, shading is usually helpful.

The Introduction of Graphical Notation

When should new graphical notation be introduced into a model? It is possible to add notation to a model for almost any construct, but we must be careful to balance economy of notation against the natural urge to have notation for every concept. The answers to the following questions can help us decide whether to introduce notation for a concept. (1) How often does the concept arise in typical application models? If the concept is seldom used, we should be very hesitant to add new notation. (2) Is it easy to agree on a notation? If not, we should not believe that others would adopt it readily. (3) Are there complications that would make the notation complex? Complex notation is rarely successful. (4) How difficult is it to express the concept another way—using a general constraint, for example. Most notational conventions represent constraints. If there is a simple way to express the constraint textually, we should be wary about creating a possibly more complex way to express the constraint graphically.

Two examples of notation we have chosen to add for OSM, which would otherwise be unnecessary, are roles and aggregation. Both roles and aggregations are templates and therefore can be expressed in terms of other OSM constructs. In both cases the concepts arise often and the notation is straightforward. The alternative notation, especially for aggregation, is more complex, so that both roles and aggregations provide a simplified expression.

An example of a possible notation we could provide, but do not, is a generalization/specialization for relationship sets. Although it would seem that we could simply connect relationship sets with a clear triangle as we do for object sets, it turns out not to be so simple—mainly because we also have to worry about properly matching pairs of object sets for the places in the n-tuples. The alternative here is also simple because we can easily give a general constraint that describes what we want. Furthermore, we do not often find a need for specialization for relationship sets.

Because we want high-level constructs to be well formed, we must obey some rules. If a high-level object set S includes a relationship set R, S must include all object sets connected to R. One of these object sets may be the high-level object set itself. We see in Fig. 4.15a, for example, that the high-level *Person* object set includes two aggregations, which are templates for several relationship sets as we discussed earlier. Thus the high-level

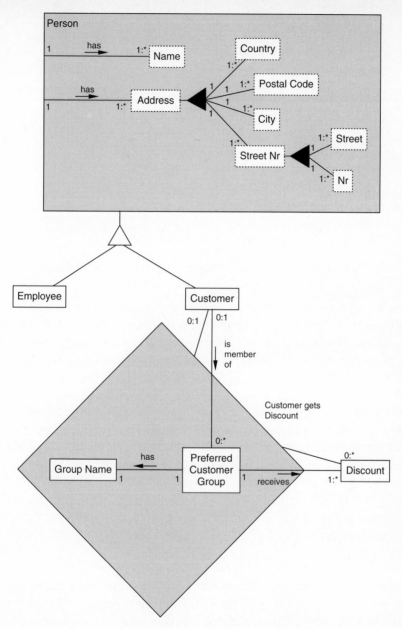

(a) Exploded with detail exposed.

Figure 4.15   High-level object and relationship sets.

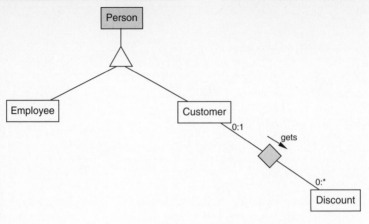

(b) Imploded with detail hidden.

Figure 4.15 (cont.) High-level object and relationship sets.

Person object set must (and does) include the *Address* object set and all the object sets constituting the address. The high-level object set *Person* also includes the *Person has Name* relationship set. Thus *Person* and *Name* must also be included. *Person*, however, is included as the high-level object set itself.

A high-level object set may include an object set on its inside that connects by a relationship set to one or more object sets on the outside. In its exploded form, we make the connection as usual between *Item* and *Department* (see Fig. 4.16a). In the imploded form, however, an outside object set cannot connect to an inside object set because the inside object set is hidden. So as not to lose the connection completely, OSM provides a dashed connecting line from the outside object set (or object sets) to the imploded high-level object set (see Fig. 4.16b). The dashed connection indicates that there is a connection to an inside object set and that, to see it, the object set should be exploded.

For high-level relationship sets, the rule for being well formed is complementary to that for high-level object sets. If a high-level relationship set *R* includes an object set *S*, *R* must include the relationship sets connected to *S*. In Fig. 4.15, we see that the high-level relationship set includes *Preferred Customer Group*. Thus the high-level relationship set must (and does) include the *has*, *receives*, and *is member of* relationship sets.

In OSM, high-level constructs are first-class in the sense that they are semantically the same as atomic constructs. Both high-level and atomic object sets represent a set of objects. *Person* in Fig. 4.14 is semantically the

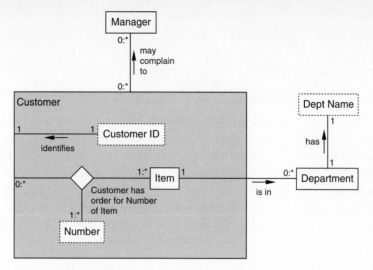

(a) Exploded with boundary-crossing relationship set.

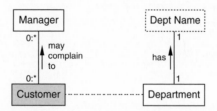

(b) Imploded with dashed connector.

Figure 4.16 High-level object set with an inside object set connected to an outside object set.

same as *Person* in Fig. 4.15. The difference lies not in the semantics of the object sets, but in our ability to form a view either by grouping with the contents exposed, as in Fig. 4.15a, or by grouping and imploding to remove low-level detail, as in Fig. 4.15b.

Similarly, both high-level and atomic relationship sets represent sets of relationships. Unlike the objects in a high-level object set, which are present implicitly, we must compute the relationships in a high-level relationship set. In the absence of an explicitly given computation rule, we compute these relationships by the join operator ($\bowtie$) over the connecting object sets. Thus, for example, if a customer c belongs to a preferred-customer group that receives a discount d, then the relationship *Customer(c) gets Discount(d)* is a relationship in the high-level *gets* relationship set. We can express other derivation rules using the formal notation developed in previous and subsequent chapters.

4.2   Object Behavior Modeling

In OSM we model individual object behavior using OBM (Object-Behavior Model) components. Many objects in the real world exhibit rich and varied individual behavior. To model real-world objects well, a behavior model for an object should be able to describe an object from creation to destruction, including concurrent and serial behavior, deterministic and nondeterministic behavior, and normal and exceptional behavior. In addition, behavior descriptions sometimes require constraints that restrict possible behavior, such as real-time or priority constraints. OBM constructs can express all these aspects of individual behavior.

4.2.1 States and Transitions

We specify the behavior of an object in an object set by a network of transitions among states. We therefore call a behavior specification a *state net*. Figure 4.17 shows a state net for an inventory controller. Observe that the state net is embedded directly in the *Inventory Controller* object set. As such, the names of states and the identifiers for transitions are local to the object set and can be reused in state nets for other object sets. Every object set has a state net, but for passive objects, the state net is a simple default state net that merely allows for object creation and insertion, object update, and object removal and destruction. For active objects, we specify the behavior explicitly.

Figure 4.17 shows the behavior for an inventory controller in terms of its potential states and transitions. Transition 1, an *initial transition*, creates the model's representation of an inventory controller and places it in the *Ready* state. Transition 2, a *final transition*, destroys an inventory controller object. Transition 3 resets inventory thresholds when requested. Transition 4 takes place when the number on hand for an item is less than the threshold and the item is not already on order. During the execution of transition 4, an inventory controller determines the amount to order, gets the supplier information, and fills out an order form. It then enters the *Waiting for Authorization to Place Order* state. When an authorization notification is received, an inventory controller places an order and marks the item as being on order.

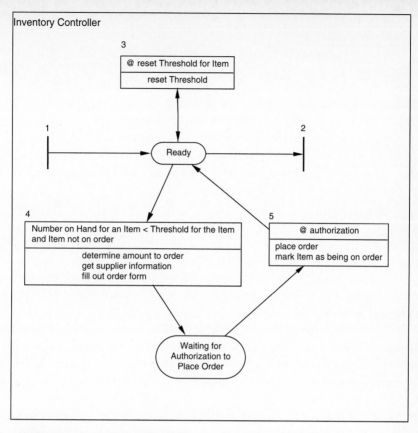

Figure 4.17   Basic state net.

In general, a transition consists of a *trigger* and an *action*. In our graphical notation, we represent a transition as a rectangle with a horizontal line that divides the trigger above the line from the action below the line. A trigger may be an event, a condition, or both an event and a condition. When not specified, the default trigger is the condition *true*. We denote events by an *at* symbol (@) followed by a description of the event. In Fig. 4.17, @ *authorization* and @ *reset Threshold for Item* are events. Conditions are Boolean expressions, for example,

Number on Hand for an Item < Threshold for the Item and Item not on order

in transition 4. An action describes an activity that takes place during the transition. The activity may consist of several steps, in which case we may more naturally say actions or activities. We need not specify an action if we are merely making a transition from one state to another.

In its most common pattern in a state net, a transition has one prior state and one subsequent state. In this pattern, a transition *fires* for an object *x* if *x* is in the prior state and the trigger holds. If the trigger is a condition, the trigger holds if it evaluates to *true*. If the trigger is an event, the trigger holds if the event occurs. Events are considered to be instantaneous. If no object can respond to an event when it occurs, nothing happens. If the trigger is both an event and a condition, the trigger holds if the event occurs and the condition evaluates to *true*. When a transition fires, any specified actions take place. Then, for the simple pattern with one subsequent state, the object enters the subsequent state. We discuss more complex patterns as we continue our discussion of state nets.

If there is no prior state for a transition, the transition is an *initial transition*. Initial transitions can have triggers and actions, but often we merely wish to bring an object into existence. The default trigger for an initial transition is @ *create*. The default action creates the object, which is implied in every initial transition and need never be written. We denote this default initial transition in a state net by a bar with a subsequent state. Transition *1* in Fig. 4.17 is an initial transition.

If there is no subsequent state for a transition, the transition is a *final transition*. Like initial transitions, final transitions can have triggers and actions, which are often specified only as defaults. We denote a default final transition by a bar with a prior state. Transition *2* in Fig. 4.17 is an example. The default trigger for a final transition is @ *destroy*, and the default action destroys a thread (perhaps the only thread) of an object. As discussed in the next section, objects can have multiple concurrent threads. When the last thread is destroyed, the object no longer exists.

4.2.2 Concurrency

Each object in an object set behaves independently and concurrently according to the object set's state net. Objects in other object sets also behave independently and concurrently according to their state nets. In this way, OSM manifests *inter-object concurrency*.

OSM also possesses *intra-object concurrency*. A single object may have multiple threads of control. We can create multiple threads of control for a single object in two ways: (1) by spawning a new thread of control when a transition fires or (2) by splitting a thread of control and entering multiple subsequent states. Figure 4.18 shows examples of both possibilities.

In Fig. 4.18, when transition *4* fires, the system creates a new thread of control to place an order. The half-circle on the tail of the arrow coming

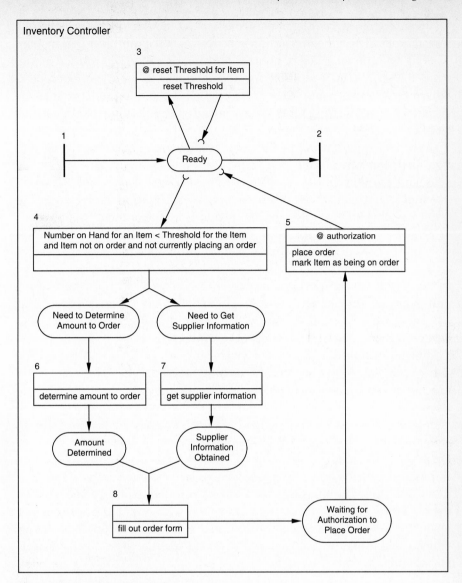

Figure 4.18 State-net concurrency.

from the *Ready* state denotes the spawning of a new thread. A thread also remains in the state from which a new thread is spawned, and thus in the state net in Fig. 4.18, a thread of control remains in the *Ready* state. Hence, an inventory object could simultaneously be in the *Ready* state and be placing an order. The added condition *not currently placing an order* in transition *4*, along with the marking of an item as being on order in transition *5*, prevents the spawning of multiple threads of control to order an item repeatedly. Presumably, an employee is alternatively requesting that the stock be checked and authorizing orders, and may also be requesting that thresholds be reset.

When leaving transition *4* in Fig. 4.18, the thread of an object splits into two more threads, placing one in the *Need to Determine Amount to Order* state and the other in the *Need to Get Supplier Information* state. Thus an inventory controller can work simultaneously on figuring out how much to order and obtaining supplier information to place the order.

A state net merges threads of control in two ways: (1) by requiring multiple prior states or (2) by a special reentry into a state in which a thread of control for the object already exists. Transition *8* in Fig. 4.18 requires that a thread of control for an object be present in both of its prior states. Thus only after the amount has been determined and the supplier information has been obtained is an inventory object ready to fill out an order form. When transition *8* fires, the threads of control merge.

Inventory-controller threads of control also merge when they reenter the *Ready* state. If a thread of control is already present in the *Ready* state when another thread of control enters the *Ready* state from either transition *3* or *5*, the thread of control merges with the existing thread of control so that there is only one. We denote this merge by a half-circle on the head side of an incoming arrow (see Fig. 4.18). Although this is what we want for the state net in Fig. 4.18, in other cases we may wish to retain several threads of control for the same object in the same state. If so, we simply enter in the normal way. Thus threads merge only when indicated explicitly, either when they synchronize before entering a transition with multiple prior states or when they make a special reentry, indicated by a half-circle on the in-arrow, which causes them to be deleted if a thread for the object in the state is already present.

When an incoming arrow entering a transition has multiple tails, as with the incoming arrow to transition *8*, we call it a *prior-state conjunction* because it requires threads for an object to be in *all* its tail states. Similarly, when an arrow leaving a transition splits a thread, as for the arrow leaving transition *4*, we call it a *subsequent-state conjunction* because it places a thread of control in *all* its head states. Occasionally we refer to a single prior state or single subsequent state, respectively, as a prior-state conjunction or a subsequent-state conjunction—they are degenerate conjunctions, having only one state.

4.2.3 Exceptions

State nets provide for two kinds of exceptions—transition exceptions and state exceptions. A *transition exception* causes a transition to abort for an object thread and places the thread in a state. A *state exception* causes an object thread to leave a state and enter a transition. Semantically, state exceptions are no different from a normal exit from a state except that they are declared to be exception exits. Transition exceptions, on the other hand, require triggering events or conditions and, when triggered, cause the processing of the transition's action to cease, abort, and roll back for the object thread for which the exception occurs.

Figure 4.19, which gives a state net for an *Order Taker* for our on-line store, contains both kinds of exceptions. We indicate that an arrow for a path in a state net is an exception by placing a bar across its tail. In Fig. 4.19, the arrow emanating from transition *1* is a transition exception, and

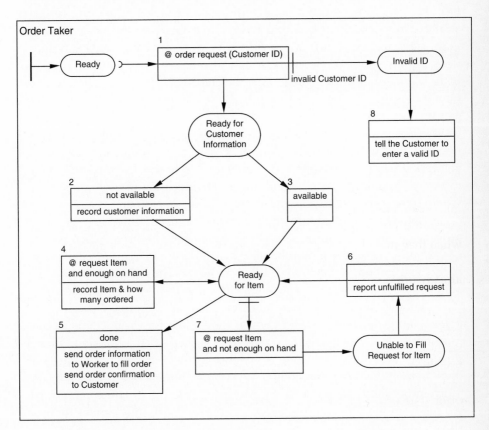

Figure 4.19   Exceptions in state nets.

the arrow emanating from the *Ready for Item* state is a state exception. The trigger for the state exception is the trigger in transition 7. For transition exceptions, we provide a trigger, which consists of events and conditions just like a trigger in a transition. The condition *invalid Customer ID* is the trigger for the transition emanating from transition 1.

4.2.4 Priority and Real-Time Constraints

To constrain the behavior of an object in a state net, we can declare priority constraints and real-time constraints. Priority constraints provide a precedence order for activities whose order may otherwise be chosen randomly. Real-time constraints can restrict the time that an object's thread may be in a state or transition or in a sequence of states and transitions.

OSM state nets sometimes allow random nondeterministic behavior, which means that a random choice can be made among several possibilities. We can constrain this nondeterministic behavior with priority constraints. In Fig. 4.20, for example, when a manager is in the *Ready to handle Email* state, the email list may contain both customer complaints and questions from workers; furthermore, it may also be time to decide what to do. If there were no priority constraints, the choice of which transition to take would be made randomly. We can constrain this behavior by labeling the exit arrows from the *Ready to handle Email* state and specifying a partial ordering over the labels. In Fig. 4.20, the ordering is $x > y > z$, which specifies that the first priority is handling customer complaints, followed by answering worker questions and deciding what to do. If the partial ordering were [$x, y > z$] instead, handling complaints and answering questions would have equal priority, followed by deciding what to do.

As another example of potential nondeterministic behavior in Fig. 4.20, a manager who is deciding what to do has several choices, which we can constrain by designating a probability distribution. In Fig. 4.20, the probability distribution is [$a(50\%)$, $b(40\%)$, $c(10\%)$]. Thus the a-exit happens about 50% of the time; the b-exit, about 40%; and the c-exit, about 10%.

In another form of nondeterminism, state-net patterns also allow for prior-state disjunctions, and in general they allow for disjunctions of conjunctions. *Prior-state disjunctions* allow us to specify that a transition fires if threads of an object are in one of several different sets of prior states. If there is more than one possibility, the system chooses one prior-state conjunction randomly. If we wish to prioritize these prior-state conjunctions, we can label the conjunctions and give priority constraints similar to those shown in Fig. 4.20.

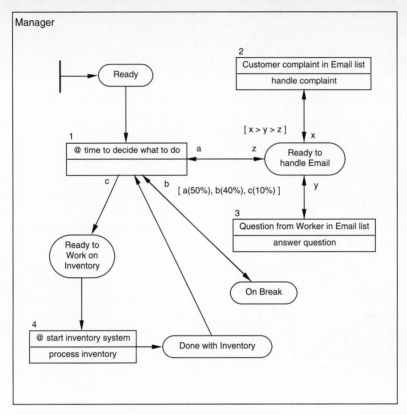

Figure 4.20 Priority constraints in state nets.

Priority constraints, like roles and aggregations, are templates. At the expense of adding more complexity, we can rewrite a state net with priority constraints as a state net without priority constraints. For example, instead of having three exits from the *Ready to handle Email* state we can have one subsequent state S with a transition T that fires when any one of the triggers in transitions *1*, *2*, or *3* is true. Then, in transition T, we can have an action that sorts out what to do based on the priority rule we wish to enforce and sets conditions for three additional transitions T_1, T_2, and T_3. These transitions must contain the actions of transitions *1*, *2*, and *3* in Fig. 4.20; all would become subsequent transitions for the new state S that follows transition T. After fixing a few connections, we can get what we want. Priority constraints for the other priority cases have similar constructions. Because the necessary complexity is cumbersome to write each time we need a priority constraint, we use priority templates as already explained.

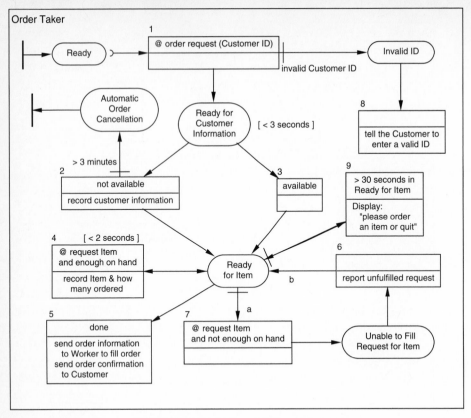

Figure 4.21 Real-time constraints in state nets.

Real-time constraints in OSM are either hard or soft. A *hard real-time constraint* appears in a trigger—in a transition trigger if it is a real-time constraint for a state or in an exception trigger if it is a real-time constraint for a transition. Such triggers cause object threads to react to hard real-time constraints. When a time constraint for an object's thread is violated, the thread either aborts and leaves a transition or it leaves a state. *Soft real-time constraints*, on the other hand, cause no behavior changes. They state that an activity should obey a time constraint but do not enforce the constraint. (An internal record may be kept of soft real-time violations, but this does not affect the observable behavior of the system.)

Figure 4.21 depicts the *Order Taker* state net of Fig. 4.19 augmented by several real-time constraints. The real-time constraint > *3 minutes* on transition 2 is a hard real-time constraint that aborts transition 2 for a thread if the thread remains in the transition more than three minutes. Not supplying customer information within three minutes causes the order taker to pass through the *Automatic Order Cancellation* state and then abort. The real-time trigger in transition *9* is a hard real-time constraint that initiates an action to display a prompt if the order-taker thread servicing a customer waits in the *Ready for Item* state for more than 30 seconds. After the prompt, the thread returns to the *Ready for Item* state, and the timer for the real-time constraint is reset.

The real-time constraint on transition *4* in Fig. 4.20 is a soft real-time constraint. It suggests that the recording of a request for an item should take less than two seconds. The real-time constraint on the *Ready for Customer Information* state, also soft, suggests that a thread should be able to determine whether a customer's information is already available in the system within three seconds.

The real-time constraint *a TO b < 2 seconds* is a soft real-time path constraint. It is a path constraint because it pertains to a sequence of transitions and states. We declare real-time path constraints by labeling the beginning and ending arrow of a path of arrows through states and transitions and then using the labels to designate the path in specifying the real-time constraint. Real-time path constraints can only be soft. We can make them hard, however, by making a high-level state or transition that spans the path and then adding a real-time exception trigger for the state or transition. High-level states and transitions are discussed next.

4.2.5 High-Level States and Transitions

High-level states and transitions have two purposes. They provide views to hide low-level detail, and they provide a way to specify high-level exits from low-level states and transitions.

Figure 4.22 shows how we use high-level states and transitions as views. Figure 4.22a shows an exploded view; Fig. 4.22b, an imploded view. The *Obtaining Information* state in Fig. 4.22b is a high-level abstraction of transitions *6* and *7* and their prior and subsequent states. Likewise, the high-level transition in Fig. 4.22b is a high-level abstraction of transitions *5* and *8*, the *Waiting for Authorization to Place Order* state. In the high-level transition in Fig. 4.22b we write a high-level description of the activities. Similar to dashed connecting lines for high-level object sets, the dashed arrows connecting to high-level states and transitions indicate that there is a connection to the inside, which can be seen only by exploding the view.

To specify exits from anywhere within a group of low-level states and transitions, we can specify a high-level state or transition and provide an

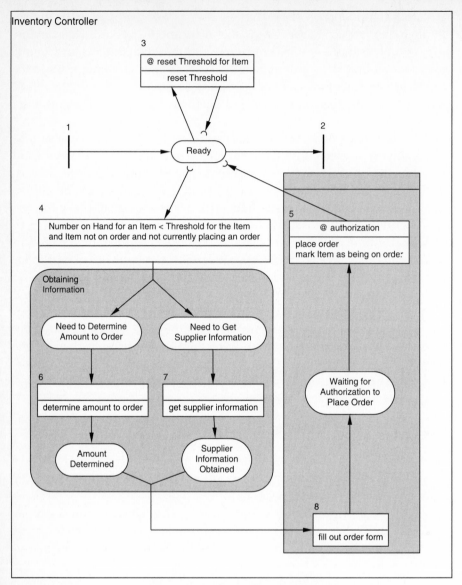

(a) Exploded with detail exposed.

Figure 4.22   High-level states and transitions as views.

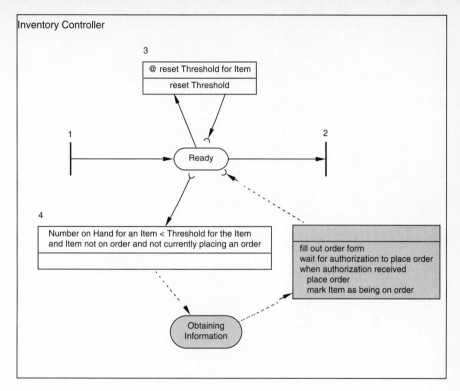

(b) Imploded with detail hidden.

Figure 4.22 (cont.) High-level states and transitions as views.

exit condition. For transitions, these exits are exceptions. For states, the exits are usually exception exits, although they need not be. Figure 4.23 shows an exit using a high-level state, while Fig. 4.24 shows an exception exit using a high-level transition. In Fig. 4.23, if a lamp is unplugged, it does not matter whether the lamp was off, whether it was on in the dim or bright state, or whether it was in a transition between states—the lamp is now unplugged. Similarly, in Fig. 4.24, when a robot is moving toward an object and becomes stuck, it becomes idle.

More complex patterns for high-level states and transitions are possible. For both high-level states and high-level transitions, we may specify an entry. In that case, the high-level state or transition behaves like an atomic state or transition. For high-level states there is an entry transition; for high-level transitions, an entry state. Based on this entry state or transition, we can further provide any low-level state net for the high-level state or

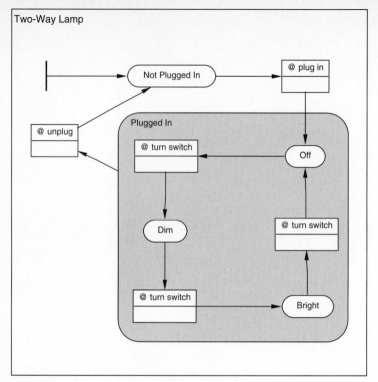

Figure 4.23   Exit from a high-level state.

transition. To terminate this low-level state net, we need an exit transition for high-level states and an exit state for high-level transitions. In simple cases with only one first and last transition, the initial and final states for a transition can be omitted.

Figure 4.25 presents an example of entry and exit states for a high-level transition. When a weather forecaster in the *Waiting for Forecast* state receives a forecast, the forecaster enters the high-level transition and thus enters the *Ready to Prepare Broadcast* state, which is the entry state for the high-level transition. The weather forecaster then behaves as specified by the low-level state net and finally enters the *Finished Preparing Broadcast* state, which is the exit state for the high-level transition.

Like high-level object and relationship sets, high-level states and transitions must obey some construction rules. Basically, any state net must have a pattern that alternates between states and transitions. If no connections exist to or from a high-level state (transition) or only exception or exception-like exits exist, the high-level state (transition) must begin and end

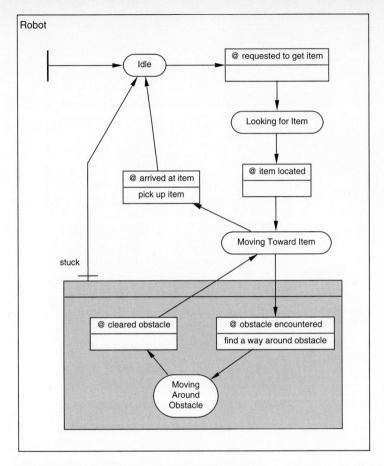

Figure 4.24   Exit from a high-level transition.

with states (transitions). If there are connections that directly enter a high-level state (transition), there must be an entry and exit transition (state). As mentioned, however, the entry and exit states for high-level transitions may be implicit when there is only one first transition and one last transition.

4.2.6 Behavior Generalization-Specialization

For any generalization/specialization hierarchy, there can only be one state net. This is the case because for each object in an *isa* hierarchy, there is

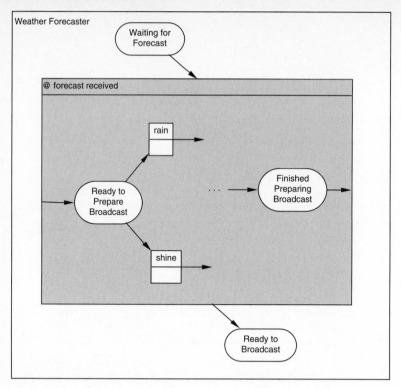

Figure 4.25   High-level transition with an entry and exit state.

logically only one object even though it may be located in several of the hierarchy's object sets. Often, we describe the behavior of an object in an *isa* hierarchy in the root generalization. We may, however, modularize the behavior and distribute it throughout the object sets in the *isa* hierarchy.

In distributing the behavior among the object sets, we need a way to reconstruct the (one and only) state net for the *isa* hierarchy. In OSM, we label connecting states and transitions in such a way that by superimposing these labeled states and transitions we can construct the state net for the *isa* hierarchy. Labels have the form

> *object-set_name.state_name* or
> *object-set_name.transition_name*

where *object-set_name* designates the object set in which the connecting state or transition is located and *state_name* or *transition_name* designates the state or transition within the designated object set. By the way, state names and transition names always have this long form with the object-set name as a prefix, but we need not use the full name unless we refer to the state or transition outside the context of its object set.

An example appears in Fig. 4.26. We can easily merge the *Order Taker* behavior with the *Backorder Taker* behavior into a single state net. We merge *Backorder Taker.8* in *Order Taker* with transition *8* in *Backorder Taker*, and we

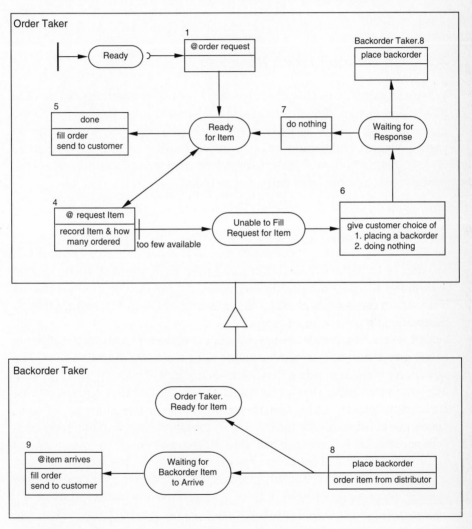

Figure 4.26   Behavior generalization/specialization.

merge *Order Taker.Ready for Item* in *Backorder Taker* with the *Ready for Item* state in *Order Taker*. The purpose of modularizing *Order Taker* and *Backorder Taker* as in Fig. 4.26 is to clearly separate the behavior pertaining to a backorder from the behavior pertaining to a regular order. Just as backorder taking is a special kind of order taking, *Backorder Taker* is a specialization of *Order Taker*, and the behavior of backorder taking is a specialization of the behavior of order taking. Each thread of a backorder taker monitors a backorder. Thus, a thread of a backorder taker waits for the arrival of a backorder. When it arrives, the thread of the backorder taker takes responsibility for sending it to the customer who ordered it.

4.3   Object-Interaction Modeling

Whereas a state net models the behavior of objects in isolation, we use OIM (Object-Interaction Model) components to model joint behavior. Objects may interact in many different ways, such as by sending information to each other, receiving information from each other, asking the system to update information, and causing events or changes in conditions that trigger an action in some other object's transition.

4.3.1 Interactions

We denote an OIM interaction in OSM by a lightning-bolt arrow. Figure 4.27 shows a basic example. In the figure, the interaction specifies that an order taker can send a message to an inventory controller, stating that so much of an item has been ordered.

An interaction has an origin, a destination, and an activity description, and it may also specify any information to be shared in the interaction. The tail of an interaction arrow designates the origin—*Order Taker* in Fig. 4.27. The head of an interaction arrow designates the destination—*Inventory Controller* in the figure. The activity description is the name given to the interaction—*item ordered* in the figure. The information shared in the interaction is in parentheses—*(Item Nr, Amount)* in the figure.

In Fig. 4.27, any order-taker object may initiate the interaction, and any inventory-controller object may process the interaction. We can be more specific about which objects initiate and process interactions, but in the absence of further specification, an interaction arrow denotes that any object in the origin object set can initiate an interaction, and any object in

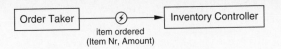

Figure 4.27 Basic interaction.

the destination object set can process the interaction. If more than one object is ready to process the interaction, one object is chosen randomly.

For an interaction, we may omit either the origin object set or the destination object set but not both, and we may also omit the activity description. If we omit the origin, the interaction is an input interaction. If we omit the destination, the interaction is an output interaction. If we omit the activity description, it defaults to *send*. Figure 4.28 shows an example. The default *send* interaction outputs the string *"please place an order for an item"*. The *order item* interaction is an input interaction. Its purpose here is to place an order for a certain amount, *Amount*, of an item whose item number is *Item Nr*.

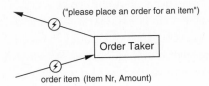

Figure 4.28 Input/output interactions.

Interactions can pass information in both directions; those that do are called *two-way* interactions. (In this context, we sometimes refer to regular interactions as *one-way* interactions.) In two-way interactions the origin object that initiates an interaction waits for a reply from the destination object that processes the interaction. Figure 4.29 shows a two-way interaction. The parenthetical information to the right of a return arrow is the information returned. Here the order taker is asking the inventory controller if there is enough stock on hand to fill an order. The *response*, for which the order taker is waiting, is a *yes/no* indicator, which the order taker can use for further processing.

Figure 4.29 Two-way interaction.

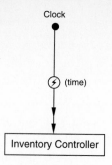

Figure 4.30   Continuous interaction.

Many activities in the real world are continuous. In OSM, we can indicate that an interaction is continuous by a double arrowhead. Figure 4.30 shows a clock that continually sends the time to an inventory controller. The behavior of an inventory controller determines which of these messages are received; presumably an inventory controller receives the time message only when it wishes to look at the clock. Continual interactions allow us to model the real world as it is, but in computer implementations we eventually make such interactions discrete and efficient.

An origin object may broadcast an interaction to multiple receiving objects. Figure 4.31 depicts an inventory controller that broadcasts its end-of-the-month report to all managers. The multiple heads indicate that the interaction is a broadcast interaction. All members of the destination object set who are ready for the interaction receive it.

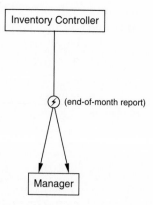

Figure 4.31   Broadcast interaction.

4.3.2 Interaction Sequences

We often wish to capture a sequence of interactions among two objects at a high level of abstraction. An OSM interaction sequence lets us describe an interaction scenario quickly. To specify an interaction sequence between two objects, we give the object set for each object and a sequence of interactions.

Figure 4.32 illustrates a sample interaction sequence between an order taker and an inventory controller. An order taker asks if there is enough inventory in stock, presumably to satisfy an order. The inventory controller responds with a *"yes"* or *"no"*. If enough stock is on hand, the order taker lets the inventory controller know that an item is being ordered. Presumably, if not enough is on hand, the order taker takes a different course of action. On receiving the *item ordered* request from the order taker, the inventory controller presumably adjusts totals and confirms or denies the action. Presumably, the inventory controller would deny the order only if there were not enough items on hand, which should not happen unless in the meantime some other concurrently executing object updated the number of items on hand.

The previous paragraph contains a lot of presumptions. Much detail has been omitted, but the interaction sequence captures the essence of the central interaction between an order taker and an inventory controller.

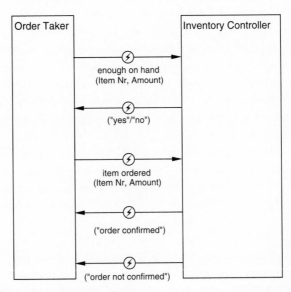

Figure 4.32 Interaction sequence.

Omitting the detail makes the interaction abstract. Indeed, all the interactions we have been discussing are abstract in this sense. To make them
concrete, we must provide lower level details, which we do in two ways.
For active objects, we provide a state net and connect interactions to triggers and actions appropriately. For passive objects, we provide a small
number of predefined interactions. The next two sections explain how to
make abstract interactions concrete, first for active objects and then for passive objects.

4.3.3 Active Object Interactions

In OSM interactions for active objects are made concrete by connecting
these interactions to state-net components. We can connect either the head
or the tail of an interaction to a state or a transition. Connecting the head of
an interaction i to a transition t and placing the activity description and
information parameters in the trigger part of t makes i an event that can
trigger t. Connecting the tail of an interaction i to a transition t indicates
that one of the activities in the action part of t initiates i. Connecting the
head or tail of an interaction to a state does little more than connect the
head or tail to an object set because the specification is still abstract. A state
connection merely specifies more exactly what part of the state net initiates
or processes an interaction. To make the interaction concrete, there would
have to be a connection to a transition within the (high-level) state.

Figure 4.33 shows how to make the active objects in Fig. 4.32 concrete.
Instead of connecting heads and tails of interaction arrows in Fig. 4.33 to
object sets, we connect them directly to transitions. An order taker initiates
the *enough on hand* interaction in transition 1. An inventory controller
receives and processes this interaction in transition a. Observe that the trigger in transition a matches the interaction description. Similarly, all the
interactions in Fig. 4.33 start in transition-action bodies and match the triggers of receiving transitions.

The text in the state nets in Fig. 4.33 has a more formal appearance than
does the text in the state nets presented earlier. Even so, the text is still not
fully formal. We do not say, for example, exactly when to initiate the *get Nr
On Hand* interaction in transition a, although clearly this must come before
the *if* statement. The state net is also incomplete because, for example, there
is no initial transition for the *Inventory Controller* state net. We delay until
Chapter 6 a full discussion of the syntax and semantics of the textual components of OSM. Here we point out that we are utilizing our principle of
tunable formalism, with some features formal and other features still

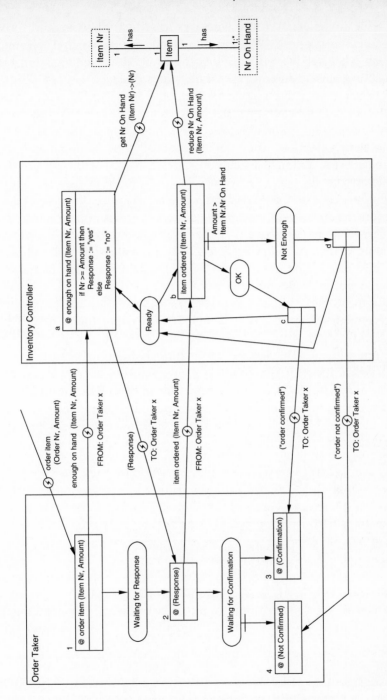

Figure 4.33 Interactions for active and passive objects.

informal. In general, we use whatever level of completion and formality best suits our purpose. When we are being incomplete and informal, we can say whatever we wish, conforming to OSM conventions, but leaving some things unsaid and others said more as notes.

Continuing our discussion of some of the details of Fig. 4.33, we turn to the *TO* and *FROM* clauses in the interactions. These clauses dynamically restrict origin and destination object sets, often to a single item within the origin and destination. They can also statically restrict origin and destination object sets, although usually this is better done with specialization in *isa* hierarchies. In Fig. 4.33, we use *TO* and *FROM* clauses to control the flow of messages to the proper order takers. There could be several order-taker objects and several inventory-controller objects. When an order-taker object asks if enough stock is on hand, it passes along its identity to the receiving inventory-controller object. The inventory-controller object then uses this information to return its answer to the order taker that asked the question, not any other order taker.

For the example in Fig. 4.33 and for many examples, what is needed can be accomplished using two-way interactions rather than *TO* and *FROM* clauses. Figure 4.34 shows the *Order Taker* state net rewritten using two-way interactions. The *FROM* information is built-in because the return message always comes to the initiator, and waits are also built-in because a sender automatically waits for a reply. As an exception, an originator can set a timer and wait for only a certain period of time before proceeding without a reply. Later we discuss this further in our consideration of real-time constraints for interactions.

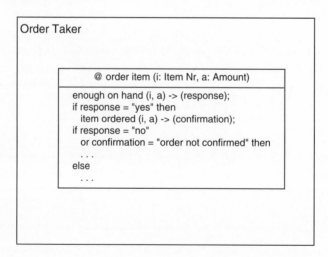

Figure 4.34 Two-way interactions in a more formal notation.

Observe that Fig. 4.34 contains even more formality than does Fig. 4.33. For example, we have added variable names for the parameters and used them as both formal and actual parameters. We have also added statement sequences and Boolean expressions in *if-then-else* statements. In general, we can informally use any notation we wish; common programming conventions are good choices. Indeed, the formal syntax we introduce in Chapter 6 utilizes the common syntax and semantics found in many computer programming languages.

4.3.4 Database Update Interactions

OSM makes interactions for passive objects concrete by providing four kinds of predefined interactions that allow us to insert, delete, modify, and query objects and relationships. There is a formal syntax and semantics for these interactions, but we may also use all the notations informally. We proceed informally here; the formal syntax and semantics are given in Chapter 6.

Figure 4.33, which we have been discussing, also presents a sample query and modification. Given an item number, the query retrieves the number on hand for that item. The modification reduces the number on hand for an item by a given amount. The form of an interaction is the same for passive objects as for active objects. It makes sense, however, for passive objects to be only on the destination side of an interaction because passive objects never initiate interactions.

The major difference between active objects and passive objects is in the way they receive and process interactions. At the lowest level of OSM modeling, there is a built-in default state net for every passive object set and for every passive relationship set (relationship sets are only passive). These default state nets handle insertion and deletion and can yield the identity of objects in an object set and the identities of objects in a relationship of a relationship set. Modification is a higher level operation that is built from basic insertion and deletion operations. Default state nets are discussed in Chapter 6.

Although low-level operations exist, it is not easy to specify typical interactions at that level of detail. If we were to specify the insertion of a new item given an item number n and the number on hand h at this basic level of detail for the very simplistic ORM diagram in Fig. 4.33, we would have to specify a state net that controls activities to do the following:

1. Retrieve an object identifier x from *Object*, the set of all available objects.

2. Query *Item* to make sure that $x \notin Item$. (If it is, repeat 1 and 2.)

3. Query *Item Nr* to make sure that $n \notin Item Nr$. (If it is, abort.)

4. Insert x in *Item*.

5. Insert n in *ItemNr*.

6. Insert $<x, n>$ in *Item has Item Nr*.

7. Query *Nr On Hand* for the existence of h.

8. If $h \notin Nr On Hand$, insert h in *Nr On Hand*.

9. Insert $<x, h>$ in *Item has Nr On Hand*.

Because of the tedium of this detail, we prefer to specify interactions for passive objects at a higher level of abstraction, even when we are being fully formal.[†] At this higher level of abstraction, we assume that "the system" knows how to take care of the low-level details for our basic four kinds of operations: insertion, deletion, modification, and query. We further assume that if we provide sufficient information to specify these operations, the system can determine which object and relationship sets to access. Thus it really does not matter where we attach the destination arrowhead for an interaction. By convention, we attach it to any object set we consider central to the operation being performed.

For the *get Nr On Hand* interaction in Fig. 4.33, for example, we attach the interaction to the *Item* object set. We assume that the system takes care of determining that it needs to (1) find the item number in the *Item Nr* object set, (2) use the item number to traverse the *Item has Item Nr* relationship set to obtain the item of interest, (3) use the item of interest to traverse the *Item has Nr On Hand* relationship set to find the associated number on hand, and (4) return it as *Nr* in the interaction.

Figure 4.35 depicts how we could specify item deletion and item insertion. Observe that for item insertion, there is enough information to satisfy all the constraints of the ORM application model. For the deletion, we need only identify the item, which is most naturally done by giving the item number. During the deletion, the item number and the relationship between the item and item number are removed. The relationship that connects the number on hand to the item is also removed. The number-on-hand object, however, is removed only if it does not connect to some other item object.

[†] If the specifications are fully formal, we can compile the low-level details.

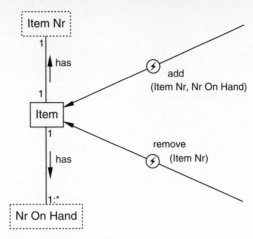

Figure 4.35   Sample add and remove interactions.

4.3.5 High-Level Interactions

Similar to other high-level features, OSM also provides high-level interactions. We may group a sequence of one-way or two-way interactions into a high-level interaction. This provides a higher level view of an interaction, one that suppresses the intermediate details about how the interaction is carried out.

Figure 4.36 provides an example. Figure 4.36a is the exploded view; Figure 4.36b, the imploded view. In the imploded view, we see what we might expect for the situation being modeled—an order taker interacts with an item to place it on order. The idea that an order taker works through an inventory controller to place the item on order is suppressed.

4.3.6 Real-Time Interactions

Real-time constraints for interactions are similar to real-time constraints for state nets. We may place a real-time constraint on an interaction or a path of interactions. As with state nets, the constraint is soft unless we provide a way to handle a violation, in which case it is hard. Since interaction initiation and response are observable events, we use standard transition and exception triggers to handle violations.

Some soft real-time interaction constraints are shown in Fig. 4.37. The real-time constraint on the *order item* interaction suggests that the confirmation be received within three seconds. The real-time path constraint

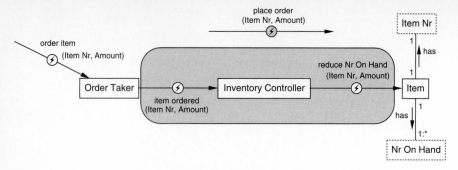

(a) Exploded with detail exposed.

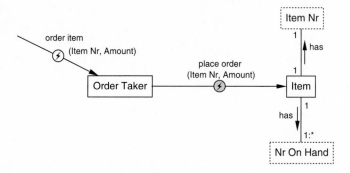

(b) Imploded with detail hidden.

Figure 4.36   High-level interaction.

suggests that the inventory controller be implemented in such a way that it can receive and process an order request in less than two seconds. Observe that since we can use the interaction names in the real-time specification, we need not introduce new names to label the interactions.

In Fig. 4.38, we see an example of a hard real-time constraint for an interaction. If an inventory controller does not respond within five seconds, the order taker ceases to wait for the inventory controller and reports the problem to the ordering customer and to a manager.

4.4   Summary Example

Figure 4.39 provides a larger example, with components of ORMs, OBMs, and OIMs integrated into a coherent whole. The example shows that these components do indeed integrate into a single OSM application model. In particular, observe that although *Order Taker* is an object set for active

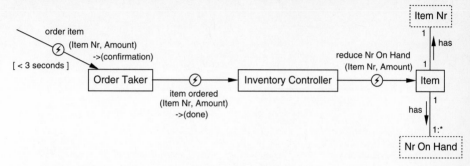

Figure 4.37 Soft real-time interaction constraints.

objects, it is nevertheless also an ordinary object set. It has, for example, a relationship set *gets orders from* that connects it to the *Customer* object set. Observe also that some of the interactions span ORM components and state net components; we can connect interactions freely in this way. The interactions whose origins or destinations are outside the OSM application model could all be connected to *Customer*, but this relationship can be modeled either way.

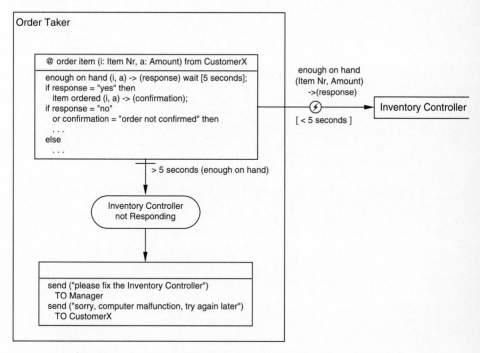

Figure 4.38 A hard real-time interaction constraint.

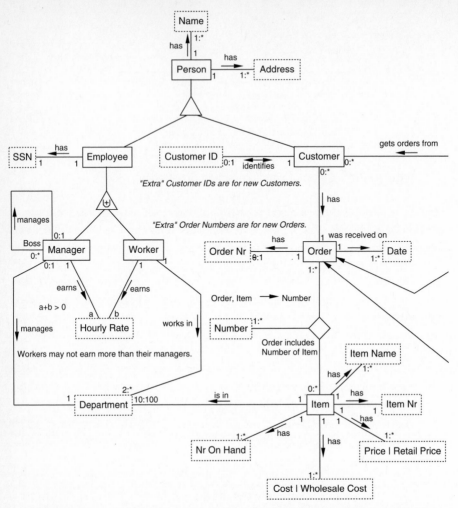

Figure 4.39 Summary example that shows ORMs, OBMs, and OIMs together.

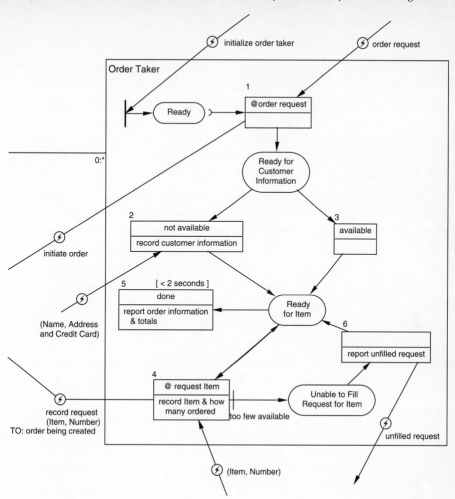

Figure 4.39 (cont.) Summary example that shows ORMs, OBMs, and OIMs together.

4.5 Chapter Summary

Topic Summary

- OSM provides a way to model real-world objects, both concrete and conceptual, and a way to model their relationships with other objects, their individual behavior, and their interactions with other objects. Because OSM takes an ontological approach to modeling, real-world objects and their behavior correspond directly to OSM representations of objects and their behavior.

- Constraints limit possible object configurations and behaviors to those that satisfy the specified constraints. Some constraints are implicit in the modeling constructs; others are explicit.

- Two particular constraints of interest are participation constraints and co-occurrence constraints. Participation constraints limit the number of times an object can participate in a connected relationship set. Co-occurrence constraints limit the number of different objects or object tuples that can appear with an object or tuple of objects in a relationship set.

- All OSM objects behave individually and concurrently; this behavior is known as inter-object concurrency. Objects may themselves perform multiple tasks at the same time; this behavior is known as intra-object concurrency. Objects may interact by sending and receiving interaction messages. Interactions may be one-way or two-way. When an interaction is one-way, an object sends a message and continues. When it is two-way, an object sends a message and waits for a reply.

- High-level constructs can reduce complexity because they can represent many lower level constructs as a single one. High-level constructs have the same semantics as their lower level counterparts. Thus, there is only one semantic meaning for an object set, a relationship set, a state, a transition, and an interaction.

- Templates provide a shorthand notation for common patterns of modeling constructs. They provide a higher level notation for communication.

Question Summary

- How do constraints help determine the semantics of an application model?

Constraints, both implicit and explicit, constitute the semantics of an application model. It is the implicit constraints, such as that an object in an object set *Person* is a person, and the explicit constraints, such as that a person participates exactly once in a *Person has Name* relation, that define what an application model means.

- How do real-world concepts of objects and relationships among objects correspond to OSM representations of objects and relationships?

  If we can observe or imagine a real-world object, we can represent it directly as an object in an object set. If real-world objects have a relationship, we can represent that relationship directly in a relationship set that connects object sets that contain representations for the related objects.

- How does real-world object behavior correspond to OSM representations of object behavior?

  If we can observe or imagine the behavior of an object as being in one of several states and as making transitions among the states, we can directly represent the behavior of an object in a state net.

- How do real-world object interactions correspond to OSM representations of object interactions?

  In the real world, objects, such as persons or computers, communicate in a variety of ways. An object may send a message to another object. An object may send a message to a group of objects, for either all of them or any one of them. An object may send a message and wait for a response. An object may observe or change a passive object. We can represent each of these interactions directly using OSM interactions.

- How do high-level constructs help reduce the information overload for large application models?

  A high-level object or relationship set can include other object and relationship sets, even other high-level object and relationship sets. By imploding these high-level object and relationship sets, we can hide all included object and relationship sets and thus can control the level at which we view an ORM diagram. Similarly, high-level states, transitions, and interactions can be used to control the level at which we view OBM and OIM diagrams.

- Why is it helpful for high-level constructs to have the same semantics as their atomic counterparts?

Because high-level constructs are first-class in OSM, they have the same semantics as their atomic counterparts. This makes it possible to read and understand high-level diagrams in the same way that we read and understand atomic diagrams. Sometimes details are hidden in a diagram with high-level constructs, but we can explode such a construct to make the hidden details available. At all levels of abstraction, the constructs have the same meaning.

4.6   Bibliographic Notes

The particular model on which we base OSM, the ontological model for this book, is OSA, Object-oriented Systems Analysis [Embley92]. Several other books have a similar thrust, all presenting models for object-oriented analysis that include both object interrelationships and object behavior. These include [Booch94, Coad91, Coleman94, de Champeaux93, Henderson-Sellers92, Jacobson92, Martin92, Rumbaugh91, Shlaer92, Wirfs-Brock90].

The OSM data model is similar to most mainstream data models [Firesmith95]. OSM departs from many of the others in two main ways: (1) it has a richer than usual collection of cardinality constraints [Liddle93] and (2) it does not include attributes as a fundamental modeling construct [Liddle94a]. This second difference agrees with the viewpoint of the vocal minority represented by [Halpin95].

Conceptual behavior modeling differs widely among conceptual models. The approach taken in OSM has some similarities to finite state machines [Gill62], statecharts [Harel87], and petri nets [Reisig85].

4.7   Exercises

4.1   Figure 4.40 shows an ORM diagram for stores that have gas pumps with automated point-of-sale, bank-card machines that act as automated clerks that can handle gas sales. Draw a diagram that shows individual objects and relationships like the one in Fig. 4.3 that shows one store with two gas-pump groups, each with three pumps.

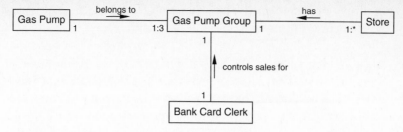

Figure 4.40   Automated gas-pump example.

4.2   Draw an ORM diagram that describes the interactive display and key pad for the bank-card clerk for the automated point-of-sale gas pumps. Assume that there is a display for messages, 10 digit buttons, and an enter button.

4.3   Let *r* be a binary relation from *A* to *B*. An element *c* of *C*, where *C* is either *A* or *B*, *participates n times in r with respect to C* if *c* appears as a *C* component in *n* and only *n* of the ordered pairs in *r*. The "with respect to *C*" may be omitted when it is clear from the context.

a. How many times does *John* participate in the relation *has_name*: {Person1, Person2, Person3} → {Alice, John, Mary, Zed} = {(Person1, John), (Person3, Alice), (Person2, John)}?

b. Give the minimum and the maximum number of times a person participates in the relation *is_taking* : {Person1, Person2, Person3} → {CS100, Math100, Chem100} = {(Person1, CS100), (Person1, Math100), (Person1, Chem100), (Person2, Chem100), (Person3, CS100), (Person3, Math100)}.

c. Give the minimum and the maximum number of times a person participates as the first person in the relation *is_married_to*: {Person1, Person2, Person3, Person4} → {Person1, Person2, Person3, Person4} = {(Person1, Person3), (Person2, Person4), (Person3, Person1), (Person4, Person2)}.

d. Give the minimum and the maximum number of times a person participates as the second person in the preceding *is_married_to* relation.

e.* Prove or disprove: If *r* is a binary relation from *A* to *B* and every element *a* ∈ *A* participates once in *r* with respect to *A*, then *r* is a function.

f.* Prove or disprove: If f is a function from A to B, then every element $a \in A$ participates once in f with respect to A.

4.4 An *n-ary relation* $(n > 2)$ *over sets ordered* A_1, ..., A_n is a set of ordered *n*-tuples $(a_1, ..., a_n)$ such that $a_i \in A_i$, $1 \leq i \leq n$. (Sometimes $n = 2$ is allowed. In this case, note that a 2-ary relation over sets ordered A_1, A_2 is the same as a binary relation from A_1 to A_2.)

a. Construct a meaningful sample 4-ary relation over sets ordered *Student_ID*, *Course*, *Semester*, and *Grade* that contains at least three tuples. What does your relation mean? Will everybody's 4-ary relation necessarily mean the same thing? Explain.

b. Generalize "participates" for *n*-ary relations.

c.* Consider generalizing "1-n" for *n*-ary relations. Give a reason why this is likely to be harder than generalizing "participates" for *n*-ary relations.

4.5 Let r be an *n*-ary relation over sets ordered A_1, ..., A_n. Consider two sets A_i and A_j, $i \neq j$, and an element $e \in A_i$. The element e *co-occurs* with *n* elements of A_j in r if in those tuples of r that contain e for A_i, there are n and only n distinct elements for A_j.

Consider the following ternary relation:

A	B	C
1	4	7
2	4	8
1	4	9
2	5	8
2	5	7

a. With how many *B*-values does the 1 in *A* co-occur? The 2 in *A*?

b. With how many *A*-values does the 4 in *B* co-occur? The 5 in *B*?

c. What are the minimum and maximum number of values an element of *C* co-occurs with the values in *A*?

4.6   Provide an ORM diagram that describes card customers, banks, and bank cards. A customer has a name and address that together identify him or her uniquely. A customer has at least one bank card and may have several. A bank card is issued by a bank. A bank card has an expiration date. There are two kinds of bank cards, credit cards and debit cards. Credit cards have a credit limit and an interest rate. Debit cards are issued only to customers who have an account at the bank issuing the card. The account has a balance and an account number. Account numbers consist of three numbers: a bank ID number, the year opened, and a card number. Banks have names, addresses, and ID numbers. For the exercise, use a generalization/specialization to model the two different types of bank cards, and have only a single object set for addresses for both banks and customers.

4.7   Devise a template for associations. An *association* is a set/member relationship in which an object represents a set of objects whose elements are members of some other object set. For example, if employees organize themselves into special-interest groups such as groups interested in hiking, skiing, or chess, we can have objects that represent each of these special interest groups.

     a.   Appendix A gives a graphical notation for an association template. What must the notation mean?

     b.   Use the graphical notation for association in an ORM diagram to say that employees are organized into special-interest groups. A particular employee may be in any number of groups including none.

     c.   Provide a translation for an association into fundamental OSM concepts.

4.8   Devise a template for relational object sets. A *relational object set* lets us view a relationship set as an object set by providing a one-to-one correspondence between the n-tuples in the relationship set and the objects in an object set. Since the object set may relate to other object sets in usual ways, such as by relationship sets and in generalization/specialization hierarchies, we can view the relationships as objects participating in these ways.

a. Appendix A gives a graphical notation for a relational object set. What must the notation mean?

b. Use the graphical notation for a relational object set to say that particular couples, which are employee-spouse relationships, are responsible for hosting company parties on particular dates.

c.* Provide a translation for a relational object set into fundamental OSM concepts.

4.9 Give a high-level relationship set that relates *Gas Pump*, *Store*, and *Bank Card Clerk* for the ORM diagram in Fig. 4.40. Be sure to provide a proper name and the proper participation constraints.

4.10 Use high-level object sets to reduce the ORM diagram of Exercise 4.6 to only four object sets: one for customers, one for bank cards, one for banks, and one for accounts.

4.11 Give a state net for automated gas-pump bank-card clerks. The automated clerk should interact with a customer to select Pump 1, 2, or 3 in a group of pumps, read the customer's card, allow the customer to pump gas, and print a receipt.

4.12 Augment the state net for automated bank-card clerks by adding the following additional features to the state net of Exercise 4.11.

a. Verify with the bank's computer that the card is not in an overdrawn or stolen status and thus can be used to make the gas purchase. If the bank card cannot be used, then as an exception ask the customer to use a different card. Give the customer the option of cancelling the transaction.

b. Have the automated clerk handle more than one transaction simultaneously.

c. Provide real-time checks for each step. If customers and banks do not respond in a reasonable amount of time, give them a second chance. If the gas does not start pumping in a reasonable amount of time after pumping is initiated, abort the transaction. If a receipt does not print in a reasonable amount of time, display a message to the customer that a written receipt can be obtained from the human clerk in the store.

4.13 Use a state net to describe the workflow for a store manager. Assume that the manager is responsible for handling customer complaints, ordering items for sale in the store, assigning workers tasks to complete, doing advertising, and signing paychecks. If a customer has a complaint, the manager must stop whatever task is currently being done, except handling another customer's complaints, and handle the complaint. If several tasks are to be worked on, the manager observes the following precedence. Signing paychecks has the highest precedence. Assigning workers tasks to complete has the next-highest precedence. Ordering items and doing advertising have the lowest precedence and have equal precedence, so that the manager may simply choose which of these tasks to do. Every few minutes, the manager should reevaluate what should be done. Occasionally, there may be nothing to do.

4.14 Consider the task of ordering items for sale in Exercise 4.13 as a high-level transition. Provide low-level details for this high-level transition. These details should include checking the amount on hand, deciding how much to order, deciding which supplier to use, finding the supplier information needed to fill out an order form, and filling out and sending an order form. It should not matter whether the manager first checks the amount on hand and decides how much to order or first decides which supplier to use and obtains the supplier information.

4.15 Provide explicit interactions for the state net of Exercise 4.11.

4.16 For the state net of Exercise 4.11, abstract the sequence of interactions between the customer and the automated clerk as a high-level interaction.

4.17 Provide the following interactions for a database of accounts. Each account has an account number and an account balance. In the interactions, provide all information about all data being transferred back and forth.

　a. Given an account number, query the current account balance of the account.

　b. Given an account number and a debit amount, debit the current balance of the account.

    c. Open a new account with a given account balance. The system assigns a new account number, which is returned.

4.18   Add real-time constraints for the interactions of Exercise 4.15. Choose reasonable time constraints for these interactions.

Chapter 5

Theoretical Preliminaries

This chapter reviews predicate calculus and presents the theoretical foundations of database systems from the perspective of model theory and proof theory. It gathers together and summarizes the results needed for our study of object database theory.

We use predicate calculus to study databases in two primary ways: (1) to express integrity constraints for databases and (2) to express database queries. As a language for integrity constraints, predicate calculus can be used to express key constraints, referential integrity constraints, and domain constraints, the three common kinds of constraints directly supported by commercial database systems. Predicate calculus defines these constraints in a long-standing, well-formed syntax and semantics of mathematical logic that is concise, precise, and independent of any commercial database system. When we use predicate calculus as a language for queries, we call it *relational calculus*. Relational calculus opens the door to the idea of a nonprocedural query language, which lets users formulate queries by specifying *what* they want rather than *how* to get it. Relational calculus also has immediate practicality because it helps explain how to formulate some complex SQL queries. Without an understanding of relational calculus, or its equivalent expressed in SQL, it is difficult, if not impossible, to formulate these kinds of complex SQL queries.

Model theory and proof theory provide a solid foundation for database application development. Model theory gives us a way to represent a database and its integrity constraints in a clean, concise, and straightforward way. We rely on this representation to guarantee that the design transformations defined in later chapters of this book preserve both information and constraints. Proof theory gives us a way to derive implied facts from given facts. In essence, this is exactly what we want to know when we pose a query to a database; that is, relative to a question of interest, we wish to know what facts (given or implied) answer the question. *Datalog*, a query language based on proof theory, lets us use this idea directly to query a database. As a side benefit, Datalog provides some wonderful insights

179

Nonprocedural Query Languages

Nonprocedural languages allow programmers to write programs by specifying *what* rather *how*. Instead of giving a computer a sequence of steps to reach a goal, nonprocedural programming languages let us specify the goal directly; the computer then figures out the steps required to reach the goal. In effect, the computer writes the procedural program required to reach the goal based on the nonprocedural specification. The computer should also optimize the program for efficient execution. This process raises the level of abstraction and lets a programmer specify a task in terms of the problem to be solved rather than by traditional imperative programming—an objective that has long been a goal of programming language developers. It is easier to state this objective, however, than to achieve it. Nonprocedural query languages, represented by both relational calculus and Datalog as described in this chapter, are good examples of our efforts to move in this direction.

---

into how to do proofs in general, as well as into how automatic theorem provers do proofs.

The following topics in this chapter are particularly important:

- The definition of well-formed formulas, especially the semantics of existential ($\exists$) and universal ($\forall$) quantifiers and the definition of logical operators, implication ($P \Rightarrow Q$) in particular.

- Closed formulas and their use in specifying database integrity constraints.

- Open formulas and their use in specifying database queries.

- The idea of a least-fixed point for recursive queries.

- Inference rules, especially modus ponens and modus tollens.

- Unification and resolution as a proof technique.

The following questions should also be kept in mind:

- How is the notion of substitution used both to check database integrity constraints and to provide results for database queries?

- What is the possible relationship between counting quantifiers and OSM participation and co-occurrence constraints? (In this chapter, try to guess the relationship; we follow up in the next chapter.)

- What is the relationship between a valid interpretation and a database?

- How does relational calculus allow us to specify queries nonprocedurally?

- How does Datalog allow us to specify queries nonprocedurally?

5.1   Predicate Calculus

First-order predicate calculus is a formal language that allows us to make statements that are *true* or *false* and to reason with and about these statements. The formal language consists of statements known as well-formed, first-order formulas, or more simply as well-formed formulas (WFFs) or even just formulas when the context is clear.

5.1.1 Syntax

We define the syntax of a first-order WFF, which consists of symbols, terms, atoms, and formulas, as follows:

Symbols

1. Truth values: *T* for *true* and *F* for *false*; alternatively, *true* for *true* and *false* for *false*.

2. Constants: Non-negative integers and real numbers as well as symbols in double quotation marks are constants (e.g., 1, 2.5, "a",

---

Variations in Predicate Calculus

Several variations in the form of WFFs are possible. We use the variation defined in this book as our first-order predicate calculus. Some variations of predicate calculus have more power than others in the sense that they can specify a larger set of statements that are true or false. A class of WFFs that, in addition to what is presented here, also allows quantification of predicate symbols and function symbols is an example of a predicate calculus with more power than first-order predicate calculus. This calculus is called second-order predicate calculus. Although second-order predicate calculus is more powerful, it can become unwieldy in that we cannot make certain guarantees. For practical use, first-order predicate calculus, as defined here, has become the de facto standard.

"abc"). Other symbols may also be declared as constants (e.g., π, e, and user-defined constants).

3. Variables: Any symbol so designated may be a variable (e.g., x, x', x_1).

4. Functions: Any symbol so designated may be a function (e.g., f, $+$, avg). All functions have at least one argument and may be written in prefix, infix, or postfix form. Functions with n arguments are said to have n *places* or to be *n-ary*, where *unary* and *binary* commonly replace 1-ary and 2-ary, respectively.

5. Predicates: Any symbol so designated may be a predicate (e.g., p, $\subseteq$, *isa*). Like functions, all predicates have at least one argument; may be prefix, infix, or postfix; and are said to have one place (be unary), have two places (be binary), have three places (be ternary or be 3-ary), and so forth.

6. Logical connectors: $\neg$, $\wedge$, $\vee$, $\Rightarrow$, and $\Leftrightarrow$. These symbols are called negation, conjunction, disjunction, implication, and equivalence, respectively, and are read as *not, and, or, implies,* and *is equivalent to*, respectively.

7. Quantifiers: $\exists$ and $\forall$. These symbols are called existential and universal quantification, respectively, and are read as *there exists* and *for all* or *for every*, respectively.

8. Parentheses: (and). An overabundance of parentheses can be annoying. By convention, some need not be written explicitly. Permissible omissions are explained when parentheses are introduced in formulas that follow.

Terms

1. Each variable and each constant is a term.

2. If f is an n-ary function symbol and t_1, ..., t_n are terms, $f(t_1, ... t_n)$ is a term, called a function.

Atoms

1. T and F are atoms; alternatively, we may use the longer *true* and *false*.

2. If p is an n-ary predicate symbol and t_1, ..., t_n are terms, $p(t_1, ..., t_n)$ is an atom, called a predicate. The common comparison predicates $=$, $\neq$, $>$, $\geq$, $<$, and $\leq$ are built-in predicate symbols.

Formulas

1. Each atom is a formula.

2. If P and Q are formulas, so are $(\neg P)$, $(P \wedge Q)$, $(P \vee Q)$, $(P \Rightarrow Q)$, and $(P \Leftrightarrow Q)$. We may omit the outermost parentheses. We may also omit parentheses for consecutive formulas for the associative operators $\wedge$, $\vee$, and $\Leftrightarrow$ (e.g., $(P \wedge Q) \wedge R = P \wedge (Q \wedge R) = P \wedge Q \wedge R$). Other parentheses may be omitted by following the precedence order: $\neg$, $\wedge$, $\vee$, $\Rightarrow$, $\Leftrightarrow$.

3. If x is a variable that appears at least once as a term in a formula P, then $\exists x(P)$ and $\forall x(P)$ are formulas. The occurrence(s) of x in P is (are) *bound*, and any other variable in P is *free* (*bound*) if it is *free* (*bound*) in P. The *scope* of a bound variable x is the subformula enclosed within the parentheses associated with $\exists x$ or $\forall x$, except that the scope may be occluded by a reintroduction of x by $\exists x$ or $\forall x$ within the scope of x. Free variables in a formula have *global scope*. A formula is *open* if it has free variables and *closed* if it has no free variables. By convention, parentheses for consecutive quantifiers may be omitted, in which case the grouping is to the right (e.g., $\forall x \exists y(P) = \forall x(\exists y(P))$).

As an example of symbols and atoms, consider the predicates *Grandchild has Grandparent*(c, p) and *Grandchild*(c) *has Grandparent*(p). For both of these predicates, *Grandchild has Grandparent* is the predicate symbol. Note that we allow white space to be part of a symbol. These predicates are two-place or binary predicates because they have two arguments, c and p. The first predicate is in the common prefix form; the second, in infix form. Throughout the text, usually we use the prefix form for abstract predicates and the infix form for sample application predicates. Conversion between the two forms is straightforward. The advantage of the infix form is that it can provide a connotative connection between an argument and its role in a predicate. For example, in the preceding predicates the role of c as the grandchild and p as the grandparent is more direct in the second predicate than in the first.

As an example of functions, terms, built-in predicates, and formulas, consider the well-formed formula $\forall x \exists y(x + y = 0)$. Here, x and y are variables and therefore terms, and 0 is a constant and thus also a term. The binary infix function $x + y$ is also a term. The infix binary predicate $x + y = 0$ is an atom and thus also a formula. Other formulas are $\exists y(x + y = 0)$ and $\forall x(\exists y(x + y = 0))$, where the implied parentheses have been added in this

---

White Space in Symbols

Although a particular implementation may be more restrictive, we prefer the increased readability of embedded white space wherever possible, a preference in harmony with our desire to support a broad range of development activities. During analysis, for example, we wish to be as expressive as possible. Often this requires phrases and sentences that are awkward to express as single strings without intervening blanks. Even using underscore characters becomes unwieldy, especially for descriptive sentences consisting of more than a couple of words. A disadvantage of strings of characters with embedded white space is that tools must become more sophisticated in their ability to form tokens from such strings.

---

last formula. Since x and y are bound, the formula is closed. The scope of y is the subformula $(x + y = 0)$, and the scope of x is the subformula $(\exists y(x + y = 0))$.

As another example, consider the WFF

$$\forall x(P(x, y) \vee \exists z(Q(x, y, z)) \wedge \exists x(R(w, x, y, z)))$$

Here, the precedence of $\wedge$ over $\vee$ implies the existence of parentheses around $\exists z(Q(x, y, z)) \wedge \exists x(R(w, x, y, z))$. Both w and y are free in the formula, and thus, since all variables are not bound, the formula is open. The scope of the variable x introduced by $\forall$ is occluded within the formula by the appearance of $\exists x$ within the scope of x. Thus the x in R is not the same x as the x in P and Q. For computer programmers, it is useful to realize that if quantifiers are thought of as analogous to variable declarations and parentheses are thought of as analogous to begin-block and end-block symbols, the rules for occlusion are the same in formulas as in blocks of block-structured languages such as Pascal or C. It is always possible to completely avoid occlusion by renaming variables.

5.1.2 Semantics

To define the semantics of a WFF W, we explain how to evaluate W so that the result is either T or F. The evaluation of W depends on a given domain of values, a chosen substitution of values from the domain for unbound variables, the predefined meaning of the logical operators and quantifiers, and the predefined or user-defined meaning of the constants, functions, and predicates.

The predefined meaning of the logical operators appears in the following truth table:

P	Q	$\neg P$	$P \wedge Q$	$P \vee Q$	$P \Rightarrow Q$	$P \Leftrightarrow Q$
F	F	T	F	F	T	T
F	T	T	F	T	T	F
T	F	F	F	T	F	F
T	T	F	T	T	T	T

In addition, Table 5.1 provides some useful equivalences, which we commonly use to simplify expressions or to convert from one form to a more convenient form.

Table 5.1. Some Useful Logical Equivalences	
Double negation:	$\neg\neg P \Leftrightarrow P$
Commutative laws:	$P \vee Q \Leftrightarrow Q \vee P$ $P \wedge Q \Leftrightarrow Q \wedge P$
Associative laws:	$(P \vee Q) \vee R \Leftrightarrow P \vee (Q \vee R)$ $(P \wedge Q) \wedge R \Leftrightarrow P \wedge (Q \wedge R)$
Distributive laws:	$P \vee (Q \wedge R) \Leftrightarrow (P \vee Q) \wedge (P \vee R)$ $P \wedge (Q \vee R) \Leftrightarrow (P \wedge Q) \vee (P \wedge R)$
Idempotent laws:	$P \vee P \Leftrightarrow P$ $P \wedge P \Leftrightarrow P$
Identity laws:	$P \vee \text{false} \Leftrightarrow P$ $P \vee \text{true} \Leftrightarrow \text{true}$ $P \wedge \text{false} \Leftrightarrow \text{false}$ $P \wedge \text{true} \Leftrightarrow P$
Negation laws:	$P \vee \neg P \Leftrightarrow \text{true}$ $P \wedge \neg P \Leftrightarrow \text{false}$
DeMorgan's laws:	$\neg(P \vee Q) \Leftrightarrow \neg P \wedge \neg Q$ $\neg(P \wedge Q) \Leftrightarrow \neg P \vee \neg Q$
Contrapositive:	$P \Rightarrow Q \Leftrightarrow \neg Q \Rightarrow \neg P$
Implication:	$P \Rightarrow Q \Leftrightarrow \neg P \vee Q$

For quantifiers, we first give the predefined meaning for finite sets. Let $X = \{x_1, x_2, ..., x_n\}$ be a finite set and let P be a one-place predicate over X, which means that for every $x \in X$, $P(x) = T$ or $P(x) = F$. Then, $\exists x(P(x))$ is equal to $P(x_1) \vee P(x_2) \vee ... \vee P(x_n)$, and $\forall x(P(x))$ is equal to $P(x_1) \wedge P(x_2) \wedge ... \wedge P(x_n)$. If X is the empty set, $\exists x(P(x)) = F$ and $\forall x(P(x)) = T$.

We extend quantification to an infinite set $X = \{x_1, x_2, ... \}$ by letting $\exists x(P(x))$ be equal to $P(x_1) \vee P(x_2) \vee ...$ and $\forall x(P(x))$ be equal to $P(x_1) \wedge P(x_2) \wedge ...$. Since we cannot write these infinite sequences, however, we say that $\exists x(P(x))$ is T if there exists an $x \in X$ such that $P(x)$ is *true*—otherwise we say that $\exists x(P(x))$ is F. We also say that $\forall x(P(x))$ is T if for no $x \in X$ is $P(x)$ *false*—otherwise we say that $\forall x(P(x))$ is F. Table 5.2 provides some useful equivalences for formulas with quantifiers.

When $P(..., x, ...)$ is an n-place predicate, we hold the other places fixed, as either constants or variables, and pass over the domain in the usual way. Thus $\exists x(P(..., x, ...) = P(..., x_1, ...) \vee P(..., x_2, ...) \vee ...$ and $\forall x(P(..., x, ...)) = P(..., x_1, ...) \wedge P(..., x_2, ...) \wedge ...$.

We assume the usual meaning of common constants, functions, and predicates. Literal numbers and strings denote themselves. Built-in arithmetic functions include $+$, $-$, $*$, and $/$ or $\div$, as well as some standard aggregate functions such as *avg*, *sum*, *min*, and *max*. Built-in predicates include $=$, $\neq$, $<$, $\leq$, $>$, and $\geq$, which apply to numbers and the standard lexical ordering of strings, and they include the standard set operators $\in$, $\subset$ (for proper subset), $\subseteq$, $\supset$ (for proper inclusion), $\supseteq$, and $|S|$ (cardinality of a set S).

Assuming these built-in standard constants, functions, and predicates and the standard meaning for quantifiers and logical connectors, we now

Table 5.2. Some Useful Equivalences and Implications for Formulas with Quantifiers
$\forall x \forall y P(x, y) \Leftrightarrow \forall y \forall x P(x, y)$ $\exists x \exists y P(x, y) \Leftrightarrow \exists y \exists x P(x, y)$ $\exists x \forall y P(x, y) \Rightarrow \forall y \exists x P(x, y)$ $\neg \forall x P(x) \Leftrightarrow \exists x \neg P(x)$ $\neg \exists x P(x) \Leftrightarrow \forall x \neg P(x)$ $\exists x(P(x) \vee Q(x)) \Leftrightarrow \exists x P(x) \vee \exists x Q(x)$ $\forall x(P(x) \wedge Q(x)) \Leftrightarrow \forall x P(x) \wedge \forall x Q(x)$ $\forall x P(x) \vee \forall x Q(x) \Rightarrow \forall x(P(x) \vee Q(x))$ $\exists x(P(x) \wedge Q(x)) \Rightarrow \exists x P(x) \wedge \exists x Q(x)$

give the semantics of a closed, well-formed formula as an *interpretation*. An *interpretation* consists of the following:

1. The specification of a domain D of values.

2. The assignment of values in D as follows:

Constants:

Each constant is assigned a value in D. For constants, we make the *unique-name assumption*, which means that literal numbers and strings may be assigned only to themselves. User-defined application constants may be assigned to any value in D (e.g., a user may define *naught* to be the value 0).

N-ary Functions:

Each n-ary function is assigned to a function from D^n to D.

N-ary Predicates:

Each n-ary predicate is assigned to a predicate from D^n to $\{T, F\}$.

As an example, let the domain D for an interpretation I be the set of all integers (i.e., $D = \{..., -1, 0, 1, 2, ...\}$). Then, $\forall x \exists y(x + y = 0) = T$ and $\exists y \forall x(x + y = 0) = F$. Suppose we change the domain D to consist of only the nonnegative integers (i.e., $D = \{0, 1, 2, ... \}$). Then we have another interpretation I', in which the answers are different. For I', $\forall x \exists y(x + y = 0) = F$ and $\exists y \forall x(x + y = 0) = F$. Suppose we change D again, this time letting $D = \{0\}$. Then we have yet another interpretation I'', in which the answers are again different. For I'', $\forall x \exists y(x + y = 0) = T$ and $\exists y \forall x(x + y = 0) = T$.

Observe that every function for an interpretation is total. Since D may be finite, however, many functions such as $+$ and $\div$, which are partial on a finite domain, must be made total. This is similar to the problem we have in computer implementations in which addition may overflow or underflow and division results may be rounded off. For functions in interpretations we may use these same techniques. One typical technique is to add an undefined value to the domain, say the question mark symbol (?), and map all undefined results to this undefined value.

A similar problem occurs because mixed-type domains are common, especially for database applications. We may have a domain that includes some integers, some reals, some strings, and some user-defined constants (e.g., {0, 1, 2, 3, 2.5, "abc", π, *naught, blue*}). In this case, although functions like 1+2 are well defined, functions like 2.5 + "abc" are not. Here again, a common solution is to add a symbol to the domain that represents "undefined" and to let the results of functions whose arguments are nonsensical yield the undefined symbol as a result. Thus, 1+2 = 3 and 2.5 + "abc" = ?.

For open well-formed formulas, in addition to an interpretation, we need a substitution of values from the domain for the free variables. A *substitution s* is a function from a set of variables (e.g., the set of free variables in a formula or the set of free variables in a set of formulas) to the domain D of an interpretation I. Given s and I, we substitute the values for the variables according to s, which turns each free variable into a constant and thus turns the open formula into a closed formula, which we can evaluate.

As an example, consider the open formula $\exists y(x + y = 0)$ in the context of an interpretation I whose domain D is the set of integers. The only free variable is x, which we may map to any value in D, say 17. With this substitution, our formula becomes $\exists y(17 + y = 0)$, which is now closed and can therefore be evaluated.

5.1.3 Counting Quantifiers

A syntactical augmentation to predicate calculus, which we use heavily, is the counting quantifier, or more precisely, a numerically bounded existential quantifier. When applied to a WFF, the existential quantifier yields *true* if there exist one or more elements in the domain that satisfy the formula. Often we do not care how many elements of the domain satisfy a formula, but sometimes we do. For example, we may want exactly one element, or more than 10, or between 3 and 5. We handle these cases with counting quantifiers.

A *numerically bounded existential quantifier* or *counting quantifier* has the form

$$\exists^{\theta n} x(P(x))$$

where n is a nonnegative integer and θ is =, ≠, >, ≥, <, ≤, or may be omitted, in which case it is assumed, by default, to be =. For example, $\exists^{1} x(P(x))$ is *true* only if there is exactly one element in the domain for which $P(x)$ is *true*, $\exists^{>10} x(P(x))$ is *true* only if there are more than 10 elements in the domain for which $P(x)$ is *true*, and $\exists^{\geq 3} x(P(x)) \wedge \exists^{\leq 5} x(P(x))$ is *true* only if there are between 3 and 5 elements in the domain for which $P(x)$ is *true*.

This augmentation to predicate calculus is strictly a convenience because we can obtain the results we want without the counting quantifier. For example:

$$\exists^0 x(P(x)) \Leftrightarrow \neg\exists x(P(x))$$

$$\exists^1 x(P(x)) \Leftrightarrow \exists x(P(x)) \wedge \forall x \forall y(P(x) \wedge P(y) \Rightarrow x = y)$$

$$\Leftrightarrow \neg\exists^0 x(P(x)) \wedge \forall x \forall y(P(x) \wedge P(y) \Rightarrow x = y)$$

$$\exists^2 x(P(x)) \Leftrightarrow \neg\exists^0 x(P(x)) \wedge \neg\exists^1 x(P(x)) \wedge$$

$$\forall x \forall y \forall z(P(x) \wedge P(y) \wedge P(z) \Rightarrow (x = y \vee x = z) \vee (y = z))$$

$$\exists^n x(P(x)) \Leftrightarrow \neg\exists^0 x(P(x)) \wedge \cdots \wedge \neg\exists^{n-1} x(P(x))$$

$$\wedge \forall x_1 \cdots \forall x_{n+1}(P(x_1) \wedge \cdots \wedge P(x_{n+1}) \Rightarrow (x_1 = x_2 \vee \cdots \vee x_1 = x_{n+1})$$

$$\vee (x_2 = x_3 \vee \cdots \vee x_2 = x_{n+1})$$

$$\cdots$$

$$\vee (x_n = x_{n+1}))$$

$$\exists^{\leq 1} x(P(x)) \Leftrightarrow \exists^0 x(P(x)) \vee \exists^1 x(P(x))$$

$$\exists^{\leq 2} x(P(x)) \Leftrightarrow \exists^0 x(P(x)) \vee \exists^1 x(P(x)) \vee \exists^2 x(P(x))$$

$$\exists^{\leq n} x(P(x)) \Leftrightarrow \exists^0 x(P(x)) \vee \cdots \vee \exists^n x(P(x))$$

$$\exists^{\geq 1} x(P(x)) \Leftrightarrow \exists x(P(x))$$

$$\exists^{\geq 2} x(P(x)) \Leftrightarrow \exists x(P(x)) \wedge \neg\exists^1 x(P(x))$$

$$\exists^{\geq n} x(P(x)) \Leftrightarrow \exists x(P(x)) \wedge \neg\exists^1 x(P(x)) \wedge \cdots \wedge \neg\exists^{n-1} x(P(x))$$

$$\exists^{\neq 0} x(P(x)) \Leftrightarrow \exists^{\geq 1} x(P(x)) \Leftrightarrow \exists x(P(x))$$

$$\exists^{\neq 1} x(P(x)) \Leftrightarrow \exists^{\leq 0} x(P(x)) \vee \exists^{\geq 2} x(P(x))$$

$$\exists^{\neq 2} x(P(x)) \Leftrightarrow \exists^{\leq 1} x(P(x)) \vee \exists^{\geq 3} x(P(x))$$

$$\exists^{\neq n} x(P(x)) \Leftrightarrow \exists^{\leq n-1} x(P(x)) \vee \exists^{\geq n+1} x(P(x))$$

As these examples show, counting quantifiers can provide a useful shorthand to avoid particularly long and awkward expressions.

As a further convenience, we may replace the n in

$$\exists^{\theta n} x(P(x))$$

not only with a nonnegative integer but with anything that yields a fixed nonnegative integer. Thus we can replace n with nonnegative integer constants and functions whose results are nonnegative integers. More specifically, what we are really doing is allowing interpretations in which a count value in a counting quantifier may be a constant or a function so long as it maps to a nonnegative integer.

For example, we may have $\exists^{nil} x(P(x))$, where the user-defined constant *nil* maps to 0 for the interpretation under consideration. We may also have $\exists^{20|S|} x(P(x))$ or $\exists^{2*|S|} x(P(x))$, where $|S|$ is the cardinality of a set S of interest.

5.2   Theoretical Foundations for Databases

One standard theoretical view of a database is model-theoretic; another view is proof-theoretic. Both of these views are based on first-order predicate calculus. In the model-theoretic view, we create an application model that satisfies a set of given constraints; we then query this model to obtain information. In the proof-theoretic view, we create a set of facts and rules, which we then use as the basis for deducing additional facts. Roughly speaking, the model-theoretic view gives us relational databases, and the proof-theoretic view gives us deductive databases. In the proof-theoretic view, we should also augment our perspective beyond simple deductive databases, gaining the ability to prove implications of a more general nature than the restricted types commonly used in deductive databases.

In this text, we rely heavily on the model-theoretic view of a database, and we refer occasionally to the proof-theoretic view of a database. These foundational points of view are introduced in the following subsections.

5.2.1   Model Theory

For a model-theoretic view of a relational database, we let relation names be predicates that have one place for each attribute, and we write integrity constraints as closed well-formed formulas. Then, for interpretations, we make a variety of simplifying assumptions. We assume that the domain is the union of the given domains of the attributes in all the relations, and we make the *domain-closure assumption*, which means that only elements of the domain may be substituted for variables and that quantifiers range over the domain and only over the domain. If the domains for each attribute are not explicitly given, we let the set of values in the relations be the domain. The unique-name assumption ensures that in any interpretation constants map only to themselves. For convenience, we allow ourselves to use standard, built-in predicates and functions without having to enumerate the results for each substitution of elements of the domain. Finally, we make the *closed-world assumption*; that is, when we substitute the values in their proper places for a tuple $t \in r$ for the current database instance, then for any interpretation, the substitution yields *true*, and all other substitutions yield *false*.

Figure 5.1 presents a model-theoretic view of a relational database. *Mgr manages Dept* is a relation with attributes *Mgr* and *Dept*. Its corresponding two-place, infix predicate is *Mgr( ) manages Dept( )*. *Item in Dept costs Price* is a relation with attributes *Item*, *Dept*, and *Price*, and its corresponding three-place, infix predicate is *Item( ) in Dept( ) costs Price( )*. The key constraints ensure that both *Mgr* and *Dept* are keys for *Mgr manages Dept* and that *Item* is a key for *Item in Dept costs Price*. The referential-integrity constraint

Relations:

Mgr manages Dept	
Pat	Toy
Chris	Hardware
Lynn	Clothing

Item in Dept costs Price		
ball	Toy	$10
game	Toy	$20
blocks	Toy	$10
hammer	Hardware	$30
saw	Hardware	$25

Integrity Constraints:

Key Constraints:

$$\forall x \exists^{\leq 1} y (Mgr(x) \text{ manages } Dept(y))$$
$$\forall x \exists^{\leq 1} y (Mgr(y) \text{ manages } Dept(x))$$
$$\forall x \exists^{\leq 1} <y, z> (Item(x) \text{ in } Dept(y) \text{ costs } Price(z))$$

Referential-Integrity Constraints:

$$\forall x \forall y \forall z (Item(x) \text{ in } Dept(y) \text{ costs } Price(z) \Rightarrow \exists w (Mgr(w) \text{ manages } Dept(y)))$$

Attribute-Domain Constraints:

$$\forall x \forall y (Mgr(x) \text{ manages } Dept(y) \Rightarrow x \in \{Pat, Chris, Lynn\}$$
$$\wedge\ y \in \{Toy, Hardware, Clothing\})$$
$$\forall x \forall y \forall z (Item(x) \text{ in } Dept(y) \text{ costs } Price(z) \Rightarrow x \in \{ball, game, blocks,$$
$$hammer, saw\}$$
$$\wedge\ y \in \{Toy, Hardware, Clothing\} \wedge z \in \{\$10, \$20, \$25, \$30\})$$

Figure 5.1 A model-theoretic view of a relational database instance.

ensures that each *Dept* in *Item in Dept costs Price* is a *Dept* in *Mgr manages Dept*.

For this example, the attribute domains are defined tightly. It is common to define attribute domains more generically, for example, as *String, Integer, Real, Money,* or *Time*. These domains are theoretically infinite, of course, and they are finite but very large when implemented on a computer. We will allow ourselves to use these designations for these sets either to mean the theoretically infinite sets for which they stand or to designate their corresponding finite implementations. Often, to make our points about domains clear, however, we will resort to small finite domains of user-defined constants, as in Fig. 5.1.

The domain *D* for the interpretation in Fig. 5.1 is

$$D = \{Pat, Chris, Lynn, Toy, Hardware, Clothing, ball, blocks, hammer,$$
$$saw, \$10, \$20, \$25, \$30\}$$

which is the union of the domains of all the attributes in the database and, for this example, is also the set of values in the relations. By our closed-world assumption, we assign the eight tuple substitutions implied by the eight tuples in Fig. 5.1 to be *true* and all other substitutions to be *false*. Thus, for example, *Mgr(Pat) manages Dept(Toy)* = *T* and *Item(saw) in Dept(Hardware) costs Price($25)* = *T*, whereas *Mgr(Toy) manages Dept(Pat)* = *F*, *Mgr(Pat) manages Dept(Hardware)* = *F*, and *Mgr($25) manages Dept($25)* = *F*. Note that we must assign every possible substitution a truth value, whether or not it makes sense intuitively. Thus, although it intuitively makes sense to say that "Pat does not manage the Hardware department" and although it makes no sense to say that "Toy does not manage the Pat department" or that "$25 does not manage the $25 department," nevertheless we must map each possibility to *T* or *F*. There are thus 14∗14 = 196 possible substitutions for *Mgr manages Dept*, only three of which map to *T*, and 14∗14∗14 = 2744 possible substitutions for *Item in Dept costs Price*, only five of which map to *T*.

Since we are interested in the validity of a database instance, we want to ensure at least that all the integrity constraints hold. We do not want, for example, the tuple <blocks, *Automotive*, $90> to be added to the *Item in Dept costs Price* relation, for then several of our integrity constraints, including a key constraint, the referential-integrity constraint, and an attribute-domain constraint, would be violated. We can ensure that the integrity constraints hold by checking them. Observe that all our integrity constraints are closed formulas. Thus, given an interpretation, they each evaluate to *true* or *false*. We say that an interpretation is *valid* if all the closed formulas are *true*.

Models in Model Theory

In standard model theory, an interpretation in which all closed formulas are *true* is called a "model." Since we are already using "model" in several different ways, adding yet another meaning is not in our best interest here. We therefore refer to a "model" in the classic, model-theoretic sense as a "valid interpretation."

To see whether the interpretation implied by the database instance in Fig. 5.1 is valid with respect to the given integrity constraints, we must check each of the six formulas. The quantifiers range over the entire domain D and thus, for each formula, we must check every combination of substitutions. For example,

$$\forall x \forall y (Mgr(x) \; manages \; Dept(y) \Rightarrow x \in \{Pat, Chris, Lynn\}$$
$$\wedge \; y \in \{Toy, Hardware, Clothing\})$$

$$= Mgr(Pat) \; manages \; Dept(Pat) \Rightarrow Pat \in \{Pat, Chris, Lynn\}$$
$$\wedge \; Pat \in \{Toy, Hardware, Clothing\}$$
$$\wedge \; Mgr(Pat) \; manages \; Dept(Chris) \Rightarrow Pat \in \{Pat, Chris, Lynn\}$$
$$\wedge \; Chris \in \{Toy, Hardware, Clothing\}$$
$$...$$
$$\wedge \; Mgr(Pat) \; manages \; Dept(Toy) \Rightarrow Pat \in \{Pat, Chris, Lynn\}$$
$$\wedge \; Toy \in \{Toy, Hardware, Clothing\}$$
$$...$$
$$\wedge \; Mgr(\$30) \; manages \; Dept(\$30) \Rightarrow \$30 \in \{Pat, Chris, Lynn\}$$
$$\wedge \; \$30 \in \{Toy, Hardware, Clothing\}$$

is *true*: most of the conjunctive terms are *true* vacuously because the left-hand side of the implication ($\Rightarrow$) is *false*, and the rest are *true* because when the left-hand side is *true*, the right-hand side is also *true*. As a second example, consider

$$\forall x \exists^{\leq 1} y (Mgr(x) \; manages \; Dept(y))$$

which is *true* since for each $x \in D$, there are either no y's or exactly one y such that $<x, y> \in Mgr \; manages \; Dept$ (i.e., for *Pat*, *Chris*, and *Lynn* there is exactly one department, and for any other value in D, there is no department).

5.2.2 Relational Calculus

For the model-theoretic approach to databases, open formulas are queries. Each substitution for which the formula evaluates to *true* is a tuple in the result. It is typical to denote queries as $\{<x_1: A_1, \dots\ x_n: A_n> \mid F(x_1, \dots, x_n)\}$, where $x_1, \dots\ x_n$ are the free variables of formula F, and where $A_1, \dots\ A_n$ are the attributes for $x_1, \dots, x_n$, respectively. We usually omit the attributes when they can be inferred from F, as will be shown in the following examples. Alternatively, we can replace the generic n-tuple with an n-place, infix predicate.

In the following series of instructive examples, we assume the sample database instance in Fig. 5.1. Each example includes a query statement in English, a relational-calculus query, and the result. We comment on the query to provide additional insight into relational calculus.

Query 1.   List all items that cost more than \$15 along with their department.

$$\{< x, y > \mid \exists z(Item(x) \ in \ Dept(y) \ costs \ Price(z) \wedge z > \$15)\}$$

Item	Dept
game	Toy
hammer	Hardware
saw	Hardware

When we substitute *game* for x and *Toy* for y, there indeed exists a z in the domain, namely \$20, such that the formula evaluates to *true*. *Item(game) in Dept(Toy) costs Price*(\$20) evaluates to true because \$20 > \$15 and because *<game, Toy, \$20>* is a tuple for *Item in Dept costs Price* in our valid interpretation. Similarly, when we substitute *hammer* or *saw* for x and *Hardware* for y, there exists z such that the formula evaluates to *true*. All other substitutions of values for x and y from the domain fail. The substitution $x = Pat$ and $y = Pat$ fails, for example, because there is no z such that *<Pat, Pat, z>* is a tuple in *Item in Dept costs Price*, and $x = ball$ and $y = Toy$ fails because although *<ball, Toy, \$10>* is a tuple in *Item in Dept costs Price*, \$10 > \$15 does not hold.

We infer attribute names for the result table by taking the object-set names from the infix predicates. In Query 1, the object-set name for x is

Item; the object-set name for *y* is *Dept*. If a variable associates with more than one object-set name or if we prefer a different name, we must declare the attribute. For example, we could rewrite Query 1 as

$$\{< x, y: Department > \ | \ \exists z(Item(x) \ in \ Dept(y) \ costs \ Price(z) \wedge z = \$15)\}$$

which yields the following result:

Item	Department
game	Toy
hammer	Hardware
saw	Hardware

We may also provide an infix predicate in place of the tuple constructor and write

$$\{Item(x) \ costing \ more \ than \ \$15 \ is \ in \ Department(y)$$
$$| \ \exists z(Item(x) \ in \ Dept(y) \ costs \ Price(z) \wedge z = \$15)\}$$

which yields the following result:

Item costing more than $15 is in Department	
game	Toy
hammer	Hardware
saw	Hardware

As a notational simplification, we sometimes give one-letter names for relations and use the order of the attributes in the table in an interpretation as an implicit specification of attributes. Suppose that we let $m(\_,\_)$ represent *Mgr manages Dept*, with *Mgr* as the attribute for the first place and *Dept* as the attribute for the second place, and that we let $p(\_,\_,\_)$ represent *Item in Dept costs Price*, with *Item*, *Dept*, and *Price* as attributes for the respective places. We can now write Query 1 more succinctly as follows:

$$\{< x, y > \ | \ \exists z(p(x, y, z) \wedge z > \$15)\}$$

We assume these more succinct representations for the rest of our discussion on relational calculus.

Query 2. List the item and department for items that cost $10.

$$\{< x, y > \mid p(x, y, \$10)\}$$

Item	Department
ball	Toy
game	Toy

When the only free variables are those in the tuple constructor, there is no need for any quantifier. Observe that the constant $10 is used in place of a variable in a predicate. This limits the tuples that satisfy the predicate to those whose corresponding value matches the constant.

Query 3. List the names of managers who manage departments with an item that costs $10.

$$\{< x > \mid \exists y \exists z(m(x, y) \wedge p(y, z, \$10))\}$$

Mgr
Pat

The variable y, which is common to both m and p, ensures that the department of the manager is the same as the department with an item that costs $10. This is the way we join tables together using relational calculus.

Query 4. List pairs of items in the toy department that cost the same. Do not list the same item twice as a pair and do not list items once in one order and again in the opposite order.

$$\{< x: Item1, y: Item2 > \mid \exists z(p(x, Toy, z) \wedge p(y, Toy, z) \wedge x < y)\}$$

Item1	Item2
ball	blocks

We can evaluate this expression by substituting any tuple from the toy department for the first predicate p and any other tuple from the toy department for the second predicate p. In general, the tuples would not have to be different, but because $x < y$ the tuples cannot be the same. Then, if the z value for the chosen tuples is the same, that is, if they both cost the same, we list the x-y pair, but only if x comes alphabetically before y. Substituting all possible pairs of tuples for the two predicates yields the result we want.

Query 5.   List the departments that do not have an item that costs \$10.

$$\{< x_1 > \mid \exists x_2(m(x_2, x_1) \wedge \neg\exists x_3(p(x_3, x_1, \$10)))\}$$

Dept
Hardware
Clothing

Much can be learned about relational calculus by carefully considering Query 5. If we substitute any value in the domain for x_1 other than one of the departments in m (e.g., if we substitute *hammer* for x_1), the formula evaluates to *false* because $m(x_2, x_1)$, which is connected conjunctively to the rest of the formula, is *false*. If we substitute *Toy* for x_1, x_2 can be *Pat*, which makes $m(x_2, x_1)$ *true*. Thus, because of the conjunction, the formula will be *true* only if $\neg\exists x_3(p(x_3, Toy, \$10))$ is *true*. Since there exists a value for x_3, namely *ball*, that makes $\exists x_3(p(x_3, Toy, \$10))$ *true*, however, $\neg\exists x_3(p(x_3, Toy, \$10))$ is *false*. Hence, *Toy* is not in the result. When we substitute *Hardware* for x_1, on the other hand, there is no value for x_3 that makes $\exists x_3(p(x_3, Hardware, \$10))$ *true*, and thus, since $\exists x_3(p(x_3, Hardware, \$10))$ is *false* for any substitution for x_3, $\neg\exists x_3(p(x_3, Hardware, \$10))$ is *true*. Similarly, substituting *Clothing* for x_1 makes $\neg\exists x_3(p(x_3, Clothing, \$10))$ *true*. Indeed, there are no tuples in p with *Clothing* as the department and thus surely no tuple in p that has a clothing item that costs \$10.

By using one of the equivalences in Table 5.2, namely $\neg\exists x P(x) \Leftrightarrow \forall x \neg P(x)$, we can rewrite Query 5 as

$$\{< x_1 > \mid \exists x_2(m(x_2, x_1) \wedge \forall x_3(\neg p(x_3, x_1, \$10)))\}$$

This version of Query 5 has a universal quantifier, which emphasizes that we must consider every tuple in p for each x_1 value we test. In particular, the universal quantifier on x_3 requires that for any possible substitution of a value into x_3 from the domain there must not be a tuple that holds. Thus, when we fix x_1 to be one of the departments, there must not be a tuple with an item for that department that costs \$10—exactly what we want.

In addition to these two ways of expressing Query 5 correctly in relational calculus, there are many ways to express Query 5 incorrectly. Two of these ways are subtly incorrect and are worth discussing. First consider

$$\{< x_1 > \mid \exists x_2 \exists x_3 (p(x_2, x_1, x_3) \wedge x_3 \neq \$10)\}$$

which yields the following result:

Dept
Toy
Hardware

Toy is in the result because $<game, Toy, \$20>$ is a tuple in p whose price is not \$10. We want departments for which none of the items cost \$10, not departments for which some item does not cost \$10. Thus, we must consider all of the items in each department, which means that we need a universal quantifier, or equivalently, the negation of an existential quantifier.

Next consider the query

$$\{< x_1 > \mid \neg \exists x_2 (p(x_2, x_1, \$10)))\}$$

which yields the following (strange) result.

Dept
Pat
Chris
Lynn
Hardware
Clothing
ball
game
blocks
hammer
saw
\$10
\$20
\$30
\$25

Notice that the only value in the domain that is not on the list is *Toy*. Indeed, this expression computes the complement of

$$\{< x_1 > \mid \exists x_2 (p(x_2, x_1, \$10)))\}$$

with respect to the entire domain. To limit the result to just the departments, we conjoin the formula involving m and write the original solution for Query 5.

Query 6.   List the managers who are responsible for every item that costs $10.

$$\{< x_1 > \mid \exists x_2(m(x_1, x_2) \wedge \forall x_3 \forall x_4(p(x_3, x_4, \$10) \Rightarrow x_2 = x_4))\}$$

$$\frac{Mgr}{Pat}$$

We can understand Query 6 by reading it as follows: a manager x_1 whose department is x_2 satisfies this query if for every $10 item in *Item in Dept costs Price* the departments match (i.e., if for every tuple $<x_3, x_4, \$10>$ in *Item in Dept costs Price*, $x_2 = x_4$).

Another way to understand Query 6 is to use the implication rule in Table 5.1 and rewrite it as

$$\{< x_1 > \mid \exists x_2(m(x_1, x_2) \wedge \forall x_3 \forall x_4(\neg p(x_3, x_4, \$10) \vee x_2 = x_4))\}$$

Here we can see that, for the formula to be true, every pair of values from the domain that we substitute for x_3 and x_4 (and we emphasize that we must substitute all possible pairs, including those that may seem silly, such as $x_3 = Pat$ and $x_4 = Clothing$, and identical ones, such as $x_3 = \$30$ and $x_4 = \$30$), either the tuple formed is not in p or the departments must match. This is exactly what we want because for any manager x_1 who should be in the result, all substitutions of values for x_3 and x_4 must either cause the tuple $<x_3, x_4, \$10>$ not to be in p or cause the departments to match, so that the manager's department has all the $10 items.

If we make another adjustment, we can look at Query 6 in one more way. Using double negation from Table 5.1, the equivalence rule $\neg \exists x P(x) \Leftrightarrow \forall x \neg P(x)$ from Table 5.2, and DeMorgan's law from Table 5.1, we can write Query 6 as follows:

$$\{< x_1 > \mid \exists x_2(m(x_1, x_2) \wedge \neg \exists x_3 \exists x_4(p(x_3, x_4, \$10) \wedge x_2 \neq x_4))\}$$

In this form, we can see that we want a manager for a department if it is not the case that there exists a $10 item such that the item is not in the manager's department.

Most people do not understand double negations readily in English (or any other natural language). Hence, we do not consider this formulation of Query 6, with not exists and not equal, to be intuitive. The form is nevertheless particularly useful for developing an SQL solution for Query 6 because it translates directly to SQL as follows:

```
select Mgr
from m
where not exists
    (select *
    from p
    where p. Price = $10 and m. Dept != p. Dept
```

The other solutions do not have direct translations to SQL, and because of the nonintuitive double negation, most people have difficulty coming up with this SQL solution to Query 6 directly. Thus SQL queries that involve universal quantification may be written in relational calculus using universal quantifiers, like the first two solutions for Query 6. Then the equivalences in Tables 5.1 and 5.2 may be used to translate such queries into queries with negations of existential quantifiers, like the last solution. Finally, using this form, the queries may be translated directly into SQL, as this example shows.

5.2.3 Proof Theory and Datalog

Another standard view of a database is a proof-theoretic view, which provides us with deductive databases and also with a way to do proofs. We begin by discussing deductive databases, focusing later in this section more on proofs.

Although various deductive database systems have been defined for first-order predicate calculus, we confine our interest in deductive databases to Datalog, more specifically to *Datalog with negation*, which we refer to as Datalog. We begin, however, by describing *pure Datalog*, without negation, which is characterized by closed formulas of the form

$$\forall x_1 \forall x_2 \cdots \forall x_m (\neg P_1 \vee \cdots \vee \neg P_n \vee Q)$$

where $m, n \geq 0$ and the P_i's and Q are atomic predicates, each of which may have a different number of places for arguments, and where each argument is a constant or one of the variables $x_1, ..., x_m$ such that any variable that appears in Q must also appear in at least one of the P_i's.

Before giving an example, let us make several observations and provide several simplifying assumptions and conventions. We observe first that all Datalog formulas are written in a standard form in which all variables are quantified by universal quantifiers that appear at the beginning. We normally write these formulas without the universal quantifiers. Thus we write

$$\neg P_1 \vee \cdots \vee \neg P_n \vee Q$$

which is equivalent to

$$P_1 \wedge \cdots \wedge P_n \Rightarrow Q$$

(Since the meaning of "without negation" may be confusing, we point out that the phrase has reference to this last form, in which there are no negation symbols.)

We further observe that when $n = 0$, the formula must have the form $Q(c_1, \ldots, c_k)$, where each c_i is a constant; otherwise, it would include a variable that does not appear in at least one of the P_i's (of which there are none, since $n = 0$). Formulas of this form are called *facts*. When $n > 0$, the formula has the form $P_1 \wedge \cdots \wedge P_n \Rightarrow Q$. These formulas express *deductive rules*. When expressing deductive rules, we usually write these formulas as $Q :- P_1, P_2, ..., P_n$.

The simplifying assumptions we make include the unique-name assumption, the closed-world assumption, and the domain-closure assumption. These assumptions, respectively, guarantee that all constants are unique and that they represent themselves, that all facts not explicitly given as *true* are *false*, and that only elements of the given domain may be substituted for variables. When not enumerated explicitly, the domain is the set of constants mentioned in the facts. For convenience, we also allow ourselves to assume that standard, built-in predicates and functions are available and have their usual meaning.

Generally, a convention is also established to distinguish between variables and constants. Although a common choice is to let variables start with capital letters and constants start with small letters, we choose instead to let variables be single letters, with or without subscripts or primes, and to let constants be multiple-letter sequences. When a constant must be a single letter, we prefix it with a backslash. As a further notational convenience, we usually elide so-called "don't care" variables, which are variables that match with no other variables in a deductive rule.

Figure 5.2 shows a pure Datalog database instance. Since a pure Datalog database instance maps directly to first-order predicate calculus, we can

Facts:

Mgr(Pat) manages Dept(Toy)	*Mgr(Tracy) supervises Emp(Deon)*
Mgr(Chris) manages Dept(Hardware)	*Mgr(Tracy) supervises Emp(Kelly)*
Mgr(Lynn) manages Dept(Clothing)	*Mgr(Kelly) supervises Emp(Pat)*
	Mgr(Deon) supervises Emp(Chris)
	Mgr(Kelly) supervises Emp(Lynn)
	Mgr(Lynn) supervises Emp(Jerry)
	Mgr(Lynn) supervises Emp(Kim)

Item(ball) in Dept(Toy) costs Price($10)
Item(game) in Dept(Toy) costs Price($20)
Item(blocks) in Dept(Toy) costs Price($10)
Item(hammer) in Dept(Hardware) costs Price($30)
Item(saw) in Dept(Hardware) costs Price($25)

Deductive Rules:

Emp(x) is directly responsible to Mgr(y) :− *Mgr(y) supervises Emp(x)*

Emp(x) is responsible to Mgr(y) :− *Emp(x) is directly responsible to Mgr(y)*
Emp(x) is responsible to Mgr(y) :−
$\qquad$ *Emp(x) is directly responsible to Mgr(z),*
$\qquad$ *Emp(z) is responsible to Mgr(y)*

Mgr(x) is responsible for Emp(y) :− *Emp(y) is responsible to Mgr(x)*

Mgr(x) is directly responsible for Item(y) :−
$\qquad$ *Mgr(x) manages Dept(z),*
$\qquad$ *Item(y) in Dept(z) costs Price( )*

Mgr(x) is responsible for Item(y) :− *Mgr(x) is directly responsible for Item(y)*
Mgr(x) is responsible for Item(y) :−
$\qquad$ *Mgr(x) is responsible for Emp(z),*
$\qquad$ *Mgr(z) is directly responsible for Item(y)*

Figure 5.2 A proof-theoretic view of a pure Datalog database instance.

define its semantics using an interpretation. It is more common, however, to use either *proof semantics* or *least-fixed-point semantics*, both of which we discuss now.

For *proof semantics*, we assume that the formulas in the database instance, both the facts and the deductive rules, are given as formulas that hold (or are always *true*), and we use them to derive other formulas. We derive formulas by means of a *derivation sequence*, consisting of a sequence of formulas, each of which is given or is implied by those already in the sequence by an *inference rule*. If we use only inference rules that are *sound*, then any formula derived from the given formulas is *true* in any valid interpretation, and if the set of inference rules we use is *complete*, then any formula that is *true* in a valid interpretation can always be derived from the inference rules.

Table 5.3 shows some sound, commonly used inference rules. The notation that describes the rules means that if there are formulas in a derivation sequence of the form of those above the line, then a formula of the form of the one below the line is inferred and thus may be added to the derivation sequence. Any logical equivalences or implications in Tables 5.1 and 5.2 may also be used as inference rules.

In addition to inference rules and logical equivalences and implications, we may also use the principle of *instantiation*. Since each of the variables in all the formulas we are using here is quantified universally over the given domain, any *true* formula is *true* for any substitution of constants for variables. Thus, since any formula f in a derivation sequence is *true*, either because f is given and thus assumed to be *true* or because f is *true* by implication, f is also *true* for any particular substitution. When we substitute one or more variables in a formula with a constant, we *instantiate* the formula. Thus we may produce a new formula for a derivation sequence by instantiating any formula already in the derivation sequence.

Figure 5.3, an example of a derivation sequence, proves that Pat is directly responsible for games. Note that we use standard predicate-calculus notation here rather than the :− notation of Datalog. There is a reason for the Datalog notation, which we will come to shortly, but for the moment we wish to focus more on proofs than on Datalog. Observe that the derivation sequence in Fig. 5.3 is of the form we require for a proof.

Table 5.3. Some Useful Inference Rules				
Modus ponens	Modus tollens	Transitivity	Conjunction	Simplification
P	$\neg Q$	$P \Rightarrow Q$	P	
$P \Rightarrow Q$	$P \Rightarrow Q$	$Q \Rightarrow R$	Q	$P \wedge Q$
Q	$\neg P$	$P \Rightarrow R$	$P \wedge Q$	P

1. *Mgr(Pat) manages Dept(Toy)*   given
2. *Item(game) in Dept(Toy) costs Price($20)*   given
3. *Mgr(Pat) manages Dept(Toy)* ∧
    Item(game) in Dept(Toy) costs Price($20)   conjunction (1, 2)
4. *Mgr(x) manages Dept(z)* ∧
    Item(y) in Dept(z) costs Price( ) ⇒
    Mgr(x) is directly responsible for Item(y)   given
5. *Mgr(Pat) manages Dept(Toy)* ∧
    Item(game) in Dept(Toy) costs Price($20) ⇒
    Mgr(Pat) is directly responsible for Item(game)   instantiation (4)
6. *Mgr(Pat) is directly responsible for Item(game)*   modus ponens (3, 5)

Figure 5.3 A derivation sequence proving that *Mgr(Pat) is directly responsible for Item(game)*.

Each formula is either given in Fig. 5.2, like the ones on lines 1, 2, and 4, or derived by a rule from the preceding formulas. We derive the formula on line 6, for example, by the modus-ponens rule in Table 5.3 using the formulas on lines 3 and 5.

Before leaving the proof in Fig. 5.3, we point out that mathematical proofs are often written less formally, in more of a narrative style. This narrative captures the idea of a derivation sequence without having to follow the rules in a strict form. It must always be possible, however, to reconstruct a strict derivation sequence. Figure 5.4 provides an example of how the proof in Fig. 5.3 might be written in narrative style.

When people write proofs, they often proceed nonsystematically, skipping nonessential rules and facts, using only instantiations that yield results, and jumping immediately to the main idea. If we want a computer to write our proofs, we need a more systematic way of covering all the possibilities. We could simply try every possible derivation sequence systematically, backing up when we run into a dead end. This approach works, but it entails two problems: (1) unless our inference rules and logical equivalences are minimal, we will generate many sequences that prove the same facts over and over, and (2) although we will arrive at our goal eventually,

Since Mgr(Pat) manages Dept(Toy) and Item(game) in Dept(Toy) costs Price($20), and since Mgr(x) manages Dept(z) and Item(y) in Dept(z) costs Price( ) implies that Mgr(x) is directly responsible for Item(y), Mgr(Pat) is directly responsible for Item(game).

Figure 5.4 A narrative-style proof of *Mgr(Pat) is directly responsible for Item(game)*.

the process is not goal directed and therefore has the tendency to wander over many facts and rules before concluding.

Robinson's resolution principle helps us solve these problems. The principle solves the first problem because it uses only one inference rule, modus tollens, which, along with instantiation and conjunction (which the resolution procedure eventually will let us ignore), constitutes a complete set of inference rules. Robinson's resolution principle solves the second problem because it is goal directed in that it starts with the fact to be proved and works backward to determine whether there is a derivation sequence that leads to the result.

In using Robinson's resolution principle, we observe that it is always possible to write each of the given facts and deductive rules in the database at the beginning of a derivation sequence. Thus, since every formula in a derivation sequence is implied by the preceding formulas, and since the transitivity rule holds, we can write $R \Rightarrow Q$, where R is a conjunction of all the given facts and rules and Q is any formula in a derivation sequence, usually the last. $R \Rightarrow Q$, however, is equivalent to $R \wedge \neg Q \Rightarrow$ *false*. We may thus prove that Q is true given R by negating Q and placing it in our derivation sequence as the starting formula. We then proceed using modus tollens (see Table 5.3), searching for a rule whose conclusion matches Q, after instantiation if necessary. The result is the negation of the antecedent, $\neg P$. Then, in addition to $\neg Q$, we also have $\neg P$ to work with. We continue in this fashion either until we encounter a fact F_i (rather than a rule) that matches a $\neg F_i$ in the derivation sequence, or until we have exhausted all the possibilities without encountering such an F_i. If we encounter F_i, having already established $\neg F_i$, then by conjunction, we have $F_i \wedge \neg F_i$, which is equivalent to *false*. Since we then have $R \wedge \neg Q \Rightarrow$ *false*, which is equivalent to $R \Rightarrow Q$, we have proved that Q is *true* given R. If not, since we are using a complete set of inference rules, we can conclude that the fact we are trying to prove does not follow logically from R. Figure 5.5 presents an example.

Observe in Fig. 5.5 that our proof uses conjunction as well as modus tollens and instantiation. We can always ignore the final conjunction by convention once we have a fact F_i and its negation $\neg F_i$ in the derivation sequence. Removing the other way in which conjunction arises is a matter of making an observation about the deductive rules, which all have the form

$$P_1 \wedge P_2 \wedge ... \wedge P_n \Rightarrow Q$$

Observe that whenever we apply modus tollens to a deductive rule with $\neg Q$, the result is

$$\neg(P_1 \wedge P_2 \wedge \ldots \wedge P_n)$$

When $n = 1$, the result has the form $\neg P_1$, which has no conjunction, and therefore needs no conjunction of facts to continue. If, on the other hand, $n > 1$, then by DeMorgan's law, the form of the result is

$$\neg P_1 \vee \neg P_2 \vee \ldots \vee \neg P_n$$

which leads to a contradiction only if *all* the individual disjunctive terms lead to a contradiction. Thus, so long as we systematically follow *every* derivation sequence (beginning with one of the disjunctive terms) to see that it leads to a contradiction, we may consider each disjunctive term one at a time, as if it were a formula in the derivation sequence. An example appears in Fig. 5.6.

Observe that in Fig. 5.6 conjunction is no longer necessary. We can simplify the derivation sequence further by putting our deductive rules in the form used in a deductive database. In this form, we write the conclusion on the left of the symbol :– and call it, in this context, the *head* of the deductive

1.	¬*Mgr(Pat) is directly responsible for Item(game)*	negation of the conclusion
2.	*Mgr(x) manages Dept(z)* ∧ *Item(y) in Dept(z) costs Price( )* ⇒ *Mgr(x) is directly responsible for Item(y)*	given
3.	*Mgr(Pat) manages Dept(Toy)* ∧ *Item(game) in Dept(Toy) costs Price($20)* ⇒ *Mgr(Pat) is directly responsible for Item(game)*	instantiation (2)
4.	¬(*Mgr(Pat) manages Dept(Toy)* ∧ *Item(game) in Dept(Toy) costs Price($20)*)	modus tollens (1, 3)
5.	*Mgr(Pat) manages Dept(Toy)*	given
6.	*Item(game) in Dept(Toy) costs Price($20)*	given
7.	*Mgr(Pat) manages Dept(Toy)* ∧ *Item(game) in Dept(Toy) costs Price($20)*	conjunction (5, 6)
8.	¬(*Mgr(Pat) manages Dept(Toy)* ∧ *Item(game) in Dept(Toy) costs Price($20)*) ∧ (*Mgr(Pat) manages Dept(Toy)* ∧ *Item(game) in Dept(Toy) costs Price($20)*)	conjunction (4, 7)
9.	*F*	negation (8)

Figure 5.5 A resolution proof of *Mgr(Pat) is directly responsible for Item(game)*.

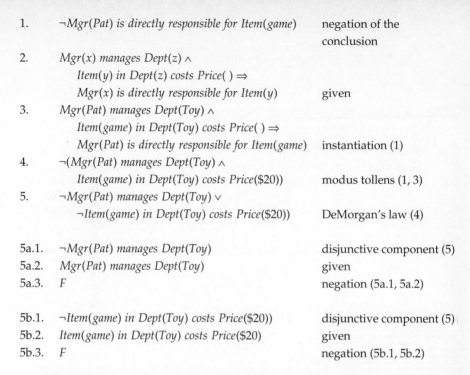

1.	¬*Mgr(Pat) is directly responsible for Item(game)*	negation of the conclusion

2.	*Mgr(x) manages Dept(z)* ∧
	    Item(y) in Dept(z) costs Price( ) ⇒
	    Mgr(x) is directly responsible for Item(y)
		given

3.	*Mgr(Pat) manages Dept(Toy)* ∧
	    Item(game) in Dept(Toy) costs Price( ) ⇒
	    Mgr(Pat) is directly responsible for Item(game)
		instantiation (1)

4.	¬(*Mgr(Pat) manages Dept(Toy)* ∧ *Item(game) in Dept(Toy) costs Price($20)*)	modus tollens (1, 3)
5.	¬*Mgr(Pat) manages Dept(Toy)* ∨ ¬*Item(game) in Dept(Toy) costs Price($20)*)	DeMorgan's law (4)

5a.1.	¬*Mgr(Pat) manages Dept(Toy)*	disjunctive component (5)
5a.2.	*Mgr(Pat) manages Dept(Toy)*	given
5a.3.	*F*	negation (5a.1, 5a.2)

5b.1.	¬*Item(game) in Dept(Toy) costs Price($20)*)	disjunctive component (5)
5b.2.	*Item(game) in Dept(Toy) costs Price($20)*	given
5b.3.	*F*	negation (5b.1, 5b.2)

Figure 5.6   A resolution proof without conjunction.

rule; we write the antecedent on the right and call it the *body* of the deductive rule. Furthermore, we list the negated atomic predicates in a derivation sequence without writing their negation symbol and hence have an immediate contradiction once we arrive at a fact in the database. Whenever we use a rule whose body has n terms, $n > 1$, we simply initiate n derivation sequences and check them all (see Fig. 5.7 for an example).

We observe that instantiation can be done systematically by substituting all elements of the domain one at a time for each of the variables. In addition, we can use the formulas already introduced in a derivation sequence to reduce greatly the number of elements we substitute.

By making one additional observation, we can turn proofs into queries. If we wish to prove a fact, as we have just done, we simply run our resolution procedure as outlined—the answer is either "yes" or "no" depending on whether the procedure proves the fact or fails to prove the fact. If, on the other hand, we wish to pose a query, we replace one or more of the constants with variables. In this context, we can imagine that the system can substitute all combinations of values systematically from the domain for

1.	*Mgr(Pat) is directly responsible for Item(game)*	conclusion (without negation)

2.	*Mgr(x) is directly responsible for Item(y)* :–
	    Mgr(x) manages Dept(z),
	    Item(y) in Dept(z) costs Price( )
		given

3.	*Mgr(Pat) is directly responsible for Item(game)* :–
	    Mgr(Pat) manages Dept(Toy),
	    Item(game) in Dept(Toy) costs Price($20)
		instantiation

4a.1	*Mgr(Pat) manages Dept(Toy)*	disjunctive component after modus tollens (1, 3)
4a.2	*F*	fact (4a.1)
4b.1	*Item(game) in Dept(Toy) costs Price($20)*	disjunctive component after modus tollens (1, 3)
4b.2	*F*	fact (4b.1)

Figure 5.7   A resolution proof using Datalog notation.

each of the variables. It can then prove or disprove each of these facts. Any and all substitutions for which a fact is proven true can then be returned as the results of the query.

We can make the substitution procedure more efficient by a process called *unification*. Unification determines whether we can make two atomic predicates match. Two atomic predicates match if they have the same predicate name and if, for each corresponding argument place, they have the same constant or variable. Two atomic predicates that do not match can be *unified* (made to match), if, by properly renaming one or more variables, they can be made to match. We *properly rename* a variable in a fact or rule by replacing each occurrence of the variable in the fact or rule by some variable name not already mentioned in the fact or rule. Sometimes several proper renamings are necessary to unify two atomic predicates. Unification makes the substitution procedure more efficient because we delay substituting constants until we encounter facts. When we substitute a constant for a variable, we then propagate the substitution back through the unified atomic predicates. Thus the variables in the initial query obtain values by unification.

Figure 5.8 shows a sample query along with its resolution and unification. The query extracts all items for which Pat is responsible {*ball, game, blocks*}. Thus we infer the following facts:

> *Mgr(Pat) is directly responsible for Item(ball)*
> *Mgr(Pat) is directly responsible for Item(game)*
> *Mgr(Pat) is directly responsible for Item(blocks)*

An alternative view of this process provides us with least-fixed-point semantics. In this view, we think of each variable in a rule as being associated with a set. We then add constants to the set, one at a time, so long as each yields a provable substitution. The maximal set obtained in this way is the *least-fixed point*. Thus, for example, for the query in Fig. 5.8, we add *ball*, *game*, and *blocks* to the solution set for x for *Item(x) in Dept(Toy) costs Price( )* to obtain the following:

$$\text{Item}(\{ball, game, blocks\}) \text{ in Dept}(Toy) \text{ costs Price}( )$$

The least-fixed-point idea also helps us see how to do disjunctive queries. Consider, for example, adding the following deductive rules

1. *Mgr(Pat) is directly responsible for Item(x)*
2. *Mgr(Pat) is directly responsible for Item(x)* :–   unified by
    Mgr(Pat) manages Dept(z),   substituting Pat for
    Item(x) in Dept(z) costs Price( ) x and x for y

3a.1 *Mgr(Pat) manages Dept(Toy)*   unified: Toy for z

3b.1 *Item(ball) in Dept(Toy) costs Price($10)*   unified: Toy for z
                                                         unified: ball for x
                                                         "don't care" variable
                                                         substitution: $10
      $x = ball$ part of the result since
                                                         x is in the query

3c.1 *Item(game) in Dept(Toy) costs Price($20)*   unified: game for x
                                                         "don't care" variable
                                                         substitution: $20
      $x = game$ part of the result since
                                                         x is in the query

3d.1 *Item(blocks) in Dept(Toy) costs Price($10)*   unified: blocks for x
                                                         "don't care" variable
                                                         substitution: $10
      $x = blocks$ part of the result since
                                                         x is in the query

Figure 5.8   A query that yields all items for which Pat is responsible.

High-cost or Hardware Item(x) :– *Item(x) in Dept( ) costs Price(y), y > \$15*
High-cost or Hardware Item(x) :– *Item(x) in Dept(Hardware) costs Price( )*

to the rules in Fig. 5.2 and then issuing the query

High-cost or Hardware Item(x)

As an aside, we point out that this is how we also do queries in a deductive database. We add the rules to derive the desired results and then issue a query corresponding to the head of the rule that represents these results.

Returning to our discussion of least-fixed-point semantics, we now try to put each value of the domain into the set systematically. If we let $x = $ *saw*, for example, we can unify *High-cost or Hardware Items(saw)* with the second rule to obtain *Item(saw) in Dept(Hardware) costs Price(\$25)*, which is a fact in Fig. 5.2. Thus, we add *saw* to our result set. Continuing, if we let x = *hammer*, we see similarly that we should add *hammer* to our result set since *Item(hammer) in Dept(Hardware) costs Price(\$30)* is a fact in Fig. 5.2. If we let x = *game*, we can unify with the first rule just stated to obtain *Item(game) in Dept(Toy) costs Price(\$20)* and \$20 > \$15, which satisfies this deductive rule and thus adds *game* to the result. Any other substitution for x fails to satisfy either rule—either the price is not greater than \$15 or the department is not *Hardware*. Thus, the least-fixed point is {*saw, hammer, game*}, which is the result for our query.

We can see that the result includes any item that satisfies either the first or the second of the two deductive rules stated earlier. Thus, in order to do disjunctive queries, we make several rules with the same head, each covering one of the cases of interest. Here, the first rule yields the high-cost items; the second, the *Hardware* items.

Least-fixed-point semantics are also useful for recursive queries. Consider, for example, the query

Emp(x) is responsible to Mgr(Tracy)

This rule can be unified with two of our deductive rules:

Emp(x) is responsible to Mgr(y) :– *Emp(x) is directly responsible to Mgr(y)*
Emp(x) is responsible to Mgr(y) :–
     Emp(x) is directly responsible to Mgr(z),
     Emp(z) is responsible to Mgr(y)

Unifying with the first rule yields the formula

$$Emp(x) \text{ is directly responsible to } Mgr(Tracy)$$

which can be unified with

$$Emp(x) \text{ is directly responsible to } Mgr(y) \; :- \; Mgr(y) \text{ supervises } Emp(x)$$

to yield the formula

$$Mgr(Tracy) \text{ supervises } Emp(x)$$

The least-fixed-point set for x here is $\{Deon, Kelly\}$, which we can read directly from the facts in Fig. 5.2. Thus by substituting this set for x in the original we have

$$Emp(\{Deon, Kelly\}) \text{ is responsible to } Mgr(Tracy)$$

To obtain the least-fixed-point solution, we must now try to enlarge this set. In this case we succeed in enlarging the set by using the second rule

$$Emp(x) \text{ is responsible to } Mgr(y) \; :-$$
$$Emp(x) \text{ is directly responsible to } Mgr(z),$$
$$Emp(z) \text{ is responsible to } Mgr(y)$$

which, by unification with what we have so far, is

$$Emp(x) \text{ is responsible to } Mgr(Tracy) \; :-$$
$$Emp(x) \text{ is directly responsible to } Mgr(\{Deon, Kelly\}),$$
$$Emp(\{Deon, Kelly\}) \text{ is responsible to } Mgr(Tracy)$$

Unifying as before now yields $x = \{Pat, Chris, Lynn\}$, which, by our least-fixed-point semantics, augments the solution set to be $\{Deon, Kelly, Pat, Chris, Lynn\}$. Repeating the process again, we now consider

$$Emp(x) \text{ is responsible to } Mgr(Tracy) \; :-$$
$$Emp(x) \text{ is directly responsible to } Mgr(\{Deon, Kelly, Pat, Chris, Lynn\}),$$
$$Emp(\{Deon, Kelly, Pat, Chris, Lynn\}) \text{ is responsible to } Mgr(Tracy)$$

which yields two additional values for x, *Jerry* and *Kim*. Since another repetition yields no new values, the least-fixed point is

$$\{Deon, Kelly, Pat, Chris, Lynn, Jerry, Kim\}$$

which is the set of employees responsible to *Tracy*.

Pure Datalog is not quite powerful enough for our needs. Let us add negation to obtain the version of Datalog we desire.

Consider, as an example, the deductive rule

People only Mgr(x) :– *Mgr(x) supervises Emp( )*, ¬*Mgr(x) manages Dept( )*

Here, we seek those managers who manage only people, that is, managers who supervise some other employee(s) but do not manage a department. *Tracy*, *Kelly*, and *Deon* satisfy the query *People only Mgr(x)*. Using least-fixed-point semantics, we can obtain this result as follows. The set of values for x satisfying *Mgr(x) supervises Emp( )* is {*Tracy*, *Kelly*, *Deon*, *Lynn*}. The set of values for x satisfying *Mgr(x) manages Dept( )*, the negated atomic predicate without negation, is {*Pat*, *Chris*, *Lynn*}. The answer is the difference: {*Tracy*, *Kelly*, *Deon*, *Lynn*} - {*Pat*, *Chris*, *Lynn*}.

To make negation work properly, we must ensure that every variable mentioned in an atomic negated predicate is also mentioned in the same rule body in some atomic predicate that is not negated. We must also ensure that at the time we evaluate the rule in which one or more atomic negated predicates appear, each predicate can be evaluated completely as a nonnegative predicate. In the preceding example, the x, which appears in the negated atomic predicate *Mgr(x) manages Dept( )*, also appears in the nonnegated atomic predicate *Mgr(x) supervises Emp( )*. Furthermore, the predicate *Mgr(x) manages Dept( )*, which is negated, can be evaluated as a nonnegated atomic predicate.

In general, we can guarantee that a negated atomic predicate can be evaluated as a nonnegative atomic predicate if the set of deductive rules is *stratified*. To determine whether a set of deductive rules is stratified, we construct a directed graph of atomic predicates in which there is a directed edge from an atomic predicate p to an atomic predicate q if p appears in the body of a rule of which q is the head. Then the set of deductive rules is *stratified* if no cycle in the graph includes a negative atomic predicate.

Given that a set of deductive rules is stratified, we can evaluate negated atomic predicates by evaluating them as nonnegated atomic predicates and then taking the complement. Since we require at least one nonnegative atomic predicate to include every variable mentioned in a negative atomic predicate, the complement is taken relative to those values that satisfy the nonnegative atomic predicates.

5.3   Chapter Summary

Topic Summary

- Formulas of the first-order predicate calculus use logical connectors and quantifiers to make statements that are true or false about a domain of values over a given collection of functions and predicates. Functions yield domain values and predicates are true or false for every possible substitution of domain values.

- A universal quantifier ($\forall$) succinctly expresses a conjunction of subformulas over all domain values. An existential quantifier ($\exists$) succinctly expresses a disjunction of subformulas over all domain values.

- A model-theoretic view of a database is an interpretation for a set of predicates over a domain of values. We write such an interpretation as a set of relations, each representing the true facts for one of the predicates, and a set of closed formulas, each representing a database integrity constraint. If all the integrity constraints hold, the interpretation is valid, and the database is considered to be in a valid state.

- We use closed predicate-calculus formulas to specify database integrity constraints and open predicate-calculus formulas to specify database queries. Any substitution of domain values in a closed formula is true or false, and thus we can check the integrity of a database by substituting database values into closed formulas. Likewise, any substitution of values in an open formula is also true or false. For open formulas, we retain the substituted values that make the formula true as the answer to a database query.

- Model theory and proof theory are two different views of the same thing. Model theory is a view in which predicates form tuples as rows of data in tables and formulas represent integrity constraints that a database must satisfy. Proof theory is a view in which each predicate represents a fact and formulas allow us to prove implications and derive implied facts from given facts.

- By using logical equivalences and inference rules such as modus ponens and modus tollens, we can prove facts that follow from a given set of ground facts expressed as a valid interpretation for a model-theoretic view of a database.

- Datalog uses the ideas of unification and resolution and least-fixed-point evaluation to determine automatically which facts of interest can be proved. It returns these facts as the result of a query.

- Neither relational calculus nor Datalog requires us to specify how to obtain the results of a query. Both languages let us express queries by saying what is wanted rather than how to get it. Since the meaning of a query expressed in terms of what a user wants is well defined, the underlying system can determine how to execute the query. Thus, queries expressed in relational calculus or Datalog are expressed nonprocedurally (by saying what is wanted) rather than procedurally (by saying how to get it).

Question Summary

- How is the notion of substitution used both to check database integrity constraints and to provide results for database queries?

  Substitution of domain values is the basis for the semantics of predicate calculus formulas. Closed formulas, which we use for database integrity constraints, hold if the substitution of domain values as directed by the quantifiers makes the formulas true. Open formulas, which we use for database queries, return the values substituted for the free variables for substitutions that make the formulas true.

- What is the possible relationship between counting quantifiers and OSM participation, and co-occurrence constraints? (In this chapter, try to guess the relationship; we follow up in the next chapter.)

  Counting quantifiers let us assert that some formula holds for at least a minimum number of values and at most a maximum number of values. We will see in the next chapter that we can use these quantifiers to assert that an object in an object set participates between a minimum and a maximum number of times in a relationship set. Thus, we will be able to use counting quantifiers directly to specify both participation and co-occurrence constraints.

- What is the relationship between a valid interpretation and a database?

  A valid interpretation and a relational database for which the integrity constraints hold are the same. The tuples in a relation specify which substitutions of the domain values make the predicate for the relation true. The closed-world assumption lets us assume that all other substitutions of domain values make the predicate for a relation false. Integrity constraints are closed formulas. When all closed formulas hold over the domain values, the integrity constraints for the database hold.

- How does relational calculus allow us to specify queries nonprocedurally?

  In relational calculus, we use open predicate-calculus formulas to specify queries. Instead of giving a sequence of operations, to say how to compute the result, as in relational algebra, we express the conditions that characterize the result we want. Thus, rather than being procedural, as is relational algebra, relational calculus is nonprocedural. In relational calculus, we say what we want, not how to get it.

- How does Datalog allow us to specify queries nonprocedurally?

  Similar to relational calculus, Datalog can be used to express queries nonprocedurally. A Datalog query uses rules, which are logical implications, and facts, which are instantiated predicates, to prove or disprove whether a fact expressed by a query follows deductively from the information in a database. For queries with variables, the common case, we obtain as a result all substitutions of domain values for which we can prove that the fact formed follows from the deductive database.

5.4 Bibliographic Notes

For more information about first- and second-order predicated calculus see [Enderton72] and [Manna74]. Our counting quantifier, which we use freely with our first-order predicate calculus, is a variation of the counting quantifier in [Gries85]. Codd presented the first paper on relational calculus in [Codd72]. This paper also includes a proof of the equivalence between relational calculus and relational algebra. The idea for the model-theoretic and proof-theoretic views of databases appears in [Reiter78]; [Atzeni93] provides a good summary of these ideas. Much of logic programming and databases finds its roots in a series of papers in [Gallaire78]. A description of logic programming as discussed here is in [Maier88]. More complete discussions of the underlying theory for databases and for logic programming can be found in [Abiteboul95, Atzeni93, Maier83].

5.5   Exercises

5.1   Let P and Q be propositions (i.e., statements that are true T or false F). Use a truth table to determine whether each of the following is a tautology (i.e., holds for all combinations of T and F):

a. $(P \Rightarrow Q) \Leftrightarrow (\neg P \vee Q)$.

b. $\neg(P \vee Q) \Leftrightarrow (\neg P \wedge \neg Q)$.

c. $\neg(P \wedge Q) \Leftrightarrow (\neg P \vee \neg Q)$.

d. $(P \Leftrightarrow Q) \Leftrightarrow ((P \Rightarrow Q) \wedge (Q \Rightarrow P))$.

e. $(P \Rightarrow Q) \Leftrightarrow (Q \Rightarrow P)$.

f. $(P \Rightarrow Q) \Leftrightarrow (\neg Q \Rightarrow \neg P)$.

g. $(P \Rightarrow Q) \Leftrightarrow ((P \wedge \neg Q) \Rightarrow F)$.

h. $(P \Rightarrow (Q \Rightarrow R)) \Leftrightarrow ((P \wedge Q) \Rightarrow R)$.

5.2   Consider the predicate $P(a, b, c, d)$, which we define as $a = b \Rightarrow c = d$, and which we read as "if a equals b then c equals d."

a.   Evaluate $P(1, 2, 3, 4)$.

b.   Evaluate $P(1, 2, 3, 3)$.

c.   Evaluate $P(1, 1, 3, 3)$.

d.   Evaluate $P(1, 1, 3, 4)$.

e.   Can we conclude anything definite about $a = b \Rightarrow c = d$ when $a \neq b$? If yes, what? If no, why not?

f.   Can we conclude anything definite about $a = b \Rightarrow c = d$ when $c \neq d$? If yes, what? If no, why not?

5.3   Let $X = \{x_1, x_2, \dots x_n\}$ be a nonempty, finite set and let P be a one-place predicate over X; that is, for every $x \in X$, $P(x) = T$ or $P(x) = F$. $\exists x \in X(P(x))$ is equal to $P(x_1) \vee P(x_2) \vee \dots \vee P(x_n)$. $\forall x \in X(P(x))$ is equal to $P(x_1) \wedge P(x_2) \wedge \dots \wedge P(x_n)$. We may omit "$\in X$" if the universe of objects over which we are applying $\exists$ and $\forall$ is stated or is clear from the context.

For the following problems, let $A = \{1, 2, 3, 4, 5\}$ and $B = \{1, 3, 5\}$:

a.   Write $\forall a \in A(2 - a > 0)$ as a conjunction and evaluate it.

  b. Write $\exists a \in A(2 - a > 0)$ as a disjunction and evaluate it.

  c. Write $\exists a \in A(\forall b \in B(a = b))$ using conjunctions and disjunctions and evaluate it.

  d. Write $\forall b \in B(\exists a \in A(a = b))$ using conjunctions and disjunctions and evaluate it.

5.4* Generalize DeMorgan's laws for any number of predicates (instead of just two). Use induction to prove that these generalized laws hold.

5.5* For the following problems, let $X = \{x_1, x_2, x_3\}$ and let P be a one-place predicate defined over the universe U for this problem, where $U = X \cup \{x_4\}$.

  a. Prove (by converting the left-hand side to the right-hand side): $\forall x \in X(P(x)) \Leftrightarrow \neg \exists x \in X(\neg P(x))$.

  b. Prove (by converting the left-hand side to the right-hand side): $\exists x \in X(P(x)) \Leftrightarrow \exists x(x \in X \wedge P(x))$. Hint: recall that $P(x) \Leftrightarrow F \vee P(x)$ and that $P(x) \Leftrightarrow T \wedge P(x)$.

  c. Prove (by converting the left-hand side to the right-hand side): $\forall x \in X(P(x)) \Leftrightarrow \forall x(x \notin X \vee P(x))$.

  d. Prove (by converting the left-hand side to the right-hand side): $\forall x \in X(P(x)) \Leftrightarrow \forall x(x \in X \Rightarrow P(x))$.

5.6* For the following problems, let $X = \{x_1, x_2, x_3\}$ and $Y = \{y_1, y_2\}$. Also, let P be a one-place predicate defined over X and let Q be a two-place predicate defined over $X \times Y$. Hint: for these problems the associative, commutative, distributive, and idempotent laws are useful.

  a. Prove (by converting the left-hand side to the right-hand side): $\exists x \in X(P(x) \vee \exists y \in Y(Q(x, y))) \Leftrightarrow \exists x \in X(\exists y \in Y(P(x) \vee Q(x, y)))$.

  b. Prove (by converting the left-hand side to the right-hand side): $\forall x \in X(P(x) \wedge \forall y \in Y(Q(x, y))) \Leftrightarrow \forall x \in X(\forall y \in Y(P(x) \wedge Q(x, y)))$.

  c. Prove (by converting the left-hand side to the right-hand side): $\exists x \in X(P(x) \wedge \exists y \in Y(Q(x, y))) \Leftrightarrow \exists x \in X(\exists y \in Y(P(x) \wedge Q(x, y)))$.

  d. Prove (by converting the left-hand side to the right-hand side): $\forall x \in X(P(x) \vee \forall y \in Y(Q(x, y))) \Leftrightarrow \forall x \in X(\forall y \in Y(P(x) \vee Q(x, y)))$.

  e. What do these proofs indicate about the placement and movement of quantifiers in predicate calculus expressions?

5.7* For the following problems, let $X = \{x_1, x_2, x_3\}$ and $Y = \{y_1, y_2\}$. Also, let P be a two-place predicate defined over $X \times Y$.

    a. Prove or disprove: $\exists x \in X(\exists y \in Y(P(x, y))) \Leftrightarrow$
$\exists y \in Y(\exists x \in X(P(x, y)))$.

    b. Prove or disprove: $\exists x \in X(\forall y \in Y(P(x, y))) \Leftrightarrow$
$\forall y \in Y(\exists x \in X(P(x, y)))$.

    c. Prove or disprove: $\forall x \in X(\forall y \in Y(P(x, y))) \Leftrightarrow$
$\forall y \in Y(\forall x \in X(P(x, y)))$.

    d. Prove or disprove: $\forall x \in X(\exists y \in Y(P(x, y))) \Leftrightarrow$
$\exists y \in Y(\forall x \in X(P(x, y)))$.

5.8 Use counting quantifiers to say that Pat owns two, three, or four cars.

5.9 Use counting quantifiers to say that Store XYZ offers more than 100 items.

5.10 Without using counting quantifiers, give an expression for $\exists^3 x(P(x))$.

5.11** Prove:

$$\exists^n x(P(x)) \Leftrightarrow \neg\exists^0 x(P(x)) \wedge \cdots \wedge \neg\exists^{n-1} x(P(x)) \wedge$$
$$\forall x_1 \cdots \forall x_{n+1}(P(x_1) \wedge \cdots \wedge P(x_{n+1})$$
$$\Rightarrow (x_1 = x_2 \vee \cdots \vee x_1 = x_{n+1})$$
$$\vee (x_2 = x_3 \vee \cdots \vee x_2 = x_{n+1})$$
$$\cdots$$
$$\vee (x_n = x_{n+1}))$$

5.12 Using only constant superscripts (i.e., without using $\leq$ or $\geq$ in superscripts), give an expression for $\exists^{\leq 3} x(P(x))$.

5.13* Prove by induction: $\exists^{\leq n} x(P(x)) \Leftrightarrow \exists^0 x(P(x)) \vee \cdots \vee \exists^n x(P(x))$.

5.14 Using only constant superscripts (i.e., without using $\leq$ or $\geq$ in superscripts), give an expression for $\exists^{\geq 3} x(P(x))$.

5.15* Prove by induction: $\exists^{\geq n} x(P(x)) \Leftrightarrow \exists x(P(x)) \wedge \neg\exists^1 x(P(x)) \wedge \cdots \wedge \neg\exists^{n-1} x(P(x))$.

5.16 Consider the following model-theoretic view of a relational database instance.

$r =$	(A	B)
	1	2
	2	4
	3	5

$s =$	(A	D	E)
	1	3	5
	1	5	7
	1	6	6
	2	8	9
	2	1	3

$$\forall x \exists^{\leq 1} y (r(x, y))$$
$$\forall x \exists^{\leq 1} <y, z> (s(x, y, z))$$
$$\forall x \forall y \exists^{\leq 1} z (s(z, x, y))$$
$$\forall x \forall y \forall z (s(x, y, z) \Rightarrow \exists w (r(x, w)))$$

a. Give the domain for this model-theoretic view.

b. Assuming that the closed-world assumption holds, is $r(2, 4)$ *true* or *false*? What about $r(3, 2)$?

c. Assuming that the closed-world assumption does not hold, is $s(1, 5, 7)$ *true* or *false*? What about $s(5, 5, 5)$?

d. What constraint does the formula $\forall x \exists^{\leq 1} y (r(x, y))$ impose? Is it *true* for this interpretation?

e. What constraint does the formula $\forall x \exists^{\leq 1} <y, z> (s(x, y, z))$ impose? Is it *true* for this interpretation?

f. What constraint does the formula $\forall x \forall y \exists^{\leq 1} z (s(z, x, y))$ impose? Is it *true* for this interpretation?

g. What constraint does the formula $\forall x \forall y \forall z (s(x, y, z) \Rightarrow \exists w (r(x, w)))$ impose? Is it *true* for this interpretation?

h. Is this interpretation valid? Explain.

5.17* Suppose we wish to define a relational database with three relations $r_1(AB)$, $r_2(ACD)$, and $r_3(CE)$. Let A be a key for r_1, AC be a key for r_2, and C be a key for r_3. A and C are foreign keys in r_2 so that referential integrity must hold.

a. Give closed formulas for the key constraints.

b. Give closed formulas for the referential-integrity constraints.

c. Explain why the following relational-database view of an interpretation is invalid with respect to the formulas for (a) and (b). The explanation should include a counterexample for each formula that does not hold.

$r_1 =$	A	B
	1	2

$r_2 =$	A	C	D
	3	4	5
	3	4	9

$r_3 =$	C	E
	6	7

d. Change/add the minimal number of values in the preceding interpretation so that it becomes valid.

5.18 Let $r(ABC)$ be a relation and let the domains for A, B, and C be the integers.

a.* Show that the constraint

$$\forall x \exists^{\leq 1} <y, z>(r(x, y, z))$$

makes A a superkey for r for any valid interpretation (i.e., ensures that for any valid interpretation $t[A] \neq t'[A]$ for distinct tuples t and t' in r).

b.** Show that the constraint

$$\forall x \exists^{\leq 1} y \exists^{\leq 1} z(P(x, y, z))$$

is not equal to the constraint in (a) and thus that the constraint in (b) does not make A a superkey for r for any valid interpretation.

5.19 Consider the following database scheme:

> *student(ID, Sname, Major, GPA) key: ID*
> *faculty(SSN, Fname, Dept, Salary) key: SSN, key: {Fname, Dept}*
> *is_teaching(SSN, CourseNum) key: Course*
> *is_taking(ID, CourseNum) key: {ID, CourseNum}*

Using this scheme, write relational-calculus expressions for the following:

a. Find the names of faculty members in the Math department.

b. Find the name and major for all students who are taking CS1.

c. Find the names of faculty members who are teaching some course and make less than $50,000.

d. Find the names of students who are taking a course being taught by Johnson in the CS department.

e. Find the names and ID-SSN pairs for students and faculty members who have the same name.

f. Find the ID and CourseNum for each student who is taking a course from a faculty member whose name is the same as the student's name.

g.* Find the names of students taking all the courses being taught by Johnson in the CS department.

5.20* For Query (g) in Exercise 5.19, convert the relational-calculus expression to an expression with no universal quantifiers (if it is not already in this form) and then write the query in SQL.

5.21 Consider the following database scheme:

supplier(*Sname, Saddress*) *key*: *Sname*
item(*ItemNumber, ItemName, Color, Weight*) *key*: *ItemNumber*
shipment(*Sname, ItemNumber, Quantity, ShipDate*) *key*: {*Sname,*
    ItemNumber}

Using this scheme, write relational-calculus expressions for the following queries:

a. Find the names and numbers of all blue items.

b. Find the names and addresses of suppliers who have shipments in quantities greater than 500.

c. Find the names of suppliers who have shipments of items that weigh more than 50.

d. Find the name and item number of shipments that have a quantity less than 200 or a weight greater than 20.

e. List pairs of item numbers of items that have the same color. Do not list an item number with itself, and do not list a pair of item numbers in both orders.

f.* Find names of suppliers who supply all items.

g.* Find names of suppliers who supply all green items that weigh less than 50.

5.22*   For Queries (f) and (g) in Exercise 5.21, convert the relational-calculus expressions to expressions with no universal quantifiers (if they are not already in this form) and then write the queries in SQL.

5.23**   In general, the results of a query may depend on the domain. Consider, for example, the query

$$\{NoItem\ Dept(x)\ |\ \neg \exists y \exists z(Item(y)\ in\ Dept(x)\ costs\ Price(z)\}$$

for the database instance in Fig. 5.1 that yields all the values in the domain D except *Toy* and *Hardware*, including, for instance, *Pat*, *Clothing*, *saw*, and $10. Not only is this not likely to yield what is intended, but if we extend the domain by adding another item to D such as *pliers*, then the answer changes and is thus dependent on the domain. Usually, however, we prefer that the results of a query be domain independent. We can ensure that they are domain independent and at the same time solve the problem of generating nonsense complements by ensuring that the results include only certain values in the database. For our example here, if we want to limit the answer to existing departments managed by someone, we would write

$$\{NoItem\ Dept(x)\ |\ \exists w(Mgr(w)\ manages\ Dept(x)$$
$$\land \neg \exists y \exists z(Item(y)\ in\ Dept(x)\ costs\ Price(z)))\}$$

The result of this query contains only *Clothing*, a reasonable answer. Moreover, if we change the domain by adding *pliers* or *Appliance*, the answer does not change. Relational-calculus queries that do not depend on the domain are referred to as *domain-independent* queries and are also sometimes called *safe* queries.

Let $r(ABC)$, $s(CD)$, and $q(DE)$ be relation schemes for a relational database, and let the domain of all attributes be the integers between 0 and 9 inclusive. Determine whether the following queries are domain dependent or domain independent. For those that are domain dependent, give an example that shows that if some domain is altered the result is different. For those that are domain independent, write an equivalent relational-algebra expression.

(a) $\{x\!:\!C \mid x = 3 \vee x = 7\}.$

(b) $\{x\!:\!C \mid \exists y(y > 3 \wedge x < 7)\}.$

(c) $\{x\!:\!E \mid \exists y(q(y, x) \wedge (x = 3 \vee x = 7)\}.$

(d) $\{x\!:\!A, y\!:\!B, z\!:\!C, w\!:\!D \mid r(x, y, z) \vee s(z, w)\}.$

(e) $\{z\!:\!C \mid \exists x(\exists y(r(x, y, z) \wedge \forall u(\forall v(q(u, v) \wedge \exists w(s(z, w))))))\}.$

5.24** Prove that relational algebra and domain-independent relational calculus are equally powerful. That is, show that for any given relational database scheme, every relational-algebra expression can be written as a domain-independent relational-calculus expression and vice versa.

5.25* Let $P_1, ..., P_n,$ and Q be propositions. Use induction to prove that $\neg P_1 \vee \cdots \vee \neg P_n \vee Q$ is equivalent to $P_1 \wedge \cdots \wedge P_n \Rightarrow Q.$

5.26* Prove that modus ponens in Table 5.3 is a sound inference rule. That is, prove that $(P \wedge (P \Rightarrow Q)) \Rightarrow Q$ is a tautology.

5.27* Prove that modus tollens in Table 5.3 is a sound inference rule.

5.28* Prove that transitivity in Table 5.3 is a sound inference rule.

5.29* Let $A, B,$ and C be sets. Using the inference rules in Table 5.3 and known facts about sets, prove or disprove the following:

a. $A \cup B = A$ implies $B \subseteq A$ and conversely.

b. $A \cap B = A$ is necessary and sufficient for $A \subseteq B.$

c. $A \subseteq B$ and $B \subseteq C$ if and only if $A \cap B \cap C = A.$

d.   The empty set is unique.

5.30* Consider the following proof-theoretic view of a Datalog database instance.

Facts:

Person(P1) has Name(Pat)	*Person(P1) is parent of Person(P2)*
Person(P2) has Name(Chris)	*Person(P1) is parent of Person(P3)*
Person(P3) has Name(Lynn)	*Person(P2) is parent of Person(P4)*
Person(P4) has Name(Tracy)	*Person(P2) is parent of Person(P5)*
Person(P5) has Name(Kelly)	*Person(P2) is parent of Person(P6)*
Person(P6) has Name(Deon)	*Person(P5) is parent of Person(P7)*
Person(P7) has Name(Jerry)	

$$Person(P1) \; owns \; Item(I1) \qquad Item(I1) \; has \; value(\$100)$$
$$Person(P1) \; owns \; Item(I2) \qquad Item(I2) \; has \; value(\$500)$$
$$Person(P2) \; owns \; Item(I3) \qquad Item(I3) \; has \; value(\$200)$$
$$Person(P3) \; owns \; Item(I2) \qquad Item(I4) \; has \; value(\$300)$$
$$Person(P4) \; owns \; Item(I4) \qquad Item(I5) \; has \; value(\$500)$$
$$Person(P5) \; owns \; Item(I4)$$
$$Person(P6) \; owns \; Item(I5)$$

Deductive Rules:

$Person(x) \; has \; child \; who \; owns \; \$500 \; Item(y) \; :-$
$\qquad\qquad Person(x) \; is \; parent \; of \; Person(z),$
$\qquad\qquad Person(z) \; owns \; Item(y),$
$\qquad\qquad Item(y) \; has \; value(w).$

Following the derivation of ideas in Section 5.2.3, do the following:

a. Give a derivation sequence that proves *Person(P1) has child who owns $500 Item(I3)*. In the derivation sequence use standard predicate-calculus notation. The proof should be similar to the one in Fig. 5.3.

b. Give a narrative-style proof of *Person(P1) has child who owns $500 Item(I3)* similar to the proof in Fig. 5.4.

c. Give a resolution proof of *Person(P1) has child who owns $500 Item(I3)* that uses conjunction and negation and is similar to the proof in Fig. 5.5.

d. Give a resolution proof of *Person(P1) has child who owns $500 Item(I3)* that does not use conjunction and is similar to the proof in Fig. 5.6.

e. Give a resolution proof of *Person(P1) has child who owns $500 Item(I3)* that uses Datalog notation and is similar to the proof in Fig. 5.7.

f. Give the derivation for the query *Person(x) has child who owns $500 Item(y)*. The derivation should be similar to the derivation in Fig. 5.8.

5.31   Using the Datalog database instance in Exercise 5.30, write Datalog queries for the following. (All queries must work even if there is a change to the facts in the database. The fact schemes, of course, do no change.)

a.   Find the names of people who own items whose value is $200.

b.   Find the names of the children of Chris.

c.   Find the names of parents whose children own items valued at $100 or $300.

d.   Find the names of people who own items valued at $400 or who have children who own items valued at $400.

e.   Find the names of people who own items valued at $400 but whose children own no items valued at $400.

f.   Find the names of people who do not own any item.

g.   Find all the descendents of Pat.

h.   Find all the ancestors of Jerry.

5.32   Determine whether each of the following is stratified:

a.   *Person(x) owns* :− ¬*Person(x) owns Item()*.

b.   *Person(x) owns $500 Item(y)* :− *Person(x) owns Item(z)*,
Item(z) has value($500).

Person(x) owns no $500 Item :− *Person(x) has Name()*,
¬*Person(x) owns $500 Item()*.

c.   *Person(x) owns $500 Item(y)* :− *Person(x) owns Item(z)*,
Item(z) has value($500).

Person(x) owns no $500 Item :− *Item() has value(z)*,
¬*Person(x) owns $500 Item()*.

Chapter 6

Modeling Theory

We begin our study of modeling theory for OSM by showing how to convert an ORM application model into a set of predicates and closed predicate-calculus formulas. The predicates become schemes for relations in a model-theoretic view of a database; the formulas become integrity constraints for the database. The conversion is automatic, and the result corresponds directly to the OSM application model. Based on this direct correspondence, we use model theory to give a valid interpretation for the application model. Every valid interpretation is a valid application-model database.

An application-model database generated in this way almost surely does not have the best set of relations or the best set of constraints for an efficient implementation. Many of the relations are likely to be redundant in the sense that we can discard them without losing information. Similarly, many of the constraints are likely to be extraneous in the sense that other constraints imply them, which means that we can discard them, as well. Further, it is likely that we can combine several of the relations without losing information and without introducing other problems such as redundant data. It is also likely that we can reorganize the constraints so that they can be checked more efficiently. This is what we do in designing a database. Thus, the conversion of an OSM application model to predicates and constraints establishes the basis for design.

During the design stage, we use the direct correspondence between an OSM application model and the underlying predicates and constraints to ensure that our designed database is faithful to our OSM application model. The design process is transformational; we make sure that every transformation preserves information and constraints with respect to the underlying model-theoretic view of the database. Thus, because the correspondence between the OSM application-model view and the underlying model-theoretic view is direct and because all transformations preserve information and constraints, we can be sure that the designed database is faithful to our OSM application model.

In the second part of this chapter, we use the conversion to predicate calculus and the notion of a valid interpretation to define the syntax and semantics of OSM formally. We express this formal definition of OSM in terms of OSM and call it the OSM metamodel—an application model that describes OSM. The formal definition is a natural consequence of treating application models as data, resulting in a metamodel that defines as valid interpretations all possible application models.

At the end of the chapter we also present an abstract-machine formalization for OSM object behavior. This formalization describes the behavior of a state net as a state net. Because the formalization is operational, it allows us to simulate object behavior.

The following topics in this chapter are particularly important:

- The relationship between generated predicates and database relation schemes.

- The relationship between generated predicate-calculus formulas and database integrity constraints.

- The OSM metamodel and an interpretation for the OSM metamodel.

- The formalization of application-model syntax as a valid interpretation for the OSM metamodel.

- Temporal logic, including temporal predicates and temporal formulas.

- The formalization of application-model semantics as a valid interpretation for an OSM metamodel with temporal predicates and formulas.

- The abstract-machine formalization of OSM.

The following questions should also be kept in mind:

- How do generated predicates correspond to OSM application-model object sets and relationship sets?

- How do generated formulas correspond to OSM application-model constraints, both implicit constraints and explicit ones?

- How does a valid interpretation for a collection of generated predicates and formulas correspond to a database?

- What is the practical significance of a formal definition for OSM?

- What are some practical applications for the abstract-machine semantics for OSM?

6.1   Application-Model Formalization *

Our first task is to map an arbitrary OSM application model to first-order predicate calculus. Before beginning, however, we adjust for any recursive relationship sets and expand any templates, such as aggregations and roles, into their underlying meaning in terms of simpler OSM constructs. We also check every relationship-set name to ensure that it includes the names of each of its object sets. This is automatic for binary relationship sets that have a reading direction arrow; for all other relationship-set names, we must ensure that this condition holds.

Recursive relationship sets are those with more than one connection to the same object set. To distinguish among the connections, we must know the role of each one. We therefore insist that for every relationship set, every connection of the relationship set to an object set, except one, have a role name. Furthermore, as part of expanding templates, we convert every role into a specialization object set of the object set to which the role is connected and change any zero-minimum participation constraint in the connecting relationship set to be one. This conversion guarantees that there are no role names and that each *n*-ary relationship set connects to *n* distinct object sets.

In the following discussion, we use as an example the application model in Fig. 6.1. This application model satisfies our requirements: there are no recursive relationship sets, all templates have been expanded, and each relationship-set name includes the names of each of its object sets. Observe that *Spouse* and *Boss*, which could be roles, are specializations and that *Address*, which could be an aggregation, has simple relationship sets connecting it to its subparts.

6.1.1 Application-Model Predicates

Application-model predicates are atomic formulas derived from object and relationship sets. In this context, we usually refer to them simply as predicates. We derive predicates from an OSM application model *M* as follows:

1. Each object set of *M* maps to one one-place predicate for each of its names. If *N* is a name of an object set, we write the predicate *N*(x). (In our notation, we use variables such as x, y, and z as place markers.) Examples from Fig. 6.1 include *Person*(x), *SSN*(x), *Item*(x), *Cost*(x), *Wholesale Cost*(x), and *Boss*(x).

* Embley/Kurtz/Woodfield, *Object-Oriented Systems Analysis: A Model-Driven Approach*, 1992 pp. 253–263. Reprinted by permission of Prentice Hall, Upper Saddle River, NJ.

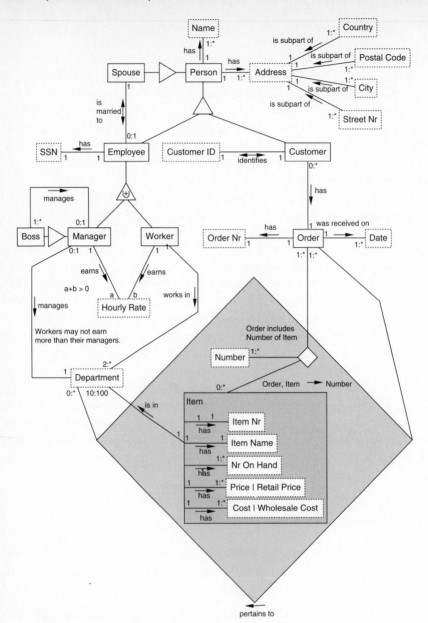

Figure 6.1 A sample application model for illustrating predicates and rules.

2. Each *n*-ary ($n \geq 2$) relationship set of *M* maps to one *n*-place predicate for each of its names. Examples from Fig. 6.1 include *Employee(x) has SSN(y)*, which is a two-place predicate derived from the *Employee has SSN* relationship set. *Order(x) includes Number(y) of Item(z)* is a three-place predicate. *Item(x) has Price(y)* and *Item(x) has Retail Price(y)* are two predicates for the same relationship set.

3. There are no predicates for generalization/specialization hierarchies, only rules.

6.1.2 Application-Model Rules

Application-model rules are closed formulas derived from model assumptions and constraints. In this context, we usually refer to these closed formulas simply as rules. We derive rules from an OSM application model *M* as follows:

1. For each object set with multiple names $N_1, ..., N_n$, we write the rules

$$\forall x (N_i(x) \Leftrightarrow N_j(x))$$

for $1 \leq i < j \leq n$. Since these rules define an equivalence class over the predicates for an object set, we can use any object-set name in place of another. Therefore, from here on we refer to *the* name of an object set to mean any one of its names. For example, we derive $\forall x(Cost(x) \Leftrightarrow Wholesale\ Cost(x))$ as one of the rules for the application model in Fig. 6.1. We can refer to this object set as either the *Cost* or the *Wholesale cost* object set.

2. We write equivalence-class rules for each *n*-ary relationship set with multiple names $N_1, ..., N_m$ as follows. Since the names do not necessarily reference the connections to the object sets in the same order, we are careful to associate the proper quantified variable with each connection in a relationship-set name. For an *n*-ary relationship set name, we will universally quantify the *n* variables $x_1, ..., x_n$ in the rules. To order these *n* variables in the rules properly, we associate each variable with a connection for the relationship set. We then let X_i represent these *n* variables written in their proper connection order for the relationship set named N_i, and we write the rules

$$\forall x_1 \cdots \forall x_n (N_i(X_i) \Leftrightarrow N_j(X_j))$$

for $1 \leq i < j \leq m$. Since these rules define an equivalence class over the predicates for a relationship set, we can use any relationship-set name in place of any other. Therefore, from here on we refer to *the* name of a relationship set to mean any one of its names.

For example, we derive the rule $\forall x_1 \forall x_2 (Employee(x_1)$ *is married to Spouse$(x_2) \Leftrightarrow$ Spouse(x_2) is married to Employee(x_1)* as one of the application-model rules for Fig. 6.1. Here we associate the universally quantified variable x_1 with the connection to *Employee* and x_2 with the connection to *Spouse*.

3. For each *n*-ary ($n \geq 2$) relationship set r, we write a rule to ensure referential integrity. Let N_r be the name of r, and let S_i be the name of the object set connected to r in the ith position. We then write the rule

$$\forall x_1 \cdots \forall x_n (N_r(x_1, \ldots, x_n) \Rightarrow S_1(x_1) \wedge \cdots \wedge S_n(x_n))$$

For the sample application model in Fig. 6.1, for example, we have $\forall x \forall y (Person(x)$ *has Name$(y) \Rightarrow$ Person$(x) \wedge$ Name(y))* for the *Person has Name* relationship set.

4. For each generalization/specialization, we write one or more rules. To accommodate multiple generalizations and multiple specializations for object sets, we let $G_1, \ldots, G_m$ be the names of the generalization object sets and $S_1, \ldots, S_n$ be the names of the specialization object sets. If a generalization/specialization has a union constraint or a partition constraint, it can have only one generalization, and if a generalization/specialization has an intersection constraint, it can have only one specialization. These constraints must be checked before beginning, and, if they fail, adjustments must be made. (We did not mention these requirements earlier because they apply only to this special case.)

For each generalization/specialization, we write the following rule:

$$\forall x (S_1(x) \vee \cdots \vee S_n(x) \Rightarrow G_1(x) \wedge \cdots \wedge G_m(x))$$

If the generalization/specialization has a mutual-exclusion or partition constraint, we also include the rules

$$\forall x(S_i(x) \Rightarrow \neg S_j(x))$$

for $1 \le i, j \le n$, and $i \ne j$. If the generalization/specialization has a union constraint or a partition constraint, we also include the rule

$$\forall x(G_1(x) \Rightarrow S_1(x) \vee \cdots \vee S_n(x))$$

where G_1 is the one generalization, as required. If the generalization/specialization has an intersection constraint, we also include the rule

$$\forall x(G_1(x) \wedge \cdots \wedge G_m(x) \Rightarrow S_1(x))$$

where S_1 is the one specialization, as required.

Figure 6.1 includes one partition generalization/specialization constraint. For this generalization/specialization, we thus write the following rules:

$$\forall x(\mathit{Manager}(x) \vee \mathit{Worker}(x) \Rightarrow \mathit{Employee}(x))$$
$$\forall x(\mathit{Manager}(x) \Rightarrow \neg \mathit{Worker}(x))$$
$$\forall x(\mathit{Worker}(x) \Rightarrow \neg \mathit{Manager}(x))$$
$$\forall x(\mathit{Employee}(x) \Rightarrow \mathit{Manager}(x) \vee \mathit{Worker}(x))$$

We also have three generalization/specializations with no constraints. We therefore also write the following rules:

$$\forall x(\mathit{Employee}(x) \vee \mathit{Customer}(x) \Rightarrow \mathit{Person}(x))$$
$$\forall x(\mathit{Spouse}(x) \Rightarrow \mathit{Person}(x))$$
$$\forall x(\mathit{Boss}(x) \Rightarrow \mathit{Manager}(x))$$

5. We write a rule to reflect each participation constraint. To form participation-constraint rules, we let c be the participation constraint in the ith place connecting to an object set named S for an n-ary ($n \ge 2$) relationship set named N_r. We assume that c has the form $c_1, ..., c_m$ where each c_i, $1 \le i \le m$, either has the form $min_i\!:\!max_i$ or is a numeric designator d_i. The rule we write has the form

$$t_1 \vee \cdots \vee t_m$$

where each t_i, $1 \le i \le m$, is a formula formed for $min_i\!:\!max_i$ or d_i as follows:

5a. If c_i is min_i: max_i and $min_i = 0$ and $max_i = *$, the term t_i is *true* and, therefore, so is disjunction $t_1 \lor \dots \lor t_m$. Hence, we discard the rule. In Fig. 6.1, for example, there is no rule for the *0:** participation constraint for the *Customer* connection in the *Customer has Order* relationship set.

5b. If c_i is min_i: max_i and min_i is a positive integer and max_i is *, the term is

$$\forall x_i(S(x_i) \Rightarrow \exists^{\geq min_i} < x_1, \dots, x_{i-1}, x_{i+1}, \dots, x_n > (N_r(x_1, \dots, x_n)))$$

where the tuple constructor in the counting quantifier means that we count tuples rather than individual values. Note that using a tuple with one variable is the same as using the variable without a tuple constructor. In this case we opt for the simpler notation and omit the angle brackets. In Fig. 6.1, for example, we write the *1:** constraint in the *Person has Name* relationship set as

$$\forall x(Name(x) \Rightarrow \exists^{\geq 1} y(Person(y) \ has \ Name(x)))$$

which asserts that for each name there is at least one person with that name. Notice that there is no need for the tuple notation here. We need the tuple notation, however, when we write the *1:** constraint for *Order* in the *Order includes Number of Item* relationship set. Here the constraint is

$$\forall x(Order(x) \Rightarrow \exists^{\geq 1} < y, z > (Order(x) \ includes \ Number(y) \\ of \ Item(z)))$$

5c. If c_i is min_i: max_i and $min_i = 0$ and max_i is a positive integer, we write

$$\forall x_i(S(x_i) \Rightarrow \exists^{\leq max_i} < x_1, \dots, x_{i-1}, x_{i+1}, \dots, x_n > (N_r(x_1, \dots, x_n)))$$

In Fig. 6.1, for example, we write the *0:1* constraint in the *Employee is married to Spouse* relationship set as

$$\forall x(Employee(x) \Rightarrow \exists^{\leq 1} y(Employee(x) \ is \ married \ to \ Spouse(y)))$$

5d. If c_i is min_i: max_i and min_i and max_i are both positive integers, we write the following rule:

$$\forall x_i(S(x_i) \Rightarrow \exists^{\geq min_i} < x_1, \dots, x_{i-1}, x_{i+1}, \dots, x_n > (N_r(x_1, \dots, x_n))) \\ \land \forall x_i(S(x_i) \Rightarrow \exists^{\leq max_i} < x_1, \dots, x_{i-1}, x_{i+1}, \dots, x_n > (N_r(x_1, \dots, x_n)))$$

which combines the cases for rules 5b and 5c. An example from Fig. 6.1 is the participation constraint *10:100* in the *Item is in Department* relationship set. We write this constraint as

$$\forall x(Department(x) \Rightarrow \exists^{\geq 10} y(Item(y) \text{ is in } Department(x)))$$
$$\land \forall x(Department(x) \Rightarrow \exists^{\leq 100} y(Item(y) \text{ is in } Department(x)))$$

5e. If c_i is the numeric designator d_i and d_i is a positive integer, the term is

$$\forall x_i(S(x_i) \Rightarrow \exists^{d_i} < x_1, \ldots, x_{i-1}, x_{i+1}, \ldots, x_n > (N_r(x_1, \ldots, x_n)))$$

For example, we write the participation constraint for *Order* in the *Order has Order Nr* relationship set as

$$\forall x(Order(x) \Rightarrow \exists^1 y(Order(x) \text{ has } Order\ Nr(y)))$$

5f. If c_i includes a variable or a function, we first decide for each variable whether it is type 1 or type 2. A variable is *type 1* if it is included in the participation constraints for a single object set and does not appear elsewhere as part of a cardinality constraint (i.e., does not also appear in a participation constraint of some other object set and does not also appear in a co-occurrence constraint or an object-set cardinality constraint). A variable is *type 2* if it is not *type 1*. For example, both *a* and *b* in Fig. 6.1 are type-1 variables. There are no type-2 variables. Although such a variable is not motivated particularly easily in the application model in Fig. 6.1, we could create a type-2 variable *c* by replacing the *'s in the participation constraints on *Wholesale Cost* and *Retail Price* by *c*'s. This would assert that the upper bound on the number of wholesale costs and retail prices is the same.

Note that the differentiating test here is not the number of times a variable appears in participation constraints, but the number of object sets with which it associates. As another example of a type-1 variable we could replace the *2:** and the *10:100* on *Department*, respectively, by *d* and *10d:10d + 9*. This constraint would assert that the number of workers in a department is equal to the number of items divided by 10 when any remainder in the division is discarded. Note here that there are three *d*'s, but that they all associate with a single object set. Note also that in addition to their appearance in participation constraints, type-1 variables may appear elsewhere, as do the a and b, which appear in the constraint $a + b > 0$. Type-1 variables, however, cannot appear in other cardinality constraints—neither object-set cardinality constraints, co-occurrence constraints, nor participation constraints for some other object set.

We assign each type-1 variable v a one-place function f_v. If by chance there is already a function with this name, we add 1, or 2, or ... as needed to make the function names unique. In Fig. 6.1 (augmented here by the examples in the preceding paragraph), we would therefore have functions $f_a(x)$, $f_b(x)$, and $f_d(x)$, but we would not have a function $f_c(x)$ because c is a type 2 variable.

With this preparation, if c_i is the numeric designator d_i, we write

$$\forall x_i(S(x_i) \Rightarrow \exists^{\geq d'} < x_1, \ldots, x_{i-1}, x_{i+1}, \ldots, x_n > (N_r(x_1, \ldots, x_n)))$$

where d'_i is d_i with the function $f_v(x_i)$ substituted for each type-1 variable v in min_i, if any. If c_i is $min_i : max_i$ and min_i is nonzero, we write

$$\forall x_i(S(x_i) \Rightarrow \exists^{\geq min'_i} < x_1, \ldots, x_{i-1}, x_{i+1}, \ldots, x_n > (N_r(x_1, \ldots, x_n)))$$

where min'_i is min_i with the function $f_v(x_i)$ substituted for each type-1 variable v in min_i, if any. And, if max_i is not *, we write

$$\forall x_i(S(x_i) \Rightarrow \exists^{\leq max'_i} < x_1, \ldots, x_{i-1}, x_{i+1}, \ldots, x_n > (N_r(x_1, \ldots, x_n)))$$

where max'_i is max_i with the function $f_v(x_i)$ substituted for each type-1 variable v in max_i, if any. If we have a rule for both min_i and max_i, we conjoin them by $\wedge$. Note that type-2 variables remain as they are and become constants in the rules we are deriving. Any functions given in a participation constraint also remain as they are—our only alteration is to replace type-1 variables by functions. In Fig. 6.1 (augmented by the examples in the earlier paragraph), we would derive the following participation-constraint rules for the participation constraints containing a, b, c, and d, respectively:

$$\forall x(Hourly\ Rate(x) \Rightarrow \exists^{f_a(x)}y(Manager(y)\ earns\ Hourly\ Rate(x)))$$

$$\forall x(Hourly\ Rate(x) \Rightarrow \exists^{f_b(x)}y(Worker(y)\ earns\ Hourly\ Rate(x)))$$

$$\forall x(Price(x) \Rightarrow \exists^{\geq 1}y(Item(y)\ has\ Price(x)))$$
$$\wedge\ \forall x(Price(x) \Rightarrow \exists^{\leq c}y(Item(y)\ has\ Price(x)))$$
$$\forall x(Cost(x) \Rightarrow \exists^{\geq 1}y(Item(y)\ has\ Cost(x)))$$
$$\wedge\ \forall x(Cost(x) \Rightarrow \exists^{\leq c}y(Item(y)\ has\ Cost(x)))$$

$$\forall x(Department(x) \Rightarrow \exists^{f_d(x)}y(Worker(y)\ works\ for\ Department(x)))$$
$$\forall x(Department(x) \Rightarrow \exists^{\geq 10f_d(x)}y(Item(y)\ is\ in\ Department(x)))$$
$$\wedge\ \forall x(Department(x) \Rightarrow \exists^{\leq 10f_d(x)\,+\,9}y(Item(y)\ is\ in\ Department(x)))$$

Note that we have used only one of the names for *Price* and *Cost*. Because of the equivalence classes established previously in Cases 1 and 2, it is unnecessary to use more than one name.

Observe that by adding variables and functions to our counting quantifiers, we have increased the complexity. Although more complex, the basic meaning remains the same. For type-2 variables, in any interpretation, we will map the variable to a nonnegative integer. For example, in the formula $\forall x\exists^{\geq a}yP(x, y)$, if we map a to 2, we have the formula $\forall x\exists^{\geq 2}yP(x, y)$, which we know how to evaluate. For type-1 variables, in any interpretation, the function will map each constant in the domain to a nonnegative integer in its range. As an example, consider $\forall x\exists^{f_a(x)}yP(x, y)$. If our domain is $\{1, 2, 3\}$, we might let $f_a(1) = 1$, $f_a(2) = 3$, and $f_a(3) = 1$. Then,

$$\forall x\exists^{f_a(x)}yP(x, y) = \exists^1 yP(1, y) \wedge \exists^3 yP(2, y) \wedge \exists^1 yP(3, y)$$

Any interpretation that does not map variables in this context to nonnegative integers or that does not map the final result of functions in this context to a range of all nonnegative integers is undefined. We treat any undefined formula as *false*, which is sufficient to invalidate any interpretation.

5g. If c_i has any other form, it has no meaning. Thus we generate *false*, which is sufficient to invalidate any interpretation.

6. For each co-occurrence constraint we write a rule as follows. Let c be a co-occurrence constraint for relationship set r. If the numeric part of the constraint for c is absent, it is assumed to be 1 by default. With this understanding, the numeric part of the constraint for c has the form $c_1, ..., c_q$, where each c_i, $1 \le i \le q$, is either a numeric designator d_i or has the form $min_i : max_i$. Let N_r be the name of r. Let c have n object sets of r listed for its left-hand side and m object sets of r listed for its right-hand side, and let p be the number of object sets of r not listed in either the left-hand side or the right-hand side. We require that neither n nor m be zero, although p may be zero, and we require that the set of n left-hand-side object sets has no intersection with the set of m right-hand-side object sets. Further, we assume, without loss of generality, that the order of the arguments for r is as follows: the n left-hand-side object sets, followed by the m right-hand-side object sets, followed by the p unlisted object sets. With these assumptions, the rule for a co-occurrence constraint has the form

$$t_1 \vee \cdots \vee t_q$$

where each t_i, $1 \le i \le q$, is a formula formed for d_i as

$\forall < x_1, ..., x_n >$
$\quad (\exists < y_1, ..., y_m, z_1, ..., z_p > (N_r(x_1, ..., x_n, y_1, ..., y_m, z_1, ..., z_p)$
$\quad \Rightarrow$
$\quad \exists^{d_i} < y_1, ..., y_m > (N_r(x_1, ..., x_n, y_1, ..., y_m, z_1, ..., z_p))))$

or formed for $min_i : max_i$ as

$\forall < x_1 \cdots x_n >$
$\quad (\exists < y_1 \cdots y_m \, z_1 \cdots z_p > (N_r(x_1, ..., x_n, y_1, ..., y_m, z_1, ..., z_p)$
$\quad \Rightarrow$
$\quad \exists^{\ge min_i} < y_1, ..., y_m > (N_r(x_1, ..., x_n, y_1, ..., y_m, z_1, ..., z_p))))$
$\wedge$
$\forall < x_1 \cdots x_n >$
$\quad (\exists < y_1 \cdots y_m \, z_1 \cdots z_p > (N_r(x_1, ..., x_n, y_1, ..., y_m, z_1, ..., z_p)$
$\quad \Rightarrow$
$\quad \exists^{\ge max_i} < y_1, ..., y_m > (N_r(x_1, ..., x_n, y_1, ..., y_m, z_1, ..., z_p))))$

For the $min_i : max_i$ formula we omit the second conjunct if max_i is *. We do not omit the first conjunct, however, because min_i should not be zero. For the co-occurrence constraint in Fig. 6.1, which has the default constraint 1, we write the rule

$$\forall <x, y> (\exists z(Order(x) \text{ includes } Number(z) \text{ of } Item(y))$$
$$\Rightarrow \exists^1 z(Order(x) \text{ includes } Number(z) \text{ of } Item(y)))$$

7. For each object-set cardinality constraint, we write a rule as follows. Let S be the name of an object set with a cardinality constraint c. We assume that c has the form $c_1, ..., c_q$ where each c_i, $1 \leq i \leq m$, is either a numeric designator d_i or has the form min_i: max_i. With these assumptions, the rule for an object-set cardinality constraint has the form

$$t_1 \vee \cdots \vee t_n$$

where each t_i, $1 \leq i \leq m$, is a formula formed for d_i as

$$\exists^{d_i} x S(x)$$

or formed for min_i: max_i as

$$\exists^{\geq min_i} x(S(x) \wedge \exists^{\leq max_i} x S(x))$$

For the min_i: max_i formula we may omit the first conjunct if $min_i = 0$, and we may omit the second conjunct if $max_i = $ *. If both are omitted, of course, we omit the term. In Fig. 6.1, we have no object-set cardinality constraints. Suppose we decide that there must be at least two departments. Then, we would place 2:* in the upper right of the *Department* object set. We might also place 10 | Department | :* in the upper right of the *Item* object set since we then also know that there must be at least ten items in each department. We would then write the rule

$$\exists^{\geq 2} x(Department(x))$$

for the first of these two constraints and

$$\exists^{\geq 10 \ | Department |} x(Item(x))$$

for the second.

8. For each high-level relationship set r whose construction is not given explicitly, and thus by default is the join of the included relationship sets, we write a rule as follows. Let N_r be the name of an n-ary high-level relationship set. Note that N_r must include the names of the object sets connected to, but outside of, N_r. Let

$N_{r_1}, ..., N_{r_p}$ be the names of the relationship sets included in r. We then write the rule

$$\forall x_1 \cdots \forall x_n \forall y_1 \cdots \forall y_m (N_{r_1}(Z_1) \wedge \cdots N_{r_p}(Z_p)$$
$$\Rightarrow N_r(x_1, ..., x_n))$$

where the x_i's pertain to the object sets connected to, but outside of, N_r, the y_i's pertain to the object sets included in N_r, and where, without loss of generality, we may assume that the order of the arguments in r is consistent with the placement of the associated object sets, and where Z_i, $1 \leq i \leq p$, represents the proper selection of the appropriate number of bound variables from among $x_1, ..., x_n, y_1, ..., y_m$ for each relationship set. In Fig. 6.1, the rule for the high-level relationship set *Order pertains to Department* is

$$\forall x_1 \forall x_2 \forall y_1 \forall y_2 \forall y_3 \forall y_4 \forall y_5 \forall y_6 \forall y_7($$
$$\wedge \, Order(x_1) \; includes \; Number(y_1) \; of \; Item(y_2)$$
$$\wedge \, Item(y_2) \; is \; in \; Department(x_2)$$
$$\wedge \, Item(y_2) \; has \; Item \; Name(y_3)$$
$$\wedge \, Item(y_2) \; has \; Item \; Nr(y_4)$$
$$\wedge \, Item(y_2) \; has \; Price(y_5)$$
$$\wedge \, Item(y_2) \; has \; Cost(y_6)$$
$$\wedge \, Item(y_2) \; has \; Nr \; On \; Hand(y_7)$$
$$\Rightarrow Order(x_1) \; pertains \; to \; Department(x_2))$$

9. A general constraint recognized as a closed, well-formed formula is included as a rule; otherwise it is included as *false*. If there are no type-1 variables in the formula, we include it directly. If there are n type-1 variables, $n \geq 1$, associated with object sets named S_1, ..., S_n, and if g is the general constraint, we write the rule

$$\forall x_1 \cdots \forall x_n (S_1(x_1) \wedge \cdots \wedge S_n(x_n) \Rightarrow g')$$

where g' is g with functions substituted for type-1 variables as explained earlier in Rule 5. Here we must also be sure, however, to match properly the universally quantified variables for the functions and the object-set names. In Fig. 6.1 the general constraint $a + b > 0$ is a well-formed formula with two type-1 variables. Thus we write

$$\forall x(Hourly \; Rate(x) \Rightarrow f_a(x) + f_b(x) > 0)$$

Simplification of Expressions

We observe that the expression for the high-level relationship set *Order pertains to Department* simplifies to

$$\forall x_1 \forall x_2 \forall y_1 \forall y_2 (Order(x_1) \text{ includes } Number(y_1) \text{ of } Item(y_2)$$
$$\wedge\ Item(y_2) \text{ is in } Department(x_2)$$
$$\Rightarrow Order(x_1) \text{ pertains to } Department(x_2))$$

This is because all relationship sets attached to *Item* have a *1* participation constraint and are otherwise unattached. We do not make this simplification, however, because it is not our purpose here to find the simplest expression, only a correct one; we are looking for a straight-forward translation, not necessarily the most efficient one. When we do design, we simplify and eliminate expressions whenever possible.

6.1.3 Valid Interpretations

When we complete a translation for an OSM application model, the result is a set of predicates and rules. The predicates are well-formed, open, atomic formulas, and the rules are well-formed, closed formulas. Figure 6.2 exhibits an application model M, while Figs. 6.3 and 6.4, respectively, show the predicates and rules generated for M.

Observe that the ORM diagram in Fig. 6.2 really does match the predicates and rules in Figs. 6.3 and 6.4. For example, the ORM diagram has 11 object sets, but there are 12 object-set predicates because one of the object sets has two names. There are also (by chance) 11 relationship sets but 12 relationship-set predicates because one of the relationship sets has two names due to the duplication of names for one of its connected object sets. These multiple names are equivalent, as Case 1 and Case 2 of Fig. 6.4 demonstrate. The list of referential integrity constraints in Case 3 is long but straightforward. We note, however, that for object and relationship sets with multiple names, we use only one of the names for all of the rules after Case 2. Thus, for example, there is no referential-integrity rule for the relationship set named *Item has Retail Price*. The only generalization/specialization in Fig. 6.2 is a partition. Thus, in Case 4 we observe that the second rule makes *Manager* and *Worker* specializations of *Employee*, the third and fourth rule make the *Manager* and *Worker* object sets mutually exclusive, and the fifth rule makes *Employee* the union of *Manager* and

Worker. Except for Case 5f, the participation-constraint rules in Case 5 are straightforward. The participation constraint on *Department* in the *is in* relationship set, for example, generates the rules in Case 5d where we see that we must have between 1 and 3 or between 10 and 100 items for each department. We say more about the functions f_a and f_b in Cases 5f and 9 after we provide an interpretation for the application model in Fig. 6.2, or equivalently for the set of predicates and rules in Figs. 6.3 and 6.4.

We provide an interpretation for an application model in the usual way by specifying a domain D and assigning values in D to constants and functions and truth values to predicates. We make the usual assumptions, including (1) the unique-name assumption so that literal numbers and strings are assigned to themselves, (2) the closed-world assumption so that tuples not listed in the assigned relation for a predicate are assigned to *false*, and (3) the standard function assumption so that common arithmetic

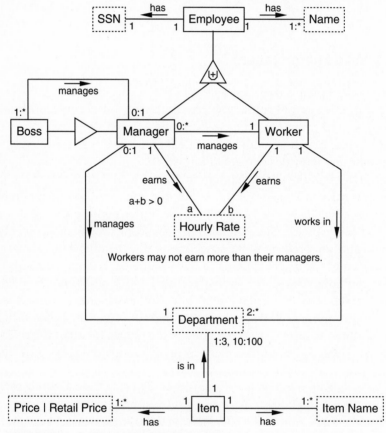

Figure 6.2   A sample application model.

Case 1—Object Sets:

>*SSN(x)*
>
>*Employee(x)*
>
>*Name(x)*
>
>*Boss(x)*
>
>*Manager(x)*
>
>*Worker(x)*
>
>*Hourly Rate(x)*
>
>*Department(x)*
>
>*Price(x)*
>
>*Retail Price(x)*
>
>*Item(x)*
>
>*Item Name(x)*

Case 2—Relationship Sets:

>*Employee(x) has SSN(y)*
>
>*Employee(x) has Name(y)*
>
>*Boss(x) manages Manager(y)*
>
>*Manager(x) earns Hourly Rate(y)*
>
>*Worker(x) earns Hourly Rate(y)*
>
>*Manager(x) manages Department(y)*
>
>*Worker(x) works in Department(y)*
>
>*Item(x) is in Department(y)*
>
>*Item(x) has Price(y)*
>
>*Item(x) has Retail Price(y)*
>
>*Item(x) has Item Name(y)*
>
>*Manager(x) manages Worker(y)*

Figure 6.3　Predicates for the application model in Fig. 6.2.

Case 1—Object Sets with Multiple Names:

$$\forall x(Price(x) \Leftrightarrow Retail\ Price(x))$$

Case 2—Relationship Sets with Multiple Names:

$$\forall x \forall y(Item(x)\ has\ Price(y) \Leftrightarrow Item(x)\ has\ Retail\ Price(y))$$

Case 3—Referential Integrity for Relationship Sets:

$\forall x \forall y(Employee(x)\ has\ SSN(y) \Rightarrow Employee(x) \wedge SSN(y))$
$\forall x \forall y(Employee(x)\ has\ Name(y) \Rightarrow Employee(x) \wedge Name(y))$
$\forall x \forall y(Boss(x)\ manages\ Manager(y) \Rightarrow Boss(x) \wedge Manager(y)$
$\forall x \forall y(Manager(x)\ earns\ Hourly\ Rate(y) \Rightarrow Manager(x) \wedge Hourly\ Rate(y))$
$\forall x \forall y(Worker(x)\ earns\ Hourly\ Rate(y) \Rightarrow Worker(x) \wedge Hourly\ Rate(y))$
$\forall x \forall y(Manager(x)\ manages\ Department(y) \Rightarrow Manager(x) \wedge Department(y))$
$\forall x \forall y(Worker(x)\ works\ in\ Department(y) \Rightarrow Worker(x) \wedge Department(y))$
$\forall x \forall y(Item(x)\ is\ in\ Department(y) \Rightarrow Item(x) \wedge Department(y))$
$\forall x \forall y(Item(x)\ has\ Price(y) \Rightarrow Item(x) \wedge Price(y))$
$\forall x \forall y(Item(x)\ has\ Item\ Name(y) \Rightarrow Item(x) \wedge Item\ Name(y))$
$\forall x \forall y(Manager(x)\ manages\ Worker(y) \Rightarrow Manager(x) \wedge Worker(y))$

Case 4—Generalization/Specialization:

$\forall x(Boss(x) \Rightarrow Manager(x))$
$\forall x(Manager(x) \vee Worker(x) \Rightarrow Employee(x))$
$\forall x(Manager(x) \Rightarrow \neg Worker(x))$
$\forall x(Worker(x) \Rightarrow \neg Manager(x))$
$\forall x(Employee(x) \Rightarrow (Manager(x) \vee Worker(x)))$

Case 5a—Nonconstraining Participation Constraints: none

Case 5b—Constrained Minimum-Participation Constraints:

$\forall x(Name(x) \Rightarrow \exists^{\geq 1} y(Employee(y)\ has\ Name(x)))$
$\forall x(Boss(x) \Rightarrow \exists^{\geq 1} y(Boss(x)\ manages\ Manager(y)))$
$\forall x(Department(x) \Rightarrow \exists^{\geq 2} y(Worker(y)\ works\ in\ Department(x)))$
$\forall x(Item\ Name(x) \Rightarrow \exists^{\geq 1} y(Item(y)\ has\ Item\ Name(x)))$
$\forall x(Price(x) \Rightarrow \exists^{\geq 1} y(Item(y)\ has\ Price(x)))$

Figure 6.4   Rules for the application model in Fig. 6.2.

Case 5c—Constrained Maximum-Participation Constraints:

$\forall x(Manager(x) \Rightarrow \exists^{\leq 1} y(Boss(y)\ manages\ Manager(x)))$

$\forall x(Manager(x) \Rightarrow \exists^{\leq 1} y(Manager(x)\ manages\ Department(y)))$

Case 5d—Constrained Minimum- and Maximum-Participation Constraints:

$\forall x(Department(x) \Rightarrow \exists^{\geq 1} y(Item(y)\ is\ in\ Department(x)))$

$\quad \wedge\ \forall x(Department(x) \Rightarrow \exists^{\leq 3} y(Item(y)\ is\ in\ Department(x)))$

$\vee\ \forall x(Department(x) \Rightarrow \exists^{\geq 10} y(Item(y)\ is\ in\ Department(x)))$

$\quad \wedge\ \forall x(Department(x) \Rightarrow \exists^{\leq 100} y(Item(y)\ is\ in\ Department(x)))$

Case 5e—Positive-Integer Participation Constraints:

$\forall x(SSN(x) \Rightarrow \exists^{1} y(Employee(y)\ has\ SSN(x)))$

$\forall x(Employee(x) \Rightarrow \exists^{1} y(Employee(x)\ has\ SSN(y)))$

$\forall x(Employee(x) \Rightarrow \exists^{1} y(Employee(x)\ has\ Name(y)))$

$\forall x(Manager(x) \Rightarrow \exists^{1} y(Manager(x)\ earns\ Hourly\ Rate(y)))$

$\forall x(Worker(x) \Rightarrow \exists^{1} y(Worker(x)\ earns\ Hourly\ Rate(y)))$

$\forall x(Worker(x) \Rightarrow \exists^{1} y(Worker(x)\ works\ in\ Department(y)))$

$\forall x(Manager(x) \Rightarrow \exists^{1} y(Manager(y)\ manages\ Department(x)))$

$\forall x(Item(x) \Rightarrow \exists^{1} y(Item(x)\ is\ in\ Department(y)))$

$\forall x(Item(x) \Rightarrow \exists^{1} y(Item(x)\ has\ Price(y)))$

$\forall x(Item(x) \Rightarrow \exists^{1} y(Item(x)\ has\ Item\ Name(y)))$

$\forall x(Worker(x) \Rightarrow \exists^{1} y(Manager(y)\ manages\ Worker(x)))$

Case 5f—Participation Constraints with Variables or Functions:

$\forall x(Hourly\ Rate(x) \Rightarrow \exists^{f_a(x)} y(Manager(y)\ earns\ Hourly\ Rate(x)))$

$\forall x(Hourly\ Rate(x) \Rightarrow \exists^{f_b(x)} y(Worker(y)\ earns\ Hourly\ Rate(x)))$

Case 6—Co-occurrence Constraints: none

Case 7—Object-Set Cardinality Constraints: none

Case 8—High-Level Relationship Sets with Default Constructions: none

Case 9—General Constraints:

$$\forall x(Hourly\ Rate(x) \Rightarrow f_a(x) + f_b(x) > 0)$$

Figure 6.4 (cont.) Rules for the application model in Fig. 6.2.

and set functions have their usual meaning. For computer representations and when we wish to be very precise in our discussion, we must be concerned with completing partial functions and dealing with overflow, underflow, and round-off error, but for most of our simple examples we can ignore these technicalities. Figure 6.5 provides an interpretation for the predicates and rules in Fig. 6.3 and 6.4.

Object-Set Relations:

SSN	Employee	Name	Boss
111-11-1111	$Employee_1$	Tracy	$Employee_1$
222-22-2222	$Employee_2$	Deon	
333-33-3333	$Employee_3$	Kelly	
444-44-4444	$Employee_4$	Pat	
555-55-5555	$Employee_5$	Chris	
666-66-6666	$Employee_6$	Lynn	
777-77-7777	$Employee_7$	Jerry	

Manager	Worker	Hourly Rate	Department
$Employee_1$	$Employee_4$	$20	Toy
$Employee_2$	$Employee_5$	$15	Hardware
$Employee_3$	$Employee_6$	$10	
	$Employee_7$		

Price Retail Price	Item	Item Name
$10	$Item_1$	ball
$20	$Item_2$	game
$30	$Item_3$	blocks
$25	$Item_4$	hammer
	$Item_5$	saw

Relationship-Set Relations:

Employee has SSN		Employee has Name	
$Employee_1$	111-11-1111	$Employee_1$	Tracy
$Employee_2$	222-22-2222	$Employee_2$	Deon
$Employee_3$	333-33-3333	$Employee_3$	Kelly
$Employee_4$	444-44-4444	$Employee_4$	Pat
$Employee_5$	555-55-5555	$Employee_5$	Chris
$Employee_6$	666-66-6666	$Employee_6$	Lynn
$Employee_7$	777-77-7777	$Employee_7$	Jerry

Figure 6.5 An interpretation for the predicates and rules in Figs. 6.3 and 6.4.

Boss manages Manager	
Employee$_1$	*Employee$_2$*
Employee$_1$	*Employee$_3$*

Manager earns Hourly Rate	
Employee$_1$	$20
Employee$_2$	$15
Employee$_3$	$15

Worker earns Hourly Rate	
Employee$_4$	$10
Employee$_5$	$10
Employee$_6$	$10
Employee$_7$	$10

Manager manages Department	
Employee$_2$	*Toy*
Employee$_3$	*Hardware*

Worker works in Department	
Employee$_4$	*Toy*
Employee$_5$	*Toy*
Employee$_6$	*Hardware*
Employee$_7$	*Hardware*

Item is in Department	
Item$_1$	*Toy*
Item$_2$	*Toy*
Item$_3$	*Toy*
Item$_4$	*Hardware*
Item$_5$	*Hardware*

Item has Price
Item has Retail Price

Item has Retail Price		Item has Item Name		Manager manages Worker	
Item$_1$	$10	*Item$_1$*	*ball*	*Employee$_2$*	*Employee$_4$*
Item$_2$	$20	*Item$_2$*	*game*	*Employee$_2$*	*Employee$_5$*
Item$_3$	$10	*Item$_3$*	*blocks*	*Employee$_3$*	*Employee$_6$*
Item$_4$	$30	*Item$_4$*	*hammer*	*Employee$_3$*	*Employee$_7$*
Item$_5$	$25	*Item$_5$*	*saw*		

Functions:

$f_a = \{(\$20, 1), (\$15, 2), (\$10, 0), \dots\}$

$f_b = \{(\$20, 0), (\$15, 0), (\$10, 4), \dots\}$

The remaining pairs for f_a and f_b do not matter.

The functions for + and >, which we need here, are standard.

Figure 6.5 (cont.) An interpretation for the predicates and rules in Figs. 6.3 and 6.4.

In Fig. 6.5 we assume that the domain consists of all values mentioned in the relations and functions, plus all necessary numeric values for the standard functions we use. It is common, especially for database systems, to define the domain in this way.

To allay potential concerns, we make two further comments about our interpretation. First, for the moment we are not concerned about the obvious inefficiencies in the implied data store. We can prove here, for example, that all the object-set relations can be discarded without losing any information, and we can combine the relationship-set relations in ways that reduce value replication. These are examples of design decisions, which will be important for us later. For now we are concerned only with theoretical foundations and conceptual views.

Second, our convention for providing lexical incarnations of nonlexical values is to represent them by an object-set name with a subscript. For nonlexical object sets in degenerate *isa* hierarchies (i.e., object sets with no generalizations or specializations), we use any one of the object-set names as the basis for providing these lexical incarnations. For nondegenerate *isa* hierarchies, we use the root of the hierarchy. Thus, for example, in Fig. 6.5 both *Worker*s and *Manager*s are referred to as *Employee*s. In the rare cases in which there is no root, we simply choose a name, usually one that mnemonically denotes the implied root that characterizes the objects in the *isa* hierarchy. Although a system can be implemented that observes these naming conventions for object identifiers, we by no means wish to imply that such a system is necessary or expected. Furthermore, since this convention is meant merely as a communication convenience, there is no harm in abbreviating the names. For example, we could use E in place of *Employee* and I in place of *Item*.

Let us conclude this section by observing that the interpretation in Fig. 6.5 is valid because all the closed formulas (the rules) are *true* with respect to the domain and the mappings for predicates and functions. As examples, we select several of the rules and show that they all hold, as follows.

For the referential-integrity rule

$$\forall x \forall y (Item(x) \text{ has } Price(y) \Rightarrow Item(x) \wedge Price(y))$$

we can observe that for any x and y in the domain, but not in the *Item has Price* relation (e.g., $x = Employee_3$ and $y = Kelly$, or $x = Item_4$ and $y = \$10$), the implication is *true* because the left-hand side of $\Rightarrow$ is *false*. When *Item*(x) *has Price*(y) is *true*, however, we can see that both *Item*(x) is *true* and *Price*(y) is *true* because each item in the *Item has Price* relation is in

Is It Obvious How to Design, to Decide Which Relations to Discard and Which to Combine?

Some of the inefficiencies we mention for the example in Figs. 6.2, 6.3, and 6.4 are obvious—for example, discarding all object-set relations—so why not simply fix these obvious inefficiencies? One answer is that not all the transformations are obvious. In our example, for instance, we can also discard the *Manager manages Worker* relationship-set relation. This is not immediately obvious, but with a little thought we can see that managers manage only one department and workers work in only one department. Thus if managers manage workers who work in their department, we can always recompute the *Manager manages Worker* relation by joining the *Manager manages Department* and *Worker works in Department* relations and projecting on *Manager* and *Worker*. Even the earlier example of discarding an object-set relation *r* is not so obvious when we realize that some objects in *r* may be lost unless the relationship-set relations always include all objects in *r*. For example, suppose we have *0:** in place of *1:** in the *Item has Item Name* relationship set in Fig. 6.2, perhaps because we wish to name some items that we do not carry. By discarding the *Item Name* relation, we would lose the names of items we do not carry.

Besides deciding which relations to discard, we must also decide which relationship-set relations should be joined together, also not immediately obvious. If we join too few, there will be unnecessary multiple copies of objects. If we join too many, we can create unnecessary duplicate copies of objects. Consider joining *Worker works in Department* and *Item is in Department*, for example. The result creates tuples for every worker-item pair in a department. This creates a relation with the cross product of workers and items for a department, which we surely should not do.

Another reason we do not simply fix some of the obvious inefficiencies is that we would lose the one-to-one correspondence with our OSM application model. As we see later, we can discard unnecessary relations and combine others and still retain the correspondence we want.

the *Item* relation and each price in the *Item has Price* relation is also in the *Price* relation. Thus the implication is true for all x and y in the domain.

For the generalization/specialization rules

$$\forall x(Manager(x) \lor Worker(x) \Rightarrow Employee(x))$$
$$\forall x(Manager(x) \Rightarrow \neg Worker(x))$$
$$\forall x(Worker(x) \Rightarrow \neg Manager(x))$$
$$\forall x(Employee(x) \Rightarrow Manager(x) \lor Worker(x))$$

we see that whenever a domain value x satisfies *Manager*(x) or *Worker*(x), x also satisfies *Employee*(x) (i.e., the union of the managers and workers is a subset—not necessarily proper—of the employees). We also see that whenever a domain value x satisfies *Manager*(x), x does not satisfy *Worker*(x), and whenever a domain value x satisfies *Worker*(x), x does not satisfy *Manager*(x) (i.e., no manager is a worker—joke not intended—and no worker is a manager). Finally, we see that whenever a domain value x satisfies *Employee*(x), x also satisfies either *Manager*(x) or *Worker*(x) (i.e., every employee is either a manager or a worker).

For the minimum participation-constraint rule

$$\forall x(Department(x) \Rightarrow \exists^{\geq 2} y(Worker(y) \text{ works in } Department(x)))$$

we see that each department has two, and thus ≥ 2, workers. *Employee*$_4$ and *Employee*$_5$ work in the *Toy* department, and *Employee*$_6$ and *Employee*$_7$ work in the *Hardware* department.

For the participation constraints with variables and the accompanying general constraint

$$\forall x(Hourly\ Rate(x) \Rightarrow \exists^{f_a(x)} y(Manager(y) \text{ earns } Hourly\ Rate(x)))$$
$$\forall x(Hourly\ Rate(x) \Rightarrow \exists^{f_b(x)} y(Worker(y) \text{ earns } Hourly\ Rate(x)))$$
$$\forall x(Hourly\ Rate(x) \Rightarrow f_a(x) + f_b(x) > 0)$$

we see that $f_a(\$20) = 1$, $f_a(\$15) = 2$, and $f_b(\$10) = 0$, and also that $f_b(\$20) = 0$, $f_b(\$15) = 0$, and $f_b(\$10) = 4$. Thus $f_a(x) + f_b(x) > 0$ for $x = \$20$, $\$15$, and $\$10$, and hence the implication (*Hourly Rate*$(x) \Rightarrow f_a(x) + f_b(x) > 0$) holds for these values of x. For all other values of x, *Hourly Rate*(x) is *false*, and thus the implication also holds.

6.2　Metamodel Formalization

Having established the basis for our formal syntax description of OSM, we now show how to define the syntax and semantics of OSM in terms of OSM itself. In Section 6.2.1 we formalize the syntax by presenting an ORM diagram that defines all the constructs of OSM. Any valid interpretation for the diagram is a syntactically correct OSM application model. In Section 6.2.2 we indicate how to formalize the semantics in terms of temporal logic, although we do not give all the details. We also provide an alternative formalism by presenting a state net that defines the behavior of a state net.

6.2.1 Static Formalization of Syntax

Since OSM is a thing, we can model it using OSM. Figure 6.6 presents the *OSM metamodel*, which, when understood properly, defines the syntax of OSM formally. A proper understanding of the ORM diagram in Fig. 6.6 requires the following:

1. A BNF (Backus-Naur Form) definition for each lexical object set,

2. A predicate-calculus formula for each natural-language constraint,

3. A derivation of the predicates and rules from the ORM diagram,

4. An interpretation based on an application model, and

5. An evaluation of the rules (closed predicate-calculus formulas) with respect to the interpretation based on the application model.

With these in hand, an application model is *syntactically correct* if the interpretation based on the application model is valid.

The BNF definitions declare user-defined strings for the lexical object sets in the metamodel. These user-defined object sets remain constant over all application models. Figure 6.7 provides some of these definitions; all of them appear in Appendix B.

Figure 6.6 includes many natural-language constraints. As examples, we convert three constraints to predicate calculus—one from Fig. 6.6a, another from Fig. 6.6b, and the third from Fig. 6.6c.

> **Constraint**: *For every Connection, each Relationship-Set Name of the connected Relationship Set must include an Object-Set Name of the connected Object Set; conversely, if an Object-Set Name appears in a Relationship-Set Name, then the Object-Set Name must name the Object Set to which it is connected.*

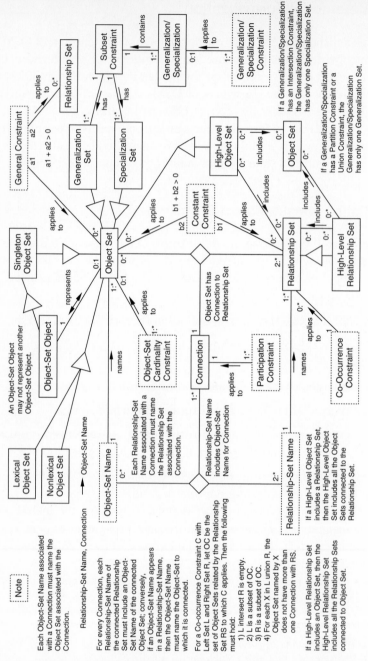

(a) OSM metamodel for ORMs.

Figure 6.6 OSM metamodel. Used with permission of Dr. Stephen Liddle. *Object-Oriented Systems Implementation: A Model-Equivalent Approach*, pp. 232–234.

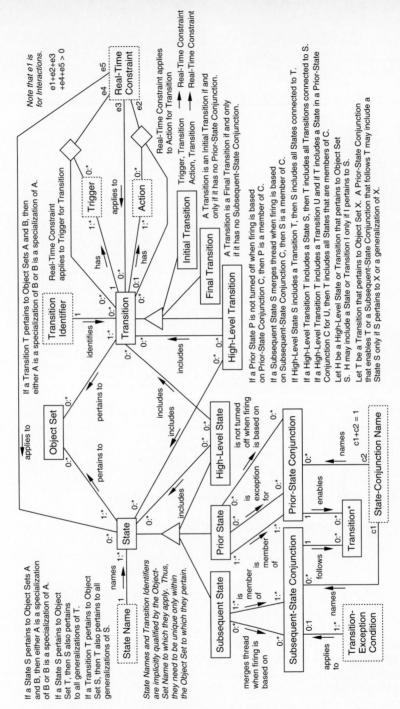

(b) OSM metamodel for OBMs.

Figure 6.6 (cont.) OSM metamodel.

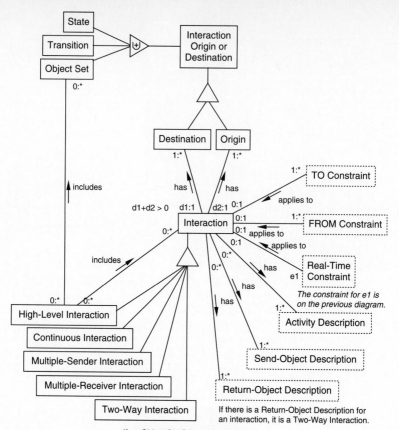

(c) OSM metamodel for OIMs.

Figure 6.6 (cont.)   OSM metamodel.

Participation Constraint ::= *Cardinality Constraint*

Object-Set Cardinality Constraint ::= *Cardinality Constraint*

Cardinality Constraint ::= *Cardinality Term* [**,** *Cardinality Term*] ...

Cardinality Term ::= Non-negative Integer Expression
    [**:** Non-negative Integer Expression | *****]

Co-occurrence Constraint ::= *Object-Set Name List* { → | **->**
  | *Cardinality Constraint*
      →
  | **-[** *Cardinality Constraint* **]->** }
  Object-Set Name List
Object-Set Name List ::= Object-Set Name [**,** Object-Set Name] ...

Generalization/Specialization Constraint ::= ∪ | ∩ | **+** | ⊎

Figure 6.7 BNF definitions for some lexical object sets in the OSM metamodel.

Conversion:

$\forall x_1 \forall x_2 \forall x_3 \forall x_4 \forall ($
    Object Set(x_1) has Connection(x_2) to Relationship Set(x_3)
    $\land$ *Relationship-Set Name(x_4) names Relationship Set(x_3)*
    $\Leftrightarrow \exists x_5 ($
        Relationship-Set Name(x_4) includes Object-Set Name(x_5) for Connection(x_2) $\land$ Object-Set Name(x_5) names Object Set(x_1)))

Constraint: *A Transition is an Initial Transition if and only if it has no Prior-State Conjunction.*

Conversion:

$\forall x_1 ($*Initial Transition(x_1)* $\Leftrightarrow$ *Transition(x_1)* $\land$
    $\neg \exists x_2 ($*Prior-State Conjunction(x_2) enables Transition(x_1)))*

Constraint: *If there is a Return-Object Description for an interaction, it is a Two-Way Interaction.*

Conversion:

$\forall x_1 \forall x_2 ($*Interaction($x_1$) has Return-Object Description(x_2)*
    $\Rightarrow$ *Two-Way Interaction(x_1))*

The derivation of the predicates and rules from the ORM diagram was defined in Section 6.1. Examples of predicates derived from the metamodel in Fig. 6.6 are as follows:

> *Object Class*(x)
> *Prior State*(x)
> *Interaction*(x) *has Activity Description*(y)
> *Object Set*(x) *has Connection*(y) *to Relationship Set*(z)

Examples of rules are as follows:

Sample Referential-Integrity Rule:
$$\forall x_1 \forall x_2 (Transition(x_1) \text{ has } Action(x_2) \Rightarrow Transition(x_1) \wedge Action(x_2)$$

Sample Generalization/Specialization Rule:
$$\forall x (High-Level \ Object \ Set(x) \Rightarrow Object \ Set(x))$$

Sample Participation-Constraint Rules:
$$\forall x (Relationship \ Set(x) \Rightarrow$$
$$\exists^{\geq 2} <y, z> (Object \ Set(y) \text{ has } Connection(z) \text{ to}$$
$$Relationship \ Set(x)))$$
$$\forall x (General \ Constraint(x) \Rightarrow \exists^{f_{a1}(x)} y (General \ Constraint(x) \text{ applies to}$$
$$Object \ Set(y)))$$
$$\forall x (General \ Constraint(x) \Rightarrow \exists^{f_{a2}(x)} y (General \ Constraint(x) \text{ applies to}$$
$$Relationship \ Set(y)))$$

Sample Co-occurrence-Constraint Rule:
$$\forall <x, y> (\exists z (Relationship\text{-}Set \ Name(x) \text{ includes } Object\text{-}Set$$
$$Name(z) \text{ for } Connection(y))$$
$$\Rightarrow \exists^{1} z (Relationship\text{-}Set \ Name(x) \text{ includes } Object\text{-}Set \ Name(z)$$
$$\text{for } Connection(y)))$$

Sample General-Constraint Rule:
$$\forall x (General \ Constraint(x) \Rightarrow f_{a1}(x) + f_{a2}(x) > 0)$$

Observe also that after all the general constraints have been converted to predicate-calculus formulas, these formulas all become rules. Thus, for example, we also have the three rules given earlier, which we obtained by converting natural-language statements to predicate calculus.

Figure 6.8 provides an application model and its interpretation. The interpretation has a relation for every object and relationship set in the metamodel, but in Fig. 6.8 we show only the non-empty relations. For

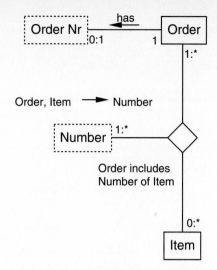

(a) A small application model.

Figure 6.8 An application model and its interpretation.

Object Set	Object-Set Name	Connection	Lexical Object Set
O_1	Order	C_1	O_1
O_2	Item	C_2	O_3
O_3	Number	C_3	
O_4	Order Nr	C_4	
O_5	String	C_5	

Relationship Set	Relationship-Set Name	Nonlexical Object Set
R_1	Order includes Number of Item	O_2
R_2	Order has Order Nr	O_4

Participation Constraint	Co-occurrence Constraint
1: *	Order, Item $\rightarrow$ Number
0: *	
1	
0: 1	

Object Set Name names Object Set		*Object Set has Connection to Relationship Set*		
Order	O_1	O_1	C_1	R_1
Item	O_2	O_1	C_4	R_2
Number	O_3	O_2	C_2	R_1
Order Nr	O_4	O_3	C_3	R_1
		O_4	C_5	R_2

Relationship-Set Name names Relationship Set

Order includes Number of Item	R_1
Order has Order Nr	R_2

Relationship-Set Name includes Object-Set Name for Connection

Order includes Number of Item	*Order*	C_1
Order includes Number of Item	*Item*	C_2
Order includes Number of Item	*Number*	C_3
Order has Order Nr	*Order*	C_4
Order has Order Nr	*Order Nr*	C_5

Participation Constraint applies to Connection

1: *	C_1
0: *	C_2
1: *	C_3
1	C_4
0: 1	C_5

Co-occurrence Constraint applies to Relationship Set

Order, Item $\rightarrow$ *Number*	R_1

(b) Interpretation for the application model.

Figure 6.8 (cont.) An application model and its interpretation.

lexical object sets, the figure shows the syntactically correct string defined by our BNF, and for nonlexical object sets the figure shows a chosen object identifier for each object.

We can guarantee that the application model in Fig. 6.8a is syntactically correct by convincing ourselves that the interpretation in Fig. 6.8b is valid. To convince ourselves of the validity of the interpretation, we evaluate each of the rules over the given domain (the values in the relations). For example, we must check each referential-integrity constraint, one of which is

$\forall x \forall y$(*Object-Set Name(x) names Object-Set(y)* $\Rightarrow$ *Object-Set Name(x)* $\wedge$ *Object Set(y)*)

which holds for every x and y in the domain. It holds for most combinations of x and y because the left-hand side of the implication is *false*, which makes the implication *true*. When the left-hand side is *true*—for example, when $x = Order$ and $y = O_1$—then the right-hand side is also *true*; here, for example, both *Object-Set Name(Order)* and *Object Set(O_1)* are *true*. As another example, we must also check each participation constraint, one of which is

$\forall x$(*Connection(x)* $\Rightarrow$ $\exists^1 y$(*Participation Constraint(y) applies to*
      Connection(x)))

This constraint holds because for each connection—C_1, C_2, C_3, C_4, and C_5—there is exactly one participation constraint. As yet another example, we must also check each general constraint, one of which is

$\forall x_1 \forall x_2 \forall x_3 \forall x_4 \forall ($
    Object Set(x_1) has Connection(x_2) to Relationship Set(x_3)
    $\wedge$ *Relationship-Set Name(x_4) names Relationship Set(x_3)*
    $\Leftrightarrow \exists x_5 ($
        Relationship-Set Name(x_4) includes Object-Set Name(x_5)
        for Connection(x_2)
        $\wedge$ *Object-Set Name(x_5) names Object Set(x_1)*))

This constraint holds because whenever we select a tuple from the *Object Set has Connection to Relationship Set* relation (e.g., the first tuple in the relation in Fig. 6.8b), a tuple from the *Relationship-Set Name names Relationship Set* relation with the same relationship set as in the first chosen tuple (e.g., the first tuple), then there is a tuple in the *Relationship-Set Name includes Object-Set Name for Connection* relation with the same relationship name as in the second chosen tuple and the same connection as in the first chosen tuple (e.g., the first tuple) and a tuple in the *Object-Set Name names Object Set* relation with the same name as in the third chosen tuple and the same object set as in the first chosen tuple (e.g., the first tuple). Furthermore, the converse is also *true*. Consider, as one more example,

$\forall x$(*Initial Transition(x)* $\Rightarrow$ *Transition(x)*)

which seemingly has nothing to do with our primary example. We must ensure, however, that all constraints hold. Constraints such as this one hold trivially, however, since for every value in the domain, the left-hand side of the implication is *false*.

It can become tedious to check each of these constraints, and of course they should be checked by a computer. If we wish to check them ourselves, we can do so at a higher level of abstraction. Instead of generating a rule to check and then evaluating it, we can read the metamodel symbols, understand what they mean, and use this understanding to check the constraints. For example, we can see in Fig. 6.6a that the *Specialization* object set is a specialization of the *Object Set* object set. We therefore know that the elements in *Specialization* must be a subset of the elements in *Object Set*. It is easy to check that the *Specialization* relation is a subset of the *Object Set* relation. As another example, we can check the 1 participation constraint on the *Connection* object set in the *Object Set has Connection to Relationship Set* relationship set by observing that each connection in the *Object Set has Connection to Relationship Set* relation associates with one and only one *Object-Set / Relationship-Set* pair and thus identifies uniquely both the object set and the relationship set to which it applies.

We can use the metamodel in a similar way to answer questions about what constitutes correct application models. For example, we can ask whether there can be more than one participation constraint for a connection, and can answer the question negatively by observing that the participation constraint for *Connection* in the *Participation Constraint applies to Connection* relationship set is *1*. As another example, we might ask whether an interaction can stand alone without either a destination or an origin. By considering the variable participation constraints on the relationship sets that connect *Interaction* to *Destination* and *Origin* in Fig. 6.6c and the related general constraint, we can answer this question negatively. Suppose that an interaction I has neither a destination nor an origin. Then $d1 = 0$ and $d2 = 0$, which violates the general constraint $d1 + d2 > 0$.

Since the metamodel is an OSM application model, we can also query it in the same way we query any other application model. For example, we can find the participation constraints of the object sets in the *Order has Order Nr* relationship set with the following OSM-SQL query:

> **select** *Object-Set Name, Participation Constraint*
> **from** *Relationship-Set Name includes Object-Set Name for Connection R,*
>   *Participation Constraint applies to Connection PC*
> **where** *R. Connection = PC. Connection*
>   **and** *Relationship-Set Name = "Order has Order Nr"*

> **OSM-SQL**
>
> OSM-SQL is an SQL query language that uses the notation of OSM to express SQL queries. OSM-SQL uses object- and relationship-set names in place of relation names and object-set names and object-set names within relationship-set names as attribute names. Otherwise, the language is the same as SQL.

Assuming the interpretation in Fig. 6.7, we obtain the following result for this query:

Object-Set Name	Participation Constraint
Order	1
Order Nr	0: 1

6.2.2 Dynamic and Temporal Formalization of Semantics

We can provide semantics for an OSM application model in two ways:

1. Augment the OSM syntax definition with time parameters, add temporal predicates and rules, produce an interpretation, and check its validity.

2. Define an abstract machine that simulates the execution of an OSM application model.

The first way, although elegant conceptually, is unwieldy in practice. The second has the standard problem of all automatons—an automaton behaves exactly as defined, but whether this is exactly what is intended is not known. If we could prove that an OSM abstract machine M always generates only valid interpretations for any temporal-augmented OSM application model, we would know that M behaves as intended. However, this is currently an open problem.

Since the equivalence proof is an open problem, and since the full definition of both the temporal-augmented semantics and the abstract-machine semantics is lengthy and beyond the scope of what we wish to accomplish here, we do not give all the details. Instead, we explain enough of the temporal predicates and rules to make it possible to see how valid temporal interpretations can define the semantics formally, and we give a basic OSM abstract machine that shows how to simulate an OSM application model.

In both cases, we ignore the thorny issue of transition exceptions, and for our temporal-augmented semantics, we ignore intra-object concurrency. These assumptions simplify our discussion considerably.

We begin with the temporal-augmented semantics, explaining how to add temporal components to OSM predicates and rules by giving an example. Our explanation of the temporal-augmented semantics is restricted to this example. Figure 6.9 shows a simple credit-card fuel dispenser. The

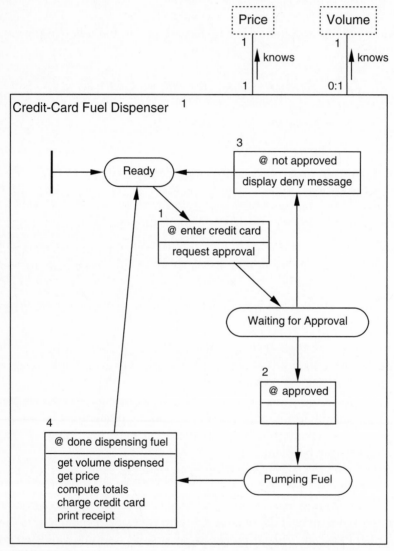

Figure 6.9   An example to illustrate OSM temporal-augmented semantics.

Credit-Card Fuel Dispenser object set is active—when it receives an approved credit card, it allows fuel to be purchased.

We convert an application model to temporal, first-order logic by adding zero, one, or two time places to each predicate. We add two time places for predicates and rules about objects and relationships. The two times designate the beginning and ending times of the existence of an object or relationship. We add one time place for events and add zero for any time-invariant predicates and rules. To distinguish syntactically the time places from any other places in a predicate, we add them in a pair of parentheses at the end of the predicate.

For the application model in Fig. 6.9, there are three object sets and thus three object-set predicates:

$$Credit\text{-}Card\ Fuel\ Dispenser(x)(t_1, t_2)$$
$$Price(x)(t_1, t_2)$$
$$Volume(x)(t_1, t_2)$$

These predicates assert not only that x exists as an object, but that x exists as an object between times t_1 and t_2, inclusively. For the two relationship sets in Fig. 6.9, the two relationship predicates are

$$Credit\text{-}Card\ Fuel\ Dispenser(x)\ knows\ Price(y)(t_1, t_2)$$
$$Credit\text{-}Card\ Fuel\ Dispenser(x)\ knows\ Volume(y)(t_1, t_2)$$

Similar to temporal object-set predicates, these temporal relationship-set predicates assert that the relationship holds from time t_1 to time t_2.

From the application model in Fig. 6.9, we generate several rules similar or identical to the rules we discussed earlier, including the following referential-integrity rules:

$$\forall x \forall y \forall t_1 \forall t_2 (Credit\text{-}Card\ Fuel\ Dispenser(x)\ knows\ Price(y)(t_1, t_2)$$
$$\Rightarrow \exists t_3 \exists t_4 \exists t_5 \exists t_6 (Credit\text{-}Card\ Fuel\ Dispenser(x)(t_3, t_4)$$
$$\wedge\ Price(y)(t_5, t_6) \wedge t_3 \leq t_1 \wedge t_2 \leq t_4 \wedge t_5 \leq t_1 \wedge t_2 \leq t_6))$$

$$\forall x \forall y \forall t_1 \forall t_2 (Credit\text{-}Card\ Fuel\ Dispenser(x)\ knows\ Volume(y)(t_1, t_2)$$
$$\Rightarrow \exists t_3 \exists t_4 \exists t_5 \exists t_6 (Credit\text{-}Card\ Fuel\ Dispenser(x)(t_3, t_4)$$
$$\wedge\ Volume(y)(t_5, t_6) \wedge t_3 \leq t_1 \wedge t_2 \leq t_4 \wedge t_5 \leq t_1 \wedge t_2 \leq t_6))$$

These rules assert that during the time a relationship exists between a credit-card fuel dispenser and a price, the fuel dispenser and price must exist. Similarly, during the time a relationship exists between a credit-card fuel dispenser and a volume, the fuel dispenser and volume must exist. The participation constraints in the application model in Fig. 6.9 are time invariant. The rules for participation constraints therefore have zero time places and are the same as the participation-constraint rules discussed previously.

With temporal predicates, we can also generate predicates and rules for state nets and interactions. This, of course, is the interesting addition that makes it possible to define formally the behavior of objects over time. We now explain how to generate the most important predicates and rules for the application model in Fig. 6.9.

Predicates

1. For each state, we write a predicate that lets us assert that an object is in the state. One of the state predicates is *Credit-Card Fuel Dispenser(x) in state Pumping Fuel*(t_1, t_2).

2. For each transition, we write several predicates that let us trace the phases involved in processing a transition. For transition *1* we write

   Credit-Card Fuel Dispenser(x) transition 1 inactive(t_1, t_2)
   Credit-Card Fuel Dispenser(x) transition 1 enabled(t_1, t_2)
   Credit-Card Fuel Dispenser(x) transition 1 committed(t_1, t_2)
   Credit-Card Fuel Dispenser(x) transition 1 executing(t_1, t_2)
   Credit-Card Fuel Dispenser(x) transition 1 finishing(t_1, t_2)

3. For each trigger of each transition, we write a predicate that lets us determine when the trigger is true. For the trigger in transition *1* we write *Credit-Card Fuel Dispenser transition 1 trigger true*(t_1, t_2). Since the trigger in transition *1* is an event, $t_1 = t_2$ must hold here and we can simplify this predicate. In general, however, we need a duration for when a trigger holds. Observe also that this predicate is object independent—a trigger can hold whether there is an object or not.

4. For each interaction, we write a predicate that lets us assert the time an interaction occurs. For the *done dispensing fuel* interaction, we write *done dispensing fuel*(t_1). Observe that an interaction is also object independent.

Rules

1. We must guarantee that any object that participates in the behavior for an object set is a member of the object set when it participates in the behavior. Thus, for example, we write

    $$\forall x \forall t_1 \forall t_2 (\textit{Credit-Card Fuel Dispenser}(x) \textit{ in state Pumping}$$
    $$\textit{Fuel}(t_1, t_2) \Rightarrow \textit{Credit-Card Fuel Dispenser}(x)(t_1, t_2)$$

    We must write similar rules for objects that are in transitions.

2. Every object in an object set must be in one and only one of the phases of every transition in the state net. Since an object can be in at most one transition at a time (recall that we are assuming that there is no intra-object concurrency), the object will be in the *inactive* phase for all but one transition, and for that transition the object can be in only any one of the five phases—*inactive, enabled, committed, executing,* or *finishing*. This takes several rules. To ensure that an object is in one of the phases for transition *1*, for example, we write

    $$\forall x \forall t_1 \forall t_2 (\textit{Credit-Card Fuel Dispenser}(x)(t_1, t_2) \Rightarrow$$
    $$\forall t_3 ((t_1 \le t_3 \land t_3 \le t_1) \Rightarrow$$
    $$\textit{Credit-Card Fuel Dispenser}(x) \textit{ transition 1 inactive}(t_3, t_3)$$
    $$\lor \textit{Credit-Card Fuel Dispenser}(x) \textit{ transition 1 enabled}(t_3, t_3)$$
    $$\lor \textit{Credit-Card Fuel Dispenser}(x) \textit{ transition 1 committed}(t_3, t_3)$$
    $$\lor \textit{Credit-Card Fuel Dispenser}(x) \textit{ transition 1 executing}(t_3, t_3)$$
    $$\lor \textit{Credit-Card Fuel Dispenser}(x) \textit{ transition 1 finishing}(t_3, t_3)$$

3. Capturing the idea of when and how a transition fires is central to defining state-net semantics. We capture this idea by requiring a rule that ensures that if a transition is enabled for an object and the transition's trigger is true, then there exists a future time at which the transition is committed for the object. We can express this rule for transition *1* in Fig. 6.9 as follows:

    $$\forall t_1 (\exists x (\textit{Credit-Card Fuel Dispenser}(x) \textit{ transition 1 enabled}(t_1, t_1)$$
    $$\land \textit{ enter credit card}(t_1))$$
    $$\Rightarrow (\exists t_2 (t_2 > t_1 \land \textit{Credit Card Fuel Dispenser}(y) \textit{ transition 1}$$
    $$\textit{committed}(t_2, t_2))))$$

Our predicates and rules give us a way to reason about the behavior of state nets. As indicated by the discussion in the preceding rule, we can be sure that a transition will fire if an object is in a prior state of a transition and if the trigger for the transition holds. With a complete set of rules, we would also be able to reason about the opposite possibility. If no object is in a prior state of a transition or the trigger is not true, then the transition does not fire.

The predicates and rules also provide a way to find a valid interpretation. Proceeding as before for static application models, we specify a domain D and assign values in D to constants, functions, and predicates. We must, of course, include time in D for a temporal application model. We then evaluate all the rules. If they all hold, the interpretation is valid.

We now turn to OSM abstract-machine semantics. We define an OSM abstract machine in terms of OSM—that is, we give a state net that describes the behavior of a state net. Only a simplified OSM abstract machine is discussed here. We continue to assume that there are no exceptions, but now we allow for intra-object concurrency. Further, we present the OSM abstract machine for only a single object. For multiple objects we would have the same state nets, but we would have to keep track of the states and transitions of each object, as well as to handle inter-object concurrency.

Under these assumptions, Fig. 6.10 presents the OSM abstract machine. Figure 6.10a defines the behavior of a state; Fig. 6.10b, the behavior of a transition.

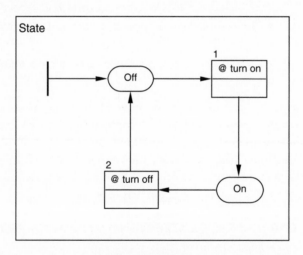

(a) Basic state behavior.

Figure 6.10   Basic OSM abstract machine for a single object.

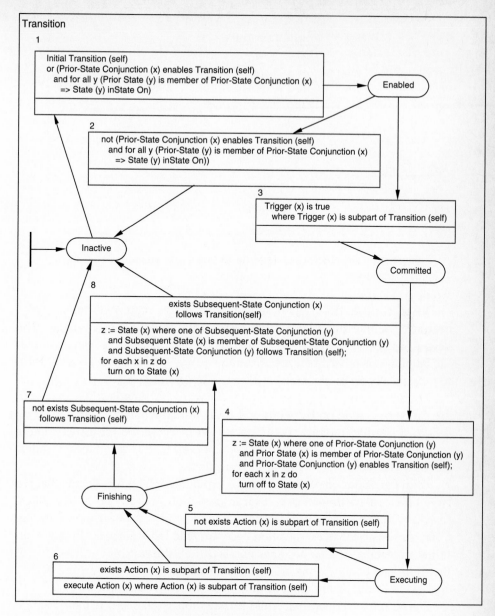

(b) Basic transition behavior.

Figure 6.10 (cont.)   Basic OSM abstract machine for a single object.

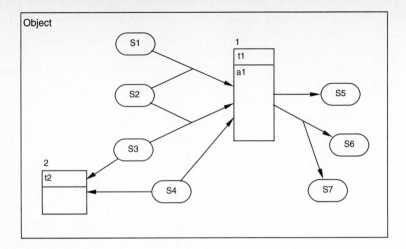

Fig. 6.11   An abstract state net with prior- and subsequent-state conjunctions.

To be formal, the triggers and actions in the state nets of the OSM abstract machine must be written in a formal, executable language. The language is OSM-L, which we do not define until Chapter 8. Here we treat the language as an abstract specification and say only enough about OSM-L to provide a basic understanding of the state net in Fig. 6.10b.

The state net in Fig. 6.10a is straightforward. A state is either on or off. We can turn a state on by sending a *turn on* interaction, and turn it off by sending a *turn off* interaction. The state net in Fig. 6.10b for a transition is more complex; we use the abstract state net in Fig. 6.11 as an aid to understanding the reasons for some of the complexity.

For a particular object—and for our explanation here we assume that we have only one—a transition is itself in transition or is in one of five states: *Inactive, Enabled, Committed, Executing,* or *Finishing*. As transition 1 in Fig. 6.10b shows, an inactive transition becomes enabled automatically if it is an initial transition. It also becomes enabled if all the states in at least one of its prior state conjunctions are on. For example, transition 1 in Fig. 6.11 is enabled if *S1* and *S2* are on, if *S2* and *S3* are on, or if *S4* is on.

Figure 6.10b shows that while a transition is enabled, it may become inactive without firing. This happens if one or more of the states in an enabling prior state conjunction is turned off. For example, if transition 2 in Fig. 6.11 fires based on *S4*, *S4* is turned off. This may disable transition 1 because *S4* may have been the only state turned on and thus the only state enabling transition 1. Similarly, if transition 1 fires based on *S3*, one of the states in the *S2-S3* prior-state conjunction for transition 1 would be turned off. If none of the other prior-state conjunctions for transition *1* were on, transition *1* would no longer be enabled.

Transition *3* in Fig. 6.10b specifies that if the trigger of an enabled transition is true, the transition becomes committed. Once committed, a transition always executes. Before executing, prior states in one of the prior-state conjunctions must be turned off. Often there is only one prior-state conjunction, but there may be several (see Fig. 6.11). When several prior-state conjunctions enable a transition, a decision must be made about which states to turn off. Suppose, for example, that states *S1*, *S2*, *S3*, and *S4* in Fig. 6.11 were all on. Then, as the **one of** clause in transition *4* in Fig. 6.10b specifies, one of these prior-state conjunctions is chosen randomly. Each of the states in this prior-state conjunction is then turned off.

Execution takes place if there is an action, as transitions *5* and *6* in Fig. 6.10b show. After execution, the transition is in the *finishing* state. If there are no subsequent states, nothing need be done, as transition *7* shows. If there are subsequent states, the action in transition *8* selects one of the subsequent-state conjunctions and turns on all its states.

6.3 Chapter Summary

Topic Summary

- A valid interpretation for a generated model-theoretic view of an OSM application model represents a valid database state for the OSM application model. The representation is almost never efficient, but, as shown later in this book, we can transform an inefficient model-theoretic view of an OSM application model into an efficient model-theoretic view that is information- and constraint-equivalent to the inefficient generated view.

- The OSM metamodel describes the set of all syntactically correct OSM application models. If we attach a temporal duration to each object and relationship and add a time line, we can describe all valid future states for all objects and relationships and for the behavior of all objects. This future "history" defines the semantics of an application model.

- As a practical matter, the formal definition of OSM tells us exactly what each construct in OSM means. It also tells us whether an OSM application model is correct and lets us answer questions about the construction process. For example, we can decide whether some construct is optional or required and what syntactic form some construct must have.

- Although the formal syntactic and semantic definition of OSM can help us answer questions about what constructs mean and about whether an application model is correct, it is an unwieldy operational definition. The temporal-semantics definition is unwieldy because it describes all possible future executions—usually far too many to comprehend. The abstract-machine formalization of OSM, on the other hand, provides an operational definition that we can use to simulate the execution of OSM application models.

Question Summary

- How do generated predicates correspond to OSM application-model object sets and relationship sets?

  Each object and relationship set has a predicate for each of its names. If each object and relationship set has one name (as is often the case), then there is a one-to-one correspondence between generated predicates, on the one hand, and object and relationship sets, on the other hand.

- How do generated formulas correspond to OSM application-model constraints, both implicit constraints and explicit ones?

  Generated formulas capture application-model constraints precisely. The explicit constraints include cardinality constraints, generalization/specialization constraints, and general constraints. Each explicit constraint generates one or more formulas to capture the constraint. The implicit constraints include multiple-name constraints, referential-integrity constraints, and high-level relationship constraints, plus the basic object-set and relationship-set predicates, which assert that an object or relationship is a member of a particular object or relationship set. Each implicit constraint generates a formula to capture the constraint.

- How does a valid interpretation for a collection of generated predicates and formulas correspond to a database?

  With assumptions such as the closed-world assumption, we can represent an interpretation as a set of predicates with their instantiations that are true, plus a set of closed formulas. If the closed

---

The One-to-One Correspondence between OSM Application Models and Their Generated Model-Theoretic Views

One-to-one correspondences imply that mappings exist in both directions. Thus, not only is it possible to generate a model-theoretic view from an OSM application model, but it is also possible to generate an OSM application model from a model-theoretic view of a database. Indeed, we use this idea when we define our model-equivalent language OSM-L in chapter 8. We cannot create an OSM application model, however, from any arbitrary set of predicates and predicate-calculus formulas—the predicates and formulas must correspond to an OSM application model. Since we always start with OSM application models and generate model-theoretic views, this is not a problem, and the inverse transformation is available to us.

---

formulas hold for the instantiations, the interpretation is valid. The predicate instantiations correspond directly to relations with an attribute for each place in the predicate, and the closed formulas correspond directly to integrity constraints. Thus, a valid interpretation corresponds directly to a relational database for which the integrity constraints hold.

- What is the practical significance of a formal definition for OSM?

There is frequent disagreement about the interpretation of the representation of some concept, or, even worse, there may be no realization that a discrepancy exists. In practice, since the formal definition for OSM provides for only one meaning for the representation of a concept, we can resolve differences by appealing to the formal definition. The formal definition is also practical in the sense that it provides a solid foundation on which to build tools and methodologies to aid in application development.

- What are some practical applications for the abstract-machine semantics for OSM?

Abstract-machine semantics provide for a simulation of object behavior. Therefore, the abstract machine directly provides the basis for testing the validity of state nets in an application model. Building on this validity checking, the abstract machine directly provides the basis for building a rapid-prototyping tool for OSM.

6.4 Bibliographic Notes

An early version of the formal syntactic definition for OSM was presented in appendix A of [Embley92]. A full formal definition of OSA, which is nearly the same as OSM, appears in [Clyde93]. Examples of other similar formalizations are in [Kifer95], and [Maier86]. Based on the formal semantics, several experimental tools have been built, including a tool that checks the syntax of an application model [Clyde93] and a rapid prototyping tool that simulates the execution of state nets according to the abstract-machine semantics for OSM [Jackson94, Jackson95].

6.5 Exercises

6.1 Translate the ORM diagram in Fig. 6.12 into the set of predicates and rules that characterize it, as follows:

    a. Give the object-set predicates.

    b. Give the relationship-set predicates.

    c. Give the referential-integrity rules.

    d. Give the generalization/specialization rules.

    e. Give the participation-constraint rules.

6.2 Suppose that we have a ternary relationship set connecting object sets A, B, and C. Translate the co-occurrence constraint $AB \rightarrow C$ into an application-model rule.

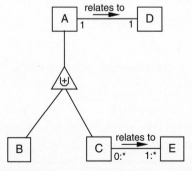

Figure 6.12 ORM diagram for generating predicates and rules.

6.3** The ORM diagram in Fig. 6.13 includes aggregation and relational object sets, both of which are templates. Convert the ORM diagram into the set of predicates and rules that characterize it, as follows:

   a. Convert the aggregation template into basic ORM components.

   b. Convert the relational object set into basic ORM components.

   c. Give the object-set predicates.

   d. Give the relationship-set predicates, including predicates of relationship sets generated in 6.3(a) and 6.3(b).

   e. Give the equivalence-class rules for object sets and relationship sets with multiple names.

   f. Give the referential-integrity rules for relationship sets, including generated relationship sets.

   g. Give the rules for participation and co-occurrence constraints.

   h. Give the general-constraint rules for the generated general constraints.

6.4* Translate the ORM diagram in Fig. 6.14 into the set of predicates and rules that characterize it, as follows:

   a. Give the object-set predicates.

   b. Give the relationship-set predicates.

   c. Give the referential-integrity rules.

   d. Give the participation-constraint rules.

   e. Give the object-set cardinality constraint rules.

   f. Give the high-level relationship set derivation rule.

6.5 Give a valid interpretation for the ORM diagram in Fig. 6.12, written as a model-theoretic view of a database similar to Fig. 6.5. The interpretation should be minimal but must have one value for B and one for E, which must relate to two values in C.

6.6 For Fig. 6.12, explain why there must be a value for D if there is a value for C. Base the argument on the generated predicated-calculus rules and show that at least one rule must be violated if there is not a value for D when there is a value for C.

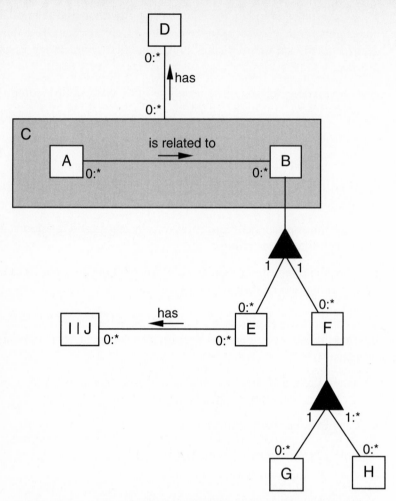

Figure 6.13 ORM diagram for generating predicates and rules.

6.7*   Give a valid interpretation for the ORM diagram in Fig. 6.13, as follows: Convert the templates for the aggregation and the relational object set to basic ORM components. Then write the interpretation as a model-theoretic view of a database similar to Fig. 6.5. The interpretation should be minimal but must have one relationship in *A is related to B*, two *J* values, and two *H* values.

6.8   Give a valid interpretation for the ORM diagram in Fig. 6.14. Write the interpretation as a model-theoretic view of a database similar to Fig. 6.5. The interpretation should be minimal but must

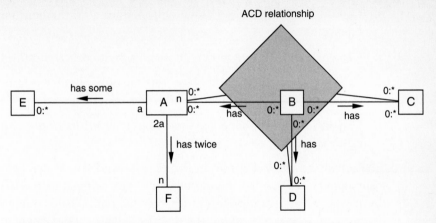

Figure 6.14 ORM diagram for generating predicates and rules.

have two relationships in *A has some E* and one in *ACD relationship*. The built-in multiplication function need not be provided.

6.9 Answer the following questions. Provide a justification for each answer by referring to the OSM metamodel in Fig. 6.6 (i.e., say specifically which constraints are relevant and how they answer the question).

a. Can a co-occurrence constraint apply to more than one relationship set?

b. Can the left-hand and right-hand sets of a co-occurrence constraint have a nonempty intersection?

c. Can a participation constraint be omitted from the connections of a relationship set in an ORM diagram?

d. If the name of an object set fails to appear in the name of a connected relationship set in an ORM diagram, is the ORM diagram valid?

e. If a generalization/specialization has a union constraint, can there be more than one generalization set?

f. Must a transition have a transition identifier?

g. Can a prior state be part of more than one prior-state conjunction?

h. Can a subsequent-state conjunction follow more than one transition?

    i. Can an interaction stand alone with neither a destination nor an origin?

    j. Can we have an interaction without an activity description?

    k. Are states, transitions, and object sets the only possible origins or destinations for an interaction?

    l. Can an interaction have the same object set for its origin and destination?

6.10* Show that the ORM diagram in Fig. 6.12 is valid (i.e., is syntactically correct in the sense that it obeys the rules of the metamodel) by giving a valid interpretation for the diagram. Use a model-theoretic database to provide the answer, which should have an appearance similar to Fig. 6.8b. Omit empty object and relationship sets. Make up mnemonic surrogate values for nonlexical object sets and use the given lexical values for lexical object sets. Does each generated constraint hold?

6.11* Repeat Exercise 6.10 for the OSM diagram in Fig. 6.10a.

6.12* Formalize the following general constraints from the metamodel in Fig. 6.6:

    a. *Each Object-Set Name associated with a Connection must name the Object Set associated with the Connection.*

    b. *If a High-Level Object Set includes a Relationship Set, then the High-Level Object Set includes all the Object Sets connected to the Relationship Set.*

    c. *If a Generalization/Specialization has an Intersection Constraint, the Generalization/Specialization has only one Specialization Set.*

    d. *A Transition is a Final Transition if and only if it has no Subsequent-State Conjunction.*

    e. *If a High-Level Transition T includes a State S, then T includes all Transitions connected to S.*

    f. *Let H be a High-Level State or Transition that pertains to Object Set S. H may include a State or Transition I only if I pertains to S.*

6.13* Give a partial temporal predicate-calculus formalization for the OSM application model in Fig. 6.15, as follows:

    a. Give all the ORM predicates.

b. Give all the ORM rules.

c. Give the state predicates.

d. Give the transition predicates for all phases of a transition for transition 2.

e. Give the trigger predicate for transition 1.

f. Give the interaction predicate.

g. Give the constraints that guarantee that a smoke alarm must exist to behave like a smoke alarm, but only for the *Ready* state and for transition 3.

h. Give the rules to guarantee that an enabled transition fires. Give the rules only for transition 4.

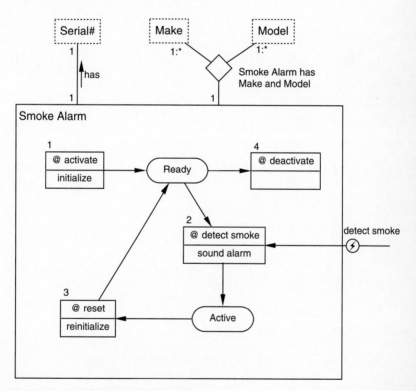

Figure 6.15   OSM application model.

Chapter 7

Analysis

Systems analysis is the study of a system, whether real or imagined. Its purposes are to gain and document user requirements and knowledge about the system under study and to promote a common understanding among system developers, analysts, and clients. The key ideas in analysis are studying, understanding, and documenting, all highly human activities.

An analysis of user requirements includes a broad understanding of the application context—what problems are being addressed and how the system can help solve these problems—and a more specific understanding of the potential costs and benefits of system development. Knowledge about the system includes not only what the system is and how it operates, but also information about pertinent parts of the system's environment and how it interacts with its environment. Ideally, synergism among clients and developers during systems analysis leads not only to understanding, but also to new insights that would not have been obtained by either clients or developers in isolation.

In the OSM development process, analysis is object oriented, and thus we take an object point of view to guide us as we study, document, and understand a system. In particular, we observe and capture knowledge directly about objects, their relationships with other objects, their individual behavior, and their behavior as they interact with other objects. This holds true for understanding user needs and assessing feasibility as well as for analyzing system and environment characteristics.

We begin with a discussion about determining client needs and assessing system feasibility. Entire books and countless papers have been written on this subject alone. Our purpose here is not to consider all the possibilities, but instead to provide some insight into what is involved and to demonstrate how we can use OSM both to describe a particular view of a needs and feasibility assessment and to capture the desired information. This approach has several advantages, which are explained and illustrated in the discussion.

We next consider ways to do analysis. Again, much has been written on this subject, some of the best of it is in the proprietary, guarded secrets of consulting firms. It may be fair to conclude that, in general, there may be no one best way to proceed. We therefore only briefly mention a few of the ideas and techniques that have been used. We then describe three generic ways to proceed: (1) a data approach when objects and relationships are central, (2) an object-behavior approach when individual object behavior is central, and (3) an object-interaction approach when interaction among objects is central. We illustrate these three approaches by developing some additional component parts for our running on-line shopping example.

For systems that are too large for an analyst or an analysis group to handle as a single unit, the work must be divided into smaller units. Analysts must then integrate these units to create a single system view. In describing a common approach to the integration process, we also finish developing the application model for our running example.

Finally, we consider how to analyze the results of an analysis. How good is it? How can we determine whether it is correct and complete? Our objective here is to check, as best we can, that the application model created during analysis properly reflects a full and complete understanding of the information pertinent to the system under study.

We do not assume, as some have, that when we satisfactorily "finish" our analysis, it is done. It is the nature of software development that as we formalize our application model during specification, design, and implementation, we learn more about the application itself. As we do, we also need to capture these insights in the application model. Allowing ourselves to capture these insights later shifts the focus of analysis (and our other development activities) to what we are doing. If we are learning and documenting knowledge about the system for the purpose of promoting a common understanding among clients and developers, we are doing analysis. It does not matter if we do this before, during, or after some other development activity. We must do much of this work up front, but not all of it.

The following topics in this chapter are particularly important:

- The purpose of analysis and the difficulties involved in being a successful analyst.

- Diagram comparison, conformance, and merge for model integration.

- Black-box and white-box approaches to reviewing application analysis models.

- Congruency, including understatements and overstatements.

- Object properties, including explicitly defined properties for object sets and common properties.

The following questions should also be kept in mind:

- Why is an ontological model well suited for doing analysis and reviewing application analysis models?

- What advantage can we gain by using OSM to model system needs and feasibility?

- What kinds of applications best fit an object-relationship approach to modeling? An object-behavior approach? An object-interaction approach?

- How do high-level constructs help provide an integration framework?

- What are some ways to determine whether an application model is satisfactory?

- How does object-set congruency help ensure the cohesiveness of objects in an object set?

7.1 System Needs and Feasibility Assessment

An assessment of business needs and alternative ways to meet these needs, along with an assessment of the feasibility of the alternatives, is often the most important part of analysis. Rarely are decisions to build database systems so clear that this assessment is unnecessary. There are usually many considerations, including the risks and payoffs for the business, the cost and scheduling of system construction, and technology and human issues—themselves hard to quantify. How much assessment should be done depends on several factors, such as the magnitude of the project and the availability of resources that can be devoted to the analysis. Indeed, the needs and feasibility assessment itself could also be the subject of an analysis.

How to proceed in developing the needs and feasibility assessment and what the results should be also depend on several factors. The dominant factor is likely to be the desires (and even the whims) of upper-level management, who must make the ultimate decisions, but the desires of personnel involved in the analysis and the application also should be considered.

Given the high variability of what results are wanted and who and what might be involved, one way to proceed is to start with a model of assessment that can be tailored, as necessary, for a particular project and manage-

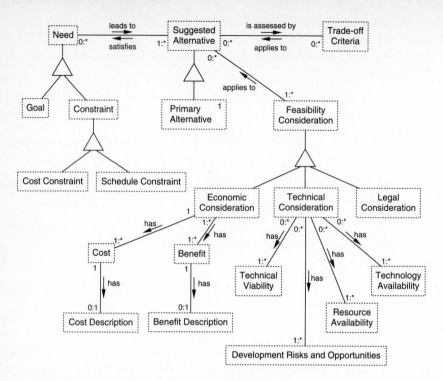

Figure 7.1 A rudimentary assessment model.

ment group. The assessment model can serve as a guide for completing the assessment, as well as a repository for the results. Moreover, if the results are captured on-line, they can be queried to obtain answers to various questions needed for decision making.

Figure 7.1 displays some rudimentary aspects of a possible OSM assessment model. This assessment model would have to be expanded greatly for a detailed analysis, of course, and it should be tailored to meet the needs of a particular project. Nevertheless, it shows some basic considerations and the relationships among them.

The assessment model in Fig. 7.1 shows, for example, that needs are either goals or constraints and that they lead to suggested alternatives. Feasibility considerations apply to the alternatives, which can be assessed by trade-off criteria. Feasibility considerations can be complex, consisting of economic, technical, and legal considerations. Each economic consideration has a cost and one or more benefits. Ultimately, economics is the bottom line in terms of costs and benefits that matters most, but technical and legal considerations must also be properly taken into account. These latter factors include the skills and availability of personnel for the project, how the project might position the company for future changes and to take advantage of future technology, and the impact of current and future laws. These additional considerations can make a big difference in the eventual success of a project.

Figure 7.1 also shows several other details, including the idea of a primary alternative, that is, the suggested alternative currently being considered for adoption. Not shown, however, are the data values for the object and relationship sets. In addition to the framework and guideline for assessment provided by an assessment model, it is also possible to prepopulate some of the object sets with values of interest. The trade-off criteria, for example, may be established in advance and may carry over from project to project. Some of the cost and benefit descriptions may also exist in advance; they might help guide the various costs and benefits that should be considered.

Given an assessment-model framework tailored for a particular project, possibly with some prepopulated object sets, assessment analysts complete their work by carefully and thoughtfully determining the information requested in the assessment model. They usually do this by asking questions. To assess needs, for example, an analyst might begin by asking some of the following questions: What are your goals and objectives for the system? What are your expectations? Why do you think the system will help you in your business? What constraints are likely to be imposed on development? What is the expected budget? When should the system be operational? In asking these questions, it is important to probe deeply enough to distinguish between needs and wants and to try to distill the essential needs of the project.

Once we populate an assessment model, we can browse the results. Moreover, we can pose queries and write information-yielding programs to help in the assessment process. As an example, Fig. 7.2 shows an OSM-SQL query that lists the total costs of the alternatives in ascending order, with the least expensive alternative first. Results, such as this cost list and other desired summary information, can be presented to upper-level management for a final decision. Furthermore, since management will most likely

> **select** *Suggested Alternative, sum(Cost)* **as** *Total Cost*
> **from** *Feasibility Consideration applies to Suggested Alternative,*
>   *Economic Consideration has Cost*
> **where** *Feasibility Consideration = Economic Consideration*
> **group by** *Suggested Alternative*
> **order by** *Total Cost*

Figure 7.2   An OSM-SQL query to obtain assessment information.

ask for information not provided in the summary, additional information can be gleaned from the assessment model—or, if necessary, gathered into the assessment model and then summarized.

We conclude this section by summarizing several advantages of using an appropriate assessment model for assessing needs and feasibility:

1. An assessment model can serve as a framework for and a guide to assessing needs and feasibility.

2. We can develop standard assessment models and make them available for general use.

3. We can tailor an assessment model for use in a particular project.

4. We can populate object sets with preestablished information that can be used for several projects or that provides a basis for establishing desired relationships.

5. We can obtain information by querying an assessment model either with ad hoc queries or with predeveloped programs.

6. We can use the same modeling paradigm for the assessment model as for the application model.

7.2   Analysis Methods

We now turn our attention to analyzing application-model characteristics, including pertinent interactions with the environment. There is a natural question to ask here: How should an analysis be done? Since analysis is knowledge discovery, it is essentially a learning task; like most learning tasks, it requires a deep involvement with the information. Knowledge discovery, especially in the face of vague and sometimes contradictory information, is difficult at best, but ultimately it can be obtained by those who make the effort. Experience counts, and the more often a person engages in analysis with genuine effort, the better he or she becomes at accomplishing the task.

Although experienced analysts may have individual approaches, some general guidelines can be followed. One general guideline is that analysis can be carried out by asking questions, observing activities, reading documents, and gleaning information from business forms. As bits and pieces of information are obtained, they should be recorded. Careful consideration of these recorded items and their interrelationships can also lead to additional insights. Furthermore, as many have observed, we learn by writing, especially formal writing such as the type required to specify a system well enough eventually so that it can be designed and implemented.

Several experienced analysts have advocated their own approaches. Their methods include CRC cards (Class/Responsibility/Collaborator cards), responsibility-driven analysis, scenarios, and use cases. These approaches usually involve business users heavily, thus providing a good opportunity for the analyst to glean insight from those who will be the eventual users of the system being developed. The bibliographic notes in this chapter reference these methods for the interested reader.

Most of these approaches present a step-by-step method of doing analysis. An alternative approach, which we explore in greater depth here, is model driven. A model-driven approach is like using a map to reach a destination, rather than following step-by-step directions (which almost always end with "you can't miss it"). Once a person knows the map symbols and their meaning and once he or she can orient a map, a destination can be reached by following a preplanned path. If obstacles prevent the person from following the preplanned path, an alternative route can be chosen. Similarly, a modeling approach to analysis requires a person to know and understand the symbols of the model and their meaning; then once he or she is oriented (i.e., has learned enough about the application to begin recording), the remainder of the application model can be created using the modeling paradigm to record the information gleaned from the analysis.

For a model-driven approach, the choice of model makes a difference because the model provides us with the abstract concepts we use to communicate. These abstract concepts can both expand and limit our potential. They expand our potential when they allow us to capture all aspects of a system and its environment easily and directly; they limit it when they cause us to shoehorn our square ideas into round holes or to miss pertinent parts of the analysis because the model does not provide a way to record some types of information. Although we sometimes believe we can rise above a modeling paradigm, more often than not we tend to think only in terms of the model.

A model-driven approach provides a great deal of flexibility in how to approach an analysis task—sometimes so much that it is difficult to decide how to begin. For OSM modeling, there are three basic approaches:

1. The ORM (Object-Relationship Model) approach.

2. The OBM (Object-Behavior Model) approach.

3. The OIM (Object-Interaction Model) approach.

By assessing the characteristics of an application or the part of the application under study, an analyst should decide whether the components of interest are dominated by object and object-relationship characteristics, by individual object behavior, or by object-interaction behavior. The decision may not be clear-cut, but this does not matter; what does matter is that, as a general rule, the most important characteristics of an application component should be considered first.

We now provide three examples, one to illustrate each approach. We also expand our running example by adding components for inventory control and customer payments.

As a first example, consider customer information, including information about customer payments. Let us assume the following. Either customers walk into a store and buy items or they order them using a home computer. If they buy in the store, they pay before leaving, and we do not keep any information on these customers. If they wish to become home-computer buyers, however, they must register as customers, in which case they are assigned a customer identification number, and they must provide credit-card information to make purchases.

This information consists mainly of objects related to customers. We therefore proceed by creating an ORM diagram for the mentioned objects and the implied relationships among these objects. The object and relation-

---

The Practical Significance of Analyzing Cardinality Constraints

Experienced OSM analysts often say that they gain more insight by a careful analysis of cardinality constraints, especially participation constraints, than by any other way. Participation constraints carry much of the meaning of an ORM diagram. They tell us in Fig. 7.3a, for example, whether every customer is expected to have a credit card. Figure 7.3a insists that they do, but is this really how the business operates? This same cardinality constraint states that a customer has only one credit card, but certainly some customers have more than one. This may not matter, however, if the business runs by using exactly one credit card for each customer—perhaps the one chosen when filling out a form to become a customer. Figure 7.3a also states that every credit card belongs to a customer—certainly there are other credit cards, but with respect to the application, this specific limitation to only those credit cards that belong to the customers in the application is probably exactly what is wanted. Figure 7.3a also states that we know the address of every Customer. Do we really always know? Do we care? Maybe it would be better to have a *0:1* participation constraint on *Customer* for *Customer has Address*.

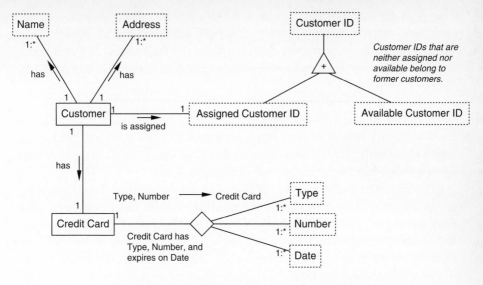

(a) Additional ORM components for customers.

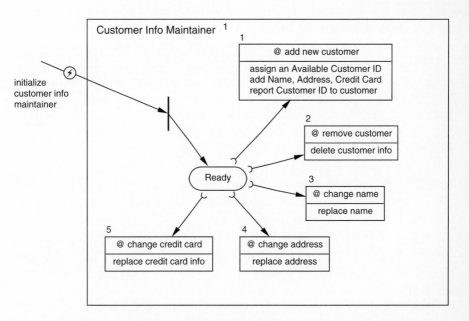

(b) Behavior needed to obtain and maintain customer information.

Figure 7.3 An ORM-dominant application-model component.

ship sets in Fig. 7.3a are the results. Note that each customer has an assigned customer ID and a name, address, and credit card, which has a type, number, and expiration date. Further, there are some available customer IDs for new customers and some expired customer IDs belonging to former customers.

Given this ORM diagram, we can immediately see what activities are necessary to obtain and maintain this customer information. Basically, we need to supply interactions to add a customer, delete a customer, and (possibly) change the information once it is established. The state net in the *Customer Info Maintainer* in Fig. 7.3b shows the result.

For our next example, we consider inventory control. Here, we may judge the individual behavior of an inventory system to be dominant, and thus we begin by first developing the OBM state nets in Fig. 7.4a. The system must watch the stock as items are sold. If the number on hand for an item decreases below a reorder threshold, new stock should be ordered, and a note should be made about the order so that the system does not continue blindly to reorder more of the item. A natural question is, "How is the threshold set?" The answer may be, "A manager often sets the threshold, but if not, we order 10% more than we sold a year ago." Although at first glance this statement may seem satisfactory, when we look more closely, as is typical, it leaves a lot to be desired. Exactly what is meant by "a year ago"? What if the item is brand new, or has been offered for only a few months? With better answers to these questions, we can record what is wanted more precisely, as transition 2 in Fig. 7.4a shows. Also, as part of answering to this question, we may learn that a history of sales is needed. Current sales should accumulate, and at the beginning of each new calendar month, several actions must be taken to update and maintain the history, including adjusting it and reinitializing monthly amounts sold and inventory thresholds. Since the history controller and inventory must coordinate these reinitializations so that the right monthly values are used, we provide an interaction between the two objects to ensure that the thresholds are set only after making the end-of-month adjustments to the inventory history. Finally, in addition to watching and reacting as items are sold, the system should also watch and react to items as they arrive. As items arrive, the system should increase the number on hand and should also notify the appropriate department manager and delete the notes about the items being on order.

The state nets in Fig. 7.4a reflect this behavior. Considering these state nets, we can next develop an appropriate ORM diagram for items from an inventory point of view. In transition 1, for example, the trigger refers to the number on hand, the threshold, and whether the item is already on

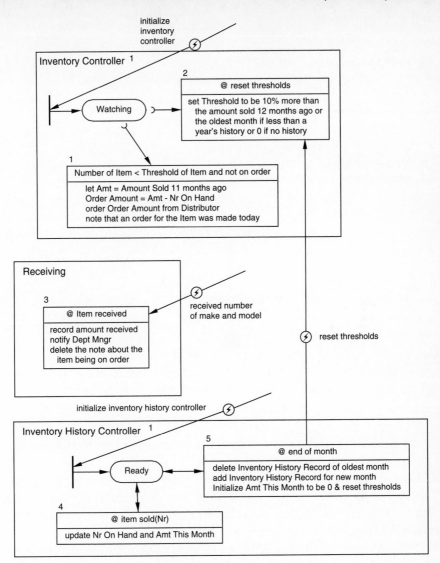

(a) State nets to control inventory.

Figure 7.4   An OBM-dominant application-model component.

order. As a result, we add the object and relationship sets for *Item has Number On Hand, Item has Threshold,* and *Item is on order from Distributor as of Date.* Considering the action for transition *1,* we see that we also need an inventory history that has a record of the amount sold for each month. In addition, we need the information necessary for making an order, including the make and model to identify the item and the distributor name and

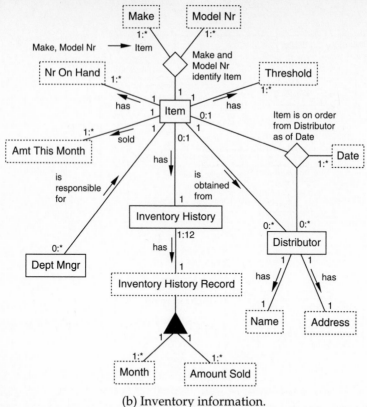

(b) Inventory information.

Figure 7.4 (cont.) An OBM-dominant application-model component.

address to mail the request. Further considerations of the state nets in Fig. 7.4a lead to the necessity of a department and department manager and a way to keep track of the amount sold during the current month. The result is the ORM diagram in Fig. 7.4b.

We could also add to this diagram explicitly the other interactions mentioned, such as notification of a department manager when an item is received. These interactions are already captured well enough, however, in the text of the transition actions. If we wish to emphasize the interactions, we may add them anyway, but since the dominant characteristic here is the inventory system behavior, we may wish to omit them. Figure 7.4a reflects this latter choice.

In our last example, we show how to begin by first considering the interactions, and thus initially we take an OIM perspective. When considering how a home-computer customer might place orders, we are likely to focus on the interactions between the customer and the automated order

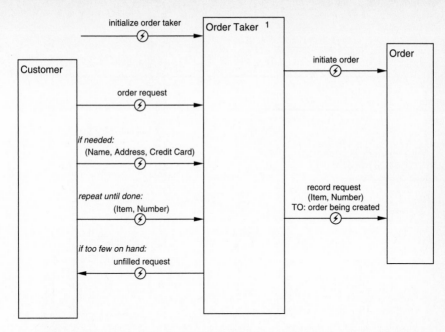

Figure 7.5 Interaction sequences for an OIM-dominant application-model component.

taker and between the order taker and the data store representing the order. Figure 7.5 shows a high-level representation of these interaction sequences. When we write interaction sequences in this way, we imply that, unless otherwise noted, the interactions occur one after another in the order shown. In Fig. 7.5, we note that two of the interactions are conditional and that one is repeated until the order is complete. Although interaction sequences provide only a rough high-level view, they are a useful way to start, especially when the dominant behavior is an interaction between two objects.

We can use an interaction sequence as a guide in developing state nets, which provide the conditionals and loops only hinted at by the notes in the interaction sequence. Figure 7.6 shows how we developed the state net for the order taker. Here, we have dropped the *Customer* object set to show that we are thinking of the customer who is making an order as being outside the system. Observe that the interactions in Fig. 7.5 are the same as the interactions in Fig. 7.6. What is different is that we have filled in the details for the behavior of an *Order Taker* by giving its state net, which tells when and how each of the interactions takes place, at least as far as an order taker is concerned.

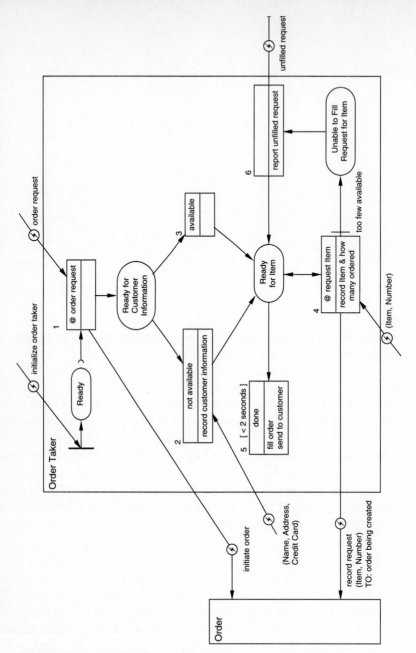

Figure 7.6 Application-model component developed from the
interaction sequences in Fig. 7.5.

7.3   Application-Model Integration

When an analysis task becomes too large for one individual, several analysts can work together to accomplish it. Each analyst is responsible for part of the system and is also responsible for assisting in the integration. Analysts can develop smaller components using techniques such as those described in the previous section. Larger components and eventually the full application model can be obtained by integrating these smaller components. The number of analysts who should be involved depends on the magnitude of the task. Be aware, of course, that dividing the task among too many analysts can eventually be counterproductive—the integration problem can become larger than the analysis problem.

Integration works best if done systematically. We therefore first consider a standard approach to integration, which we then illustrate by integrating the components we have developed for our running example.

7.3.1 An Approach to Integration

Our approach to integration for OSM is similar to the process of schema integration in database systems. We directly adopt these schema integration techniques for ORM diagrams, and we adapt these same techniques for integrating OBM and OIM diagrams.

OSM has some features of its own that make it particularly suitable for integration. For example, it provides us with high-level components, which give us views, which in turn lead to a framework for doing top-down integration. Top-down development encourages an appropriate divide-and-conquer approach to the development of large systems. Once a high-level view is in place, we are able to make reasonable decisions about how to divide the analysis task among a group of analysts so that each can develop a reasonably independent subpart for a large system. Top-down development also simplifies later integration and helps ensure that the integrated result will indeed model the entire system.

We therefore begin with an integration framework, which guides the division of labor among the analysts as well as later integration of the diagrams they produced. Using the integration framework to guide us in choosing which diagrams to integrate, we integrate diagrams in three steps: (1) compare diagrams, (2) conform diagrams, and (3) merge diagrams.

Diagram Comparison   We compare diagrams to identify components that correspond. Corresponding components may or may not have conflicts. If conflicts exist, they will be either name conflicts or structural conflicts.

Name conflicts arise because of synonyms or homonyms. If the same component has two or more names in different diagrams, we have a synonym conflict. For example, we may have an object set named *Dept Mngr* in one diagram and the same object set named *Manager* in another diagram. If different components have the same name, we have a homonym conflict. For example, *Date* may be the expiration date of a credit card in one ORM diagram, the date an order is received in another diagram, and the date an item was ordered from a distributor in yet another diagram.

Structural conflicts in an application model arise either because different types of structures represent the same concept or because of conflicting constraints. One way different types of structures can represent the same concept is when a concept is described in one diagram at a high level of abstraction and in another diagram at a low level of abstraction. We may, for example, have a direct relationship between managers and items for which they are responsible in one diagram, while in another diagram we may have an indirect relationship through a department that a manager manages. In the first case, the "is responsible for" relationship is a high-level abstraction that has suppressed the details about which department is involved. Another common example is an aggregate object, such as an *Address* object set, which may be represented in one diagram as just the aggregate and in another as the aggregate with multiple subparts, each of which may also be an aggregate with multiple subparts.

Constraint conflicts occur when there are inconsistencies in constraints. A common example in OSM integration is conflicting participation constraints. A participation constraint in one diagram may specify, for example, that department managers are responsible for at least one item, whereas in another diagram, we may have a stronger requirement stating that they are responsible for at least 10 items and at most 100 items.

No Structural Conflicts between Object Sets and Attributes in OSM

Structural conflicts between object sets and attributes occur often when integrating models such as the ER model that require analysts to distinguish between entities and attributes. Since OSM does not require analysts to distinguish between attributes and object sets, the common difficulty of deciding whether something should be modeled as an object or as an attribute disappears. It is thus impossible to have a component in one ORM diagram described as an object set and in another ORM diagram as an attribute. This feature alone simplifies OSM model integration greatly.

Diagram Conformance Once we have identified conflicts, we resolve them. To resolve them, we conform diagrams. In the process of conforming diagrams, we must make sure that the resulting model remains consistent with reality. Sometimes this means that we should return to our sources of information to validate the newly conformed model.

We resolve synonym and homonym conflicts by changing names or allowing aliases as best suits our needs. Synonym conflicts can be resolved by retaining all the names as aliases for one another, by choosing one of the synonym names as the name, or by choosing a different name altogether. For example, if we have *Manager* in one diagram and *Dept Mngr* in another diagram, we may rename *Dept Mngr* as *Manager*. We can resolve homonym conflicts by selecting different names for all, or at least for all but one, of the homonyms in conflict. For example, we can rename *Date* for credit cards as *Expiration Date*, rename *Date* for customer orders as *Order Date*, and rename *Date* for orders to distributors as *Stock Order Date*.

Resolution of structural conflicts is more difficult than resolution of name conflicts. In general, by adding, deleting, replacing, and combining diagram elements, we make alterations so that diagrams conform. The process is not automatic and usually requires insight and understanding by both analysts and clients. For our aggregate address example, the adjustment is easy. We can choose to have the full subpart breakdown, not to have any breakdown, or to have partial breakdown. For the indirect versus direct association between managers and items, we would likely choose to add the *Department* object set because it conveniently allows us to record several details about associations with items, managers, and workers.

Diagram Merge Once diagrams conform, we can merge them. Two or more components considered to be conceptually identical become one component in the merged diagram. After merging common components on all diagrams, we may be finished, but usually there are two more considerations:

1. A straightforward merge often yields unsatisfactory results. Two typical unsatisfactory results are redundant information that is not wanted and missing generalizations that are wanted.

2. By doing the integration, we are likely to have gained more knowledge and insight. As a result, we may need to make some changes.

Redundant information arises naturally because several facts in one diagram may imply a single fact in another diagram. In one diagram, for example, we may have several facts about customers and how they relate to customer IDs—some customer IDs may be assigned to customers, others may be available, and still others may be unassigned and unavailable. In another diagram, there may be a simple fact that associates customer IDs to customers, but this fact would most likely be implied by the facts about customer IDs in the first diagram. When we merge the two diagrams, the redundant fact may be seen as superfluous and uninformative, in which case it should be removed. We emphasize, however, that we are not generally concerned about redundancy during analysis; we want to remove redundancy in an application analysis model only if it does not help us understand and communicate.

Missing generalizations also arise naturally. We may, for example, have employees with names and addresses in one diagram and have customers with names and addresses in another diagram. In a merged diagram we can generalize by creating an object set for persons who have names and addresses. Similar cases arise regularly, and we can handle them in the same way.

It is hard to predict what additional insights might be gained during integration, but they almost always appear. We incorporate this new knowledge in the same way we incorporate any new knowledge into an application analysis model—by adding missing information or changing existing information to make it conform to our improved understanding.

7.3.2 Integration Example

We now present an example that illustrates OSM model integration. We also develop our running example further.

Let us begin by giving an integration framework. Figure 7.7 shows a high-level view of our application. For this example, subcomponents fall out naturally by observing high-level interactions. Thus we have a customer-information maintainer that maintains customer information, an order taker that takes orders from customers and produces order information (which includes the items ordered), an inventory control system that watches items and orders and receives stock, and interactions to add, delete, and maintain information about employees and items.

The customer-information component is in Fig. 7.3; the inventory-control component, in Fig. 7.4. Figure 7.6 gives the basic order-taking component, but it is incomplete because it is missing both order information and backorder details. Figure 7.8 provides the missing information about orders, and Fig. 7.9 provides the missing backorder details. Also missing is the component about employees and their relationship to items; this information is provided in Fig. 7.10.

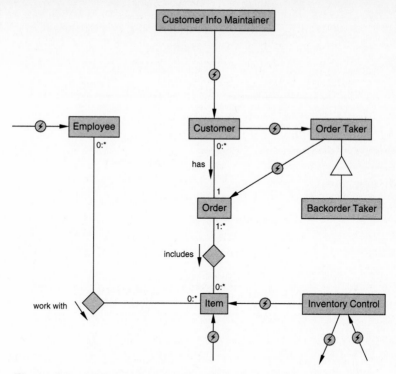

Figure 7.7 High-level application view and integration framework.

Using our integration framework, we can see that the central part of the integration task is to link the path from object set *Employee* to object set *Customer*. Therefore we first integrate the ORM diagrams in Figs. 7.8 and 7.10. In comparing the diagrams, we see that the object sets *Item*, *Item Name*, *Item Nr*, and *Nr On Hand* all match. We also see that the intended price of an order should match the retail price, and we decide to resolve the name conflict by keeping both names—*Retail Price* is more descriptive, but *Price* is a short name we expect to use often. For this same reason we also decide to add *Cost* as a name for *Wholesale Cost*. Having conformed the diagrams, we now merge them. The result is almost what we want, with the only problem being the *Name* and *Address* object sets associated with both employees and customers. Realizing that there is a missing generalization, we add *Person* and promote *Name* and *Address* to be associated only with *Person*. The result is the ORM diagram in Fig. 7.11. (By the way, observe that if we were to expand *Order Taker* in Fig. 7.11 with the *Order Taker* state net in Fig. 7.6, we would have the OSM diagram in Fig. 4.39.)

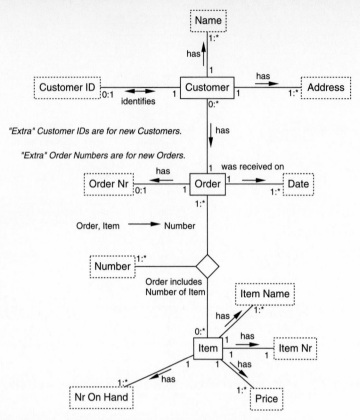

Figure 7.8 ORM diagram for order information.

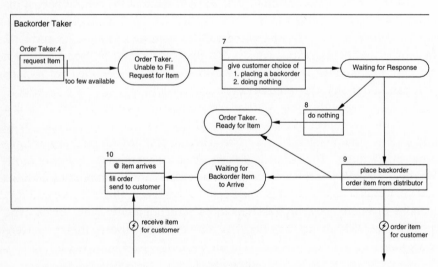

Figure 7.9 OBM diagram for backorders.

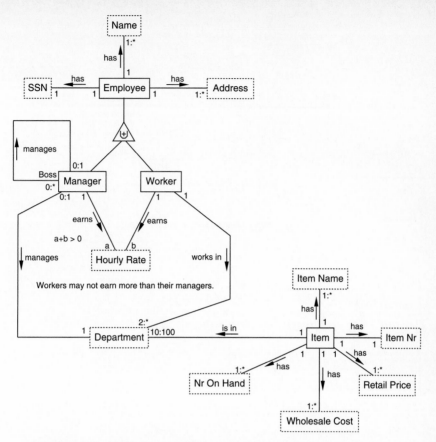

Figure 7.10 ORM diagram for employee and item information.

We next consider the state net in Fig. 7.9, which we must integrate with the state net in Fig. 7.6. In comparing the state nets, we observe that there are explicit given matches for two of the states and one of the transitions. With some consideration, we see further that the state net in Fig. 7.9 completely subsumes the exception loop in Fig. 7.6 and that we should thus remove transition 6, its prior state, and the exception exit from transition 4 from the state net in Fig. 7.6. If we now rename the state between transitions 4 and 7 in Fig. 7.9 as *Unable to Fill Request for Item*, we can merge the two diagrams immediately by doing nothing. In essence, we have modularized the behavior by placing the behavior we associate with taking backorders in the *Backorder Taker* state net. The connection between the two state nets is through transition 4, which initiates a backorder when the exception path is taken, and the state *Ready for Item*, which is the resumption state for

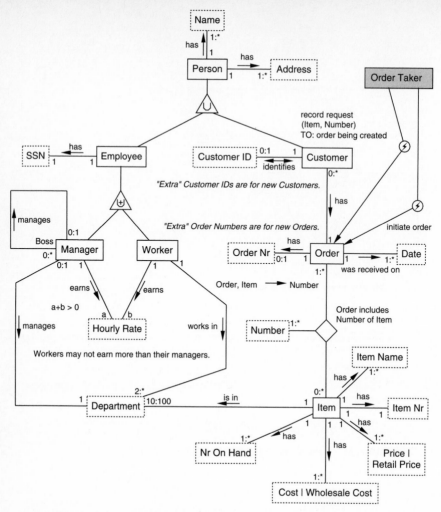

Figure 7.11   Initial ORM integration.

the general order taker. Observe that the object splits into two threads when leaving transition *9*, one to resume regular order taking and one to await the arrival of the item on backorder. Figure 7.12 shows these revisions.

We next integrate the information from the view of the customer-information maintainer. In comparing the diagrams in Figs. 7.3 and 7.11, we see that there is a homonym conflict for *Date*. We rename the *Date* for

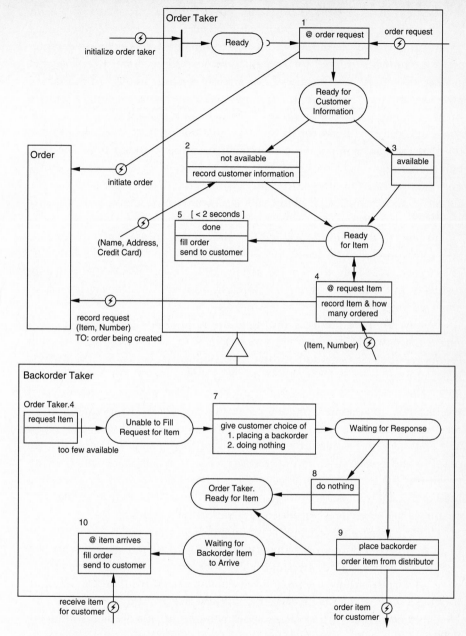

Figure 7.12   Merged state nets representing the full state net

the credit card as *Expiration Date* and the *Date* of the order as *Order Date*. We also observe a homonym conflict for *Number,* and choose to rename the credit-card *Number* as *Card Nr,* but not to rename the *Number* that represents the number ordered for an item. We next observe that the *Name* and *Address* object sets on *Customer* have already been promoted to the *Person* object set in Fig. 7.11. Since this is where we want them, we simply remove them from Fig. 7.3 before merging. Next we observe that although there are some interesting differences in the way customer IDs are represented, we see that they are compatible semantically and that nothing need be done before merging. After merging, however, we see in Fig. 7.13, which shows only this part of the merge, that the *identifies* relationship set between the *Customer* and *Customer ID* object sets is not only redundant, but probably also confusing. We therefore delete it. We might, however, prefer the name "identifies" to the name "assigned to" and choose to use it for the one-to-one correspondence between the *Customer* and the *Assigned Customer ID* object sets. We show this choice in Fig. 7.14, the full ORM diagram that results from the merge. There is nothing to do with the *Customer Info Maintainer* state net, so we leave it as it is in Fig. 7.3.

Finally, we integrate the ORM diagram in Fig. 7.4 with that in Fig. 7.14. The resulting ORM diagram appears as Fig. 7.15. In integrating these diagrams we first observe and resolve two homonym conflicts. We rename *Name* of *Distributor* as *Distributor Name* and *Address* of *Distributor* as *Distributor Address.* Recalling that *Date* would have been a homonym conflict if we had not done some previous renaming, we decide to rename *Date* as *Stock Order Date.* We next observe the synonym conflict between *Dept Mngr* and *Manager* and resolve it by renaming *Dept Mngr* as *Manager.* Finally, we observe and resolve a structural conflict. The *is responsible for* relationship set in Fig. 7.4 includes the object set *Department* and two of its associated relationship sets. Instead of restructuring, the easiest way to make this change is to delete the *is responsible for* relationship set in Fig. 7.4.

Having integrated all our component diagrams, we now assess the results. By comparing our integration framework in Fig. 7.7 with our results, we notice that the two high-level interactions into *Employee* and *Item* have no corresponding interactions in our integrated results. We therefore provide low-level details for these interactions in Fig. 7.16.

Other observations that result in adjustments are also possible. Indeed, there is still much to check in our application model. Since we wish to do this checking by using a systematic engineering approach rather than an ad hoc one, however, we postpone these observations and adjustments until the next section.

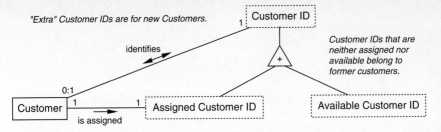

Figure 7.13 An unwanted redundancy.

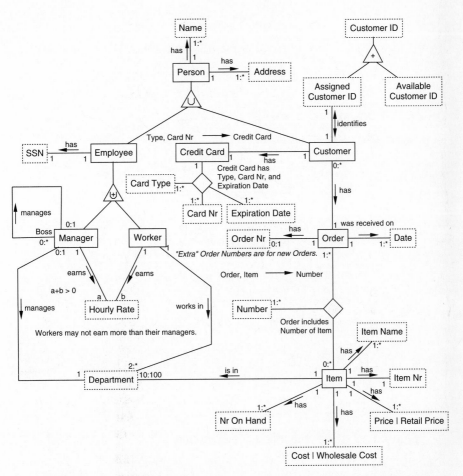

Figure 7.14 ORM diagram obtained by integrating the ORM diagrams in Figs. 7.3 and 7.11.

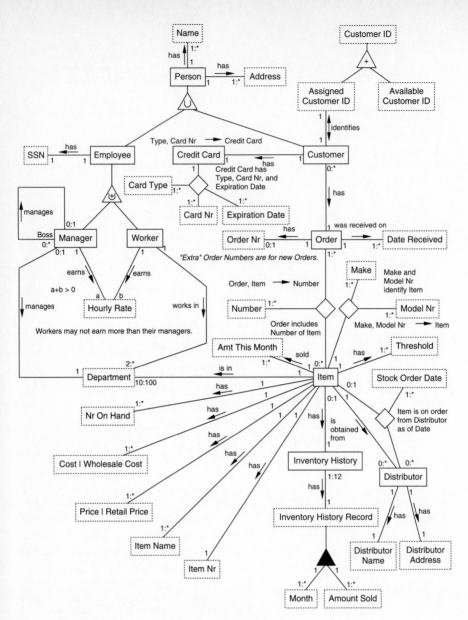

Figure 7.15 Final integrated ORM diagram.

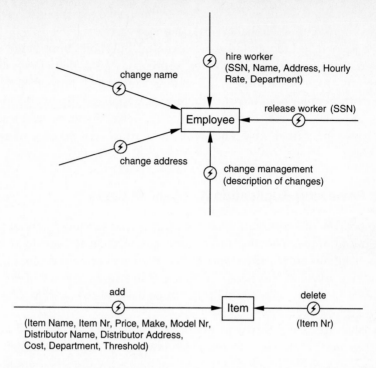

Figure 7.16 Interaction details for maintenance of employee and item data.

7.4 Analysis Validation

How can we determine whether our application model is complete and correct? This is a difficult question with no easy answer. Although both this chapter and the the next are devoted to this question, we only begin to scratch the surface. In this chapter we emphasize information discovery; in Chapter 8, information formalization. Although the ideas in both chapters provide some answers, we should recognize that analysis and specification are highly human activities that require a great deal of skill and insight. However, some helpful techniques are available.

In this section we explore two techniques for analyzing an application analysis model. The first is a formal technical review, which, from the perspective we take here, is similar to program testing except that there is no execution. Even without execution, we can still propose interaction sequences, behavior scenarios, and ad hoc queries about objects and their interrelationships, and can check whether the developed application model appears robust enough to handle the proposed cases.

The second technique addresses a central question about being object oriented. In taking an object-oriented approach, we say that objects should be grouped together if they have similar properties. Is there a way to measure the similarity of objects formally? We shall see that such a method exists and that we can consider object similarity in terms of structural properties, individual object-behavior properties, and object-interaction properties.

7.4.1 Reviewing Application Analysis Models

We do not describe techniques for conducting formal reviews, although the bibliographic notes contain some references that cover how to organize review meetings and to apply specific techniques to achieve desired results. Instead, we take an OSM perspective here, showing how some of the ideas of software testing combined with the three basic views of OSM provide a basis for making reviews successful.

Broadly speaking, there are two main approaches to software testing: black box and white box. In black-box testing, we treat the system as a black box whose inside is hidden. We then interact with the system to see if it responds appropriately. Since an application analysis model does not yet execute, however, we have to provide the execution ourselves. In some sense, this is like white-box testing, in which we scrutinize the inside of the box. We adapt the essence of the idea of black-box testing, however, by considering possible interactions independent of what is in our application model, whereas we use white-box ideas by considering directly the interactions, triggers, and actions given in the application model.

In approaching reviews from a black-box perspective, OSM provides three ways to generate appropriate interactions for consideration:

1. From an ORM perspective, we may consider ad hoc queries to which the system should respond. If the ORM diagram for the application model cannot answer successfully all the reasonable queries asked of it, there are missing object or relationship sets that should be added.

2. From an OIM perspective, we may consider interactions or inter-action sequences that should be handled by the behavior of objects within the system. Reasonable interactions that should be handled but to which the system has no response show where the analysis is lacking.

3. From an OBM perspective, we may consider the receiving end of interactions initiated from outside the system. In particular, we look for any incoming interactions that involve more than a set of simple updates but for which there is no state net.

We now illustrate each of these three OSM black-box approaches.

As an example of ad-hoc queries, we list some questions customers might ask:

How many mountain bikes do you have on hand?

I'd like to browse the information you have about barbecue grills. I'd like their descriptions, and I'd like to see any pictures you have.

What is the status of my backorders?

We may now try to formulate these as application-model queries, say in OSM-QL (see the accompanying box). OSM-QL works well here because it specifies queries in terms of the application model we are investigating. Neither exact syntax nor exact results are needed, but rather just the assurance that the needed object and relationship sets exist. Figure 7.17 shows the first query. There is no way to formulate the second and third queries, however, because the information requested is not present. Figure 7.18 shows the object sets and relationships we must add to satisfy these queries.

As examples of interactions, we might consider the preceding two customer queries, and wonder whether we need a customer-question-answering subsystem. Indeed, we probably do. With further consideration, we see that it is possible to classify customer interactions as placing orders, asking questions about orders, and browsing the catalog. Other interactions, such as returning items for refund or exchange or reporting

---

OSM-QL

OSM-QL is a graphical query language that uses the notation of OSM to express constraints to describe desired results. An OSM-QL query is a view created by manipulating an ORM diagram until it represents the data wanted for the query. The manipulations include removing, and sometimes adding, object sets and relationship sets, and removing, adding, and adjusting constraints. Underlined object-set names designate object sets whose contents after execution hold the results of the query.

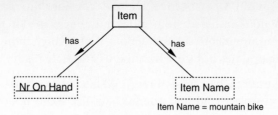

Figure 7.17 OSM-QL query for mountain bikes.

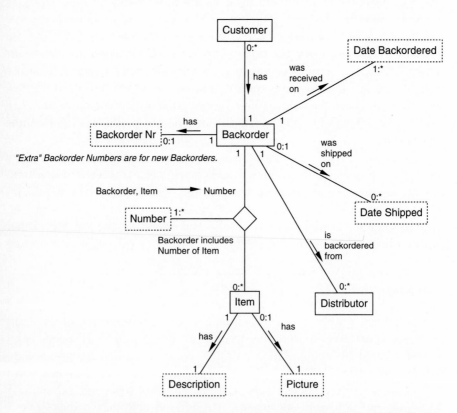

Figure 7.18 Additional object and relationship sets for the application model.

Large Diagrams

Note that if we try to merge the ORM diagram in Fig. 7.18 with the diagram in Fig. 7.15, the result starts to become too large in the sense that it is difficult to include all the information at once. Large diagrams can be managed by views, by OSM-L textual representations, by a set of separate diagrams such as those in Figs. 7.15 and 7.17, or by a combination of these techniques.

---

discrepancies in orders and deliveries, may be considered outside the scope of our application. Having made these decisions, we now see that there are two missing two-way interactions, one to access order information given a customer ID and one to browse item information. Figure 7.19 shows these additions under the assumption that the ORM diagrams in Figs. 7.15 and 7.18 have been merged.

As examples of missing behavior, we consider each of the interactions that come from outside the application model. All but one enter a state net, which handles them; or are queries; or consist merely of receiving straightforward update information. The one interaction of interest here is the *change management* interaction in Fig. 7.16. It requires either a complex description (as implied in Fig. 7.16) or a state net to guide a user through the changes. Figure 7.20 shows a state net for making these management changes.

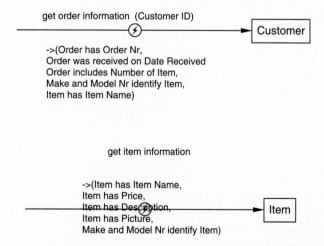

get order information (Customer ID)

Customer

->(Order has Order Nr,
Order was received on Date Received
Order includes Number of Item,
Make and Model Nr identify Item,
Item has Item Name)

get item information

->(Item has Item Name,
Item has Price,
Item has Description,
Item has Picture,
Make and Model Nr identify Item)

Item

Figure 7.19 Additional interactions for the application model.

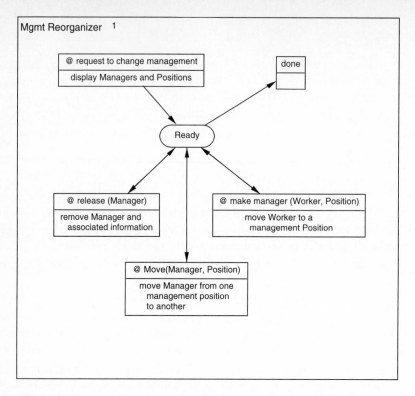

Figure 7.20 Additional behavior for the application model.

Turning now to a white-box approach for doing reviews, we can consider each state net separately. White-box reviews are particularly appropriate after model integration because assumptions made about the expected behavior in other components can be checked. A white-box approach is also appropriate after adjustments are made as a result of a black-box review or after adjustments are made by a prior white-box review.

As an example of cross-checking after integration, consider the inventory-control subsystem, which expects the sales subcomponent to update the number on hand as items are sold, and the sales subcomponent, which expects the inventory-control subsystem to update the number on hand as items are received. Checking these assumptions, we see that a receiving object in Fig. 7.4 does indeed record the amount received. Although an *Order Taker* object does not adjust the number on hand explicitly, it is easy to see how to add this as a second statement in transition 4 in Fig. 7.6. We should also, of course, increase the amount sold during a month for each item purchased.

A more important oversight than the failure of the order taker to make stock adjustments is that nowhere within the application model is there a way to update the number on hand and the amount sold for in-store sales. Moreover, this raises the question of coordination between stock sold by customer orders and stock sold off the shelf. We resolve all these questions first by deciding to allow orders to come only from stock in the back room. This way we avoid the problem of believing we have enough on hand when we do not because an in-store customer has picked up but not yet purchased some of the item. Figure 7.21 shows these changes: instead of giving the full *Order Taker* state net, we provide only the replacement transition for transition 4. Note that in addition to updating values for sales, these changes show that we have considered and taken care of moving items from the back room to restock in-store shelves.

As a final example of review through white-box testing, consider the ripple effect that occurs from adding backorder status information. The

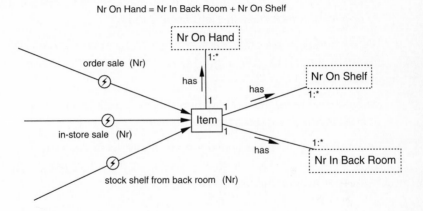

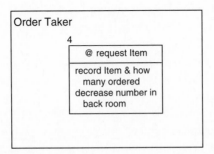

Figure 7.21   Needed adjustments for sales.

state net for backorders in Fig. 7.9 must now record this information. We thus add a statement to transition *9* to record the backorder, and we add a statement to transition *10* to fill in the date shipped.

7.4.2 Object Classification

We turn now to the question of object classification. Before explaining how we measure similarity, however, we point out several reasons why the consideration of object classification is a useful way to validate an analysis:

1. In trying to classify objects, we may discover new sets of objects that should be part of our analysis, and perhaps some that are but should not be part of our analysis.

2. We may find relationship sets that would be better attached to generalizations or to specializations to make the presentation of an application model clearer and more succinct.

3. We may reorganize state nets in a generalization/specialization hierarchy better to reflect the behavior of the various roles an object plays.

4. We may also reorganize interactions better to reflect how an object interacts with other objects and with its environment.

5. In making these adjustments, we are likely to understand better the system we are analyzing; as a result, we are often in a position to make some general improvements.

We measure the similarity of objects in an object set by considering their properties, both structural and behavioral. The more properties two objects have in common, the more similar they are. In an ideal classification, object sets would consist only of objects that all have the same kinds of properties. Thus, in an ideal classification, all objects in an object set would have the same kinds of relationships to other objects, would have the same individual behavior, and would interact with other kinds of objects and with the environment in the same way.

We call this principle of similarity *congruency* because it refers to how objects correspond, coincide, or agree with respect to their properties. We say that an object set is *congruent* if the common properties of the objects in an OSM object set *S* coincide with the properties explicitly defined for *S*. Congruency measures the cohesiveness of an object set. A congruent object set is cohesive and better reflects a system component than does an incongruent object set because its definition represents the common properties of its instances accurately.

Before further pursuing the idea of congruency, we must say what we mean by the notion of a *property*. A relationship to another object, a state, a transition, and an object interaction all can be properties of an object. An object has a relationship property if it participates in a relationship with another object. A hammer, for example, has a price, and thus having a price is a property of a hammer. A state or transition is a property of an object if the object is or can be in the state or transition. An order taker, for example, can be ready to receive an order or can be recording information for an ordered item. Thus an order taker can have the property of being in the ready state or in the transition where ordered items are recorded. An interaction is a property of an object if the object can participate in the interaction. A backorder taker, for example, can receive an item for a customer and thus can have the property of being able to receive an item backordered for a customer.

A relationship property is a common property of several objects if they all participate in the same relationship. A behavior property is common among several objects if they can all be in the same state or transition or can all participate in the same interaction. Observe that for relationship properties, the property must currently hold, whereas for behavior properties, the property must only have taken place, be taking place, or be possible.

A property is defined explicitly for an object set if it is part of the application model for the object set. Specifically, a relationship property for an object set S is any relationship set that connects to S or any generalization of S. A state or transition property for an object set S is any state or transition in the state net of S or any of its generalizations. An interaction property for S is any interaction connected to S or to a state or transition of S, or connected to any of its generalizations or to any state or transition in any of its generalizations.

Incongruencies arise for one of two reasons. Either a property is given explicitly for an object set but is not common among all its objects, or it is not given explicitly but is common among all its objects. We call the former an *overstatement* because too much has been stated; the latter an *understatement* because too little has been stated. To illustrate congruency and incongruency, we now give several examples of overstatements and understatements.

Relationship-property overstatements are usually easy to spot because most of them arise when a participation constraint has a zero minimum. In Fig. 7.15, for example, consider the *0:1* participation constraint on the object set *Manager* in the relationship set *Manager manages Department*. The *Manager* object set is incongruent because the connected relationship set *manages* need not contain a relationship for each of the managers. Presumably, some managers manage other managers rather than departments. This tells us that there is an implied specialization of *Manager*, which we might call *Department Manager*. Having discovered a new object set, we can now decide whether it should be part of the application model; it should if it communicates additional worthwhile information. Judging whether the information is worthwhile is subjective. Here, for example, we might consider whether department managers differ from managers in any significant way with respect to the system we are developing. If so, we should separate them. We may also wish to separate them simply to provide a meaningful designation for a subset of the managers. Here, for example, we may decide that *Department Manager* is an additional label that is both natural and useful for discussion and thus add it. Similarly, we also add *Shipped Backorder* in Fig. 7.18 as a specialization of *Backorder*.

Figures 7.15 and 7.18 contain several other relationship-property overstatements. Analyzing them individually increases our understanding and may convince us to change our application model. For example, we see that both *Order Nr* and *Backorder Nr* have 0:1 participation constraints, and, upon further consideration, we see that we could introduce constructs similar to the *Customer ID* generalization/specialization hierarchy. We may decide that we would be better off not to be concerned about available numbers and IDs and change them all to 1-1 *identifies* relationship sets. Continuing, we may decide that all other 0:1 participation constraints are reasonable, but that we should soften all the names of the relationship sets so that they are more indefinite—changing, for example, *has* to *may have*. For the 0:* participation constraints, we may decide that those on *Customer* and *Item* are satisfactory, for when read in context, they say exactly what we wish to convey—"Customer has zero or more Orders," for example. Those 0:* participation constraints on *Distributor* (two in Fig. 7.15 and one in Fig. 7.18), however, probably mean more than is apparent initially. If only distributors from whom items are obtained are of interest, we should change the constraints to c, d, and e and add $c + d + e > 0$, but if a list of distributors is wanted even if the distributors are not supplying items actively, we should probably make several adjustments (e.g., the items they could supply or the reason a particular supplier is chosen might be recorded). For our application, we mean the former, and thus make the change. Figure 7.22 shows Figs. 7.15 and 7.18 as altered by these congruency considerations.

Relationship-property understatements also tend to follow a common pattern. Figure 7.23 gives an example. It shows a possible ORM diagram

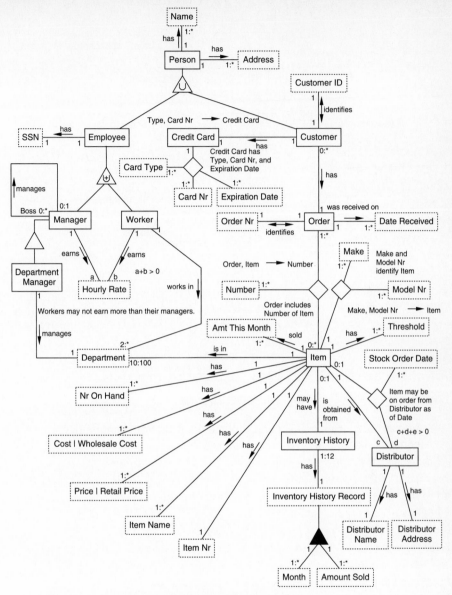

(a) Adjustments for Fig. 7.15.

Figure 7.22 Some ORM adjustments resulting from congruency considerations.

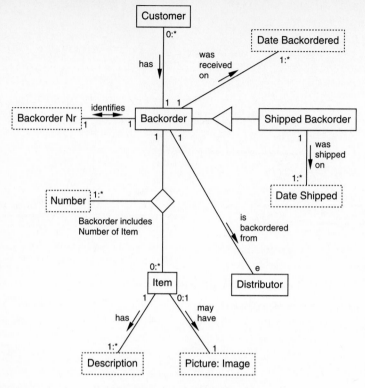

(b) Adjustments for Fig. 7.18.

Figure 7.22 Some ORM adjustments resulting from congruency considerations.

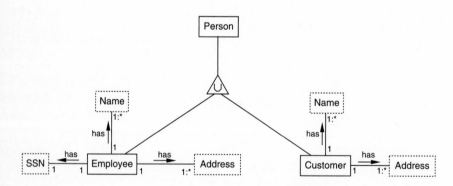

Figure 7.23 An ORM diagram with understatements.

Should Diagrams Always Be Congruent?

We are not suggesting here that congruency is an essential property. In practice, there are often anonymous object sets that serve no practical purpose. A student, for example, may or may not have a phone number, may or may not have both a permanent and local address, and may or may not have a declared major. Rather than split students several ways—students with phones; students with two addresses; students with majors; students with phones and two addresses; students with phones and majors; students with two addresses and majors; and students with phones, two addresses, and majors—normally we would put all students in a single object set and recognize that there can be incongruencies.

What we are suggesting is that by analyzing congruency, we can often discover new object sets that are of interest to the application and can find adjustments that may improve the application model. In Chapter 9 we will also find that congruency helps us make decisions about semantic equivalence, which we need to do design transformations.

---

resulting from a merge of parts of the diagrams in Figs. 7.8 and 7.10, followed by the introduction of the *Person* object set, which generalizes *Customer* and *Employee*. Observe that in Fig. 7.23 the union constraint for the generalization ensures that all persons are either employees or customers. Observe also that all employees and all customers have names and addresses. Thus having a name and having an address are both common properties of persons. The *Person* object set, however, has no connecting relationship sets to accommodate these name and address relationships. Hence the *Person* object set is incongruent. We can rectify this incongruency, of course, by promoting *Name* and *Address*, as when we merged Figs. 7.8 and 7.10 to become the ORM diagram in Fig. 7.11.

Generally, incongruencies in OBM and OIM components can generally be found by asking some straightforward questions. Let S be an object set. Then, to find OBM overstatements, we ask for each state or transition X in S:

$$\text{Does each object } s \in S \text{ enter } X?$$

If not, there is an incongruent overstatement. To find OIM overstatements, we ask for each interaction Y whose destination is S:

$$\text{Does } Y \text{ affect each object } s \in S?$$

Again, if not, there is an incongruent overstatement. To find OBM and OIM understatements, we let *S* be a specialization of a generalization object set *G*. Then, to find OBM understatements, we ask for each state or transition *X* in *S*:

Does every object *g* enter *X*, where $g \in G$?

If so, there is an incongruent understatement. To find OIM understatements, we ask for each interaction *Y* whose destination is *S*:

Does *Y* affect every object *g*, where $g \in G$?

Again, if so, there is an incongruent understatement. Using these questions, we investigate the behavior in Fig. 7.12 as an example. The result of our investigation appears in Fig. 7.24, to which we refer as we reorganize the behavior in Fig. 7.12.

When we ask whether every order taker enters transition 2 of the state net in Fig. 7.12, we realize that only those who are not already customers will go this way. Since the *Customer Info Maintainer* state net in Fig. 7.3 should handle new customers, we can discard this path, except that we should do something about persons who try to place an order without entering a customer ID or who enter an invalid customer ID. Having discarded the path through transition 2, we also realize that there is no need for transition 3 and no need for the *Ready for Customer Information* state. Hence we discard them also. We can see the results of these changes in Fig. 7.24. Observe that there is no *Ready for Customer Information* state and that there are no transitions with *available* and *not available* triggers. Instead, after transition 1, the order taker is in the *Ready for Item* state unless the ID, which is now explicitly passed in, is invalid or missing, in which case there are exception handlers.

Continuing our investigation, we consider the specialization *Backorder Taker*. If we ask whether all backorder takers enter transition 9 in Fig. 7.12, we see that a backorder taker either does or does not make a backorder. This is strange since the name *Backorder Taker* implies that an object in this class should make backorders. Only transitions 9 and 10 in Fig. 7.12 and the state between them pertain to all objects that actually take backorders. Hence we should reduce the specialization state net to include only these states and transitions, as Fig. 7.24 shows. Observe, by the way, that the states *Order Taker.Ready for Item* and *Order Taker.Waiting for Response* are not states of the *Backorder Taker* object set. These states provide only notational context, making it possible to piece the state net together from its components.

Continuing, we now consider where we should place transition 7 of Fig. 7.12, which asks the customer whether an unavailable item should be back-

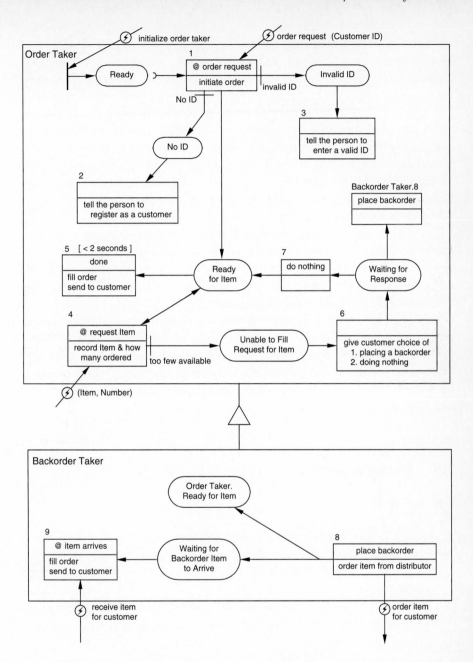

Figure 7.24 Adjustments for *Order Taker* and *Backorder Taker*.

ordered. Transition 7 does not belong in *Backorder Taker*, as we have said, but if we make it a transition in the *Order Taker* object set, there will be an incongruency since not all order takers ask customers this question. Indeed, we have discovered that there must be another specialization object set—order takers who find that too few items are available to fill a request. We may not consider this specialization to be useful enough, however, to merit including it in our application model. We therefore decide to place this part of the state net in the generalization, leaving only those states and transitions that pertain to backorder takers in the specialization. This makes the specialization congruent, which is better in this case because our decision to have a specialization is based on backorder activities. Figure 7.24 reflects these adjustments.

In examining the final result in Fig. 7.24, we see that the two other exception paths in *Order Taker* for missing and invalid IDs are also incongruent. Like the behavior for deciding what to do about too-few-available exceptions, we realize that the implied specializations are unimportant. We therefore leave the behavior as it is in Fig. 7.24.

As can be seen from these examples, our congruency questions tend to uncover many more possible specializations than we may wish. We are under no obligation to add these specializations to our application model. The important observation is that these congruency questions give us a useful way to discover additional object sets that should be considered, and that they can lead us to develop better application models.

7.5   Chapter Summary

Topic Summary

- Analysis is difficult. It is a highly human activity that involves understanding and documenting understanding, both difficult tasks. An ontological model whose constructs match well with the real world can make the task easier because a good ontological model reduces the gap between the real world and the application model's abstract representation of it. This makes it easier both to record the abstractions and to review them.

- Model integration is useful for large projects because it allows several analysts to work independently and later integrate the results of their work. We can use high-level object and relationship sets and states and transitions to map out an overall plan for integration. The details of integration require that we compare diagrams to find commonalities and conflicts, conform diagrams by resolving conflicts, and then merge diagrams. Usually we also need to make some final adjustments so that the result is a cohesive, well-structured diagram that represents an application nicely.

- Analysts can validate their work by reviewing their results with clients carefully and by applying techniques such as congruency tests. To test for correctness, we can consider each constraint carefully and can perform a white-box execution of each behavior path in an application model. Testing for completeness is difficult. In addition to asking ourselves if we have forgotten something, we can use black-box techniques to probe our application model with questions and interactions to which it should be able to respond, and we can find understatements and overstatements that indicate what object sets may be missing.

- Besides giving us a way to find missing object sets that may be of potential interest and helping us adjust application models after merging them, congruency provides a formal test for cohesiveness—the better the match between the common properties of objects in an object set and the explicitly defined properties for the object set, the more cohesive the object set. For active objects, we gain further cohesiveness when we ensure that all objects in an object set behave uniformly according to their state net, as well as when each object responds to the same set of interactions.

Question Summary

- Why is an ontological model well suited for doing analysis and reviewing application analysis models?

  Ontological models with a rich set of features can directly reflect an application as seen in the real world or as conceptualized as part of the real world. This direct correspondence facilitates both the creation and the understanding of an application model because each real-world object corresponds directly to a conceptual application object and has the same relationships to other objects as it does in the real world, the same states and transitions for behavior as it does in the real world, and the same interactions with other objects as it does in the real world.

- What advantage can we gain by using OSM to model system needs and feasibility?

  Using the same modeling paradigm to model needs and feasibility as for application model specification and development has two primary advantages: (1) There is a common language for communication among all people connected with the project. (2) Tools, such as diagram-drawing packages and query languages, apply to all aspects of the project.

- What kinds of applications best fit an object-relationship approach to modeling? An object-behavior approach? An object-interaction approach?

  Data-intensive applications, such as traditional business data processing or information storage and retrieval, best fit an ORM approach to modeling. Behavior-intensive applications that simulate the behavior of active objects, such as controllers for mechanical systems or systems that automate routine human activities, best fit an OBM approach to modeling. Interaction-intensive applications, such as cooperating processes or interactive information exchange where message passing is critical, best fit an OIM approach to modeling.

- How do high-level constructs help provide an integration framework?

  An integration framework should divide the integration work as cleanly as possible so that each division is highly cohesive and there are few, if any, connections among the divisions. Creation of high-level constructs should follow these same principles. Thus, creating effective high-level constructs and providing an integration framework can be thought of as the same kind of activity.

- What are some ways to determine whether an application model is satisfactory?

  Several techniques apply, including application-model reviews, black-box testing, white-box testing, and congruency testing. Joint application development, in which clients and developers sit down together to produce application models, is also a good way to produce satisfactory application models.

- How does object-set congruency help ensure the cohesiveness of objects in an object set?

If an object set is congruent, the properties common to all objects in the object set match perfectly with the properties declared as possible properties for the objects in the object set. Thus, with respect to an application model, congruent object sets have the highest possible degree of cohesiveness.

Checklist for Analysis

☐ Obtain assessment model and let it guide the project.

☐ Gather information from all available sources (e.g., forms, legacy systems, business procedures).

☐ Elicit information from knowledgeable personnel (use techniques such as expected sample data and question-answer sessions).

☐ Match analysis approach with application characteristics.

   ☐ Use an ORM approach for data intensive application components.

   ☐ Use an OBM approach for application components with intensive individual object behavior.

   ☐ Use an OIM approach for application components with intensive interactive behavior.

☐ Apply application model integration for large projects.

   ☐ Divide into highly cohesive, loosely coupled integration components.

   ☐ Do analysis for each integration component.

   ☐ Compare, conform, and merge integration components.

   ☐ Adjust merged components to improve global comprehensibility.

☐ Validate and improve analysis application model.

   ☐ Conduct formal reviews.

   ☐ Apply black-box and white-box review techniques.

   ☐ Apply congruency tests.

   ☐ Use overstatements and understatements to look for significant missing object sets.

7.6 Bibliographic Notes

Systems analysis is a broad and difficult topic. Much has been written, but it is hard to find a definitive publication. General software engineering books such as [Pressman92] cover the topic. Some books such as [Davis90] address the topic of analysis specifically. Others advocate specific ways to do analysis. These include the use of CRC cards [Wilkinson95] responsibility-driven analysis [Wirfs-Brock90], model-driven analysis [Embley92], and scenarios and use cases [Jacobson92].

The needs and feasibility diagram presented in this chapter is based on comments in Chapter 5 of Pressman's book [Pressman92], which also includes information on technical reviews and testing strategies. A comprehensive survey of schema integration can be found in [Batini86]; both [Batini92] and [Embley92] include a chapter on the topic of integration. [Freedman90] covers all aspects of formal reviews. The idea of congruency, as presented in this book, is new and comes from [Clyde96]. A full description of OSM-QL, including its formal definition, a proof that it is relationally complete, and a description of its prototype implementation, appears in [Embley97].

7.7 Exercises

7.1 For each of the following applications, decide whether to take an ORM approach, an OBM approach, or an OIM approach to analysis. Explain why.

   a. An automatic teller machine.

   b. Student records at a university.

   c. Airline reservations.

   d. A semaphore at a cross walk.

   e. Parts stored at a warehouse.

   f. A scoreboard.

7.2* Integrate the ORM diagrams in Fig. 7.25. Point out synonyms and homonyms, conflicting constraints, and structural conflicts, and explain their resolution.

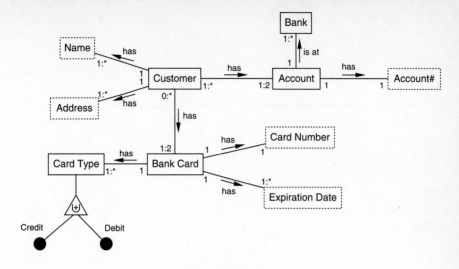

(a) Customer information.

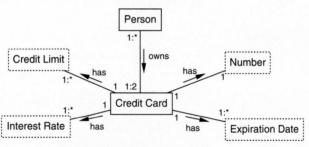

(b) Debit-card information.

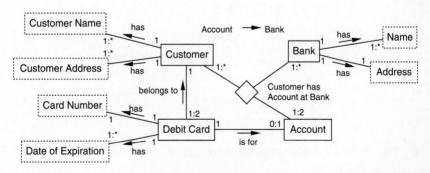

(c) Credit-card information.

Figure 7.25 ORM diagrams for integration.

7.3 Integrate the state nets in Fig. 7.26. Point out the conflicts and explain their resolution.

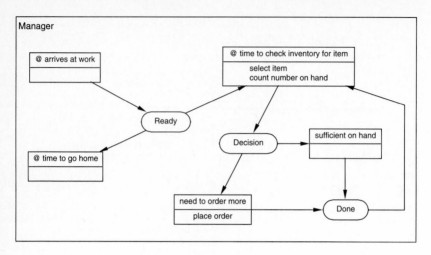

(a) Workflow for inventory.

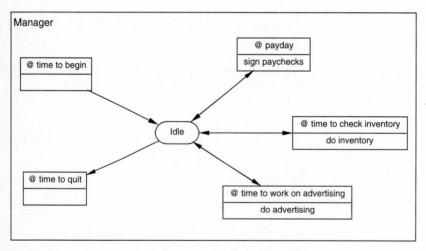

(b) Workflow for manager tasks.

Figure 7.26 State nets for integration.

7.4* Consider the ORM diagram in Fig. 7.27. Determine whether the ORM diagram has sufficient information for answering each of the the following questions. If so, give an OSM-QL query to answer the question. If not, augment the diagram so that the question can be answered and then give an OSM-QL query to answer the question. Provide a final augmented ORM diagram that answers all the questions.

   a. What is the current volume of gas tank 2?

   b. Who usually supplies gas?

   c. Which supplier last supplied gas for gas tank 1 and when was the gas supplied?

   d. What was the volume for gas tank 2 when it was last checked?

   e. When was gas tank 1 last filled and which supplier supplied the gas?

   f. How long will it take each of the suppliers to supply gas, and what is the current wholesale price of the gas?

7.5* There are some errors in the *Stop Watch* state net in Fig. 7.28. The stop watch has two buttons, one to turn it on and off; the other to start, stop, and reset the timer. When the stop watch is in the ready state, it should display the time 0:00:00. When the on/off button is pressed from any state, the stop watch should go to the *Off* state. Turning the watch off while it is timing or displaying a nonzero time should be treated as an exception. Simultaneous button presses are mechanically impossible. Find the errors and fix them.

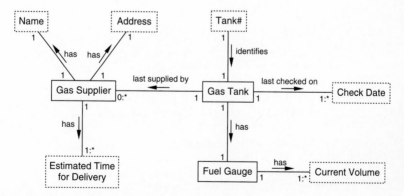

Figure 7.27 ORM diagram for black-box testing.

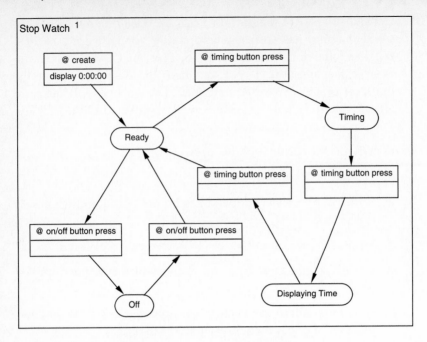

Figure 7.28 ORM diagram for white-box testing.

Exercises 7.6–7.12 build and then use a formal definition for congruency of object sets. To simplify the definitions, we assume that there are no recursive relationship sets. For our exercises on congruency, we make use of the application model in Fig. 7.29 and one of its valid interpretations in Fig. 7.30.

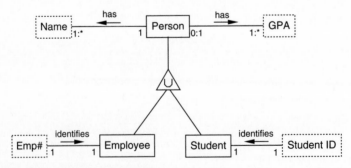

Figure 7.29 Application model.

Person	Name	Employee	Student
$Person_1$	Pat	$Person_1$	$Person_2$
$Person_2$	Lynn	$Person_2$	$Person_3$
$Person_3$	Kelly	$Person_5$	$Person_4$
$Person_4$	Tracy		
$Person_5$	Chris		

Emp#	Student ID	GPA
111	222	4.0
222	333	3.0
555	444	

Person has Name		Person has GPA	
$Person_1$	Pat	$Person_2$	3.0
$Person_2$	Lynn	$Person_3$	3.0
$Person_3$	Kelly	$Person_4$	4.0
$Person_4$	Tracy		
$Person_5$	Chris		

Emp# identifies Employee		Student ID identifies Student	
111	$Person_1$	222	$Person_2$
222	$Person_2$	333	$Person_3$
555	$Person_5$	444	$Person_4$

Figure 7.30 A valid interpretation for the application model in Fig. 7.29.

7.6 We call the elements of the domain of an interpretation *objects*. (Recall that when not separately specified, the domain for an interpretation is the set of values mentioned in the relations.) Let x be an object in the domain for an interpretation; then, any fact that mentions x is a *fact about* x. For example, $Person(Person_2)$ *has* $Name(Lynn)$ is a fact about $Person_2$ and is also a fact about *Lynn*. $Name(Lynn)$ is another fact about *Lynn*.

a. How many facts are there about $Person_1$? $Person_4$? *Kelly*? 3.0?

b. List all facts about $Person_5$.

c. List all facts about $Person_2$.

d. List all facts about 333.

e. What is the relationship between the number of facts about an object and the number of appearances of an object in an interpretation?

7.7 Let F be a fact about x and let P be the predicate name for F. Then, P is a *property* of x. For example, the properties of $Person_1$ are *Person, Employee, Person has Name,* and *Emp# identifies Employee.*

    a. List all properties of $Person_5$.

    b. List all properties of 333.

7.8 Let A be an application model and let P_N be the set of names of generated predicates for A. Let N be the name of an object set S in A. The *immediate properties* of S are the predicate names in P_N that include N as an object-set name. *Student,* for example, has two immediate properties—*Student* and *Student ID identifies Student.*

    a. List the immediate properties of *Person.*

    b. List the immediate properties of *Name.*

7.9 Let A be an application model and let P_N be the set of names of generated predicates for A. Let S be an object set in A and let G be a generalization of S (either direct or indirect). If P is an immediate property of G, then P is an *inherited property* of A. For example, the inherited properties of *Student* are *Person, Person has Name,* and *Person has GPA.* For readability, we sometimes substitute the name of a specialization object set for the name of a generalization object set in inherited properties. Thus, we may read the inherited property *Person has Name* for *Student* as *Student has Name,* and we may read *Person has GPA* as *Student has GPA.* This is merely for readability, however, and is not a way to introduce more properties or to give properties different names in our formal presentation of congruency.

    a. List the inherited properties of *Employee.*

    b. Suppose that *Person has Address* is an inherited property of *Employee* in application model in Fig. 7.29. Write the inherited property more readably by substituting the specialization name for the generalization name.

7.10 Let x and y be objects in a valid interpretation I of an application model A. The *common properties of x and y with respect to I* are the elements in the intersection of the properties of x and the properties of y. If $x_1, ..., x_n$ are the objects in an object set S in A, then the *common properties of S with respect to I* are the properties in $\overset{n}{\underset{i=1}{\cap}} P_{x_i}$

where P_{x_i} is the set of properties of x_i with respect to I. Let A be an application model and let S be an object set in A. Let I_S be the (possibly infinite) set of all valid interpretations for application model A in which there is at least one object in S (i.e., in each interpretation we are considering, the set of objects in S is nonempty). Let C_S be the set of all common-property sets of S with respect to the interpretations in I_S. Then, the *common properties of S* are the properties in $\underset{C \in C_S}{\cap} C$. For example, the common properties of *Person* are *Person* and *Person has Name*. This follows because when there is a person object x in *Person*, *Person(x)* is a fact, and, because of the *1:** participation constraint, for every object x in *Person* there exists an object y in *Name* such that *Person(x) has Name(y)* is a fact. There are no other common properties of *Person* because for all other predicates P, there is a valid interpretation with an object x in *Person* such that P is not a property of x. The interpretation in Fig. 7.30 is a counterexample for all other possible common properties of *Person*. For example, *Person$_1$* is in *Person*, but *Person has GPA* is not a property of *Person$_1$*.

a. List the common properties of *Person$_1$* and *Person$_2$* with respect to the interpretation in Fig. 7.30.

b. List the common properties of 4.0 and 3.0 with respect to the interpretation in Fig. 7.30.

c. List the common properties of the object set *Student* with respect to the interpretation in Fig. 7.30.

d. List the common properties of the object set *Emp#* with respect to the interpretation in Fig. 7.30.

e. List the common properties of the object set *Employee* in Fig. 7.29. Explain why each listed common property is a common property, and explain why there are no other common properties.

f. List the common properties of the object set *GPA* in Fig. 7.29. Explain why each listed common property is a common property.

7.11* We can use the generated predicates for an application model to write a formal proof that a property is a common property. For example, we can prove that *Person has Name* is a common property of *Employee* as follows. Let x be an object in *Employee*, then *Employee(x)* is a fact about x and thus *Employee(x)* holds. Since *Employee* is a direct specialization of *Person*, we have $\forall x(Employee(x) \Rightarrow Person(x))$. Thus, since *Employee(x)* holds, *Person(x)* holds. Since *Person has Name* has a *1* participation constraint for *Person*, we have $\forall x(Person(x) \Rightarrow \exists^1 y(Person(x)$ has *Name(y)))*. Thus, since *Person(x)* holds, $\exists^1 y(Person(x)$ has *Name(y)))* holds and thus there exists an object y such that *Person(x) has Name(y)* holds. Since *Person(x) has Name(y)* holds, *Person(x) has Name(y)* is a fact for x and thus *Person has Name* is a property of x. Since x was chosen arbitrarily from *Employee*, however, every object $x \in Employee$ has the property *Person has Name*. Thus, *Person has Name* is a common property of *Employee*.

a. Prove that *Student ID identifies Student* is a common property of *Student*.

b. Prove that *Person has Name* is a common property of *Student*.

c. Prove or disprove: *Person has GPA* is a common property of *Student*.

d. Prove or disprove: *Emp# identifies Employee* is a common property of *Person*.

7.12 Let the union of the immediate and inherited properties of an object set S be called the *explicitly defined properties* of S or simply the *explicit properties* of S. Let EP_S be the explicit properties of an object set S, and let CP_S be the set of common properties for S. An object set S is *congruent* if $EP_S = CP_S$ and is otherwise *incongruent*. The set of *overstatements* for an object set S is the set $EP_S - CP_S$. The set of *understatements* for an object set S is the set $CP_S - EP_S$. The set $EP_{Person} = \{Person, Person\ has\ Name, Person\ has\ GPA\}$, but the set $CP_{Person} = \{Person, Person\ has\ Name\}$. Therefore, *Person* is incongruent. Its set of overstatements is $\{Person\ has\ GPA\}$, and its set of understatements is $\{\ \}$.

a. List the congruent object sets in Fig. 7.29.

b. Explain why the *Student* object set in Fig. 7.29 is incongruent.

c.** Add a general constraint to the application model in Fig. 7.29 to make *Person has GPA* a common property of *Student*. Then, using the general constraint, prove that *Person has GPA* is a common property of *Student*. Finally, given this general constraint, explain why *Student* is congruent.

d.* Suppose we add an object set *ID#* to the application model in Fig. 7.29 along with the following general constraints:

$\forall x \forall y (Emp\#(x)$ *identifies Employee*$(y) \Rightarrow ID\#(x)$ *identifies Person*$(y))$

$\forall x \forall y (Student\ ID(x)$ *identifies Student*$(y) \Rightarrow ID\#(x)$ *identifies Person*$(y))$

$\forall x (Person(x) \Rightarrow \exists y (Emp\#(y)$
    identifies Employee$(x) \vee Student\ ID(y)$
    identifies Student$(x))$

Prove that *ID# identifies Person* is a common property of *Person*.

e.* Given the general constraints in Exercise 7.12d, provide the set of overstatements and the set of understatements for the *Person* object set.

f. Given the general constraint requested in 7.12c and the given general constraints in 7.12d, reorganize the ORM diagram in Fig. 7.29 so that every object set is congruent and every constraint is captured.

7.13   Consider the application model in Fig. 7.31.

a. Give a valid interpretation for the application model in Fig. 7.31 that has three persons P_1, P_2, and P_3 such that P_1 and P_2 are employees and P_2 and P_3 are customers, P_2 is married to P_3, and P_3 has two orders. Make up any other needed values.

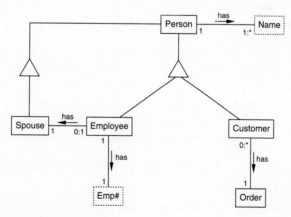

Figure 7.31   Application model.

Make the interpretation minimal in the sense that no value or tuple can be removed from any relation while still satisfying the requirements of the problem.

b. List all facts about P_2.

c. List all properties of P_2.

d. List the common properties of P_1 and P_2 with respect to the interpretation.

7.14 Consider the *Employee* object set in Fig. 7.31.

a. List the immediate properties of *Employee*.

b. List the inherited properties of *Employee*.

7.15 List the common properties of the objects in the set *Spouse* in Fig. 7.31 and explain why each is a common property.

7.16 The application model in Fig. 7.31 is not congruent.

a. List the incongruent object sets.

b. For each incongruent object set, give the set of overstatements and the set of understatements.

c. Transform the application model into a congruent application model. (Do not change the semantics except as minimally necessary to make the application model congruent.)

7.17 Consider the three ORM diagrams in Fig. 7.32, which are rudimentary application models for a business that rents tools. Observe that all three ORM diagrams in Fig. 7.32 are congruent.

a. Merge the three ORM diagrams by merging object sets with the same names. (The result should have six object sets.) Do not assume that every customer who has a reservation for a tool is currently renting a tool or vice versa; do not assume that the sets of rented, reserved, and available tools are the same; and do assume that every tool has a description.

b. Find the incongruencies and label them as overstatements or understatements.

c. Resolve any understatements, adding generalizations and making adjustments so that there are no understatements.

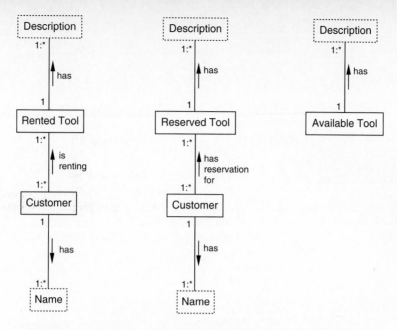

Figure 7.32 ORM diagrams for integration and congruency testing.

d. Resolve any overstatements, adding specializations and making adjustments so that there are no understatements.

e.* Using this example, make a general statement about how understatements are likely to arise when integrating ORM diagrams and what to do about them.

f.* Using this example, make a general statement about how overstatements are likely to arise when integrating ORM diagrams and what to do about them.

Chapter 8

Specification

System specification, the development of a detailed and precise proposal for a system, provides the technical basis for a contractual agreement between clients and developers. Ideally, the detail and precision of the proposal should (1) enable clients to validate that the proposed system will meet their needs and (2) establish a basis for developers to verify that the system will perform as expected.

In practice, both validation and verification are hard to achieve. *Validation* means checking a specification to see that the proposed system will meet a client's needs. Validation is about solving the right problem. *Verification* means showing that a design or an implementation is equivalent to a specification. Verification is about solving the problem right. It is difficult to validate a system as proposed in a specification because the system is not yet built. Typically, validation is accomplished by anticipating client needs and checking the application model to see that it meets these needs. It is difficult to verify a system because we must show formally that the design or implementation is equivalent to a specification. Typically, verification is accomplished by thoughtful inspection and testing.

To improve the chances of successful validation and verification, a formal specification is needed. Formalization helps facilitate validation

---

Validation

Often we think of analysts and developers as having the primary responsibility for validation. An alternative that makes sense is Joint Application Development (JAD), in which clients and developers share responsibility equally. As a team, clients and developers carry out systems analysis, write specifications, and validate the results. Some members of the JAD team have the responsibility of documenting the work, but all members of the team are trained and expected to be proficient in the models, techniques, and tools used in analysis, specification, and validation. The client members of the team become the final authority on the completeness and accuracy of the specifications.

---

because it increases precision in specification and makes an application model executable. Executable application models are particularly useful because they allow a client to interact with the system and view the results of execution, providing a better way to check a proposed system than mere inspection. Formalization also helps facilitate verification because it increases precision; in addition, it can provide the basis for establishing equivalence transformations and proving program correctness. Precision is particularly important for developers, who without it are forced to make their own (often wrong) assumptions about what something means.

Unfortunately, there is a down side to formalization. It is hard to do and, when done, is hard to read and understand. Thus its use in software development is controversial: theoreticians claim that formalism is necessary to establish sound engineering practices, while practitioners claim that formalism hinders productivity and does not help in constructing real-world applications in a reasonable amount of time. One possible compromise in this debate is to allow the formalism to be "tunable." *Tunable formalism* lets users work with different levels of formalism, ranging from completely informal to fully mathematical. OSM supports tunable formalism because it is sufficiently expressive for informal use, it allows various levels of detail and completion, and yet it also has a formally defined syntax and semantics and can support fully formalized application models.

The purpose of this chapter is to explain how to develop systematically a sufficiently formal OSM specification that will provide a firm basis for contractual agreement and further development. The specification should be formal enough to enable validation and verification to the extent agreed upon by client and developer. Here we do not attempt to determine what this agreed-upon extent is. Rather, since OSM supports tunable formalism, it lets a client and developer carry the formalism to whatever extent they deem necessary. OSM also allows the formalism for one part of a system

---

Verification

During design and implementation, if we only make transformations that preserve information, constraints, and behavior, we will have verified that our implementation is faithful to our specification. In a transformational approach, verification depends on whether we can prove that every transformation does indeed preserve information, constraints, and behavior. We strive to achieve this ideal in Chapters 9–12, where we describe information-preserving, constraint-preserving, and behavior-preserving transformations.

to be developed more fully than the formalism for another part of a system. One of the possible desired outcomes is a fully formal specification; we show in this chapter how this can be done.

We develop a formal specification for an analysis version of an OSM application model in three parts, as follows:

1. We establish the system automation boundary.

2. We formalize the functional specification.

3. We formalize system interface specifications.

Each part is discussed in detail. In addition, between the first and second parts, we introduce the language used here for specification formalization. This language, called OSM-L, is an OSM model-equivalent language, by which we mean that it is a textual-representation language that matches OSM, concept for concept. Thus, OSM-L is a language in which we can give a formal, textual view of an OSM application model.

The following topics in this chapter are particularly important:

- System automation boundary.

- Mitosis.

- The one-to-one correspondence between OSM diagrams and OSM-L.

- The similarities and differences between OSM-L and programming languages.

- Boundary-crossing interactions and interface forms.

The following questions should also be kept in mind:

- How does the principle of tunable formalism allow us to strike a balance between practical realities and theoretical, idealistic expectations for specifications?

- What are the advantages of using a model-equivalent language as a specification language? Are there disadvantages?

- How does a formal functional specification help both raise and resolve detailed questions that must be answered about an application?

- How do interface-specification forms both help make a specification more readable and help ease the amount of detail that must be written for a boundary-crossing interaction?

8.1   System Boundary

The automation boundary for a system specifies the division between the system environment and the system to be implemented. So far, we have ignored this division totally, modeling environment objects in the same way we model system objects. Indeed, because of the ontological view we take for OSM, it does not matter whether objects are abstract or concrete or whether they are represented in a software system or are real-world objects.

In OSM, we designate the boundary by specifying a high-level object set. We restrict this special high-level object set, however, so that the only constructs that cross its boundary are interactions. These boundary-crossing interactions constitute the system interface.

Sometimes it is easy to establish a system boundary. It is easy, for example, when the analysis happens to be done so that (1) all object and relationship sets are part of the database, (2) all states and transitions are part of the system behavior, (3) all interactions with an origin and destination are internal to the system, and (4) all interactions that have only an origin or only a destination are interface interactions. Our analysis results in the previous chapter satisfy these conditions. It is therefore easy to establish the system boundary for our analysis application model. Figure 8.1a shows the system boundary as the high-level object set called *System*. Observe that the only boundary-crossing constructs are interactions.

Since in this chapter we will use the behavior developed thus far in our discussion extensively, we have gathered together all the state nets in Chapter 7. Figures 8.1b–8.1e show these state-net details. In gathering these state nets together, we have omitted internal interactions and added explicitly the external interactions that previously were only implied by event triggers. We do not copy the ORM diagram in Fig. 7.22, which includes the object and relationship sets to be represented in the database. Instead we represent all the object and relationship sets in Figs. 7.22a and 7.22b as the high-level *Database* object set in Fig. 8.1a, and we show only the atomic object sets in the database that participate as origins or destinations for boundary-crossing interactions.

Creating system boundaries is not always so easy. One other case, however, is almost as simple. That case is an analysis application model in which the automation boundary cuts only through interactions even though there may be object and relationship sets and state nets on both sides of the boundary. For such a case, relationship sets may connect object sets inside the boundary and may connect object sets outside the boundary, but no relationship set spans the boundary. Similarly, state nets may reside in object sets both inside and outside the boundary, but no state net has a

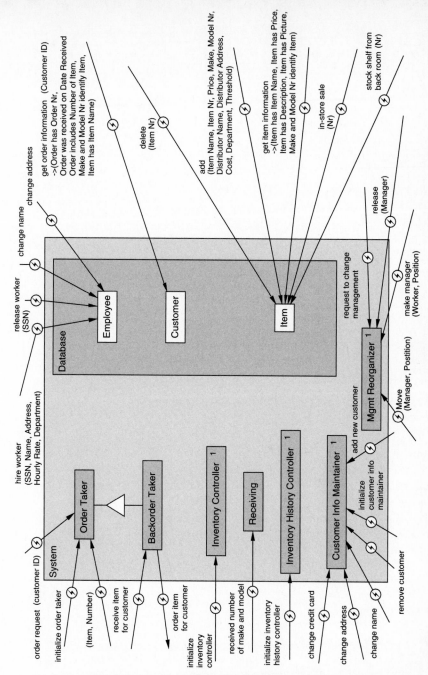

(a) System boundary for the sample application model.

Figure 8.1 System boundary and state-net details for the sample application model.

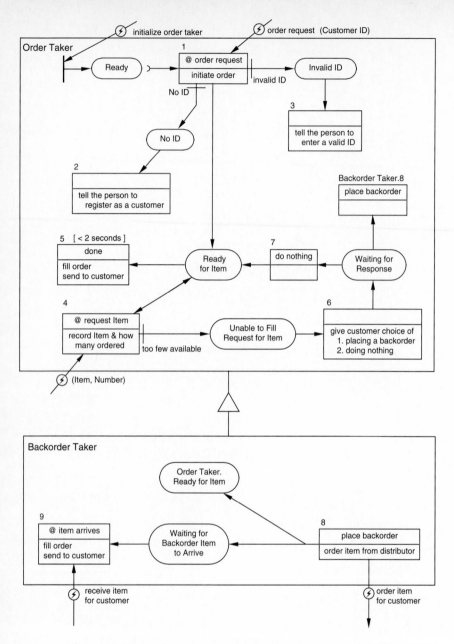

(b) Order-taker state net for the sample application model.

Figure 8.1 (cont.)   System boundary and state-net details for the sample application model.

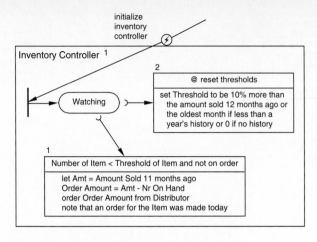

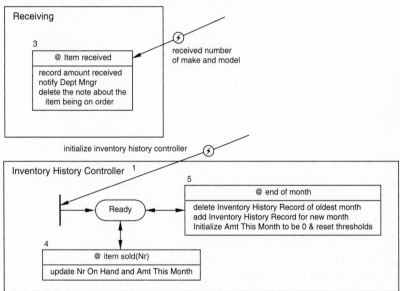

(c) Inventory state nets for the sample application model.

Figure 8.1 (cont.)   System boundary and state-net details for the sample application model.

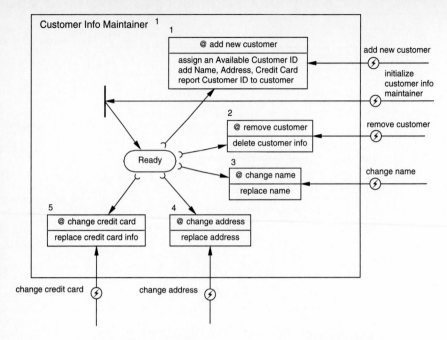

(d) Customer information-maintainer state net for the
sample application model.

Figure 8.1 (cont.) System boundary and state-net details for the
sample application model.

connection that crosses the boundary. The *Order Taker* and *Backorder Taker*
object sets in Fig. 8.1b, for example, both would have to be outside or
inside, for if one were on one side and the other were on the other side, the
(single) state net for the *isa* hierarchy would span the automation boundary.

Having established these two cases, the first of which is a special case of
the second, we can often do some simple transformations to obtain proper
automation boundaries. Suppose we establish a working automation
boundary that (1) passes through any relationship sets whose connecting
object sets span the boundary and (2) in addition to passing through all
interactions that naturally cross the automation boundary, also touches all
interactions that should cross the boundary but cannot because both the origin and destination are inside the boundary. Suppose further that the
working automation boundary need not pass through the middle of a state
net in some object set or, if it does, that we have already resolved this case
as explained next. Then we can transform the application model into an
application model with a proper automation boundary, as follows.

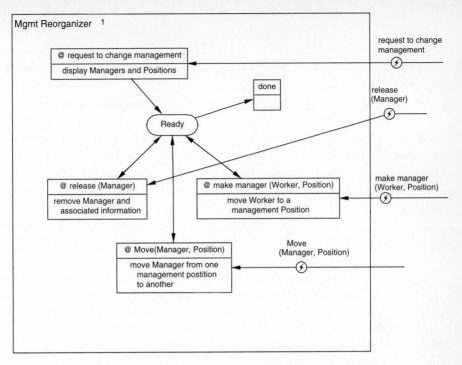

(e) Management reorganizer state net for the sample
   application model.

Figure 8.1 (cont.)   System boundary and state-net details for the
sample application model.

For interactions that should cross the system boundary but whose origin and destination object sets both are inside the system automation
boundary, we sever the origin or destination connection that should be outside the boundary and place it outside. For example, since a customer originates an order request, the origin of the *order request* interaction in Fig. 8.1b
could have been attached to the *Customer* object set, which is inside the
automation boundary because it contains data to be stored in the database.
If the origin of the *order request* were attached inside, we would have had to
sever the origin from the *Customer* object set to create the *order request* interaction, as Fig. 8.1b shows. Similarly, since we order an item for a customer
from a distributor, the destination of the *order item for customer* interaction in
Fig. 8.1b could have been attached to the *Distributor* object set, which is
inside the boundary (not shown, but inside the high-level *Database* object
set). Hence, we would have severed the destination from the *Distributor*
object set, which would have resulted in the *order item for customer* in Fig.

8.1b. In general, what is happening in these examples is that we have a real customer and a real distributor outside the automation boundary, but we also have a representation of the customer and distributor inside the boundary. Since the interactions in our examples must go to real customers and distributors, we sever the connections to the database representations and make them cross the boundary to the real customers and distributors.

For relationship sets that cross the automation boundary, if the relationship set is to be stored in the database for the application, then we must transform it so that all connections are on the inside. Figure 8.2 depicts the basic idea of the transformation for a binary relationship set. For *n*-ary relationship sets, we repeat the basic transformation for each of the outside connections. In Fig. 8.2a we see that if one of the connections that crosses to the outside connects to an object set that is already also inside, then we sever the outside connection and reconnect it to the inside object set. If the connecting object set is not already also inside, then we make a copy of it on the inside and make the connection as Fig. 8.2b shows. For example, suppose that we had placed the object set *Customer* only on the outside (perhaps because it is the origin and destination of several interactions). Then, any relationship sets connected to *Customer* would cross the boundary, and thus we would place a duplicate copy of *Customer* on the inside and move all the boundary-crossing relationship-set connections to the inside copy. If a boundary-crossing relationship set need not be stored in the database for the application, then we can either discard the relationship set or transform it to the outside in the same way as we transformed it to the inside.

We now attack the most difficult case—when the boundary splits a state net. We call the process of splitting a state net *mitosis* because it is in some ways similar to biological cell division, which involves a complex halving of chromosomes. A developer may approach the process of mitosis in any way that works. To give some guidance, however, we present one systematic way to proceed:

1. Identify an object set whose state net should be split across the automation boundary and establish an inside object set and an outside object set.

2. Identify the roles that an inside object and an outside object play to support the activity of the original state net.

3. Identify the synchronization interactions necessary to coordinate the activities of objects in the inside and outside object sets.

4. Write the state nets for the two object sets and the interactions between them. These interactions become automation boundary-crossing interactions for this part of the system interface.

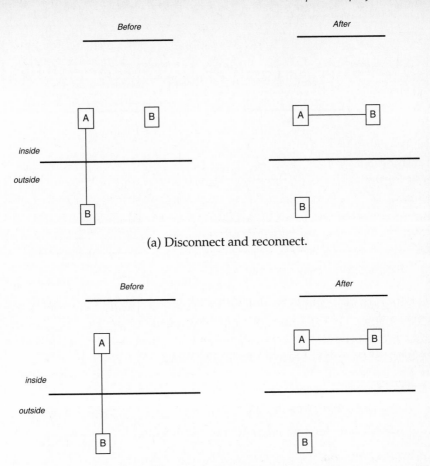

(a) Disconnect and reconnect.

(b) Split, then disconnect and reconnect.

Figure 8.2   Transformations that resolve boundary-crossing relationship sets.

As an example, we consider a calendar, needed for our application model to signal the end of each month for the inventory history controller. Figure 8.3 shows a state net for our calendar. The calendar assumes that time passes automatically and that it can recognize the end of each month automatically. It can even recognize the possibility of its clock being reset and know whether it has missed an end-of-month notification. Unfortunately, these assumptions are beyond the ability of an application object unless it has access to a clock. Since clocks are provided by operating systems, which are in the environment of the application but not in the application, we have a state net that should be split across the system application boundary.

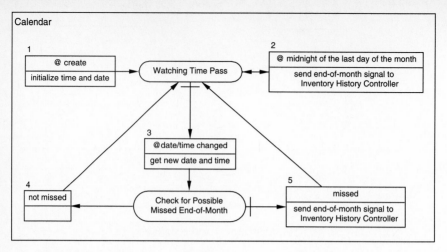

Figure 8.3   A calendar state net.

Using our guidelines for mitosis, we split the *Calendar* state net in Fig. 8.3 as follows. We first decide to call the inside object set *Calendar*—the same as the original—and to call the outside object set *Operating System*. We then list the roles of each of these object sets:

Calendar

> notify inventory controller

> decide how long to wait until next notification

Operating System

> provide date and time

> allow date and time to be reset

> register a waiting process

> restart a waiting process

Next, we identify the synchronization interactions necessary to coordinate the calendar and the operating system:

To "decide how long to wait," the calendar must retrieve the date and time.

To "register a waiting process," the calendar must notify the operating system.

To "restart a waiting process," the operating system must notify the calendar.

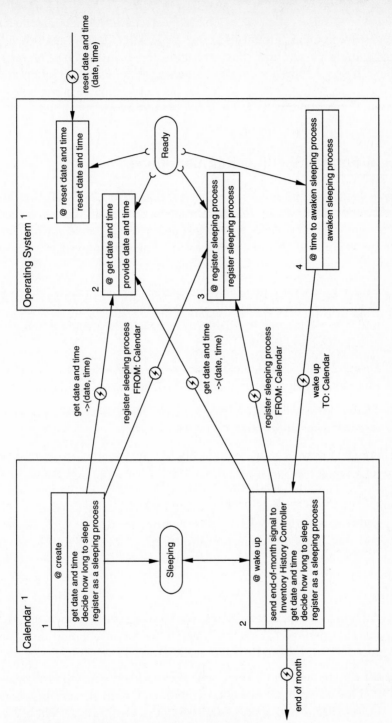

Figure 8.4 Results of mitosis transformation.

Finally, we write the state nets for the two object sets and include the interactions between them. Figure 8.4 shows the result. Observe that the application boundary can now pass through the coordinating interactions between these two object sets. Observe also, by the way, that by no means have we defined all the behavior of an operating system in the *Operating System* state net, but only the behavior of interest for our application.

8.2   A Formal Specification Language

Once we have an application boundary for our system, we can specify formally the part of the system to be automated and the logical interface to the system's environment. Before we begin, however, we need a language in which to write our formal specification. The advantages of a textual language for specification include the following:

1. Unlike graphical representations, textual representations scale up to any size. This is particularly important for detailed specification because we are not likely to be able to represent a detailed specification graphically.

2. Because the textual language scales up, it also lets us add more precision without becoming notationally cumbersome.

3. Textual specifications are also closer to code, which is the eventual target of a specification.

Although presumably we could choose any well-defined textual language for writing our specification, we should be careful about our choice. If we select a standard programming language, we will no doubt begin our implementation even before we have completed our design. What we need is a specification language such as Z or Paisely. We do not wish, however, to have to translate our application model into some "foreign language" that is unrelated to OSM. What we need is an OSM model-equivalent language, one equivalent to OSM, so that the following advantages are present:

1. We can use immediately all the work we did during analysis. We can either convert directly to the textual representation or leave part or all of the graphical representation as is.

2. We can convert the textual language back into a graphical notation for use in higher level presentations for clients and for when we must return to analysis to learn more about the system being specified.

A language *L* is *model equivalent* with respect to a model *M* if for every application model *A* of *M*, there exists a program *P* of *L* whose semantics are one-to-one with *A*; conversely, for every program *P* of *L*, there exists an application model *A* of *M* whose semantics are one-to-one with *P*. By "semantics are one-to-one with" we mean that for every construct in a program, there is a corresponding construct in the application model and vice versa. A program written in a model-equivalent language is nothing more than an alternative view of some application model and vice versa. Consequently, every program written in a model-equivalent language is fully integrated and fully compatible with an application model.

OSM has a model-equivalent language, which we introduce in this section as a language for writing fully formal specifications and which we call OSM-L. Since OSM-L is model equivalent, we can represent every graphical construct textually. However, we need not write in a fully textual style. Since OSM-L is fully compatible and fully integrated with OSM, we can mix the graphical and textual notation as we wish. This has the advantage of leaving the basic analysis structure in place as we proceed with specification. In this section, we concentrate mainly on the textual representation. In the following sections, when we return to writing formal specifications for our application model, we will intermix graphical and textual notation freely.

8.2.1 Declarations

Since we can use OSM-L to write any OSM diagram textually, we can, in particular, write any ORM diagram textually. As an example, Fig. 8.5 shows a simple ORM written both diagrammatically (Fig. 8.5a) and textually (Fig. 8.5b). The complete syntax definition for OSM-L appears in appendix B. Here we motivate the syntax by examples.

An OSM-L program is a sequence of statements. A semicolon marks the end of each statement. Declaration statements correspond to ORM components; for declaration statements, the order of appearance is immaterial.

The first statement in Fig. 8.5b represents directly the *Order has Order Nr* relationship set in Fig. 8.5a. Participation constraints for the relationship set are in square brackets; in OSM-L all constraints are denoted by being placed in square brackets. The second statement represents directly the *Order includes Number of Item* relationship set, including its co-occurrence constraint.

Although we can represent object sets directly, we often represent them only indirectly as part of a relationship-set declaration. If we wish to represent object sets directly, we write their names followed by semicolons:

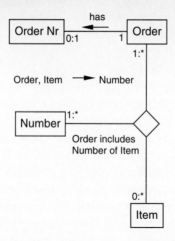

(a) Representation as an ORM diagram.

Order [1] *has Order Nr* [0:1];
Order [1:*] *includes Number* [1:*] *of Item* [0:*]
    [*Order, Item* − > *Number*];

(b) Representation as OSM-L.

Figure 8.5   An ORM diagram and its equivalent representation in OSM-L.

Order; Order Nr; Number; Item;. This is needed if an object set stands alone (such as the *Mgmt Reorganizer* in Fig. 8.1e), if it has a cardinality constraint, or if it has multiple names. To give an object set a cardinality constraint, for example, we would write

Calendar [1]

to specify that the *Calendar* object set in Fig. 8.4 has exactly one calendar. Then, if we include this in a relationship set, such as

Calendar [0:*] *not operational between Down Time* [1] *and Up Time* [1]

we do not (indeed, may not) repeat the object-set cardinality constraint.

    Throughout the text we use an initial upper- and lowercase convention to distinguish between object-set names and other text in a relationship-set name. We can use this convention to find object-set names embedded in relationship-set declarations. The first word of an object-set name in a relationship-set declaration begins with an uppercase letter; usually we capitalize every word to help us recognize object-set names visually. Other

object *On-line Store;*

Employee [1] *works* for *On-line Store* [1: *];*

Person [1] *has Name: String* [1: *];*

Person [1] *has Address: String* [1: *];*

Spouse **isa** *Person;*

Employee, Customer **isa** *Person;*

Manager, Worker **isa[partition]** *Employee;*

Boss **isa** *Manager;*

Boss [1: *] manages Manager* [0: 1];*

Employee [1] *has SSN: String* [1];*

Employee [0: 1] *is married to Spouse* [1] | *Spouse is married to Employee;*

Customer [1] *identifies Customer ID: String* [1] | *Customer ID identifies Customer;*

Customer [0: *] has Order* [1];*

Order [1] *has Order Nr: String* [0: 1];*

Order [1] *was received on Date Received: String* [1: *];*

Order [1: *] includes Number: String* [1: *] *of Item* [0: *]*

    [*Order, Item* → *Number*];*

Item **includes**

    Item [1] *has Item Name: String* [1: *];*

    Item [1] *has Item Nr: String* [1: *];*

    Price | *Retail Price;*

    Item [1] *has Price: String* [1: *];*

    Cost | *Wholesale Cost;*

    Item [1] *has Cost: String* [1: *];*

    Item [1] *has Nr On Hand: String* [1: *];*

    end;*

Order [1: *] pertains to Department* [0: *];*

Order(x) *pertains to Department*(y) :− *Order*(x) *includes Number*() *of Item*(),

    Item(x) *has Item Name*(), *Item*(x) *has Item Nr*(), *Item*(x) *has Price*(),

    Item(x) *has Cost*(), *Item*(x) *has Nr On Hand*(), *Item*(x) *is in Department*(y);

Item [1] *is in Department: String* [10: 100];*

Worker [1] *works in Department* [2: *];*

Manager [0: 1] *manages Department* [1];*

Manager [1] *earns Hourly Rate: String* [a];*

Worker [1] *earns Hourly Rate* [b];*

[$a + b > 0$];

[<< *Workers may not earn more than their managers.* >>];

(a) OSM-L declarations.

Figure 8.6 OSM-L declarations and corresponding ORM diagram.

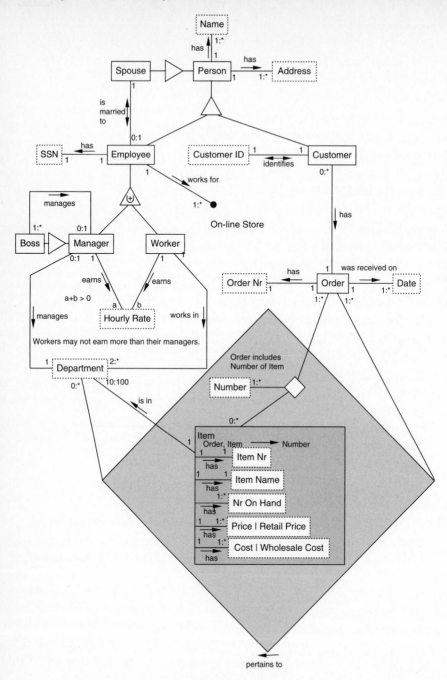

(b) ORM diagram.

Figure 8.6 (cont.) OSM-L declarations and corresponding ORM diagram.

conventions are also possible, but we use only this one in this text. We also allow white space within a name, but not leading or trailing white space within a name. This can cause some parsing headaches, but once we are given the object- and relationship-set names in the declarations, we can recognize them in other contexts without much difficulty.

Another example that illustrates additional declaration features appears in Fig. 8.6a, which gives the OSM-L statements for the ORM diagram in Fig. 8.6b. After our discussion of Fig. 8.6, it should be clear that there is indeed a one-to-one correspondence between the declaration features of OSM and the declaration features of OSM-L—an observation that underscores the idea that OSM-L is nothing more than a way to represent an OSM application model textually.

As we begin our discussion of Fig. 8.6, we make three minor but important points. First, OSM diagrams allow informal components. Most of the ORM diagram in Fig. 8.6b is formal, but there is one informal constraint: *Workers may not earn more than their managers*. We enclose informal components within double-angle brackets, << and >>. Using this technique, we can distinguish between formal and informal textual components. If we wish, we can also use these double-angle brackets in OSM diagrams.

The second point is that some words we wish to use in our application model may be reserved words in the language. The keyword **includes** is an example. We distinguish keywords from regular words by placing keywords in boldface type. In Fig. 8.6a, for example, *includes* appears both as a regular word in the relationship-set declaration

Order [1: *] *includes Number: String* [1: *] *of Item* [0: *]

and as a keyword in the high-level object set declaration

Item **includes** ... **end**.

When we do not have the luxury of using boldface, we prefix non-keywords with the escape symbol, a backslash (\). Thus "*includes*" is the regular word "*includes*".

The third point we wish to make is that OSM-L has three types of comments. A double dash "--" makes the rest of a line a comment, and anything enclosed in the brackets "/-" and "-/" is a comment. The first two types of comments represent notes in an OSM diagram; the third type is a question mark "?", which stands for a single-character comment consisting only of "?". We use this second type of comment to denote anything that is questionable—something to discuss with the client. We may also use question marks in OSM diagrams if we wish.

We distinguish lexical object sets from nonlexical object sets by declaring each lexical object set to be a specialization of a built-in representable object set, such as *String*, *Integer*, or *Real*. Logically, *String* contains all possible strings over an assumed alphabet, and *Integer* and *Real* contain all possible integer and real numbers. The dotted rectangle in an OSM diagram denotes lexicalization. By default, a lexical object set in an OSM diagram is a specialization of *String*. In OSM-L, we specify this by appending "*: String*" to the object-set name. If the lexical object set is to be a specialization of some other built-in object set *X*, we append "*: X*" to the object-set name. For example, if we wish to say that *Nr On Hand* is an integer, rather than a string, we write *Nr On Hand: Integer* in place of *Nr On Hand* in the dotted rectangle in the OSM diagram, and we write

$$Item~[1]~has~Nr~On~Hand:~Integer~[1:*]$$

in place of

$$Item~[1]~has~Nr~On~Hand:~String~[1:*]$$

for OSM-L.

In addition to these standard built-in object sets, we also assume the existence of some common, but not always standard, built-in object sets. These include some subsets of the integers and reals: *Positive Integer*, *Nonnegative Integer*, *Positive Real*, *Nonnegative Real*. They also include *Date*, *Time*, *Time Period*, and *Money*—with specializations such as *US$*, *AUD$*, *CAN$*, *DM*, and *Yen*—as well as units of measure such as *Inch*, *Centimeter*, *Quart*, and *Liter*. Along with these built-in object sets, we have the expected built-in operators such as exchange rates and unit conversions, as well as

---

Literals for a Wide Range of Types

The real world has a wide range of types—everything from ID numbers to part numbers to country and city names to monetary amounts. Especially in context, we recognize literals of these types with relative ease. For analysis and specification, we would not like to be bothered by having to turn these literals into strings or with having to mark them as being special in any way. We therefore simply use them as they appear naturally in an application.

For tools and eventual implementation, however, this simple usage can cause problems. Thus, to make the process work out and look right, we can consider literals of extended built-in types or literals of application types to include special invisible markers—inserted, for example, by a syntax-directed editor at the time they are created. We do not show these special markers here, nor do we concern ourselves with them further.

other common operators such as *Positive Integer * US$* = *US$* and *Time – Time = Time Period*.

In addition to the standard (and the nonstandard) object sets, users may declare object sets of their own. We provide several ways to specify the contents of these sets, including enumeration, set specification by a predicate, and grammars. For an enumeration, we list the elements that should be in the set. For example, we may have

$$Primary\ Color = \{red, yellow, blue\}$$

which declares *Primary Color* as an object set that contains three nonlexical objects; red, yellow, and blue. For set specification by a predicate, we use the Datalog notation as discussed in Chapter 5. For example, we may specify the set of even numbers between 1 and 99 as

$$One\ And\ TwoDigit\ Even\ Integers(i) :- Integer(i), 1 < i, i < 99$$

For grammars, we use standard BNF, restricted to regular expressions. To provide a connection between the BNF and OSM-L, we allow object-set names to be nonterminals, and any new nonterminals we introduce become names of new object sets. For example, we may declare social security numbers to be

```
Social Security Number = {
    Social Security Number ::=
        Digit Digit Digit-Digit Digit-Digit Digit Digit Digit
        | Digit Digit Digit Digit Digit Digit Digit Digit Digit
    Digit ::= 0 | 1 | 2 | 3 | 4 | 5 | 6 | 7 | 8 | 9
    }
```

If *Digit* were already declared as an object set with the values 0 through 9, we would not have needed the last line in the preceding declaration, which is equivalent to

$$Digit = \{0, 1, 2, 3, 4, 5, 6, 7, 8, 9\}$$

written as an enumeration.

OSM-L denotes generalization/specialization either by **isa** or by a colon. The specializations are comma-separated object-set names on the left of the **isa** or colon, and the generalizations are comma-separated object-set names on the right. To specify the generalization/specialization constraints intersection, union, mutual-exclusion, or partition, we add them to the **isa** or colon. Using **isa**, for example, we would write **isa[intersection]**, **isa[union]**, **isa[mutex]**, and **isa[partition]**, respectively.

As a convention in this text, we use **isa** in OSM-L where we would use an open triangle in an ORM diagram, and we use a colon for generalizations for lexical object sets and for roles. In the example in Fig. 8.6b, we explicitly write the role *Boss* as a specialization—for indeed, all roles are specializations. We may, however, write the role name near a connection. Then, in OSM-L, we would write

$$Boss: Manager\ [1:*]\ manages\ Manager\ [0:1]$$

Despite these notational differences, the semantics of generalization/specialization is always the same.

OSM-L has high-level declarations for high-level object sets and for high-level relationship sets. The basic pattern for these declarations is the same, consisting of the name of the high-level component, followed by a keyword or symbol that distinguishes the kind of high-level component, followed by an inner declaration of subcomponents. The distinguishing designator is **includes** for high-level object sets and the Datalog symbol : – for high-level relationship sets. For high-level relationship sets, the declaration is a Datalog rule. This gives us a way to specify the derivation of a high-level relationship set precisely. There is no special semantics for high-level object sets.

8.2.2 General Constraints

Although we often write general constraints informally, using a natural language, we must convert them to a formal language for a formal specification. Formal general constraints in OSM diagrams are closed formulas. Notationally, we write constraints as closed, first-order, well-formed formulas, as defined in Chapter 5 and used in Chapter 6. In OSM-L, we write them in the same way except that we must convert several of the symbols to ordinary text. Table 8.1 shows the correspondence between predicate-calculus symbols and OSM-L symbols and keywords.

For the application model in Fig. 8.6b, for example, if we wish to assert that the retail price for an item must always exceed the wholesale price for the item, we would write

$$\textbf{for all}\ x\ \textbf{for all}\ y\ \textbf{for all}\ z\ ((Item(x)\ has\ Price(y)\ \textbf{and}$$
$$Item(x)\ has\ Cost(z)) => y > z)$$

Table 8.1. Symbol Correspondence

Predicate Calculus	OSM-L
true	**true**
false	**false**
$\neg$	**not**
$\wedge$	**and**
$\vee$	**or**
$\Rightarrow$	**=>**
$\Leftrightarrow$	**<=>**
$\exists$	**exists**
$\exists^c$	**exists[c]**
$\forall$	**for all**
(	(
)	)
$\geq$	**>=**
$\leq$	**<=**
other function symbol (e.g., +, -, >)	other function symbol (e.g., +, -, >)

If we wish to ensure that when there are at least five departments, then there is a boss, we would write

$$\textbf{exists}[5: *]\ x\ (Department(x)) = > \textbf{exists}[1: *]\ y\ (Boss(y))$$

The general constraint $a + b > 0$ in Fig. 8.6b is formal as it stands. However, the general constraint

> *Workers may not earn more than their managers*

is not. As is often the case with informal statements, this statement is ambiguous. Does it mean that a worker in a department may not earn more than the manager of that department? Or does it mean that a worker may not earn more than any supervisor in the management chain all the way to the top? Or does it mean that no employee along any management chain may earn more than the manager who supervises that employee directly? If it means that a worker in a department may not earn more than the manager of that department, we would write

for all $x1$ **for all** $x2$ **for all** $x3$ **for all** $x4$ **for all** $x5$ *(Worker($x1$) earns*
    Hourly Rate($x2$)
and *Manager($x3$) earns Hourly Rate($x4$)* **and** *Manager($x3$)*
    manages Department($x5$)
and *Worker($x1$) works in Department($x5$)* $=> x2 < x4$)

If the statement means that a worker may not earn more than any supervisor in the management chain all the way to the top, we would first produce a high-level relationship set consisting of all the managers of an employee by writing

Manager(x) manages Employee(y) : $-$ *Manager(x) manages Manager(y)*;
Manager(x) manages Employee(y) : $-$ *Manager(x) manages Department(z),*
    Worker(y) works in Department(z);
Manager(x) manages Manager(y) : $-$ *Boss(x) manages Manager(y)*;
Manager(x) manages Manager(y) : $-$ *Boss(x) manages Manager(z),*
    Manager(z) manages Manager(y);

We would then write the general constraint

for all $x1$ **for all** $x2$ **for all** $x3$ **for all** $x4$ **for all** $x5$ *(Employee($x1$) earns*
    Hourly Rate($x2$)
and *Manager($x3$) earns Hourly Rate($x4$)* **and** *Manager($x3$)*
    manages Employee($x1$)
$=> x2 < x4$)

If the statement means that no employee along any management chain may earn more than the manager who supervises that employee directly, we would write

for all $x1$ **for all** $x2$ **for all** $x3$ **for all** $x4$ **for all** $x5$ *(Worker($x1$) earns*
    Hourly Rate($x2$)
and *Manager($x3$) earns Hourly Rate($x4$)* **and** *Manager($x3$)*
    manages Department($x5$)
and *Worker($x1$) works in Department($x5$)* $=> x2 < x4$)
and
for all $x1$ **for all** $x2$ **for all** $x3$ **for all** $x4$ *(Manager($x1$) earns*
    Hourly Rate($x2$)
and *Manager($x3$) earns Hourly Rate($x4$)* **and** *Boss($x3$)*
    manages Manager($x1$)
$=> x2 < x4$)

8.2.3 Queries and Expressions

OSM-L queries return sets. Here again, we use predicate calculus directly. As explained in Chapter 5, we can use open formulas for queries by writing

$$\{ <x_1, \dots x_n> \mid F(x_1, \dots, x_n) \}$$

where $x_1, \dots x_n$ are the free variables of a formula F. Notationally, in OSM-L we write the bar (|) as **where** and we write the target list of free variables in the result $<x_1, \dots x_n>$ as a predicate. If there is one free variable in the result, we may think of the result as an object set; if there are two or more free variables, we may think of the result as a relationship set. Often, we use predicate names of existing object or relationship sets. In this case, the result is either the object or relationship set itself or a subset of the object or relationship set.

As an example, we can obtain the social security numbers and names of workers in the toy department by the query

Name(x) and SSN(y) **where exists** *z (Employee(z) has Name(x),*
Employee(z) has SSN(y), Worker(z) works in Department(Toy))

As another example, we can obtain the list of departments by the query

Department(x)

Observe here that when the predicate is simply **true**, we omit the **where** clause. We can also omit the *x* and the parentheses and simply write

Department

to express the same query.

We may simplify complex queries by using *path expressions*, so-called because they traverse a path in an ORM diagram. We use a dot operator to represent traversal through an object-relationship graph. Here are several sample dot queries:

Person. Address
ItemName(ball). Price
Order(x). Item Name

A dot query finds the shortest path between its left-hand and right-hand sides. In the relational-algebra sense, it then joins the relationship sets along the path, selects using any given argument(s), and projects on the right-most predicate. Thus, given the application model of Fig. 8.6b, the first expression just given returns the address of a customer and, since every customer is a person, is equivalent to

$$\pi_{Address}(Person\ has\ Address)$$

The second expression returns the price of the item named *ball* and is equivalent to

$$\pi_{Price}\sigma_{Item\ Name\ =\ ball}(Item\ has\ Item\ Name\ \bowtie\ Item\ has\ Price)$$

The third expression returns the item names of the orders, restricted to orders in the set *x*, and is equivalent to

$$\pi_{Item\ Name}\sigma_{Order\ \in\ x}(Order\ includes\ Number\ of\ Item\ \bowtie\ Item\ has\ Item\\ Name)$$

If the shortest path happens to be ambiguous, we may specify more of the path in the dot query. For example, if we want the names of items associated with a person, it is unclear whether this means items a customer has ordered, items a manager is responsible for, or items a worker handles. We can make this clear by adding *Customer* or *Worker* or *Manager* to the dot query. For example, *Name(Kelly). Manager. Item Name* requests the names of items for which the manager named *Kelly* is responsible. This dot query is equivalent to

$$\pi_{Item\ Name}\sigma_{Name\ =\ Kelly}\sigma_{Manager\ =\ Person}\\ (Person\ has\ Name\ \bowtie\ Manager\ manages\ Department\ \bowtie\ Item\ is\ in\\ Department\ \bowtie\ Item\ has\ Item\ Name)$$

When a path traverses (part of) a generalization/specialization hierarchy, the **isa** relationship dictates that an equality selection be used to traverse the path, as this example shows.

Besides standard queries and dot queries, queries also include standard expressions, which may yield sets, but often yield singleton sets, which can denote scalars. Thus, for example, we may have the following expressions:

> *Boss − Manager*
> *Boss + Worker*
> *2 + 3*
> *Boss* **subset** *Spouse. Employee*
> *SSN*(111-11-1111). *Manager. Hourly Rate*
> $\quad$ < *SSN*(222-22-2222). *Manager. Hourly Rate*

The first expression, the set difference of *Boss* and *Manager*, yields those managers who are bosses. The second, the union of *Boss* and *Worker*, yields the set of employees who are bosses or workers. The third is a standard arithmetic expression that yields 5—technically {5}, which we write as 5. The fourth asks whether the set of bosses is a subset of of the set of employees who have spouses, and the fifth asks whether the hourly rate of the manager whose social security number is *111-11-1111* is less than the hourly rate of the manager whose social security number is *222-22-2222*. The fourth and fifth expressions yield either **true** or **false**—technically {**true**} or {**false**}, which we treat as scalars. Note also that the less-than operator in the last expression applies to two singleton sets, which we treat as scalars. In general, when a singleton set appears in a scalar context, OSM-L treats it as a scalar.

8.2.4 State Nets

Since OSM-L is a model-equivalent language, we can write any state net textually. For example, Fig. 8.7 shows how we write the *Inventory History Controller* state net from Fig. 8.1c in OSM-L. We write state nets textually by listing each transition as a transition statement. Basically, a transition statement specifies an event in an event clause (also called an @ clause because we denote events by @), prior states in a **when** clause, a condition in an **if** clause, an action in a **then** clause, and subsequent states in an **enter** clause. Any transition identifier precedes a transition statement. If there are no prior states, a new object with a thread of control is created. The default initial transition, denoted graphically by a bar with only an out-arrow, represents the event @ *create*. If there is no subsequent state, we terminate a thread of control. When all threads of control for an object terminate, the object ceases to exist. The default final transition, denoted graphically by a bar with only an in-arrow, represents the event @ *destroy*. The order of the transition statements is immaterial.

As a larger example of OSM-L, Fig. 8.8 shows the *Order Taker* state net from Fig. 8.1b. There are several additional features in this state net.

Inventory History Controller **includes**

@ *create*
enter *Ready;*
end;

4
when *Ready*
@ *item sold(Nr)* **then**
    <<*update Nr On Hand and Amt This Month*>>
enter *Ready;*
end;

5
when *Ready*
@ *end of month* **then**
    << *delete Inventory History Record of oldest month*
    add Inventory History Record for new month
    Initialize Amt This Month to be 0 & reset thresholds >>
enter *Ready;*
end;

end;

Figure 8.7   OSM-L *Inventory History Controller* state net.

Order Taker **includes**

@ *initialize order taker*
enter *Ready;*
end;

1
when *Ready* **new thread**
@ *order request* **then**
    <<*initiate order*>>
enter *Ready for Item;*
exception <<*No ID*>> **enter** *No ID;*
exception <<*Invalid ID*>> **enter** *Invalid ID;*
end;

Figure 8.8   OSM-L *Order Taker* state net.

2

when *No ID* **then**
    << *tell the person to*
        register as a customer >>
end;

3

when *Invalid ID* **then**
    << *tell the person to*
        enter a valid ID >>
end;

4

when *Ready for Item*
@*request Item* **then**
    << *record Item & how*
        many ordered >>
enter *Ready for Item*;
exception <<*too few available*>> **enter** *Unable to Fill Request for Item*;
end;

5

when *Ready for Item*
if <<*done*>> **then**
    << *fill order*
    send to customer >>
end;

6

when *Unable to Fill Request for Item* **then**
    << *give customer choice of*
        1. *placing a backorder*
        2. *doing nothing* >>
enter *Waiting for Response*;
end;

7

when *Waiting for Response*
if <<*do nothing*>> **then**
enter *Ready for Item*;
end;

Figure 8.8 (cont.) OSM-L *Order Taker* state net.

> *Backorder Taker.8*
> **when** *Waiting for Response*
> **if** *<<place backorder>>*
> **end**;
>
> **end**;

Figure 8.8 (cont.)   OSM-L *Order Taker* state net.

Observe that unlike creation, which always creates a new object, thread termination does not necessarily destroy an object. An object is destroyed only when all its threads terminate. New threads for an object arise in one of two ways:

1. A thread does not leave a prior state when a transition fires if a **new thread** condition qualifies a state, as it does for transition *1* in Fig. 8.8.

2. A thread splits when it leaves a transition, as it does when it leaves transition *8* in Fig. 8.1b.

In this case our OSM-L *enter* clause would read

> **enter** *Waiting for Backorder Item to Arrive* **and** *Order Taker. Ready for Item*

Figure 8.8 shows how we write exceptions in OSM-L. Observe that we write a transition exception by adding an **exception** clause following the **enter** clause. For Transition *1*, for example, we have

> **enter** *Ready for Item*;
> **exception** *<<No ID>>* **enter** *No ID*;
> **exception** *<<Invalid ID>>* **enter** *Invalid ID*;
> **end**;

for the two transition exceptions. For state exceptions, we add **exception** to the state name (conjunction of state names) in a transition that is considered to be an exception for the state (conjunction of states).

Null triggers are also new in Fig. 8.8. A null trigger, which is always true, is indicated by the absence of both an @ clause and an **if** clause. Figure 8.8 also shows how we designate a connection to another part of the state net in a generalization or specialization. We use special transition names as transition identifiers, and we give the trigger, but nothing else. The special name has the form *<object – set name>.<transition identifier>*. In Fig. 8.8, *Backorder Taker.8* designates transition *8* in the *Backorder Taker* state net. For state connections we use full names of the form *<object – set name>.<state name>* in place of state names that normally need not include *<object-set name>* because the context provides this part of the name.

Our final observation here leads to the need for the next sections of our formal specification language. Observe that the triggers and actions in the OBM diagram in Fig. 8.8 are still informal. Indeed, we have simply copied them from the diagram and set them off with our informal-statement brackets, << and >>. Eventually they must be made formal if we are to have a fully formal specification.

8.2.5 Update and Assignment Statements

OSM-L provides for updates by using interactions—either built-in interactions for default state nets or user-defined interactions, which are based ultimately on built-in interactions. Building here from the ground up, we first discuss initial and final transitions, then default state nets for object sets without a user-defined state net, and finally assignment statements, which provide for high-level specification of low-level update operations.

An *initial transition* is a transition in a state net that has no prior state. In Fig. 8.1c, transition *4* in the *Inventory History Controller* state net and transition *3* in the *Receiving* state net are examples, as are all the unlabeled transition bars such as in *Order Taker* in Fig. 8.1b. When an initial transition in the state net for an object set S executes successfully, it creates a new object and adds it to S. In this sense, initial transitions are already formal, and nothing further need be done to formalize the notion of inserting an object into an object set. Some parts of our sample initial transitions have been informal, of course, but these informal parts have to do with auxiliary initialization, not with the addition of an object to an object set.

A *final transition* is a transition in a state net that has no subsequent state. In Fig. 8.1b, transition *5* in the *Order Taker* state net is an example. Transition *3* in the *Receiving* state net in Fig. 8.1c is both an initial and a final transition. When a final transition executes for an object x, it always terminates the thread of x that executes the final transition. When the last thread for x terminates, x ceases to exist and is thus deleted. As with initial transitions, final transitions formalize deletion, and nothing further need be done.

For object sets that have no user-defined state net, OSM-L provides a default state net. Figure 8.9 presents the basic default state net, which we will augment as we proceed. The initial transition responds to an **add** event by placing a new object in the *Exists* state for the object set *A*. A final transition responds to a **remove** event by removing an object from the *Exists* state, effectively destroying the object. The object to be removed is usually identified specifically in the **remove** interaction, either as a literal or in a **to** or **where** clause. All object sets that are not in *isa* hierarchies have this basic behavior. The system also provides the equivalent of this default state net for every relationship set. Since there are only default state nets for relationship sets, we provide no notation for them.

For a default state net in an *isa* hierarchy, we must ensure that when the system adds an object to a specialization *S*, it also adds the object to all generalizations of *S*, if the object is not already there. We must also ensure that when the system removes an object from a generalization *G*, then the system is also removes the object from all specializations of *G*. Figure 8.10 shows a default state net for a simple *isa* hierarchy. If we add a new object to the specialization *B* in Fig. 8.10, the state net adds it automatically to *A*. If an object is already in *A*, adding it again does nothing, since all object sets are sets. If we remove an object from *A*, the state net removes it automatically from *B*, if it is there. Basic default state nets for *isa* hierarchies with several object sets are more complex, but they follow the same pattern; this ensures that adding an object to a specialization adds it to any generalization in which it is not already found, and removing an object from a generalization removes it from all specializations.

Since stand-alone lexical object sets are automatically specializations of the built-in *String* object set, their state net behaves like a default specialization state net. Since all strings already logically exist in *String* and since the system neither adds strings to nor removes them from this built-in set, we

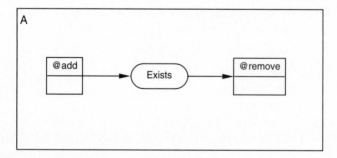

Figure 8.9 Default state net.

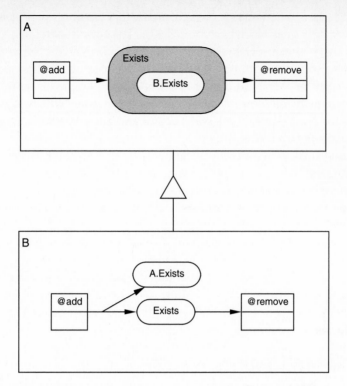

Fig. 8.10 Default state net for a generalization/specialization hierarchy.

can also think of stand-alone lexical object sets as having the behavior of a stand-alone nonlexical object set.

The following sample **add** and **remove** statements show the range of possible basic updates for OSM-L:

> **add** *Item*;
> **add** *Item(x), Order(y), Order(x) includes Number(3) of Item(y)*;
> **add** *Customer(x) has Order(y), Order(y) has Order Nr(999)*
>   **where** *Customer(x) has Customer ID(123)*;
> **remove** *Employee(x)* **where** *Employee(x) has SSN(777-77-7777)*;
> **remove** *Spouse(x)* **where** *Person(x) has Name(Pat)*;

The first **add** statement here creates a new object for the *Item* object set. The second creates a new item, a new order, and a new relationship in the *Order includes Number of Item* relationship set that relates the new item, the new order, and the number *3*. The third statement adds a new order, order number *999*, for the customer, whose customer ID is *123*. Observe that this third statement has a **where** clause, which provides a defining predicate in the same way as it does elsewhere in OSM-L. The fourth statement removes the employee whose social security number is *777-77-7777*. Note that this statement also removes the employee from at least one of the specializations *Manager* or *Worker* and may also remove the employee from *Boss*. It does not remove the employee from *Person*, however, which is what we would want if the employee is still a customer. The last statement removes any spouse whose name is *Pat*.

We now turn to assignment statements, which are built from **add** and **remove** statements. An assignment statement has the form *l-value := r-value*, where *l-value* defines a subset *S* of an object or relationship set, and *r-value* is an expression that provides a set of values *S'* to replace *S*. Since queries yield subsets, both l-values and r-values may be queries. In addition, an r-value may be an expression. The assignment statement in OSM-L generalizes standard assignment statements found in most programming languages because it works with sets rather than scalars and maintains the relationship context for replaced values. The details of the OSM-L assignment statement are complex, but its normal usage is straightforward.

Here are some examples:

Hourly Rate($10) := $11

SSN(444-44-4444). *Name* := *Kim Carter*

Item Nr(123-45). *Nr On Hand* := *Item Nr*(123-45). *Nr On Hand* + 10

SSN(555-55-5555). *Hourly Rate*

   := *SSN*(555-55-5555). *Hourly Rate*

   + 0.1 * *SSN*(555-55-5555). *Hourly Rate*

The first assignment statement changes the hourly rate, *$10*, to *$11* for all employees who earn $10 per hour. The second statement changes the name for the employee whose social security number is *444-44-4444* to *Kim Carter*. The third increases by 10 the number on hand for the item whose item number is *123-45*. The last gives the employee whose social security number is *555-55-5555* a 10% raise, where we are assuming the declaration

Hourly Rate: US$;

and that *US$ + US$* and *Real * US$* are built-in operators.

8.2.6 Interactions, Parameters, and Local Declarations

OSM-L has two ways to initiate interactions and one way to respond to interactions. We may initiate an interaction as either a one-way or a two-way interaction. An event monitor in a transition trigger receives an initiated interaction and allows the action in the transition to provide the response.

A one-way interaction-initiation statement lets a user specify which interaction is being initiated by naming the interaction and what data values, if any, are being sent by providing a parameter list. The parameter-passing mechanism is like pass-by-value in the sense that copies of objects or sets of objects passed as parameters are given to the receiver. Besides naming an interaction and designating parameters, an interaction-initiation statement also lets a user specify the set of objects eligible to receive the interaction and whether only one object should receive it or whether all who are ready can receive it.

Here are some examples of one-way interactions:

> *unfilled request* **from** *Order Taker* **to** *Manager*(*x*)
> **where** *Manager*(*x*) *manages Department*(*Toy*)
> *initialize order taker* **to** *Order Taker*
> *order request* (123) **to** *Order Taker*
> *reset date and time* (7 *Aug* 95, 15: 43) **to** *Operating System*
> *pay raise* (0. 10) **to all** *Worker*

The first interaction sends an *unfilled request* from an order taker to a manager, but only to the manager of the toy department. The second interaction sends a request, *initialize order taker*, to create an order taker, or another order taker if one or more already exist. The third interaction sends an *order request* to any one of the order takers to initiate an order, while the fourth sends a request to the operating system (since there is only one) to reset the date and time. The last interaction sends a pay raise to all workers.

When we write interaction statements in context, we can simplify them. For example, if we initiate an interaction from within a transition of a state net in an object set *S*, we know that the **from** clause must be **from** *S*. We therefore need not write it. Also, if the interaction name is unique and is found in the state net of the destination object set, we can omit the **to** clause because it must designate the object set in which the interaction is received. As a further convenience, we allow the destination to be a prefix for the operation name. This makes an interaction look syntactically like message passing or a procedure call in many common languages. In the context of the *Order Taker* state net in Fig. 8.1b, for example, we may thus write the first three preceding interactions as

> *Manager*(x). *unfilled request* **where** *Manager*(x) *manages*
>   *Department*(*Toy*)
> *Order Taker*. *initialize order taker*
> *order request* (123)

where we are assuming that the first interaction originates within the *Order Taker*.

A two-way interaction is like a one-way interaction except that it waits for a response, which is returned in a second parameter list. There may also be a **wait** clause that specifies a length of time to wait, beyond which the two-way interaction no longer waits for a response. Also, unlike one-way interactions, two-way interactions may interact with only one object—thus, there is no **to all** clause. Another difference is that a two-way interaction may be invoked either as a statement or in an expression. When invoked as a statement, a two-way interaction is like a procedure call. When invoked in an expression, a two-way interaction is like a function. In that case, the return list, which is implicit, must have exactly one parameter.

Here are some examples of two-way interactions:

> *get date and time* () → (*d*: *Date*, *t*: *Time*);
> *d* := *MonthFromDate*(*d*);
> *register waiting process*(*wait time*(*d*, *t*));
> *get item for order from customer* () → (*i*: *Item Nr*, *n*: *Number*) [**wait**
>   *5 minutes*];
> *get order information* (95123) → (
>   *order information Order has Order Nr*: *Order has Order Nr*,
>   *Order was received on Date*: *Order was received on Date Received*,
>   *Count of Ordered Item is in Customer Order*:
>   *Order includes Number of Item*
>   **where** *Count*: *Number*, *Ordered Item*: *Item*, *Customer*
>   *Order*: *Order*,
>   *Item has Make & Model*: *Make and Model Nr identify Item*,
>   *Item has Item Name*: *Item has Item Name*
>   )

The first two-way interaction invokes the *get date* and *time* interaction, which is handled by the operating system. It takes no input parameters, but returns two parameters, one for the date and one for the time. Observe that the formal parameters have the form *A*: *B*, which looks like a type specification in an ordinary programming language but in actuality is an **isa** statement for a generalization/specialization in OSM-L. Just as for ORM declarations, the object set before the colon is the specialization, while the object set after the colon is the generalization. There are no variables in OSM-L, but there are object sets, which are containers that are like variables. Moreover, containers that have a single element are like scalar variables.

The second statement in the preceding examples invokes a two-way interaction that returns an object and is thus like a function—we are assuming here that *MonthFromDate* takes an input date and returns a result date. The third statement is a one-way interaction, *register waiting process*, that includes as an actual parameter the two-way interaction *wait time*, which we are assuming takes a date and a time and returns the time we need for our running example—the number of milliseconds to the beginning of the next month. The fourth statement shows a two-way interaction with a **wait** clause. Here we are asking the customer for the item number of an item being ordered and the number wanted. If the customer does not respond within five minutes, the interaction does not take place.

The last statement in the preceding set of examples shows that we can pass and receive relationships as well as objects in parameter lists. We declare relationship sets in the same way as we declare object sets, using a colon, which denotes generalization/specialization or subset. (The corresponding graphical representation uses a subset constraint specified as a general constraint.) For object sets, since there is only one place in the predicate, there is no difficulty matching places. For relationship sets, however, there are at least two places, and we must match the places explicitly, one for one. We do so either by matching object-set names or by specifying generalizations explicitly for the object sets in a relationship set in a **where** clause. In the example under discussion we show the various ways this can be done. In the first declaration we use direct name matching—*Order* matches *Order* and *Order Nr* matches *Order Nr*. In the second declaration, we match directly the names of all but one—*Order* matches *Order* and thus by the process of elimination *Date* must match *Date Received*. In the third declaration, we use an explicit **where** clause. The fourth declaration is like the second, and the last is like the first.

The receiving side of both a one-way and a two-way interaction is an event component in a trigger. In a trigger, we write the @ symbol, which designates an event, followed by the interaction name, followed by a formal parameter list, which may be omitted when no parameters are passed. Syntactically, a formal parameter list is like a return parameter list for a two-way interaction in that it may also specify "variable" names and "types." If the interaction being received is two-way, then there is also a return parameter list, which syntactically is like a formal parameter list for both one-way and two-way interactions. As examples, we give the receiving event specification for some of the sample one-way and two-way interactions just considered.

> @ *initialize order taker*
>
> @ *order request* (*id*: *Customer ID*)
>
> @ *get date and time* → (*d*, *t*)
>
> @ *MonthFromDate* (*d*: *Date*) → (*d*)
>
> @ *get order information* (*id*: *Customer ID*) → (*retrieved Order has Order Nr*,
>   *retrieved Order was received on Date Received*,
>   *retrieved Order includes Number of Item*,
>   *retrieved Make and Model Nr identify Item*,
>   *retrieved Item has Item Name*)

OSM-L treats formal parameters like local variables. The scope of these object and relationship sets declared in formal parameter lists is the transition in which they are declared. Thus, for example, if the trigger for a transition T is

$$@ \; order \; request(id: Customer \; ID)$$

then the local object set (local variable) *id* is known only within T. Furthermore, there is a different copy of every local object and relationship set for each object thread that executes a transition. Thus, if several order takers are in transition T simultaneously, each has its own copy of the local *id* object set.

Besides local object and relationship sets declared in formal parameter lists, we may also declare local object and relationship sets in any transition. We declare these local object and relationship sets in the same way as we declare them globally, by specifying ORM components. A local ORM application model represents transient information, whereas a global ORM application model represents persistent information. Transient information for a transition T comes into existence for the thread of an object x when x enters T and passes out of existence for T when x leaves T.

There can be several nested scopes since low-level transitions may be nested in higher level transitions. As should be expected, standard occlusion rules apply, so that a local object or relationship set occludes a more global object or relationship set with the same name.

To conclude this section, let us mention one special local name that is declared implicitly, that is, **self**. This name is always available in every transition. It designates the object identifier or lexical value of an object whose thread is being executed.

8.2.7 Control Structures

OSM-L has four control structures:

1. a statement sequence,

2. an **if then elseif ... else** statement,

3. a **while** statement, and

4. a **for each** statement.

In our model-equivalent language OSM-L, these control structures are one-to-one with particular state-net patterns. Figure 8.11 presents these patterns along with the syntax for the statements. Figures 8.11a–8.11c each show a textual statement in a transition, as well as this textual statement expanded. Figure 8.11d shows two expansions, an intermediate one and a full one.

All these patterns except the last are straightforward; the **for each** statement requires some sophisticated OSM-L machinery. The essential idea of a **for each** statement is that it executes a sequence of statements for each element of a set. The set for a **for each** statement is an object or relationship set, which may be either given or derived by an OSM-L Datalog-like logic statement. In all cases a predicate with n arguments defines the set over which the iteration takes place. If $n = 1$, we are iterating over an object set, and if $n > 1$, we are iterating over a relationship set. In Fig. 8.11d, we use *X1 ... Xn Predicate* and its variation with explicit places to designate the object or relationship set over which the iteration takes place.

The full expansion of the **for each** shows the control flow for the embedded **while** statement and the embedded statement sequences. It also shows the local declarations explicitly. Transitions nested inside transitions provide for nested local declarations. In the intermediate expansion, observe that the **while** statement defines a local scope in which local declarations can reside. Indeed, all the control statements define local scopes, as the expansions in Figs. 8.11b–8.11d show.

The intermediate expansion of the **for each** is basically textual. By explaining each of these textual statements, we will have also explained each of the textual statements in the full expansion. We therefore turn our attention to the intermediate expansion of the **for each** statement.

The transition for the **for each** statement consists of two declaration statements and an initialization statement followed by a **while** loop. The condition in the **while** along with the first and last statements in the body of the loop cause the body of the **while** loop to execute for each element in the set whose name is $X1 \ldots Xn$. The **one of** operator is a built-in operator that arbitrarily selects one element of an object or relationship set. The body of the **while** loop contains n declaration statements, n assignment statements, and the m given statements in the body. Once we select one of the elements of $X1 \ldots Xn$, we assign the object for Xi to xi $(1 \le i \le n)$ and execute the statements in the body of the **for each** statement. We then remove the element selected from $X1 \ldots Xn$ so that it cannot be selected on subsequent iterations.

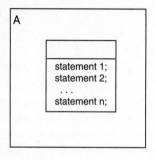

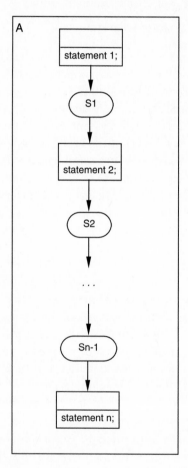

(a) OSM-L statement sequence.

Figure 8.11   OSM-L control structures.

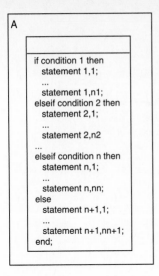

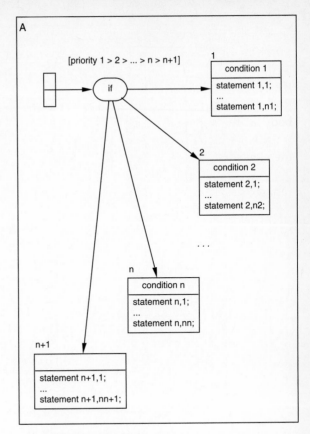

(b) OSM-L **if** statement.

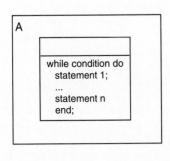

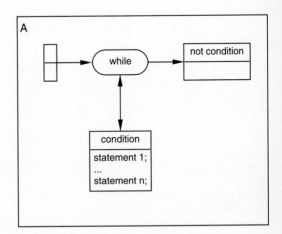

(c) OSM-L **while** statement.

Figure 8.11 (cont.) OSM-L control structures.

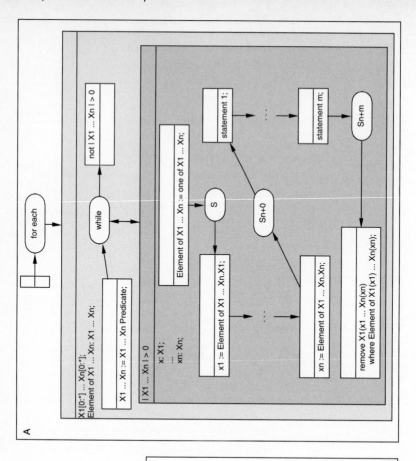

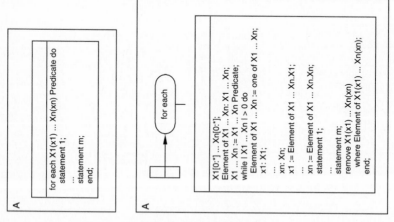

(d) OSM-L **for** statement.

Figure 8.11 (cont.) OSM-L control structures.

Figure 8.12 provides an example of OSM-L control structures by giving a completely formal specification for transition 2 of the *Inventory Controller* in Fig. 8.1c. The example assumes the existence of the ORM application model in Fig. 7.22a. The **for each** statement selects each item one at a time and sets the threshold. The **if** statement selects the case: no history exists, less than a full year's history exists, or a full year's history exists. The cases are straightforward except when there is less than a full year's history. For this case, the **while** statement finds the earliest month with a history. We are assuming here that *Today* is built-in and that it returns today's date in the form *day month year*, that *month(d)* returns the month part of date *d* (one of *Jan, Feb, ..., Dec*), and that *nextMonth(m)* returns the month after month *m*. We are assuming also, as for the application model in Fig. 7.22a, that there are at most 12 months of history.

for each *Item*(x) **do**

> -- *if there is no history, set the threshold at 0*
> **if not exists** y(*Item*(x). *Inventory History*(y)) **then**
>> *Item*(x). *Threshold* := 0;
>
> -- *if there is less than a year's history, set the threshold at*
> -- 10 *percent more than the amount sold during the earliest month*
> -- *for which there is a history*
> **elseif** (*Item*(x). *Month*(*month*(*Today*)) = { }) **then**
>> *m*: *Month*;
>> *m* := *nextMonth*(*month*(*Today*));
>> **while** (*Item*(x). *Month*(*m*) = { }) **do**
>>> *m* := *nextMonth*(*m*);
>>> **end**;
>>
>> *Item*(x). *Threshold* := 1. 1∗(*Month*(*m*). *Amount Sold*);
> -- *otherwise, we set the threshold at* 10
> **else**
>> *Item*(x). *Threshold* := 10;
>> **end**;
>
> **end**;

Figure 8.12 Formal specification for setting thresholds.

OSM-L as an Implementation Language and as a Rapid Prototyping Language

With the addition of an optimizing compiler that would generate both database structures and functional code, OSM-L could be a database programming language. Providing an optimizing compiler is a major task. For the data side, the compiler should automate the design procedures described in Chapters 9 and 10; for the behavior side, the design procedures described in Chapter 11. This would just be the beginning, however, because a successful optimizing compiler would have to apply many further optimizations to make it produce industrial-strength code.

As a rapid prototyping language, OSM-L could make an immediate contribution. It is always possible to execute any OSM application model by executing OSM-L. Informal parts, of course, can be "executed" only by displaying them. But the possibility of direct execution makes it easy to develop prototypes rapidly and to turn partly functioning prototypes into fully functioning ones.

8.3   Functional Specification

To a large extent, the purpose of a formal functional specification is to clear up questions that arise because of the inherent, often unexpected ambiguity in natural-language statements. The formal specification for setting thresholds in Fig. 8.12, for example, clears up several possible questions: Exactly what does "12 months ago" mean? (It means exactly one year prior to the date on which the transition is invoked.) Exactly what does "oldest month" mean? (It means the earliest month for which there is a history.) Does the 10% apply only to the amount sold 12 months ago, or does it also apply to the oldest month? (It applies to both.) What happens if there is no history? (The threshold is set at 10.)

The example in Fig. 8.12 also shows the amount of detail needed to formalize a statement fully. Producing this much detail for a specification requires a lot of work. We emphasize again, however, that it may not be desirable or necessary to formalize all components fully, although it should always be possible.

Producing a formal specification, especially for transitions, also looks much like coding. Indeed it is, but there are some important differences:

1. We are using a model-equivalent language, which allows us to narrow our focus to only those OSM components written in natural language, exactly the parts that are likely to be troublesome.

2. We need not be concerned about efficiency—this comes later during design or implementation.

3. The formality of the specification lends itself to automatic conversion. If appropriate tools are available (or even if they are not), the work of formalization done during specification can carry over into design and implementation.

Since we wish to formalize an application model more completely, we should ask whether there is a systematic way to proceed. To a large extent, every OSM application model is already executable. Thus, one way to proceed is by rapid prototyping. A tool can be built to simulate the execution of an application model. While executing, this tool may encounter an informal trigger, action, interaction, or constraint. The tool could then allow a specifier to formalize the encountered informal component and proceed— or even proceed without formalizing the component, but with the consequence that the component would then be ignored in the execution. In this way, a specifier can turn an informal specification into a formal one. Furthermore, and perhaps even more important, the model-execution tool could evaluate the results of execution and report constraint violations, allowing formal specifications to be fixed. Finally, if the tool displays values crossing outside the automation boundary and allows a specifier to invoke ad hoc queries to view resulting object and relationship sets, a meaningful validation can be carried out.

But what if no such model-execution tool exists? We can still proceed largely in the same way. We can choose an interaction. If the interaction is incomplete or informal, we can make it complete and formal. We can then see if the transition trigger and action for the interaction exists and is formal. If not, we can make it formal. If the action causes an update, we should see which constraints apply. If any of these constraints are informal, we can formalize them. We can then check whether the results should satisfy the constraints. If not, adjustments should be made. Continuing in this way from interaction to interaction, we can formalize as much of the application model as we wish.

We proceed with some examples. Suppose we wish to formalize the *Customer Info Maintainer* in Fig. 8.1d, a particularly good place to start because we need not assume anything about any data already being in the database. Furthermore, we need consider only a small part of the

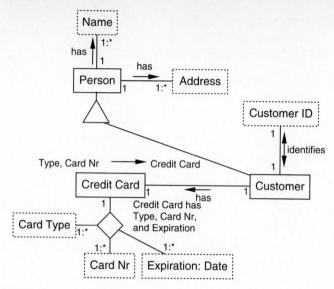

Figure 8.13   Relevant ORM components for *Customer Info Maintainer.*

application-model ORM, that is, the part in Fig. 8.13. When considering only a small part of the ORM, we must be careful, of course, not to omit some component mistakenly that is relevant, for then our results may not hold when we consider the entire database. We can reason here, however, by considering the generalization *Person* and the participation constraints on the connecting relationship sets for *Customer* and *Person* that only names, addresses, credit-card information, and customer IDs need be part of the reduced ORM—neither orders nor backorders are necessary because of the *0:** participation constraints.

Figure 8.14 provides the results of the formalization. Our presentation of how we arrived at these results consists of listing and answering the questions that would arise naturally by considering each interaction. Our purpose here is to show that by considering each interaction systematically and answering the questions it presents, we can formalize a state net.

1. Is the initial transition formal?

    Yes. Nothing need be done.

2. Is the @ *add new customer* interaction complete?

    No, because it sends no information. When a customer is added, the constraints require that a name, address, customer ID, and

Customer Info Maintainer **includes**

> @ *initialize customer info maintainer* **then**
> **enter** *Ready*
> **end**;

> 1
> **when** *Ready* **new thread**
> @ *add new customer* (*name: String, address: String, cardType: String,*
>   *cardNr: String, expiration: Date*) → (*id: Customer ID*) **then**
>   *Last Customer ID* := *Last Customer ID* + 1; -- *make new customer ID*
>   *id* := *Last Customer ID*;
>   *customer: Customer*;
>   *creditCard: Credit Card*;
>   **add** *Customer ID*(*id*) *identifies Customer*(*customer*),
>   *Person*(*customer*) *has Name*(*name*),
>   *Person*(*customer*) *has Address*(*address*),
>   *Customer*(*customer*) *has Credit Card*(*creditCard*),
>   *Credit Card*(*creditCard*) *has Card Type*(*cardType*),
>   *Card Nr*(*cardNr*), *and Expiration*(*expiration*);
> **end**;

> 2
> **when** *Ready* **new thread**
> @ *remove customer* (*id: Customer ID*) **then**
>   **remove** *Customer ID*(*id*) *identifies Customer*(*x*),
>   *Person*(*x*) *has Name, Person*(*x*) *has Address,*
>   *Customer*(*x*) *has Credit Card*(*y*),
>   *Credit Card*(*y*) *has Card Type, Card Nr, and Expiration;*
> **end**;

> 3
> **when** *Ready* **new thread**
> @ *change name* (*id: Customer ID, name: String*) **then**
>   *Customer ID*(*id*). *Name* := *name*;
> **end**;

> 4
> **when** *Ready* **new thread**
> @ *change address* (*id: Customer ID, address: String*) **then**
>   *Customer ID*(*id*). *Address* := *address*;
> **end**;

Figure 8.14 Formalization of the *Customer Info Maintainer* state net.

5

when *Ready* **new thread**

@ *change credit card* (*id*: *Customer ID*, *cardType*: *String*, *cardNr*: *String*,
      expiration: *Date*) **then**

    Customer ID(*id*). *Card Type* : = *cardType*;
    Customer ID(*id*). *Card Nr* : = *cardNr*;
    Customer ID(*id*). *Expiration* : = *expiration*;
  end;

end;

    Figure 8.14 (cont.)   Formalization of the *Customer Info Maintainer* state net.

credit-card information also be added. Where does the system get this information?

It is not hard to see that the real customer outside the system should supply everything but the customer ID. Thus we need to add *name, address, cardType, cardNr,* and *expiration* as input parameters for the interaction, as transition *1* in Fig. 8.14 shows. Observe that the object-set generalizations for these parameters are *String* (for all but *Expiration*) and *Date* (for *Expiration*). We take the constraints directly from the ORM diagram in Fig. 8.13. Note that *Expiration* in Fig. 8.13 is different from what it was in previous figures—since we see here that the expiration date should be a date, we choose to let *Expiration* be a specialization of a more specific object set than *String*.

3. How do we provide the customer ID?

   Figure 8.14 shows a modification we can make to allow the system to supply customer IDs. Observe here, as with the addition of *Date* previously, that in formalizing our application model we are learning more about it and continuing to enhance it.

4. How do we report the new customer ID to the customer?

   We must give the ID back to the customer. Thus we should make the interaction two-way and return the generated ID. Figure 8.14 shows this return parameter in transition *1*.

5. Is the @ *remove customer* interaction adequate?

   No, because the system does not know which customer to remove. In answering how the system gets this information, we see that a customer-ID parameter should be added to the interaction. Transition 2 in Fig. 8.14 shows this change. Once we have the ID to identify the customer to be removed, the participation constraints in Fig. 8.13 make it obvious that when we remove a customer, we must also remove the customer's ID, credit-card information, name, and address. Transition 2 shows this modification.

6. For transitions 3, 4, and 5 we also ask, How does the system know which customer information to change?

   Again, we see that the interaction must supply the customer ID.

7. How does the system know the new information?

   The obvious response is that the real customer must supply it. Transitions 3, 4, and 5 in Fig. 8.14 provide this formalization.

In the following example, we formalize the *Order Taker* and *Backorder Taker* activities in Fig. 8.1b. The resulting formal specification appears graphically in Fig. 8.15a and textually in Fig. 8.15b, except that we omit the text of the actions for the transitions in Fig. 8.15a, providing them only in Fig. 8.15b. Observe that there is only a state net for *Order Taker* and that the state net subsumes the *Backorder Taker* state net. Since there is always only one state net for a generalization/specialization hierarchy, we can always write our state nets this way. Here, however, there is another reason—we must form a high-level transition that includes most of the states and transitions in the two state nets so that we can introduce some local variables (object sets) to carry information across all states and transitions in the state net. We need the customer ID (supplied by the customer in the *order request* interaction) so that we can communicate information back to the customer if a backorder possibility arises, and we need to carry the information about an item being backordered from transition 4 to transition 8, where we use it to make the backorder if the customer wishes. As Fig. 8.15a shows, we introduce a local state net inside a high-level transition by beginning and ending with transitions. Textually, *Entering* denotes an implicit initial state within a high-level transition, and *Exiting* denotes an implicit final state. In our example, we do not need the *Exiting* state because the high-level transition itself is a final transition.

We emphasize again that it is in doing the formalization that questions arise, particularly about interactions, information passed in interactions, the exact meaning of triggers and actions, and the information stored in the database. Once these questions arise, they can be answered. A common

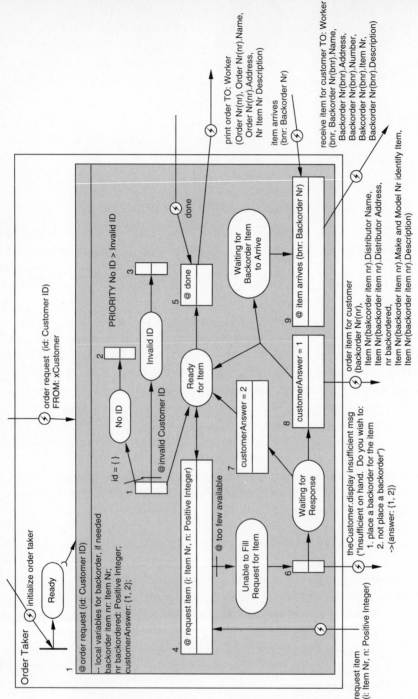

(a) Graphical formalization of the *Order Taker* state net.

Figure 8.15 Formalization of the *Order Taker* state net.

Order Taker **includes**

> @ *initialize order taker*
> **enter** *Ready*;
> **end**;
>
> **when** *Ready* **new thread**
> @ *order request* (*id*: *Customer ID*) **from** *theCustomer* **then**
>
>> -- *local variables for backorder, if needed*
>> *backorder item nr*: *Item Nr*;
>> *nr backordered*: *Positive Integer*;
>> *customerAnswer*: {1, 2};
>>
>> 1
>> **when** *Entering* **then**
>>> *Last Order Nr* := *Last Order Nr* + 1; -- *make new order number*
>>> *nr*: *Order Nr*;
>>> *nr* := *Last Order Nr*;
>>> **add** *Customer*(*x*) *has Order*(*y*),
>>>> *Order*(*y*) *identifies Order Nr*(*nr*),
>>>> *Order*(*y*) *was received on Date Received*(*Today*)
>>>> **where** *x* = *Customer ID*(*id*). *Customer*;
>>
>> **enter** *Ready for Item*
>> **exception** *id* = { } **enter** *No ID*
>> **exception** *invalid Customer ID* **enter** *Invalid ID*
>> [**priority** *No ID* > *Invalid ID*];
>> **end**;
>>
>> 2
>> **when** *No ID* **then**
>>> *theCustomer. display no id* ("*No Customer ID entered.*" +
>>>> "*You must be registered as a customer and enter a*
>>>>> *customer ID.*");
>>
>> **end**;
>>
>> 3
>> **when** *Invalid ID* **then**
>>> *theCustomer. display invalid id* ("*Invalid Customer ID.*" +
>>>> "*You must be registered as a customer and enter a valid*
>>>>> *customer ID.*");
>>
>> **end**;

Figure 8.15 (cont.)   Formalization of the *Order Taker* state net.

4

when *Ready for Item*
@ *request item (i: Item Nr, n: Positive Integer)* **then**
    if *n > Nr In Back Room* **then**
        backorder item nr := i;
        nr backordered := n;
        too few available;
        add *Order(x) includes Number(n) of Item(y) at Unit Price(z)*
            where *x = Order Nr(nr). Order*
                and *y = Item Nr(i). Item*
                and *z = Item Nr(i). Price;*
      Item Nr(i). Amt This Month := Item Nr(i). Amt This Month + n;
      Item Nr(i). Nr In Back Room := Item Nr(i). Nr In Back Room − n;
enter *Ready for Item*
exception *too few available* **enter** *Unable to Fill Request for Item;*
end;

5

when *Ready for Item*
@ *done* **then**
    if *Order Nr(nr). Order includes Number of Item ≠ { }* **then**
        Nr(x) Item Nr(y) Description(z) :−
            Order Nr(nr) identifies Order(t),
            Order(t) includes Number(x) of Item(s) at Unit Price(w),
            Item(s) has Item Nr(y),
            Item(s) has Description(z);
        Worker. print order (Order Nr(nr), Order Nr(nr). Name,
                Order Nr(nr). Address, Nr Item Nr Description;
end;

6

when *Unable to Fill Request for Item* **then**
    theCustomer. display insufficient msg
        "("Insufficient on hand. Do you wish to:" +
        "1. place a backorder for the item" +
        "2. not place a backorder")" +
        "→ (answer: {1, 2});
    customerAnswer := answer;
enter *Waiting for Response;*
end;

Figure 8.15 (cont.)   Formalization of the *Order Taker* state net.

7

when *Waiting for Response*
if *customerAnswer* = 2
enter *Ready for Item;*
end;

8

when *Waiting for Response*
if *customerAnswer* = 1 **then**
 Last Backorder Nr := *Last Backorder Nr* + 1;
 nr: *Backorder Nr;*
 nr := *Last Backorder Nr;*
 add *Backorder Nr(nr) identifies Backorder(x);*
 add *Backorder(x) includes Number(nr backordered) of*
    Item(y) at Unit Price(z)
  where *x = Backorder Nr(nr). Backorder*
   and *y = Item Nr(backorder item nr). Item*
   and *z = Item Nr(backorder item nr). Price;*
 add *Backorder(x) was received on Date Backordered(Today)*
  where *x = Backorder Nr(nr). Order;*
 add *Responsible Order Taker(self) is responsible for Backorder(x)*
  where *x = Backorder Nr(nr). Order;*
 order item for customer (Backorder Nr(nr),
  Item Nr(backorder item nr). Distributor Name,
  Item Nr(backorder item nr). Distributor Address,
  nr backordered,
  Item Nr(backorder item nr). Make and Model Nr identify Item,
  Item Nr(backorder item nr). Description);
enter *Waiting for Backorder Item to Arrive* **and** *Ready for Item;*
end;

9

when *Waiting for Backorder Item to Arrive*
@ *item arrives (bnr: Backorder Nr)* **then**
 Worker. receive item for customer (bnr, Backorder Nr(bnr). Name,
  Backorder Nr(bnr). Address, Backorder Nr(bnr). Number,
  Backorder Nr(bnr). Item Nr, Backorder Nr(bnr). Description;
end;

end;

(b) Textual formalization of the *Order Taker* state net.

Figure 8.15 (cont.) Formalization of the *Order Taker* state net.

problem, however, is that without a formal specification, pertinent questions often are not asked until well into design. Then designers tend to answer them without consulting clients, often making incorrect assumptions. We illustrate the kinds of questions that arise and show their resolution in regard to interobject behavior, then individual object behavior, and finally the database.

By comparing Fig. 8.1b with Fig. 8.15a, we can observe that after our formalization of interactions, we have added six more boundary-crossing interactions, altered three of the five existing boundary-crossing interactions, altered both existing internal interactions, and added several new internal interactions. We show the boundary-crossing interactions graphically in Fig. 8.15a, but we give the internal interactions only textually in Fig. 8.15b. Every **add** statement and every assignment statement here represents an internal interaction. We now discuss these changes.

To determine whether an order is complete, we replace *done* in transition 5 with @ *done*, which means that real customers simply say they are done. (Exactly how they say they are done is part of the interface specification, which we discuss in the next section.)

To determine where to return messages to interact with a customer, we add a **from** clause, which we use to direct messages to a specific customer.

To determine what it means to fill an order and send it to a customer, we add outgoing print interactions, both for orders in transition 4 and backorders in transition 9.

To determine exactly how to find out whether a customer wishes to place a backorder, we display a choice question and receive a 1 or a 2 in response (see transitions 5, 7, and 8 in Fig. 8.15).

To determine exactly what information is needed for sending and receiving backorders, we add parameters to both the *order item for customer* and *receive item for customer* interactions (see Fig. 8.15).

By realizing that the right object thread must receive the backorder from a distributor, we see that we need a **to** clause for the *receive item for customer* interaction. We thus add *TO: Backorder Nr(backorder nr).Responsible Order Taker*, as Fig. 8.15a shows. Note that we have no way to record this information in Fig. 8.15b. This is because the origin state net supplies the restriction captured in a **to** clause of an interaction. In this case, however, since the interaction crosses the automation boundary, describing how this is done is part of the interface specification, which we discuss in Section 8.4.

By a simple observation, we see that the interaction and trigger in transition 4 do not match and we fix them, as Fig. 8.15 shows.

By considering the *order request* interaction, we see that we must add the two assignment statements and the **add** statement in transition 1 in Fig. 8.15b. These statements initialize an order in the database.

Similarly, by considering the *request item* interaction, we see that we need to check to see whether there is enough on hand, and if so, then record the order with the **add** statement in transition 4 and adjust the database.

Finally, we see that several additional assignment and **add** statements, which were not even mentioned in any interaction or in the original state net, are also needed to complete our formalization.

Besides making transition 1 high level, as discussed earlier, we have made two other state-net changes. One change explains exactly how the *too few available* exception should be handled. In transition 4 we check to see whether enough of the requested item is in the back room, and, if not, we then set the proper values in the *backorder item nr* and *nr backordered* variables in anticipation of a possible backorder. We then signal the event *too few available*. To make the event cause the exception to fire, we also change the exception condition *too few available* to the exception event @ *too few available*. The other change consists of adding a priority ordering for the exceptions. Since an empty customer ID is also invalid, we wish to give priority for handling the error to entering the *No ID* state over entering the *Invalid ID* state. We do so with the priority statement

[**priority** 2 > 3]

where, as usual, the brackets mean that the enclosed feature is a constraint.

In connection with handling invalid input for *Customer ID*, we should also ask what happens for any other invalid input such as for *Item Nr* and *Positive Integer* in transition 4. When there is any parameter-value violation caused by an input value that is not an element of a generalization object set as specified, the system automatically signals the event *invalid G*, where *G* is the name of the generalization object set. If there is a handler for the exception, as for *invalid Customer ID* in transition 1 for example, the handler is invoked. If not, as is the case for *Item Nr* and *Positive Integer* in transition 4, then nothing happens, and the system remains in the state in which it was when the interaction was sent—it is as if the interaction was never sent.

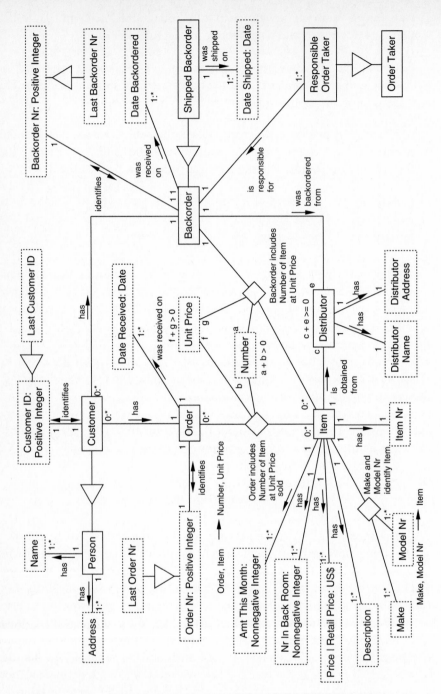

Figure 8.16 ORM changes that result from formalizing behavior.

As a result of formalizing the behavior, several ORM changes as well as OBM and OIM changes have taken place. Figure 8.16, which consists only of the part of the database that pertains to making orders, shows these changes. The figure shows that we have added a *Unit Price* object set. In making an order, we realize ("out of thin air," which is where we get many of our realizations) that the price of an item is likely to change regularly. Thus we need to record the price at the time a customer places an order or backorder. In the ORM, we have also added *Responsible Order Taker* as a result of formalizing the backorder interactions with the distributor. We also need object sets for *Last Customer ID*, *Last Order Nr*, and *Last Backorder Nr* to hold the last generated customer ID, order number, and backorder number, respectively. There is also a small but significant change in the participation constraint for orders. By formalizing the state net as we have, we realize that it is possible for an order to have no items, either because all items are backordered or because the event *done* occurs before any items are ordered. We could have chosen to remove such "orders," but we have assumed that our clients have told us that for various management reasons they wish to see these orders explicitly. Finally, as part of formalizing state nets, we typically make lexical object sets specializations of subsets of more specific object sets. Thus we have added *Positive Integer*, *US$*, and *Date* to designate several existing lexical object sets more specifically.

In our next example, we show how formalizing a state net can sometimes lead to creating additional object sets with state nets. We often encounter parts of a behavioral specification that are identical. When we encounter these identical behavioral specifications, we should ask whether an additional object set with this special behavior is warranted. For example, consider the *decide how long to wait* action in transitions 1 and 2 of the *Calendar* object set in Fig. 8.4. Figure 8.17 provides a formalization of these actions as a new object set, *Milliseconds To Wait Determiner*. Note that the *Milliseconds To Wait Determiner* object set is a singleton object set and can thus be thought of as an object whose sole function is to compute the number of milliseconds to the end of the month. Sometimes, even in an object-oriented approach, we need a routine that appears to be strictly functional. Singleton object sets with state nets that perform these functions give us a way to provide these routines.

In connection with this discussion about identical behavioral specifications, we mention that the actions in transitions 5 and 9 in Fig. 8.1b appear to be identical. The formalization in Fig. 8.15, however, shows that they are different. Thus we see an example of how providing formalization details helps us resolve the ambiguity and vagueness so often present in informal specifications. As it turns out, the two *decide how long to wait* phrases in

Milliseconds To Wait Determiner [1] **includes**

    @ *get milliseconds to wait* (*d*: *Date*, *t*: *Time*)

        → (*msecTime*: *Time Period*) **then**

      Month [1] *has Days* [1:*];

      add *Month*(*Jan*) *has Days*(31);

      add *Month*(*Feb*) *has Days*(28);

      add *Month*(*Mar*) *has Days*(31);

      add *Month*(*Apr*) *has Days*(30);

      add *Month*(*May*) *has Days*(31);

      add *Month*(*Jun*) *has Days*(30);

      add *Month*(*Jul*) *has Days*(31);

      add *Month*(*Aug*) *has Days*(31);

      add *Month*(*Sep*) *has Days*(30);

      add *Month*(*Oct*) *has Days*(31);

      add *Month*(*Nov*) *has Days*(30);

      add *Month*(*Dec*) *has Days*(31);

      Leap Year: *Boolean*;

      if *year*(*d*) **mod** 400 = 0 **then**

        Leap Year := **true;**

      elseif *year*(*d*) **mod** 100 = 0 **then**

        Leap Year := **false;**

      elseif *year*(*d*) **mod** 4 = 0 **then**

        Leap Year := **true;**

      else

        Leap Year := **false;**

        end;

      if *Leap Year* **then**

        Month(*Feb*) *has Days*. *Days* := 29;

        end;

      msecTime := (*Month*(*month*(*d*)) *has Days*. *Days*

        − *day*(*d*)) * 24 * 60 * 60 * 1000

        + (24 − *hours*(*t*)) * 60 * 60 * 1000

        + (60 − *minutes*(*t*)) * 60 * 1000

        + (60 − *seconds*(*t*)) * 1000;

    end;

  end;

Figure 8.17 Functional specification in an object-oriented approach.

transitions *1* and *2* of *Calendar* are identical, whereas the two *fill order* phrases in both transitions *5* and *9* of *Order Taker*, as well as *send to customer*, also in both transitions *5* and *9* of *Order Taker*, only appear to be identical.

We leave additional formalization of the user-defined state nets in Fig. 8.1 as exercises and turn our attention to a formalization of the interactions with object sets that do not have user-defined state nets. We first consider the *Item* object set in the database in Fig. 8.1a. Since we have provided no state net for *Item*, its state net is the default state net. By considering the default state net in Fig. 8.9, however, we can see that none of these interactions has a proper formalization because much more is happening than merely a simple creation or destruction.

For analysis, we tend to make numerous assumptions. These *Item* interactions are examples, in which we are assuming that we basically interact with items—getting information about them, changing them, and creating new ones. In reality, however, we are interacting with the properties of an item. Since we are actually interacting with the properties of an item and not an item itself, we need to make some changes to formalize these interactions. We can either supply a state net for *Item* to service them (similar to the state net for maintaining customers in Fig. 8.14), or we can break the interactions apart, redirect them, and sequence them to utilize default state nets or simpler state nets we define. We take the latter approach here.

For example, consider the state nets for *in-store sales* and *stock shelf from back room*, which are similar. Figure 8.18 depicts a graphical state net for an in-store sale; Fig. 8.19, a textual state net for stocking the shelf. In both cases, the question about what happens if *Nr* is too large arises. Again, we mention that the formalization helps us to understand better and to ask pertinent questions. Here, we choose to do nothing, anticipating that the numbers will be generated automatically (by scanning at the checkout counter) or will be adjusted manually by workers who check for consistency.

Properties

In essence, we can think of the "properties" of an object set as the relationship sets either immediately attached to an object set or inherited from a generalization. (See the exercises in Chapter 7 for an explanation about exactly what we mean by properties.) Further, taking only a little liberty with the formal idea of a property, we can think of the properties of an object set as the object sets associated with these immediate and inherited relationship sets. Thus, for example, some of the properties of *Item* are *Price*, *Item Nr*, *Make*, *Model*, and *Distributor*.

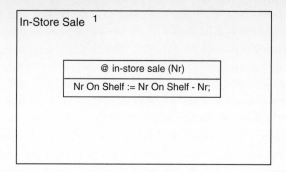

Figure 8.18   State net for *In-Store Sale*.

As a last example before we consider interface specifications and continue our discussion of default state net interaction formalization, we consider the *delete* interaction for *Item* in Fig. 8.1a. Deletion is particularly interesting because it is not always immediately clear that a deletion should even be allowed, and if allowed, what its extent should be. By considering the constraints in the ORM diagram in Figs. 7.21 and 7.22, however, we can answer these questions. For item deletion, we can see by the one-to-one binary constraints that we should also delete the item number (which must exist) and the item's inventory history and picture (if they exist). The one-to-one constraint with *Make* and *Model Number*, however, is not so simple because either the make or the model number might be associated with some other item. This is also the case for all other properties of *Item*. Except for its *Order*, *Backorder*, *Department*, and *Distributor* properties, we also wish to delete all the item's properties when the only association to them is with the item we are deleting. We must, for example, delete the price *p* of the deleted item if *p* is not the price of any other item. For *Department*, the deletion of an item may cause the number of items in a depart-

Stock Shelf [1] **includes**;

> @ *stock shelf from back room* (*Nr*: *Positive Integer*) **then**
> > *Nr On Shelf* := *Nr On Shelf* + *Nr*;
> > *Nr In Back Room* := *Nr In Back Room* − *Nr*;
> **end**;

end;

Figure 8.19   State net for *Stock Shelf*.

ment to drop below the minimum of 10. In this case, we cannot delete the item and maintain the constraint, so we should not do the deletion. For *Order* and *Backorder*, we may cause problems either with filling orders or handling backorders, and thus if there are any orders or backorders that include the item, we should not make the deletion. Similarly, we should not delete the item if it is currently on order from a distributor.

Taking these considerations into account, Fig. 8.20 shows the formalization of the *delete* interaction. The formal specification of *Item Deletion* here is lengthy and intricate. Fortunately, use of an interface specification as discussed in the next section provides an easier way.

Item Deletion [1] **includes**

> @ *delete item* (*nr*: *Item Nr*) **then**
>
>> -- *let i represent the item to be deleted*
>> *i*: *Item*;
>> *i* := *Item Nr*(*nr*). *Item*;
>>
>> -- *make a set of items in the same department as the*
>>   *item being deleted*
>> *item set*: *Item*;
>> *item set*(*x*) :− *Item*(*x*), *Item*(*y*) *has Item Nr*(*nr*), *Item*(*y*) *is in*
>>   *Department*(*z*),
>> *Item*(*x*) *is in Department*(*z*);
>>
>> -- *don't delete item if there is an outstanding order for the item*
>> -- *or if there is an outstanding backorder for the item*
>> -- *or if there is an order from a distributor for the item*
>> -- *or if there would be less than 10 items left in its department*
>> -- *or if there is a backorder associated with the distributor of*
>> --   *the item, if the distributor would be removed*
>> **if not**(**exists** *x* (*Item Nr*(*nr*). *Order*(*x*))
>>   **or exists** *x* (*Item Nr*(*nr*). *Backorder*(*x*))
>>   **or exists** *x* (*Item Nr*(*nr*). *Stock Order Date*(*x*))
>>   **or** | *item set* | ≤ 10
>>   **or** (| *i*. *Distributor*. *Backorder was*
>>   *backordered from Distributor* | ≥ 1 **and**
>> | *Item is obtained from Distributor*(*i*. *Distributor*) | = 1))
>>   **then**
>>
>>> -- *remove property values of item i, but only if they*
>>> -- *are not attached to some other item.*

Figure 8.20   State net for item deletion.

if | *Item has Amt This Month*(*i. Amt This Month*) | = 1 **then**
  remove *i. Amt This Month*;
if | *Item has Nr On Hand*(*i. Nr On Hand*) | = 1 **then**
  remove *i. Nr On Hand*;
if | *Item has Nr On Shelf*(*i. Nr On Shelf*) | = 1 **then**
  remove *i. Nr On Shelf*;
if | *Item has Nr In Back Room*(*i. Nr In Back Room*) | = 1 **then**
  remove *i. Nr In Back Room*;
if | *Item has Cost*(*i. Cost*) | = 1 **then**
  remove *i. Cost*;
if | *Item has Price*(*i. Price*) | = 1 **then**
  remove *i. Price*;
if | *Item has Item Name*(*i. Item Name*) | = 1 **then**
  remove *i. Item Name*;
if | *Item has Description*(*i. Description*) | = 1 **then**
  remove *i. Description*;
if | *Item is obtained from Distributor*(*i. Distributor*) | = 1 **then**
  remove *i. Distributor Name*;
  remove *i. Distributor Address*;
  remove *i. Distributor*;
if | *Item has Threshold*(*i. Threshold*) | = 1 **then**
  remove *i. Threshold*;

-- *remove the make, but only if it is not the make*
-- *for some other item*
Item(*x*) *has Make*(*y*) : −
  Make(*y*) *and Model Nr*(*z*) *identify Item*(*i*),
  Make(*y*) *and Model Nr*(*w*) *identify Item*(*x*);
if | *Item has Make* | = 1 **then**
  remove *i. Make*;

-- *remove the model number, but only if it is not the model*
-- *number for some other item*
Item(*x*) *has Model Nr*(*y*) : −
  Make(*z*) *and Model Nr*(*y*) *identify Item*(*i*),
  Make(*w*) *and Model Nr*(*y*) *identify Item*(*x*);
if | *Item has Make* | = 1 **then**
  remove *i. Model Nr*;

-- *remove the inventory history and inventory history records*
-- *for the item (if any), and remove the months and amounts*

Figure 8.20 (cont.)   State net for item deletion.

-- *sold for the item, but only if these months and amounts*
-- *sold do not pertain to another item*
for each *i. Month*(*m*) **do**
    if | *Month*(*m*) *is subpart of*
            Inventory History Record | = 1 **then**
        remove *m*;
    end;
for each *i. Amount Sold*(*a*) **do**
    if | *Amount Sold*(*a*) *is subpart of*
            Inventory History Record | = 1 **then**
        remove *a*;
remove *i. Inventory History Record*;
remove *i. Inventory History*;

-- *remove the picture (if any), the item number, and*
-- *finally, the item itself*
remove *i. Picture*;
remove *i. Item Nr*;
remove *Item*(*i*);

    end;

    end;

end;

Figure 8.20 (cont.) State net for item deletion.

8.4   Interface Specification

OSM interface specifications have three purposes:

1. They provide a higher level, simpler, and more direct formalization of individual deletion, insertion, modification, and retrieval interactions that cross the automation boundary.

2. They provide a way to group boundary-crossing interactions together into a logical interface activity.

3. They provide a way to match external user actions and inputs with internal events and values.

Our interface specifications do not provide the "look and feel" characteristics of end-user interfaces. Development of end-user interfaces is a separate activity that normally should be done with a user-interface management system. Since interface development is a broad topic, enough by itself to fill an entire book and more, we do not include it as part of this text.

8.4.1 Insertion Interactions

Figure 8.21 presents an example that formalizes the interaction in Fig. 8.1a that adds an item. The formalization has the appearance of an ordinary business form and is much more intuitive and straightforward than its formalization in OSM-L in Fig. 8.22. The two, however, are equivalent.

```
                              @ add item
                                (add)


Item _____ (new)


Item Nr _____ (new)              Item Name _____


Make _____                       Model Nr _____


Description _____                Picture _____ (optional)


Retail Price _____              Wholesale Cost _____


Nr In Back Room _____           Nr On Shelf _____


Nr On Hand _____ ( = Nr In Back Room +
    Nr On Shelf)


Amt This Month 0                  Threshold _____


Department _____ (connect only)


Distributor Name _____ (connect only)
```

Figure 8.21 Interface specification for item insertion.

Item Insertion [1] **includes**

> @ *add item* (*itemNr*: *String*, *itemName*: *String*,
>> *make*: *String*, *modelNr*: *String*, *description*: *String*,
>> *picture*: *Image*, *retailPrice*: *US$*, *wholesaleCost*: *US$*,
>> *nrInBackRoom*: *Nonnegative Integer*,
>> *nrOnShelf*: *Nonnegative Integer*,
>> *threshold*: *Nonnegative Integer*, *department*: *Department*,
>> *distributorName*: *Distributor Name*) **then**

> *newItem*: *Item*;
>
> **add** *Item*(*newItem*);
>
> **if** *Item Nr* (*itemNr*) **then** ≪ *error* ≫
>
> **else add** *Item*(*newItem*) *has Item Nr*(*itemNr*) **end**;
>
> **add** *Item*(*newItem*) *has Item Name*(*itemName*):
>
> **add** *Make*(*make*) *and Model Nr*(*modelNr*) *identify Item*(*newItem*);
>
> **add** *Item*(*newItem*) *has Description*(*description*);
>
> **if exists** *x* (*picture*(*x*)) **then**
>> **add** *Item*(*newItem*) *has Picture*(*picture*);
>> **end**;
>
> **add** *Item*(*newItem*) *has Retail Price*(*retailPrice*);
>
> **add** *Item*(*newItem*) *has Wholesale Cost*(*wholesaleCost*);
>
> **add** *Item*(*newItem*) *has Nr In Back Room*(*nrInBackRoom*);
>
> **add** *Item*(*newItem*) *has Nr On Shelf*(*nrOnShelf*);
>
> **add** *Item*(*newItem*) *has Nr On Hand*(*nrInBackRoom* + *nrOnShelf*);
>
> **add** *Item*(*newItem*) *has Amt This Month*(0);
>
> **add** *Item*(*newItem*) *has Threshold*(*threshold*);
>
> **add** *Item*(*newItem*) *has Department*(*department*);
>
> **add** *Item*(*newItem*) *is obtained from Distributor*(*distributor*)
>> **where** *Distributor*(*distributor*) *has Distributor*
>>> *Name*(*distributorName*);

> **end**;

end;

Figure 8.22 Formal specification for item insertion.

We explain the equivalence of the high-level interface specification in Fig. 8.21 and the low-level interface specification in Fig. 8.22 by describing how we can generate the formal specification in Fig. 8.22 from the specification in Fig. 8.21 automatically. The first entry on the form is the interaction name—note, by the way, that we have changed the name of the interaction from *add* as given in Fig. 8.1 to *add item* as given in Figs. 8.21 and 8.22. The second entry tells what kind of form it is by giving the default command for each field. Here, **add** is the default command assumed to apply to each field with no command. As we shall see, the only default field commands for our forms are **add** and **remove**, which designate the built-in OSM-L interactions **add** and **remove**; **modify**, which designates the OSM-L assignment statement; **input** and **output**, which designate the input and output parameters for two-way interactions; and **keep**, which is the complement of **remove** in a deletion context.

The fields follow the form heading. There are 16 fields in the form in Fig. 8.21, another change from the original in Fig. 8.1a because we have recognized in our formalization that more information is needed. Field names must match object-set names in the application model. Fields may have commands and command modifiers, which determine how to generate the OSM-L formalism. Fields with no modifier have only the default **add** command. For each field f, if the corresponding object set is lexical and the field does not have a given value (e.g., *Amt This Month* has the given value 0) or an expression to compute a value (e.g., *Nr On Hand* can be computed), we include a parameter $x: G$, where x is a local variable name and G is a generalization. If f is modified by **connect only**, G is the object set corresonding to f; otherwise G is the object set corresponding to f is an immediate parent generalization object set of x. The variable names can be chosen arbitrarily, but we have made them mnemonic for our example by using object-set names, except that the initial letter is lowercase and blanks have been elided. The generalizations must be part of the application model—*String* for lexical object sets unless there is a more specific designation such as *US$* or *Positive Integer*. We have taken the liberty of assuming that, in addition to all specifically given specifications earlier, we also have more specific designations for *Wholesale Cost*, *Nr On Shelf*, and *Threshold*.

For each field with no modifier, we include an **add** statement that helps build the connections needed to satisfy the interaction. These connections come from the relationship sets in the application model, that is, those that connect the object sets for the fields in the form. We must have a starting place, however, for inserting objects and building connections. A **new** modifier provides a starting place.

The **new** modifier requires a new object for the field. In Fig. 8.21, **new** modifies the fields *Item* and *ItemNr*, and thus there must be a new item and item number added according to this specification. For new, nonlexical fields, there is an **add** statement with a declared but uninitialized variable. The first two statements in the transition in Fig. 8.22,

newItem: *Item*;
add *Item*(*newItem*);

show what is generated for the *Item* field in Fig. 8.21. The informal specification <<*error*>> is still incomplete here. To complete it, we would need to add further detailed specification. For new, lexical fields, we make sure that the item does not exist and then add it as follows:

> **if** Item Nr(itemNr) **then** <<error>>
> **else add** Item(newItem) has Item Nr(itemNr);

An **optional** modifier means that a value need not be present. Thus the generated specification includes an **if** statement for each optional field to add a value, but only if one is provided. For the *Picture* field in Fig. 8.21, we generate the code

> **if exists** x $(picture(x))$ **then**
> > **add** *Item(newItem) has Picture(picture)*;
> **end**;

Finally, a **connect only** modifier means that the value must already exist in the object set with which the field is associated. As stated, the object set for the input parameter for these fields is not a generalization, but is the object set itself. Since interactions check every input parameter automatically to see whether it is in the designated set, we get an automatic check for existence for connect-only values. As for <<*error*>>, we need further detail to handle these errors. In fact, we really need transaction processing, but we stop short here because we do not discuss transaction processing in OSM-L until Chapter 11.

8.4.2 Retrieval Interactions

Figure 8.23 shows an example that formalizes the interaction in Fig. 8.1a that obtains the order information for a customer. Again, the formalization has the appearance of an ordinary business form and is much more intuitive and straightforward than the equivalent formalization in OSM-L (see Fig. 8.24).

Retrieval interactions are queries. From the given input, we must provide the requested output. As with dot queries, we take the shortest path from input to output, and we require that the paths be unambiguous. We could compute each field independently, but this could easily prevent objects from being grouped naturally into tables and nested tables. We therefore allow and support grouping.

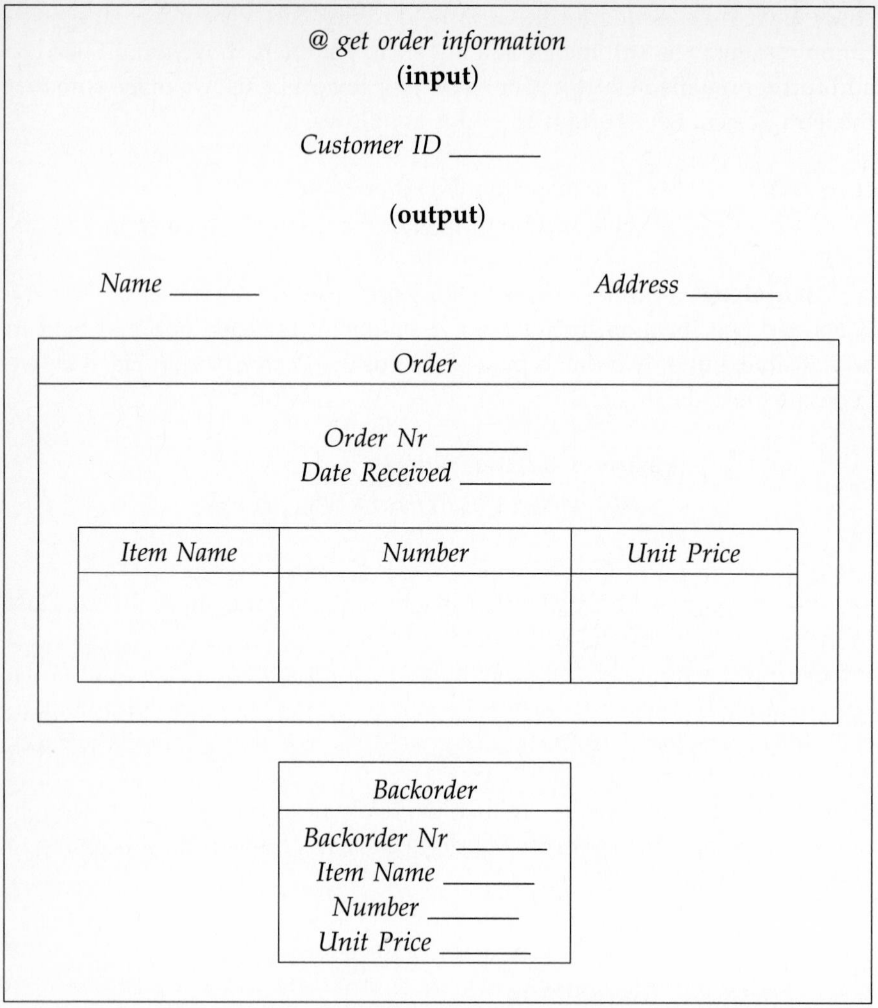

@ *get order information*
(input)

Customer ID _____

(output)

Name _____   *Address* _____

Order

Order Nr _____
Date Received _____

Item Name	Number	Unit Price

Backorder
Backorder Nr _____
Item Name _____
Number _____
Unit Price _____

Figure 8.23   Interface specification for obtaining order information.

With these principles in mind, we interpret a form as follows. A retrieval interaction is a two-way interaction, with input parameters for each field in the **input** section and output parameters for each field in the **output** section. The output fields, however, may be grouped by giving multiple-entry specifications. An example in Fig. 8.23 is the grouping subfield inside *Order* that groups multiple entries for *Item Name*, *Number*, and *Unit Price*. *Order* and *Backorder* are both degenerate multiple-entry groups in the sense that there is only one repeating field—the order itself and the back-

Order Information Retrieval [1] **includes**

> @ *get order information (customerID: Customer ID)* →
>> *(name: Name, address: Address,*
>>> *orderInformation: Order and Order Nr and Date Received and*
>>>> *Item Name and Number and Unit Price relationship set,*
>>> *backorderInformation: Backorder and Backorder Nr and Item Name*
>>>> *and Number and Unit Price relationship set*
>>) **then**
>> *name* := *customerID. Name;*
>> *address* := *customerID. Address;*
>> *orderInformation(order, orderNr, dateReceived, itemName, number,*
>>> *unitPrice)* : −
>> *Customer ID(customerID) identifies Customer(x1),*
>> *Customer(x1) has Order(order),*
>> *Order Nr(orderNr) identifies Order(order),*
>> *Order(x1) was received on Date Received(dateReceived),*
>> *Order(x1) includes Number(number) of Item(x2) at*
>>> *Unit Price(unitPrice),*
>> *Item(x2) has Item Name(itemName);*
>> *backorderInformation(backorder, backorderNr, itemName, number,*
>>> *unitPrice)* : −
>> *Customer ID(customerID) identifies Customer(x1),*
>> *Customer(x1) has Backorder(backorder),*
>> *Backorder(backorder) includes Number(number) of Item(x2) at*
>>> *Unit Price(unitPrice),*
>> *Item(x2) has Item Name(itemName);*
> **end**;

end;

Figure 8.24   Formal specification for obtaining order information.

order itself. We also see that within a multiple-entry field, we may specify a subform. Thus, for example, an *Order* may repeat many times, and each *Order* has an *Order Nr*, a *Date Received*, and a multiple-entry group consisting of *Item Name*, *Number*, and *Unit Price*.

To retrieve the information for a top-level, multiple-entry group, we join all lower fields together to form a single high-level relationship set and return it. Sometimes this does not give the results wanted, however, because there may be embedded optional items, which may cause the join to be empty even though there are higher level items. For example, we allow an order to be empty in the sense that no items may be ordered for the order. (The participation constraints on *Order* in Fig. 8.16 allow this possibility.) In this case the fields *Item Name*, *Number*, and *Unit Price* are all empty, and the join would fail to return the *Order Nr* and *Date Received*. If this is not what we want, we must write the formal specification using OSM-L.

8.4.3 Deletion Interactions

Figure 8.25 provides an example that formalizes the interaction in Fig. 8.1a to delete an item. Again, the formalization is much more intuitive and straightforward. The equivalent formalization in OSM-L was given in Fig. 8.20.

Like a retrieval query, the **input** along with the **remove** part identifies the objects to be removed (unconditionally). The **optional** modifier on *Picture* in Fig. 8.25 means that there may be no object to delete. Beyond the

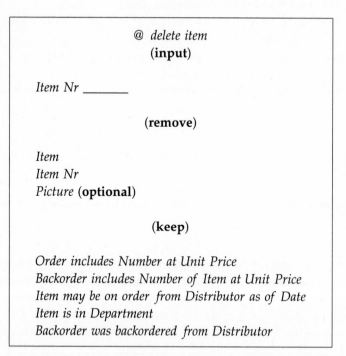

@ delete item
(input)

Item Nr _____

(remove)

Item
Item Nr
Picture **(optional)**

(keep)

Order includes Number at Unit Price
Backorder includes Number of Item at Unit Price
Item may be on order from Distributor as of Date
Item is in Department
Backorder was backordered from Distributor

Figure 8.25 Interface specification for deleting item information.

```
┌─────────────────────────────────┐
│  @  change employee address     │
│            (input)              │
│                                 │
│     SSN _____                │
│                                 │
│          (modify)               │
│                                 │
│     Address _____            │
└─────────────────────────────────┘
```

Figure 8.26 Interface specification for changing an employee address.

initial deletion, the main question to ask is how far to propagate the deletion. We give the extent of the deletion by listing in the **keep** part of the specification the relationship sets to be kept. No relationship in a relationship set in the **keep** part may be deleted. All other relationships connected to removed items are removed; in addition, all connecting objects that may no longer satisfy constraints are removed. This removal continues along a path until the end of the path is reached or until a relationship set in the **keep** part is reached.

8.4.4 Modification Interactions

Figure 8.26 presents an example that formalizes the interaction in Fig. 8.1a that changes the address for an employee; Fig. 8.27 shows the OSM-L formalization. The difference in complexity between the interface form and the OSM-L formalization is less dramatic here than in the other examples. Nevertheless, the interaction form has a nice intuitive appeal.

Employee Address Change [1] **includes**

    @ *change employee address*(*sSN*: *SSN*, *address*: *String*) **then**
        sSN. *Address* := *address*;
    end;

end;

Figure 8.27 Formal specification for changing an employee address.

Semiautomatic Generation of Interface Forms from Informal and Incomplete Interactions

Because of the correspondence between an ORM diagram and an update or retrieval interaction, it should be largely possible to generate an interface form from a given informal and incomplete boundary-crossing interaction. For example, we can generate the retrieval form in Fig. 8.23 from the ORM diagram in Fig. 8.16 automatically, as follows. If we specify that *Customer ID* is the input, then we can generate fields for the lexical object sets by observing the cardinality constraints. We know, for example, that there is only one *Name* and *Address*; that there can be many orders, each of which has one *Order Nr* and one *Date Received*; and that for each order there are zero or more items, each of which has an *Item Name*, *Number*, and *Unit Price*. We can continue following paths in this way and generate a form. What we do not know automatically, is when to stop. Thus, if a user indicates the end in some way, such as by marking the object sets to be displayed or the relationship-set paths that should not be taken, then starting with the given user input, we can generate an interface form automatically.

8.5 Chapter Summary

Topic Summary

- Adding formalism to an application model provides precision. Tunable formalism allows developers and clients to tune the amount of formalism and thus the amount of precision in a specification to suit the needs of an application.

- OSM-L is a model-equivalent language that allows us to specify any OSM application model fully. Some features of OSM-L are unique, such as having variables and types based on object sets. Other features, such as control structures, local and global declarations, assignment statements, and procedure calls, make OSM-L look much like an ordinary programming language. Direct "execution" of OSM-L provides a way to simulate a functioning OSM application model.

- An automation boundary marks the line between an automated software system and the system's environment. Only interactions cross the system automation boundary. These boundary-crossing interactions specify the interface between the automated system and its environment.

- When part of an object's behavior is inside the automation boundary and part is outside, we use the process of mitosis to split the behavior into inside and outside behavior, connected by boundary-crossing interactions.

- Interface forms facilitate the specification of boundary-crossing interactions. The familiar two-dimensional layout of a form whose fields are to be filled makes it easy to see what values pass in and out of the system to satisfy an interaction. The statement of function—insertion, deletion, modification, retrieval—and the field information make it largely possible to generate a detailed OSM-L specification automatically for these update and query boundary-crossing interactions.

Question Summary

- How does the principle of tunable formalism allow us to strike a balance between practical realities and theoretical, idealistic expectations for specifications?

  Since tunable formalism lets us add formalism, ranging from entirely informal to fully formal, our specification can have whatever level of formality we wish. Furthermore, we can tune the formalism up or down for any part of our specification independent of the level of formalism for other parts. We can thus have the level of formal specification we desire for our application in general and for any aspect of our application in particular.

- What are the advantages of using a model-equivalent language as a specification language? Are there disadvantages?

  There are four advantages: (1) A model-equivalent language lets us transition smoothly from analysis to specification because we can capture an analysis application model directly in the language. The language is simply an alternative textual representation that can be used in place of a graphical representation for an application model. (2) The compact textual representation of a language scales up more easily than does the graphical representation, making it easier to add specification detail to the application model that we need for further development. (3) We can transform the textual specification, or any coherent part of the it, back into a graphical notation. This is often useful for design, as we shall see in the next three chapters, where we use a graphical notation to guide our transformations. (4) Following design, the textual representation is particularly suitable for transforming into code (see Chapter 12).

There appear to be no clear disadvantages to the use of a model-equivalent language as a specification language. As a practical matter, however, this idea is new and lacks widespread acceptance and good support tools.

- How does a formal functional specification help both raise and resolve detailed questions that must be answered about an application?

Formalization requires careful thought and rigorous documentation. As a natural byproduct of these activities, issues surface that can then be resolved and documented formally.

- How do interface-specification forms both help make a specification more readable and help ease the amount of detail that must be written for a boundary-crossing interaction?

Interface-specification forms provide a higher level of abstraction for interactions that is both more easily read and less encumbered with detail. When detail becomes overwhelming, a higher level of abstraction helps because it lets us omit some of the details. If the omitted details can be generated, as is the case for interface-specification forms, then we can work with a more readable, higher-level abstraction, and still obtain the details without having to provide them explicitly.

8.6   Bibliographic Notes

Many software engineering books include chapters on specification; see [Pressman92] as an example. [Davis90] is more specifically devoted to specification is Formal specification languages, starting with [Balzer82, Zave82] have been around for some time, but these languages have not been generally accepted and used for software specification. [Blum94] presents a succinct, comprehensive view of software development methods,

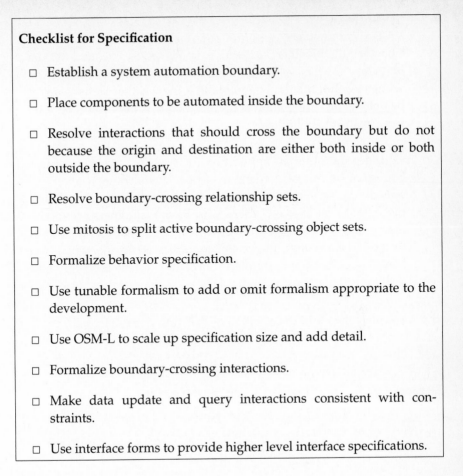

Checklist for Specification

☐ Establish a system automation boundary.

☐ Place components to be automated inside the boundary.

☐ Resolve interactions that should cross the boundary but do not because the origin and destination are either both inside or both outside the boundary.

☐ Resolve boundary-crossing relationship sets.

☐ Use mitosis to split active boundary-crossing object sets.

☐ Formalize behavior specification.

☐ Use tunable formalism to add or omit formalism appropriate to the development.

☐ Use OSM-L to scale up specification size and add detail.

☐ Formalize boundary-crossing interactions.

☐ Make data update and query interactions consistent with constraints.

☐ Use interface forms to provide higher level interface specifications.

ties conceptual and formal specification to analysis and design, and argues for a new approach to validation and verification.

Several topics in this chapter—including joint application development (JAD), interface forms, tunable formalism, mitosis, rapid prototyping, the model-equivalent language OSM-L, and interface forms—are either new or take a new twist as presented here. For a book that discusses JAD in general see [Wood95], and for an article that discusses JAD in relation to OSM see [Jackson96]. Interface forms are an outgrowth of some earlier work on forms query languages [Embley89a]. Tunable formalism [Clyde92], mitosis [Clyde93b], a method of doing rapid prototyping with OSM application models [Jackson95], and the model-equivalent language OSM-L [Liddle95] were all developed as part of the OSM research effort.

8.7   Exercises

8.1   Consider the weather application in Fig. 8.28. Create a system boundary for this application. Assume that the monitor is to be within the automation boundary, that the weather stations are to be outside the automation boundary, and that the ID numbers are to be inside the boundary.

8.2*   Consider the librarian application in Fig. 8.29. Create a system boundary by mitosis. There are to be several human librarians outside the system; they choose catalog numbers for books and place books on shelves. There is to be one automated librarian; the automated librarian receives the catalog number and stores it in the database, and also answers queries about the status of a book given its catalog number. Show the system boundary and the interactions crossing the boundary.

8.3   Translate the ORM diagram in Fig. 8.30 into OSM-L.

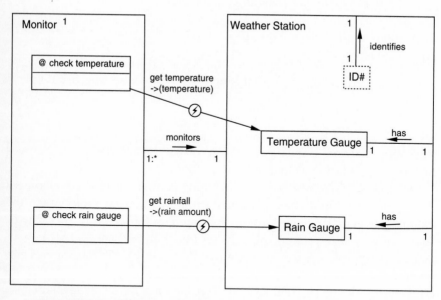

Figure 8.28   Weather application.

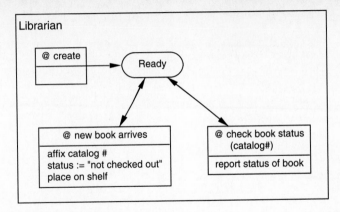

Figure 8.29 Librarian application.

8.4 Translate the following OSM-L specification into an ORM diagram. (Note: **object** specifies a "black dot.")

> **object** *On – Line Store*;
> *On – Line Store* [100: *] *offers Item* [1];
> *Item* [1] *sells* for *Price*: *String* [0: *];
> *Description*: *String* [1: *] *describes Item* [1];
> *Make* [50: 75];
> *Make* [1: *] *and Model Nr* [1: *] *identify Item* [1]
>   [*Make, Model Nr ->Item*];

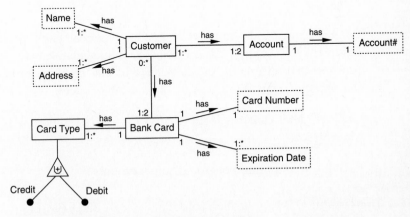

Figure 8.30 Bank-card application model.

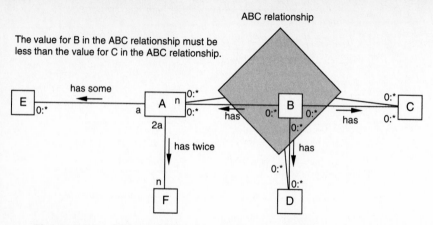

Figure 8.31 ORM diagram for converting to OSM-L.

8.5* Translate the ORM diagram in Fig. 8.31 into OSM-L. As part of the translation, formalize the general constraint.

8.6 For the bank-card application model in Fig. 8.30, write OSM-L queries to answer the following questions. Make use of dot queries where appropriate.

    a. List all expiration dates.

    b. List the names and addresses of customers who have credit cards.

    c. List the names and addresses of customers whose bank cards have expired. Assume that *Current Date* is an available built-in function that returns the current date and that there are built-in comparison operators ($<, <=, =, !=, >=, >$) for dates.

    d. Give the debit card numbers (if any) for Zed who lives at 12 Main Street.

    e. Give the account numbers for all joint accounts.

8.7 Translate the OSM application model in Fig. 8.32 into OSM-L.

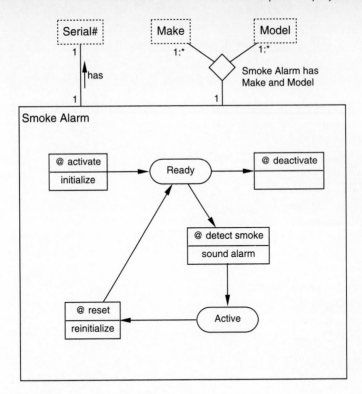

Figure 8.32 OSM application model.

8.8 Translate the following OSM-L specification to an OSM diagram.

Motion Sensor [1] **includes**

> @ *create*(*Delay Time*) **then**
>   << *set timer* >> ;
>   << *set delay* >> ;
> **enter** *Monitoring Delay*;
> **end**;

> **when** *Monitoring Delay* or *Not Monitoring Delay*
> @ *motion* **then**;
>   << *reset timer* >> ;
>   *turn on*;
> **enter** *Monitoring Delay*;
> **end**;

> **when** *Monitoring Delay*
> **if** << *delay time exceeded* >> **then**
>   *turn off;*
> **enter** *Not Monitoring Delay;*
> **end;**

end;

Automatic Light [1] **includes**

> @ *install*
> **enter** *Off;*
> **end;**

> **when** *Off*
> @ *turn on*
> **enter** *On;*
> **end;**

> **when** *On*
> @ *turn off*
> **enter** *Off*
> **end;**

end;

8.9 For the bank-card application model in Fig. 8.30, write update statements for the following. Use assignment statements where appropriate.

a. Change Pat Smith's name to Pat Jones (the Pat Smith who lives at 12 Main Street).

b. Change the expiration date for all bank cards that expire today to two years from today. Assume that *Current Date* is an available built-in function and that there are built-in date binary addition operators (+ n days, + n months, + n years).

c. Add a new customer whose name is Kelly Adams, whose address is 5 Elm Street, and whose new account has account number 12345-1.

d. Delete all information about the customer whose name is Pat Johnson and whose address is 15 Oak Street.

    e. Remove all credit cards for Jerry Blackburn.

    f. Add a debit card for the customer(s) whose account number is 55555-2. The card number is to be 48-7777-21 and the expiration date is to be two years from today. Assume built-in functions and operators as specified in Exercise 8.9b.

8.10   Translate the OSM application model in Fig. 8.33 into OSM-L.

8.11   Translate the following OSM-L code into states and transitions such that there are no textual control structures and there is at most one statement per transition.

$$N1 := 1;$$
$$N2 := 1;$$
while $N2 < 100$ **do**
    if $N2$ **mod** $2 = 0$ **then**
        output$(N2)$;
    $N3 := N1 + N2;$
    $N1 := N2;$
    $N2 := N3;$
    end;

8.12   For the bank-card application model in Fig. 8.30, write OSM-L code to check the expiration date of each bank card. If the card has expired, output the name and address of the customer with the note "expired." If the card expires within the next two weeks, output the name and address of the customer with the note "about to expire." Assume that *Current Date* is an available built-in function, that there are built-in date binary addition operators (+ n days, + n months, + n years), and that there are built-in comparison operators (<, <=, =, !=, >=, >) for dates.

8.13   Write a formal specification for the *Receiving* state net in Fig. 8.1a.

8.14   Write a formal specification for the *Inventory Controller* state net in Fig. 8.1c.

8.15   Write a formal specification for the *Inventory History Controller* state net in Fig. 8.1c.

8.16   Write a formal OSM-L specification for the *change name* interaction in Fig. 8.1d.

8.17   Give a form interface specification for the *hire worker* interaction in Fig. 8.1a.

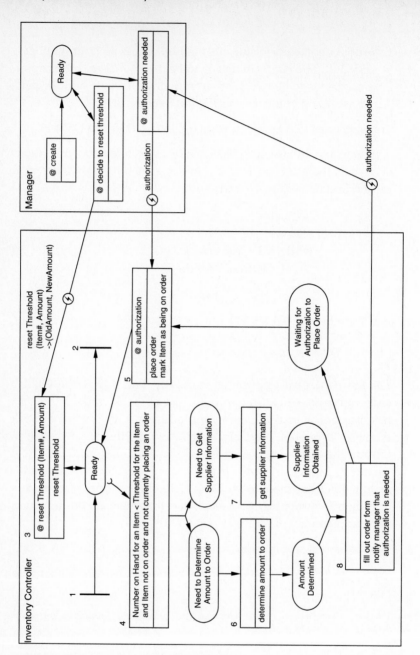

Figure 8.33 OSM application model.

8.18 For the *release worker* interaction in Fig. 8.1a, do the following:

    a. Give a form interface specification.

    b. Write a formal OSM-L specification.

8.19 Give a form interface specification for the *get item information* interaction in Fig. 8.1a.

Chapter 9

Data Design—Reduction

The purpose of design is to organize a system to achieve particular goals, such as efficiency, maintainability, extensibility, and portability. In this chapter, we focus mostly on efficiency, showing how to organize a system with the objective of reducing time and space. By "organize," we mean transform from one form into another. Thus, for us, the purpose of design is to transform a specification into a form ready for efficient implementation.

During design usually we also "discover" that our analysis or specification is not as complete or as detailed as it should be. When we discover these "shortcomings" during the design phase, we add the necessary information. We do not consider this addition of analysis and specification information during the design phase to be design, but rather additions to our analysis and specification. We view design strictly as organization, and we transform only what has been specified into a form ready for implementation. As we shall see, the product of our design is a set of object modules with scheme definitions for data and service-signature definitions for operations, along with detailed information about the implementation of the data and operations.

There are several technical dimensions to our efficiency objective of reducing time and space in design, including (1) the general time-space trade-off itself, (2) reduction of time and space with respect to data structure, data integrity, and operational behavior, and (3) designer-directed versus tool-supported optimizations:

1. When we can reduce both time and space easily, we do so unquestioningly. Often, however, we are forced into a trade-off between space and time. In such cases designers really "earn their pay"—the proper decisions often depend on many variables, including application characteristics, management objectives for the application, computing theories of what is and is not possible, and management-imposed deadlines.

421

2. Design is usually such a large task that it is necessary to focus on some smaller aspect such as data design, constraint design, function design, control design, or interaction design. By focusing on only one aspect, however, we may neglect to consider its impact on some other aspect. Ultimately, to achieve the best possible solution, we must produce a certain harmony among all aspects of design.

3. Ideally, we would like to push as many optimization decisions as possible to tool support. Optimizing compilers, for example, do a much better job of optimizing low-level operations than do programmers. On the other hand, high-level tools such as database normalizers often make improper decisions because they are blind to everything but their normalization objectives.

Given these technical dimensions, we take the following approach to design. We divide the design task roughly into data design (organizing data efficiently) and behavior design (organizing operations efficiently). We then subdivide data design further into general reduction transformations, general synthesis transformations, and several other specific transformations. In making these task divisions, we follow the long-standing tradition in database design of organizing data separately from organizing operations on the data. Further, since in database design the data-design part is by itself a large task, we subdivide it by following a common approach used in the design of relational databases—we apply reduction transformations first and then synthesize what remains into schemes that are as large as possible but do not violate basic design guidelines. We then follow these transformations by adjustments based on an application-dependent cost analysis, and we make several other transformations concerning computed data and special data types.

We discuss design reductions for data in this chapter; design synthesis and cost-analysis adjustments Chapter 10; and computed data, special data types, and behavior design in Chapter 11. Our approach is systematic and disciplined, giving algorithms and theoretical results that form a solid foundation for tool and environment support. Also, however, we explain the role of designers in resolving uncertainties and design trade-offs. As a result, we show how tools, theory, and designers can work synergistically to produce the best possible system design.

The systematic approach enhances the verification goal described in Chapter 8. If we have a formal specification, and if we can prove that every organizational transformation we do during design preserves the speci-

---

Relational Dependency Theory

The reader who already understands relational dependency theory should see that this chapter presents that theory from an interesting perspective, a graphical one. This perspective ties relational dependency theory directly to ORM diagrams. Even more important, however, we do *not* make the usual assumptions about having a universal-relation scheme, and we do *not* assume that somehow all functional, multivalued, and join dependencies are given initially. We prefer instead to work from the information given in an ORM diagram, without requiring that the diagram satisfy the universal-relation-scheme assumption and without assuming that developers have provided any dependencies consciously. We derive dependencies from what is written. Thus an analyst's task is to capture the application faithfully as an OSM application model, not to specify the functional, multivalued, and join dependencies.

---

fication, then we can verify that our design meets the specification. A number of these organizational transformations are presented, along with explanations of why each of them preserves the semantics of the specification.

Turning now to data design, we first give a brief overview of the topics in this chapter. Since we are focusing on data, all our organizational transformations are ORM transformations (transformations on OSM's Object-Relationship Model). We begin by discussing the correspondence between ORMs and functional and nonfunctional relationships. We then introduce one of our reduction transformations and use it as a motivational example for the next section, in which we discuss the theory of functional dependencies. We then describe the remaining reduction transformations.

The following topics in this chapter are particularly important:

- The correspondence between ORM diagrams and ORM hypergraphs.

- Definitions for functional dependencies, the closure of a set of functional dependencies, and the closure of a set of attributes with respect to a set of functional dependencies.

- The direct correspondence between a directed hypergraph and a set of functional dependencies.

- The direct correspondence between derivation sequences and functional closure for a set of object sets in an ORM hypergraph.

- Reductions: tail reduction, head reduction, edge-component consolidation, lexicalization, and nonfunctional edge reduction.

- Properly embedded functional dependencies.

The following questions should also be kept in mind:

- How do we ensure that a transformation preserves information?

- How do we ensure that a transformation preserves constraints?

- How do relevant edge sets and roles help resolve questions about semantic equivalence?

- How do reductions relate to changes in the underlying model-theoretic database view?

- Why do properly embedded, functional-edge reductions require a high-level relationship set with a functional dependency?

- In what sense can we view reduction transformations as patterns for design?

9.1   Hypergraphs

Our first task is to extract the features of interest from an ORM diagram. For the most part, we are interested in cardinality constraints, particularly participation and co-occurrence constraints. We ignore general constraints, except to carry them along as they are, and thus any general constraint that can be expressed as a participation or co-occurrence constraint should be expressed that way. We present and work with these features of interest in the form of a hypergraph, which we introduce next.

A *graph* consists of two sets, a set of vertices V and a set of edges E. In its simplest form (which disallows loops and parallel edges), an edge $e \in E$ is a two-element set of V. Like a graph, a *hypergraph* consists of two sets, a set of vertices V and a set of edges E. However, an edge $e \in E$ is a subset of V with two or more elements. As for graphs, this defines only the simplest type of hypergraph, one without loops and parallel edges.

The reason we need hypergraphs, rather than just graphs, is to accommodate *n*-ary relationship sets in ORM diagrams. If there are no recursive relationship sets and no two relationship sets connecting the same object sets, we can convert the object and relationship sets of any ORM diagram to a hypergraph immediately—the object sets are the vertices of the hypergraph and the relationship sets are the edges. We can remove recursive relationship sets easily, by requiring all, except possibly one, of the connections of a relationship set to an object set to have a role name. We therefore accept this restriction and do not concern ourselves further with recursive relationship sets. We must allow, however, for multiple edges that connect the same group of object sets because occasionally we do have different relationship sets that connect the same object sets. We do so in the same way we allow for parallel edges in ordinary graphs—by adding labels to the the sets of vertices that would otherwise be ambiguous.

Similar to the concept of a *directed graph* or *digraph*, in which the edge set E is a set of ordered pairs of vertices, we also have *directed hypergraphs*. Of course, we must generalize this idea for edges with more than two vertices. We do so by dividing the sets of vertices into tails and heads. For a directed hyperedge, there can be multiple tails, multiple heads, or both multiple tails and multiple heads.

To accommodate multiple edges with the same set of vertices and to accommodate directed edges, we augment our notion of a hypergraph as follows. A *generalized hypergraph* consists of two sets, a nonempty set of vertices V and a set of edges E. An edge e in E has one of the three following forms:

$$n: v_1, \cdots v_n$$

or

$$n: v_1, \ldots, v_n \to v_{n+1}, \ldots, v_m$$

or

$$n: v_1, \ldots, v_n \leftrightarrow v_{n+1}, \ldots, v_m$$

where n names the edge and may be omitted if not needed to distinguish among edges that connect the same object sets, and where $v_1, \ldots, v_n, \ldots, v_m$ are unique vertices of V. Some edges are not directed (no arrow), some are (singly) directed (one-way arrow), and some are bidirectional (two-way arrow). A bidirectional edge is merely a notational convenience, denoting two one-directional edges, one in each direction.

Based on the idea of a generalized hypergraph, we define a *generalized hypergraph for an ORM of an application model M* to be a generalized hypergraph in which the vertices are the object sets of M and the edges are relationship sets of M. An *ORM hypergraph*, which is what we want, is a generalized hypergraph for an ORM of an application-model M with three additions:

1. We distinguish the vertices as lexical or nonlexical, as they are in *M*.

2. We mark the vertex v of an edge e with an "O" as being *optional* if the objects in the object set represented by v need not participate in a relationship of the relationship set represented by e, that is, if there is a zero-minimum participation constraint for the connection between v and e.

3. We add the *isa* connections of *M* to the generalized hypergraph to express subset/superset, union, intersection, mutual-exclusion, and partition constraints.

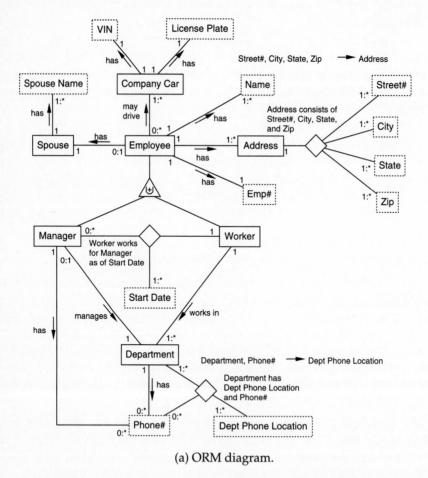

(a) ORM diagram.

Figure 9.1 ORM diagram and corresponding ORM hypergraph.

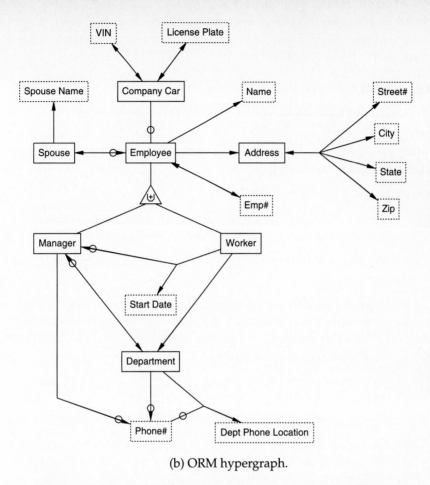

(b) ORM hypergraph.

Figure 9.1 (cont.) ORM diagram and corresponding ORM hypergraph.

We draw an ORM hypergraph for an application model M by replacing each relationship set of M with directed, bidirected, or nondirected edges with optional specifications, if needed. We discard all participation constraints and co-occurrence constraints; usually we also discard names for relationship sets; and sometimes we discard general constraints. Figure 9.1 presents an example. Figure 9.1a is an ORM diagram, while Fig. 9.1b is the ORM hypergraph for the ORM diagram in Fig. 9.1a.

In general, we obtain an ORM hypergraph from an ORM diagram according to Algorithm 9.1. The input to Algorithm 9.1 requires an ORM application model with no templates and whose only participation constraints are *0:*, *0:1*, *1:1*, *1*, and *1:*, and whose co-occurrence constraints all have default cardinality constraints, namely *1*. This does not restrict the

possible application models in any way, but it does require some preprocessing. In particular, if there are templates such as aggregations or roles,
we transform these templates into their basic ORM components. If there

Algorithm 9.1

Input: an ORM application model M with no templates and whose only
participation constraints are $0{:}*$, $0{:}1$, $1{:}1$, 1, and $1{:}*$, and whose co-
occurrence constraints all have the cardinality constraint 1, which is the
default cardinality constraint.

Output: an ORM hypergraph H.

1. The vertices of H are the object sets of M, including information
   about whether the object set is lexical or nonlexical.

2. For each relationship set r of M, generate one or more edges of H, as
   follows:

   2.1. For each connection with a participation constraint that allows a
        maximum of one (i.e., for 1, $1{:}1$, and $0{:}1$), add a directed edge
        whose tail is the object set for the connection and whose head(s)
        are all the other object sets of r.

   2.2. For each co-occurrence constraint $A_1, ..., A_p \rightarrow B_1, ..., B_q$ associ-
        ated with r, add a directed edge whose tail(s) are the object sets
        $A_1, ..., A_p$ and whose head(s) are the object sets $B_1, ..., B_q$.

   2.3. As a notational simplification, we may replace any pair of
        directed edges $A_1, ..., A_p \rightarrow B_1, ..., B_q$ and $B_1, ..., B_q \rightarrow A_1, ..., A_p$
        with a single bidirected edge $A_1, ..., A_p \leftrightarrow B_1, ..., B_q$.

   2.4. If no edge has been generated that includes *all* object sets of r,
        add a nondirected edge connecting every object set in r. (Note
        that in Step 2.2 one or more edges for an n-ary relationship set r
        of degree less than n may have been generated. Step 2.4 applies
        unless an n-ary edge—one connecting *every one* of the n object
        sets of r—has been generated.)

3. Mark any edge connection that has optional participation (i.e., one
   whose participation constraint has a zero-minimum, either $0{:}*$ or $0{:}1$)
   with an "O."

4. Retain generalization/specialization declarations and generaliza-
   tion/specialization constraints as they are, as well as any other
   general constraints.

Potential Ambiguity between Heads and Tails

When we draw a bidirectional edge in an ORM hypergraph that has multiple heads or tails, we can create an ambiguity. Since this is merely a convenient shorthand, we can avoid the ambiguity if we do not superimpose the edges. Alternatively, we can superimpose the edges, but ensure that we always make a small enough acute angle spanning all heads for one directed edge (tails for the other) so that the angle clearly marks a group. In Fig. 9.1b, for example, *Street#*, *City*, *State*, and *Zip* clearly form a group in the bidirectional edge between these object sets and *Address*. Note that this ambiguity occurs only in a drawing. In the underlying semantics, we simply record the two directed edges.

---

are participation constraints or co-occurrence constraints not of the required form, we translate them into general constraints according to the derivation for application-model rules presented in Chapter 6, and we replace any translated participation constraints with *0:*.

We obtained the ORM hypergraph in Fig. 9.1b from the ORM application model in Fig. 9.1a by using Algorithm 9.1. In Step 1 we obtained all the vertices, which are the object sets of the application model. In Step 2.1 we added one or two directed edges for every relationship set except for the relationship sets *Employee may drive Company Car* and *Department has Dept Phone Location and Phone#*. For example, in Step 2.1 we obtained the directed edge from *Worker* to *Department* because of the *1* participation constraint on *Worker*. For most of the relationship sets we added only one directed edge, but for the relationship sets *Company Car has VIN*, *Company Car has license Plate*, *Employee has Emp#*, and *Manager manages Department*, we added two directed edges. In Step 2.2 we added directed edges for the two co-occurrence constraints, resulting in one directed edge for *Department has Dept Phone Location and Phone#* and a second directed edge for *Address consists of Street#, City, State, and Zip*. In Step 2.3 we created bidirectional edges for all the relationship sets with two directed edges. The edge between *Employee* and *Emp#* in Fig. 9.1b, for example, has one bidirectional edge rather than two one-directional edges. Note, by the way, that the reading-direction arrow in Fig. 9.1a has nothing to do with the direction of the edge—in general, a reading-direction arrow can point in the same direction or the opposite direction, be two-way when the edge is one-way, and be one-way when the edge is two-way. In Step 2.4 we generated the nondirected binary edge for *Employee may drive Company Car*. There are no examples in Fig. 9.1 for which we have only a partial edge generated in Step 2.2. Suppose, however, that the co-occurrence constraint for *Department has Dept Phone Location and Phone#* had been *Department → Dept Phone Location*. Then in Step 2.2 we would have generated a directed edge with only the two object sets *Department* and *Dept Phone Location*. In this case, the binary edge would not have connected all three object sets of the ternary edge. Thus in Step 2.4 we would have added a nondirected ternary edge connecting *Department*, *Phone#*, and *Dept Phone Location*. In Step 3, we added the seven O's, marking optional connections on the edges corresponding to the participation constraints with zero minimums—three on *Phone#*, two each on *Manager* and *Employee*. For Step 4, observe that the *isa* connection that makes *Employee* a partitioned generalization of *Manager* and *Worker* is left intact in Fig. 9.1b, unchanged from its appearance in Fig. 9.1a.

There are no cardinality constraints that are not of the required form, and no general constraints. Suppose that in Fig. 9.1 we had had the participation constraint *1:12* in place of *1:** in the *Employee may drive Company Car* relationship set, as well as the general constraint

> *If a worker works in a department and a manager manages that department, then the worker works for the manager as of some start date.*

Then we would have replaced the *1:12* by *0:** and added the closed formulas

$$\forall x(Company\ Car(x) \Rightarrow \exists^{\geq 1} y(Employee(y)\ may\ drive\ Company\ Car(x)))$$

and

$$\forall x(Company\ Car(x) \Rightarrow \exists^{\leq 12} y(Employee(y)\ may\ drive\ Company\ Car(x)))$$

These closed formulas are those generated for the *1:12* participation constraint as discussed in Chapter 6. Because of the zero minimum for the new *0:** participation constraint, we would have also marked the *Company Car* connection for the nondirected edge between *Employee* and *Company Car* with an "O." We would then have carried these closed formulas along with the stated informal general constraint directly into the ORM hypergraph. The stated informal constraint could have been formalized first as

$$\forall x \forall y \forall z(Worker(x)\ works\ in\ Department(y)$$
$$\land\ Manager(z)\ manages\ Department(y)$$
$$\Rightarrow \exists w(Worker(x)\ works\ for\ Manager(z)\ as\ of\ Start\ Date(w)))$$

before being carried into the ORM hypergraph.

Automatic Generation of an ORM hypergraph

As a practical matter, a tool should generate a hypergraph and all the constraints automatically. All preprocessing should also be automatic. The tool should expand any templates into their basic components and should generate closed formulas for all participation and co-occurrence constraints that are not of the required form.

9.2 Functional Dependencies

Having defined ORM hypergraphs, we are nearly ready to begin presenting our reduction transformations. First, however, we must introduce the idea of a functional dependency and show that it corresponds precisely to a directed edge in an ORM hypergraph.

Let R be the relation scheme for a relation r. Let $X \subseteq R$, and let t be a tuple in r. The *restriction* of t to X, written $t[X]$, is the projection of the tuple t onto X. For example, if we consider the relationship set *Department has Dept Phone Location and Phone#* in Fig. 9.1a, the scheme is the set of object sets {*Department, Dept Phone Location, Phone#*}, the relation is the relation in some valid interpretation, say

Department has Dept Phone Location and Phone#		
Department$_1$	*2ndFloorSWCorner*	222-2222
Department$_2$	*1stFloorCenter*	222-3333
Department$_3$	*2ndFloorSWCorner*	222-2222

and tuple t is one of the rows in the relation, say the first one (i.e., t = <*Department*$_1$, *2ndFloorSWCorner*, 222-2222>). Then, if we let X = {*Dept*

Relation Schemes

Recall that we defined a relation scheme in Chapter 2 to be a set of attributes, and we defined an attribute to be an object-set name in the name of a relationship set. Thus, when we say that R is the relation scheme for a relation r—also written $r(R)$—we are saying that R is the set of object-set names of the object sets that r connects. Furthermore, recall that we usually shorten "object-set name" to "object set" in this context and that we also often refer to an object set as an "attribute."

Phone Location, Phone#}, then $t[X]$ = <2ndFloorSWCorner, 222-2222>, and if X = {*Phone#*}, then $t[X]$ = <222-2222>, which since the tuple is degenerate we also write as 222-2222.

Let R be a relation scheme, and let $X \subseteq R$ and $Y \subseteq R$. A statement of the form $X \to Y$ is called a *functional dependency* or an *FD*. A relation r on R *satisfies* an FD $X \to Y$ (or *holds*) if for any two tuples t_1 and t_2 in r, $t_1[X]$ = $t_2[X] \Rightarrow t_1[Y]$ = $t_2[Y]$. Alternatively, $X \to Y$ holds if for every tuple x in $\pi_X r$, | $\sigma_{X=x} \pi_{XY} r$ | = 1. Here, $X = x$ means $A_1 = a_1 \wedge ... \wedge A_n = a_n$, where X = {$A_1, ..., A_n$} is a set of n object sets and x = <$a_1, ..., a_n$> is an n-element tuple.

As a matter of notational convenience, it is common in database theory to write the set {$A_1, A_2, ..., A_n$} as $A_1 A_2 \cdots A_n$. This works particularly well for generic object sets with one-letter names. If some of the object sets have more than one symbol, it is common to separate them by a space. For OSM, we may have spaces in our object-set names, so we allow ourselves to separate the object-set names by commas. (Ultimately, this may be ambiguous since we also allow commas in names, but we simply choose not to have object-set names with commas, and we rename any that do when we use them in this way.) As a further notational convenience, if X and Y both represent sets of object sets, XY denotes the union $X \cup Y$ of X and Y. For example, if $X = ABC$ and $Y = CD$, then $XY = ABCD$.

We can show that any directed edge obtained in Algorithm 9.1 is an FD. Then, since any directed edge in an ORM hypergraph is an FD, we sometimes refer to it as an FD edge or simply as an FD.

Theorem 9.1.

Let M be an ORM application model, and let H be an ORM hypergraph produced from M by Algorithm 9.1. Let $e: A_1, ..., A_n \to B_1, ..., B_m$ be a directed edge of H obtained from a relationship set R of M. Then, in any valid interpretation for M, if r is the relation for R, then the FD $A_1...A_n \to B_1...B_n$ holds in r.

9.3 Motivational Example

Before diving into functional-dependency theory, we wish to provide some motivation and an example to which we can refer while discussing FD theory. Consider the FD edge *Worker* $\to$ *Manager, Start Date* in Fig. 9.1b. We claim, and we will show eventually, that we can reduce this FD edge to *Worker* $\to$ *Start Date*. Notice that we have removed an object set from the head side of the FD, motivating the term "head reduction," which we use to refer to this particular type of ORM transformation. Notice also that this removal is equivalent to removing the head component of the FD edge in Fig. 9.1b that points to *Manager*.

When reducing, we must ensure that our transformations preserve both the information and the constraints of the application model. An ORM *transformation* is a function that maps one ORM application model M along with any interpretation for M to another application model M' along with its corresponding interpretation. An *ORM reduction transformation* is a transformation in which one or more object sets are discarded, one or more relationship sets are discarded, or part of one or more relationship sets are discarded by discarding one or more columns by projection. We show in the exercises that all of our ORM reduction transformations map ORM application models with valid interpretations to other ORM application models with valid interpretations, and we assume this throughout our discussion. A reduction transformation T from ORM application model M to ORM application model M' *preserves information* if there exists a procedure P that for any valid interpretation I_M for M computes I_M from the interpretation $I_{M'}$ for M' computed from I_M by T. To match the names, procedure P may directly use names of object sets and relationship sets in M. Furthermore, if P generates object identifiers for a nonlexical object set S that match one-to-one with object identifiers in I_M for S, we may substitute the object identifiers in I_M for their corresponding generated object identifiers. Let C be the constraints in an application model M, and let C' be the constraints in an application model M' transformed from M by some transformation T. T *preserves constraints* if C' implies C.

As an example, we claim that the head reduction that removes *Manager* from the head side of the FD edge *Worker → Manager, Start Date* in Fig. 9.1b is both information and constraint preserving. It preserves information because

Worker works for Manager as of Start Date =
$\pi_{Worker,Manager,StartDate}$(*Worker works in Department*
⋈ *Manager manages Department* ⋈ *Start Date Worker relation*)

where *Start Date Worker relation* is the name for the new head-reduced relation. (In general, we may provide new names for reduced relationship sets explicitly, but in the absence of a given name, we use the space-separated concatenation of the object-set names followed by *"relation"*, followed by a distinguishing integer 1, 2, ..., if needed to distinguish ambiguous cases. The name *Start Date Worker relation* in the expression we are discussing is an example.) This head reduction also preserves constraints. It preserves the lost FD

$$Worker \rightarrow Manager, Start\ Date$$

because three of the remaining FDs

$$Worker \rightarrow Start\ Date$$
$$Worker \rightarrow Department$$
$$Department \rightarrow Manager$$

imply the lost FD.

9.4   Functional Dependency Theory

The theory of functional dependencies allows us to make the preceding claims about information and constraint preservation for the particular head reduction we were considering. In this section, we consider the general conditions that are both necessary and sufficient for making reductions based on FDs. Among the considerations are FD implication, semantic equivalence, and roles, which we discuss in turn.

9.4.1 Functional Dependency Implication

Let R be a scheme for a relation r, and let F be a set of FDs over R, by which we mean that if an FD $X \rightarrow Y$ is in F, then $XY \subseteq R$. We say that r *satisfies* F,

---

Model Theory and Diagram Reductions

When we reduce a diagram by discarding an edge or part of an edge, we are optimizing the underlying model-theoretic view of our database. In our motivating example, when we discard the connection to *Manager* in *Worker works for Manager as of Start Date*, we are really discarding the *Manager* column for any table for any valid interpretation in our underlying model-theoretic view. If we discard an edge, we discard an entire table for any valid interpretation. To complete the optimization, we must also combine relation schemes in our underlying model-theoretic view, as addressed in Chapter 10. This chapter is basically about what we can discard, and the next is basically about what we can combine.

or alternatively that r is a *valid* relation for F, if each FD in F holds for r. Given a set of FDs F over R, there may also be FDs not in F that always hold for any relation $r(R)$ that satisfies F. We say that F *implies* an FD $X \to Y$ (whether in F or not in F) if $X \to Y$ holds for every relation that satisfies F.

For example, let R be the set of object sets A, B, C, and D, written $R = ABCD$. Let $F = \{A \to B, B \to C\}$. Then, if r is the relation

A	B	C	D
1	1	1	1
2	1	1	2
2	1	1	3
3	2	1	4

r satisfies F. We can use the definition of FDs to check this claim. For example, if we let t_1 be the first tuple and t_2 be the second tuple, then $t_1[B] = t_2[B] \Rightarrow t_1[C] = t_2[C]$ holds and thus for these tuples $B \to C$ holds. Also, $t_1[A] = t_2[A] \Rightarrow t_1[B] = t_2[B]$ holds vacuously since the left-hand side of $\Rightarrow$ is *false*, and thus for these tuples $A \to B$ holds. Similarly, the FDs of F all hold for all pairs of tuples. Even more interesting, however, the FD $A \to C$ also holds. Moreover, $A \to C$ always holds in any relation $r(R)$ that satisfies F. This is because for any two tuples t_1 and t_2 where $t_1[A] = t_2[A]$, since $A \to B$ holds, $t_1[B] = t_2[B]$ and thus since $B \to C$ holds, $t_1[C] = t_2[C]$. Hence, $A \to C$ holds. Note, therefore, that F implies not only $A \to B$ and $B \to C$, but also $A \to C$. Other FDs are also implied—$AD \to B$, for example, and $BD \to CD$ and many more. There are also many that are not implied—$B \to A$, for example, and $C \to D$.

Given a set of object sets U and a set of FDs F over U, the set of all FDs over U that are implied by F is called the *closure* of F, which we denote by F^+.

We now introduce three implication rules to derive the closure of a given set of FDs. For these rules, we assume that R is a relation scheme with $WXYZ \subseteq R$ and that the given set of FDs over R is F. Furthermore, as a common notational convenience, whenever we assert an FD $X \to Y$, we are saying that $X \to Y \in F^+$ for some set of FDs F. We use this shorthand whenever it is unclear which set of FDs is meant. Usually, however, it is clear, and we can simply assert the FD.

(trivial implication) If $Y \subseteq X$, then $X \to Y$

(accumulation) If $X \to Y$, $W \to Z$, and $W \subseteq Y$, then $X \to YZ$.

(projection) If $X \to Y$ and $Z \subseteq Y$, then $X \to Z$.

This set of FD implication rules is sound and complete. Let R be a scheme, F be a set of FDs over R, and r be a relation on R that satisfies F. A set of FD implication rules is *sound* if every FD derived by these rules holds for r and is *complete* if there is no FD that holds for every valid relation r on R that is not derived by these rules.

Theorem 9.2.

(Soundness) Trivial implication, accumulation, and projection are sound FD implication rules.

Theorem 9.3.

(Completeness) Trivial implication, accumulation, and projection constitute a complete set of FD implication rules.

Since trivial implication, accumulation, and projection are sound and complete, we can use them to derive FDs in F^+ by applying them to FDs in F and to FDs derived by these rules. A *derivation sequence* for deriving an FD $X \rightarrow Y$ from a given set of FDs F is a sequence of FDs ending with $X \rightarrow Y$ such that each FD in the sequence is either an FD in F or is derived from the FDs already in the sequence by one of the FD implication rules. For example, let $R = ABC$ and $F = \{A \rightarrow B,\ B \rightarrow C\}$; then we can derive $A \rightarrow C$ by the following derivation sequence:

1.	$A \rightarrow A$	trivial implication
2.	$A \rightarrow B$	given
3.	$A \rightarrow AB$	accumulation, 1 and 2
4.	$B \rightarrow C$	given
5.	$A \rightarrow ABC$	accumulation, 3 and 4
6.	$A \rightarrow C$	projection, 5

We almost have what we want now—a set of sound and complete FD-implication rules that we can use in a derivation sequence to determine whether a given set of FDs implies some particular FD of interest. What we need, however, is a slightly stronger result that ensures that we need apply our trivial-implication rule only once, at the beginning, and that we need apply our projection rule only once (if at all), at the end. In between, we may apply our accumulation rule as many times as we wish (or not at all). Furthermore, whenever we apply our accumulation rule, we can always apply it using a given FD as its second antecedent (i.e., using a given FD as the one whose left-hand side is a subset of the right-hand side of the other).

Observe as an example that the preceding derivation sequence has this form. The derivation sequence starts with trivial implication, ends with projection, and uses accumulation based on given FDs in between. Of course, we can move the steps that list given FDs in the derivation to the beginning. We use this form in Theorem 9.4, which guarantees that we can always find a derivation sequence that states the given FDs first, uses trivial implication next, then uses zero or more applications of accumulation based only on the given FDs, and finally uses one application of projection. We note that we may need only some, possibly none, of the given FDs and that we may not need the projection at the end. We can simplify our statement about the form of the derivation sequence, however, if we allow ourselves to add these (sometimes) redundant steps.

Theorem 9.4.

Let R be a relation scheme, and let $F = \{X_1 \rightarrow Y_1, ..., X_n \rightarrow Y_n\}$ be a given set of FDs over R. Let $X \rightarrow Y \in F^+$. Then there exists a derivation sequence for $X \rightarrow Y$ having the following pattern:

1.	$X_1 \rightarrow Y_1$	given
2.	$X_2 \rightarrow Y_2$	given
	...	
n.	$X_n \rightarrow Y_n$	given
$n+1$.	$X \rightarrow X$	trivial implication
$n+2$.	$X \rightarrow XY_{i_1}$	accumulation, $n+1$ and i_1
$n+3$.	$X \rightarrow XY_{i_1}Y_{i_2}$	accumulation, $n+2$ and i_2
	...	
$n+m$.	$X \rightarrow XY_{i_1}Y_{i_2} \cdots Y_{i_{m-1}}$	accumulation, $n+m-1$ and i_{m-1}
$n+m+1$.	$X \rightarrow Y$	projection, $n+m$

where $i_1, ..., i_{m-1}$ is a sequence of $m-1$ unique derivation-step numbers between 1 and n inclusive. We call this pattern a *TAP derivation sequence—T* because we apply trivial implication first, *A* because we apply accumulation next, and *P* because we apply projection last.

As an example, the derivation sequence we just gave for deriving $A \rightarrow C$, given $R = ABC$ and $F = \{A \rightarrow B, B \rightarrow C\}$, can be written in the precise form stated in Theorem 9.4 as follows:

1.	$A \rightarrow B$	given
2.	$B \rightarrow C$	given
3.	$A \rightarrow A$	trivial implication
4.	$A \rightarrow AB$	accumulation, 3 and 1
5.	$A \rightarrow ABC$	accumulation, 4 and 2
6.	$A \rightarrow C$	projection, 5

As a result of Theorem 9.4, observe that we can determine whether an FD $X \rightarrow Y$ is in F^+ by writing the sequence of right-hand sides

$$X$$
$$XY_{i_1}$$
$$XY_{i_1}Y_{i_2}$$
$$XY_{i_1}Y_{i_2}\cdots Y_{i_{m-1}}$$

from steps n through $n + m$. We formalize this shorthand idea as follows. Let R be a relation scheme, and let F be a set of FDs over R. Let $X \subseteq R$; then the *closure of a set of object sets X with respect to F*, denoted by X^+, is the maximal set of object sets Y such that $X \rightarrow Y$ can be derived from F by trivial implication and accumulation. This definition implies certain properties about X^+—(1) $X \rightarrow X^+$, (2) $X \subseteq X^+$, and (3) X^+ is unique. This closure definition also leads to Theorem 9.5, which finally provides us with what we need.

Theorem 9.5.

Let U be a set of object sets, and let F be a set of FDs over U. Let X and Y be subsets of U. $X \rightarrow Y \in F^+$ if and only if $Y \subseteq X^+$.

Using Theorem 9.5, we can determine whether $X \rightarrow Y$ holds in a hypergraph whose edges represent a given set of FDs F. We mark the initial vertices in X and then repeatedly mark the heads of each FD whose tails are all marked until either all the vertices in Y are marked or until no more vertices can be marked. If all the vertices in Y are marked, $X \rightarrow Y \in F^+$; otherwise, $X \rightarrow Y \notin F^+$. It should be clear that determining whether an FD is implied is equivalent to asking whether we can reach the right-hand side from the left-hand side in a directed hypergraph. For example, given

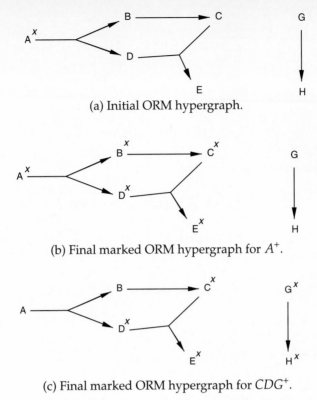

(a) Initial ORM hypergraph.

(b) Final marked ORM hypergraph for A^+.

(c) Final marked ORM hypergraph for CDG^+.

Figure 9.2   Testing FD implication using an ORM hypergraph.

$R = ABCDEGH$ and $F = \{A \to BD, B \to C, CD \to E, G \to H\}$, if we wish to test whether $A \to E \in F^+$, we start with the hypergraph in Fig. 9.2a[†] with A marked, and then proceed to mark B and D because of $A \to BD$, C because of $B \to C$, and finally E because of $CD \to E$, yielding the marked hypergraph in Fig. 9.2b. Since E is marked, $A \to E \in F^+$. Or, as another example, given the same scheme R and the same set of FDs F, if we wish to test whether $CDG \to A \in F^+$, we mark C, D, and G initially and then proceed by marking H and E. Since we can mark no more vertices and since A is not marked, as the result for this example in Fig. 9.2c shows, $CDG \to A \notin F^+$.

The same idea applies to an ORM hypergraph except that there are a few more complications, as we will discuss shortly. Suppose we are given

---

[†] In generic ORM hypergraphs (ones whose nodes or object sets are all single letters of the alphabet), when we do not care whether object sets are lexical or nonlexical, we drop the object-set box and let the object-set name alone denote the object set.

the ORM hypergraph in Fig. 9.3, which is the ORM hypergraph in Fig. 9.1b except that the hyperedge

$$Worker \rightarrow Manager, Start\ Date$$

has been reduced to

$$Worker \rightarrow Start\ Date$$

If we wish to determine whether

$$Worker \rightarrow Manager, Start\ Date$$

is implied by the ORM hypergraph in Fig. 9.3, initially we mark *Worker*, then *Start Date* and *Department* because of

$$Worker \rightarrow Start\ Date$$

and

$$Worker \rightarrow Department$$

and then *Manager* because of

$$Department \rightarrow Manager$$

Indeed, the hypergraph does imply

$$Worker \rightarrow Manager, Start\ Date$$

This gives us what we need for our transformations. In our example, we can do the head reduction by transforming the ORM hypergraph in Fig. 9.1b to the ORM hypergraph in Fig. 9.3 because the FDs

$$Worker \rightarrow Start\ Date$$
$$Worker \rightarrow Department$$
$$Department \rightarrow Manager$$

imply the FD

$$Worker \rightarrow Manager, Start\ Date$$

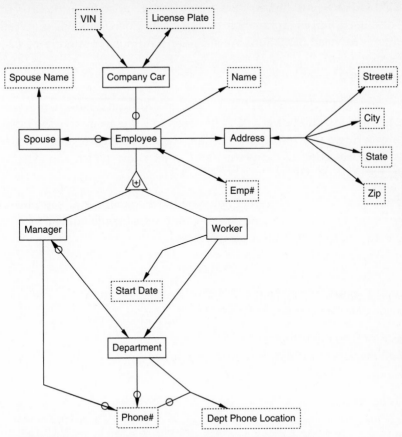

Figure 9.3 An ORM hypergraph after a head reduction.

The FD implication guarantees that there is a maximum of one manager for any worker, and thus we preserve the one-maximum constraint on the *Worker* object set in the *Worker works for Manager as of Start Date* relationship set in Fig. 9.1a. The path based on

$$Worker \rightarrow Start\ Date$$
$$Worker \rightarrow Department$$
$$Department \rightarrow Manager$$

tells us that we can preserve information based on the join

$$Start\ Date\ Worker\ relation\ \bowtie\ Worker\ works\ in\ Department$$
$$\bowtie\ Manager\ manages\ Department$$

Before discussing the complications that may arise from the procedure just discussed, let us summarize by stating the necessary FD-implication conditions for head reduction. We state our conditions as Algorithm 9.2:

Algorithm 9.2

Input: an ORM hypergraph H and a designated head connection C of a directed hyperedge D of H. (If D happens to come from an edge notationally written as a bidirectional edge, we must be clear about which one-directional edge D represents, and must know which connections are its head(s) and tail(s).)

Output: "yes" or "no", meaning yes, the head connection C can potentially be removed (pending an investigation of semantic equivalence as discussed next), or no, it cannot be removed.

Mark all the tails of the directed hyperedge D.

Remove the head connection C from hypergraph H, and if C is the only
head connection, remove D from H.

Repeat until no more changes:
If all the tails of a directed edge E are marked
mark all the heads.

If C is not marked
Output "no".
Else
Output "yes".

9.4.2 Semantic Equivalence

FD implication is necessary for head reduction and some other reductions; unfortunately, it is not sufficient. The problem is that in defining FD implication, we assumed that we were dealing with one relation scheme, with only one meaning. In general, this may not be true, particularly for ORM hypergraphs.

Consider the following example. In the ORM hypergraph in Fig. 9.3, we have *Manager* → *Department* and *Department* → *Phone#*. These FDs imply *Manager* → *Phone#*. Thus, we may think that we can do a head reduction and discard the relationship set *Manager has Phone#*. The reduction assumes that the phone number for the manager can be recovered by finding the phone number of the department the manager manages. Suppose, however, that the *Manager has Phone#* relationship set represents the home phone number of a manager, which has nothing to do with the phone number of the phone for the department the manager manages. Since there is more than one meaning for the relationships between a manager and a phone number, the assumption that the relationship among *Manager*, *Department*, and *Phone#* has only one meaning fails. Thus, since the assumption for FD implication fails, FD implication itself fails. As a consequence, if we do the reduction and discard the *Manager has Phone#* relationship set, we certainly will lose information, since there will be no way to recover the home phone number for a manager.

In general, to make a transformation information preserving, we must be sure that the relationship set or the part of the relationship set being discarded can be recomputed from the information that remains. In the phone example, the relationship set being discarded must be equivalent semantically to the projection onto *Manager Phone* of the join of the relationship sets *Manager manages Department* and *Department has Phone#*. This holds only if *Manager has Phone* denotes the phone number of the phone of the department the manager manages.

Determining semantic equivalence is sometimes easy because we may know the meaning of the relationship sets involved. Often, however, we do not know the exact meaning of relationship sets, and sometimes we may not even realize that we do not know. It is best to check with our client. Clients also may not know the exact meaning of a relationship set, however, or may perceive the meaning to be somewhat different from what it really is. Often there are subtleties that become evident only after careful scrutiny of the application model.

We continue our discussion of semantic equivalence by presenting some ways to scrutinize an application model to determine whether a reduction transformation is information preserving. The techniques we discuss include the notion of a universal relation, a universal relation with nulls, and a relevant-edge set. After this discussion, we will be able to say more precisely what we mean by semantic equivalence.

Considering our example again, along with the implicit assumption that FD implication holds when we have one relation with only one meaning, we first discuss what we must do to reconcile several relations as one. The several relations we must reconcile as one are relations in a valid interpretation that correspond to the relationship sets of interest in an application model. For our phone example, we must reconcile relations for the relationship sets *Manager manages Department*, *Department has Phone#*, and *Manager has Phone#*. Furthermore, we must reconcile relations for relationship sets not just for some valid interpretation but for all possible valid interpretations.

Reconciling several relations as one is possible if, for any valid interpretation, we can join the relations together losslessly. Let $r_1(R_1), ..., r_n(R_n)$ be relations in a valid interpretation and let $q = r_1 \bowtie ... \bowtie r_n$. If $\pi_{R_i} q = r_i$, $1 \le i \le n$, then $r_1, ..., r_n$ *join losslessly*. Further, if $r_1, ..., r_n$ join losslessly, then $q = r_1 \bowtie ... \bowtie r_n$ is said to be a *universal relation* for $r_1, ..., r_n$.

Figure 9.4 depicts three relations from a valid interpretation: a *manages* relation, a *Department has Phone#* relation, and a *Manager has Phone#* relation. If we join these three relations together, we obtain an empty relation. Thus, any projection is empty, and we cannot recover the original relations. Hence, there is no universal relation. Since we cannot reconcile these relations as one, we cannot apply our head-reduce transformation.

Figure 9.5a also shows three relations from a valid interpretation: a *manages* relation, a *works in* relation, and a *Worker works for Manager as of Start Date* relation. Figure 9.5b shows their join, which is a universal relation for the relations in Fig. 9.5a. Given this universal relation, if we project on *Manager* and *Department*, we obtain the original *manages* relation. Similarly, if we project on *Worker* and *Department*, we obtain the original *works in* relation, and if we project on *Worker*, *Manager*, and *Start Date*, we obtain the original *Worker works for Manager as of Start Date* relation. This by itself does not ensure that for any valid interpretation, the join of these three relations will always yield a universal relation, but at least we cannot use this particular interpretation as a counterexample.

When there is a universal relation for a set of relations for any valid interpretation, we say that the *universal-relation assumption* holds for these relations. When a universal relation exists for all interpretations, FD implication holds. Sometimes, however, this condition is too strong. As an example, let us consider Fig. 9.3 with a different meaning. Suppose that *Manager has Phone#* designates the manager's work phone number and that

Manager manages Department		Department has Phone#	
$Manager_1$	$Department_1$	$Department_1$	222-1111
$Manager_2$	$Department_2$	$Department_2$	222-2222

Manager has Phone#	
$Manager_1$	123-3333
$Manager_2$	123-4444

Figure 9.4 Relations with no universal relation.

Manager manages Department	
Manager$_1$	Department$_1$
Manager$_2$	Department$_2$

Worker works in Department	
Worker$_1$	Department$_1$
Worker$_2$	Department$_2$
Worker$_3$	Department$_2$

Worker works for Manager	as of Start Date	
Worker$_1$	Manager$_1$	15 Jun
Worker$_2$	Manager$_2$	15 Jun
Worker$_3$	Manager$_2$	30 Jun

(a) Three sample relations.

Manager	Department	Worker	Start Date
Manager$_1$	Department$_1$	Worker$_1$	15 Jun
Manager$_2$	Department$_2$	Worker$_2$	15 Jun
Manager$_2$	Department$_2$	Worker$_3$	30 Jun

(b) A universal relation for the three relations.

Figure 9.5   Three relations that have a universal relation.

for managers who manage departments this phone number is also the department's phone number. Bosses who manage only managers also have a work phone, but since these bosses do not manage departments, the phone numbers for these bosses are not department phone numbers. Figure 9.6a presents some possible relations for a valid interpretation. Note that the phone numbers all are now department phone numbers and that Manager$_3$ has a work phone but does not manage a department.

Beware of the "Hidden" Universal-Relation Assumption

Database theorists make the universal-relation assumption when they discuss dependency theory, often with little, if any, discussion. This "hidden" assumption often fails in practice. Thus students who understand textbook dependency theory find that they cannot apply it as practitioners. They almost never realize that it is the assumption, not the theory, that fails. Even if they happen to realize that the problem is with the assumption, they usually do not know what to do because they have not been taught.

Manager manages Department	
Manager$_1$	Department$_1$
Manager$_2$	Department$_2$

Department has Phone#	
Department$_1$	222-1111
Department$_2$	222-2222

Manager has Phone#	
Manager$_1$	222-1111
Manager$_2$	222-2222
Manager$_3$	222-9999

(a) Relations with no universal relation.

Manager	Department	Phone#
Manager$_1$	Department$_1$	222-1111
Manager$_2$	Department$_2$	222-2222

(b) The join of the three relations.

Manager	Department	Phone#
Manager$_1$	Department$_1$	222-1111
Manager$_2$	Department$_2$	222-2222
Manager$_3$	$\perp$	222-9999

(c) A universal relation with nulls.

Figure 9.6   Three relations that have a universal relation with nulls.

Figure 9.6b shows the join of the three relations in Fig. 9.6a. The relation in Fig. 9.6b is not a universal relation because when we project on *Manager Phone#*, we do not obtain the *Manager has Phone#* relation in Fig. 9.6a. In particular, we do not obtain the tuple <*Manager$_3$*, 222-9999> because this tuple does not participate in the join. A tuple that does not participate in a natural join of two relations is called a *dangling tuple*. Although not a universal relation, the relation in Fig. 9.6b nevertheless has the properties we need to be able to discard the relationship set *Department has Phone#*. Observe that the projection of the relation in Fig. 9.6b onto *Department Phone#* yields the *Department has Phone#* relationship set in Fig. 9.6a.

For the example in Fig. 9.6, we can consider reconciling the three relations in Fig. 9.6a as one by using an outer join rather than a natural join. The outer join ensures that there are no dangling tuples by padding tuples that would be dangling with nulls. We define the outer join as follows. Let

> **Nulls**
>
> In general, nulls may have several meanings, such as "does not exist," "must not exist," "exists, but is not known," or "it is unknown whether a value exists." This is problematic enough, but the situation is even worse because two unknown values may be the same, and we may either know this or not know this. When we know that nulls represent the same unknown value, we mark these nulls with subscripts and call them *marked nulls*. If the subscripts are the same, the unknown values are the same. When nulls are not subscripted, it is assumed that they are all different. But, as mentioned, this assumption may be wrong. In general, all of this makes it difficult to deal with nulls effectively. We hasten to point out, however, that for specific cases there may be no real problem, and nulls can be convenient place holders whose meaning causes no problems for the application.

r be a relation on scheme R and s be a relation on scheme S. Then, the *outer join* of r and s, denoted by $r \otimes s$, is

$$\{t(RS) \mid t \in r \bowtie s\}$$
$$\cup \ \{t(RS) \mid t(R) \in r \wedge t(R) \notin \pi_R(r \bowtie s) \wedge t(S - R) = < \perp, \cdots \perp >\}$$
$$\cup \ \{t(RS) \mid t(R - S) = < \perp, \cdots \perp > \wedge t(S) \in s \wedge t(S) \notin \pi_S(r \bowtie s)\}$$

The symbol $\perp$ denotes a *null*, which for the outer join means "does not exist." Figure 9.6c is the outer join of the relations in Fig. 9.6a. If we now project the relation in Fig. 9.6c once for each of the object sets of the three relations in Fig. 9.6c and discard any tuples that contain a null, we obtain the three relations in Fig. 9.6a. We may thus refer to the relation in Fig. 9.6c as a "universal relation with nulls."

This weaker condition helps, but it still does not solve the problem of having to check all interpretations, which is generally impossible. We must somehow be able to reason about the ORM application model and determine whether the universal-relation assumption or the weaker assumption of the existence of a universal relation with nulls holds for the relationship sets of interest. One approach is to imagine constructing universal relations (with nulls, if necessary) and to convince ourselves that they exist for every possible valid interpretation. For the last example, where the manager's phone is the department's phone when the manager manages a department, we should be able to see that for any valid interpretation, the projection onto *Department Phone#* of the join of the relations for *Manager manages Department* and *Manager has Phone#* will always yield the relation in the same interpretation for *Department has Phone#*. Another approach is to reason as follows. If we consider any department *d* and find the phone number *n* of *d* in the *Department has Phone#* relationship set, this is always the same phone number as the phone number we would find if we start with department *d*, find the manager *m* for *d* in the *manages* relationship set, and then find the phone number for *m* in the *Manager has Phone#* relationship set.

Observe that in our discussions in this section, we have selected only the relevant edges in the ORM hypergraph, not all the edges. In the simple examples we have considered so far, we knew, mostly by intuition, which edges were relevant. If intuition gets the job done quickly, easily, and correctly, we should use it. Sometimes, however, we need a more systematic way—either because the situation is complex or because we want an automatic tool to do the work for us.

Consider, for example, the edge set we would obtain in running Algorithm 9.2 on Fig. 9.1b when attempting to head reduce

$$Worker \rightarrow Manager, Start\ Date$$

by removing the connection to *Manager*. After removing the head that is connected to *Manager* as in Fig. 9.3, we would start with *Worker* and subsequently mark *Start Date*, *Department*, *Manager*, *Phone#*, and *Dept Phone Location*. The directed-edge set used in this marking could be either

$$Worker \rightarrow Start\ Date$$
$$Worker \rightarrow Department$$
$$Department \rightarrow Manager$$
$$Manager \rightarrow Phone\#$$
$$Department,\ Phone\# \rightarrow Dept\ Phone\ Location$$

or

$$Worker \rightarrow Start\ Date$$
$$Worker \rightarrow Department$$
$$Department \rightarrow Manager$$
$$Department \rightarrow Phone\#$$
$$Department,\ Phone\# \rightarrow Dept\ Phone\ Location$$

where the only difference between the two sets of FDs is on the left-hand side of the fourth FD. In either case, we can eliminate superfluous edges systematically by eliminating right-hand-side object sets that are not the target object set (*Manager* in this example), and that are not used subsequently on a left-hand side. *Dept Phone Location*, for example, is not the target and is not used subsequently on a left-hand side. If all the right-hand-side object sets are removed for an edge, the edge can be removed. We can continue this process until there are no more changes. Observe that for our example, both rule sets reduce to

$$Worker \rightarrow Department$$
$$Department \rightarrow Manager$$

which is precisely the relevant edge set we want.

Unfortunately, this simple procedure does not always yield the relevant edge set. Consider, for example, the ORM diagram in Fig. 9.7a and the corresponding ORM hypergraph in Fig. 9.7b. Now, when attempting to head reduce

$$Worker \rightarrow Manager, Start Date$$

in Fig. 9.7 by removing *Manager*, one of the directed edge sets we obtain is

$$Worker \rightarrow Start Date$$
voted for: $Worker \rightarrow Manager$
works in: $Worker \rightarrow Department$
can help in another: $Worker \rightarrow Department$
$Worker \rightarrow Dept Name$
$Dept Name \rightarrow Department$
$Department \rightarrow Manager$
$Manager \rightarrow Phone\#$
$Department, Phone\# \rightarrow Dept Phone Location.$

Reducing this set by removing systematically right-hand-side object sets that are neither the target nor used in subsequent markings yields

voted for: $Worker \rightarrow Manager$
works in: $Worker \rightarrow Department$
can help in another: $Worker \rightarrow Department$
$Worker \rightarrow Dept Name$
$Dept Name \rightarrow Department$
$Department \rightarrow Manager$

Our problem here is that there are several possible relevant edge sets. When this happens, we may need to find several, and often all, relevant

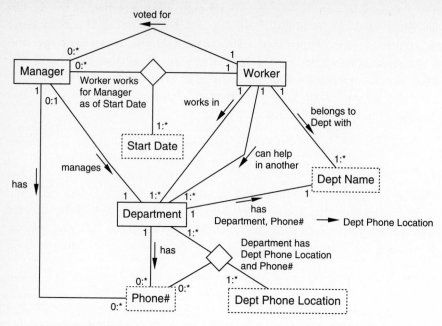

(a) An ORM diagram that allows several relationships among the same objects.

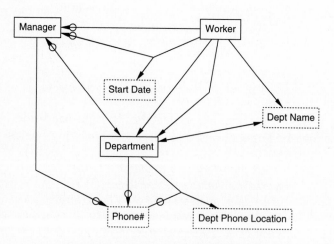

(b) A corresponding ORM hypergraph.

Figure 9.7 An application model with several relevant edge sets for the same reduction.

edge sets and consider each individually. For this example, the relevant edge sets include the following:

voted for: *Worker* → *Manager*

works in: *Worker* → *Department*
Department → *Manager*

can help in another: *Worker* → *Department*
Department → *Manager*

Worker → *Dept Name*
Dept Name → *Department*
Department → *Manager*

In the exercises we ask for an algorithm that finds relevant edge sets systematically. By utilizing a backtracking procedure, this algorithm can find each path that leads from an initial marked set of object sets to a target set of object sets.

Once we obtain relevant edge sets, we can evaluate each to see whether we can make a reduction. Let *s* be a relevant edge set for a proposed reduction transformation that reduces an edge *e*. If there is a universal relation or a universal relation with nulls over *s* and *e*, we say that we have *semantic equivalence* over *s* and *e*. If we have semantic equivalence, then the part of *e* we discard (which may be all of *e*) is *semantically equivalent* to the projection onto the object sets for the discarded part of *e* of the join over the relations for *s* and what remains of *e*, if anything, in any valid interpretation. Seman-

---

Synergistic Discovery of Redundancy

As a practical matter, a tool should help discover redundant connections and help developers check semantic equivalence. By initially assuming semantic equivalence, a tool can find relationship sets that potentially could be reduced or eliminated. Once found, the tool should locate a relevant edge set and then highlight it in such a way that a developer, with any necessary client input, can determine easily whether semantic equivalence holds. This is synergism at its best—based on the underlying theory, a tool does everything it can to help, but since the tool does not know everything, it lets a user complete the task of checking semantic equivalence, which is not captured in the theory.

tic equivalence is what makes our transformations information preserving. We continue to explore the idea of semantic equivalence and information-preserving transformations in the remainder of this chapter.

Returning to our example, if we have semantic equivalence, we can make a reduction. Someone who knows, presumably our client, must give us the answers we seek. We assume that we are told that workers need not vote for their own manager; thus semantic equivalence does not hold for the relevant-edge set

$$voted \ for: Worker \rightarrow Manager$$

which is the first of the four relevant-edge sets just discussed. Note, by the way, that if we are looking at actual data and workers tend to vote almost exclusively for their own manager, we may not run across a counterexample in some sample data, which underscores the reason we may need to consult someone who really knows. Semantic equivalence does hold for the second relevant-edge set, which is

$$works \ in:Worker \rightarrow Department$$
$$Department \rightarrow Manager$$

This is the example we discussed earlier. Since we assume that we are told that the other department in which a worker can help must not be a worker's own department, semantic equivalence does not hold for the third relevant-edge set, which is

$$can \ help \ in \ another: Worker \rightarrow Department$$
$$Department \rightarrow Manager$$

For the fourth relevant-edge set, which is

$$Worker \rightarrow Dept \ Name$$
$$Dept \ Name \rightarrow Department$$
$$Department \rightarrow Manager$$

semantic equivalence does hold—it does not matter whether we determine a worker's department directly (as we do in the second set) or indirectly through the department name (as we do in this fourth set). When we have a choice, we should use a relevant edge set with as few edges as any other choice. Thus the preferred edge set for our reduction here is

$$works \ in:Worker \rightarrow Department$$
$$Department \rightarrow Manager$$

9.4.3 Roles and Congruency

As a preprocessing step to Algorithm 9.1, we converted explicit roles into explicit *isa*'s. So far we have ignored implicit roles. Not only do we have the explicit specializations of the *Employee* object set in Fig. 9.1, which can be thought of as roles, but we also have implicit role specializations for every optional connection. By definition, these optional connections correspond to relationship-set connections that have zero-minimum participation constraints. As explained in Chapter 7, whenever we have a zero-minimum participation constraint, we have an incongruency because the common properties of the objects in an object set need not coincide with the properties defined explicitly for the object set.

Suppose we make all the object sets in Fig. 9.7a congruent by adding explicit role specializations for every zero-minimum participation constraint. Figure 9.8a shows the result, while Fig. 9.8b shows the corresponding ORM hypergraph. Now observe that some of the semantic-equivalence problems tend to resolve themselves. In particular, we see much more clearly that the *Manager has Home Phone#* relationship set is not redundant. Here a manager's home phone number is obviously not a manager's department's phone number, as might be assumed (incorrectly) from the ORM diagram and hypergraph in Fig. 9.7. It is also clear that the *Worker voted for Favorite Manager* relationship set cannot be implied by any other relationship set. In addition, it becomes clearer that the *Worker works for Department Manager as of Start Date* relationship set can be head reduced because we do not have to be concerned about whether the subset of managers who manage departments is the same as the subset of managers for whom workers work.

Although congruency helps solve many of our problems, it does not solve them all. The analysis of the relationship sets that connect *Worker* and *Department* is still the same as before, as is the analysis of the relationship sets that connect to *Dept Name*.

Since congruency helps in many cases, we might ask ourselves, Why not require that all application models be congruent before checking for reductions? This is a possibility, but it does not always help, and the imposition of this requirement might become burdensome. Instead, we take the position that we may make any part of an application model congruent before, during, or after reductions. When we find a potential reduction that involves an incongruency, however, we should resolve the congruency question as part of determining whether semantic equivalence holds. Thus, for example, if we are analyzing the potential reduction in Fig. 9.7b of removing

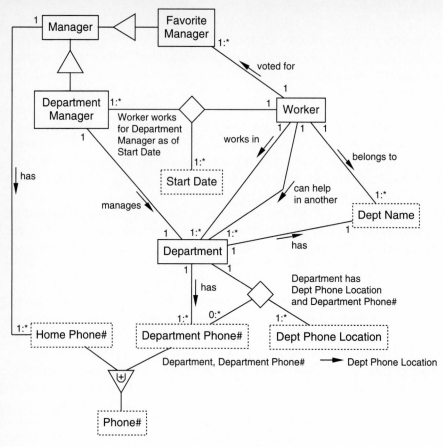

(a) A congruent ORM diagram.

$$Manager \rightarrow Phone\#$$

based on

$$Manager \rightarrow Department$$
$$Department \rightarrow Phone\#$$

we should resolve the incongruencies for this part of the diagram as in Fig. 9.8b, which would tell us immediately that semantic equivalence does not hold. Other parts of the diagram need not be congruent to make this determination.

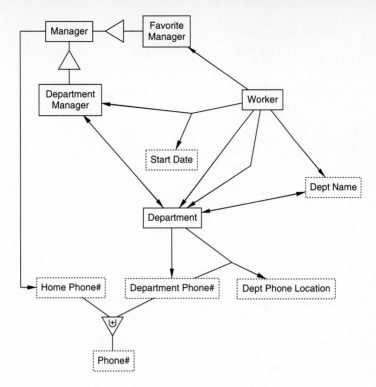

(b) A corresponding ORM hypergraph.

Figure 9.8 An application model with congruent object sets.

Congruency can also help answer some other questions about potential reductions. In general, for an ORM hypergraph derived from a congruent application model, there can be no head reduction of a head connection to an object set *S* unless there is at least one other head connection to *S*. In Fig. 9.8b, for example, there is only one head connection to *Favorite Manager*, and thus there can be no reduction.

If the application model is incongruent, however, this assertion does not necessarily hold because we may be able to move heads (or tails) up or down *isa* hierarchies. In Fig. 9.9a, for example, there is only one head on *Manager*, but we can still head reduce. If we make the diagram congruent as in Fig. 9.9b, the reduction becomes clear. We are assuming here, of course, that the implicit role for the optional connection to *Manager* is exactly the explicit role *Department Manager*. And we are also assuming that the reason we have optional connections on *Department* is because some department may be staffed by only long-time employees or by only

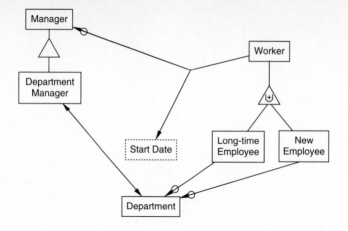

(a) An incongruent ORM hypergraph.

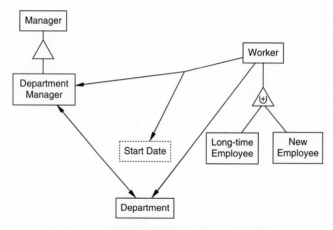

(b) Congruent version of the ORM hypergraph.

Figure 9.9 An incongruent ORM hypergraph with reductions.

new employees. Every department is staffed by some worker, however, so that when we consolidate the two optional connections to *Department* and attach them to *Worker* in making the diagram congruent, the optional designation disappears. Once we have made these congruency transformations, we have the two required heads for head reduction on *Department Manager*. We also have the closure beginning with *Worker*, which without the direct connection to *Department Manager* still includes *Department Manager*.

If we do not address congruency issues properly, we may overlook some potential reductions. The problem is that the potential reductions may be "hidden" in the sense that we have to pass through one or more *isa* connections to find them. In Fig. 9.9a, for example, if we remove the head connection to *Manager*, mark the tail, and run our closure algorithm, we mark only *Worker* and *Start Date*. Since *Manager* is not marked, we should conclude that we cannot make a head reduction because FD implication fails. Any generalization/specialization, however, constitutes a one-to-one relationship between a generalization object set and a specialization object set. This is because every object in a specialization maps to itself in the generalization, and every object in a generalization either maps to itself in the specialization or does not have a corresponding object in the specialization. Since the relationship is one-to-one, there is a functional dependency in both directions, with the generalization side being optional. Figure 9.10 shows the ORM hypergraph in Fig. 9.9a explicitly augmented with *isa* FDs. With these FDs in place, when we now run our closure algorithm, we mark every object set in Fig. 9.10, and we mark *Manager* in particular. In general, for incongruent ORM hypergraphs we may have to search across every encountered *isa* hierarchy to determine whether FD implication holds.

Finding potential reductions is not the only problem. We also wish to ensure that our reductions are information preserving. As indicated earlier, when we make a head reduction based on some relevant set of edges, then by simply joining these edges together and projecting on the origin and target object sets, we can recover the information removed in the reduction.

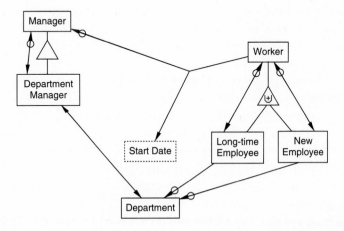

Figure 9.10 An incongruent ORM hypergraph with explicit FDs over *isa* hierarchies.

This breaks down if we include *isa* FDs. However, once we find a head reduction, if we make the relevant part of the diagram congruent, we can again simply join edges and project on the origin and target object sets. For example, if we convert the ORM hypergraph in Fig. 9.10 to the congruent ORM hypergraph in Fig. 9.9b, we can then use

$$\pi_{Worker, \, Manager} \textit{Worker works in Department}$$

$$\bowtie \textit{Department Manager manages Department}$$

to compute the information lost by projecting *Worker works for Department Manager as of Start Date* on *Worker* and *Start Date* for the head reduction.

Besides helping resolve questions of semantic equivalence, helping find potential reductions across *isa* hierarchies, and making reductions information preserving, congruency also leads to a reduction of isolated root generalizations that have union constraints. An *isolated root generalization with a union constraint* is an object set that is the root (top) of an *isa* hierarchy, has no connecting relationship sets, and has specialization object sets whose union is equal to the root object set. In Fig. 9.8, *Phone#* is an isolated root generalization with a union constraint. It is the root of the *isa* hierarchy over phones; it has no connecting relationship sets; and it is equal to the union of its specializations, *Department Phone#* and *Home Phone#*.

We can always discard an isolated root generalization that has a simple union constraint. This transformation preserves information because we can reestablish the root by taking a union of the specializations. The transformation is also constraint preserving because the construction of the union itself guarantees that the established *isa* triangle has a union constraint. Thus, we may assume that the transformed application model has this union constraint, as it does implicitly for any group of object sets over which we take the union.

If the isolated root generalization has a partition constraint, as does our example in Fig. 9.8, then in the transformation we must generate a general constraint to guarantee that the specializations are mutually exclusive. This mutual-exclusion constraint is the closed formula we generate for partition and mutual-exclusion constraints as discussed in Chapter 6, that is,

$$\forall x(S_i(x) \Rightarrow \neg S_j(x))$$

where $S_1, ..., S_n$ are the specializations and $1 \leq i, j \leq n$ and $i \neq j$. Thus, when we discard the *Phone#* object set in Fig. 9.8, we must add the general constraints

$$\forall x(\text{Home Phone\#}(x) \Rightarrow \neg\text{Department Phone\#}(x))$$

and

$$\forall x(\text{Department Phone\#}(x) \Rightarrow \neg\text{Home Phone\#}(x))$$

With this addition, the partition constraint is implied—the union as before and the mutual exclusion because it is retained and is thus given.

To discover isolated root generalizations with a union constraint in an ORM hypergraph, we need consider only object sets whose connections are all optional. If there is a nonoptional connection, the generalization cannot be isolated. In Fig. 9.7b, for example, we see that all the connections to *Phone#* are optional. *Manager* in the same ORM hypergraph could not be discarded because one of its four connections is not optional. Once we identify an object set that has a potential isolated root generalization with a union constraint, we add explicit roles and then consolidate them in a single *isa* hierarchy and add a union or partition constraint, if applicable. If a union or partition constraint applies, then the object set can be discarded.

9.5   Head Reduction

We now revisit our motivational transformation, which is a head reduction. Because the motivational example was simple, it did not cover all the relevant cases. In particular, to make our transformation information preserving, sometimes we must add an edge when we remove one. Consider, for example, the ORM hypergraph in Fig. 9.11. (Here, and whenever we have examples with generic object-set names A, B, ..., we assume semantic equivalence and, unless a connection is marked specifically as optional, we also assume that there are no incongruencies.)

Observe that we can head reduce $AB \rightarrow C$ and thus remove this edge. Using Algorithm 9.2, we mark AB, then remove the edge $AB \rightarrow C$, and then mark D and E because of $A \rightarrow D$ and $B \rightarrow E$, and then C because of $D \rightarrow C$. If we now transform the diagram in Fig. 9.11a just by removing the ternary edge, however, we may *not* preserve information.

Figure 9.12 provides some sample data, which we use to show that this transformation is not information preserving. Figure 9.12a shows the original data for the edges. Since the relevant edge set is $\{A \rightarrow D, D \rightarrow C\}$, we should presumably join r_2 and r_3 in Fig. 9.12a. Since there is no B, however, we certainly cannot recover r_1; thus the transformation definitely is not information preserving. Even if we join r_4 in an attempt to recover the

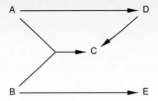

(a) Initial head-reducible ORM hypergraph.

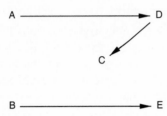

(b) ORM hypergraph with the head-reducible edge discarded.

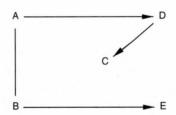

(c) ORM hypergraph properly head reduced.

Figure 9.11   A head reduction needing a nonfunctional relationship-set connection.

information for B, we still cannot recover r_1, because $\pi_{ABC}(r_2 \bowtie r_3 \bowtie r_4) \neq r_1$, as Fig. 9.12b shows. No other join or combination of any of these relations works either. Hence, there is no way to recover the lost information. What is missing is the connection between A and B. Figure 9.11c shows the addition of an AB connection to the hypergraph. The data for this edge is the projection of the discarded functional edge onto the tails. Letting this addition be r_5, Fig. 9.12c shows the r_5 relation for our sample data. If we now join this r_5 relation with the relations of the relevant edge set, that is, r_2 and r_3, and project onto ABC, we obtain r_1.

$$r_1 = \quad \begin{array}{ccc} A & B & C \\ \hline 1 & 2 & 3 \\ 1 & 3 & 3 \\ 2 & 4 & 5 \\ 2 & 3 & 5 \end{array}$$

$$r_2 = \quad \begin{array}{cc} A & D \\ \hline 1 & 6 \\ 2 & 7 \end{array} \qquad r_3 = \quad \begin{array}{cc} D & C \\ \hline 6 & 3 \\ 7 & 5 \end{array} \qquad r_4 = \quad \begin{array}{cc} B & E \\ \hline 2 & 8 \\ 3 & 9 \\ 4 & 9 \end{array}$$

(a) Original sample data.

$$\pi_{ABC}(r_2 \bowtie r_3 \bowtie r_4) = \quad \begin{array}{ccc} A & B & C \\ \hline 1 & 2 & 3 \\ 2 & 2 & 5 \\ 1 & 3 & 3 \\ 2 & 3 & 5 \\ 1 & 4 & 3 \\ 2 & 4 & 5 \end{array}$$

(b) The result is not r_1.

$$r_5 = \quad \begin{array}{cc} A & B \\ \hline 1 & 2 \\ 1 & 3 \\ 2 & 4 \\ 2 & 3 \end{array}$$

(c) Data for the nonfunctional edge, the AB relation.

Figure 9.12 Sample data for a head reduction.

In general, when we head reduce a single-headed, multiple-tail edge e, we must connect the tails with a nonfunctional edge e' among all the tails. The participation constraints for the connections are all *1:**. We populate e' with the values of the projection of e onto the tails. This new relationship set then becomes one of the relationship sets joined in the expression used to recover e after the reduction. Thus, if we generate e' and we let r' be the populated relation for e' and if r_i, $1 \leq i \leq m$ are the relations for the relationship sets in the relevant edge set, and A_1, ..., A_n are the n object sets that e connects, the expression to recover e is

$$\pi_{A_1 \cdots A_n}(r' \bowtie r_1 \bowtie \ldots \bowtie r_m)$$

If the edge e that we head reduce is single-headed and has only one tail, then the recovery expression is

$$\pi_{A_1 \cdots A_n}(r_1 \bowtie \ldots \bowtie r_m)$$

And if the edge e that we head reduce is multiple-headed, and the head we remove is A_n, then the recovery expression is

$$\pi_{A_1 \cdots A_n}(r \bowtie r_1 \bowtie \ldots \bowtie r_m)$$

where r is the projection of the relation for e onto $A_1 \ldots A_{n-1}$.[†] Thus, for example, the recovery expression for the reduction in Fig. 9.11, which is single-headed with multiple tails, is

$$\pi_{ABC}(AB \text{ relation} \bowtie AD \text{ relation} \bowtie DC \text{ relation})$$

To illustrate the second case, which is single-headed with a single tail, consider the head reduction in which we removed the edge *Worker belongs to Dept Name* based on the relevant edge set *Worker* $\rightarrow$ *Department* and *Department* $\rightarrow$ *Dept Name*. Here the recovery expression is

$$\pi_{Worker, \, Dept \, Name}(Worker \text{ works in Department}$$
$$\bowtie Department \text{ has Dept Name})$$

For the third case, we consider the original motivational example, in which we head-reduced *Manager*, leaving a functional edge *Worker* $\rightarrow$ *Start Date*, which we called *Start Date Worker relation*. Thus the recovery expression is

$$\pi_{Worker, \, Manager, \, StartDate}(Start \text{ Date Worker relation}$$
$$\bowtie Worker \text{ works in Department} \bowtie Manager \text{ manages Department})$$

[†] Observe that if we do not care whether we have the most efficient expression, we can always use the single expression $\pi_{A_1 \cdots A_n} s \bowtie r_1 \bowtie \ldots \bowtie r_n)$ where s is the projection of the relation for e onto $A_1 \cdots A_{n-1}$. (For the first case $A_1 \cdots A_{n-1}$ are all on the tail side, and for the second case $n = 2$ and A_1 is guaranteed to be included in one of the relation schemes of r_i, $1 \leq i \leq m$.)

We leave for the exercises the proof that head reduction is information preserving and that therefore we can always recover the data discarded. We also leave for the exercises the proof that head reduction is constraint preserving.

9.6 Tail Reduction

We begin with an example of our tail-reduction transformation. Consider the *Department has Dept Phone Location and Department Phone#* relationship set in Fig. 9.8a. We claim that the corresponding FD edge in Fig. 9.8b, which is

$$Department, Department\ Phone\# \rightarrow Dept\ Phone\ Location$$

can be reduced to

$$Department \rightarrow Dept\ Phone\ Location$$

Notice that we have removed an object set from the tail side of the FD, thus motivating the term "tail reduction."

The reduction preserves information because

$$Department\ has\ Dept\ Phone\ Location\ and\ Department\ Phone\# =$$
$$(Department\ has\ Department\ Phone\#$$
$$\bowtie Department\ Dept\ Phone\ Location\ relation)$$

where *Department Dept Phone Location relation* is the new relationship set formed in the reduction.

The reduction also preserves constraints. Since our application model in Fig. 9.8a is congruent, the one-minimum constraints are automatic, as are the referential-integrity constraints. The only other constraint is the co-occurrence constraint

$$Department, Department\ Phone\# \rightarrow Dept\ Phone\ Location$$

which is preserved because it can be derived from FDs in the reduced ORM hypergraph, as follows:

1. *Department, Department Phone#* → *Department, Department Phone#*, by trivial implication.

2. *Department → Dept Phone Location*, given (i.e., this is the new FD relationship set).

3. *Department, Department Phone# → Department, Department Phone#, Dept Phone Location*, by accumulation from 1 and 2.

4. *Department, Department Phone# → Dept Phone Location*, by projection from 3.

Evolving General Constraints with Design Transformations

If we have general constraints that apply to an object set or relationship set that is discarded or altered in a reduction transformation, we must alter the general constraint. If the general constraint is informal, we may wish to reword it. If the general constraint is formal, we can transform it automatically to a new general constraint. Since our transformations preserve information, we can replace a reference to a discarded or altered object or relationship set by the expression required to compute the object or relationship set. For example, we earlier gave the general constraint

$\forall x \forall y \forall z$(*Worker*($x$) *works in Department*($y$) $\wedge$ *Manager*(z) *manages*
   Department(y)
$\Rightarrow \exists w$(*Worker*(x) *works for Manager*(z) *as of Start Date*(w)))

which applies to the *Worker works for Manager as of Start Date* relationship set, which we reduced subsequently in a head reduction. Since the expression to reconstitute this relationship set is

$\pi_{\text{Worker, Manager, StartDate}}$(*Start Date Worker relation*
   $\bowtie$ *Worker works in Department* $\bowtie$ *Manager manages Department*)

we can replace *Worker*(x) *works for Manager*(z) in the general constraint by $\exists u$(*Worker*(x) *works in Department*(u) $\wedge$ *Manager*(z) *manages Department*(u) $\wedge$ *Worker*(x) *Start Date relation*). After substitution, we can simplify the expression to

$\forall x \forall y \forall z$(*Worker*($x$) *works in Department*($y$)
   $\wedge$ *Manager*(z) *manages Department*(y)
   $\Rightarrow \exists w$(*Worker*(x) *Start Date*(w) *relation*))

Figure 9.13 shows this change in an ORM diagram. It also shows all the other changes we have been discussing. In general, at any time we can return to a standard ORM diagram and view the application-model ORM as transformed during design. Observe, for example, that we have reduced the union-constrained isolated root generalization and have added the general constraint that ensures mutual exclusion for the partition. The general constraints are written in OSM-L, rather than in predicate calculus. Figure 9.13 also shows some names chosen for the new relationship sets formed by the reductions. Since one of these new names, *Worker started on Start Date*, is in a general constraint, the general constraint includes this name rather than *Worker Start Date relation*. If we are clever, we notice that the general constraint for workers is implied by the constraints of the ORM hypergraph since for every worker there exists a start date, and thus we can discard the general constraint.

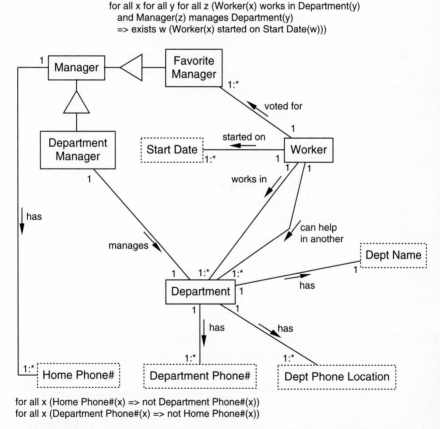

for all x for all y for all z (Worker(x) works in Department(y)
and Manager(z) manages Department(y)
=> exists w (Worker(x) started on Start Date(w)))

for all x (Home Phone#(x) => not Department Phone#(x))
for all x (Department Phone#(x) => not Home Phone#(x))

Figure 9.13 A revised ORM diagram based on tail and head reductions.

In general we can determine whether a tail reduction satisfies FD implication by Algorithm 9.3. The basic idea is that if we do not need one of the tails to arrive at the heads, we can remove the tail. For our example in Fig. 9.8b, we can test whether the tail connection to *Department Phone#* in

$$Department, Department\ Phone\# \rightarrow Dept\ Phone\ Location$$

can be removed by marking *Department*, then *Department Phone#* because *Department → Department Phone#*, and *Dept Phone Location* because of

$$Department, Department\ Phone\# \rightarrow Dept\ Phone\ Location$$

Other object sets, including *Dept Name* and *Department Manager*, would also be marked in the closure step of Algorithm 9.3.

Algorithm 9.3

Input: an ORM hypergraph H congruent over the edges of interest and a designated tail connection T of a directed hyperedge D of H. (If D happens to come from an edge notationally written as a bidirectional edge, we must be clear about which one-directional edge D represents and must know which connections are its head(s) and tail(s).)

Output: "yes" or "no", meaning yes, the tail connection T potentially can be removed or no, it cannot be removed.

Mark all the tails of the directed hyperedge D except T.

Repeat until no more changes:
    If all the tails of a directed edge E are marked,
        mark all the heads.

If all the heads of D are marked
    Output "yes".
Else
    Output "no".

After using Algorithm 9.3 to determine that a potential tail reduction is possible, we can find all relevant edge sets for the reduction. For our example, there is only one relevant edge set:

$$Department \rightarrow Department\ Phone\#$$
$$Department, Department\ Phone\# \rightarrow Dept\ Phone\ Location$$

We use this relevant edge set to test semantic equivalence. If there are several relevant edge sets, we test each one. To test semantic equivalence for our example, we could ask, on an abstract level, whether the phone number determined by the department is the same as the phone number used to determine the location of the department phone. Since it is, we can do the reduction.

Before leaving tail reduction, we give a few more examples, which show some additional patterns for tail reduction, as well as some interdependencies between tail and head reduction and the general procedure for reconstituting the reduced relationship set.

Figure 9.14 provides an example in which we indirectly determine one left-hand-side object set from another (rather than directly as in the preceding example). For Algorithm 9.3, since we are removing the connection to B in the ternary relationship set, we mark A in Fig. 9.14a, then D because of $A \rightarrow D$, then B because of $D \rightarrow B$, and finally C because of $AB \rightarrow C$. We can reconstitute $AB \rightarrow C$ from $A \rightarrow D$, $D \rightarrow B$, and $A \rightarrow C$, the FDs in Fig. 9.14b, by

$$\pi_{ABC} \ AD \ relation \bowtie DB \ relation \bowtie AC \ relation$$

In the example shown in Fig. 9.15, there is both a tail and a head reduction, but only if we do the tail reduction first. Suppose we try to head

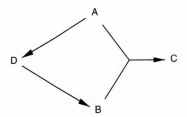

(a) Initial ORM hypergraph.

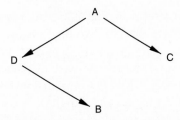

(b) Tail-reduced ORM hypergraph.

Figure 9.14   A tail reduction with indirect determination of a left-hand-side object set.

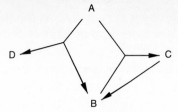

(a) ORM hypergraph that is initially not head-reducible.

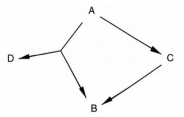

(b) Tail-reduced ORM hypergraph.

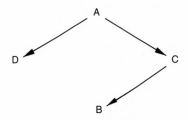

(c) Head-reduced ORM hypergraph.

Figure 9.15 A tail reduction followed by an initially impossible head reduction.

reduce the ORM hypergraph in Fig. 9.15a by head reducing $A \rightarrow BD$ to $A \rightarrow D$. In running Algorithm 9.2, we temporarily remove the head connection to B in $A \rightarrow BD$, mark A, and then mark D based on $A \rightarrow D$, but we cannot mark B directly and we cannot mark C, which would lead to B indirectly, because we need B. Thus FD implication fails, so we cannot head reduce. Now suppose we try tail reducing $AB \rightarrow C$ to $A \rightarrow C$. Using Algorithm 9.3, we mark A, then B and D based on $A \rightarrow BD$, then C based on $AB \rightarrow C$. We thus succeed and make the reduction, shown in Fig. 9.15b. Now, however, we can head reduce $A \rightarrow BD$ to $A \rightarrow D$. By removing this connection to B in Fig. 9.15b, when we now run Algorithm 9.2 starting with

A, we also mark C and D, respectively, because of $A \rightarrow C$ and $A \rightarrow D$ and then mark B because of $C \rightarrow B$. The result of these reductions is the ORM hypergraph in Fig. 9.15c. In general, if we first do all tail reductions and then all head reductions, we will have done all possible tail reductions. If we reverse this, however, and do all head reductions first and then all tail reductions, we still may be able to do some additional head reductions.

As with head reduction, we must be careful in some cases that we do not lose information. Let us examine Fig. 9.11 again; this time we will consider a tail reduction instead of a head reduction. We can tail reduce $AB \rightarrow C$ to $A \rightarrow C$. Using Algorithm 9.3, we mark A, then D because of $A \rightarrow D$, and then C because of $D \rightarrow C$. No other object sets are marked. If we now transform the diagram in Fig. 9.11a by just removing the tail connection to B in $AB \rightarrow C$, however, we may lose information. Consider again the data in Fig. 9.12. This time, however, we also have the data for edge $A \rightarrow C$, which is

$$r_1' = \quad \begin{array}{cc} A & C \\ \hline 1 & 3 \\ 2 & 5 \end{array}$$

As before, with head reduction, no combination of joins of relations r_2, r_3, r_4, or r_1' with a final projection onto ABC yields r_1. Hence, there is no way to recover the lost information.

Again, what is missing is the connection between A and B. The relation r_5 in Fig. 9.12c is the required relation. If we now join this relation with the relations used for FD implication, namely r_2 and r_3, and project onto ABC, we obtain r_1.

In general, for a tail reduction, if the edge e being tail reduced is not in the relevant set, then before reducing we add an n-ary relationship with all $1{:}{*}$ participation constraints connecting the n tails of e and populate the edge with the values of the projection of e onto the tails. This new relationship set also becomes one of the relationship sets joined in the expression used to recover e after the reduction. Thus, if the relevant set includes the edge e being tail reduced and r_i, $1 \le i \le m$ are the relationship sets in the relevant set (so that $e = r_i$ for some i, $1 \le i \le m$), and A_1, ..., A_n are the n object sets that e connects, the expression to recover e is

$$\pi_{A_1 \cdots A_n}(r_1 \bowtie \cdots \bowtie r_m)$$

If the relevant set does not include the edge e and the relationship sets in the relevant set are r_i, $1 \le i \le m$, then the recovery expression is

$$\pi_{A_1 \cdots A_n}(r' \bowtie r_1 \bowtie \cdots \bowtie r_m)$$

where $r' = \pi_{A_{j1} \cdots A_{jk}} e$ is the new relation formed from e, where $A_{j1} \ldots A_{jk}$ is the subset of $A_1 \ldots A_n$ that constitutes the tail components of e. Thus, for example, the recovery expression for the reduction in Fig. 9.14b, which uses the reduced edge, is

$$\pi_{ABC}(AC\ relation \bowtie AD\ relation \bowtie DB\ relation)$$

And the recovery expression for the reduction in Fig. 9.11b, which does not use the reduced edge, is

$$\pi_{ABC}(AB\ relation \bowtie AD\ relation \bowtie DC\ relation)$$

where *AB relation* is the new relation and is equal to $\pi_{AB} ABC$ *relation*, where *ABC relation* is the relationship set in Fig. 9.11a that connects *A*, *B*, and *C*. We leave for the exercises the proof that tail reduction preserves information and constraints.

9.7   Equivalence-Class Transformations

Equivalence-class transformations capitalize on the idea that we may be able to find two or more object sets, or sets of object sets, that are in a one-to-one correspondence and thus in an equivalence class. Then, based on an equivalence class, we may be able to do some interesting transformations, including

1. A reduction in the number of connections in a relationship set,

2. A reduction of the number of object sets, and

3. Further head reduction, which otherwise would have been impossible.

After defining what we mean by an equivalence class, we explore each of these transformations in turn.

Let X and Y be subsets of a relation scheme R and let F be a set of FDs over R. X and Y are *equivalent* if $X \rightarrow Y \in F^+$ and $Y \rightarrow X \in F^+$. If $X \rightarrow Y$ and $Y \rightarrow X$, we write $X \leftrightarrow Y$. The relation $\leftrightarrow$ over subsets of R is an equivalence relation because the relation is reflexive, symmetric, and transitive. For any equivalence relation formed from the relation $\leftrightarrow$, we can form a set of pairwise nonintersecting sets of object sets, where each set of object sets determines every other set functionally. We call this set an *equivalence class*. For example, let $R = ABCDEGHI$ and let $F = \{A \rightarrow B,\ B \rightarrow C,\ C \rightarrow A,\ DE \rightarrow GH,\ G \rightarrow DEI\}$. Then, $\{A, B, C\}$ and $\{DE, G\}$ are equivalence classes.

These equivalence classes also have a minimum number of elements in each set included within them in the sense that if we remove any one attribute (object set), then the result is no longer an equivalence class; they are hence called *minimal-set equivalence classes*. For example, if we remove D from DE, $\{E, G\}$ is not an equivalence class since $E \rightarrow G$ does not hold. $\{AB, B, C\}$ and $\{DEH, GEI\}$ are also equivalence classes but not minimal-set equivalence classes because we can remove B from AB, H from DEH, and EI from GEI and still have equivalence classes. We are interested only in minimal-set equivalence classes.

Sometimes we are interested in equivalence classes with only a single set of attributes. These equivalence classes are *trivial* because they always satisfy the definition no matter what set of attributes we choose since $X \rightarrow X$ for any set of attributes. For trivial equivalence classes, we are sometimes interested in multiple-attribute sets even though they are not minimal-set equivalence classes.

As examples of equivalence classes in ORM hypergraphs, we list the nontrivial minimal-set equivalence classes in Fig. 9.8b:

{*Department Manager, Department, Dept Name*}

and in the top half of the ORM hypergraph in Fig. 9.1b:

{*VIN, Company Car, License Plate*}
{*Emp#, Employee*}
{*Address, Street# City State Zip*}

Even though this last equivalence class involves five object sets, we note that it has only two elements: (1) the singleton set of object sets *Address* and (2) the 4-ary set of object sets *Street# City State Zip*.

As is the case for head and tail reduction, we cannot be sure that we have the equivalence classes we want by FD implication alone. We must also ensure that semantic equivalence holds over the one-to-one relationship sets used to form the equivalence class. Suppose, for example, that in Fig. 9.8b we have an additional bidirectional edge between *Department Manager* and *Department* and that this relationship set represents an alternate manager for a department when the manager is not on duty. Figure

Department Manager manages Department

M_1	D_1
M_2	D_2
M_3	D_3

Department Manager secondarily manages Department

M_1	D_2
M_2	D_3
M_3	D_1

Department has Dept Name

D_1	*Toy*
D_2	*Hardware*
D_3	*Clothing*

Figure 9.16 Some relations that show that semantic equivalence does not hold.

9.16 provides some possible data for the relevant relations. Observe that their join is the empty relation and thus that there is no universal relation. As Fig. 9.17 shows, we can resolve this problem. Here we have supplied additional object sets and made them equivalent to sets we already have by making a generalization/specialization that goes in both directions. This forces each set to be a subset of the other, making the sets equivalent. We now have two equivalence classes

{Department Manager, Department}

and

{Alternate Manager, Secondary Department}

Having defined what we mean by an equivalence class and by an equivalence class over which semantic equivalence holds, we now discuss some transformations enabled by having equivalence classes. We first consider how equivalence classes can reduce the number of connections in a relationship set. Figure 9.18a depicts an ORM hypergraph with an equivalence class in which *Address* is in a one-to-one correspondence with the set of object sets {*Street#, City, State, Zip*}. It also shows a 5-ary relationship set that connects *Street#, City, State,* and *Zip* to *Neighborhood Status*. Because of the equivalence class, we can consolidate the tails of the 5-ary relationship

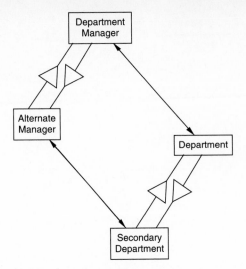

Figure 9.17 Splitting an equivalence class when semantic equivalence fails.

set and move them to *Address*, as seen in Fig. 9.18b. This reduces the 5-ary relationship set to a binary relationship set. We call this reduction *minimal consolidation* because we consolidate edges minimally to one element of an equivalence class.

Our next transformation shows how equivalence classes may allow the number of nonlexical object sets to be reduced. Consider, for example, the two object sets *Emp#* and *Employee* in Fig. 9.1a. Since these two object sets are in an equivalence class, the objects in these sets are in a one-to-one correspondence. Furthermore, one of these object sets, namely *Employee*, is a nonlexical object set, which means that its elements are represented by system-chosen, object identifiers. Because of the one-to-one correspondence, we may choose instead to represent employees by their employee number, discarding the object identifiers.

In general, if we have an equivalence class with at least one nonlexical object set N and at least one lexical object set L, we can discard N and any one-to-one relationship sets used to form the equivalence that connect N and L directly and can move any relationship-set connection on N to L. Furthermore, if N is in an *isa* hierarchy H, we make all the object sets in H lexical. The generalization of this transformation to sets of object sets in an equivalence class is immediate, but cumbersome to describe.

We call this transformation *lexicalization* because we are choosing to represent a set of nonlexical objects by a set of lexical objects. Our lexical trans-

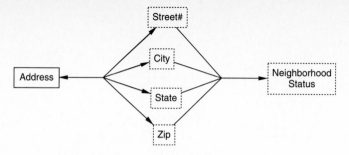

(a) A relationship set with five connections.

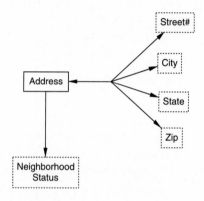

(b) The same relationship set with only two connections.

Figure 9.18 Reduction of the number of connections in a relationship set.

formation is information preserving because we can provide a nonlexical object set *N* for any lexical object set *L*, create a relationship set between *N* and *L*, and add constraints to ensure that *N* and *L* are in a one-to-one correspondence. This also guarantees that we have a one-to-one correspondence with the object identifiers discarded when we lexicalized. Thus, according to our convention about renaming object identifiers, which we stated when we defined information-preserving transformations, we can replace the generated objects for *N* by the original objects and recover the original interpretation precisely.

Figure 9.19 displays a full lexicalization of Fig. 9.1b. Here we have lexicalized *Employee* with *Emp#*, *Company Car* with *VIN*, and *Address* with its components *Street#*, *City*, *State*, and *Zip*. We have also renamed some of the object sets. Notice that in the renaming we have retained the original name

---

Object Identity

Object-oriented purists may object to lexicalization because it discards object identifiers and thus destroys true object identity. To the purist we say that lexicalization is not required. Our design method fully supports true object identity—all other transformations apply in the same way and all the results we obtain in the next chapter hold, except the minimality result on lexicalization itself, which tells only that we can discard object identifiers as described here. To the nonpurist, we also say that we can have object identity in exactly those situations where it matters. We simply keep the nonlexical object sets when we are not sure that we will always have a one-to-one correspondence between a lexical and nonlexical object set or when it may be more efficient to store object identifiers as keys and foreign keys rather than potentially space-expensive nonlexical identifiers. To the pragmatist, we further point out that we can always introduce a lexical object set and place it in a one-to-one correspondence with any nonlexical object set so that we can always lexicalize every nonlexical object set.

---

as part of the new name, helping the reader to recall what the lexicalized object sets were previously. As a standard renaming convention, we add "(*of X*)" to the name where *X* is the name of the lexicalized object set. Thus, when we lexicalize *Employee* with *Emp#*, the name becomes *Emp#* (*of Employee*). Observe also that we have propagated the lexicalization down the employee *isa* hierarchy so that *Manager* and *Worker* also became lexical based on *Emp#*.

In addition to reducing the number of object sets by lexicalization, where one of the object sets in the one-to-one correspondence is lexical and the other is nonlexical, we can also do a reduction when two nonlexical object sets are in a one-to-one correspondence. In this case we have two sets of object identifiers that identify one set of objects. We can combine the two by letting only one set represent the set of objects, giving this new object the names of both nonlexical object sets, and connecting all relationship sets of the two nonlexical object sets to the new object set. For example, suppose that in Fig. 9.19 there was an additional object set called *Partner* that was in a one-to-one correspondence with *Spouse*. Then we could combine the two into a single object set called *Spouse | Partner* and connect it with the relationship sets *Spouse Name*, *Couple*, and *Emp#(of*

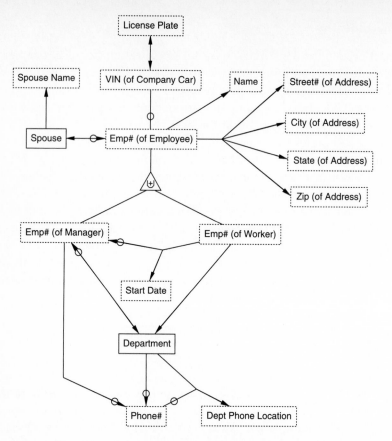

Figure 9.19   Full lexicalization of the ORM diagram in Fig. 9.1b.

Employee), discarding both *Spouse* and *Partner*. We call this transformation *object-set merge*.

For our last equivalence transformation, we show how equivalence classes themselves sometimes may be reduced by linking elements of an equivalence class by FD edges circularly and then discarding the original FDs that link the elements of the equivalence class. More significantly, we also show that this circular linking can lead to additional head reductions that otherwise are not possible.

Once we have an equivalence class in an ORM hypergraph, we can connect the object sets or sets of object sets in an equivalence class circularly by adding FD edges, proceeding in any ordered sequence from element to element of the equivalence class and from the last element of the sequence to the first. Observe that if we link an equivalence class with two elements circularly, then this is the same as having a bidirectional edge linking the two elements. After linking the elements of an equivalence class circularly, we can discard all other FD edges that link elements of the equivalence class.

In some cases, connecting object sets in an equivalence class circularly leads to a reduction in the number of FD edges. In Fig. 9.8b, for example, we have the equivalence class

$$\{Department\ Manager,\ Department,\ Dept\ Name\}$$

In place of the four FD edges

$$Department\ Manager \rightarrow Department$$
$$Department \rightarrow Department\ Manager$$
$$Department \rightarrow Dept\ Name$$
$$Dept\ Name \rightarrow Department$$

we can link the elements of this equivalence class circularly with the three FDs

$$Department\ Manager \rightarrow Department$$
$$Department \rightarrow Dept\ Name$$
$$Dept\ Name \rightarrow Department\ Manager$$

or any other circular list of these names. In any case we need only three edges, one less than the original four in Fig. 9.8b.

Figure 9.20 provides another example of how we can make additional head reductions after circularly connecting sets of object sets in an equivalence class. In the figure, we first observe that no tail reductions are possible. If we mark D in an attempt to remove either the tail connection to E or the tail connection to F, we can make no further marks. If we mark E or F in an attempt to remove the tail connection to D, likewise we can make no further marks. No other tail reductions are possible since in a congruent hypergraph we can never tail reduce an FD edge with a single tail. We next observe that no head reductions are possible. If we attempt to remove the head connection to D from C, we can further mark only E and F, which is insufficient. If we attempt to remove the head connection to D from A, we can make no further marks. No other head reductions are possible since D is the only object set with multiple head connections. However, $AB \rightarrow C$ is given and we can derive $C \rightarrow AB$ by marking C, which then allows us to mark D, E, and F, and finally A and B. Thus, since we are assuming semantic equivalence, we have the equivalence class $\{AB, C\}$. Hence, we can circularly add the edge connection from C to AB (see Fig. 9.20b). The only

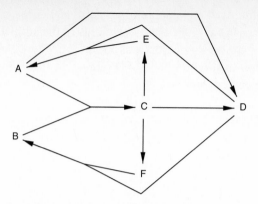

(a) ORM hypergraph with no possible head reductions.

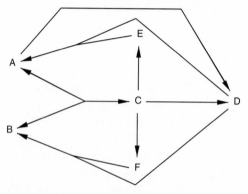

(b) Connected equivalence-class object sets leading to head reductions.

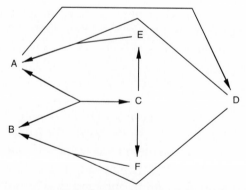

(c) Head-reduced ORM hypergraph.

Figure 9.20   An ORM hypergraph in which head reductions are possible only after connecting object sets circularly in an equivalence class.

differences between Fig. 9.20a and Fig. 9.20b are the two arrowheads that point to A and B, representing a bidirectional (circular) edge and thus the new edge from C to AB. With this new ORM hypergraph in Fig. 9.20b, we can head reduce $C \rightarrow D$. If we remove this edge and mark C, we can now mark A and B because of the new edge we just added, and since A is marked we can mark D because of $A \rightarrow D$. Figure 9.20c shows this reduction. (Additional reductions apply to the ORM hypergraph in Fig. 9.20c, including some that we have not yet discussed. We follow up on these reductions in the exercises.)

9.8 Redundant Nonfunctional Relationship Sets

Consider the ORM hypergraph in Fig. 9.21, which is the ORM hypergraph of Fig. 9.8b after all tail reductions, head reductions, and equivalence-class transformations, including the lexicalization of *Department* by *Dept Name*. In addition, the ORM hypergraph has a new functional edge from *Item* to *Department* and a new nonfunctional edge between *Worker* and *Item—Worker is responsible for Item*. We assume here that this new edge represents the relationships between workers and items in which each worker is responsible for many items and each item has many workers responsible for it. If we assume that workers are responsible for items that are in the departments for which they work, then this new nonfunctional edge is redundant. This is because

$$\textit{Worker is responsible for Item} = \pi_{\textit{Worker, Item}}(\\ \textit{Worker works for Department} \bowtie \textit{Item is in Department})$$

Removal of this *is responsible for* relationship set preserves information because we can reconstruct it by the expression on the right-hand side. It is also constraint preserving because there are no optional edge connections and thus the one-minimum participation constraints hold, and also because the relationship set is many-many and thus unconstrained by maximum participation constraints. Referential integrity is immediate since only workers in *Worker* and items in *Item* can be in the projection of the join in the recovery expression.

An important observation to make about this redundant *is responsible for* relationship set is that it participates in a cycle with the *works for* and *is in* relationship sets, which are those relationship sets whose join and projection are equivalent to the relationship. Indeed, a relationship set can be redundant only if it is in a cycle. We hasten to point out, however, that

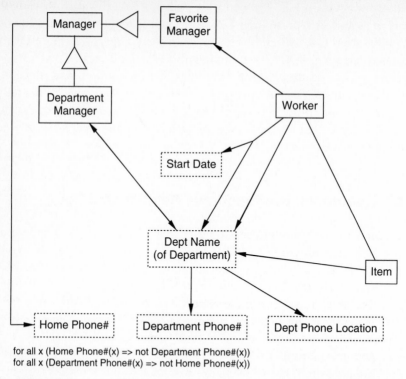

for all x (Home Phone#(x) => not Department Phone#(x))
for all x (Department Phone#(x) => not Home Phone#(x))

Figure 9.21 An ORM hypergraph with a nonfunctional relationship set of interest.

being in a cycle does not mean that a relationship set is redundant, only that it is potentially redundant. If instead of being *is responsible for*, the non-FD relationship set in Fig. 9.21 is *has special knowledge about* and not every worker has special knowledge about every item in the worker's department, then the relationship set would not be redundant.

Cycles in regular graphs are well understood, but what exactly do we mean by a cycle in an ORM hypergraph? Recall that in an ORM hypergraph each edge is a set of two or more object sets (since we insist that recursive edges have roles for all but one edge, we have no one-element edge sets or multisets). Two edges with the same set of object sets can be named to resolve ambiguity. For our purpose here, let us also assume that *isa* edges in *isa* hierarchies are edges. (It turns out that we can ignore these *isa* edges, but then we would have to insist that our ORM diagrams be congruent. Since this constraint is sometimes too restricting, we allow *isa* edges in our cycles.)

In an ORM hypergraph, we define a *path* to be a sequence of unique edges such that each successive pair has a nonempty intersection. The three-edge sequence

1. {*Worker, Start Date, Manager*}
2. {*Manager, Phone#*}
3. {*Department, Phone#, Dept Phone Location*}

in Fig. 9.7b, for example, is a path because the first and second sets intersect on *Manager* and the second and third sets intersect on *Phone#*. A *cycle* in an ORM hypergraph is a path whose first and last edge sets have a nonempty intersection. If we extend the preceding path by adding

4. {*Department, Dept Name*}
5. {*Dept Name, Worker*}

we have a cycle because the third and fourth edges intersect on *Department*, the fourth and fifth edges intersect on *Dept Name*, and finally, to complete the cycle, the fifth and first edges intersect on *Worker*.

Rather than search exhaustively for cycles, we can reduce the search space by first applying our reduction transformations—tail reduction, head reduction, and equivalence-class transformations—and then by removing any parts of the hypergraph that are not part of some cycle. By our preceding definitions, we can see that if an object set is in at most one edge, it cannot be in an intersection of two paths and thus cannot participate in connecting two edges for a path in a cycle. If we are looking for cycles, we may thus eliminate the object set. If the elimination of an object set causes an edge to have fewer than two object sets or deletes the only generalization or specialization in an *isa* edge, we can also eliminate the edge. We repeat this process until no more changes are possible. If no object sets remain after this process, the graph is *acyclic*; otherwise it is *cyclic*. We call a cyclic ORM hypergraph reduced in this way a *reduced cyclic ORM hypergraph*.

Applying these reductions to the ORM hypergraph in Fig. 9.21, we obtain the ORM hypergraph in Fig. 9.22. Since the ORM hypergraph in Fig. 9.21 is congruent, we can remove all the *isa* edges immediately. Then, if we remove all the object sets in at most one edge, we have the reduced cyclic ORM hypergraph in Fig. 9.22 immediately. Recall that a bidirectional edge is really two edges—one going in one direction; the other, in the other direction. Thus the edge between *Department Manager* and *Dept Name* (*of Department*) is indeed a cycle, although it may appear otherwise deceptively in the diagram.

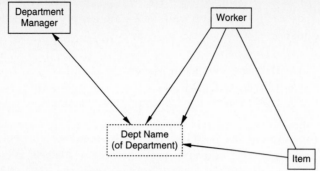

Figure 9.22 A reduced cyclic ORM hypergraph.

Given a reduced cyclic ORM hypergraph, we can begin to search for redundant edges. We search only for non-FD edges, leaving our FD edge reductions to other transformations. Thus, the only edge we consider in Fig. 9.22 is the *is responsible for* edge between *Worker* and *Item*. If we now exhaustively look for all the cycles involving this edge, we find two:

> {*Worker, Item*}
> {*Item, Dept Name (of Department)*}
> *works in*: {*Worker, Dept Name (of Department)*}

and

> {*Worker, Item*}
> {*Item, Dept Name (of Department)*}
> *can help in another*: {*Worker, Dept Name (of Department)*}

To determine whether the *is responsible for* relationship set is redundant, the questions we now ask become simple:

- For the first set we ask, "Are the items a worker is responsible for the same as the items in the department in which a worker works?"

- For the second set we ask, "Are the items a worker is responsible for the same as the items in the other department in which a worker can help?"

If we get a "yes" answer for a cycle, the nonfunctional edge under consideration is redundant and can be deleted. The deletion is information preserv-

---

Nonredundant Edges in Cycles

Although an edge we are considering as possibly being redundant must exist in its entirety in a cycle, this is not true of other edges in a cycle. Indeed, in our example here, the *works in* edge is incomplete because *Start Date* is missing, as can be seen by referring to Fig. 9.21. In this case we are not concerned because the edge does not participate in the join as an intersecting object set and also does not participate in the projection as an object set in the relationship set to be deleted.

---

ing because it can be computed by projecting on the object sets in the deleted edge after joining all the other relationship sets in the cycle. It is constraint preserving because neither the discarded participation constraints nor any discarded co-occurrence constraint can be violated if the edge is indeed the proper projection of the join of all other relationship sets in the cycle.

As a further simplification, we observe that if a nonfunctional edge has itself been reduced in creating a reduced cyclic ORM hypergraph, it can never be redundant. Assume, for example, that the nonfunctional edge in Fig. 9.21 had been the ternary edge *Worker is responsible for Item with a certain Priority Order*, where *Priority Order* is a connected object set that participates in no other edge. Since it participates in only one edge, it will have been removed in the reduction, again leaving us with the ORM hypergraph in Fig. 9.22. This time, however, because we cannot recover the priority order, we cannot compute the ternary edge from the information on hand. Generalizing, we observe that the complete edge of the edge we are testing for removal must be in the reduced cyclic ORM hypergraph. This observation further reduces the cycles we need to consider. In general, we need not consider an edge as possibly being redundant unless it is completely in a cycle and nonfunctional. If part of an edge is in a cycle, the edge may be reducible, as we shall see in the next section, but not discardable.

9.9　Reducible Nonfunctional Relationship Sets

Some non-FD *n*-ary relationship sets can be replaced by two or more relationship sets of degree less than *n*. Consider, as an example, the ORM diagram in Fig. 9.23. The *is responsible for* edge is redundant immediately because it is a projection of the ternary edge *Worker is responsible for Item*

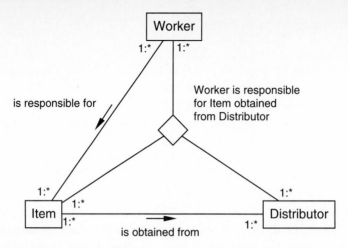

Figure 9.23 An ORM diagram with a redundant n-ary relationship set.

obtained from Distributor.[†] Likewise, the *is obtained from* edge is redundant immediately because it is also a projection of the ternary edge. Before discarding these edges too quickly, however, we must consider one other possibility—that the ternary edge itself may be redundant. Indeed it is, because the join of the *is responsible for* edge and the *is obtained from* edge yields the ternary edge precisely. We cannot, of course, remove all three edges, but we can either remove the *is responsible for* edge and the *is obtained from* edge, or we can remove the ternary edge. We may be tempted to remove the two and keep the one, but it is usually better to remove the ternary edge, as we will see in the next chapter. Figure 9.24 shows the proposed reduction.

Now suppose that we had been given only the ternary relationship set in Fig. 9.23, and not either of the binary relationship sets. In this case, we should try to find binary projections, whose join reconstructs the ternary relationship set. Then we can still make the reduction. In general, we should consider every non-FD *n*-ary relationship set, $n \geq 2$, to see if it can be decomposed into two or more relationship sets, all of which have fewer than *n* object sets.

For a given *n*-ary relationship set, a decomposition may or may not be possible. Whether or not it is possible depends on the semantics of the application. It is possible for the ternary relationship set in Fig. 9.23, but not

---

[†] We are assuming, of course, that we have been told by a reliable source that this is the case (i.e., that we have semantic equivalence). We make this assumption in this section for all our other assertions like this so that it is not necessary to repeat this important assumption each time.

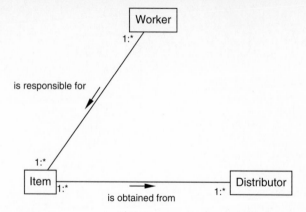

Figure 9.24 An ORM diagram reduced by removing an n-ary relationship set.

possible, for example, for the ternary relationship set in Fig. 9.25. We can determine that it is not possible for a ternary relationship set by considering all pairs of binary relationship sets plus the possibility of three binary relationship sets. To consider the possibilities, we can draw data from the application in a search for counterexamples. In this case, we can see that there is no possible decomposition by considering the four relationship sets in Fig. 9.26. In the figure, the relation labeled r_1 represents the ternary relationship set. The binary projection onto *Worker* and *Department* is the relation r_2; the projection onto *Department* and *Start Date* is r_3; and the projection onto *Worker* and *Start Date* is r_4. Our story here is slightly different from the one we have been assuming, but it is not unusual. We are assuming that a worker may be assigned to one or more departments on the same or on different starting dates. Now observe that

$$r_1 \neq r_2 \bowtie r_3,$$
$$r_1 \neq r_2 \bowtie r_4,$$
$$r_1 \neq r_3 \bowtie r_4, \text{ and}$$
$$r_1 \neq r_2 \bowtie r_3 \bowtie r_4$$

Hence, since we have chosen a valid ternary relation r_1, we have a counterexample to every possible decomposition. Thus the ternary relationship set in Fig. 9.25 cannot be decomposed.

Our next example shows that sometimes, even when it is impossible to decompose a ternary relationship set by any pair of projected binary relationship sets, it may still be possible to decompose the ternary relationship

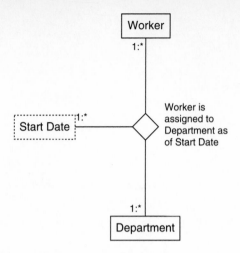

Figure 9.25 An ORM diagram with a nonreducible ternary relationship set.

$r_1 =$	Worker	Department	Start Date
	W_1	D_1	May 1
	W_2	D_2	May 1
	W_1	D_2	May 8

$r_2 =$	Worker	Department
	W_1	D_1
	W_2	D_2
	W_1	D_2

$r_3 =$	Department	Start Date
	D_1	May 1
	D_2	May 1
	D_2	May 8

$r_4 =$	Worker	Start Date
	W_1	May 1
	W_2	May 1
	W_1	May 8

Figure 9.26 Relations that serve as counterexamples for decomposition.

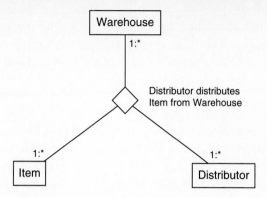

Figure 9.27 A decomposable ternary relationship set.

set by using all three projections. Figure 9.27 presents an example. To make this example work, we need a semantic reason for it to be decomposable. The rule we are assuming is as follows:

(1) a distributor supplies an item,
(2) a distributor stores items in a warehouse, and
(3) an item is stocked in a warehouse

if and only if

a distributor distributes an item from a warehouse.

This rule is quite reasonable since we would expect a distributor to supply an item if that item is available in a warehouse in which the distributor stores items. What might be unusual here is that the participation constraints allow more than one distributor to share a single warehouse.

Figure 9.28 displays an example of a possible relation for the ternary relationship set in the ORM diagram in Fig. 9.27. If we decompose it into the three relations for *Distributor-Item, Item-Warehouse,* and *Distributor-*

Distributor	Item	Warehouse
D_1	I_1	W_1
D_2	I_1	W_2
D_1	I_2	W_2
D_1	I_1	W_2

Figure 9.28 A relation to illustrate a three-way decomposition.

Warehouse and then join all three back together, we get the original in Fig. 9.28. Notice that we cannot join any pair of the relations to get the original; thus the relation in Fig. 9.28 serves as a counterexample for decomposing the ternary relationship set into any pair of binary relationship sets. How do we know, however, that there are no counterexamples for decomposing the ternary relationship set into three relationship sets, as we are proposing? The example alone does not tell us; we must reason by the given semantic rule. For example, if we try to create a counterexample by removing the last tuple, we violate the semantic rule. Note first that if we do remove the last tuple, then we would have a counterexample because the join of the three projections does not yield the original. The counterexample is invalid, however, because it does not satisfy the semantic rule. It does not satisfy the rule because from the first three tuples we have (1) D_1 supplies I_1, (2) I_1 is stocked in W_2, and (3) D_1 stores items in W_2. Therefore, by our semantic rule we must have D_1 distributes I_1 from W_2 as a fact. But this is the last tuple, so we cannot delete it as we had supposed. In general, only a semantic reason or rule can ensure that a decomposition is always lossless.

9.10 Properly Embedded Functional Dependencies

We observe in this section that we can reduce an FD n-ary edge or an equivalence class when an FD is embedded in the edge or equivalence class in a certain way. In particular, if R is a set of object sets from an ORM hypergraph H such that R constitutes an edge or the object sets of an equivalence class over which semantic equivalence holds, then we can make a reduction transformation if the following conditions hold:

1. XY is a set of object sets such that $XY \subseteq R$.
2. $X \cap Y = \varnothing$.
3. $X \rightarrow Y$ is an FD given in H or implied by the FD edges of H.
4. Semantic equivalence holds for $X \rightarrow Y$ with respect to R.
5. $X^+ \not\supseteq R$.

We call an FD $X \rightarrow Y$ that satisfies these conditions a *properly embedded FD*. $X \rightarrow Y$ is embedded because Condition 1 requires $XY \subseteq R$. $X \rightarrow Y$ is properly embedded because Conditions 3 and 5 require that XY must be a proper subset of R. There must be at least one object set in R that is not in XY because $X \rightarrow Y$ implies $XY \subseteq X^+$, but X^+ does not include all of R.

These conditions also imply some other properties of R, which we explore in the exercises. Some of these properties are as follows. If we have already done all other transformations discussed in this chapter, we need consider only two cases: (1) R constitutes the object sets of a single FD edge or (2) the object sets that constitute R are the elements of a nontrivial equivalence class. Furthermore, if R is an FD edge, it must have multiple tails and Y must be a proper subset of the tail object sets.

We first consider FDs that are properly embedded in an n-ary FD edge. In the application model in Fig. 9.29a, a salesperson services one or more customers, but a customer is assigned only one salesperson. In addition, salespersons can have one or more appointments with customers on various dates and at various times. However, a salesperson can meet with only one customer on any date at a particular time.

Figure 9.29b is the ORM hypergraph for the ORM diagram in Fig. 9.29a. *Customer* $\rightarrow$ *Salesperson* is properly embedded in *Salesperson has appointment with Customer at Time on Date* because we have semantic equivalence, because *Customer*$^+$ $\not\supseteq$ *Salesperson Date Time Customer*, and because the rest of the conditions are clearly satisfied. Observe also that there are no head reductions, no tail reductions, and no nontrivial equivalence classes. Observe further that the FD edge *Salesperson Date Time* $\rightarrow$ *Customer* has the additional properties we expect: its tail is composite, and its right-hand-side object set is an element of the composite tail.

By analyzing our example, we can see that if we let r represent the *Salesperson has appointment with Customer at Time on Date* relationship set and s represent the *Salesperson services Customer* relationship set, then

$$r = s \bowtie \pi_{Date, \, Time, \, Customer} r$$

This holds because if we take any appointment date, time, and customer triple, then since there is only one salesperson for a customer, we can determine who the salesperson must be. Thus if we replace the *Salesperson has appointment with Customer at Time on Date* relationship set by the non-FD n-ary relationship that is equal to the projection of this relationship set onto *Date*, *Time*, and *Customer*, then we can still recover the information. Thus this transformation is information preserving.

The transformation is not constraint preserving, however, because we no longer have or can imply the FD

$$\textit{Salesperson, Date, Time} \rightarrow \textit{Customer}$$

To make the transformation constraint preserving, we must add a high-

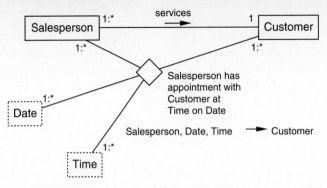

(a) ORM diagram with an FD embedded in an n-ary FD.

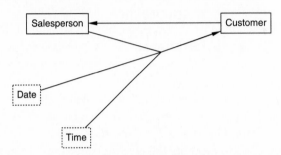

(b) ORM hypergraph for the ORM diagram.

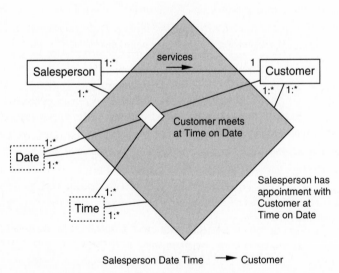

(c) High-level relationship set for the embedded FD.

Figure 9.29   Sample transformation for an FD embedded in an n-ary FD.

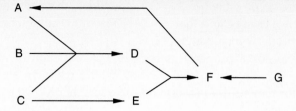

(a) ORM hypergraph with an implied properly embedded FD.

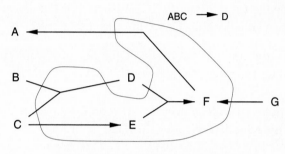

(b) Reduced ORM hypergraph.

Figure 9.30   Sample transformation for an implied properly embedded FD.

level relationship set that is equal to the join of the *Salesperson services Customer* relationship set and the new relationship set, which is the projection onto *Date, Time,* and *Customer* of the *Salesperson has appointment with Customer at Time on Date* relationship set. Figure 9.29c shows this high-level relationship set. Given this high-level relationship set, we can specify the co-occurrence constraint

$$Salesperson\ Date\ Time \rightarrow Customer$$

With this addition, the transformation is now also constraint preserving.

Figure 9.30 illustrates some additional possibilities. In Fig. 9.30a we can determine that $CD \rightarrow A$ is an implied FD by starting with CD, taking the closure which is $CDEFA$, and observing that A is in the closure. Assuming semantic equivalence, we see that $CD \rightarrow A$ is a properly embedded FD: $CDA \subseteq ABCD$, $CD \cap A = \varnothing$, and $CD^+ \not\supseteq ABCD$. We can observe further that there are no possible head or tail reductions, that there are no nontrivial equivalence classes, and that $ABC \to D$ is an FD edge whose tail is composite and properly includes A.

In general, for a properly embedded FD reduction of an FD edge R where $X \to Y$ is the embedded FD and where we have already done all other transformations discussed in this chapter, we proceed as follows:

1. Create a non-FD edge that is the projection of R onto $R - Y$.

2. Create a high-level relationship set over this new edge and the relevant edge set that yields $X \to Y$ such that the object sets in this high-level relationship set are the object sets in R.

3. Specify the original FD in the FD edge as the co-occurrence constraint for the high-level relationship set.

For our example, we first project $ABCD$ onto BCD. We then create a high-level relationship set that includes the relationship sets BCD (the new edge) and the relevant edge set $\{C \to E, DE \to F, F \to A\}$ such that the connecting object sets are A, B, C, and D. (Note that the edge $G \to F$ is not included. In drawing high-level relationship sets, we do not include an edge unless its midpoint is within the high-level relationship set.) Finally, we specify the co-occurrence constraint $ABC \to D$ for the high-level relationship set. Figure 9.30b shows the result.

After applying a properly embedded FD reduction, we may still need to apply other reductions. In particular, we may still be able to reduce the non-FD edge created in the transformation. We can minimize the number of subsequent reductions by ensuring that Y is initially maximal. See the exercises for illustrations of these further reductions.

As an example of an FD that is embedded properly in an equivalence class, we consider Fig. 9.31a, an ORM hypergraph that has the equivalence class $\{AB, AC, D\}$. We can see that the given edge $B \to C$ is properly embedded in this equivalence class as follows. We are assuming semantic equivalence, and we can observe that $BC \subseteq ABCD$, $B \cap C = \emptyset$, and $BC_+ \not\supseteq ABCD$. Figure 9.31b shows the transformation for this example. This transformation is information preserving because we can compute the information for the only missing edge $AC \to D$ by $\pi_{ACD}(r \bowtie s)$, where r and s are edges for ABD and BC, respectively. The transformation is constraint preserving because $\{AB \to D, D \to AB, B \to C, AC \to D\}$ implies $\{B \to C, AC \to D, D \to AB\}$. In the exercises, we explore algorithms for removing FDs that are embedded properly in equivalence classes.

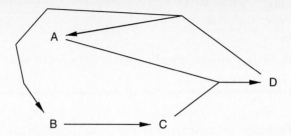

(a) ORM hypergraph with an implied FD embedded in an n-ary FD.

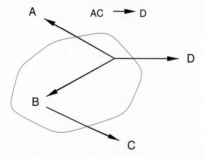

(b) High-level relationship set for the implied FD.

Figure 9.31 Another sample transformation for an implied FD embedded in an n-ary FD.

9.11 Chapter Summary

Topic Summary

- Given an ORM diagram for an application, we can generate an ORM hypergraph directly. An ORM hypergraph is a view of an ORM diagram that represents directly the FDs of the application. There is therefore no need for a developer to specify the FDs for an application separately, only the need to capture objects and relationships properly in an ORM diagram.

- Two sets of FDs are equivalent if their closures are the same—that is, if the sets of FDs implied by each are identical. If the FDs in one set imply the FDs in another set and conversely, the closures of the two sets are the same. TAP (Trivial-implication/Accumulation/Projection) derivation sequences provide an easy way to determine whether a set of FDs implies a given FD.

- Because of the direct correspondence between sets of FDs and hypergraphs, we can manipulate hypergraphs rather than sets of FDs to do reductions. For a given hypergraph, a reduction produces a new hypergraph with fewer components, but with the same information capacity and the same implied constraints as the given hypergraph. Head reductions remove a head component from a hyperedge; tail reductions remove a tail component; minimal consolidation can reduce the arity of a hyperedge; lexicalization removes a node and an edge; object-set merge combines two nodes and removes an edge; and nonfunctional edge reduction reduces the arity of or removes a nonfunctional hyperedge. Properly embedded FD reductions remove edge components, but at the expense of adding FDs that apply to high-level relationship sets spanning two or more edges.

- When we do a reduction transformation, we must ensure that the transformation preserves information and constraints. When we transform one application model to another, we preserve information if, for any valid interpretation, there is a way for us to recover all the information in the valid interpretation from the transformed interpretation of the transformed application model. We preserve constraints if the constraints of the transformed application model imply the constraints of the application model before the transformation. All our transformations preserve information and constraints.

- Our transformations assume semantic equivalence over relevant edge sets. Semantic equivalence depends on the meaning of the application model. Developers must check semantic equivalence for each proposed reduction. Relevant edge sets, universal relations restricted to relevant edge sets, congruency, and roles all help developers resolve semantic-equivalence questions. Relevant edge sets let developers focus on only those edges that have any bearing on the question of semantic equivalence. Universal relations over relevant edge sets let developers present examples and possible counterexamples to clients. Properly chosen examples help lead to a resolution of semantic equivalence. Congruency and roles provide valuable clues to semantic-equivalence resolution.

Question Summary

- How do we ensure that a transformation preserves information?

  Our transformations are all reduction transformations, in the sense that they discard one or more components. Thus, to make our transformations preserve information, we ensure that we can compute the data discarded with the component from the data of the remaining components.

- How do we ensure that a transformation preserves constraints?

  Except for embedded FD reductions and discarding union-covered isolated root generalizations, our transformations only discard constraints. Thus to make our transformations preserve constraints, we make sure that the constraints that remain after the transformation imply the discarded constraints. For embedded FD reductions and for discarding isolated root generalizations with partitions, we add constraints—without the additions, the remaining constraints would not imply the discarded constraints.

- How do relevant edge sets and roles help resolve questions about semantic equivalence?

  If the objects under consideration play different roles in the relationship sets of a relevant edge set where they should play the same role, then semantic equivalence does not hold over the relevant edge set. Naming these roles and making them explicit often provides enough information to let us resolve semantic-equivalence questions.

- How do reductions relate to changes in the underlying model-theoretic database view?

  Removal of a relationship set or object set in a reduction corresponds to removal of a relation in the underlying model-theoretic database view. Removal of a component of a relationship set corresponds to projecting out the columns of the underlying relation that no longer participate in the relationship set, or, equivalently, projecting on the columns of the underlying relation that are still connected in the relationship set. Decomposing a relationship set into two or more relationship sets corresponds to decomposing the underlying relation into two or more relationship sets by projecting on the columns of the connected components of the decomposed relationship set. Consolidating connections on a single element of an equivalence class corresponds to replacing a column or columns of an underlying relation by the column or columns of another underlying relation in such a way that the one-to-one correspondence among underlying objects is retained. The merging of nonlexical object sets whose objects are in a one-to-one correspondence can be thought of as discarding all but one of the underlying relations, giving the names of discarded relations as aliases to the remaining relation, and replacing object identifiers of discarded objects that happen to appear in other relations by the corresponding object identifiers of objects in the remaining relation. Reductions also reduce the number of constraints to check. In the underlying model-theoretic database view, this corresponds to removing some of the generated closed formulas.

- Why do properly embedded, functional-edge reductions require a high-level relationship set with a functional dependency?

  Without the high-level relationship set and FD, we would not be able to preserve constraints.

- In what sense can we view reduction transformations as patterns for design?

  Every reduction transformation is a design pattern. These patterns manifest themselves in specific ways in applications, but all can be classified as general patterns to which we can apply reduction transformations.

9.12   Bibliographic Notes

Researchers have used hypergraphs to study various aspects of database theory [Abiteboul95, Maier83]. The ORM hypergraph notation and the use of ORM hypergraphs in design transformations as presented here are unique to this book.

Many researchers have contributed to the theory of functional dependencies. Most of what is known about functional dependencies and how they apply to database design can be found in books on relational theory [Abiteboul95, Atzeni93, Maier83]. Less theoretical treatments of functional-dependency theory can be found in books on relational databases [Date95, Elmasri94, Hansen92, Helman94, Korth97, O'Neil94, Ullman97]. Although unique to this book, the derivation of functional dependencies from concep-

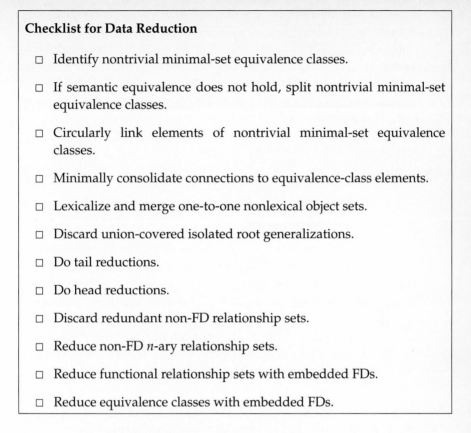

Checklist for Data Reduction

☐ Identify nontrivial minimal-set equivalence classes.

☐ If semantic equivalence does not hold, split nontrivial minimal-set equivalence classes.

☐ Circularly link elements of nontrivial minimal-set equivalence classes.

☐ Minimally consolidate connections to equivalence-class elements.

☐ Lexicalize and merge one-to-one nonlexical object sets.

☐ Discard union-covered isolated root generalizations.

☐ Do tail reductions.

☐ Do head reductions.

☐ Discard redundant non-FD relationship sets.

☐ Reduce non-FD *n*-ary relationship sets.

☐ Reduce functional relationship sets with embedded FDs.

☐ Reduce equivalence classes with embedded FDs.

tual models as presented here has some similarities with [Ram95], which describes how to derive functional dependencies from the ER model rather than from an ORM application model.

As explained in the chapter, the notion of semantic equivalence is related to the idea of a universal relation [Fagin82] and the assumption that a universal relation exists [Kent81]. Semantic equivalence is also related to a weaker assumption that the attributes have the same meaning everywhere, which is known as the universal-relation scheme assumption [Maier83]. The term "semantic equivalence" and its use in localized information- and constraint-preserving transformations is unique to this book.

Many of the hypergraph transformations presented here are based on standard nonhypergraph transformations for functional and join dependencies as presented in most books on relational database, but especially in [Atzeni93] and [Maier83]. However, head and tail reductions that require the addition of a nonfunctional edge to make the transformation information preserving and the addition of a constraint for a high-level relationship set for embedded FD transformations both are unique in this book. Our lexicalization transformation is also unique in the sense that other relational database books do not discuss it, but the idea of this transformation appeared earler in an article [Embley89b]. Transformations with a similar intent to those presented here have also been developed for the OR model [Halpin95a, Halpin95b].

9.13 Exercises

9.1 Convert the ORM diagram in Fig. 9.32 into (a) an ORM hypergraph and then into (b) a set of FDs.

9.2 Convert the set of FDs $\{A \rightarrow G,\ AB \rightarrow CD,\ D \rightarrow EF,\ BE \rightarrow FG,\ G \rightarrow C\}$ into (a) an ORM hypergraph and then into (b) an ORM diagram. Assume that each attribute represents a nonlexical object set. Be sure to supply proper participation and co-occurrence constraints. Do not give a co-occurrence constraint unless it is required (that is, give preference to specifying constraints as participation constraints). Choose names for relationship sets and be sure to make the names valid.

9.3 Consider the predicate $P(a, b, c, d)$, which we define as $a = b \Rightarrow c = d$, and suppose we know that this predicate is *true*.

    a. If $a = b$, can we conclude anything about whether c and d are equal? If yes, what? If no, why not?

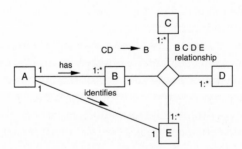

Figure 9.32 ORM diagram for conversion.

b. If $c = d$, can we conclude anything about whether a and b are equal? If yes, what? If no, why not?

c. What does this problem have to do with FDs?

9.4** Prove Theorem 9.1.

9.5 Let I and I', which follow, be valid interpretations for application models M and M', respectively. Let T be a transformation from M to M' that maps I to I'. Give a procedure to compute I from I'.

Interpretation I:

A	B	C		A	B		B	C		A	C
1	4	7		1	4		4	7		1	7
2	5	8		2	5		5	8		2	8
3	6										

Interpretation I':

A	B	C		A	B		B	C
1	4	7		1	4		4	7
2	5	8		2	5		5	8
3	6							

9.6 List *all* the nontrivial FDs satisfied by the following relation. (An FD $X \rightarrow Y$ is *trivial* if $Y \subseteq X$.)

A	B	C
1	1	1
1	1	2
2	1	1
2	1	3

9.7* Let $R = ABC$ be a relation scheme and let $F = \{A \rightarrow C\}$ be a set of FDs. List all the FDs over R that are in F^+.

9.8* Prove Theorem 9.2.

9.9* In addition to trivial implication, accumulation, and projection, the following three additional FD derivation rules are useful. For these rules, let R be a relation scheme and let $XYZ \subseteq R$.

(augmentation) If $X \rightarrow Y$, then $XZ \rightarrow YZ$.

(union) If $X \rightarrow Y$ and $X \rightarrow Z$, then $X \rightarrow YZ$.

(transitivity) If $X \rightarrow Y$ and $Y \rightarrow Z$, then $X \rightarrow Z$.

a. Use the cardinality definition of an FD (i.e., $X \rightarrow Y$ if $|\sigma_{X=x}\pi_{XY}r| = 1$) to prove that the augmentation rule is sound.

b. Use the implication definition of an FD (i.e., $t_1[X] = t_2[X] \Rightarrow t_1[Y] = t_2[Y]$) to prove that the union rule is sound.

c. Use a generic derivation sequence (i.e., one with variables X, Y, ... that stand for sets of attributes) along with trivial implication, accumulation, and projection to prove that the transitivity rule is sound.

9.10 Consider the following proposed FD derivation rule:

If $X \rightarrow Y$ and $X \rightarrow Z$, then $Y \rightarrow Z$.

Give a counterexample to show that this rule is *not* sound.

9.11** Prove Theorem 9.3.

9.12** Prove Theorem 9.4.

9.13* Prove Theorem 9.5.

9.14 Let $F = \{A \rightarrow G, AB \rightarrow CD, D \rightarrow EF, BE \rightarrow FG, G \rightarrow C\}$ be a set of FDs.

a. Give a derivation sequence using only trivial implication, augmentation, and transitivity for $BD \rightarrow C$.

b. Give a TAP derivation sequence for $BD \rightarrow C$.

c. Compute BD^+.

d. Draw the ORM hypergraph for F and mark all reachable nodes starting from BD.

e. Show that F does not imply $A \rightarrow E$.

f. Draw the ORM hypergraph for F and mark all reachable nodes starting from A.

9.15   Let F and F' be sets of FDs. If F implies each FD f' of F', F implies F', sometimes written $F \mid= F'$. If $F \mid= F'$ and $F' \mid= F$, F and F' are *equivalent*, and we write $F \equiv F'$.

Show that each of the following pairs of sets of FDs are equivalent:

a. $\{A \rightarrow BC, A \rightarrow D, D \rightarrow C\}$ and $\{A \rightarrow B, A \rightarrow D, D \rightarrow C\}$.

b. $\{AB \rightarrow C, A \rightarrow B\}$ and $\{A \rightarrow B, A \rightarrow C\}$.

c. $\{A \rightarrow B, AB \rightarrow C, B \rightarrow CD, A \rightarrow C\}$ and $\{A \rightarrow BC, B \rightarrow CD\}$.

d. $\{A \rightarrow B, CD \rightarrow A, C \rightarrow D\}$ and $\{C \rightarrow B, A \rightarrow B, C \rightarrow AD\}$.

9.16   Show that the following sets of relations either do or do not have a universal relation:

a.

$r_1 =$	A	B		$r_2 =$	B	C
	1	2			2	5
	3	4			2	6
					4	7

b.

$r_1 =$	A	B		$r_2 =$	B	C
	1	2			2	5
	3	4			2	6
	8	9			4	7

c.

$r_1 =$	A	B		$r_2 =$	B	C		$r_3 =$	A	C
	1	1			1	3			1	3
	2	1			1	4			2	4
	1	2			2	4			1	4

d.

$r_1 =$	A	B		$r_2 =$	B	C		$r_3 =$	A	C
	1	1			1	3			1	3
	2	1			1	4			2	4
	3	2			2	4			1	4

9.17   Compute $r \otimes s$ (the outer join) for r and s:

$r =$	A	B	C		$s =$	B	C	D
	1	1	1			1	1	1
	2	1	1			1	2	3
	3	4	5			6	7	8

9.18 Let R be a relation scheme. A *decomposition of R* is a set of attribute sets $\{R_1, ..., R_n\}$ such that $R = R_1 ... R_n$. (Recall that a concatenation of relation schemes denotes the union of the schemes.) Let r be a relation on R. A decomposition $R_1 ... R_n$ of R is *lossless* for r if $r = \pi_{R_1} r \bowtie ... \bowtie \pi_{R_n}$.

    a.** Let q be a relation on RS. Prove that if $R \cap S \to R$ or $R \cap S \to S$, then the decomposition $\{R, S\}$ is lossless for q.

    b.* Show that the converse of (a) is false.

    c.* Let r be a relation on $R_1 ... R_n$. Prove by induction that if $R_1 \cap R_2 \to R_2$, $R_1 R_2 \cap R_3 \to R_3$, ..., $R_1 ... R_{n-1} \cap R_n \to R_n$, then the decomposition $\{R_1, ..., R_n\}$ is lossless for r.

9.19** Develop an algorithm to find relevant edge sets. The input should be an ORM hypergraph with a designated initial set of object sets X and a target set of object sets Y, where $X \cap Y = \varnothing$. The output should be all relevant edge sets. Each relevant edge set should be a minimal collection of edges (possibly reduced to remove superfluous object sets) such that we can reach the target set Y from the initial set X.

9.20 The ORM diagram in Fig. 9.33 includes some object sets that play multiple roles.

    a. Add an appropriate role name for every connection that has a zero-minimum participation constraint.

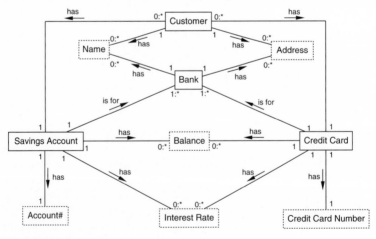

Figure 9.33 ORM diagram for roles.

b. Rework the ORM diagram so that each role added in (a) becomes an object set. These new object sets should be specializations of an object set in the diagram. Assume that each object set for which a pair of roles was added in (a) consists only of objects that participate in at least one of the roles, sometimes both. Assume that neither banks and customers have names or addresses in common. Add generalization/specialization constraints to reflect these constraints.

c. Discard union-covered isolated root generalizations.

d.* Use OSM-L to formalize any added constraints for (c).

9.21** Prove that removal of a union-covered isolated root generalization preserves information and constraints.

General note: Any hypergraph that corresponds to a set of FDs should have exactly one edge for each FD and should have no optional edge connections. Also, assume that semantic equivalence holds for any generic hypergraphs and sets of FDs—ones whose nodes or object sets are all single letters of the alphabet. Assume further that congruency holds for generic hypergraphs, except where there is a zero-minimum participation constraint or an explicitly marked optional connection.

9.22 Let $F = \{AB \rightarrow C, C \rightarrow B, A \rightarrow BD\}$.

a. Produce the ORM hypergraph corresponding to F.

b. Give the ORM hypergraph after making tail and head reductions.

c. Give the set of FDs corresponding to the reduced ORM hypergraph in (b) and show that it is equivalent to F.

9.23 Let $F = \{A \rightarrow B, B \rightarrow A, BCG \rightarrow D, C \rightarrow E, AE \rightarrow D\}$.

a. Produce the ORM hypergraph corresponding to F.

b. Give the ORM hypergraph after making tail and head reductions.

c. Show that the transformation would *not* be information preserving without adding the nonfunctional edge required as part of the reduction transformations.

9.24* Reduce the ORM hypergraph in Fig. 9.34. Be sure to adjust the general constraint as part of doing the reduction.

for all x for all y for all z for all w (A(x)C(y)D(z) relation
and D(z)E(w) relation => A(x)E(w) relation)

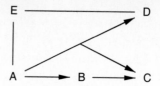

Figure 9.34 ORM diagram with a general constraint.

9.25** Prove that head reduction preserves information and constraints.

9.26** Prove that tail reduction preserves information and constraints.

9.27 Let $F = \{A \rightarrow B, B \rightarrow C, B \rightarrow D, D \rightarrow A, EJ \rightarrow C, E \rightarrow G, G \rightarrow H,$
$J \rightarrow I, HI \rightarrow E, HI \rightarrow J, A \rightarrow K, HI \rightarrow L\}$.

    a.* List all nontrivial minimal-set equivalence classes for F.

    b. Give the ORM hypergraph for F.

    c. Minimally consolidate connections to equivalence-class elements.

9.28** Prove that consolidation of connections over an equivalence class preserves information and constraints.

9.29 Consider the ORM diagram in Fig. 9.35.

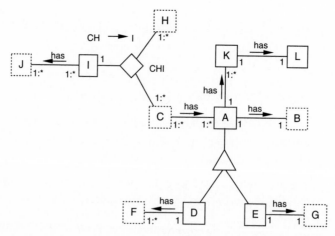

Figure 9.35 ORM diagram for lexicalization and one-to-one merge.

    a. Give the ORM hypergraph for this diagram.

    b. Lexicalize and merge one-to-one nonlexical objects sets for the ORM hypergraph obtained for (a).

9.30** Prove that merging nonlexical object sets whose elements have a one-to-one correspondence preserves information and constraints.

9.31** Prove that lexicalization for binary relationship sets preserves information and constraints.

9.32** Give an algorithm for lexicalization of a nonlexical object set whose objects are in a one-to-one correspondence with the tuples of two or more objects in lexical object sets. Prove that the algorithm preserves information and constraints.

9.33 Let $F = \{BE \rightarrow A,\ DG \rightarrow BE,\ B \rightarrow C,\ E \rightarrow H,\ D \rightarrow A,\ G \rightarrow A,\ ABH \rightarrow G,\ AEC \rightarrow D\}$.

    a. Explain why the edge $BE \rightarrow A$ cannot be head reduced in F.

    b. Find the set of left-hand sides of the FDs in F that belong together in an equivalence class (there is only one such set).

    c. Circularly link the elements of the equivalence class found for (b) in F, yielding F'.

    d. Explain why the edge $BE \rightarrow A$ can be head reduced in F'.

9.34 Let $F = \{A \rightarrow B,\ B \rightarrow A,\ BC \rightarrow D,\ C \rightarrow E,\ AE \rightarrow D\}$.

    a. Give the ORM hypergraph for F.

    b. Transform the ORM hypergraph for F by doing a head reduction of $BC \rightarrow D$.

    c.* Is the nonfunctional edge BC generated by the head reduction of $BC \rightarrow D$ redundant? If so, give an expression to compute BC. If not, give an example to show that the BC edge cannot be removed.

9.35 Let object sets *Course*, *Semester*, and *Book* be connected by a ternary relationship set.

    a. Give a meaning for this ternary relationship set so that it can be reduced to two binary relationship sets.

    b. Give a meaning for this ternary relationship set so that it cannot be reduced.

9.36** Prove that the removal of redundant nonfunctional relationship sets preserves information and constraints.

9.37** Prove that n-ary nonfunctional relationship-set reduction preserves information and constraints.

9.38 Let $F = \{AB \rightarrow C, C \rightarrow DE, E \rightarrow A, BD \rightarrow G\}$.

    a. Produce the ORM hypergraph H corresponding to F.

    b. There is an FD in F^+ that is properly embedded in one of the edges of H. Find it.

    c. Reduce H by doing an embedded FD reduction.

    d. Let H' be the ORM hypergraph produced by the reduction in (c). Give an expression in terms of H' to compute the edge in H that does not appear in H'.

    e. Let H' be the ORM hypergraph produced by the reduction in (c). Give the FDs for H and H' and showing that the FDs of H' imply the FDs of H.

9.39* Reduce the ORM hypergraph in Fig. 9.20c as far as possible.

9.40** Prove that the embedded FD reduction of an FD edge preserves information and constraints.

9.41 The conditions required for embedded FD reduction imply that several other conditions must hold. We can check many of these other conditions easily. Thus, if we know these conditions, we can usually quickly eliminate many edges as possibilities for embedded FD reduction, leaving perhaps none or only a few edges to which we must apply the full test for embedded FD reductions.

    a.* Prove that the conditions for embedded FD reduction for an edge R imply that R cannot be binary.

    b.** Prove that if an ORM hypergraph has been head and tail reduced (including head reductions with elements of nontrivial minimal-set equivalence classes linked), then the conditions for embedded FD reduction for an FD edge R imply the following two conditions:

       1. The tail side of R must be composite (i.e., its tail side must have more than one object set).

       2. For an FD $X \rightarrow Y$ embedded in R such that $X^+ \not\supseteq R$ there exists an object set $A \in Y$ that is also in the composite tail of R.

9.42 Let $F = \{ABC \rightarrow D, D \rightarrow A, D \rightarrow B\}$.

    a. Give the ORM hypergraph H for F.

    b. Apply an embedded FD reduction to H to obtain H' by using $D \rightarrow A$ as the embedded FD.

    c. Explain why the non-FD edge BCD in H' can be reduced.

    d. Explain how to reduce the non-FD edge BCD in H' so that the transformation preserves information and constraints. Give this reduction as H''.

    e. Apply an embedded FD reduction to H to obtain H''' by using the implied FD $D \rightarrow AB$ as the embedded FD.

    f. Compare H'' and H''', and explain any similarities and differences.

9.43 Let $F = \{ABCD \rightarrow EG, E \rightarrow AB, G \rightarrow D\}$.

    a. Give the ORM hypergraph H for F.

    b.* Apply embedded FD and non-FD edge reductions to H until no more reductions are possible.

9.44 Let $F = \{BC \rightarrow A, B \rightarrow G, C \rightarrow D, D \rightarrow E, EG \rightarrow B, EG \rightarrow C\}$.

    a. Give the ORM hypergraph for F.

    b. List the nontrivial, minimal-attribute-set, equivalence class for F.

    c.** Apply transformations to remove all FDs that are properly embedded in the equivalence class for F. Give the resulting hypergraph, including high-level relationship sets and constraints.

9.45** Give an algorithm for removing FDs that are properly embedded in equivalence classes. Prove that the algorithm preserves information and constraints.

9.46** Let M be an application model and let M' be an application model transformed from M by transformation T. Let I_M be a valid interpretation for M and let $I_{M'}$ be the transformed interpretation for M' for T. For each reduction transformation T in this chapter, prove that $I_{M'}$ is a valid interpretation for M'.

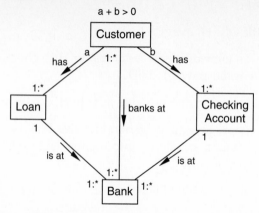

Figure 9.36 ORM diagram for observing another kind of reduction transformation.

9.47* Consider the ORM diagram in Fig. 9.36. Assume that a customer banks at a bank if the customer has a loan at the bank, has a checking account at the bank, or both.

a. Give the ORM hypergraph H for this ORM application model. (Note that the presence of the participation constraints a and b makes this interesting. To handle these constraints, replace both a and b by 0:* and add formal general constraints for these participation constraints, that is, the ones that would be generated for these constraints when the diagram is converted to predicates and rules. Also, replace $a + b > 0$ by the formal general constraint that would be generated for this expression.)

b. Explain why none of the transformations discussed in this chapter apply to H.

c. Explain why H is nevertheless reducible. In particular, explain why *Customer banks at Bank* is redundant.

d. Show that we can remove *Customer banks at Bank* and still preserve information by giving an expression that computes *Customer banks at Bank* from the other object and relationship sets.

e. Show that we can remove *Customer banks at Bank* and still preserve constraints by listing the constraints in H that are not in the transformed diagram and explaining why the constraints in the transformed diagram imply each of these constraints.

f. In addition to the transformations described in this chapter, this exercise shows that other transformations are also possible. An interesting research problem might be to find and classify additional reduction transformations. What does the particular example in this exercise suggest about the kinds of reduction transformations we might expect to find?

9.48* In a congruent ORM hypergraph, prove that any binary relationship set that connects to a singleton object set is redundant, that is, prove that we can discard such a relationship set while preserving information and constraints.

Chapter 10

Data Design—Synthesis

In the last chapter we presented several transformations to remove redundant ORM components. In this chapter we show how to synthesize data schemes for object modules, which we introduce in the next chapter as our basic unit for implementation. Informally, an *object module* consists of a data definition, which describes the data for the object module, and a behavior definition, which gives the operations for the object module. Our objective in this chapter is to show how to derive good schemes for data definitions for object modules.

In order to derive good data definitions, we must know which properties are desirable, as well as how we can tell whether our data structures satisfy these properties. Ultimately, our properties are motivated by time and space, but we also look for simpler characterizations and guidelines that generally yield good time and space characteristics.

In Section 10.1, we provide some examples to motivate our discussion. These motivating examples show that we are interested in combining schemes from an underlying valid interpretation for an application model into larger units. In Section 10.2, we discuss join dependencies, which are constraints that arise naturally and that concern us when we start combining schemes. In Section 10.3, we discuss redundancy, a major problem that can arise when we combine schemes, not only because we must store redundant data values, but also because we must spend additional time updating and enforcing constraints over these redundant data values. After laying out these concerns, we show in Section 10.4 how to synthesize flat schemes; both Sections 10.4 and 10.5 describe how to generate the intrascheme and inter-scheme constraints we must enforce. These flat schemes and constraints are the basis for standard relational and deductive databases. We then show in Section 10.6 that, with the help of the reduction transformations described in Chapter 9, we can have the basic properties we want. All is not well, however, because occasionally the properties are at odds with the goals of time and space reduction. We therefore discuss cost in Section 10.7, in an effort both to substantiate claims about the basic properties and to determine when we should make exceptions to the general rules for database design. In Section 10.8, we turn our attention to synthesizing and analyzing nested schemes, which are useful for object databases. Finally, in Section 10.9, we discuss a particularly thorny issue about time and space trade-offs for embedded FDs. We leave this until the end because we draw on both flat and nested scheme synthesis and the properties of flat and nested schemes to address this issue.

Relational Normalization Theory

The reader who already understands relational-database normalization theory will recognize that our approach has its roots in normalization theory. Our approach to normalization, however, emphasizes denormalization as much as normalization—it takes a cost-based approach to deciding whether to seek a higher normal form.

The following topics in this chapter are particularly important:

- Multivalued and join dependencies.

- The difference between actual redundancy and potential redundancy.

- The difference between having nulls and the possibility of having nulls.

- Scheme synthesis and the objectives of scheme synthesis, including minimum number of schemes, maximum size of schemes, elimination of potential redundancy, removal of potential nulls, and lossless joins.

- Interscheme dependencies: inclusion dependencies, scheme-spanning FDs, and generalization/specialization constraints.

- Canonical ORM hypergraphs.

- Properties of synthesized schemes.

The following questions should also be kept in mind:

- What distinguishes redundant data values from values that are merely the same as other data values?

- Why do we want to remove potential redundancy?

- How can we guarantee that synthesized schemes preserve information and constraints?

- What do the properties of synthesized schemes have to do with efficiency? How do the properties balance competing requirements?

- How does a cost analysis allow us to make exceptions to the general rules?

- To what extent can we automate data design? Can it be fully automatic?

- In what sense can we view synthesizing schemes as patterns for design?

10.1   Motivating Examples

We begin with some motivating examples of all the major ideas we wish to explore systematically in this chapter. Consider first the ORM diagram in Fig. 10.1a and a sample single relation *r* for the ORM diagram in Fig. 10.1b. There are several problems with *r*:

1. There are a number of redundant data values. Observe, for example, that every tuple whose *Dept* is *Toy* repeats *Pat* as the manager. Yet we know from the constraints in Fig. 10.1a that each department has only one manager. Similarly, *Chris* is repeated for every *Hardware* entry, and *Lynn* is repeated for every *Clothing* entry. Along with the repetition of the manager name, the department phone number and the department phone location are repeated. Observe also that the home phone is repeated for every duplicate manager entry. (Note, by the way, that *Pat* and *Lynn* have the same phone number—presumably they are roommates.) If there are hundreds of items in each department, as there likely would be for our application, this repetition would multiply several hundred fold.

2. Accompanying redundant data values, where we know that two occurrences of a value must be the same, is the possibility that we could have inconsistent data. If we change *Pat* to *Deon* in the first tuple, but forget to change it in the second and third tuple, we have an inconsistency and also a constraint violation since there can only be one manager. This is an example of a *modification*

anomaly. To overcome this modification anomaly, we would have to execute code that would change every duplication of a value automatically whenever we change any one of the duplicates. This could be costly, especially if the values were scattered in various different disk blocks.

3. Along with inconsistent data, we could delete some information inadvertently. Suppose, for example, that we delete the fact that *hammer* is in the hardware department and then the fact that *saw* is in the hardware department (maybe we are expecting a different type of saw and hammer to replace them later). Notice that we

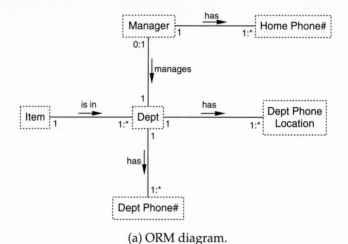

(a) ORM diagram.

$r =$

Item	Dept	Manager	Home Phone#	Dept Phone#	Dept Phone Location
ball	Toy	Pat	123-1789	222-2222	2ndFloorSWCorner
game	Toy	Pat	123-1789	222-2222	2ndFloorSWCorner
blocks	Toy	Pat	123-1789	222-2222	2ndFloorSWCorner
hammer	Hardware	Chris	123-4567	222-2222	2ndFloorSWCorner
saw	Hardware	Chris	123-4567	222-2222	2ndFloorSWCorner
shirt	Clothing	Lynn	123-1789	222-3333	1stFloorCenter
socks	Clothing	Lynn	123-1789	222-3333	1stFloorCenter
$\perp$	$\perp$	Kelly	123-9922	$\perp$	$\perp$

(b) Single-relation representation.

Figure 10.1 A motivating example.

will have removed all the entries that pertain to the hardware department. Thus we will also have deleted the information about who manages the hardware department as well as the phone numbers and location. We have now lost information we were not expecting to lose. This is an example of what is called a *deletion anomaly*. To prevent it, we would have to execute code every time we delete an item from a department to make sure that it is not the last item in a department, and if it is, to take some action—such as notifying someone or creating a tuple with a null for the item, either of which may be unsatisfactory.

4. It is also awkward to insert some types of information. Suppose we are creating a new department and that we know the manager, location, and phone numbers, but that we either do not know or are not yet ready to enter any items for the department. If we add this partial information, we will have to introduce unwanted nulls (unwanted because our application model in Fig. 10.1a requires that a department have at least one item). Having a reasonable fact to insert and not being able to insert the fact without introducing nulls is called an *insertion anomaly*. Nulls can cause problems, especially when they are unexpected and violate constraints. In this case, we may wish to prevent them, but then, because of the insertion anomaly, we also prevent the insertion we wish to make.

Now consider the set of relations in Fig. 10.2, which contains the same sample information as the relation r in Fig. 10.1b. In this relation set, the information about a manager's home phone number and about a department's manager, phone, and phone location appears once and only once. Thus there are no multiple occurrences of data values in any relation that we know must be the same and hence no extra space costs for these values and no extra time costs for keeping multiple copies consistent. We are able to overcome our deletion and insertion anomalies as well. If we wish to delete the last item(s) in a department (both hammers and saws in our example), we need not lose the information about a department since the deletion is in r_1 and the information about the department is in r_3. Similarly, we can add information about a department in r_3 without necessarily having to add information about the items in the department in r_1. We note, however, that this deletion and insertion violate the constraint $\pi_{Dept} r_1 = \pi_{Dept} r_3$. We could solve the problem by changing the constraint to $\pi_{Dept} r_1 \subseteq \pi_{Dept} r_3$. The corresponding change in the ORM diagram in Fig. 10.1a would be to change the one-minimum participation constraint on *Dept* in

$r_1 =$	Item	Dept
	ball	Toy
	game	Toy
	blocks	Toy
	hammer	Hardware
	saw	Hardware
	shirt	Clothing
	socks	Clothing

$r_2 =$	Manager	Home Phone#
	Pat	123-1789
	Chris	123-4567
	Lynn	123-1789
	Kelly	123-9922

$r_3 =$	Dept	Manager	Dept Phone#	Dept Phone Location
	Toy	Pat	222-2222	2ndFloorSWCorner
	Hardware	Chris	222-2222	2ndFloorSWCorner
	Clothing	Lynn	222-3333	1stFloorCenter

$$\pi_{Manager} r_3 \subseteq \pi_{Manager} r_2$$
$$\pi_{Dept} r_1 = \pi_{Dept} r_3$$

Figure 10.2   Multiple-relation representation.

the *is in* relation to zero, which would allow a department and its information to exist independent of the items in the department. Such a semantic change enhances the versatility of the application model and makes it easier to check the constraints. With this change, the set of relations in Fig. 10.2 overcomes all four of the problems just discussed.

Figure 10.3 presents another set of relations with the same information as in the relation in Fig. 10.1b and in the set of relations in Fig. 10.2. Here we have already taken the liberty of changing $\pi_{Dept} r_1 = \pi_{Dept} r_3$ to $\pi_{Dept} r_1 \subseteq \pi_{Dept} r_3$. The main difference between the relation sets in Figs. 10.2 and 10.3 is that there are only two relations in Fig. 10.3 because we have combined relations r_2 and r_3. Observe that there is still a resolution to all four of the problems discussed earlier—we do not have multiple occurrences of the same data values and thus no potential inconsistencies among these values, and we have no deletion anomalies and no insertion anomalies. We do, however, have nulls in r_6. Whether it is better to have these nulls, or to have the pair of relations in Fig. 10.2, depends on the application. There is more to store and more work to do to get the home phone number of a manager in Fig. 10.2, but we need not worry about what it means to have a selection-condition or a join apply to a null.

In general, when we decompose our design into several relations, if we do it right, we can overcome the data redundancies and the update anoma-

$$r_5 =$$

Item	Dept
ball	Toy
game	Toy
blocks	Toy
hammer	Hardware
saw	Hardware
shirt	Clothing
socks	Clothing

$$r_6 =$$

Dept	Manager	Home Phone#	Dept Phone#	Dept Phone Location
Toy	Pat	123-1789	222-2222	2ndFloorSWCorner
Hardware	Chris	123-4567	222-2222	2ndFloorSWCorner
Clothing	Lynn	123-1789	222-3333	1stFloorCenter
$\perp$	Kelly	123-9922	$\perp$	$\perp$

$$\pi_{Dept} r_1 \subseteq \pi_{Dept} r_3$$
$$\pi_{Dept} r_5 = \pi_{Dept} r_6$$

Figure 10.3   An alternative multiple-relation representation.

lies discussed earlier. In turn, however, we may introduce other problems, particularly the following two:

1. It may be necessary to join the relations back together to answer questions. For example, if we wish to know the number to call to ask about a *game* in the *Toy* department, we would have to join two relations for either of the relation sets in Figs. 10.2 or 10.3, but not for the single relation in Fig. 10.1b. Joining relations can be costly, especially if the information is scattered in many different blocks on the disk. Query optimizers and internal infrastructure can reduce the cost of the join. Here, for example, the system may be able to look up *game* in an index, find the *Toy* department, and then use a hash function to find the department information and retrieve the phone number.

2. Since we have decomposed the data in the original relation into separate relations, it may be necessary to consider constraints among these relations. For example, we have added the referential integrity constraints required by the application model in Fig. 10.2. Because of the zero-minimum participation constraint on *Manager* in the *manages* relation, the managers who participate in the *Manager manages Department* relationship set may be a proper

subset of the managers. On the other hand, because of the one-minimum participation constraints on *Dept*, the set of departments in the *is in* relationship set (r_1 in Fig. 10.2) must be the same as the set of departments in *Dept* in the department relationship set (r_3 in Fig. 10.2). As discussed, these constraints may be too tight for our purposes, but even changing $\pi_{Dept}r_1 = \pi_{Dept}r_3$ to $\pi_{Dept}r_1 \subseteq \pi_{Dept}r_3$ does not remove the inter-relation constraint (although it does make it less costly to check).

Before leaving this example, we consider one more idea. The department names— *Toy*, *Hardware*, and *Clothing*—appear several times in *r* in Fig. 10.1b, in r_1 in Fig. 10.2, and in r_5 in Fig. 10.3. The appearances are not redundant copies of the same value, however, because there is no constraint that guarantees us that any two must be the same. Instead, they are the same simply because there happen to be many items in a department. Rather than repeat these department-name values for every tuple in the same department, we could arrange to group the items in a department together and have only one department-name entry for the group. This leads to the idea of nested relations. Figure 10.4 provides an example of r_1 in Fig. 10.2 (or r_5 in Fig. 10.3) written as a nested relation. Observe that no data value in Fig. 10.4 appears more than once. We can implement nested relations as variable-length records, which are more difficult to manage than fixed-length records, but which have the advantage of not repeating some of the values multiple times (possibly hundreds of times).

One possible implementation of a nested relation is to replace implicit references by explicit ones. Figure 10.5, for example, shows pointers

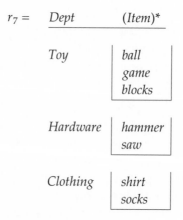

Figure 10.4 A nested relation.

$$r_7 =$$

Dept	(Item)*
$\bullet \to$ Toy	ball
	game
	blocks
$\bullet \to$ Hardware	hammer
	saw
$\bullet \to$ Clothing	shirt
	socks

Dept	Manager	HomePhone#	DeptPhone#	DeptPhoneLocation
Toy	Pat	123-1789	222-2222	2ndFloorSWCorner
Hardware	Chris	123-4567	222-2222	2ndFloorSWCorner
Clothing	Lynn	123-1789	222-3333	1stFloorCenter
$\perp_1$	Kelly	123-9922	$\perp_2$	$\perp_3$

Figure 10.5 Nested relations with pointers.

in place of values in the nested relation. In this implementation, even the repetition of values as implicit identifiers has been removed. All references to departments from other relations are explicit. The advantage, of course, is that we can access department information directly without having to look up the location of the information. The disadvantage, however, is that we may have to update the pointers if we move the information about departments to another location.

Before leaving our motivational section, let us consider one more example. Figure 10.6a displays an ORM diagram with two many-many relationship sets. An order includes several items, but an item can also be included in several orders, and a distributor supplies many items, but an item can also be supplied by many distributors.

Figure 10.6b shows a single-relation representation for some sample data for the ORM diagram in Fig. 10.6a. Here again we have several problems:

1. There are redundant data values, but the reason for the redundancy is more subtle than the reason for the redundant data values in Fig. 10.1b. To see the redundancy, observe that Fig. 10.6c graphically shows the relationships among the data values in Fig. 10.6b. Next observe that r in Fig. 10.6b is the join of the two rela-

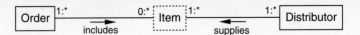

(a) ORM diagram with two many-many relationship sets.

$$
\begin{array}{cccc}
r = & \textit{Item} & \textit{Order} & \textit{Distributor} \\
\hline
& \textit{ball} & O_1 & D_1 \\
& \textit{ball} & O_1 & D_2 \\
& \textit{ball} & O_2 & D_1 \\
& \textit{ball} & O_2 & D_2 \\
& \textit{game} & O_1 & D_2 \\
& \textit{saw} & O_2 & D_3 \\
\end{array}
$$

(b) A single-relation representation.

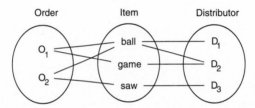

(c) A data diagram for the two many-many relationship sets.

Fig. 10.6 An application model with redundancy and update anomalies.

tionship sets *includes* and *supplies*. The join causes the relationship between the orders and the distributors with a common item connection to be multiplied unnecessarily. Thus, with respect to an item, such as *ball* in this example, we end up with a cross product of the associated orders and distributors, $\{O_1, O_2\}$ and $\{D_1, D_2\}$ in this case. Now, if we have a nontrivial cross product (one that has at least two elements in the sets from which we form the cross product), as we do for *ball*, we can see that any one of the data values participating in the nontrivial cross product is superfluous in the sense that if we did not have it we could recover it from the remaining information, knowing that a cross product exists. If, for example, we were to delete the D_1 from the first tuple in r, then by selecting the four tuples with item *ball* and projecting once on

Order to form the set $\{O_1, O_2\}$ and once on *Distributor* to form the set $\{D_1, D_2\}$ (which we get even without the first D_1 value since the D_1 is in the third tuple), we can now reconstitute the cross product with respect to *ball* and determine that the missing value must be D_1.

2. There are update anomalies. We can have modification anomalies because of the redundancy. In this case, however, replicating the modifications may not be so simple. If, for example, distributor D_2 becomes distributor D_{20}, we simply change all D_2's to D_{20}'s. If D_2 no longer supplies item *ball*, but instead D_3 does, however, we change only the D_2's associated with *ball* to D_3, not all of them. The redundancy also causes insertion anomalies. To add a new order, say O_3, that includes item *ball*, we must add two tuples:

$$< ball, O_3, D_1 >$$
$$< ball, O_3, D_2 >$$

one for D_1 and one for D_2, neither of which is pertinent to the change we are making. Finally, we also have the same kind of deletion anomalies we had before that may cause us to lose information unintentionally. If, for example, we delete the fact that D_2 no longer supplies item *game*, we also delete the fact that order O_1 includes item *game*.

Figure 10.7 shows two relations that represent the same information as does the single relation in Fig. 10.6b, but without the redundancy problems and without the update anomalies. An order appears at most once for each item in r_1, and a distributor appears at most once for each item in r_2. Thus there is no cross-product redundancy. There are also no insertion anomalies. If we wish to insert the fact that a new order, O_3, includes item *ball*, we

$r_1 =$	Item	Order		$r_2 =$	Item	Distributor
	ball	O_1			ball	D_1
	ball	O_2			ball	D_2
	game	O_1			game	D_2
	saw	O_2			saw	D_3

$$\pi_{Item} r_1 \subseteq \pi_{Item} r_2$$

Figure 10.7   A two-relation representation.

need only insert $< ball, O_3 >$ into r_1. Moreover, there are no deletion anomalies. If we delete the fact that D_2 no longer supplies item *game* by deleting the 3rd tuple in r_2, we do not lose the fact that *game* is part of order O_1. The modification anomaly is not gone entirely because we have many-many relationship sets and thus multiple occurrences of data values. Except in the smallest of cases, however, the modification anomaly is reduced because we have fewer duplicate data values since we no longer have the cross-product redundancy.

We can remove some of the data-value duplication by using nested relations. Figure 10.8 shows one nested relation r_3 that represents the same information as in relation r in Fig. 10.6b or as in the two relations r_1 and r_2 in Fig. 10.7. In the nested relation r_3 in Fig. 10.8, each item value appears at most once, whereas in r in Fig. 10.6b and in r_1 and r_2 in Fig. 10.7, some items appear more than once. In r_1 and r_2 together, an item appears as many times as the sum of the number of orders that include it and the number of distributors that supply it, and in r_3 each item value appears as many times as the product of the number of orders that include it and the number of distributors that supply it.

The motivating examples indicate that we must explore the idea of data redundancy and the problems with update anomalies that accompany data redundancy. As the examples show, redundancy arises because of constraints that force multiply occurring values to be the same. One of these constraints is a functional dependency, which we defined and explored in the last chapter. Our motivating examples also indicate, however, that cross-product redundancy can be another problem. Since we have not explained formally what we mean by the cross-product constraint that leads to potential redundancy, we begin our more formal discussion with a definition of a generalization of this cross-product idea, which is called a join dependency. We then give a definition for redundancy based on func-

$r_3 =$

Item	(Order)*	(Distributor)*
ball	O_1 O_2	D_1 D_2
game	O_1	D_2
saw	O_2	D_3

Figure 10.8 A nested-relation representation.

tional and join dependencies. With the definition of redundancy in hand, we are then in a position to define an algorithm that takes an ORM diagram and synthesizes redundancy-free schemes for object-module implementation units.

10.2 Join Dependencies

Let R be a relation scheme, and thus a set of attributes (object sets), and let $R_1, ..., R_n$ be subsets of R such that $\overset{n}{\underset{i=1}{\cup}} R_i = R$. A *join dependency* (JD) denoted $\bowtie(R_1, R_2, ..., R_n)$ holds for a relation r defined on scheme R if

$$r = \pi_{R_1} r \bowtie \pi_{R_2} r \bowtie ... \bowtie \pi_{R_n} r$$

For example, the join dependency $\bowtie(\{Item, Order\}, \{Item, Distributor\})$ holds for relation r in Fig. 10.6b. Here the projections yield the relations in Fig. 10.7, which when joined together yield r. Using our convention for writing sets of attributes, our sample join dependency here can be written more simply as $\bowtie(Item\ Order, Item\ Distributor)$. Because we allow spaces in names, sometimes this form can be ambiguous. We therefore also allow an alternative form $\bowtie(R_1; R_2; ...; R_n)$, where the R_i's are comma-separated sets of attributes. Thus we may also write our sample join dependency as $\bowtie(Item, Order; Item, Distributor)$, but we would probably prefer the simpler notation just given for this example.

The special case of a join dependency in which $n = 2$ is called a *multivalued dependency* (MVD). In this case, we can write $\bowtie(R_1, R_2)$ as $X \twoheadrightarrow Y$ or as $X \twoheadrightarrow Z$ or as $X \twoheadrightarrow Y \mid Z$, where $X = R_1 \cap R_2$, $Y = R_1 - R_2$, and $Z = R_2 - R_1$. For our example, $\bowtie(Item\ Order, Item\ Distributor) = Item \twoheadrightarrow Order = Item \twoheadrightarrow Distributor = Item \twoheadrightarrow Order \mid Distributor$.

The join dependencies of interest to us are already naturally part of ORM application models and can be extracted mechanically. Thus, as is the case for FDs, analysts and designers need not be concerned with providing JDs; they need be concerned only with modeling the data properly for an application as an ORM diagram.

The join dependencies of greatest interest to us are those that occur along acyclic paths in ORM application models. (In the exercises, we generalize this to include other JDs also.) There are two basic cases to consider: the case in which congruency holds everywhere and the case in which congruency does not hold everywhere. Although the first is a special case of the second, we give it anyway because it is instructive and because it corresponds to the more common way of thinking about JDs.

Theorem 10.1

Let M be a congruent application model. Let $R_1, ..., R_n, n \geq 2$, be any acyclic path of M such that there is exactly one object set in the intersection of successive edges (i.e., $|R_i \cap R_{i+1}| = 1$ for $1 \leq i \leq n-1$). Let $r_1(R_1), ..., r_n(R_n)$ be relations in a valid interpretation for M and let $r = \bowtie_{i=1}^{n} r_i$. Then, the JD $\bowtie(R_1, R_2, ..., R_n)$ holds for r.

By using the outer join rather than the natural join to construct our relations, we can extend Theorem 10.1 to the general acyclic case in which the application model is not necessarily congruent. Figure 10.9 indicates why the outer join gives us the result we want. Observe that the last two tuples in r_2 in Fig. 10.9a would not participate in the natural join of r_1 and r_2. We therefore pad them with the right number of marked nulls, one each in this case, and add them to the result (see Fig. 10.9b). Because the ORM diagram in Fig. 10.6a does not allow items with no distributors, we have no tuples in $r_1 \otimes r_2$ with a null for *Distributor*. Observe that if we treat nulls as ordinary values, the join dependency $\bowtie$ (*Item Order, Item Distributor*) holds because if we project on the schemes of r_1 and r_2 and then join these projections together, we get $r_1 \otimes r_2$. As Theorem 10.2 shows, this works in general.

$r_1 =$	*Item*	*Order*		$r_2 =$	*Item*	*Distributor*
	ball	O_1			ball	D_1
	ball	O_2			ball	D_2
					hammer	D_3
					shirt	D_4

(a) Two possible relations for the relationship sets in Fig. 10.6a.

$r_1 \otimes r_2 =$	*Item*	*Order*	*Distributor*
	ball	O_1	D_1
	ball	O_1	D_2
	ball	O_2	D_1
	ball	O_2	D_2
	hammer	$\perp_1$	D_3
	shirt	$\perp_2$	D_4

(b) The outer join of r_1 and r_2.

Figure 10.9 A JD with marked nulls.

Theorem 10.2

Let M be an application model. Let $R_1, ..., R_n$, $n \geq 2$, be any acyclic path of M such that there is exactly one object set in the intersection of successive edges (i.e., $|R_i \cap R_{i+1}| = 1$ for $1 \leq i \leq n-1$). Let $r_1(R_1), ...,$ $r_n(R_n)$ be relations in a valid interpretation for M and let $r = \overset{n}{\underset{i=1}{\otimes}} r_i$. Then, the JD $\bowtie(R_1, R_2, ..., R_n)$ holds for r.

We conclude this section with a few more observations about JDs. A JD for a relation scheme R is said to be *trivial* if it holds for any relation r on R. A JD $\bowtie(R_1, R_2, ..., R_n)$ on R holds for any relation $r(R)$ if $R = R_i$ for some i, $1 \leq i \leq n$. We also note that every FD is a JD. If $X \rightarrow Y$ is an FD that holds on a relation scheme R, then we can express it as a JD by writing $\bowtie(XY, X(R - Y))$.

10.3 Redundancy

Our notion of redundancy is based on the idea that an atomic data value v in a relation is redundant if we can erase v, and then, from the data that remains, and using a single FD or JD that holds, we can determine what v must have been. Our definition has two parts, one for redundancy caused by FDs and one for redundancy caused by JDs.

Let r be a relation on scheme R. Let $X \subseteq R$, $A \in R$, and $A \notin X$. If an FD $X \rightarrow A$ holds for r and there exist distinct tuples t_1 and t_2 in r such that $t_1(X) = t_2(X)$, then $t_2(A)$ is *redundant* (and, by symmetry, so is $t_1(A)$). In Fig. 10.1b, for example, the FD *Dept* $\rightarrow$ *Manager* holds. If we let t_1 be the first tuple and t_2 be the second tuple, then $t_1(Dept) = t_2(Dept)$ ($= Toy$), and hence $t_2(Manager)$ ($= Pat$) is redundant. Observe that since we have the FD *Dept* $\rightarrow$ *Manager*, we can indeed erase *Pat* in the second tuple and use the

---

A Technical Point about Relational Theory

For the relational theorist, we note the following. When F is a set of FDs generated from an ORM diagram and J is a set of JDs (including MVDs) generated from an ORM diagram, there are no FDs implied by $F \cup J$ that are not implied by F alone. This, of course, is not true for arbitrary sets of FDs and JDs. It means, however, that for our application models, FD implication alone is sufficient for determining FDs that can cause FD redundancy.

first tuple, which agrees with the second on *Dept*, to determine what it must have been. Many other data values in Fig. 10.1b are redundant.

For JD redundancy, we consider first the special case of MVDs. Let r be a relation on scheme R. Let X, Y, and Z be nonempty subsets of R such that $X \cap Y = \emptyset$, $Z = R - (XY)$, and $A \in Y$. If $X \twoheadrightarrow Y$ holds for r and there exist distinct tuples t_1 and t_2 in r such that $t_1(X) = t_2(X)$, $t_1(Y) = t_2(Y)$, and $t_1(Z) \neq t_2(Z)$, then $t_2(A)$ is *redundant* (and by symmetry, so is $t_1(A)$). In Fig. 10.6b, for example, the MVD *Item* $\twoheadrightarrow$ *Order* holds. If we let t_1 be the first tuple and t_2 be the second tuple, we have $t_1(Item) = t_2(Item)$ (= *ball*), $t_1(Order) = t_2(Order)$ (= O_1), and $t_1(Distributor)$ (= D_1) $\neq t_2(Distributor)$ (= D_2), and hence $t_2(Order)$ (= O_1) is redundant. An easy way to see that the O_1 for t_2 is redundant is to observe that the MVD *Item* $\twoheadrightarrow$ *Order* | *Distributor* forces a cross product of *Order* and *Distributor* values with respect to an *Item* value. Thus, for the first four tuples, whose item value is *ball*, we must have the cross product of $\{O_1, O_2\}$ and $\{D_1,$ and $D_2\}$. Now, even when O_1 in t_2 is missing, we still have enough information to determine the elements of the sets from which we must form the cross product. Hence, we can form the cross product and see which value must be missing.

Let r be a relation on scheme R for which the join dependency $\bowtie(R_1, ..., R_n)$ holds. Let t be a tuple in r and A be an attribute in R. Since $A \in R$, by definition of a join dependency, A is in one or more of R_i, $1 \leq i \leq n$. Assume, without loss of generality, that A is in $R_1, R_2, ...\ R_k$, $k \leq n$. Then, the data value $t(A)$ is redundant if we can find n tuples in r $t_1, ..., t_n$ (not necessarily distinct) such that, for $1 \leq i, j \leq n$

$$t_i(R_i \cap R_j) = t_j(R_i \cap R_j)$$

and

$$t(R_i) = t_i(R_i)$$

and at least one of the tuples $t_1, ..., t_k$ is distinct from t. For example, consider the relation r in Fig. 10.10. The join dependency $\bowtie(Distributor\ Item, Item\ Warehouse, Distributor\ Warehouse)$ holds for r, and we claim as an example that I_1 in the fourth tuple of r is redundant. We satisfy the definition t_1, t_2, and t_3 as the first three tuples, t as the fourth, A as *Item*, R_1 as *Distributor Item*, R_2 as *Item Warehouse*, R_3 as *Distributor Warehouse*, and k as 2. Observe that

$$t_1(Distributor) = t_3(Distributor) = t(Distributor)$$
$$t_1(Item) = t_2(Item) = t(Item)$$
$$t_2(Warehouse) = t_3(Warehouse) = t(Warehouse)$$

$$r = \quad \underline{Distributor \quad Item \quad Warehouse}$$

$$
\begin{array}{ccc}
D_1 & I_1 & W_1 \\
D_2 & I_1 & W_2 \\
D_1 & I_2 & W_2 \\
D_1 & I_1 & W_2 \\
\end{array}
$$

Figure 10.10   A relation to illustrate a three-way decomposition.

and that at least one (and indeed both) of the tuples t_1 and t_2 are distinct from t. The reason this works is that the join dependency forces the A value in t to be the same as the A value in all the other tuples where the A is in the intersection of the R_i's. So long as at least one of these tuples is different from t, we can use its value to tell us what the erased A value in t should be. Several other data values in r besides the I_1 in the fourth tuple are redundant; we leave it as an exercise to find them all.

10.4   Flat-Scheme Synthesis

Our general objectives for synthesizing schemes are as follows:

1. To minimize the number of schemes,

2. To maximize the size of each scheme,

3. To eliminate the possibility of redundancy,

4. To remove the possibility of having nulls, and

5. To ensure that we do not violate semantic equivalence.

These objectives may be tempered by cost characteristics, as discussed in section 10.7. But before making exceptions to our objectives, we first show how to balance the first two objectives against the last three. We could achieve the first two objectives by having only one scheme. As Fig. 10.1b indicates, however, such a relation is likely to have a lot of redundancy and many nulls. Furthermore, if semantic equivalence does not hold over the scheme, it may also have some internal inconsistencies, or it may be lossy. On the other hand, we could achieve the last three objectives by having one scheme for every relationship set and every object set, but this tends to maximize (rather than minimize) the number of schemes and minimize (rather than maximize) the size of the schemes. Ideally, we would like to find the happy medium where we minimize the number of schemes and maximize their size, while at the same time we allow no possible redundancy and no possible nulls, and we guarantee semantic equivalence.

Our approach is to combine relationship sets together into larger and larger schemes until adding any more yields the possibility of a redundancy, a null, or a semantic-equivalence inconsistency. We call algorithms that do this combining *synthesis* algorithms. When we combine relationship sets, we use outer join, ensuring that no tuples will be lost for any valid interpretation. We will see, however, that if the ORM hypergraphs from which we synthesize schemes are congruent, if we combine only relationship sets along a path (which must of course be connected), and if we ensure semantic equivalence, then we can use natural join rather than outer join.

We proceed now by informally motivating our synthesis algorithm for flat schemes. We first discuss the effect of nulls on the algorithm, then the effect of redundancy, and finally the effect of semantic equivalence.

Recognizing the possibility of introducing a null is straightforward. If we combine schemes that are not connected by a relationship set or if there is an incongruency within a synthesized scheme, there will be a possibility of nulls; otherwise, no nulls can arise. Thus we need merely look at the sub-ORM that constitutes a synthesized scheme. If the sub-ORM is disconnected or if there is an object set that participates in more than one relationship set and at least one of these relationship sets has a zero-minimum participation constraint for the object set, there can be nulls in a valid relation for the synthesized scheme. As an example for disconnected schemes, the sub-ORM for relations r_1 and r_2 in Fig. 10.2 consists of the two relationship sets *Item is in Dept* and *Manager has Home Phone#* in Fig. 10.1a, which are disconnected because the sub-ORM does not include the *Manager manages Dept* relationship set. The outer join $r_1 \otimes r_2$ has many nulls, one for every *Item* and *Dept* for each *Manager* and one for every *Manager* and *Home Phone#* for each *Item*. As an example for incongruencies, the sub-ORM for relation r_6 in Fig. 10.3 consists of all the relationship sets in Fig. 10.1a except the *Item is in Dept* relationship set. Observe that there is an incongruency because of the zero-minimum on *Manager* for the *manages* relationship set. This allows a manager not to be associated with a department and hence allows nulls for *Dept*, *Dept Phone#*, and *Dept Phone Location*, as relation r_6 in Fig. 10.3 shows. As another example, consider Fig. 10.6. Here, relation r in Fig. 10.6b is a possible relation for the sub-ORM (actually the whole ORM) of Fig. 10.6a. Observe that the sub-ORM has an incongruency, but that there are no nulls in the relation r. There could be a null, however, if we have an item that is not in any of the orders. It is the possibility of a null we are concerned about, not just whether some sample relation has a null.

Recognizing the possibility of introducing redundancy is not so straightforward, but does fall out naturally as a generalization of the examples in Fig. 10.11. These examples show several ways of combining two relationship sets from an ORM hypergraph. For the hypergraph in Fig. 10.11a, there is no redundancy. Because of the FDs $A \rightarrow B$ and $A \rightarrow C$, for any A value there is exactly one B value and one C value. Any attempt to add redundancy by putting another tuple in the relation with an A value of 1, for example, fails because, to be valid, the B and C values must also be 1, which means that the tuple must be <1, 1, 1>—a duplicate and therefore not allowable in the set of tuples that constitutes the relation. Thus, we can combine the AB and AC relationship sets without introducing redundancy.

This same reasoning holds for the ORM hypergraph in Fig. 10.11b. Here the constraints are even stronger because we also have $B \rightarrow A$. An interesting feature of Fig. 10.11b is that it would change neither the redundancy-free property of the ORM hypergraph nor the sample relation if the tail of the AC relationship set were changed to B. Indeed, we can observe that, with respect to redundancy, having the tail of a functional edge attached to any element in an equivalence class is the same as having it attached to any other element in the equivalence class.

Combining the two relationship sets for the ORM hypergraphs in any of the ORM hypergraphs in Figs. 10.11c, d, or e yields potential redundancy. For Fig. 10.11c, the 1's under C are redundant—they must be the same because $A \rightarrow C$ and both A values are 1. It is the fact that B values are unconstrained and therefore can differ that allows tuples to be formed with duplicate A values and hence, because of the FD, redundant C values. For Fig. 10.11d, both the edges are FDs, but the FD edges go from B to A and then from A to C, rather than both emanating from A as in Figs. 10.11a and b. Here the redundancy is again caused by the FD $A \rightarrow C$ because the B values can differ. For Fig. 10.11e, the redundancy is caused by an MVD. There are no FDs, but we do have the MVD $A \twoheadrightarrow B \mid C$. In the sample relation, all the values under B and C are redundant. We can determine any one of them by forming the cross product of the others. If we erase the first 1 under B, for example, we still have enough information to see that the cross-product sets for both B and C (with respect to the 1's under A) are both {1, 2} and thus that there must be a <1, 1> tuple, which returns us the "erased" 1 under B.

Observe that all the ORM hypergraph samples in Fig. 10.11 are reduced fully according to our transformations in Chapter 9. If we work with ORM hypergraphs that are not reduced fully, we must be even more careful. In Fig. 10.11d, for example, if we have an additional edge $B \rightarrow C$, then we might reason as we did for Fig. 8.11a that we should combine the BA and

(a) Combining two FD edges with the same tail.

(b) Combining an FD edge with an equivalence-class edge.

(c) Combining an FD edge with a non-FD edge.

(d) Combining FD edges that do not have the same tail.

(e) Combining two non-FD edges.

Figure 10.11 Some patterns whose combinations do and do not allow redundancy.

BC relationship sets. This combination, however, now also includes the *AC* relationship set, and we have the redundancy as discussed for Fig. 10.11d. The problem here is that the ORM hypergraph has not been head reduced. A head reduction would remove the edge $B \rightarrow C$, giving us back the ORM hypergraph in Fig. 8.11d, which we would then not combine, thus avoiding the redundancy.

Recognizing semantic-equivalence problems is also not straightforward, mainly because semantic-equivalence questions cannot be resolved without knowing the semantics of the application model. As it turns out, however, if we have completed the reductions in Chapter 9, it is easy to resolve the remaining semantic-equivalence problems in preparation for our synthesis algorithms.

Before we discuss how to resolve the problem, let us first show what happens when we try to combine schemes for relationship sets over which semantic equivalence does not hold. As an example, consider Fig. 10.12a, which shows an ORM application model for managers, the workers they manage, and the workers' favorite managers. For this example we assume that every manager must be some worker's favorite and that every manager manages workers. Thus, the application model is congruent. Semantic equivalence does not hold, however, because workers may have favorite managers who are different from their own managers. Figure 10.12b presents the ORM hypergraph for this application model, which shows that

$$has \ favorite: Worker \rightarrow Manager$$
$$manages: Worker \rightarrow Manager$$

Figure 10.12c contains a valid relation for the *manages* relationship sets and for the *has favorite* relationship set. If we use the natural join to join the two relations in Fig. 10.12c, we will lose tuples since we obtain only the tuples where workers favor their own managers, as Fig. 10.12d shows. On the other hand, if we use the outer join, no tuples are lost, but now we have a constraint violation since there may be two managers for a worker—one as the managing manager and one as the favorite manager. Figure 10.12e shows that worker W_1 associates with both M_1 and M_2, and thus there is an inconsistency. Moreover, if we were to discard the relations in Fig. 10.12c, which is what we intend to do when we synthesize relations, we would not even be able to tell which manager is the managing manager and which is the favorite manager.

We can resolve this problem by adding roles. First observe that if semantic equivalence holds for the ORM hypergraph in Fig. 10.12b, then we can head reduce by removing one or the other of the edges. Indeed, if

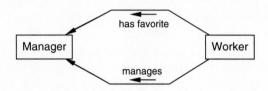

(a) Different relationships between managers and workers.

(b) ORM hypergraph for the different relationships.

manages =	*Worker*	*Manager*		*has favorite* =	*Worker*	*Manager*
	W_1	M_1			W_1	M_2
	W_2	M_2			W_2	M_2
	W_3	M_2			W_3	M_1

(c) Data that shows the different relationships.

manages ⋈ *has favorite* =	*Worker*	*Manager*
	W_2	M_2

(d) Join (= intersection) of the data.

manages ⊗ *has favorite* =	*Worker*	*Manager*
	W_2	M_2
	W_1	M_1
	W_3	M_2
	W_1	M_2
	W_3	M_1

(e) Outer join (= union) of the data.

Figure 10.12 Resolution of a semantic-equivalence problem by adding roles.

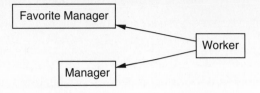

(f) ORM hypergraph with explicit roles.

Figure 10.12 (cont.) Resolution of a semantic-equivalence problem by adding roles.

semantic equivalence holds, then the two relationship sets must always have the same meaning. If we therefore assume that we have already applied our head reduction transformation to the extent possible, then we must have already addressed the semantic-equivalence question for these two edges and decided that semantic equivalence does not hold. To resolve the problem, we add explicit roles. The resulting diagram, Fig. 10.12f, was arrived at as follows: we added *Favorite Manager* and *Temp* as role names; created a union-covered isolated root generalization out of *Manager*, which we discarded; and then renamed *Temp* to again be *Manager*. In general, we can always resolve the semantic-equivalence problem by adding roles.

Based on these observations about nulls, redundancy, and semantic equivalence, we can conclude the following intuitively:

- To avoid nulls, we should synthesize congruent hypergraphs and synthesize only along paths of connected relationship sets.

- To avoid redundancy, we should put FD edges together only if their tails are the same, and we should put all non-FD edges in separate schemes.

- To avoid semantic-equivalence problems, we should synthesize only schemes over which semantic equivalence holds.

Thus, the approach we take is first to apply the reductions in Chapter 9 and make some adjustments for congruency and semantic equivalence, if necessary, and then to synthesize schemes. This approach is sometimes a little too restrictive, but, as we shall see, needed modifications can be made as part of a cost analysis.

To state precisely what characteristics we want for our synthesis algorithms, we provide the following definitions. An ORM hypergraph is

- *Congruent* if there are no optional connections;

- *Nonrecursive* if no edge has more than one connection to an object set;

- *Head reduced* if we can apply neither our simple head-reduction transformation nor our equivalence-class head-reduction transformation;

- *Tail reduced* if we cannot apply our tail-reduction transformation;

- *Object-set reduced* if we cannot apply our lexicalization transformation and cannot merge nonlexical object sets that are in a one-to-one correspondence;

- *Non-FD-edge reduced* if no non-FD edge is redundant or equivalent to some decomposition of the edge;

- *Embedded-FD reduced* if we cannot apply our embedded-FD reduction transformation either to an FD edge or to an equivalence class;

- *Separately linked* if each nontrivial minimal-set equivalence class for which semantic equivalence does not hold has been split into separate equivalence classes over which semantic equivalence holds and each of these equivalence classes, as well as each of the other nontrivial minimal-set equivalence classes, has been circularly linked;

- *Minimally consolidated* if, for every separately linked equivalence class, we have moved all the connections incident on an element of the equivalence class to one element of the equivalence class, and this one element has no more object sets than any other element in the equivalence class; and

- *Semantically head-consistent* if roles have been introduced where necessary so that no edge would have a head reduction even under the assumption that semantic equivalence holds when it does not hold.

An ORM hypergraph with all these properties is called a *canonical* ORM hypergraph. We can produce a canonical ORM hypergraph by (1) making the ORM application model congruent as discussed in Chapter 5, (2) applying the transformations discussed in Chapter 9 until no more changes are possible, and (3) adding roles as necessary to remove any recursion introduced by the transformations and to remove any edges that are not semantically head-consistent.

Algorithm 10.1

Input: a canonical ORM hypergraph.

Output: a set of flat schemes.

If the tail(s) of an FD edge F constitute an element of an equivalence class C and if F is not one of the linking FDs for C, we call F an *external* FD edge of C.

1. For each separately linked equivalence class C (including both trivial equivalence classes, which have no links, and nontrivial equivalence classes) such that there is at least one external FD edge of C:
   Form a scheme whose object sets are the union of

   1.1 the object sets in C, and

   1.2 the head object sets of all the external FD edges of C.

2. For each nontrivial equivalence class C with no external FD edge:
   Form a scheme whose object sets are the object sets in C.

3. For each non-FD edge E:
   Form a scheme whose object sets are the object sets of E.

4. For each object set S with no connecting edge:
   Form a scheme from S alone.

In practice, most equivalence classes are trivial, and those that are not almost always satisfy the semantic-equivalence assumption. As Fig. 9.17

Synthesis Algorithms Combine Most Single-Attribute Relations in the Model-Theoretic Database View

With respect to the underlying model-theoretic database view, the synthesis algorithms we present here and later in this chapter tell us how to combine relations. We combine relations as much as possible, but not so much that we introduce the possibility of redundant data values and nulls. Note in particular that, for the most part, we combine all single-attribute relations that represent object sets with attached relationship sets. Thus, we finally take care of the obviously redundant relation schemes generated by our transformation from an ORM diagram to a model-theoretic database view. We see, however, that we cannot just discard such schemes because of the few exceptions we may find in various applications where we must leave them as single-attribute relations.

shows, however, a violation is possible, in which case we must at least transform the hypergraph as explained in Section 9.7 before we apply Algorithm 10.1. When these conditions hold, and they often do, Step 1 of Algorithm 10.1 reduces simply to grouping together those FD edges that have a common tail. Thus, for many practical cases, Algorithm 10.1 is very straightforward.

To see how Algorithm 10.1 handles potential redundancy, consider the results of applying it to the ORM hypergraphs in Fig. 10.11. For the hypergraph in Fig. 10.11a, we have a trivial equivalence class $\{A\}$, with at least one external FD edge (actually two—$A \rightarrow B$ and $A \rightarrow C$). Therefore, the scheme is the union of $\{A\}$, the object sets in the equivalence class, and $\{B, C\}$, the set of heads of the FD edges whose tails are in the equivalence class. Thus the scheme is ABC, which, as explained earlier, is a relation scheme with no potential redundancy; that is, there can never be a valid interpretation for the ORM application model such that the join of the *AB relation* and the *AC relation* will have a redundant data value. For the hypergraph in Fig. 10.11b, we have a nontrivial equivalence class $\{A, B\}$ and an external FD edge $A \rightarrow C$. We therefore obtain ABC, which has no potential redundancy.

For the hypergraph in Fig. 10.11c, we have a trivial equivalence class, which yields the scheme AC, and a non-FD relationship set, which yields the scheme AB. Although the scheme ABC in Fig. 10.11c has potential redundancy—indeed the relation in Fig. 10.11c is redundant—neither scheme AB nor scheme AC has potential redundancy. For the hypergraph in Fig. 10.11d, we have two trivial equivalence classes with external FD edges. Thus, Algorithm 10.1 yields schemes AB and AC, which have no potential redundancy. For the hypergraph in Fig. 10.11e, there are no FD edges and thus no equivalence classes with external FD edges. Hence, Algorithm 10.1 yields schemes AB and AC, one for each of the non-FD edges. These schemes have no potential redundancy.

As a realistic example, we can apply Algorithm 10.1 to the ORM hypergraph in Fig. 10.13, which is the canonical ORM hypergraph for the ORM diagram in Fig. 10.1a. We have a nontrivial equivalence class $\{Dept Manager, Dept\}$ with two external FD edges. Thus from Step 1 of Algorithm 10.1, we obtain the scheme

Dept, Dept Manager, Dept Phone#, Dept Phone Location

We have one trivial equivalence class $\{Manager\}$ with an external FD edge. Thus, from Step 1 again, we obtain the scheme

Manager, Home Phone#.

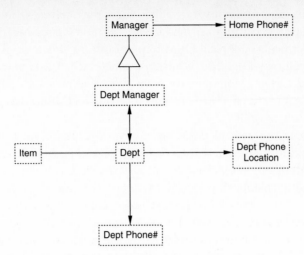

Figure 10.13   ORM hypergraph for the ORM diagram in Fig. 10.1a.

There is also one non-FD edge. Thus from Step 3 we obtain

Dept, Item

The schemes here are the schemes in Fig. 10.2, except that in r_3 *Manager* is replaced by *Dept Manager*. Once we have obtained our schemes, we may wish to do some renaming. We can rename *Dept Manager* to be *Manager*, but *Dept Manager* may even be more expressive because we do not have all managers listed under *Manager* in r_3, only all department managers.

Figure 10.2 shows some possible relations for these schemes. There is no redundancy in any of these relations, and there are no nulls. The phone numbers 123-1789 are not redundant because we cannot guarantee that *Pat* and *Lynn* have the same phone number—presumably this happens because they share an apartment, not because of any constraints in the application model. Similarly, the duplicate department phones and phone locations are not redundant because the toy department and hardware department need not share the same phone—next week we may install a new phone in a different location for the hardware department. Observe that there are also no nulls. By considering the ORM hypergraph in Fig. 10.13, we can see that there never can be any. Items must be in departments, and departments must have items. Every manager must have a home phone. Every department must have a manager, a phone, and a phone location.

To illustrate two other points about Algorithm 10.1, let us first suppose that there may be items not assigned to departments—perhaps they are new and a manager has not yet decided where they belong— and thus that the participation constraint on *Item* in Fig. 10.1a is *0:1* instead of *1*. Now, when we produce a canonical ORM hypergraph for this revised ORM, we have a new role, say *Dept Item*, which takes the place of *Item* in the schemes we generated earlier. Moreover, we have *Item* as an object set with no relationship-set connections. Thus in Step 4 of our algorithm, we generate a scheme for *Item* by itself.

To illustrate our second point, let us suppose that there is no department phone information and thus that we have the ORM hypergraph in Fig. 10.13 without the *Dept Phone#* and *Dept Phone Location* object sets and their connecting relationship sets. Now when we run Algorithm 10.1, we use Step 2 to obtain the scheme *DeptManager, Dept*. Steps 1 and 3 yield the schemes *Manager, Home Phone#*, and *Dept Item* as before.

As a final point about Algorithm 10.1, we mention explicitly that we totally ignore all generalization/specialization connections. These are not relationship sets and are therefore neither FD edges nor non-FD edges. These edges are not totally useless, however, as the following section shows.

10.5   Interscheme Dependencies

In addition to schemes, we would like to generate the referential-integrity constraints among the schemes. A referential-integrity constraint is a special case of the more general idea of an inclusion dependency, which we now define. In its simplest form, if we let A be an object set in the scheme for one relation r and B be an object set in the scheme for another relation s, then the *inclusion dependency* $r[A] \supseteq s[B]$ holds if $\pi_A r \supseteq \pi_B s$. In general, if r names a relation whose attributes are $A_1, ..., A_n$, and s names a relation whose attributes are $B_1, ..., B_m$, and if $k \leq n$, and $k \leq m$, then the *inclusion dependency* $r[A_1, ..., A_k] \supseteq s[B_1, ..., B_k]$ holds if $\pi_{A_1, ..., A_k} r \supseteq \pi_{B_1, ..., B_k} s$. The attributes in this general inclusion dependency are ordered and match one-to-one in the order specified. If both the inclusion dependency $r[A_1, ..., A_k] \supseteq s[B_1, ..., B_k]$ and $s[B_1, ..., B_k] \supseteq r[A_1, ..., A_k]$ hold, we may write $r[A_1, ..., A_k] = s[B_1, ..., B_k]$.

In canonical ORM hypergraphs, a generalization/specialization immediately gives us one or more one-attribute inclusion dependencies. Each object-set name that appears in two or more schemes generated by Algorithm 10.1 immediately gives us an equality one-attribute inclusion dependency. For multiple-attribute inclusion dependencies, we need a general constraint that imposes a subset limitation between parts of two schemes.

This subset constraint arises naturally as a result of lexicalizing a nonlexical object set with a group of lexical object sets when the nonlexical object set is the root of an *isa* hierarchy. We give an example later to show how to obtain this more complex multiple-attribute inclusion dependency. First, however, we present Algorithm 10.2, which gives a general procedure for generating inclusion dependencies from a canonical ORM hypergraph and a set of schemes generated by Algorithm 10.1.

Algorithm 10.2

Input: a canonical ORM hypergraph and a set of schemes generated by Algorithm 10.1.

Output: a set of inclusion dependencies among the schemes.

Let R and S be distinct generated schemes.
Let r designate the relation for R and s designate the relation for S.

For each generalization/specialization pair with a generalization object set A in R and a specialization object set B in S,
output the inclusion dependency $r[A] \supseteq s[B]$.

For each object set A that appears in both R and S,
output the inclusion dependencies $r[A] = s[A]$.

For each general constraint that is a subset constraint among relationship sets with $A_1, ..., A_k$ as the superset object sets all in R and $B_1, ..., B_k$ as the subset object sets all in S,
output the inclusion dependency $r[A_1, \ldots, A_k] \supseteq s[B_1, \ldots, B_k]$.

For ORM hypergraphs, we commonly have only one generalization object set A and one specialization object set B, but there could be several generalization object sets $A_1, ..., A_n$ and several specialization object sets $B_1, ..., B_m$. In this case, as Algorithm 10.2 specifies, we output an inclusion dependency for each of the nm generalization-specialization pairs (i.e., $r[A_1] \supseteq s[B_1], r[A_1] \supseteq s[B_2], ..., r[A_2] \supseteq s[B_1], ..., r[A_n] \supseteq s[B_m]$).

As an example of how Algorithm 10.2 works, consider the ORM hypergraph in Fig. 10.13. As discussed previously, Algorithm 10.1 generates the schemes

> $r_1(Dept, Dept\ Manager, Dept\ Phone\#, Dept\ Phone\ Location)$
> $r_2(Manager, Home\ Phone\#)$
> $r_3(Dept, Item)$

where for these schemes we have also provided a relation name for reference in inclusion dependencies. Since we have an *isa* hierarchy with *Manager* as the generalization object set in one scheme and *Dept Manager* as the specialization object set in another scheme, Algorithm 10.2 outputs the inclusion dependency

$$r_2[Manager] \supseteq r_1[Dept\ Manager]$$

Further, since *Dept* appears in two schemes, Algorithm 10.2 outputs the inclusion dependency

$$r_1[Dept] = r_3[Dept]$$

To illustrate the general-subset-constraint part of Algorithm 10.2 and to show how to obtain a composite inclusion dependency, we consider the ORM diagram in Fig. 10.14a and its corresponding canonical ORM hypergraph in Fig. 10.14b. We obtained the relationship set between *Name (of Person)* and *Address (of Person)* in Fig. 10.14b by lexicalizing *Person* with *Name* and *Address* in Fig. 10.14a. We then propagated this lexicalization down the *isa* hierarchy to *Employee*. The redundant binary relationship set between *Name (of Employee)* and *Address (of Employee)* that would have been generated in the lexicalization transformation has been discarded because the ternary relationship set with *Salary* subsumes it. To retain the generalization/specialization information between *Person* and *Employee*, the general constraint in Fig. 10.14b has been added. This general constraint is a subset constraint between the two relationship sets in Fig. 10.14b, which ensures that if there is a name-address-salary triple for an employee, then the name-address pair of this triple appears in the name-address relation for a person. Thus Algorithm 10.2 outputs the inclusion dependency

$$person[Name,\ Address] \supseteq employee[Name,\ Address]$$

where we assume that *person* and *employee* are the relation names for the *Person* and *Employee* relationship sets.

Besides inclusion dependencies, there are several other interscheme dependencies of interest. These include FDs generated as a result of an embedded FD reduction, as well as the partition, mutual-exclusion, union, and intersection constraints given explicitly in a generalization/specialization. We need do nothing for FDs generated as a result of an embedded FD reduction other than record them as constraints for the generated schemes. We will see later in this chapter and in Chapter 11 some alternative and

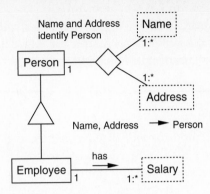

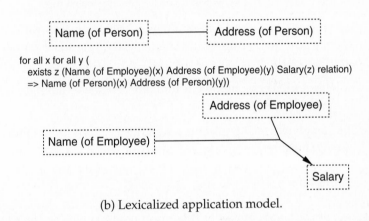

(a) Application model with a potential composite lexicalization.

for all x for all y (
   exists z (Name (of Employee)(x) Address (of Employee)(y) Salary(z) relation)
   => Name (of Person)(x) Address (of Person)(y))

(b) Lexicalized application model.

Figure 10.14 Application model with a general subset constraint among relationship sets.

sometimes better ways to organize *isa* hierarchies and also some special ways to handle generalization/specialization constraints. If we can do nothing better, we can at least always generate inclusion dependencies according to Algorithm 10.2, and we can generate closed formulas for each generalization/specialization constraint according to the generation rules for these constraints in Chapter 6.

10.6 Properties of Flat Schemes

We now wish to investigate the properties of schemes generated by Algorithms 10.1 and 10.2. Recall that in our motivating example and as we began our discussion on flat-scheme synthesis, we were interested in certain properties. We are now able to guarantee these properties. Because we assume that the input ORM hypergraph for Algorithms 10.1 and 10.2 is canonical, we can guarantee the following properties:

1. No valid relation for any of the schemes ever will have redundancy caused by FDs.

2. No valid relation for any of the schemes ever will have redundancy caused by JDs (except under certain conditions that we explain when we discuss this point).

3. No valid relation for any of the schemes will ever have a null.

4. The generated set of schemes is information preserving.

5. The number of schemes is minimal in the sense that we cannot combine any two of them and maintain the first three properties simultaneously.

6. No object set can be removed from any scheme without violating the fourth property.

7. The generated set of schemes and constraints is constraint preserving. Further, if there are no transformations that generate FDs for high-level relationship sets, the FDs are preserved by FD constraints on the schemes alone.

In the following discussion of these properties, it will be clear that for any particular property, we do not always need all the conditions of a canonical ORM hypergraph. It is possible for each of the properties to reduce the conditions to only those that are needed, but since we want all of the properties anyway and since it is somewhat confusing to try to remember all the variations, we simply assume that our input ORM hypergraph is canonical. Recognizing that particular properties do not depend on some of the conditions of canonical ORM hypergraphs is useful, however, because this tells us where we can make some adjustments without losing properties of interest. For example, we can guarantee that there is no potential redundancy without requiring lexicalization. Thus, if we want object identifiers to represent objects rather than lexical strings, we need not lexicalize. We will not have as few object sets as possible, but we will not introduce redundancy or nulls because we fail to lexicalize.

We begin our discussion of the properties of canonical ORM hypergraphs by showing an interesting result about keys, which are extremely

---

The Empty Set of Attributes Can Be a Candidate Key

If a relation can have at most one tuple in any valid interpretation, then the empty set of attributes can serve as a candidate key. Technically, to make the definition work, we define $t[\varnothing] = \lambda$ for any tuple t. Thus for any two tuples t_1 and t_2, $t_1[\varnothing] = t_2[\varnothing]$ since they both are defined to be equal to λ. Hence, if there can ever be more than one tuple in a relation, $\varnothing$ *cannot* be a key, let alone a candidate key. If there is at most one tuple t in a relation, however, $t[\varnothing] = t[\varnothing] \Rightarrow t[R] = t[R]$ holds for any scheme R and any set of FDs F. Thus $\varnothing \to R \in F$ so that the first condition of a candidate key is satisfied. Since there is no proper subset of the empty set, the second condition also holds. Thus $\varnothing$ is a candidate key when a relation can have at most one tuple in any valid interpretation.

---

important in database systems, but about which we have said nothing since Chapter 2. Let U be a set of object sets, and let F be a set of generated FDs over U. Let R, a subset of U, be a relation scheme. A subset K of R is a *superkey* of R if $K \to R \in F^+$. A subset K of R is a *candidate key* of R (also called a *minimal key* of R) if K is a superkey and there does not exist a proper subset K' of K such that $K' \to R \in F^+$. If a relation scheme has several candidate keys, we usually designate one as a *primary key*, or if it only has one, we can also call the only candidate key a *primary key*. The term *key* is often ambiguous and may mean superkey, candidate key, or primary key. Although we could choose to make key mean just one of these, we will let it be ambiguous and use one of these other terms when we must be specific.

A property of any key of a relation scheme R is that its value can designate at most one tuple in any valid relation on R. Said another way, the key value for a tuple appears at most once in a relation. In relation r_2 in Fig. 10.2, for example, *Manager* is a candidate key. We are given *Manager* $\to$ *Home Phone#* from the ORM diagram in Fig. 10.1a and thus *Manager* $\to$ *Manager, Home Phone#* holds, satisfying the first condition. The only proper subset of *Manager* is the empty set, but since the constraints allow several tuples to be in the r_2 relation, the empty set is not a key. Thus the second condition is satisfied. Observe that the manager names in r_2 are unique. If we try to put a duplicate manager into the relation, say *Pat*, we would have to add the phone number 123-1789 to satisfy the FD, but then we would have a duplicate tuple, which is not allowed.

In relation r_3 in Fig. 10.2, both *Dept* and *Manager* are candidate keys. Note that either the department name or the manager name identifies a

---

3NF, BCNF, 4NF, PJNF

For the relational-database theorist, we remark that once we have established our results about keys (Theorem 10.3) and redundancy (Theorem 10.4), we can prove as corollaries that if an ORM hypergraph is canonical, the schemes produced are in Project-Join Normal Form (PJNF), and hence also in 4th Normal Form (4NF), Boyce-Codd Normal Form (BCNF), and 3rd Normal Form (3NF). Relaxing the constraints on being canonical gives us schemes that may not be in PJNF but that are in other normal forms. We address these issues in the exercises.

---

tuple in the relation uniquely. We might choose *Dept* as the primary key. *Manager* and *Dept Phone#* together form an example of a superkey but not a candidate key since *Manager* is a proper subset of the superkey. *Manager* is a superkey as well as a candidate key. In relation r_1 in Fig. 10.7, neither *Item* nor *Order* is a key, but together *Item Order* is a candidate key.

We emphasize that a key is a property of a relation scheme, not a relation. It may just happen that for some valid relations a value identifies a tuple uniquely, but a key must always identify a tuple uniquely for *all* valid relations. For example, all the values under *Distributor* in r_2 in Fig. 10.7 are unique, but *Distributor* is still not a key because we do not have *Distributor* → *Item*; it is possible, indeed highly probable, that a distributor supplies more than one item. We thus base keys on FDs that are generated from an ORM application model, which represents the semantics of the application.

When we apply Algorithm 10.1 to an ORM hypergraph, it produces a set of schemes $\{R_1, ..., R_n\}$, where each scheme is a set of object set names. If we provide at least one primary key for each of these schemes and as many other candidate keys as we wish, and if we give these schemes names—automatically by selecting names from the ORM application model, by default, or simply by giving names to the schemes—we have what is called a *database scheme*. Thus, if we knew how to find candidate keys for the schemes generated by Algorithm 10.1, we could generate a database scheme automatically. Theorem 10.3 gives us a way to find candidate keys.

Theorem 10.3

Let H be a canonical ORM hypergraph, and let F be the set of FDs corresponding to the FD edges of H. Let $\{R_1, ..., R_n\}$ be the schemes generated from H by Algorithm 10.1 and assume that the constraints of H allow more than one tuple in each R_i, $1 \le i \le n$, and thus that $\varnothing$ is not a key for any scheme. Then, if R_i is generated by either Step 1 or

Step 2 of Algorithm 10.1, each set of object sets in the equivalence class from which R_i is formed is a candidate key for R_i; and if R_i is generated by either Step 3 or Step 4 of Algorithm 10.1, the object sets for the entire scheme together constitute a candidate key for R_i.

We can augment Algorithm 10.1 to output candidate keys as follows. If we recognize that for Steps 3 and 4, the scheme is a trivial equivalence class, we can simply add the following as Step 5:

5. For each generated scheme
    if the constraints of the ORM hypergraph allow at most one tuple
        output $\varnothing$ as the candidate key
    else output the object sets of the equivalence class for the scheme
        as the candidate keys.

It is usually easy to determine from the semantics of the application whether a scheme can have at most one tuple. In cases in which the answer is not obvious, we may need to consult with the client, who should know. We need not ask the client about other keys, however, since we can determine this information from constraints that have already been provided for the ORM application model.

Having investigated keys, we now turn to the other properties of interest, beginning with redundancy. A database scheme has *potential redundancy* if any one of the relation schemes has potential redundancy; otherwise, it has *no potential redundancy*. Theorem 10.4 tells us how to ensure that the database scheme has no potential redundancy.

Theorem 10.4

A database scheme produced by Algorithm 10.1 from a canonical ORM hypergraph H has no potential redundancy, except (possibly) for any schemes that have a nontrivial, inextricably embedded JD.

To understand Theorem 10.4, we must understand the exception about inextricably embedded JDs. A JD $\bowtie(R_1, ..., R_n)$ is *embedded* in a scheme R if $R_1...R_n$ is a proper subset of R and is *inextricably embedded* if there is no nontrivial JD $\bowtie(Q_1, ... Q_m)$ that holds for R such that $R_1...R_n$ is one of the components of D.

For example, the ORM hypergraph in Fig. 10.15a has an inextricably embedded JD. The embedded JD is $\bowtie(Item\ Distributor,\ Distributor\ Store)$, which means that if a distributor distributes an item and services a store,

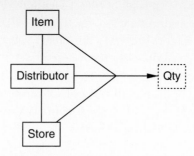

(a) ORM hypergraph with an inextricably embedded JD.

$r =$	Item	Distributor	Store	Qty
	I_1	D_1	S_1	10
	I_1	D_1	S_2	20
	I_2	D_1	S_1	30
	I_2	D_1	S_2	40
	I_1	D_2	S_1	40

(b) A relation with a lossy decomposition {*Item Distributor, Distributor Store, Item Store Qty*}.

Figure 10.15   An inextricably embedded JD.

then the distributor services the store with the item. (Although this might not be the case for arbitrary stores and items, it could very well be the case if the stores were all in a chain and the ordering was done for all the stores in the chain from a central office.) The FD

$$Item\ Distributor\ Store \rightarrow Qty$$

means that only one quantity is ordered for an item, distributor, and store. The JD is embedded in this FD since no *Qty* appears in the JD. It is inextricably embedded because every potential JD that has *Item Distributor Store* as a component is lossy. There are seven nontrivial JDs to check. Using the first letter to designate the object set, the seven are *IDS* along with (1) *Q*, (2) *IQ*, (3) *DQ*, (4) *SQ*, (5) *IDQ*, (6) *ISQ*, and (7) *DSQ*. Now we must find a relation over *IDSQ* for each of these potential JDs, one that satisfies the embedded JD and the FD but not the potential JD. As it turns out, the relation in Fig. 10.15b works for all seven. For example, if we decompose into *IDS* and *ISQ* and join, we get the extraneous tuples <I_1, D_1, S_1, 50> and <I_1, I_2, I_1, I_1>.

The redundancy for an inextricably embedded JD is the same as for a JD. For relation r in Fig. 10.15b, we have the cross product of $\{I_1, I_2\}$ and $\{S_1, S_2\}$ with respect to D_1. Hence, any one of these values is redundant. Since we cannot decompose an inextricably embedded JD without making the decomposition lossy and thus *not* information preserving, we cannot remove the redundancy.

As another example, consider a relationship set *Distributor distributes Item from Warehouse in quantities of Qty*, where the relationship set expresses that only certain quantities are allowable for distribution. Now, if we assume the JD $\bowtie$(*Distributor Item, Distributor Warehouse, Item Warehouse*), we have a JD embedded in the scheme

Distributor Item Warehouse Qty

since it does not include *Qty*, and inextricably embedded since there is no nontrivial, lossless decomposition of the relationship set. The redundancy here is the same as the redundancy in the embedded JD alone, which we explained earlier in our discussion of the relation in Fig. 10.10. Since we cannot do an information-preserving decomposition of this inextricably embedded JD, the redundancy cannot be removed.

Besides not allowing us to remove redundancy, inextricably embedded JDs also introduce another problem. The inextricably embedded JD is itself a constraint on the application model ORM. Assuming we wish to enforce all constraints, we should add this constraint to the application model ORM (unless it happens to be there already). We add it by simply giving the inextricably embedded JD as a general constraint.

We discover inextricably embedded JDs in essentially the same way we discover JDs. If we already have a canonical ORM hypergraph, then for any n-ary edge, $n > 2$, if we can remove one or more of the object sets and then guarantee that there is lossless decomposition, we have found an inextricably embedded JD. For both of the preceding examples, if we remove *Qty*, the semantics of the application model guarantee that the inextricably embedded JD holds.

A database scheme has *potential nulls* if some scheme in the database has *potential nulls*. To decide whether a scheme R has potential nulls, we consider the construction of a relation r for R from the relations in a valid interpretation I for the ORM application model. The construction consists of joining the relations of I for those object and relationship sets used to construct the scheme in Algorithm 10.1. Then, if there exists a valid interpretation I for the ORM application model such that in the construction of the relation r for R there is a relation with a dangling tuple, then R has *potential nulls*.

Theorem 10.5

A database scheme produced by Algorithm 10.1 from a canonical ORM hypergraph H has no potential nulls.

One property we always want is information preservation. We have no choice but to represent the application's objects and relationships faithfully. Since our transformations are information preserving, we can represent any valid interpretation for the application ORM faithfully. Since Algorithm 10.1 combines some relations, however, we must guarantee that the combining is done losslessly. Since we combine by joining, we must guarantee that we can losslessly join the relations in any valid interpretation that are combined by Algorithm 10.1.

Our next theorem shows that if ORM hypergraph H is canonical and thus that H is congruent and that semantic equivalence holds over the equivalence classes of H and the external FD edges for each equivalence of H, then the relations to be combined as a result of Algorithm 10.1 can be joined losslessly.

Theorem 10.6

Let H be a canonical ORM hypergraph, and let R be a scheme generated for H by Algorithm 10.1. Then, for any valid interpretation I of the ORM hypergraph, if $r_1(R_1)$, ..., $r_n(R_n)$ represent relations in I for the object and relationship sets combined by Algorithm 10.1 to form R ($= R_1...R_n$), and if $r = r_1 \bowtie ... \bowtie r_n$ is the relation on R for I, then $r_i = \pi_{R_i} r$, $1 \le i \le n$.

The following theorem shows that if the given ORM hypergraph is canonical and no scheme allows at most one tuple, then we cannot combine any two schemes without introducing either potential redundancy or potential nulls. We combine using an outer join; otherwise, we might also lose information. Thus, in the sense that no two schemes can be combined without affecting other properties negatively, Algorithm 10.1 produces a database scheme with the fewest number of schemes.

Theorem 10.7

Let H be a canonical ORM hypergraph, and let $\{R_1, ..., R_n\}$ be the set of schemes generated for H by Algorithm 10.1. Assume that no scheme allows at most one tuple. Then, any combined scheme $R = R_i R_j$, $1 \le i, j \le n$ and $i \ne j$, has either potential redundancy or potential nulls.

LTKNF

The relational theorist will recognize that when we replace a set of object sets X in a scheme by a set of object sets Y, where X and Y are in the same equivalence class and $|Y| < |X|$, we are addressing the problem solved by LTKNF (Ling-Tompa-Kameda Normal Form).

Although we cannot combine schemes to minimize the number of schemes further, we may be able to reduce the number of object sets mentioned in schemes; lexicalization is one obvious way. Of course, if the ORM hypergraph is canonical, we can do no more lexical reductions. A less obvious way to reduce the number of mentioned object sets in a scheme is to use consolidation to replace a set of object sets X in a scheme by a set of object sets Y, where X and Y are in the same equivalence class and $|Y| < |X|$. Figure 10.16 shows a specific example. The ORM hypergraph in both Figs. 10.16a and 10.16b has an equivalence class $\{AB, C\}$ with one set larger than the other. If we consolidate connections on AB, we generate the schemes in Fig. 10.16a, which has more mentioned object sets than necessary. If we consolidate the connections on C, however, we generate the schemes in Fig. 10.16b, which has a minimal number of mentioned object sets. Observe that the ORM hypergraph in Fig. 10.16b is canonical, whereas the one in Fig. 10.16a is not. If the ORM hypergraph is canonical, it is already minimally consolidated, and thus we cannot use this idea to reduce the number of mentioned object sets further.

We state these two facts about lexical reduction and minimal consolidation as propositions, which only state the obvious. We would like something stronger, namely, a theorem that states that if an ORM hypergraph is canonical, we cannot reduce the number of mentioned object sets in any scheme. This theorem, however, would not be true, since it is sometimes possible to add one to remove two or more. For the application model in Fig. 10.14a, for example, we could add an object set *Name & Address* in place of the two object sets *Name* and *Address*. Furthermore, it is difficult to guarantee that we cannot find some other way to reduce the number of mentioned object sets.

Proposition 10.1

In a database scheme generated for a canonical ORM hypergraph by Algorithm 10.1, it is not possible to use either a lexical transformation or a merge of nonlexical object sets that are in a one-to-one correspondence to reduce the number of object sets mentioned in any of the schemes.

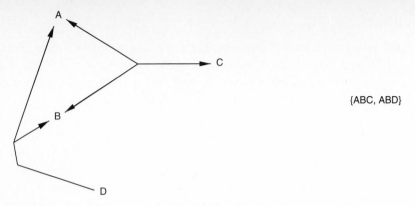

{ABC, ABD}

(a) Generated schemes with more mentioned objects sets than necessary.

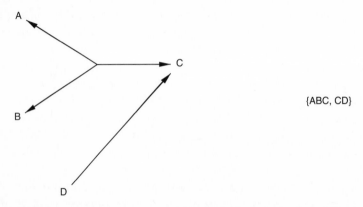

{ABC, CD}

(b) Generated schemes with a minimal number of mentioned object sets.

Figure 10.16   Schemes with and without a minimal number of mentioned object sets.

Proposition 10.2

In a database scheme generated for a canonical ORM hypergraph by Algorithm 10.1, it is not possible to use a consolidation transformation to reduce the number of object sets mentioned in any of the schemes.

Another desirable property is constraint preservation. Our transformations on ORM hypergraphs all preserve constraints. As we have discussed, we may need to carry along, occasionally generate, and possibly adjust some general constraints. If we then generate schemes and keys by Algorithm 10.1 augmented with Step 5 and inclusion dependencies by

---

Dependency Preservation

The relational theorist will recognize that when every FD constraint is embedded in at most one generated scheme, we have dependency preservation. Furthermore, if we wish to know how much redundancy we can eliminate and still have dependency preservation, we will encounter 3NF (a commonly accepted trade-off), or EKNF (Entity-Key Normal Form) (an even tighter trade-off).

Algorithm 10.2 and if we keep all general constraints in our generated database scheme, then the constraints of our database scheme imply the constraints of the given canonical ORM hypergraph. We state this result as Theorem 10.8. Then, since our reduction transformations also preserve constraints, by transitivity of implication we know that the generated database scheme preserves the constraints of the original application model.

Theorem 10.8

Let H be a canonical ORM hypergraph. Let S be a database scheme generated by Algorithm 10.1 for H, and let K be the key constraints generated by Algorithm 10.1 as augmented for keys. Let I be the set of inclusion dependencies generated by Algorithm 10.2. Let C be all other constraints carried into the database scheme, including any FD constraints for high-level relationship sets generated by embedded-FD reductions, any inextricably embedded JD constraints, any partition, mutual-exclusion, and union constraints of H converted to closed formulas, and any general constraints. Then, $K \cup I \cup C$ implies the constraints of H.

As a corollary to Theorem 10.8, we can observe that if there are no FD constraints for high-level relationship sets, then each nontrivial FD constraint is embedded in at most one generated scheme. Indeed, we can make an even stronger statement, as we do in Theorem 10.9, that all the FD constraints are implied by the key constraints. These observations are particularly important for efficient integrity checking.

Theorem 10.9

Let H be a canonical ORM hypergraph, and assume that H has no FD constraints for high-level relationship sets generated by the embedded-FD reduction. Let F be the set of FDs corresponding to the FD edges of H. Let $\{R_1, ..., R_n\}$ be the schemes generated from H by

Algorithm 10.1, and let $K_{i1}, ..., K_{in_i}$ be the candidate keys generated by Algorithm 10.1 (as augmented) for scheme R_i, $1 \le i \le n$. Let F' be the set of FDs $\overset{n}{\underset{i=1}{\cup}} \{K_{11} \to R_1, ..., K_{1n_i} \to R_1\}$. Then, $F' \equiv F$.

10.7 Cost Analysis

As stated at the beginning of Chapter 9, our objective for design is to minimize time and space. In the last section, however, our objective was stated differently. There we wanted to preserve information and constraints, eliminate redundancy and nulls, and minimize the number and size of schemes. To a large extent, these objectives are complementary:

- When we eliminate redundancy, we tend to minimize space because we do not need to store the redundant data values.

- When we eliminate redundancy, we also tend to minimize time because we do not need to check multiple values to ensure integrity and do not need to update multiple values.

- When we minimize the number and size of schemes, we tend to minimize space because we do not need to store as many schemes and because the schemes themselves are smaller; we also tend to minimize time because our searches over relations are shorter.

Furthermore, these objectives are consistent with what we generally expect of data designed for an application:

- We expect designed application data to be information and constraint preserving. We must never lose any needed information as a result of design transformations. To ensure that the representation of the application is as accurate as possible, we should keep and check the given and implied constraints that should never be violated.

- We expect application data to be informative. Nulls can cause problems unless we know exactly what they mean and exactly what is being asked in a query. By eliminating nulls, we can avoid having to interpret their meaning.

Unfortunately, there are exceptions to these general observations, and we should therefore not make our guidelines here supersede our ultimate objectives of reducing time and space. In some cases, when we eliminate redundancy, we may actually increase both space and time. We should find these exceptions and make adjustments. In other cases, when we eliminate redundancy, we may have a space/time trade-off, which we need to resolve in favor of one or the other. Furthermore, for some applications, it may simply cost too much to be fully informative or to check constraints completely. In these cases we usually choose not to enforce some of the constraints.

Consider an example. We can head reduce the 5-ary relationship set connected to address in the ORM hypergraph in Fig. 10.17a because

$$Employee\ Emp\# \rightarrow Street\#, City, State, Zip$$
$$Street\#, City, State \rightarrow Zip$$

This yields the ORM hypergraph in Fig. 10.17b, which is canonical. Given this canonical ORM hypergraph, Algorithm 10.1 generates two schemes:

$$Employee\ Emp\#\ Name\ Street\#\ City\ State$$
$$Street\#\ City\ State\ Zip$$

Now suppose, as is typical, that we store each scheme as a separate relation in the database and each relation as a separate file in the system. Under this assumption, whenever we wish to print an address for an employee, we would have to retrieve the employee's street number, city, and state from one file, and the zip code from another file, to form the address for printing. If this is the dominant use for these relations (and it likely is), then it would be better to store all of the address in a single file with the scheme

$$Employee\ Emp\#\ Name\ Street\#\ City\ State\ Zip$$

To see this analytically, we can compute the space and time cost as follows. Assuming that *Employee Emp#* takes 7 bytes, *Name* takes 20 bytes, *Street#* takes 30 bytes, *City* takes 15 bytes, *State* takes 2 bytes, and *Zip* takes 6 bytes, then if there are 100 employees, the two schemes would likely require 7400 + 5300 = 12,700 bytes, whereas the single scheme would likely require only 8000 bytes. We say "likely" because two or more employees could live in the same household, and thus the second of the two relations may have fewer bytes due to the elimination of duplicate tuples. If this is unlikely, or if company policy prohibits hiring more than one person from any household, then the difference of 4700 bytes is a reasonable estimate of the *extra* space required.

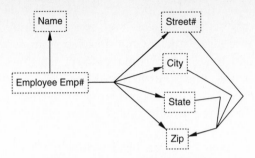

(a) Head-reducible ORM hypergraph.

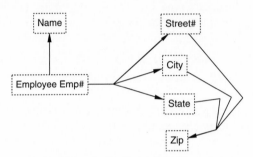

(b) Head-reduced ORM hypergraph.

Figure 10.17 Unwanted head reduction.

Time estimates depend on the algorithms and data structures used to access the data and on whether the information we need is in memory or on disk and whether it is local or distributed. Suppose we know, for example, that our files are on a disk, with an average access time of 20 milliseconds and a transfer rate of 3500 bytes per millisecond. Suppose that we also know that the files are stored by hashing on the keys and that the blocks are 90% full and that there is a 5% collision rate. Then, we would expect to retrieve an address for a given employee number from the two relations by hashing twice, each costing on the average $20*(1.05) = 21$ milliseconds to access the right block and, if the block size is 4096, 4096/3500 approximately 1 more millisecond to read the block, for a total of about 44 milliseconds, whereas we could retrieve an address from the one relation by a single hash lookup, which would cost about 22 milliseconds. Updating these files by adding a new employee would cost twice as much for each update since we not only read from disk but also write to disk. We may also be interested in producing a mailing list for all employees. In this case, if we know that the files are stored in contiguous disk blocks except for one overflow bucket for each file, and we also know that there is sufficient space in memory to store the files we read in, we can estimate the cost of producing a full list. Since the files are small, only a single access is needed for each contiguous read. To read the two files for the first case, we need four accesses, one for the main part of the file and one for the overflow bucket for each file; to read the one file for the second, we need two accesses. Since the transfer rate lets us read about one block per millisecond, and since 90% of the block size is about 3800 bytes, giving us two blocks to read for the main part of r_1 and r_2 and three for r, we can estimate $2((21+2) + (21+1)) = 90$ milliseconds for the first case versus $(21+3) + (21+1) = 46$ milliseconds for the second case.

For this address example, we can see that the elimination of redundancy, what little there is, will cost us more in terms of both time and space. Furthermore, if we try to find any potential savings, it would be because of a change in zip code, a highly unlikely occurrence. Even if a zip-code change were to occur, we would probably not recognize it as such because, for this application, we would likely receive a simple change of address request, which would happen much more often because employees move than because a zip code changes. In our design, we should join the two relations and discard the FD *Street# City State → Zip*.

In general, if we know which algorithms and data structures the system will use to access and update data and if we know the characteristics of the hardware, we can estimate time and space costs for system actions. Often, however, we do not have this information, especially at design time. Furthermore, even with this basic information, we would find it difficult to make accurate estimates because of complex interactions among the various subsystems within a database system. To see the whole picture, we would need to consider the following:

- The query-optimization system, which generates access plans and may decide to generate temporary indexes on the fly;

- The transaction-processing system, which manages concurrency, usually by locking and unlocking data;

- The crash-recovery system, which manages logs and forces log and block writes according to its algorithms;

- The cache system, which tries to make commonly used blocks available without an additional disk access; and

- The clustering and space-management systems, which try to organize and sometimes reorganize information on secondary storage efficiently.

Because of these complexities, the general strategy is to make an educated guess about what the base schemes should be and what indexing and hashing should be used. Then, once the system is implemented, if the performance is not satisfactory, we should fine-tune the system as necessary. After implementation, we can find actual bottlenecks and critical transactions that run too slowly and then make adjustments. Since fine-tuning takes place after implementation, we do not discuss it further. Instead, we consider how to make the best possible guess about how the schemes should be organized.

Even the task of making good educated guesses, however, is too complex to consider thoroughly. We therefore use the following strategy:

1. Produce a canonical ORM hypergraph from the given ORM application model.

2. Generate an initial database scheme from the canonical ORM hypergraph.

3. Use the guidelines for space and time (that we develop next) to determine whether any schemes should be combined.

We mention that the first and second steps of our strategy, by themselves, often yield a reasonable design. We further observe that our synthesis approach is conservative, yielding schemes that generally should not need any decomposition. Because of the way we synthesize schemes, further decomposition cannot remove redundancy. Thus, unless we have some unusually large objects, such as images or videos that we wish to store separately, we should only need to join schemes. As we have seen, this approach reintroduces redundancy or nulls or both, but, as our preceding address example illustrates, sometimes produces better time and space characteristics.

Our approach, therefore, is to develop some general guidelines for space and time by considering what happens when we join two schemes. We consider some particular examples, generalize from the examples, and then extract some general guidelines, which we give as summary comments at the end of our discussions of space and time.

10.7.1 Space

Consider the ORM hypergraph in Fig. 10.18. If we know the expected number of A's and the expected number of B's for A's and C's for A's, we can compute the expected number of tuples in r_1, r_2, and in $r = r_1 \bowtie r_2$. Let

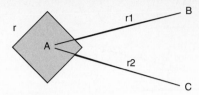

Figure 10.18　The cost of redundancy.

the expected number of A's be n_A, the average number of B's for each A be ave_B, and the average number of C's for each A be ave_C. Also, let b_S be the number of bytes required to store an object in object set S. Then, the expected number of bytes in r_1 is $(b_A + b_B)*n_A*ave_B$, the expected number of bytes in r_2 is $(b_A + b_C)*n_A*ave_C$, and the expected number of bytes in r is $(b_A + b_B + b_C)*n_A*ave_B*ave_C$. Thus, if

$$(b_A + b_B + b_C)*n_A*ave_B*ave_C < (b_A + b_B)*n_A*ave_B + (b_A + b_C)*n_A*ave_C$$

we may save space by combining r_1 and r_2.

　　Observe, as a boundary condition, that if we have FDs $A \to B$ and $A \to C$ so that ave_B and ave_A are both 1, then the inequality is $(b_A + b_B + b_C)*n_A < (b_A + b_B)*n_A + (b_A + b_C)*n_A$, which reduces to $0 < b_A*n_A$, which always holds. For this case, of course, Algorithm 10.1 combines r_1 and r_2.

　　If $A \to B$, but $A \not\to C$, so that $ave_B = 1$, we have $b_B*n_A*ave_C < b_A*n_A + b_B*n_A$, which reduces to $b_B*ave_C < b_A + b_B$. The right-hand side of this inequality is the size of a tuple in r_1, and the left-hand side is the size of the B extension of a tuple in r multiplied by the expected amount of redundant replication. Thus if the redundant replication is low while the size of an r_1 tuple is large, particularly the size of the A part of an r_1 tuple, then we might save space by combining r_1 and r_2. For example, the graph in Fig. 10.19 shows what happens when we fix b_B at, say 5, and fix ave_C at, say 10, and plot the ratio of $b_A + b_B$ to b_B and ave_C. The crossover point for this example is 45, which means that b_A should be at least 45 bytes, or 8 times the size of b_B, before we should even consider combining r_1 and r_2. If there are no FDs, then the averages ave_B and ave_C become the dominating factors in

$$(b_A + b_B + b_C)*n_A*ave_B*ave_C < (b_A + b_B)*n_A*ave_B + (b_A + b_C)*n_A*ave_C$$

Since these averages are multiplicative on the left and additive on the right, the left-hand side quickly dominates the right-hand side. Again, to get a

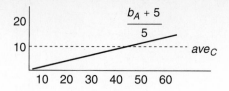

Figure 10.19 Cost of combining a functional and a nonfunctional edge.

feeling for what is happening, let us fix n_A and all the byte counts at, say 10, and let $ave_B = ave_C = ave$. Then the graph in Fig. 10.20 shows that the redundancy causes the size of r to quickly outpace the size of r_1 and r_2 as the average number of corrections increases.

When doing space analysis, a consideration that should not be overlooked is the space required by very large objects. When objects are very large, as are images or videos, we should probably never replicate them, even if there is no redundancy. For example, suppose we have *Person* → *Favorite Movie Star*. Then, if we store the names of movie stars, we probably need have no concern; but if we store pictures of movie stars, we should not store replications of Denzel Washington or Demi Moore for every person who picks them as their favorite. Instead, we can replace the image by an object identifier or pointer, storing each image only once.

We may wish to do the same even when there is no replication. For example, we may have *Item* → *Picture of Item* in our store example, and we may also have *Picture of Item* → *Item*. Since there is a one-to-one correspondence, we will have no replication. If we also wish to store other object sets with *Item* such as *Item Number*, *Price*, and so forth, however, it is still likely

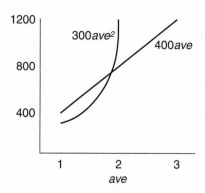

Figure 10.20 Comparison of space costs as the average increases.

to be better to have a pointer or object identifier for the image. Otherwise, the distance between records on disk is likely to be so large that the information about items would be scattered widely among the images.

Nulls are another consideration that should not be overlooked when doing space analysis. Sometimes allowing nulls or adjusting object sets in different ways to avoid nulls can save space, and often time, too. Consider, for example, the canonical ORM hypergraph in Fig. 10.21. From this hypergraph we would generate the schemes

> *distributor(Distributor#, Name, Address)*
> *distributorWithPhone(Distributor# With Phone, Phone#)*
> *item(Item#, Price, Distributor#, Dept With Items)*
> *department(Dept)*
> *seasonalItem(Seasonal Item#, Season, Start Shelf Date, End Shelf Date)*

where we have added convenient relation names for reference. Observe that we have three explicit roles *Distributor# With Phone#* (we do not have a phone number recorded for every distributor), *Dept With Items* (there may be departments with no items), and *Item On Order* (not every item is on some order). If we rename attributes so that the specialization attribute name is the same as the generalization attribute name and then use outer join to combine schemes, we introduce potential nulls. If we combine *distributorWithPhone* and *distributor*, we will have a null for every unknown distributor phone number. If we combine *department* with *item*, departments without items will have nulls for item numbers, prices, and distribu-

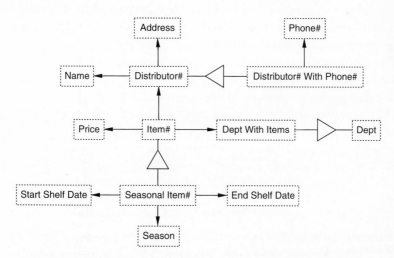

Figure 10.21 ORM hypergraph for cost analysis for nulls.

tor numbers. If we combine *item* with *seasonalItem*, for every nonseasonal item we will have a null for *Season*, *Start Shelf Date*, and *End Shelf Date*.

To see the space trade-off, we can choose some expected sizes for the object sets, and then compute the number of data items that must be stored when schemes are combined and not combined. We could obtain more accurate estimates by also working with the number of bytes required to store each type of data value, but less accurate estimates are sufficient to show the differences here. Let us assume that there are 50 departments, 2 departments without items, 10,000 items, 200 seasonal items, 1000 distributors, and 10 distributors for which we do not know the phone number.

With these assumptions, *distributor* has 3*1000 = 3000 data values, and *distributorWithPhone* has (1000 − 10)*2 = 1980 data values. The total is 4980. If we combine these two schemes, since every distributor with a phone number is a distributor, we have 4*1000 = 4000 data values, 10 of which are nulls. Thus, we would save space by combining the schemes. Furthermore, we are not likely to encounter any problems with these nulls, which represent "applicable but unknown data values." We are likely to want only to record phone numbers, perhaps change them, and look them up, and we are not likely to select or join on them. Further, we can also save considerable time by not having to join the two relations when we need the name, address, and phone information for a distributor, and by not having to update two relations when we do obtain an unrecorded phone number. Thus, we save both time and space, and we should combine the schemes.

For departments with and without items, *item* has 4*10,000 = 40,000 data values, and *department* has 50 data values. The total is 40,050. If we combine these two schemes we will have two additional tuples, each with one department value and three nulls. Thus, we will have 40,008 data values, about the same as when we do not combine schemes. The nulls in this example are "nonapplicable nulls" because there are no prices, items, and distributors for departments without items. Thus, we are not likely to update them as we do "applicable but unknown" nulls in our last example. Instead, we would want to discard the tuple with nulls when we begin adding items for the department. This operation is awkward because it represents a special case. When the schemes are not combined, we need to do only regular insertions when we begin adding items for a department. Since we save very little space by combining the schemes and since we encounter some special-case updates that will take extra time, we should not combine the schemes.

As an alternative to either combining *Dept* or leaving it separate, it should be clear that we must store separately only the 2 departments that have no items, not all 50. In terms of ORM transformations, we can see this if we make another specialization of *Dept* called *Dept Without Items* and observe that this specialization together with *Dept With Items* partition *Dept*. Thus, we have a union-covered isolated root generalization, which we can discard. As a result, we store the 2 departments in a new scheme *departmentWithoutItems* and discard the *department* scheme.

For seasonal items, we have 200*4 = 800 data values. Since *item* has 40,000 data values as just computed, we have a total of 40,800 data values when the *item* and *seasonalItem* schemes are separate. Since every seasonal item is an item, if we combine them, we will have 10,000 tuples, each with 7 data values, for a total of 70,000 data values. Of these 70,000 data values, $(10,000 - 200)*3 = 29,400$ will be null values. Combining the schemes wastes considerable space. The nulls here represent "nonapplicable nulls" because nonseasonal items do not have an associated season, and no start and end dates for being placed on and taken off a shelf. These nonapplicable nulls can cause problems because we are likely to want to select on them and possibly join on them. In these cases, we probably want to select seasonal items first before doing further processing. Since combining the schemes takes considerably more space and likely more processing time, we should not combine the schemes.

We summarize this section by listing some "rule of thumb" guidelines:

1. When we combine relations along relationship-set paths, we usually create a lot of redundancy unless the probability of redundant replication is very close to zero. Thus when we almost have functional dependencies and when data objects are all about the same size, we may consider combining edges as if they were functional dependencies.

2. When the size of the objects in the object sets common to two schemes is large compared with the size of the other objects, we may consider combining the schemes. In other words, if the size of the common objects that would be replicated by a decomposition because they would be in both schemes is large, we may wish to keep the schemes together.

3. When an object set has very large objects, we may wish to keep them in a relation of their own and use pointers or object identifiers to refer to them.

4. When we consider combining relations whose combination potentially would have null values, we can ask whether the nulls are

"applicable but unknown" or "nonapplicable." We tend to save
time and space by combining schemes with "applicable but
unknown nulls" but not by combining schemes with "nonapplicable nulls."

Returning to our address example, we see that by following the first rule of
thumb, we should probably not decompose the address for an employee
because there is likely to be almost no redundant replication. Also, by following the second rule of thumb, since the common items in the two
schemes are *Street# City State*, which together are relatively large compared
with the sizes of the other objects under consideration, we should combine
the relations for all the edges in Fig. 10.17b.

10.7.2 Time

To compare time costs, we must know which operations will be applied, the
frequency of the operations, and how much they will cost. Figure 10.22
shows more exactly what we need. To compare the cost of having combined schemes versus the cost of having separate schemes, we estimate the
relative frequency of retrieval and update operations, and we estimate the
cost of these operations for both the combined and separate cases. We then
compute an estimated weighted cost for each and compare.

Since a common and costly retrieval operation is the join, we should certainly use it in our estimations unless we know that its frequency in the
application is zero. Indeed, since the cost of the join usually dominates all
other costs, we may use it alone to get a basic cost estimation. The updates
are insertion, deletion, and value modification, which consist not only of the
basic change, but also the cost of any required integrity checking. Since we
consider both the change and the check, any one of these operations has
about the same cost as any of the others. Insertions and deletions, however,

	Frequency	Combined	Separate
Retrieval	estimated frequency	estimated cost	estimated cost
Update	estimated frequency	estimated cost	estimated cost
Totals		estimated weighted cost	estimated weighted cost

Figure 10.22   Considerations when comparing time costs.

also may introduce nulls, which need additional consideration. Therefore, a reasonable way to proceed is to estimate the cost of a join and the cost of doing an insertion, both when the schemes are separate and when they are combined. Then, using the expected frequency of these operations, we can estimate the total expected costs and compare.

Consider again the ORM hypergraph in Fig. 10.18. We first estimate the number of blocks in r, r_1, and r_2 based on the expected size of r_1 and r_2, the expected replication of redundant values in r, and the expected block size. These calculations are similar to those we have done before. Let n_r, n_{r_1}, and n_{r_2} be the number of blocks for relations r, r_1 and r_2.

We next need to know how these blocks are organized. There are several choices here, and which organization is chosen makes a difference. We illustrate the ideas using hash tables and nested-loop joins. If the application is such that we can get good estimates for the size of our files (and often it is), and if we choose a good hash function for our data, we can assume that the main parts of our hash files appear sequentially on disk in contiguous blocks and that the block chains for collision data are short.

Estimating the cost of the join for the combined case is easy because in the combined case we directly store r, which is the join $r_1 \bowtie r_2$. We find the first block in the main part of our hash file, read all the contiguous blocks sequentially, and then find the first and (assumed) only block for the collision data and read it. Assuming (as we did before) that the average access time is 22 milliseconds and that it costs 1 millisecond to read each block, our estimated time is $22+n_r+22+1 = 45+n_r$ milliseconds. This is the entry for the estimated cost for combined retrieval in Fig. 10.22.

Estimating the cost of the join for the separate case is harder because it depends on the join algorithm and the amount of space available in memory. We illustrate with a nested-join algorithm and assume that enough space is available in memory to hold m blocks, where $m \geq 2$, of course, but is usually larger. With m blocks available, our nested join algorithm proceeds as follows:

> If $b_{r_1} > b_{r_2}$:
>   Exchange the roles of r_1 and r_2. -- to have the smaller relation in the
>   -- outer loop.
> Repeat:
>   Read (up to) $m-1$ blocks of r_1.
>   For each block b of r_2:
>   Read b.
>   Join the tuples of the blocks of r_1 currently in memory with the
>   tuples of b.
> Until all blocks of r_1 have been read.

The cost of this join is the sum of the number of accesses multiplied by 22 milliseconds plus the number of blocks read (multiplied by 1 millisecond). Since we access a block of r_2 every time we access a group of $m-1$ blocks of the main part of r_1 and since we also access the collision block of r_1, the number of accesses is $\left\lceil \dfrac{n_{r_1} - 1}{m - 1} \right\rceil * n_{r_2} + 1$. Since we read each block of r_1 once and each block of r_2 as many times as it takes to put all of r_1 into memory in groups of $m-1$ at a time, the number of blocks read is $n_{r_1} + \left\lceil \dfrac{n_{r_1}}{m - 1} \right\rceil * n_{r_2}$. Thus, the entry of the estimated cost for the separate retrieval for Fig. 10.22 is

$$22 * \left(\left\lceil \frac{n_{r_1} - 1}{m - 1} \right\rceil * n_{r_2} + 1 \right) + \left\lceil \frac{n_{r_1}}{m - 1} \right\rceil * n_{r_2}$$

The cost of an insertion depends on the file organization, on whether we are inserting into r_1 or r_2 or both, and on the number of connections between A values and B values or C values. For a hashing organization, we hash on the keys, which for our example may involve one, two, or three values as input to the hash function, one or two of which may be null. For nulls and hashing, we simply treat a null as a value.

For the separate case, we hash on the key to find the block for tuple insertion. Inserting a tuple into r_1 or r_2 takes one—or if there is a collision, two—accesses to find the right block, one block read to fetch the block, and one block write to do the update. If by chance our insertion is a duplicate, we need not write, but we ignore this case. Thus, assuming a 5% collision rate and an average access time of 22 milliseconds (broken down into an average seek time of 8 milliseconds and an average rotational latency of 14 milliseconds), an average insertion into r_1 or r_2 costs 1.05*22 milliseconds for the fetch, plus 1 millisecond for the read, plus 14 milliseconds for the rotational latency before the write, plus 1 millisecond for the write. To insert a tuple into r, we decompose the tuple into two subtuples, one for r_1 and the other for r_2, and make the individual insertions. For the entry in Fig. 10.22, we take the average of the three insertions unless we have better information about the relative frequencies of these three types of updates. Thus we enter the estimate as approximately 39*4/3 = 52 milliseconds.

For the combined case, we can have nulls because we may just insert an AB tuple or a BC tuple. If nulls are a fundamental problem, we should either reject the combined case or disallow an update if it would cause a null to be inserted. For our analysis, we will assume that nulls are allowed.

	combined	separate
retrieval	545 msec	6922 msec
update	1560 msec	52 msec

Figure 10.23 Some estimates for the example.

To see what happens when we do an insertion that corresponds to an insertion into either r_1 or r_2, consider inserting *<ball, D_3>* into the *Distributor supplies Item* relation in Fig. 10.6a. In Fig. 10.6c, this corresponds to adding a link between *ball* and D_3, but in Fig. 10.6b, this corresponds to adding two tuples *<ball, O_1, D_3>* and *<ball, O_2, D_3>*. In general, when we add to the r_1 part of r, we must add as many tuples as there are connections from the *A* value of the tuple being added to the *C* values in the r_2 part of r. Thus, if we let ave_B and ave_C be the average number of connections for an *A* value in r to the *B* values and *C* values, respectively, the estimated cost of inserting into r_1 is $39*ave_C$ and into r_2 is $39*ave_B$. When inserting directly into r, we must replicate tuples for both *B* and *C*. Thus, the cost is $39*ave_B*ave_C$. Hence, as an average we have $13*(ave_B + ave_C + ave_B*ave_C)$.

To become familiar with these formulas, let us choose some numbers so that we can obtain results for each of the four estimated costs from Fig. 10.22. Then let us vary the ratio of retrievals to updates, which we call the read-write ratio, and plot a graph. We assume, for the sake of illustration, that $n_{r_1} = n_{r_2} = 50$, $n_r = 500$, $m = 10$, and $ave_B = ave_C = 10$. Substituting these numbers into our formula yields the numbers in the table in Fig. 10.23. The numbers themselves are revealing, indicating that joins are relatively costly and that additional tuple insertions for combined tables, although not as costly as a join here, are also relatively costly. Of course, if the averages ave_B and ave_C had been 25 instead of 10, the entry would have been 8775 rather than 1560. Indeed, this is the basic trade-off—the cost of the join when the tables are separate versus the cost of the redundant updates (and the extra storage as discussed in the previous section, which storage is accounted for partly by the relative size of n_r compared with n_{r_1} and n_{r_2}). To plot a graph, we let f_{read} be the read frequency, which makes $1 - f_{read}$ the write frequency. Hence we plot $545 f_{read} + 1560(1 - f_{read})$ for the combined case and $6922 f_{read} + 52(1 - f_{read})$ for the separate case. The graph in Fig. 10.24 shows the results as solid lines. We see, for this example, that the crossover point is close to 0.2, which means that if more than about 20% of the operations require the join, we might consider storing r_1 and r_2 combined as r.

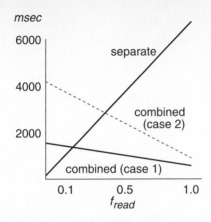

Figure 10.24 Comparison of combined and separate cases based on read frequency.

We must be careful in our interpretation here, however, because we have set arbitrary values for sizes and connection averages. For example, suppose we change the averages for the connections so that $ave_B = ave_C = 17$. Then, if we still assume that $n_{r_1} = n_{r_2} = 50$, we should change n_r to about 900 because if we have 50 tuples each in r_1 and r_2 with an average of 17 B's for A's and 17 C's for A's, we should have approximately $17*17*3 = 867$ or about 900 tuples in r. If we now recompute our estimates, we obtain $945 f_{read} + 4199(1 - f_{read})$, which we show on the graph in Fig. 10.24 as the dashed line. Now the crossover point is closer to 0.4.

We summarize this section with two "rule of thumb" guidelines:

1. Consider combining relations when the frequency of needing the relations joined is large compared with the frequency of updating them.

2. Before combining, consider the cost of other retrieval operations that may be affected adversely.

For this second point, we can compute the expected costs of other retrieval operations that may be affected using the ideas we have discussed. For our example, we should also consider the fact that selections and joins that use either r_1 or r_2, but not both, will be more expensive for the combined case.

To illustrate how to use these guidelines, let us again consider our address example. Assuming that in our application we are interested in printing individual addresses and address lists, and in updating addresses when people move or are added or deleted from the database, we should certainly combine the zip code with the rest of the address. We would always want the address combined for our assumed application, both for reading and for updating. Furthermore, we do not ever expect to use one part of the address without the other. If we really stretch our imagination, we might be able to believe that we could update the street number without having to update the zip code, but handling this as a special case would be far more trouble than it is worth.

10.8 Nested-Scheme Synthesis

In our motivating example at the beginning of this chapter, we considered nested relation schemes as well as flat relation schemes. In Figs. 10.4 and 10.5, we saw that it was possible to collapse some of the replicated (but not redundant) data values. Intuitively, it should not be necessary to repeat *Toy* for every toy in the toy department. Recording each department once followed by all the items in the department should be sufficient.

If we carry this idea too far, however, we can cause unwanted redundancy; Fig. 10.25 provides an example. Here we use the data in Fig. 10.6 but recast it in the nested framework in Fig. 10.25. Now all the D_1's and D_2's are redundant. Since, as Fig. 10.6c shows, both distributor D_1 and distributor D_2 supply balls, and since, as Fig. 10.25 shows, both order O_1 and order O_2 include *ball*, we must replicate distributors redundantly for each order with the same item.

We define redundancy in nested relations the same way we define redundancy in flat relations. If we can remove a value and determine from the constraints what the value must have been, it is redundant. We can test redundancy in nested relations by unnesting the relation so that it becomes a flat relation, then use the definition for redundancy given earlier. Then, however, when we find a pair of redundant values in the flat relation, they are redundant in the nested relation only if they map to separate places in that relation. Figure 10.26 displays the total unnesting of the nested relation in Fig. 10.25. Since the MVD *Item* $\twoheadrightarrow$ *Order* | *Distributor* holds, all the orders connected to *ball* and all the distributors connected to *ball* are redundant. The pair of O_1's and the pair of O_2's, however, each map to only one place in the nested relation, and thus neither is redundant, but the pair of D_1's and the pair of D_2's each map to separate buckets in the nested relation and are redundant. Observe also that multiple appearances alone do not make a value redundant. The D_2 for *game* is not redundant formally because it is not redundant in the flat relation in Fig. 10.26, and it is not

Order	(Item	(Distributor)*)*

O_1 — ball — D_1, D_2

game — D_2

O_2 — ball — D_1, D_2

saw — D_3

Figure 10.25 A nested relation with redundancy.

redundant informally because if we remove it from the nested relation in Fig. 10.25, there is no way to recover it since there is no other *game* value to give us the association we need.

Before giving an algorithm to generate nested relation schemes with no potential redundancy, we provide one more motivating example. Figure 10.27a shows an ORM hypergraph; Fig. 10.27b, a nested relation scheme for the hypergraph. This scheme has no potential redundancy. We can see why by considering the structure of the ORM hypergraph. The basic structure is a sequence of one-many relationship sets. For each salesperson there are many customers, and for each customer there are many orders. The key, however, is that there is only one salesperson for each customer and only one customer for each order. This prevents customers and orders from being in different buckets, for if a customer were in two buckets, then the salesperson would have to be replicated, which we disallow in nested rela-

Order	Item	Distributor
O_1	ball	D_1
O_1	ball	D_2
O_1	game	D_2
O_2	ball	D_1
O_2	ball	D_2
O_2	saw	D_3

Figure 10.26 The unnesting of the nested relation in Fig. 10.25.

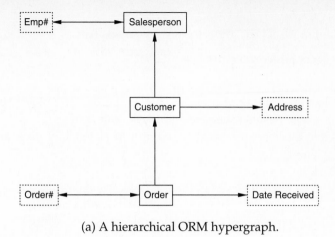

(a) A hierarchical ORM hypergraph.

Salesperson, Emp# (Customer, Address (Order, Order#, Date Received)*)*

(b) A nested relation scheme with no potential redundancy.

Figure 10.27   An ORM hypergraph and nested relation scheme.

tions, and if an order were in two buckets, then the customer would have to be in two different buckets, which we have said is not possible.

In general, because we have a strict one-many hierarchy, we can continue nesting as deeply as we wish without causing redundancy. Furthermore, any object sets in an equivalence class with any member of the one-many hierarchy can also be placed in the hierarchy without a problem. In Fig. 10.27, for example, we can place *Emp#* in the same place in the hierarchy as we place *Salesperson*, and we can place *Order#* in the same place in the hierarchy as we place *Order*. Still further, we can place object sets that depend functionally on these equivalence classes in the same place in the hierarchy. Thus, for example, we can place *Address* alongside *Customer* and we can place *Date Received* alongside *Order*. Just as in Algorithm 10.1, however, we cannot add any other FD edges. As our discussion concerning Fig. 10.25 indicates, we also cannot have more than one non-FD edge strung together in a hierarchy, although we can nest them side by side. With these observations in mind, we now present Algorithm 10.3.[†]

As an example, we can generate the nested relation scheme in Fig. 10.27b from the ORM hypergraph in Fig. 10.27a as follows. We first select

[†] Note that the algorithm works only for ORM hypergraphs whose edges are all binary. See the bibliographic notes for a general algorithm.

Algorithm 10.3 *

Input: a canonical, acyclic, binary ORM hypergraph H.

Output: a set of nested schemes.

> Repeat:
> > Select an unmarked node N in H to be the first object set of a
> > > new nested scheme S and mark N in H.
> >
> > While there is an unmarked edge E in H incident on a marked
> > > node A:
> >
> > Mark E.
> > Let B be the unmarked node in E (which is guaranteed to exist).
> > If $A \rightarrow B$ and $B \rightarrow A$:
> > > Add B to S in the same place as A is in S.
> > > Mark B.
> >
> > Else if $A \rightarrow B$:
> > > Add B to S in the same place as A is in S.
> > > If every edge incident on B is marked, mark B.
> >
> > Else if $B \rightarrow A$:
> > > Add B to S nested under the place where A is in S.
> > > Mark B.
> >
> > Else (neither $A \rightarrow B$ nor $B \rightarrow A$):
> > > Add B to S nested under the place where A is in S.
> > > If every edge incident on B is marked, mark B.
> >
> Until all nodes have been marked.

and mark *Salesperson*. There are two unmarked edges incident on the marked node *Salesperson*. Since *Salesperson* $\rightarrow$ *Emp#* and *Emp#* $\rightarrow$ *Salesperson*, we add *Emp#* alongside *Salesperson*, and we mark the edge and *Emp#*. Since *Customer* $\rightarrow$ *Salesperson*, we add *Customer* by nesting it under the place where *Salesperson* is, and we mark the edge and *Customer*. Continuing around the while loop, we see that there are two unmarked edges incident on *Customer*, which is marked. Since *Customer* $\rightarrow$ *Address*, we add *Address* alongside *Customer*, and we mark the edge and *Address*, but only because every (the only) edge incident on *Address* is already marked. (This would prevent us from adding something on this branch past *Address* if it were there.) Since *Order* $\rightarrow$ *Customer*, we nest it under the place where *Customer* is, and we mark the edge and *Order*. Continuing around the while loop, we see that there are two unmarked edges incident on *Order*, which is

---

*Used with permission of Naveen Prakash. "Theoretical and Practical Implications of a New Definition for Nested Normal Form," Mok, W., Embley, D., Ng, Y-K. in *Proceedings of the 5th International Conference on Information Systems and Management of Data*, Madras, India, 10/94.

Figure 10.28 ORM hypergraph for generating nested relations.

marked. Since *Order* → *Order#* and *Order#* → *Order*, we add *Order#* along-side *Order* and mark the edge and *Order#*. Since *Order* → *Date Received*, we also add it alongside *Order* (and *Order#*), and we mark the edge and *Date Received*, but again, only because all edges incident on *Date Received* are marked.

As a second example, we show that Algorithm 10.3 does *not* generate the nested relation scheme of Fig. 10.25, which has redundancy. Figure 10.28 provides the ORM hypergraph for the ORM diagram in Fig. 10.6a. If we start with *Order* and mark it, then we can select the only incident edge on *Order*, mark it, and nest *Item* under *Order*. Not every edge incident on *Item* is marked, however, so we do not mark *Item*. Now there is no unmarked edge incident on a marked node. Thus we drop out of the while loop and start over with a new scheme, generating either *Item* (*Distributor*)* or *Distributor* (*Item*)* as a second nested relation scheme. In any case, we cannot generate the nested relation scheme in Fig. 10.25. Observe, however, that if we start first with *Item*, then we can generate a single scheme, *Item* (*Order*)* (*Distributor*)*.

Note that the optional connection on *Item* causes no difficulties with nulls. In the scheme *Item* (*Order*)∗(*Distributor*) *, for example, it simply means that there may be an empty nested bucket for *Order*. In general, for Algorithm 10.3 we can relax "canonical" to allow optional connections any-where except on the tail-side of an FD edge.

Theorem 10.10

A nested relational database scheme produced by Algorithm 10.3 has no potential redundancy, except (possibly) for any schemes that have a nontrivial, inextricably embedded JD.

NNF

The relational theorist will recognize that, in general, to guarantee that we have no potential redundancy in nested relation schemes, we need to satisfy the conditions of Nested Normal Form (NNF). NNF is discussed further in the exercises.

We conclude by listing and discussing some advantages and disadvantages of nested relations compared with flat relations.

Advantages

- We usually save space because we need not repeat some values. For example, in the nested relation in Fig. 10.4, we need not repeat the department name. If there are 20 departments with an average of 100 items each, we save 99∗20 = 1980 repetitions of department names.

- We save time for some operations because we can store the join of relations without redundancy, relations that if flat would have redundancy. For example, rather than storing the relations for the ORM hypergraph in Fig. 10.27a in three flat relations

  1. *Order#, Order, Date Received, Customer*
  2. *Customer, Address, Salesperson*
  3. *Salesperson, Emp#*

we can store all three relations together as a single nested relation

  Salesperson, Emp# (Customer, Address (Order, Order#, Date Received)*)*

Then if we need to access something like the *Address* and the *Order* together or the *Emp#* and the *Date Received*, we need not join the relations since they are joined already in the nested relation.

- We can find a good trade-off between pointer chasing and redundancy. For large objects in object-oriented database-management systems, we often wish to access all the components at once. If we store them in flat or even nested relations, however, there may be some, perhaps even a lot, of redundancy. If we decompose the objects and still want to access them quickly, we may link the various subcomponents by pointers. If we decompose them too far, however, we will introduce excessive pointer chasing. A reasonable compromise is to use nested relations to group subcomponents as much as possible without introducing redundancy, and then use pointers to link these subcomponents together. This gives a good balance between data redundancy, on the one hand, and excessive pointer chasing, on the other.

Disadvantages

- We must maintain records of varying length. The number of data values in a bucket varies as we insert and delete items. For example, in Fig. 10.4, whenever we add a new item to or delete an item from a department, we change the size of the set of data values associated with the department. If we happen to know what the size of a bucket should be, and if the size does not vary widely, we might simply allocate enough space and let the actual size of the bucket vary within the space. Often, however, we cannot be precise enough, and we must resort to allowing overflow blocks if we exceed the space allocated. This not only makes the management of the space more difficult, but it also increases the retrieval and update time.

- Some operations take more time. When we join nested relations together, the extra overhead can slow down the operation. For example, joining two nested relations on deeply nested attributes is likely to take more time than joining two flat relations containing these attributes.

10.9 Cost Analysis for Embedded Functional Dependencies

We have observed as a corollary to Theorem 10.8 and in Theorem 10.9 that if there are no FD constraints for high-level relationship sets, then each non-trivial FD constraint is embedded in at most one generated scheme and can be checked by checking only a key constraint. Unfortunately, for some ORM hypergraphs, we either must have redundancy or we must have an FD constraint for a high-level relationship set. In these cases, we must resolve the redundancy/constraint-checking trade-off by time and space arguments based on the application or by agreeing on semantic changes to the application when we cannot afford the time and space penalties.

We illustrate these ideas by discussing further the example introduced in Chapter 9 about salespersons and their appointments with customers. Figure 10.29 shows the ORM hypergraph for this example. We first observe that the only way to remove redundancy is to remove the FD edge *Customer → Salesperson* from the *Salesperson has appointment with Customer at Time on Date* relationship set. For if we embed this FD in a scheme along with any other object set or sets, *Customer* will *not* be the key. Since it is not the key, its value can be repeated, and thus the *Salesperson* value is redundant for

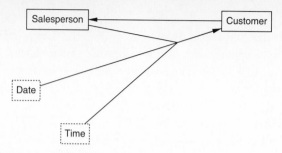

Figure 10.29   ORM hypergraph with an embedded FD.

every repeated *Customer* value. Thus we must remove either *Customer* or *Salesperson* or both from the 4-ary scheme. Since the only way to do this and still preserve information is to carry out an embedded-FD reduction, our only alternatives are to have redundancy or an FD constraint for a high-level relationship set.

We consider the following five alternatives:

1. Implement as a single flat scheme *Salesperson Date Time Customer*. Use an unsorted sequential file. To manage the free space within the file, we assume that a list of blocks with free space is kept in memory.

2. Implement as two flat schemes *Salesperson Customer* and *Date Time Customer*. Use two unsorted sequential files, each with a list of blocks with free space in memory.

3. Implement as a nested relation scheme *Salesperson (Date Time Customer)**. Use an unsorted sequence of varying length records with a single chain of overflow blocks. Since the *Salesperson* records are together physically, we also assume that we have an in-memory index on *Salesperson*.

4. Change the semantics by discarding *Customer* → *Salesperson*. Then implement as a single flat scheme *Salesperson Date Time Customer*. Use an unsorted sequential file with a list of blocks with free space in memory.

5. Change the semantics by discarding *Customer* → *Salesperson*. Then implement as a nested relation scheme *Salesperson (Date Time Customer)**. Use an unsorted sequence of varying length records with a single chain of overflow blocks. Since the *Salesperson* records are together physically, we also assume that we have an in-memory index on *Salesperson*.

To make our discussion concrete, let us assume that there are 50 salespersons, each represented by a 1-byte object identifier, and 2000 customers, each represented by a 2-byte identifier. Let us also assume that customers typically have between one and five appointments with salespersons, with two being the average, and that the customers are more or less uniformly distributed among the salespersons so that each salesperson has about 40 customers. Finally, we assume that dates and times are 2-byte integers and that the block size is 1024 bytes.

With this information we can estimate that Alternatives 1 and 4 have 4000 7-byte records, which is about 28,000 bytes of data. If we assume a 10% space overhead for deleted records not yet occupied by replacement records, we may estimate that the space requirement is about 31 blocks. For Alternative 2, we can estimate that there are 2000 3-byte records (= 6000 bytes) and 4000 6-byte records (= 24,000 bytes), which, with a 10% space overhead, requires about 7+26 = 33 blocks. For Alternatives 3 and 5, we may suppose that we reserve 40 6-byte records for each 1-byte salesperson value, and that there are, say, three overflow blocks. Thus we have approximately $1 + (40*2)*6 = 481$ bytes or less than one block for a single salesperson; for 50 salespersons, a total of 24,050 bytes, or about 24+3 = 27 blocks. Although the nested scheme has slightly fewer blocks, it is interesting to note that there is no clear winning alternative with respect to space.

To estimate time, let us assume that the operations with the highest frequency are (1) setting a new appointment for a customer, (2) deleting old appointments, and (3) requesting a list of appointments for an individual salesperson. We also assume that the relative frequency of these three operations is about equal.

Before making time estimates for these operations, we establish some basic time estimates. We assume that the sequential files are stored in contiguous blocks and that the main parts of the files of varying length records are stored in contiguous blocks.

- To read the salesperson-date-time-customer file, it takes an access (22 milliseconds) plus a transfer of 31 blocks at about 3 blocks per millisecond (11 milliseconds) for a total of 33 milliseconds.

- To read the salesperson-customer file, it takes an access (22 milliseconds) plus a transfer of 7 blocks (3 milliseconds) for a total of 24 milliseconds.

- To read the date-time-customer file, it takes an access (22 milliseconds) plus a transfer of 26 blocks (9 milliseconds) for a total of 31 milliseconds.

- To read or write an individual block, such as a block in an over-flow chain, it takes an access (22 milliseconds) plus a transfer of 1 block (1 millisecond) for a total of 23 milliseconds. If, however, we can assume that the disk head is already on the right track, we can reduce this to a rotational latency (14 milliseconds) plus a transfer of 1 block (1 millisecond) for a total of 15 milliseconds.

- To read the varying length salesperson-(date-time-customer)* file, it takes an access (22 milliseconds) plus a transfer of 1 block (1 millisecond) for a total of 23 milliseconds.

- To read the date-time-customer information for a given salesperson in the file of varying length records, it takes an access (22 milliseconds) plus a transfer of 27 blocks (9 milliseconds) plus an access and transfer of the three individual blocks in the chain (69 blocks).

We now consider the average operation time for each alternative, assuming that one-third of the operations are setting new appointments, one-third are deleting old appointments, and one-third are requesting lists of appointments for an individual salesperson.

Alternative 1. To set an appointment, we must insert a single salesperson-date-time-customer record. However, since we must also ensure that the two FDs hold so that a customer has only one salesperson and a salesperson has only one appointment for any date and time, we must read the entire file to check the constraints and then write one block to do the update. This takes 33+15 = 48 milliseconds. To delete an appointment, we must read the unsorted file to find the record and write one block. Since, on the average, we will find the record by the time we have read half of the file, this takes 33/2 + 15 = 32 milliseconds. To list the appointments for a salesperson, we must read the unsorted file, which takes 33 milliseconds. Hence the average time for an operation for Alternative 1 is 38 milliseconds.

Alternative 2. To set an appointment, we must insert a time-date-customer record; if we do not already have a salesperson-customer record for the customer, we must also insert a salesperson-customer record. As it turns out this does not matter, however, because we must already read both files to check the FDs. Furthermore, we must also do a join, but since the files are relatively small, we will assume that all the blocks from both files fit in memory and thus that the time to do the join is negligible. Thus, this insertion takes 24+31 = 55 milliseconds. (Although we are assuming that the blocks of a file are contiguous, we are not assuming that the two files are contiguous.) To delete an appointment, we must remove a record from the time-date-customer file after finding it. We should also delete the corresponding salesperson-customer record if the salesperson has no more appointments with the customer, but we will assume that the frequency of this is low and ignore the time contribution from this action. Because of this possibility, however, we must not only find the record to delete but also find another one or read to the end of the file to learn that there is no other one. Working out the probabilities here to determine the estimated fraction of the file we need to read is unnecessarily complex, and we will not be too far off in estimating that about three-fourths of the file needs to be read. Since we also need to do a block write, most likely on the cylinder we are on, we estimate that the deletion takes $15 + 31*3/4 = 39$ milliseconds. To list the appointments for a salesperson, we must join the two files. Since we are assuming that we can fit both files in memory, we estimate that this query takes $24+31 = 55$ milliseconds. Hence the average time for an operation for Alternative 2 is 50 milliseconds.

Alternative 3. To set an appointment, we must insert a date-time-customer subtuple under the right salesperson. Since we have the file indexed on salesperson, this operation would need only a block read and a block write. However, we must also check the integrity constraint *Customer* → *Salesperson*. If the customer to be inserted for the appointment already has another appointment with the salesperson, we can be sure that since the FD is assumed to hold before the update, we need not check to see whether the customer has an appointment with some other salesperson. About half the time, however, we will not have this information, so we estimate a one-block read and a one-block write half the time and a full read half the time. Thus we estimate that the insertion takes half of 23 milliseconds to read and 15 milliseconds to write for the first case and half of 69 milliseconds plus 23 milliseconds to write for the second case, for an estimate of 65 milliseconds. To delete an appointment, we need read and write only one block for a salesperson (it could be two because of records overlapping from one block to the next, but we will assume one). Thus, a deletion takes only 23 milliseconds to read and 15 milliseconds to write, for a total of 38 milliseconds. To list the appointments for a salesperson, we need access only one block. Thus, this operation takes 23 milliseconds. Hence the average time for an operation for Alternative 3 is 42 milliseconds.

Alternative 4. Setting an appointment takes the same amount of time as for Alternative 1, 48 milliseconds. Although we need not check the

Customer → *Salesperson* constraint, we still must check the *Salesperson Date Time* constraint. Thus we must read the entire file. Deleting an appointment and listing appointments for a salesperson also takes the same amount of time as for Alternative 1, 32 milliseconds and 33 milliseconds, respectively. Hence the average time for an operation for Alternative 4 is the same as for Alternative 1, 38 milliseconds.

Alternative 5. To set an appointment, since we need not check *Customer* → *Salesperson*, we need only read and write one block (at most two blocks, but we assume one) for the salesperson. This takes 23+15 = 38 milliseconds. Deleting an appointment and listing appointments for a salesperson take the same amount of time as for Alternative 3, 38 milliseconds and 23 milliseconds, respectively. Hence the average time for an operation for Alternative 5 is 33 milliseconds.

We see that if we can ignore the *Customer* → *Salesperson* FD, the clear winner is Alternative 5. We cannot change the semantics arbitrarily, however, and thus Alternatives 4 and 5 are not generally available to us. We should check the possibility, however, that the constraint need not be checked. Here, for example, it may simply be the case that customers always work with the same salesperson, but not that they are required by some policy to work with the same salesperson. The FD *Customer* → *Salesperson* may have just crept into the analysis because this is the way the business works, not because it is the way it has to work. If we cannot change the semantics, the winner is Alternative 1.

In coming to these conclusions, we must be careful—we have made several assumptions along the way. For example, we have assumed particular disk characteristics and particular file structures. It is best, of course, if we know what these characteristics and structures will be, but if not, we may need to explore several different options before making a final decision.

10.10   Chapter Summary

Topic Summary

- ORM hypergraphs represent MVDs and JDs as well as FDs. Developers need not specify these constraints separately (except for inextricably embedded JDs); they need only produce an application model that represents an application faithfully.

- A data value is redundant if it can be derived from other data values using the constraints that must hold. Potential redundancy tells us whether a relation in a valid interpretation of an underlying model-theoretic database view can have redundant data values. Redundant data values require extra storage space and extra processing time when there are database updates. Generally, we wish to remove the possibility of potential redundancy, but we may wish to retain it if a cost analysis convinces us that this would be more efficient for our application.

- Nulls can arise if we synthesize schemes whose relations may join with dangling tuples. We can use outer join to retain the dangling tuples, but we must then add nulls. Nulls may require additional storage, and they can cause difficulties for answering queries. Generally, we would like to avoid nulls, but sometimes it is more cost effective to retain them.

- Based on the property of lossless joins and the given constraints, we can synthesize a database scheme that preserves information and constraints from an ORM hypergraph. If the ORM hypergraph is canonical, our synthesis algorithms guarantee that the schemes produced have no potential redundancy (except when there are inextricably embedded JDs) and have no potential nulls. Holding to these properties, our synthesis algorithms also guarantee that the schemes are minimal, both in number and size in the sense that we cannot discard any scheme or part of any scheme, and we cannot combine schemes. We can always preserve constraints, and in the absence of scheme-spanning FDs we can guarantee global satisfaction of FDs by having to guarantee only that key constraints hold for each local scheme. We also generate inclusion dependencies, which along with key constraints capture a large share of the constraints required by most applications. In our design, we retain any other constraints we wish to enforce but realize that we must enforce them by providing code for them explicitly.

- The goal of the design process presented in this chapter and Chapter 9 is efficiency. The reduction transformations in Chapter 9 help us achieve efficiency by discarding or reducing schemes in the underlying model-theoretic database. The synthesis transformations in this chapter combine schemes losslessly and do not introduce redundancy and nulls. In the absence of other information, this increases efficiency by reducing both space and time.

We increase efficiency further by performing an application-dependent cost analysis. As a result of doing a cost analysis, we may be able to combine schemes further and reduce space and time requirements even further, or trade space for time or vice versa when this would suit our application better.

Question Summary

- What distinguishes redundant data values from values that are merely the same as other data values?

  If we can erase a data value and then from an FD, MVD, or JD and from other data values uniquely determine what the erased data value must be, the data value is redundant. Otherwise, the data value may, by chance, be the same as some other data value but not be redundant.

- Why do we want to remove potential redundancy?

  Except for some special cases, data redundancy increases both space and time. Redundant data requires more storage space because there is more of it. Redundant data requires more processing time to ensure consistency when we update redundant data values. When we update a redundant data value, for example, we must update all other copies of the data value.

- How can we guarantee that synthesized schemes preserve information and constraints?

  We must ensure that the synthesis transformation itself preserves information and constraints. If so, then since all our reduction transformations also preserve information and constraints, by transitivity our synthesized schemes preserve the information and constraints of our original application model. To ensure that the synthesis transformation itself preserves information, we must show that we can recover any valid interpretation for the input hypergraph for Algorithm 10.1. To ensure the synthesis transformation preserves constraints, we must show that the key constraints, the referential-integrity constraints, and the inclusion dependencies that we obtain, along with any general constraints we carry directly into our design, imply the constraints of the input hypergraph for Algorithm 10.1.

- What do the properties of synthesized schemes have to do with efficiency? How do the properties balance competing requirements?

  The properties include (1) no potential redundancy, (2) no potential nulls, and (3) minimality in both number and size (in the sense that no schemes can be combined, discarded, or reduced in arity). Having no redundancy generally reduces both time and space. Having no nulls eliminates query-processing ambiguities caused by uncertainties. Having nulls may require extra storage to hold the null values and may make query processing slower due to special processing for null values. Minimality reduces storage space by eliminating the need to store some values and reduces processing time for queries that might otherwise unnecessarily span two or more schemes. There is a balance among these properties because we can achieve greater minimality if we combine schemes. If we combine schemes, however, we introduce either potential redundancy or potential nulls.

- How does a cost analysis allow us to make exceptions to the general rules?

  Although observing redundancy, null, and minimality guidelines generally reduces space and time, there are no absolute guarantees. We should thus consider application characteristics and make exceptions where needed. Cost analysis consists of estimating time and space for combined schemes under expected application characteristics and choosing the design with the expected lowest cost. If estimates show that it would be cost effective to combine schemes, the schemes should be combined.

- To what extent can we automate data design? Can it be fully automatic?

  We can find all potential reduction transformations automatically, but we cannot determine semantic equivalence automatically. We can provide some help for resolving semantic-equivalence questions, however, by isolating relevant edge sets, stating the conditions that must hold for semantic equivalence in terms of the relevant edge sets, and providing possible counterexamples for consideration. Given a canonical ORM hypergraph, we can automatically synthesize schemes that have no potential redundancy, no potential nulls, and have good minimality properties, and we can automatically find keys and inclusion dependencies. We cannot decide automatically when it would be cost effective to combine schemes. We can, however, provide help for analyzing space and time costs. Given application characteristics such as the expected size of data elements, the expected size of relations, and

---

Checklist for Data Synthesis

☐ Obtain a canonical hypergraph.

   ☐ Use the checklist in Chapter 7 to perform reductions.

   ☐ Add explicit roles for any recursive relationship sets introduced in the transformations.

   ☐ Complete any unfinished work to make the application model congruent.

   ☐ Make the application model semantically head-consistent.

☐ Synthesize schemes (flat or nested).

☐ Extract key constraints and inter-scheme dependencies.

☐ Do application-dependent cost analysis.

   ☐ Apply "rule of thumb" guidelines as an aid to determining which scheme combinations to consider.

   ☐ Estimate space savings for combined schemes.

   ☐ Estimate time savings for combined schemes.

   ☐ Considering the options and trade-offs, combine schemes when appropriate.

   ☐ Scrutinize scheme-spanning FDs that come from embedded FD reductions and resolve trade-offs.

frequencies for query and update operations, we can provide time and space trade-offs between synthesized schemes versus various possible scheme combinations.

- In what sense can we view synthesizing schemes as patterns for design?

Our scheme-synthesis algorithms, as presented here, are design patterns. From a given hypergraph, our scheme-synthesis design patterns directly produce well-organized schemes for implementation.

10.11 Bibliographic Notes

Much has been written about how to design schemes for databases, especially relational databases. Relational database books, such as [Date95, Elmasri94, Hansen92, Helman94, Korth97, O'Neil94, Ullman82] provide a good introduction to database scheme design. In these books and elsewhere database scheme design is called *normalization* because scheme design is based on various normal forms—3NF [Codd72], LTKNF [Ling79], EKNF [Zaniolo82], BCNF [Codd74], 4NF [Fagin77], PJNF [Fagin79], and NNF [Mok96]. A simple guide to normalization is in [Kent83]. More theoretical treatments of normalization theory can be found in [Abiteboul95, Atzeni93, Maier83]. A good summary of relational database design theory appears in [Biskup95], which also provides an extensive bibliography not only of relational design theory but also of relational theory in general. Other aspects of relational theory that pertain to this chapter include multivalued dependencies [Fagin77], join dependencies [Aho79, Rissanen77], redundancy [Mok96, Vincent92], and inclusion dependencies [Casanova84].

The basic idea of synthesizing a relational database scheme as we do in this chapter originated with [Bernstein76]. The essence of the specific approach presented here was first explained in [Embley89b], but the full explanation for flat schemes is new in this text. For nested schemes, the algorithm for canonical hypergraphs with binary edges is from [Mok94] and a generalization to *n*-ary edges is in [Mok96b].

Techniques for performing cost analysis for database designs have been around for some time. [March83] presents a useful survey of this area.

10.12 Exercises

10.1 Show that the JD $\bowtie(AB, BC, AC)$ does not hold on the following relation:

A	B	C
1	1	2
1	2	1
2	1	1

10.2 Let R be a relation scheme and let $XY \subseteq R$. An MVD $X \twoheadrightarrow Y$ is *trivial* for R if $Y \subseteq X$ or $XY = R$. List all nontrivial MVDs that hold for the following relation:

A	B	C
1	1	1
1	1	2
2	1	1
2	1	3

10.3** Prove Theorem 10.1.

10.4** Prove Theorem 10.2.

10.5 Let $D = \{B \to C, C \twoheadrightarrow D\}$ be a set of FDs and MVDs. In the following relations, circle each data value that is redundant, as defined in Section 10.3, with respect to the FDs and MVDs in D.

A	B	C		C	D	E	F
1	1	1		1	1	1	1
2	1	1		1	2	1	1
3	2	2		1	1	1	2
4	4	4		1	2	1	2
5	4	4		2	2	2	2

10.6 Find the redundant data values in Fig. 10.10 not already given in the text. Use the definition of redundancy to explain why each is redundant.

10.7* Let $U = ABCDE$ and let $F = \{A \rightarrow BC, BD \rightarrow E, C \rightarrow D, E \rightarrow A\}$.

    a. List all candidate keys for ABC.

    b. List all candidate keys for $ABDE$.

    c. List all candidate keys for $ABCDE$.

10.8 Consider the ORM hypergraph in Fig. 10.30.

    a. Given the constraints in the application model in Fig. 10.30, explain why the scheme DJM has potential redundancy. Give an example to show that the scheme DJM can have redundancy.

    b. Given the constraints in the application model in Fig. 10.30, explain why the scheme DIJ has potential redundancy. Give an example to show that the scheme DIJ can have redundancy.

    c. Give the set of schemes produced by Algorithm 10.1. Also, add scheme names $R_1, R_2, ...$ for the schemes.

    d. Underline the candidate keys in the schemes.

    e. Give the referential integrity constraints as produced by Algorithm 10.2. Use $r_1, r_2, ...$ to designate the relations associated respectively with $R_1, R_2, ...$

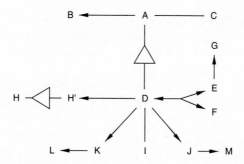

Figure 10.30 Application model.

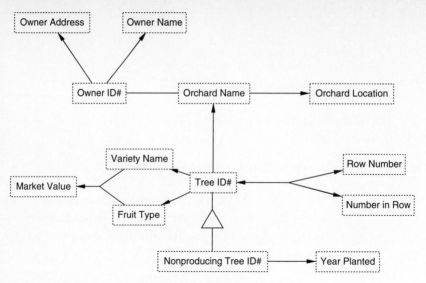

Figure 10.31 Orchard application model.

10.9   Consider the ORM hypergraph in Fig. 10.31.

   a. Give the set of schemes produced by Algorithm 10.1. Also, add reasonable scheme names. (Use initial uppercase letters for scheme names.)

   b. Underline the candidate keys in the schemes.

   c. Give the referential integrity constraints as produced by Algorithm 10.2. Use scheme names with initial lowercase letters to designate the relations associated with each scheme.

10.10** Prove Theorem 10.3.

10.11*   For each of the following relations, determine whether the relation can be used to show that $\bowtie(AB, AC)$ is an inextricably embedded JD. For those that cannot be used, explain why.

   a.

A	B	C	D
1	1	1	3
1	1	2	3
1	2	1	3
1	2	2	3
2	1	1	3

b.

A	B	C	D
1	1	1	1
1	1	2	2
1	2	1	3
1	2	2	4
2	1	1	5

c.

A	B	C	D
1	1	1	3
1	2	2	3

10.12** Prove Theorem 10.4.

10.13* Let U be a set of attributes and let F be a set of FDs over U. Let $R \subseteq U$. R is in *Boyce-Codd Normal Form* (*BCNF*) if for every non-trivial FD $X \rightarrow Y \in F^+$ such that $XY \subseteq R$, X is a superkey of R.

For each of the following schemes and sets of FDs, determine whether the scheme is in BCNF. If it is not in BCNF, produce the corresponding ORM hypergraph, then reduce the hypergraph so that it becomes canonical, and use Algorithm 10.1 to produce schemes. (Observe that the schemes produced are in BCNF.)

a. $ABCD \{AB \rightarrow D, A \rightarrow C, C \rightarrow D\}$.

b. $ABCDE \{AB \rightarrow CD, C \rightarrow AB, C \rightarrow E\}$.

c. $ABCDE \{ABC \rightarrow D, D \rightarrow E, E \rightarrow BC\}$.

d. $ABCDE \{A \rightarrow BC, BD \rightarrow E, C \rightarrow D, E \rightarrow A\}$.

10.14** Let H be a canonical hypergraph and let F be the set of FDs generated from H. Prove that if we apply Algorithm 10.1 to H, then each scheme in the result is in BCNF with respect to F.

10.15** Let H be a canonical hypergraph, and let U be the object-set names of H. Let M be the set of MVDs generated from H, as follows. If X is any subset of U, then $X \twoheadrightarrow Y$ is an MVD over U if Y is a maximal connected component of H when we remove X from H. A connected component Y is maximal if there does not exist a subset Z of U such that $Z \not\subseteq Y$ and YZ is a connected component. Prove that MVDs generated in this way are indeed MVDs over U.

10.16** Let R be a relation scheme and let D be a set of MVDs and FDs over R. R is in *Fourth Normal Form (4NF)* with respect to D if for every nontrivial MVD $X \twoheadrightarrow Y \in D^+$, X is a superkey of R.

Let H be a canonical hypergraph, and let D be the set of FDs and MVDs generated from H. Prove that if we apply Algorithm 10.1 to H, then each scheme in the result is in 4NF with respect to D.

10.17** Let H be a canonical hypergraph, and let U be the object-set names of H. Let J be the set of JDs generated from H as follows. If $R = \{R_1, ..., R_n\}$ is the set of sets of object-set names of the relationship sets of H, then each connected element $\{R_{k_1}, ..., R_{k_m}\}$ of the power set of R (excluding the empty set) is a JD $\bowtie(R_{k_1}, ..., R_{k_m})$ over $R_{k_1} R_{k_2} ... R_{k_m}$, the set of object-set names in that element. Prove that each JD $\bowtie(R_{k_1}, ..., R_{k_m})$ generated in this way is indeed a JD over $R_{k_1} ... R_{k_m}$.

10.18** Let R be a relation scheme and let D be a set of JDs (including MVDs) and FDs over R. R is in *Project-Join Normal Form (PJNF)* with respect to D if for every nontrivial JD $\bowtie(R_1, R_2, ..., R_n)$ such that $R = R_1 R_2 ... R_n$, every R_i is a superkey of R.

Let H be a canonical hypergraph, and let D be the set of FDs, MVDs, and JDs generated from H. Prove that if we apply Algorithm 10.1 to H, then each scheme in the result is in PJNF with respect to D.

10.19* Show that 4NF implies BCNF.

10.20* Show that PJNF implies 4NF.

10.21** Prove Theorem 10.5.

10.22** Prove Theorem 10.6.

10.23** Prove Theorem 10.7.

10.24** Prove Theorem 10.8.

10.25** Prove Theorem 10.9.

10.26* Let U be a set of attributes and let $R \subseteq U$. An FD $X \to Y$ *applies* to R if $XY \subseteq R$. A *decomposition* of R is a set of schemes $\{R_1, ..., R_n\}$ such that $R_i \subseteq R$ for $1 \le i \le n$ and $R_1 \cup ... \cup R_n = R$. Let F be a set of FDs over U. The *restriction* of F to R is the set of FDs $X \to Y$ in F^+ such that $X \to Y$ applies to R. Let F' be equivalent to the restriction of F to R. Let $D = \{R_1, ..., R_n\}$ be a decomposition of R, and let G be a set of FDs that is equivalent to the union of the restrictions of F to R_i for $1 \le i \le n$. D *preserves* F' on R (D is *dependency preserving* for R with respect to F') if G implies F'. (Since F' implies G, we could say "if $G \equiv F'$" instead of "G implies F'.")

Let scheme $R = ABCD$ be given along with the set of FDs $F = \{A \to BC, BC \to D, D \to B\}$. For each of the following, state whether the decomposition is dependency preserving. For dependency-preserving decompositions, give a set of FDs equivalent to F such that each FD in the set applies to a scheme in the decomposition, and for decompositions that do not preserve dependencies, list the FDs of F that are not preserved.

a. $\{ABC, BCD\}$.

b. $\{ABC, CD, DB\}$.

c. $\{AB, AC, BCD\}$.

10.27* Let U be a set of attributes and let F be a set of FDs over U. Let $R \subseteq U$. R is in *Third Normal Form* (3NF) if for every nontrivial FD $X \to Y \in F^+$ such that $XY \subseteq R$, X is a superkey of R or each attribute in $Y - X$ appears in some candidate key of R.

For each of the following schemes and sets of FDs, determine whether the scheme is in 3NF. If the scheme is not in 3NF, use the techniques in the text to decompose the scheme so that it will be in 3NF and still preserve dependencies. Say whether the resulting schemes are in BCNF. If the scheme is in 3NF, determine whether it is possible to decompose it into BCNF and still preserve dependencies. If so, do it; if not, give at least one dependency that will not be preserved by the transformation.

a. $ABCD \{AB \to D, A \to C, C \to D\}$.

b. $ABCDE \{AB \to CD, C \to AB, C \to E\}$.

c. $ABCDE \{ABC \to D, D \to E, E \to BC\}$.

d. $ABCDE \{A \to BC, BD \to E, C \to D, E \to A\}$.

10.28** Let H be a hypergraph that is canonical except that it is not necessarily embedded-FD reduced. (When we say that we apply Algorithm 10.1 to H in (a) and (b) in this exercise, we mean that we ignore the precondition on H being canonical and otherwise apply Algorithm 10.1 as given.)

a. Prove that if we apply Algorithm 10.1 to H, then each scheme in the result is in 3NF with respect to the FDs generated from H.

b. Let F be the set of FDs generated for the FD edges of H. Let $\{R_1, ..., R_n\}$ be the schemes generated from H by Algorithm 10.1 and let $K_{i1}, ..., K_{in_i}$ be the set of candidate keys for R_i as generated by Algorithm 10.1 (augmented with Step 5 for keys). Let F' be the set of FDs $\bigcup_{i=1}^{n}\{K_{11} \rightarrow R_1, ..., K_{1n_i} \rightarrow R_1\}$. Prove: $F' \equiv F$.

10.29** Show that BCNF implies 3NF.

10.30 Suppose *PersonID* $\rightarrow$ *Name BirthDate BirthPlace BirthHospital* and *BirthHospital* $\rightarrow$ *BirthPlace*. Then we can do a head reduction to remove *BirthPlace* from the 5-ary edge and produce the schemes

PersonID Name BirthDate BirthHospital

BirthHospital BirthPlace

Alternatively, we can join the schemes, but then we will have redundancy because everyone born in the same hospital will have the same birthplace.

a. Give the characteristics of an application for which the two schemes would take less space.

b. Give the characteristics of an application for which the one scheme would take less space.

c. Give the characteristics of an application for which the two schemes would take less processing time.

d. Give the characteristics of an application for which the two schemes would take more processing time.

e. Suppose that our application is a health tracking system for young children ages 0–5 years old for a large city. An occasional ad hoc query asks for the birth city for a child. Which schemes should be chosen? Why?

f. Suppose that our application is an information system for military personnel stationed at some location. Here again, an occasional ad hoc query asks for the birth city for a soldier. Which schemes should be chosen? Why?

10.31 Suppose that we have a many-many relationship set between A and B and also a many-many relationship set between A and C. Suppose further that A's each require 30 bytes of storage, B's require 10 bytes, and C's require 50 bytes; that 10,000 A's are expected; and that on the average there are twice as many C's for each A as B's for each A. As a function of the average number of B's, compute the crossover point for determining whether to store two tables AB and AC or to store one table ABC.

10.32 Suppose that we have a many-many relationship set between A and B and also a many-many relationship set between A and C. Suppose further that we have the following:

- The expected number of A's is 10,000.

- The expected number of AB relationships is 100,000, with each A value participating about an equal number of times.

- We can store 50 AB relationships per block.

- The expected number of AC relationships is 210,000, with each C value participating about an equal number of times.

- We can store 70 AB relationships per block.

- On the average, each AB tuple is expected to join with 2 AC tuples.

- We can store 30 ABC relationships per block.

- Buffer space in main memory allows for 20 blocks.

Assume that our data structures and algorithms are as in Section 10.7.2.

a. Based on the read frequency, f_{read}, plot the graphs for the separate case (AB and AC) and for the combined case (ABC).

b. Calculate the crossover point.

c. Summarize by stating when the combined case would be better and when the separate case would be better.

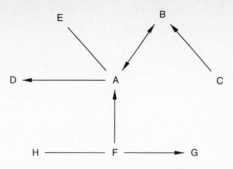

Figure 10.32 Application model for exercises on nested relations.

10.33* Consider the canonical ORM hypergraph in Fig. 10.32.

    a. Explain why the nested scheme $H(FG)^*$ has potential redundancy. As part of the explanation, give a nested relation with redundancy. Also, explain why Algorithm 10.3 does not produce this nested scheme.

    b. Explain why the nested scheme $FA(E)^*$ has potential redundancy. As part of the explanation, give a nested relation with redundancy. Also, explain why Algorithm 10.3 does not produce this nested scheme.

    c. Explain why the (nested) scheme FAD has potential redundancy. As part of the explanation, give a (nested) relation with redundancy. Also, explain why Algorithm 10.3 does not produce this (nested) scheme. What does this example indicate about redundancy in any nonnested schemes produced by Algorithm 10.3?

    d. Beginning with A, apply Algorithm 10.3 to the ORM diagram in Fig. 10.32. For any succeeding tree, select the root to be the alphabetically first name not already in some tree.

    e. Beginning with D, apply Algorithm 10.3 to the ORM diagram in Fig. 10.32. For any succeeding tree, select the root to be the alphabetically first name not already in some tree.

    f. Beginning with H, apply Algorithm 10.3 to the ORM diagram in Fig. 10.32. For any succeeding tree, select the root to be the alphabetically last name not already in some tree.

10.34** Prove Theorem 10.10.

10.35** A *scheme tree* T corresponding to a nested relation scheme R is defined recursively as follows:[†]

1. If R has the form X, then T is a single-node scheme tree whose root node is the set of attributes X.

2. If R has the form $X\ (R_1)^*\ ...\ (R_n)^*$, then the root node of T is the set of attributes X, and a child of the root of T is the root of the scheme tree T_i, where T_i is the corresponding scheme tree for the nested relation scheme R_i, $1 \le i \le n$.

Notationally, we let $Aset(T)$ denote the set of attributes in a scheme tree T. If N is a node in T, $Ancestor(N)$ denotes the union of attributes in all ancestors of N, including N. Similarly, *Descendent*(N) denotes the union of attributes in all descendants of N, including N. In a scheme tree T each edge (V, W), where V is the parent of W, denotes an MVD $Ancestor(V) \twoheadrightarrow Descendent(W)$. Notationly, we use $MVD(T)$ to denote the union of all the MVDs represented by the edges in T. By construction, each MVD in $MVD(T)$ is satisfied in the total unnesting of any nested relation for T. Since FDs are also of interest, we let $FD(T)$ denote any set of FDs equivalent to all FDs $X \to Y$ implied by a given set of FDs and MVDs over a set of attributes U such that $Aset(T) \subseteq U$ and $XY \subseteq Aset(T)$.

Let U be a set of attributes. Let M be a set of MVDs over U and F be a set of FDs over U. Let T be a scheme tree such that $Aset(T) \subseteq U$. An MVD $X \twoheadrightarrow Y$ *holds* for T with respect to M and F if $X \subseteq Aset(T)$ and there exists a set of attributes $Z \subseteq U$ such that $Y = Z \cap Aset(T)$ and $M \cup F$ implies $X \twoheadrightarrow Z$ on U. An FD $X \to Y$ *holds* for T with respect to M and F if $XY \subseteq Aset(T)$ and $M \cup F$ implies $X \to Y$ on U.

Let U be a set of attributes. Let M be a set of MVDs over U and F be a set of FDs over U. Let T be a scheme tree such that $Aset(T) \subseteq U$. T is in *Nested Normal Form* (NNF) with respect to $M \cup F$ if the following conditions are satisfied:

1. If D is the set of MVDs and FDs that hold for T with respect to $M \cup F$, then D is equivalent to $MVD(T) \cup FD(T)$ on $Aset(T)$.

2. For each nontrivial FD $X \to A$ that holds for T with respect to $M \cup F$, $X \to Ancestor(N_A)$ also holds with respect to $M \cup F$, where N_A is the node in T that contains A.

[†] Used with permission of Naveen Prakash.

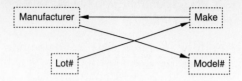

Figure 10.33 Manufacturing application model.

Let H be a canonical hypergraph, and let D be the set of FDs and MVDs generated from H. Prove that if we apply Algorithm 10.1 to H, then each scheme in the result is in NNF with respect to D.

10.36** Show that NNF implies 4NF.

10.37 Consider the ORM hypergraph in Fig. 10.33. Assume that a *Manufacturer* produces a few different *Makes*, but only one *Make* for any particular *Lot#*. *Makes* are unique for *Manufacturers*. A *Lot#* for a particular *Manufacturer* determines both the *Make* and the *Model#*, and several different *Lot#*s can have the same *Make* and *Model#*. Observe that the FD *Make → Manufacturer* is an embedded FD. Order the following implementation alternatives from best to worst. Base the order on expected usage and on a rough cost analysis, and explain what assumptions are being made. Be sure to consider how the constraints will be enforced.

a. One flat scheme: *Manufacturer Lot# Make Model#*.

b. Two flat schemes: *Make Manufacturer* and *Lot# Make Model#*.

c. One nested scheme: *Manufacturer (Make (Model# (Lot#)*)*)**.

d. Change the semantics by discarding *Make → Manufacturer* and use one flat scheme: *Manufacturer Lot# Make Model#*.

e. Change the semantics by discarding *Make → Manufacturer* and use one nested scheme: *Manufacturer (Make (Model# (Lot#)*)*)**.

Chapter 11

Object-Module Design

In this chapter, we examine the behavioral aspects of design and discuss how to group behavior and data together into object-oriented computational units. Our general objective for design is to organize the system so that it has good space and time properties, as well as other less tangible but nonetheless important properties such as understandability, extensibility, and reusability. We achieve these objectives by making our design object oriented in the classical sense. That is, we group object behavior together with object description into a unit we call an object module.

Object modules help achieve understandability, extensibility, and reusability because they constitute a conceptual building block for a system. If properly constructed, object modules have a simple interface that can be documented and protected. The documentation describes how to use the object module as a building block for a larger system. The protection ensures that the integrity of the building block will not be violated, also allowing for and encouraging an efficient underlying implementation.

In Section 11.1, we define an object module and explain how it relates to the concepts of class, type, variable, and value. We also explain the notion of encapsulation, which allows us to define a simple interface and at the same time provides for a layer of protection and an efficient underlying implementation. In Sections 11.2–11.7, we show how to transform OSM specifications into object modules. The transformations for grouping data largely have been discussed in Chapters 9 and 10; here we concentrate on adding behavior and adding other kinds of data information such as types. Section 11.8 demonstrates how the design concepts presented here and in Chapters 9 and 10 apply to our on-line shopping example.

The following topics in this chapter are particularly important:

- Object modules.
- Encapsulation and object integrity.
- Inheritance, overriding, overloading, late binding, polymorphism.
- Methods as computed relationship sets and as state-net services.

- Uniform and nonuniform service availability.

- OSM data structures.

- The view update problem.

The following questions should also be kept in mind:

- What are the similarities and differences between object modules and ADTs?

- What are the similarities and differences among classes, types, variables, and values?

- What are the similarities and differences between types in programming languages and generalization/specialization?

- How can we transform state nets into ADTs?

- What are various ways to manage the concurrency found in state nets?

- What are some reasons for limiting visibility and providing views?

- How does inheritance simplify the specification of efficient specializations?

- In what sense are the transformations in this chapter patterns for design?

11.1   Object Modules

An *object module* is a named pair $N = (D, B)$, where N is the name of the object module, D is a data description, and B is a behavior description. A *data description* D (1) defines a set of possible elements for D by giving potential lexical and nonlexical values that can be acquired by the elements of D, (2) designates a subset of the elements of D as the *current extent* or simply the *extent*, and (3) gives a set of constraints applicable to D. A *behavior description* B describes the active or passive behavior of an element of D, including (1) the events or conditions to which the behavior responds, (2) the circumstances under which it responds to these events or conditions, and (3) the responses to these events or conditions. The responses of an object module N to external events and conditions are called the *services* of

N. We usually name services by the external events or conditions that invoke them. If all the services are always available, N has *uniform service availability*; otherwise, N has *nonuniform service availability*. An object module generalizes the notion of an ADT as described in Chapter 2 by explicitly allowing constraints over the data, by explicitly recognizing an extent, and by allowing nonuniform service availability. An ADT is an object module in which D is simply a set of values and B is a set of uniformly available services, called operations.

One example of an object module is simply an OSM object set S. If S is nonlexical and has no generalization, its set of possible elements is the conceptually infinite set of object identifiers, its extent is the current set of object identifiers in the object set, and its constraints are all the ORM constraints applicable to S. Further, the state net of S, whether it is the default state net or a given state net, describes the active or passive behavior of an element in S, including the events or conditions to which an element of S responds, when an element responds to these events or conditions, and its response. The services of S are the responses to the external interactions or external conditions applicable to S, which we refer to by naming the trigger (e.g., @ request order, balance < 0).

Another example of an object module is the built-in *Integer* object set. Its possible elements and potential values and its logical extent are all the same, consisting of all possible integers in an implementation. Its state net provides for a passive response to operator invocations such as +, *, and /.

Besides being an object set, the data description of an object module can be built from an ORM application model, usually part of the application's ORM. A typical configuration is a high-level, nonlexical object set that includes several interrelated lexical object sets. In this configuration, an element consists of an object identifier for the high-level object set connected through relationship sets to values in the lexical object sets. The constraints are the constraints of the components of the high-level object set. The high-level object set may or may not have a given state net, and the included lexical object sets all have the default state net.

When we restrict this last idea to a configuration in which the interrelated lexical object sets each supply a value for an element of the high-level object set, we have a typical record configuration. If we then lexicalize and have only default state nets, we have a record-based scheme, typical of schemes for a relational database. Thus, for example,

Employee(*Emp#*, *Name*, *Address*)
key: *Emp#*

can constitute an object module whose values are employee tuples and whose behavior responds to **add**, **remove**, and query services.

11.1.1 Classes, Types, Variables, and Values

Classes, types, variables, and values can all be thought of as special types of object modules. Although not generally discussed in this way, the definitions we give here are consistent with definitions typically given for these concepts. (See the bibliographic notes in Section 11.10.)

We define a *class* as an object module with some restrictions. The exact nature of the restrictions varies considerably, depending on whether we are discussing database systems, programming languages, or conceptual modeling. One typical set of restrictions disallows active behavior and provides for only one- and two-way interactions with uniform service availability. Another typical set of restrictions is similar but also disallows an extent. Another set of "restrictions" is the complete absence of restrictions, making a class the same as an object module. Because of the wide variation in definition, we will not use the term *class* in this discussion, although it appears prominently in later chapters when we discuss specific systems. In that context, the meaning of *class* will be the meaning it has with respect to the system under discussion.

We also define a *type* as an object module that has some restrictions. Unlike classes, however, typically types have only one set of restrictions. A *type* is a named pair (D, B), where the data description D defines a set of potential values for its elements along with a (sometimes empty) set of constraints applicable to D, and where the behavior description B consists of only one- and two-way interactions with uniform service availability. In this context, the services are usually called *operations*.

It is interesting to consider a variable as an object module with constraints. A variable is a named container for a value. Likewise, an OSM object set is a container for a set of values and may be restricted to hold only one value. Further, we can assign a value to a variable, and we can ask a variable to yield its value. Likewise, the default operations for an object set allow us to remove and add values and thus to assign values to an object set, as well as to query an object set for its values. With these similarities in mind, we can define a *variable* to be an object module, and thus a named pair (D, B), restricted so that the extent for D is a single value and B consists of the default operations query, **add**, and **remove** (and assignment as a combination of **add** and **remove**). Usually, we declare a variable V to be *of some type T*, which means that the values assigned to V must come from the potential values of T and that the operations applied to V must come from the operations of T. We can give a variable a type by making an object module representing a variable a specialization of an object module representing a type.

We can also define values as object modules that have even more restrictions than variables. A *value* is an object module, and thus a named pair (D, B), restricted so that B allows only the default query operation (and thus can be read but not written), and D is a single value.

11.1.2 Encapsulation

Encapsulation, which provides a protective layer for an object module, serves several purposes:

1. Object integrity, which prevents outside objects from modifying objects inside the object module in unintended ways,

2. Interface specification, which lets the encapsulated object control which services are available and when they are available, and

3. Implementation independence, which separates an abstract external specification from its internal implementation and thus also allows the internal implementation to change without affecting the external specification.

Sometimes the implementation languages we use support encapsulation in the sense that the language makes it easy to achieve these purposes, and sometimes the implementation languages we use do not support encapsulation. Whether our implementation language does or does not support encapsulation, we should still observe these purposes, because this is what makes an object module understandable and reusable. We next discuss these purposes of encapsulation, explaining what should be done to achieve them.

Object Integrity

The most basic concept of encapsulation is that objects are protected from unwanted external influences. Object integrity embodies two concepts. First, object identity is immutable; second, objects are in control of their own behavior.

An object's identity is immutable if the identity is specific and does not change over the lifetime of the object. Both nonlexical and lexical objects have this property naturally. The danger arises when we lexicalize, allowing a lexical object to represent a nonlexical object. In and of itself, this is not a problem and it may even be beneficial, as explained in Chapters 9 and 10. However, if we allow inappropriate operations such as replacing one employee's *Emp#* by another employee's *Emp#*, we will destroy object identity. When we lexicalize, we must be careful to allow only appropriate operations.

An object is in control of its own behavior if the only way an object's behavioral configuration can change is by the object's acting according to its behavior specification. This means that no outside entity (object or system) can change the internal behavioral configuration of an object. In OSM, for example, this means that no outside entity can modify directly the status of the threads in another object—for example, by placing the object in some state arbitrarily. Objects may interact, in which case they can influence one another indirectly, but in all cases objects respond to external events according to the laws defined by their state nets.

Interface Specification

Interface specification is another way to ensure object integrity. An interface specification states what is allowed and only what is allowed. If other objects interact with an encapsulated object only through its interface, there will be no unwanted external influences.

An interface specification states either implicitly or explicitly which services may be invoked. Sometimes it also specifies when or under what conditions these services may be invoked. Unfortunately, many languages do not support interface specification, and some that do make it inconvenient to specify some services that should be available.

When there is no language support for an interface specification, we must use extra discipline to ensure that object integrity is not violated. For example, we can make comments in our design (and code) about what services should be available and then design our object modules so that we use only these services. This is easy in theory but difficult in practice because often we can see an easy way to do something by violating encapsulation. We often succumb to the temptation, especially when under a deadline.

Although being disciplined is sometimes difficult, it is even more difficult when the language supports encapsulation but makes it inconvenient to specify some services that should be available. This is especially true for object-oriented database systems where we wish to provide for ad hoc queries and for queries in general. Often language encapsulations hide the attributes and relationships of a complex object, making the attributes unavailable for queries. Exposing the attributes, on the other hand, usually opens up the possibility of violating object integrity. When the attributes are hidden, program "work arounds" are difficult to provide and are even more difficult to provide properly. Until we learn how to balance the opposing trade-offs, we are likely to have to resolve these issues through discipline and reasonable "work arounds."

Implementation Independence

One way to work around problems imposed on us by languages is to use the principle of implementation independence. Implementation independence separates specification from implementation and allows for alternative implementations that should be faithful to the specification. An example of implementation independence is found in relational database systems, where, as discussed in Chapter 2, the concept of data independence provides for the conceptual and physical models of a database to be separated.

Properly used, the principle of implementation independence lets us view and use the services of an object module in one way, while implementing the services in another way. For example, we may specify and think of a relationship set as a relation, but instead of implementing it as a set of tuples, we might be able to compute some of the column values from other column values and thus not have to store these values in the relation. In this case, to be faithful to the specification, we would also need to implement the inverses of these computations so that we maintain the full functionality of the relationship-set specification.

Another use for the principle of implementation independence is overriding and late binding for polymorphic variations of an object. In a generalization/specialization hierarchy, an operation may apply to objects in a generalization and in several specializations. Sometimes we may be able to reimplement the operation more efficiently for the specializations. For example, suppose we have an area computation and an *isa* hierarchy of polygons, rectangles, squares, and triangles. We should implement this area operation differently for each shape. Implementation independence lets us carry out the implementation any way we wish, but we should be faithful to the semantics of the operation. When we replace the implementation of a generalization operation with a different implementation, we *override* the original implementation. Then when the system executes, it

---

Abuses of Inheritance

Unfortunately, it is easy to abuse the principle of implementation independence by creating polymorphic variations that are not faithful to their specification. For example, it is easy in many object-oriented languages to inherit from an object set that has operations similar to what is wanted and then override some of the operations and change their meaning. Abusing implementation independence in this way may be the biggest deterrent to creating understandable and reusable object modules. The problem here is somewhat similar to the GOTO problem in structured programming—we can create a mess without much rational meaning. Unless we discipline ourselves to use implementation independence only to implement specifications faithfully, the object modules we create probably will behave in unexpected ways, making them hard to understand and reuse.

---

waits until run time to choose which implementation to use based on which type of object it has. This is *late binding*. The principle that lets us override an implementation and use late binding to select the most efficient implementation for an operation is called *polymorphism*.

11.2   Computations and Methods

Computations arise naturally in both OBM and ORM specifications. Computations in OBM state nets translate directly into code, but ORM computations usually require some thought and work. We therefore discuss here the design of ORM computations.

Figure 11.1 shows an ORM diagram with a potential computation. Based on an employee's hire date, we can calculate the employee's longevity. Because we can compute the longevity, we have several options:

1. Even though longevity is computable, we can choose nevertheless to implement the *Hire Date yields Longevity* relationship set as a relation in the usual way.

2. We can utilize our principle of implementation independence and implement all required default operations for the *Hire Date yields Longevity* relationship set without storing a relation.

3. We can convert the computation into an interaction.

Inheritance and Reuse

One of the advantages of object-oriented systems is that they allow us to reuse an implementation by the principle of inheritance. When we truly have a specialization, as in OSM, we can always reuse an inherited implementation, and there is never any functional need to override it except to improve efficiency. When there is no need or no way to make the operation more efficient in a specialization, we can simply reuse the implementation and gain the reuse advantage so often advertised by object-oriented systems.

If an object module has an operation similar to what we need for another object module, but there is no generalization/specialization relationship between the two object modules, we can still reuse the implementation. We should not, however, reuse the implementation by inheritance. Instead, we should make a copy of the implementation and then alter its meaning as needed to implement the similar operation. This copy and modify approach to reuse has a cost because it takes space to store the code and time to copy and modify the code. It is this cost that usually tempts us to inherit instead. In the long run, however, it may well be worth the cost because keeping inheritance hierarchies intact enhances understandability and thus maintainability and long-term reuse.

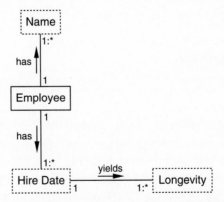

Figure 11.1   An ORM diagram with a potential computation.

4. We can drop the relationship set from the ORM diagram and have the state nets or ad hoc queries compute the longevity from the hire date when it is needed.

Which option is best depends on the application. We discuss the implications and trade-offs for this example as a typical instance of the general case.

Table Implementation

In a table implementation, we store the relationship set directly as a relation or part of a relation, which we call a table in this context. The advantage of a table implementation is that it is fully faithful to the ORM specification. For example, we can ask for the employees in a certain longevity range without having to convert our query to a query about hire dates—as we would have to do for Option 4—or to convert our query to work with interactions—as we would have to do for Option 3—or to cause some extra internal computations—as we would have to do for Option 2. The disadvantage is that we must store the information even though it can be computed, and we must update it over time (i.e., to keep the longevity table consistent, we would have to change a longevity value in the table for an employee each year on the hire date).

For this example a table implementation may not be best, but for a different example, it may be a good choice indeed. Consider an application in which we need the values for the area of various irregularly shaped polygons. If we need these values often and if we alter the polygons rarely, it may be better to use the extra space and store the area of each polygon, rather than compute the area each time it is needed.

Virtual Implementation

Like a table implementation, a virtual implementation is fully faithful to the ORM specification. It does not have the space disadvantage of a table, however, since no table is stored. On the other hand, to make the implementation faithful, we must provide several operations, including operations to simulate adding data to and removing data from both the object set and the relationship set, and operations to simulate querying the data in its various combinations. For our longevity example, we must be able to process queries such as "find all employees who have been employed over 25 years" or "find all employees who have been employed longer than their managers." Both of these queries require inverse operations that take a longevity L and find hire dates and then employees whose computed longevity exceeds L. If these inverse operations are costly to execute and must be executed often, the speed disadvantage may weigh considerably in our decision.

Providing the operations for a virtual implementation also takes programmer time. The patterns for these virtual implementations, however, tend to have a number of similarities. The **add** and **remove** are easy because we do not actually store computed objects and relationships. The inverse operations for finding an object or set of objects given a computed object either have direct implementations, which could make them all different and thus more costly to implement, or they can be computed by scanning all the objects, doing the forward computations, and keeping track of the objects that satisfy the conditions of interest. To find all employees who have been employed more than 25 years, for example, we can compute the longevity of each employee and keep those employees whose longevity is greater than 25 years.

When we choose a virtual implementation, we should be aware that it can affect our choice of schemes. If we apply the scheme-generation algorithm of Chapter 10 to the ORM in Fig. 11.1, for example, we would generate two schemes:

$$Employee, Name, HireDate$$
$$HireDate, Longevity.$$

Indeed, combining these schemes would yield redundancy whenever two or more employees have the same hire date. In a virtual implementation, however, when the objects in an object set are all computed, we do not store them. Thus, for computed objects, we have none of the space or time disadvantages of redundant data. No space is wasted because a virtual implementation takes no space for storing any of the data values. There are also no update anomalies to expend extra computation time. We should therefore combine the schemes.

Interaction Implementation

In an interaction implementation, we implement only some proper subset of the operations that would be available in a faithful table or virtual implementation. A possible disadvantage is that we no longer have the same semantics. This may not matter, however, because the application may need only the subset we provide. In our longevity example, we may need to find only the longevity given a hire date, and we may never need to find hire dates given a longevity value. If so, we can replace the relationship set *Hire Date yields Longevity* and the object set *Longevity* by an interaction that requests the longevity given a hire date.

This choice is quite common and leads to a standard object module in which we package operations, which are often called *methods* in this context, together with data. Figure 11.2 shows the ORM application model in Fig. 11.1 written as an object module. The object module in Fig. 11.2 allows all the default interactions for the *Employee has Name* and *Employee has Hire Date* relationship sets and the *Employee*, *Name*, and *Hire Date* object sets, but it allows only the interaction *get longevity* for computing a longevity value. Observe that all the other interactions implied by the ORM diagram in Fig. 11.1, such as **add** and **remove** longevity values, and all the query expressions, such as *Employee(x). Longevity* and *Employee. Longevity*(25), are not available.

Often method placement is straightforward, as in this example, but this is not always the case. In general, when all the input arguments for a method reside in one scheme, we place the method with the scheme. For the *yields* relationship set in Fig. 11.1, implemented as the method *get longevity* in Fig. 11.2, the input argument is taken from the *Hire Date* object set. According to our discussion in Chapter 10, the flat scheme we would generate for the ORM in Fig. 11.1 when we disregard the *Longevity* object set would be

Employee, Name, Hire Date

Since the input argument for the *get longevity* method is in this scheme, we would group this method with this scheme, as in Fig. 11.2.

> **object module** *Employee* **includes**
>
> > *Employee* [1] *has Name* [1: *];
> > *Employee* [1] *has Hire Date* [1: *];
> >
> > @ *get longevity* (*hireDate*) $\rightarrow$ (*longevity*);
> **end;**

Figure 11.2 An object module in which a method replaces a relationship set.

Once we have grouped a method with a scheme that contains all the method's input arguments, we can consider the method's output arguments also to be part of the scheme. Thus in our example, we would now also consider *Longevity* to be part of the scheme. If we had another method with *Longevity* as an input argument—for example, a method that computes bonuses based on longevity—then we would also group this method with the scheme.

When all the input arguments are not from a single scheme or when there are no input arguments, we have two alternatives: (1) Place the method with a scheme with which it best fits intuitively. (2) Create a new scheme for the method. The disadvantage of the first alternative is that the placement decision is arbitrary, and there may not be an "intuitive" best fit. The second placement alternative proliferates schemes but has the advantage of keeping method placement clean.

No Implementation

By not implementing an operation arising from an ORM, we shift the burden of computation to the code that needs the result—that is, to an ad hoc query or some action in a state net. For our example, the code for the ad hoc query or action would have to extract the hire date and then compute the longevity. This is not usually a good idea if the computation arises often in the application, for then we would have to specify the code for the same computation in several different places. Factoring out the code and putting it in only one place is the same as choosing one of the other alternatives. Of course, if we learn that the information we are discarding is never used in our application or that it is used only in occasional ad hoc queries, this alternative may be attractive.

11.3 Generalization/Specialization Patterns

Generalization/specialization patterns lead to several different kinds of design organizations. We have already seen how we can add roles to make ORM diagrams congruent, how we can derive inclusion dependencies from specified generalization/specializations, and how we can sometimes eliminate union generalizations covered by their specializations. Here, we further study generalization/specialization patterns and consider how they lead to enumeration types and generated value-set types.

11.3.1 Enumeration Types

Consider the ORM diagram in Fig. 11.3a, in which we have products, each one of which has one of three prespecified quality designators, *"A"*, *"AA"*, or *"AAA"*. Since the *isa* constraint in the generalization/specialization in Fig. 11.3a guarantees that these are the only possibilities for *Quality Designators*, we can rewrite our specification as

$$\textit{Quality Designator}: \{"A", "AA", "AAA"\}$$

using an enumeration (see Fig. 11.3b).

In general, an *enumeration* is a set of values for which each value of the set is given explicitly. When we specify an enumeration for an object set, as we have done here for *Quality Designator*, we turn the *isa* hierarchy upside down and let the object set be a specialization of the enumeration. This transformation turns the values for the objects in the object set into elements of the enumeration. For *Quality Designator*, this is exactly what we want since any designation must be *"A"* or *"AA"* or *"AAA"*.

A subtle shift of focus makes this enumeration transformation advantageous. Instead of viewing the generalization (*Quality Designator* in this example) as a string that is restricted to the values of its specialization, we view it directly as being one of the values in the enumeration ({*"A"*, *"AA"*, *"AAA"*} in this example). Since we still also have all the default operations,

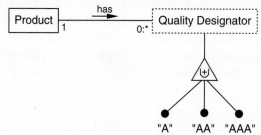

(a) An ORM diagram with a potential enumeration.

(b) An ORM diagram with an enumeration.

Figure 11.3 Transformation of a partitioned specialization of objects into an enumeration.

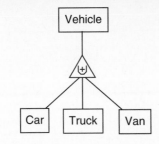

(a) Partitioned category specialization.

(b) Partitioned category specialization transformed to an enumeration.

Fig. 11.4 Transformation of a partitioned category specialization into an enumeration.

we have a set of values and a set of operations for *Quality Designator*. Hence we have a type, namely, an enumeration type. It should be clear that whenever we have an object set whose objects are *all* specified as specializations, we can turn this pattern into an enumeration type.

Enumeration types are also useful for nonlexical specializations. We can transform a nonlexical, partitioned, category specialization into an enumeration type, as in Fig. 11.4. In Fig. 11.4a we see that a vehicle must be a car, truck, or van. The transformation in Fig. 11.4b shows that we introduce a value for each category and associate each vehicle with one of these category values.

When the *isa* constraint is not a partition, we can still transform a nonlexical, category specialization into an enumeration type, except that we must relax the participation constraint. Figure 11.5 provides an example. Since there is no constraint for the generalization/specialization in Fig. 11.5a, a person may participate in zero or more of the categories as in Fig. 11.5b. That is, a person may or may not be a doctor, patient, or professor, or may be any two, or may be all three. In general, a partition constraint yields 1 as a participation constraint (as in Fig. 11.4), a mutual-exclusion constraint yields 0:1, a union constraint yields 1:*, and no constraint yields 0:* (as in Fig. 11.5).

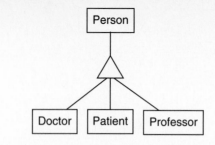

(a) Unconstrained category specialization.

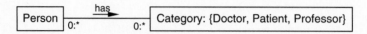

(b) Unconstrained category specialization transformed to an enumeration.

Figure 11.5 Transformation of an unconstrained category specialization into an enumeration.

11.3.2 Generated Value-Set Types

Generalization/specialization can also be used to define other types. Figure 11.6 presents an example. Here we are defining a *Skill* type. The aggregation makes each skill a pair of values (*Skill Description, Gradation*). The gradation specifies the strength of the skill for an individual in the range 1 to 5. The partition constraints on the skill-description *isa* hierarchies specify that a skill description is a standard skill (one of *"managerial"*, *"technical"*, *"clerical"*, or *"sales"*) or a language skill, which could either be a computer language skill (one of *"Ada"*, *"C"*, *"C++"*, or *"Eiffel"*) or a natural language skill (one of *"English"*, *"French"*, *"German"*, or *"Japanese"*). The operations for the type are the default operations. Both *Manager Skill* and *Worker Skill*, as the example shows, are specializations of *Skill* and therefore "of type *Skill*."

In general, we may use OSM to construct the equivalent of a grammar that describes the value set for a type. An additional part of the aggregation template for OSM, used to specify grammars, is the ability to order the subparts in an aggregation and to declare that a lexical aggregate is a composition of its subparts. To denote that the subparts are ordered, we add the keyword **seq** near the black triangle in an OSM diagram, as in Fig. 11.6. When the object sets in the aggregation are lexical, the keyword **seq** also denotes that the aggregate string is precisely the concatenation of the sub-

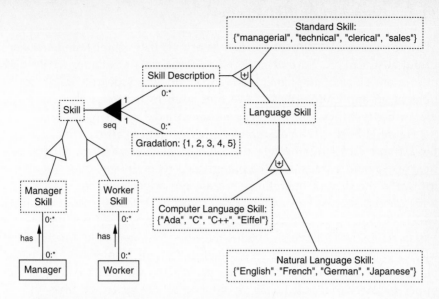

Figure 11.6 A sample generated value-set type.

part strings ordered by the sequence specification. The sequence is from left to right when the apex of the triangle is at the top or bottom and is from top to bottom when the apex of the triangle is to the left or right.

When we use OSM notation to specify a grammar, object-set names are nonterminals; *Skill, Gradation,* and *Standard Skill* in Fig. 11.6 are examples. In place of grammatical operators, we use aggregation for a sequence of tokens, partitioned generalization/specialization for an alternation of tokens, participation constraints for iteration, and recursive aggregation for recursion. Thus, in Fig. 11.6, *Skill* is a sequence of one *Skill Description* followed by a *Gradation;* a *Skill Description* is either a *Standard Skill* or a *Language Skill;* and a *Language Skill* is either a *Computer Language Skill* or a *Natural Language Skill.* The grammar description for *Skill* in Fig. 11.6 is equivalent to the following BNF grammar (where underscores are spaces in nonterminals):

> *Skill ::= Skill_Description Gradation*
>
> *Skill_Description ::= Standard Skill | Language Skill*
>
> *Language_Skill ::= Computer_Langage_Skill | Natural_Language_Skill*
>
> *Computer_Language_Skill ::= Ada | C | C++ | Eiffel*
>
> *Natural_Language_Skill ::= English | French | German | Japanese*
>
> *Gradation ::= 1 | 2 | 3 | 4 | 5*

11.4 Data-Structure Patterns

Many common data structures such as arrays, lists, graphs, and trees are useful abstractions. Furthermore, when these data structures apply they offer more efficient implementations than do direct default implementations of an application model. We thus wish to recognize them and use them whenever they apply in an application model we are designing.

Figure 11.7a shows an example of an array pattern. If we wish to access the *Distance Table* only through the interactions *create*, *destroy*, *retrieve*, and *store*, we should encapsulate the pattern as a type. In forfeiting our ability to invoke the default operations, we are no longer able, for example, to issue queries such as *From City(x) To City(y) is Distance(z) where z ≥ 1000*, which obtains pairs of cities farther apart than 1000 kilometers, or *Distance(100). To City*, which obtains the cities that are 100 kilometers from a *To City*. We gain, however, an efficient underlying implementation based on standard array layouts. For this particular example, we can use an upper- or lower-triangular array layout to save both space and time.

Figure 11.7b shows a way to specify the pattern as an array. In general, we may develop any number of useful templates and use them to designate

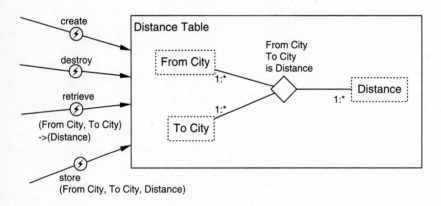

(a) An array pattern.

Array [From City, To City] of Distance

(b) An instantiated array template.

Fig. 11.7 Transformation of an array pattern into an array type.

specific data-structure patterns. Figure 11.8 presents some examples. These patterns are generic because they contain slots to be filled in by object-set names or constants for a particular usage. We designate the slots with angle brackets. In Fig. 11.7b, for example, we have instantiated the *Array* generic in Fig. 11.8 with *From City* and *To City* for < *index* 1 > and < *index* 2 > and with *Distance* for < *name* >.

Complex Objects

OSM modeling supports complex objects in the sense that we can recursively build complex objects from simpler objects. By using object sets and relationship sets and constructing higher and higher level object sets and relationship sets, we can construct an object of any complexity. Sometimes these complex objects represent well-known structures, but the construction in terms of only object and relationship sets obscures the simplicity that we have come to know and understand. We can represent an ordered list, for example, by placing the objects in an object set in a bijection with the set of positive integers. But this representation obscures the simplicity of a list by adding extra baggage to record the order of the elements in the list. We therefore provide templates in which we can represent common structures in well-known ways.

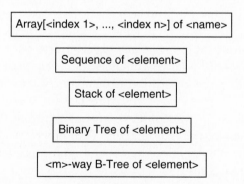

Figure 11.8 Generic templates for some well-known data-structure patterns.

11.5 State-Net Patterns

A state net can have arbitrary complexity. Multiple threads of control are possible, and the configuration of states and transitions can be any bipartite hypergraph. In practice, however, many state nets have simple patterns. In this section, we investigate how to take advantage of these patterns to design efficient implementations.

11.5.1 Abstract Data Types

Figure 11.9 displays a pattern for an abstract data type. Recall that an *abstract data type* (*ADT*) is a type, except that it is usually supplied rather than built in. Since an ADT is a type, it specifies a set of values and a set of uniformly available services. In Fig. 11.9 the object set *Object* represents the set of values. In general, any ORM component of an application model can represent the set of values. In addition, the ORM component also provides default operations to read and write ADT data values. These default operations are implicit services. (We will see later how to control the external use of these implicit operations.) In addition to these implicit operations, an object manager can provide explicit services that manipulate the values in

---

Concurrency Control

Because of the ontological nature of OSM, objects naturally behave independently and thus concurrently. They may also perform multiple tasks simultaneously. This leads to a high degree of concurrency in OSM application models. Although some common patterns lend themselves to relatively simple solutions, managing arbitrary concurrency with computer systems is nontrivial. Fortunately for database designers, much of this complexity can be passed to the database system because databases have built-in concurrency control. The transaction-processing component of a database queues transactions automatically, starts them, and ensures that they do not interfere with each other. Distributed database systems further manage concurrency in a multiprocessing environment, allowing multiple threads of control to execute simultaneously. Thus a database designer's task is reduced from the almost overwhelming one of managing all the complexities of concurrency to the simpler one of mapping the concurrency into transactions.

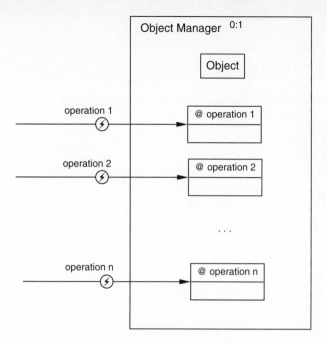

Figure 11.9 Abstract data type state-net pattern.

the ORM component. There is at most one object manager, as required by the *0:1* object-set cardinality constraint. Each transition in the object manager's state net is both an initial transition and a final transition. Thus, when we invoke a service, the object manager comes into existence, provides the service, and then passes out of existence. No concurrency is possible since we can have at most one object manager.

Figure 11.10a shows a sample ADT for a credit card. The potential values are defined by the ORM diagram in the high-level object set. The services include the implicit services provided by the default operations and the explicit services provided by the state net of the *Credit Card Clerk*, which acts as the credit-card manager. Figure 11.10b provides a textual version of the ADT. The example shows how readily these ADT patterns translate into types. The included data description represents the data and the implicit operations, and the individual initial/final transitions each represent an operation.

Some state-net patterns, such as the one in Fig. 11.10a, may already be in the right form for an ADT. Others can be mapped into this form, as seen in the examples of Fig. 11.11. The pattern in Fig. 11.11a contains an interaction

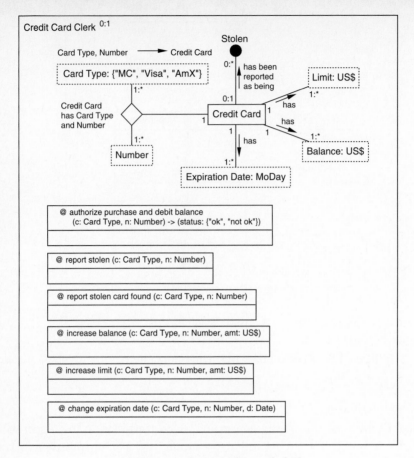

(a) Diagram for a credit-card clerk.

Figure 11.10 An ADT for a credit-card clerk.

object module *Credit Card Clerk* [0: 1] **includes**

> *Credit Card* [1] *has Card Type* [1: *] *and Number* [1: *]
>   [*Card Type, Number* → *Credit Card*];
> *Card Type*: {"*MC*", "*Visa*", "*AmX*"};
> *Number*: String;
> *Credit Card* [1] *has Expiration Date* [1];
> *Expiration Date*: MoDay;
> *Credit Card* [1] *has Limit* [1: *];
> *Credit Card* [1] *has Balance* [1: *];
> *Limit, Balance*: US$;
> **object** *Stolen*;

Credit Card [0: 1] *has been reported as being Stolen* [0: *];

@ *authorize purchase and debit balance (c: Card Type, n: Number)*
   → *(status: {ok, not ok});*
@ *report stolen (c: Card Type, n: Number);*
@ *report stolen card found (c: Card Type, n: Number);*
@ *increase balance (c: Card Type, n: Number, amt: US$);*
@ *increase limit (c: Card Type, n: Number, amt: US$);*
@ *change expiration date (c: Card Type, n: Number, d: Date);*

end;

(b) Translation to an object module.

Figure 11.10 (cont.)   An ADT for a credit-card clerk.

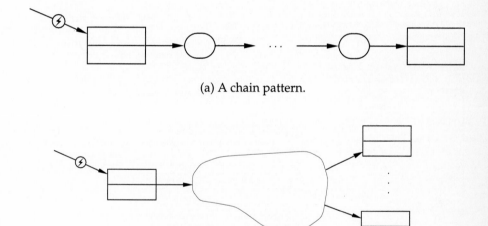

(a) A chain pattern.

(b) A single thread of control in a complex pattern.

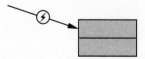

(c) High-level transition representation.

Figure 11.11   Transformation of initial-to-final services into a high-level transition.

that initiates a chain of states and transitions that starts with an initial transition and ends with a final transition. Note also that there are no intervening interactions. In the more complex variation in Fig. 11.11b, an interaction initiates an initial transition, which is followed by any single-threaded pattern with no interactions such that the single thread leads to one of several final states. We can translate both of these patterns into a high-level transition that is initiated by the interaction and is itself both an initial and a final transition. Figure 11.11c shows the resulting high-level transition, which is now in the right form for an operation in an ADT.

Under certain circumstances we can transform additional patterns into an ADT pattern. We show a variation of our credit-card example in Fig. 11.12. Here, instead of having a single credit-card clerk provide services for

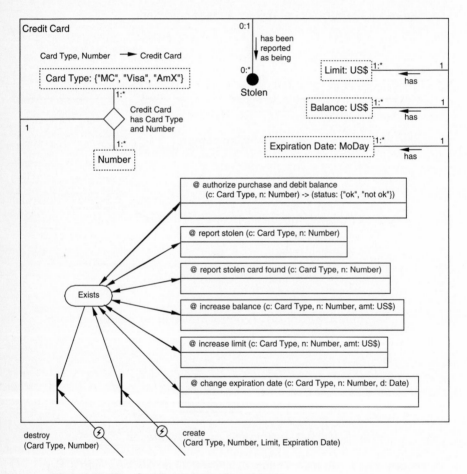

Figure 11.12 Credit card reactive objects.

credit cards, we let the credit cards themselves be reactive objectives. Now, according to the semantics, each of these cards is independent and can potentially service requests concurrently. If we know that any calling routines will send only one request at a time, however, we can transform Fig. 11.12 into Fig. 11.10a to create an ADT. To perform the transformation, we add a single object—the *Credit Card Clerk* in this example—and give it the behavior of the individual objects. In addition, we replace the *create* and *destroy* operations by explicit create and destroy operations that initialize and destroy the data for a credit card. We then delete the state —*Exists* in the example—and let all the transitions be both initial and final transitions.

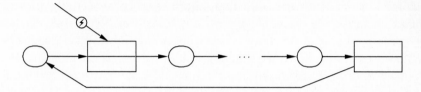

(a) A chain from and back to a state.

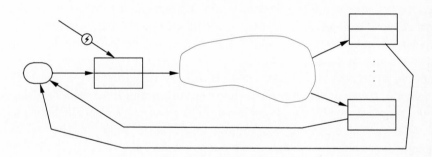

(b) A complex pattern from and back to a state.

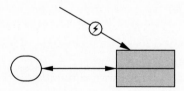

(c) High-level transition from and back to a state.

Figure 11.13 Transformation of from-and-back-to-state patterns into a high-level transition.

This transformation from multiple reactive objects to a server object is based on a state net that has one state and a special pattern of transitions. After an object comes into existence, it resides in some single state. Then it provides a service as requested and returns to the single state. It can also be destroyed. We can accommodate a broader spectrum of patterns, however, as shown in Fig. 11.13. Figure 11.13 exhibits patterns similar to those in Fig. 11.11, except that we have added a state from which we always begin and end. As in Fig. 11.11, we can transform the patterns in Figs. 11.13a and 11.13b to the pattern in Fig. 11.13c. By first making this transformation and then making a transformation like the transformation from Fig. 11.12 to Fig. 11.10, we can translate many common state nets into ADTs.

Some state-net patterns with nonuniform service availability present another circumstance under which we can transform a state net into an ADT pattern. As Fig. 11.14 shows, a stack has nonuniform service availability. When a stack is empty, we cannot pop it or ask for its top element. We can transform this stack specification into an ADT by first transforming it into a pattern with only one state (similar to the state net in Fig. 11.12) and then transforming it into an ADT, as just explained.

Before transforming the *Stack* object set to an ADT, we show the main idea for the simpler pattern in Fig. 11.15a. Observe first that we do indeed have nonuniform service availability because there are two services—one dependent on an object's being in state *S*1 and the other dependent on an object's being in state *S*2. This makes the pattern in Fig. 11.15a different from the pattern in Fig. 11.13a, which is directly transformable to an ADT. In general, a transformation for a state net with nonuniform service availability requires an additional object set and state-changing specifications to track the state changes that would have taken place. In Fig. 11.15b we see the additional object set *State*, which keeps track of the state *S*1 or *S*2. We also see that statements have been inserted to add and remove the appropriate state values as control enters and leaves transitions. The triggers are also different because they depend on the state value as well as on the interaction invocations. After the transformation, the pattern in Fig. 11.15b has one state, *Exists*, and except for the initial transition, each transition has *Exists* for both its prior and its subsequent state. This is exactly the pattern we need for further transformation into an ADT.

Figure 11.16 shows how we can use the idea in Fig. 11.15 to transform the stack specification in Fig. 11.14 into a specification with only one state. Observe that we have added an object set to keep track of the state information in the original. We have also converted the actions in several of the transitions to take the state information into account. The transitions for *is empty*, which depended solely on the state information, have been consoli-

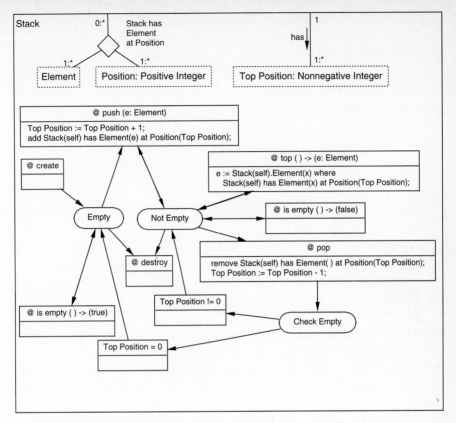

Figure 11.14 A stack.

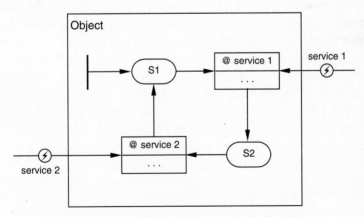

(a) A pattern of nonuniform service availability.

Figure 11.15 Transformation from nonuniform to uniform service availability.

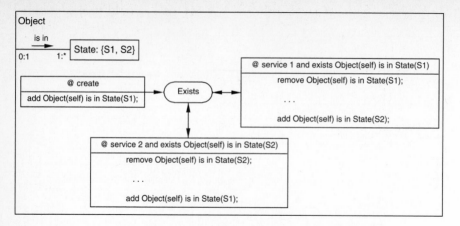

(b) A pattern of uniform service availability.

Figure 11.15 (cont.)   Transformation from nonuniform to uniform service availability.

dated to return a result dependent on the state information. We have duplicated the *push* transition because it depends on two different prior states, and we have also duplicated, but then consolidated, the *destroy* transition, which also depends on two different prior states. In general, our transformation must account for all combinations of prior and subsequent states.

Although we can use the general transformation, we are often likely to do better by making a translation of our own that achieves the same purpose. We can often consolidate some of the transitions and write them more conventionally. Also, sometimes the state information is inherent in the data structure. In such a case, we may not need to add an object set explicitly to track state changes. The stack example illustrates both consolidation and removal of the *State* object set. In Fig. 11.17, we show a more conventional stack specification that is ready to be turned into an ADT. Observe that there is no *State* object set. Instead, we make direct use of the information in *Top Position* to direct the state changes for the stack. Observe also that we have consolidated several of the transitions.

11.5.2 Queued Concurrent Requests

Suppose we still allow only one thread of control in our application, but assume that requests for services come from outside the system independently, and that they are buffered until they can be serviced. This assump-

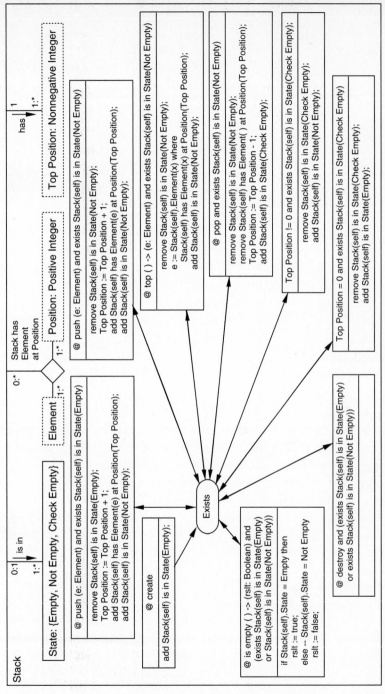

Figure 11.16   A stack ready to be turned into an ADT.

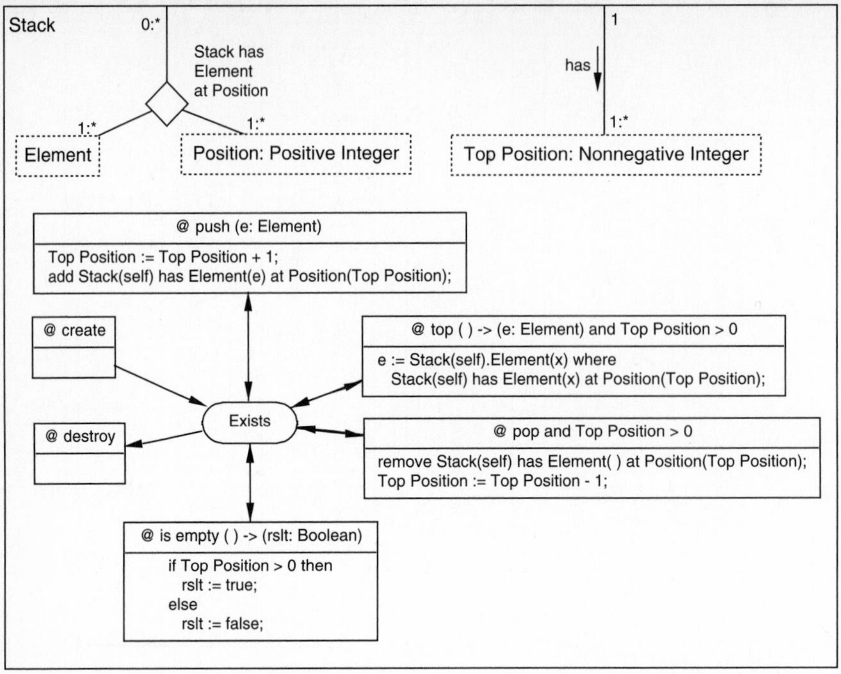

Figure 11.17 A stack ready to be turned into an ADT, but with a conventional specification.

tion allows us to relax the constraints for the patterns we have been discussing, yielding an additional pattern of interest and one additional interesting possibility, both of which we discuss in this section.

Figure 11.18 displays a pattern in which every object is always available to service a request, even when the object currently is servicing a request. If we buffer incoming requests, we can simulate this concurrency by storing the requests in a queue and servicing them one at a time. With this assumption, we can transform the pattern in Fig. 11.18a into the pattern in Fig. 11.18b, which we know how to transform into an ADT.

We make two observations here. First, we do not really have the same behavior as in the original because services do not process concurrently. The concurrent case in Fig. 11.18a, however, must properly handle the case in which requests follow one another sequentially and in which there is no concurrency. Thus by making the transformation to the pattern in Fig. 11.18b, we have simply restricted the possible execution sequences without changing the behavior of any one of the services.

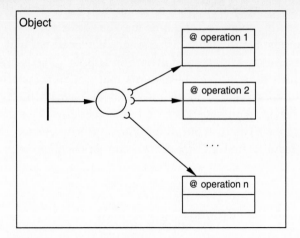

(a) Uniform service availability assuming multiple concurrent requests.

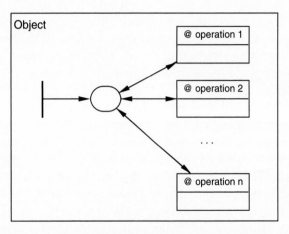

(b) Uniform service availability assuming a queue of requests.

Figure 11.18 Transformation to uniform service availability assuming a queue of requests.

Second, if the purpose of the pattern in Fig. 11.18a is to ensure that the application would service every request, queued concurrent requests with a state net transformed into an ADT may lead to a more efficient implementation than any of the alternatives. We are assuming already that the operations do not depend on any other external event and that there is only one external thread of control. If we also know that there are no secondary-storage accesses and that the operations are not prohibitively time consuming, then executing them one at a time may be sufficient. If we cannot process the requests in the queue fast enough, however, we may need some genuine concurrency, as discussed in Section 11.5.4.

Besides providing additional patterns that can be transformed into an ADT, queued concurrent requests also provide us with the possibility of prioritizing service requests. Since we buffer requests, if we provide priority information, we can turn our buffer into a priority queue. Then, instead of servicing requests first-in/first-out, we can service them in priority order.

11.5.3 Transaction Processing

Until now, we have been assuming a single thread of control. When multiple threads of control are possible, a system can quickly become complex. Usually the complexity is such that we need some system support to be successful. In this section, we assume the existence of a transaction-processing system and discuss transaction design. In the next section, we assume, in addition, the existence of a multiprocessing (possibly distributed) system and further discuss transaction design.

As explained in Chapter 3, a transaction is a program unit that preserves correctness and atomicity. To preserve correctness, a transaction must transform the database from one consistent state to another consistent state. While a transaction executes, however, the database may be inconsistent. To preserve atomicity, the transaction-processing system must ensure either that a transaction executes to completion or that it must leave the system in a state as if the transaction had not executed at all.

For short-duration transactions, we also make use of the principle of serializability, which ensures that a set of transactions will behave as if all the transactions had been executed sequentially in some order. Serializability breaks down for long-duration transactions, however, because it may not be acceptable to wait until a transaction completes to commit it. Our purpose here is not to discuss how transaction-processing systems work, but rather to give some guidelines for designing transactions. We can provide some reasonably good guidance for designing short-duration transactions, which we discuss in this section. Providing guidance for designing long-duration transactions is much harder. Basically, we must consider the relevant state nets carefully and determine how to make them not interfere with each other. We discusss an example of designing long-duration transactions in Section 11.8.

Generally, we can design short-duration transactions in much the same way as we design services for ADTs. A service is often exactly the unit that should be protected as a transaction. Suppose, for example, that we have concurrent execution of a stack, as defined in Fig. 11.17. If two threads of control invoke the push operation simultaneously, it may be possible to increment *Top Position* twice before storing an element on the stack. This action will corrupt the stack and must be prevented. Other simultaneous operator invocations, such as attempting to read the top element of the stack and pop the stack at the same time, may also corrupt the stack.

We can prevent these stack-corrupting possibilities by making each service a transaction. We mark transactions by bracketing them with **start** and **commit** statements. If we wish, we can also cause a transaction to abort by executing **abort**. Figure 11.19 shows the push operation for our stack in Fig. 11.17 written as a transaction. With this change, the transaction-processing system will now guarantee that *push* executes atomically and serially.

We can also prevent the corruption of our stack by guaranteeing that separate threads of control never invoke a stack operation simultaneously. For many applications, this may indeed be possible. Often, for example, we have only one thread of control, in which case we need not create transactions, thus avoiding the overhead caused by transaction processing.

The credit-card example in Fig. 11.12, on the other hand, is an application in which we are likely to need transaction processing. Although rare, it is certainly possible that both parties who share a joint credit card may request some service simultaneously. If both are in the process of debiting the same account, it is possible to corrupt the database. We can solve this problem by making each of the services in Fig. 11.12 transactions and thus protecting them. If we look more closely, however, we may see that with some of the operations no problem can ever arise, again perhaps because only one thread of control invokes them. For example, if only the bank can increase the limit or change the expiration date, then we may not need to protect these operations by making them transactions.

Besides the patterns we have already discussed, short-duration transactions nicely support two additional patterns. One is a simple variation on the first transaction pattern we discussed. After protecting each operation

> **start**;
> *Top Position* := *Top Position* + 1;
> **add** *Stack*(**self**) *has Element*(*e*) *at Position*(*Top Position*);
> **commit**;

Figure 11.19 The *push* operation written as a transaction.

as a transaction, we may remove the object-set cardinality constraint *0:1* and allow multiple objects to service requests simultaneously. This may be especially useful for the credit-card example of Fig. 11.10, where now we are able to have as many clerks as are needed to service requests.

The second pattern leads to yet another transformation. Figure 11.20, a variation of our pattern of nonuniform service availability in Fig. 11.15, shows how we can take advantage of the concurrency offered by transaction processing to support multiple threads of control within a single object. The semantics of the state net in Fig. 11.20a splits a thread of control when leaving the transition of *service 1*. One of these new threads always enters state *S3*, which can have many threads of control for a single object. A thread of control enters state *S2*, however, only if there is no thread of control for the object already in state *S2*. Similarly, for state *S1* there can only be one thread of control for an object. The ternary relationship set in Fig. 11.20b *Thread of Object is in State* stores the information we need to track the states for each thread of an object. We let positive integers represent the various threads. We then capture these semantics by the statements we add in Fig. 11.20b to control the *Thread of Object is in State* relationship set. For example, for states *S1* and *S2* we check first before adding a new thread of control for an object, whereas for state *S3* we always add a thread of control for an object. Also, for exiting state *S3*, we select one specific thread for removal, whereas for states *S1* and *S2*, there is only one thread of control, so we can remove "all" to remove the only one.

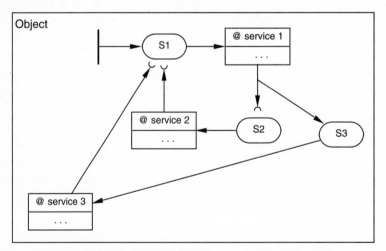

(a) A pattern of nonuniform service availability with
intra-object concurrency.

Fig. 11.20 Transformation from nonuniform to uniform service availability under intra-object concurrency.

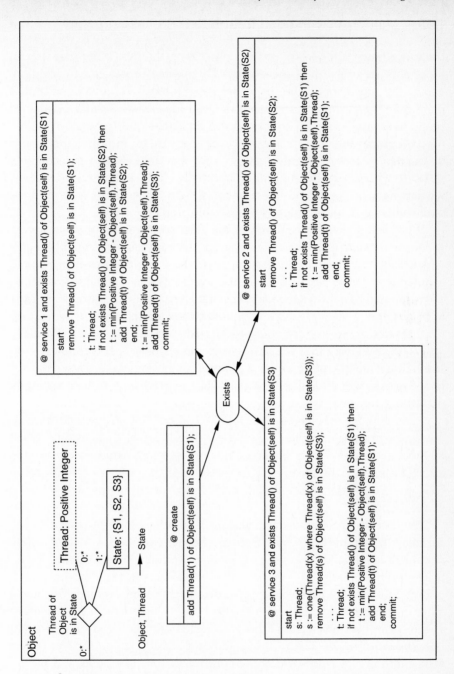

(b) A pattern of uniform service availability with intra-object concurrency.

Fig. 11.20 (cont.)   Transformation from nonuniform to uniform service availability under intra-object concurrency.

11.5.4 Multiprocessing and Distributed Processing

Multiprocessing adds to transaction processing the possibility that several processors are executing concurrently. Distributed processing, in addition, allows the processors to be dispersed geographically and recognizes that there may be various transmission delays. Ideally, we should be able to program an application without concern for either multiprocessing or distributed processing. In practice, however, software for multiprocessing and distributed systems is highly complex, and it is unlikely that this complex software will execute an application optimally. If the execution is too slow, we may have to step in and fine-tune the system. Fine-tuning is beyond the scope of this text, and we do not pursue this problem.

What we do wish to pursue is the idea of maximizing concurrency. When we maximize concurrency in design, we provide for as many concurrent threads as possible. In this way, we allow multiprocessing and distributed systems to assign these threads of control to different processors. There are two basic ways to maximize concurrency: (1) increase the number of objects and (2) increase the number of threads for objects.

Consider as an example our credit-card clerk in Fig. 11.10. We have observed previously that we can remove the *0:1* object-set cardinality constraint if we are executing under the control of a transaction-processing system. We gain very little if there is only a single processor. If there are many processors, however, we can service many requests simultaneously.

Removing the *0:1* object-set cardinality constraint is an example of maximizing concurrency by allowing multiple objects rather than a single object to process services. This is especially important if requests for services arrive faster than they can be processed or if the services require time-consuming operations such as disk reads and writes or interactions with the outside world.

Another way to maximize concurrency is to maximize intra-object concurrency by spawning as many threads of control as possible within a state net. Figure 11.18a, for example, shows how we can spawn a thread of control for each service.

Yet another way to maximize concurrency is to split threads of control whenever actions can take place simultaneously. In general, we can analyze a sequence of actions such as those in Fig. 11.21a and produce a directed "depends-on" graph. Figure 11.21b shows a possible graph for Fig. 11.21a. (The graph in Fig. 11.21b was chosen arbitrarily for illustration, and we are assuming that the actions have been analyzed to determine the dependencies.) A *depends-on* graph has an arc from an action *a* to another action *b* if

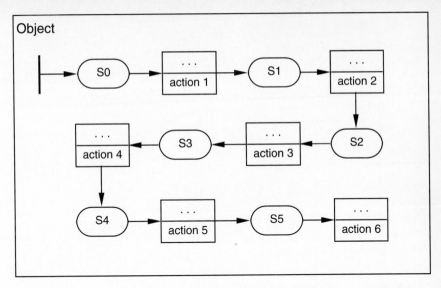

(a) State net with a sequence of actions.

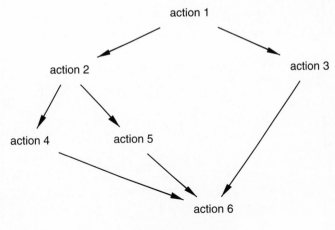

(b) A depends-on graph.

Figure 11.21 Maximizing concurrency based on a depends-on graph.

action *b* depends on the results of action *a*. Figure 11.21b, for example, shows that *action 2* and *action 3* depend on *action 1*, but not on each other. Since they do not depend on each other, they can execute concurrently.

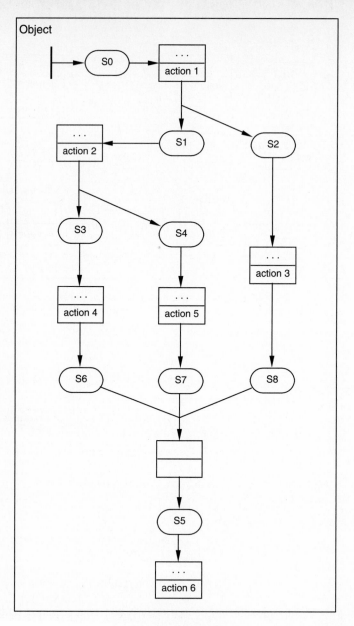

(c) Transformed actions.

Figure 11.21 (cont.)   Maximizing concurrency based on a depends-on graph.

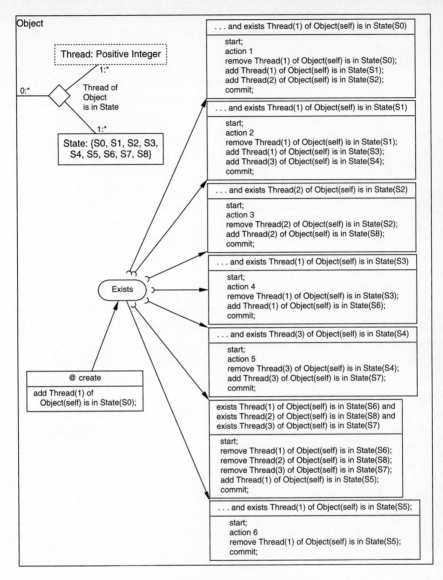

(d) Actions further transformed.

Figure 11.21 (cont.) Maximizing concurrency based on a depends-on graph.

Following the dependencies in our depends-on graph, we can reorganize our state net to maximize concurrency. Figure 11.21c shows the result of reorganizing the state net in Fig. 11.21a according to the dependencies in Fig. 11.21b to maximize concurrency.

Figure 11.21d shows how we can transform the pattern in Fig. 11.21c into a pattern like the one in Fig. 11.18a, which we can transform further, if necessary. As before, the transformation requires a *Thread of Object is in State* relationship set, as well as changes to the triggers and additional statements in the actions. Figure 11.21d shows the changes needed for our example.

We are assuming in this example that the states are simple holding places between actions and that the triggers are simple "wait for object to enter prior state" triggers. If not, then we must also consider the meaning of the states and triggers when building our depends-on graph. In any case, the general idea is to spawn as many threads of control as possible to maximize concurrency.

In principle, although we wish to spawn as many threads of control as possible, we should realize that there is an upper limit. Indeed, we may be able to spawn many more threads of control than can ever be handled by a real system. In a direct simulation of an application model, for example, we could have a processor for every thread of every object! If we have more threads of control than processors, the underlying system should properly reduce the number of threads of control. Ideally, it would do the reduction optimally. Unfortunately, with all the complexity involved, an optimal reduction is highly unlikely. We should therefore be judicious in our choices about how many and what threads of control we spawn.

As a guiding principle, we should spawn threads of control where we gain the most benefit. For example, we should not try to squeeze out some additional concurrency analyzing a sequence of atomic statements in a non-time-critical and seldom-executed action. On the other hand, we should add concurrency, for example, for queues that fill up with time-critical requests faster than objects can service those requests.

11.6 Visibility and Views

Having considered how to transform state-net patterns into ADTs and then into object modules, we now turn our attention to restricting visibility and adding views. We first discuss visibility and then views.

Consider our stack example in Fig. 11.17. Here we have the explicit operations *create*, *destroy*, *push*, *top*, *pop*, and *is empty*. We also have several implicit operations provided by the ORM components, including, for example, **add** *Element*, **remove** *Element*, and even "crazy" actions such as *Position := Position - Top Position*. Clearly, we should disallow all of the latter.

In an object module, we can disallow implicit and even explicit operations by taking them out of the *public* part of an object module and putting them in the *hidden* part. To show the public and hidden parts of an object module syntactically, we introduce a **hidden** keyword, which divides the public part of an object module (which until now is the only part we have shown) from the hidden part. Figure 11.22 shows the stack object module with the implicit operations hidden, and all the other state-net details hidden as well. Even the triggers are hidden so that there are no references to *Top Position* or to local parameter names. Only the interactions remain exposed in the public part. As a technical point, recall that when an object set such as *Stack* has a state net, the state net replaces the default state net. Thus, there is also no way to access or modify the *Stack* object set except through the operations provided.

> **object module** *Stack* **includes**
>
>> @ *create*;
>> @ *push* (*Element*);
>> @ *pop*;
>> @ *top* () → (*Element*);
>> @ *is empty* () → (*Boolean*);
>> @ *destroy*;
>
> **hidden**
>
>> *Element*: *String*;
>> *Position*: *Positive Integer*;
>> *Stack* [0: *] *has Element* [1: *] *at Position* [1: *];
>> *Top Position*: *Nonnegative Integer*;
>> *Stack* [1] *has Top Position* [1: *];
>>
>> @ *create* **then**
>> **enter** *Exists*;
>> **end**;

Figure 11.22   Object module with a hidden part.

when *Exists*
@ *push (e: Element)* **then**
    start;
    Top Position := *Top Position* + 1;
    add *Stack*(**self**) *has Element(e) at Position(Top Position)*;
    commit;
enter *Exists*;
end;

when *Exists*
@ *pop*
if *Top Position* > 0 **then**
    start;
    remove *Stack*(**self**) *has Element at Position(Top Position)*;
    Top Position := *Top Position* − 1;
    commit;
enter *Exists*;
end;

when *Exists*
@ *top*() → (*e: Element*)
if *Top Position* > 0 **then**
    start;
    e := *Stack*(**self**). *Element*(*x*) **where**
        Stack(**self**) *has Element*(*x*) *at Position(Top Position)*;
    commit;
enter *Exists*;
end;

when *Exists*
@ *is empty*() → (*rslt: Boolean*) **then**
    start;
    if *top Position* > 0 **then**
        rslt := **true**;
    else
        rslt := **false**;
    commit;
enter *Exists*;
end;

 end;

Figure 11.22 (cont.)   Object module with a hidden part.

We may not always wish to hide all ORM components. Consider, for example, the credit-card example of Fig. 11.12. Here, we may wish to read and write all the ORM components using the default operations. In this case, there may be no need for any of the explicit operations. As another alternative, we may wish to read and write only the limit and read only the expiration date, balance, card information, and stolen status. In this case, we would not need the *increase limit* operation since the default operations would allow us to modify the limit in arbitrary ways. Indeed, the reason for our encapsulation choice may be to allow decreases as well as increases to the limit.

From this example, we can see the need for three visibility categories. Besides making them public and hidden, we may also wish to make components readable but not writable (read only). For this reason, object modules have a **read only** part as well as a public part and a hidden part. Figure 11.23a shows an object module for the last alternative for the credit-card example (minus the detailed actions in the hidden part). Observe that *Limit* is the lone ORM component in the public part, making it both readable and writable. The object *Stolen*, the object sets *Expiration Date* and *Balance*, and the relationship sets *Credit Card has Card Type and Number* and *Credit Card has been reported as being Stolen* are in the read-only part.

object module *Credit Card* **includes**

@ *create (Card Type, Number, Limit, Expiration Date);*
@ *authorize purchase and debit balance (Card Type, Number) – >*
   ({"ok", "not ok"})
@ *report stolen (Card Type, Number);*
@ *report stolen card found (Card Type, Number);*
@ *increase balance (Card Type, Number, US$);*
@ *change expiration date (Card Type, Number, Date);*
@ *destroy (Card Type, Number);*
Limit;

read only

Expiration Date;
Balance;
Credit Card [1] has Card Type [1: *] and Number [1: *]
   [Card Type, Number – > Credit Card];
object *Stolen;*
Credit Card [0: 1] has been reported as being Stolen [0: *];

Figure 11.23 Object module with both a read-only and a hidden part.

hidden

> *Card Type*: {"MC", "Visa", "AmX"};
> *Limit*: US$;
> *Credit Card* [1] *has Limit* [1:*];
> *Balance*: US$;
> *Credit Card* [1] *has Balance* [1:*];
> *Expiration Date*: MoDay;
> *Credit Card* [1] *has Expiration Date* [1:*];
>
> **when** *Exists*
> @ *authorize purchase and debit balance*
>   (c: *Card Type*, n: *Number*) − > (status: {"ok", "not ok"}) **then**
>   ...
> **enter***Exists*;
> **end**;
>
> **when** *Exists*
> @ *report stolen* (c: *Card Type*, n: *Number*) **then**
>   ...
> **enter***Exists*;
> **end**;
>
> **when** *Exists*
> @ *report stolen card found* (c: *Card Type*, n: *Number*) **then**
>   ...
> **enter***Exists*;
> **end**;
>
> **when** *Exists*
> @ *increase balance* (c: *Card Type*, n: *Number*, amt: US$) **then**
>   ...
> **enter***Exists*;
> **end**;
>
> **when** *Exists*
> @ *change expiration date* (c: *Card Type*, n: *Number*, d: Date) **then**
>   ...
> **enter***Exists*;
> **end**;

end;

(a) Textual version.

Figure 11.23 (cont.)   Object module with both a read-only and a hidden part.

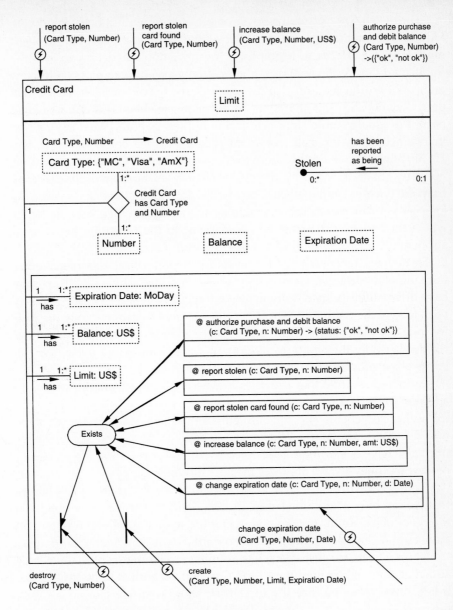

(b) Graphical version.

Figure 11.23 (cont.) Object module with both a read-only and a hidden part.

If we wish, we can represent an object module with a read-only and a hidden part graphically. Figure 11.23b shows how by presenting the object module in Fig. 11.23a in a graphical form. A horizontal line divides the public part (above the line) from the read-only and hidden parts (below the line). Within the read-only and hidden parts, a box encloses the hidden part. Relationship sets that span parts belong to their most encapsulated part. We usually write state nets in the hidden part and interactions that invoke actions in the state net as interactions on the object set, as in Fig. 11.23b, although we do this more for convenience and consistency than for necessity. State nets are by definition already encapsulated. Interactions from the outside, on the other hand, are by definition not encapsulated. As long as we can match the interactions with triggers, it does not matter where the arrowhead points—it could point to the transition to which it applies or to any part of the object module, as in Fig. 11.23b.

Sometimes when we specify visibility for an object module, we are thinking of a particular client who uses that module. Different clients may have different visibility requirements. For our credit-card example, we may wish to give the issuing bank full visibility, to give a customer only the ability to check the balance, limit, and expiration date, and to give an authorized seller only the ability to request an authorization and debit. We can create object modules that provide each of these views.

An object module that provides a view is an **object module view**. In addition to being a regular object module, an object-module view provides for authorized clients and for derived data (which we have not yet mentioned but discuss later). Whenever we have an object-module view, we must also have one or more base object modules for the view. The presence of view modules always occludes the base modules totally.

Figure 11.24 provides four object-module views. Figure 11.24a shows that we can hide everything from all clients except that we allow objects in the *Seller* object set to invoke one operation, allowing sellers to obtain an authorization and post a debit to the account.

Figure 11.24b, for customers, has a similar structure except that we have added an automation boundary, with *Customer* on both the outside and the inside. Also, observe that the **to** clauses allow customers to access only their own credit cards. In particular, the **to** clauses limit the objects to the subset that belongs to the customer, and the *Card Type* and *Number* parameters select the particular card of interest to the customer. If the intersection of the selected card and the limitation to the set of customer cards is empty, the requested information will not be returned.

To allow for several views simultaneously, we can provide them all. For example, we can put Figs. 11.24a and 11.24b in the same application

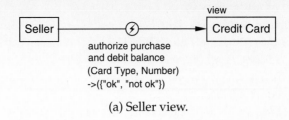

(a) Seller view.

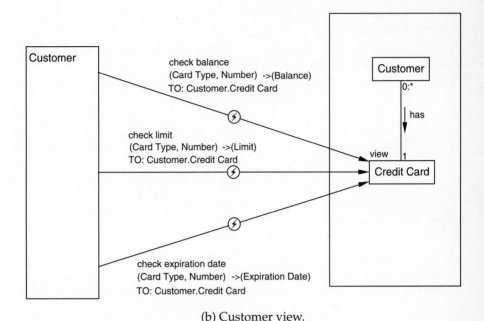

(b) Customer view.

Figure 11.24 Authorization views.

module. Indeed, unless we have several views (or derived data as discussed later), there is no need for a view module because the base module can provide the (single) view needed for all clients.

Figure 11.24c shows an alternative way to provide authorization. Here, we could give all the (default) interactions explicitly and connect the tails to the credit-card officers, but this procedure is tedious at best and overwhelming in general. The **authorized** clause takes care of the difficulty.

Figure 11.24c allows any bank credit-card officer to access and update credit-card information. This may be what we want if there is only one bank in our application. If there are several banks, each issuing its own credit cards, we would not want the officers of one bank accessing and updating the information of the credit cards of another bank. Figure 11.24d

object module view *Credit Card*
authorized sender/receiver *Bank. Credit Card Officer* **includes**
    Credit Card [1] *has Card Type* [1: *] *and Number* [1: *]
        [*Card Type, Number → Credit Card*];
    Card Type: {"MC", "Visa", "AmX"};
    Number: String;
    Credit Card [1] *has Expiration Date* [1];
    Expiration Date: MoDay;
    Credit Card [1] *has Limit* [1: *];
    Credit Card [1] *has Balance* [1: *];
    Limit, Balance: US$;
    object *Stolen;*
    Credit Card [0: 1] *has been reported as being Stolen* [0: *];

read only

hidden

    ...

end;

(c) General bank view.

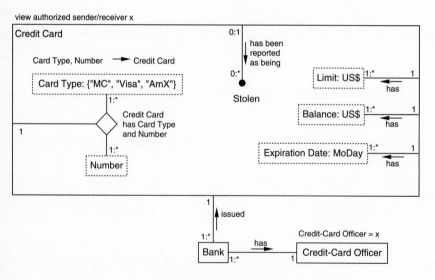

(d) Particular bank view.

Figure 11.24 (cont.)   Authorization views.

shows how we can limit the interactions properly. As usual, the **from** clause provides the identity of the sender. When this identity becomes known for an interaction invocation, we can use it to restrict the available objects. In Fig. 11.24d, we denote the identity of the sender by x and restrict the available objects by imposing the condition

Credit Card Officer = x

For data retrieval and authorization, views present no particular problem except that the specification may be tedious, as mentioned. For data update, however, some inherent problems are difficult to overcome. Historically, the view-update problem has plagued database-system developers since the inception of the idea of a view. A view update must satisfy the properties depicted by the diagram in Fig. 11.25. In the figure, D is a database and V is a view created by a query Q. U is an update to V that results in a new view, V'. Since views are virtual, we cannot update a view directly. The view-update problem is to find a translator T for U that updates D, yielding D', such that when we apply Q to D' we get V'. If there is a unique translator T, there is no ambiguity and no particular problem. Unfortunately, there may be no unique translator.

Figure 11.26 presents an example. Figure 11.26a gives a simple ORM diagram for customers, orders they make, and items included in the orders. Figure 11.26b gives a valid interpretation for the ORM diagram in Fig. 11.26a. Figure 11.26c is a view created by joining the two relationship sets, and Fig. 11.26d is the virtual interpretation, $v = \pi_{Customer,\ Item}(r_1 \bowtie r_2)$. Suppose that now we wish to update v by inserting $<C_1, I_4>$. Since v is virtual, we must find a translator. Unfortunately, there are three possibilities:

1. Insert $<O_1, I_4>$ into r_2,

2. Insert $<O_2, I_4>$ into r_2, or

3. Insert $<C_1, O_3>$ into r_1 and insert $<O_3, I_4>$ into r_2.

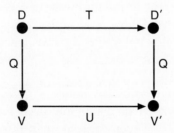

Figure 11.25   View-update requirements.

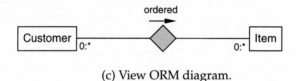

(a) Base ORM diagram.

$$r_1 = \begin{array}{c c} \underline{\text{Customer} \quad \text{Order}} \\ C_1 \quad O_1 \\ C_1 \quad O_2 \end{array} \qquad r_2 = \begin{array}{c c} \underline{\text{Order} \quad \text{Item}} \\ O_1 \quad I_1 \\ O_1 \quad I_2 \\ O_2 \quad I_1 \\ O_2 \quad I_3 \end{array}$$

(b) Interpretation for base ORM diagram.

ordered

Customer ◆ Item
0:* 0:*

(c) View ORM diagram.

$$v = \begin{array}{c c} \underline{\text{Customer} \quad \text{Item}} \\ C_1 \quad I_1 \\ C_1 \quad I_2 \\ C_1 \quad I_3 \end{array}$$

(d) Virtual interpretation for view ORM diagram.

Figure 11.26   The view-update problem.

For the third possibility, there are actually many more translators since we (or the system) could choose any object identifier for *Order* in place of O_3, but these are all isomorphic to the third case and not of particular interest. Observe that for each of the three possibilities, a reapplication of the query $\pi_{Customer, Item}(r_1 \bowtie r_2)$ yields the updated view. Thus, although we are able to satisfy the requirements stated in Fig. 11.25, we are unable to do so unambiguously.

Since the view-update problem defies a general solution, we must resolve it some other way. One commonly used procedure is to disallow view updates. Many, however, believe that this is overly restrictive. Another possibility is to let the user decide whenever there is an ambiguity, but users may not understand well enough to make a proper choice in every case. A third possibility is to have the designer decide. This may preclude some of the possibilities a user may want, but if done under the direction of the client for whom the software is being built, it should be satisfactory.

In our example, it might be reasonable to preclude the direct insertion of a tuple into v and provide, instead, an interaction that adds tuples whenever a customer places a new order. Conceptually, this means that all insertions into v would fall under a variation of Case 3, just given, where we impose a stipulation that the object identifier inserted into r_1 and r_2 must be the object identifier of the order placed by the customer.

We may also wish to disallow deletions in this example. Although still ambiguous, deletions are easier to resolve than are insertions. If we wish to delete all tuples for a customer, for example, we could delete all tuples for the customer in r_1; we could delete all orders made by the customer in r_2; or we could do both deletions. A reasonable resolution of the ambiguity would be to do both.

Continuing with our example, let us assume that we wish to disallow insertions and allow controlled deletions of a customer. With these assumptions, Fig. 11.27 shows how we would create the object-module view. The relationship set that constitutes the view is in the read-only part; its derivation is in the hidden part. We can therefore read the information in the view, but not write to the view, using the default operations. The view does expose one operation, *delete*. When invoked, this operation calls the default **remove** operation in the *Customer made Order* relationship set for

> **object module view** *Ordered Item* **includes**
>
> > @ *delete (Customer)*;
>
> **read only**
>
> > *Customer* [0: *] *ordered Item* [0: *]
>
> **hidden**
>
> > *Customer(x) ordered Item(y)* : −
> > > *Customer(x) made Order(z), Order(z) includes Item(y)*;
> >
> > @ *delete (c: Customer)* **then**
> > > **remove** *Customer(c) made Order*;
> > **end**;
>
> **end**;

Figure 11.27   View creation.

the given customer *c*, which removes the customer-order pairs for *c*. Observe that there are no states and thus no persistent objects. This is consistent with the idea that a view is virtual.

11.7   Inheritance

Inheritance is a technique that lets us specify some parts of a system incrementally. If an object module *M inherits* from another object module *M'*, then *M* initially has everything in *M'*, including all data definitions, all operations, all constraints, and all operational specifications in all sections of the object module—public, read only, and hidden. Indeed, *M* may be thought of initially as being the same as *M'*, and if nothing is specified in *M* except that it inherits from *M'*, *M* and *M'* are the same semantically for any object in *M*. In general, we can make *M* differ from *M'* by (1) adding data or behavior components, (2) subtracting data or behavior components, and (3) redefining existing behavior components. Thus, we can begin with *M* being the same as *M'* and then alter *M* incrementally. As we shall see, however, for OSM we restrict these possibilities.

Figure 11.28 presents an example. Here, *Employee* inherits from *Person*. The **inherits from** clause in an object module specifies the inheritance relationship. Since *Employee* inherits from *Person*, every employee object, as well as every person object, has a name, address, phone number, height, gender, and age, and we can compute the ideal weight for an employee as well as for a person. Objects in *Employee* also have an additional data component and additional behavior. In particular, an employee object has a hire date, and we can compute an employee's longevity (how long the employee has worked since being hired).

In OSM, we take a conceptual-modeling view of inheritance. We inherit only in *isa* hierarchies, and we treat specialization object sets as subsets of generalization object sets. In Fig. 11.29, an ORM hypergraph for the object-module inheritance in Fig. 11.28, we see that every employee object is indeed a person object. It should therefore be possible to treat every employee as either a person or an employee, and there should be no conflict in any data or behavior component.

As a consequence of taking a conceptual modeling view of inheritance, we restrict the ways in which an inheriting object module can differ from the object module from which it inherits. Because every specialization object is a generalization object, a specialization object must appear and behave like a generalization object. For OSM, if *M* inherits from *M'*, we may add data or behavior components in *M*, but we may not subtract data

object module *Person* **includes**

> *Person* [1] *has Name* [1:*];
> *Person* [1] *has Address* [1:*];
> *Person* [1] *has Phone#* [1:*];
> *Person* [1] *has Height* [1:*];
> *Person* [1] *has Gender* [1:*];
> *Person* [1] *has Age* [1:*];
>
> @ *ideal weight(Person)* → *Integer;*

end;

object module *Employee* **inherits from** *Person* **includes**

> *Employee* [1] *has Hire Date* [1:*];
>
> @ *Longevity(Employee)* → *Integer;*

end;

Figure 11.28   Object-module inheritance.

or behavior components of M', and we should not redefine existing behavior components in ways that change the meaning of a behavior component in M'. We do not subtract data or behavior for a specialization object—if we were to, the specialization object would no longer be a generalization object because it would not have the same data relationships, and it would not respond to the same operations. For the object modules in Fig. 11.28,

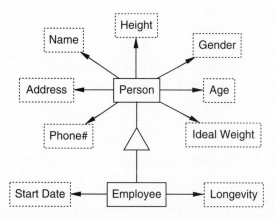

Figure 11.29   Inheritance and generalization/specialization.

for example, we cannot specify that an employee does not have a name or a height, nor can we specify that an employee does not have an ideal weight. We do not change the meaning of a behavior component—if we were to, a specialization object would not respond in the same way to an operation as it would as a generalization object, and thus it would not also be a generalization object. For the object modules in Fig. 11.28, for example, we should not specify a procedure for the *ideal weight* operation that returns something else, such as the minimum weight among all the employees in the database.

Although we should not change the meaning of an operation for an inheriting object module, we may be able to provide a more efficient specification for the operation in an inheriting object module. Suppose, for example, that the computation for ideal weight depends on age only for infants and for people above age 80. If we know that no employees are infants or above age 80 (and we probably do), we can simplify the computation for *ideal weight* in the specialization.

Figure 11.30 displays an example of how we specify a more efficient operation for an inheriting object set. In Fig. 11.30, both *Square* and *Isosceles Triangle* inherit from *Regular Polygon*. Both *Square* and *Regular Polygon* are identical to *Regular Polygon* with respect to what they export. In the hidden part of both, however, there is an alternative, more efficient specification for the *area* computation. For squares, we must square only the side length; for isosceles triangles, we have a simpler formula for the area.

object module *Regular Polygon* **includes**

> *Regular Polygon* [1] *has Number of Sides* [1:*];
> *Regular Polygon* [1] *has Side Length* [1:*];
> @ *perimeter* (*Regular Polygon*) → (*Real*);
> @ *area* (*Regular Polygon*) → (*Real*);

hidden

> @ *perimeter* (*x*: *Regular Polygon*) → (*y*: *Real*) **then**
> > *y* := *Regular Polygon*(*x*). *Number of Sides*
> > > * *Regular Polygon*(*x*). *Side Length*;
>
> **end**;

> @ *area* (*x*: *Regular Polygon*) → (*y*: *Real*);
> > *RadiansPerDegree* [1] : *Real*;
> > *RadiansPerDegree* := 0. 01745;
> > > *nrSides* [1] : *Integer*;
> > > *sideLength* [1] : *Real*;

Figure 11.30 Object-module inheritance.

nrSides := Regular Polygon(x). Number of Sides;
sideLength := Regular Polygon(x). Side Length;
y := nrSides * (sqr(sideLength)/4) * tan(RadiansPerDegree * (180
− 360/nrSides)/2);
    end;

end;

object module *Square* **inherits from** *Regular Polygon* **includes**

hidden

    @ area (x: Square) → (y: Real);
      y := sqr(Square(x). Side Length);
    end;

end;

object module *Isosceles Triangle* **inherits from** *Regular Polygon* **includes**

hidden

    @ area (x: Isosceles Triangle) → (y: Real);
      y := (sqrt(3)/4) * sqr(Isosceles Triangle(x). Side Length);
    end;

end;

Figure 11.30 (cont.)   Object-module inheritance.

11.8   Example

We summarize our design chapters by doing the design for part of our on-line shopping example. Figure 11.31 (the same as Fig. 8.16) gives the ORM diagram for our example, and Fig. 11.32 (the same as Fig. 8.15a) gives the OBM and OIM diagram for our example. As for Fig. 8.15a, the detailed formal specification of the actions for the transitions appears in Fig. 8.15b.

We begin by doing the data design for Fig. 11.31. First we adjust our ORM diagram. *Customer* is the only specialization of *Person* in Fig. 11.31. Since *Person* has no other role in this diagram and since we are doing only this part of the example, we adjust the diagram by discarding *Person* and attaching *Name* and *Address* to *Customer*.

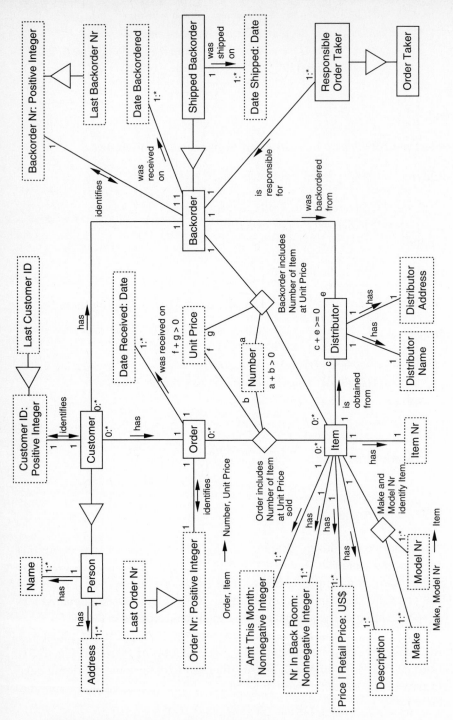

Figure 11.31 ORM diagram for the design example.

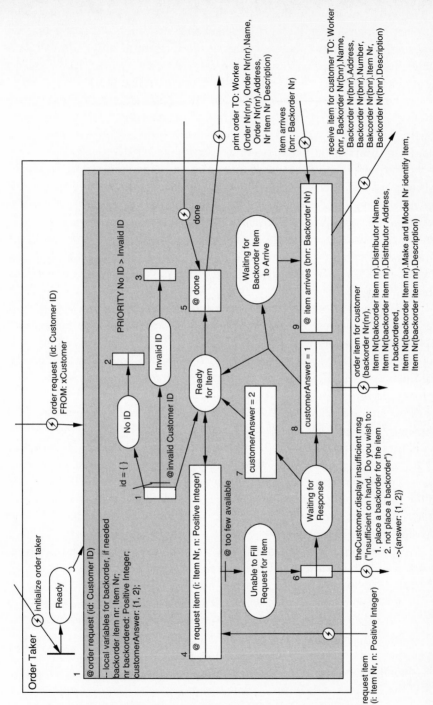

Figure 11.32 OBM/OIM diagram for the design example.

We next consider the three specializations that represent the last order number, last customer ID, and last backorder number. Realizing that we can calculate these numbers by finding the maximum order number, customer ID, and backorder number, we discard *Last Order Nr*, *Last Customer ID*, and *Last Backorder Nr* from the ORM diagram in Fig. 11.31.

We next consider the object sets *Unit Price*, *Number*, and *Distributor*, each of which has a pair of variable participation constraints. The participation constraints *a* and *b*, along with the constraint $a + b > 0$ on *Number*, tell us that every number participates either with the order relationship set or the backorder relationship set. If we add roles and a generalization to capture this information, it is easy to see that we will have a union-covered isolated generalization, which we should discard. The two other pairs of variable participation constraints are similar. We thus introduce the roles *Number for Order* and *Number for Backorder* for *Number*, *Unit Price for Order* and *Unit Price for Backorder* for *Unit Price*, and *Item Distributor* and *Backorder Item Distributor* for *Distributor* and discard the union-covered isolated generalizations.

At this point we should transform our ORM diagram into a hypergraph. First, however, let us consider the possible lexical transformations, which are seen just as easily in the ORM diagram in Fig. 11.31 as in a hypergraph. For lexicalizing *Customer*, *Order*, and *Backorder*, we have only one choice. We thus represent *Customer* by *Customer ID*, *Order* by *Order Nr*, and *Backorder* by *Backorder Nr*. For *Item* and *Distributor* we have two choices each; we choose to lexicalize *Item* by *Item Nr* rather than by *Make* and *Model Nr* together, *Distributor* by *Distributor Name* rather than by *Distributor Address*.

Figure 11.33 presents the ORM hypergraph for Fig. 11.31 as transformed by the preceding discussion. Checking the hypergraph for further reductions, we see that there are none. Thus, we apply Algorithms 10.1 and 10.2 to the ORM hypergraph in Fig. 11.33. The result is the flat schemes in Fig. 11.34. As usual, we have made some slight name adjustments. We have also added the remaining types.

We next analyze the flat schemes for time and space. Our analysis, which results in the improved schemes in Fig. 11.35, is as follows:

1. We first combine the *Shipped Backorder* and *Backorder* schemes. When we do an outer join of these two schemes, we have a possible null for *Date Shipped* that is applicable but not yet known. Since the *Backorder* scheme contains all backorders, we will save both space and time by not keeping a separate scheme that holds backorders with shipping dates.

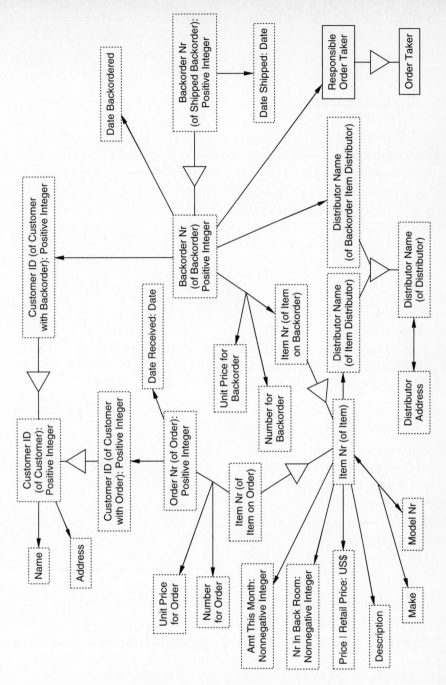

Figure 11.33   ORM hypergraph for the design example.

Customer(Customer ID: Positive Integer, Name: String, Address: String)
    key: Customer ID
Distributor(Distributor Name: String, Distributor Address: String)
    key: Distributor Name
    key: Distributor Address
Order Taker(Order Taker: OID)
    key: Order Taker
Item(Item Nr: String, Make: String, Model Nr: String,
       Distributor Name: String, Amt This Month: Nonnegative Integer,
       Nr In Back Room: Nonnegative Integer
       Price: US\$, Description: String)
    key: Item Nr
    key: Make, Model Nr
    Distributor[Distributor Name] $\supseteq$ Item[Distributor Name]
Order(Order Nr: Positive Integer, Date Received: Date, Customer ID:
    Positive Integer)
    key: Order Nr
    Customer[Customer ID] $\supseteq$ Order[Customer ID]
Ordered Item(Order Nr: Positive Integer, Item Nr: String, Number:
       Positive Integer, Unit Price: US\$)
    key: Order Nr, Item Nr
    Item[Item Nr] $\supseteq$ Ordered Item[Item Nr]
    Order[Order Nr] $\supseteq$ Ordered Item[OrderNr]
Backorder(Backorder Nr: Positive Integer, Customer ID: Positive Integer,
       Date Backordered: Date, Item Nr: String, Number: Positive Integer,
       Unit Price: US\$, Distributor Name: String,
         Responsible Order Taker: OID)
    key: Backorder Nr
    Customer[Customer ID] $\supseteq$ Backorder[Customer ID]
    Item[Item Nr] $\supseteq$ Backorder[Item Nr]
    Distributor[Distributor Name] $\supseteq$ Backorder[Distributor Name]
    Order Taker[Order Taker] $\supseteq$ Backorder[Responsible Order Taker]
Shipped Backorder(Backorder Nr: Positive Integer, Date Shipped: Date)
    key: Backorder Nr
    Backorder[Backorder Nr] $\supseteq$ Shipped Backorder[Backorder Nr]

Figure 11.34   Flat schemes for the example.

2. Next we observe that if we treat the two explicit *Customer ID* roles as implicit roles of *Customer ID*, we can use Algorithm 10.3 to nest the *Order* relation scheme and the *Backorder* relation scheme under *Customer*. Furthermore, we can nest the *Ordered Item* scheme under *Order*. Although the edge is not binary for this last nesting, we can reason that there can be no redundancy because every customer order is independent of every other customer order. In this nested scheme for customers, we will have direct access from customers to their orders and backorders without having to join several relations, saving both time and space. Updating orders by adding new ones and deleting old ones can be time consuming, however, because we must process updates for variant-length records. If instead of variant-length records with the order information, we are able to use pointers to order and backorder information, we can control the space allocation better. For this application, the number of orders and backorders is likely to be small and not vary widely among customers, making it reasonable to allocate sufficient space for the pointers. Confirming this assumption with our client, we proceed with the design. Thinking a little more, we can also see that we can enhance the design even further. It would be possible to store the information for customer orders and for customer backorders in hash tables. This way, in addition to being able to reach order information directly from customer records, we could also hash either on order numbers or backorder numbers to access the order information directly. We may also wish to add back pointers from these hash tables to customer records. Additionally, we could have a B^+-tree index on customers. We could also have a separate sequential file for collections of ordered-item records, with explicit pointers from each order to its collection of ordered-item records. This makes the order records for the order hash table all the same size and still makes the order information directly accessible without requiring a join.

3. Looking ahead, we realize that *Order Taker* will become an active object manager. Since its threads will represent its existence, we need not record the existence of the object separately in the database. Thus we simply drop the *Responsible Order Taker* and *Order Taker* schemes.

To show that we can place our design schemes in an object module, we write our adjusted database schemes in Fig. 11.35 as an object module. In

object module *Order Taker* **includes**

> *Distributor(Distributor Name: String, Distributor Address: String)*
> > *key*: *Distributor Name*
> > *key*: *Distributor Address*
>
> *Item(Item Nr: String, Make: String, Model Nr: String, Distributor Name:*
> > *String, Amt This Month: Nonnegative Integer, Nr In Back Room:*
> > *Nonnegative Integer*
> > *Price: US$, Description: String)*
> > *key*: *Item Nr*
> > *key*: *Make, Model Nr*
> > *Distributor[Distributor Name]* ⊇ *Item[Distributor Name]*
>
> *Customer(Customer ID: Positive Integer, Name: String, Address: String,*
> > *Order(Order Nr: Positive Integer, Date Received: Date,*
> > > *Ordered Item(Item Nr: String, Number: Positive Integer, Unit Price:*
> > > *US$)*)*,*
> >
> > *Backorder(Backorder Nr: Positive Integer, Date Backordered: Date, Item*
> > *Nr: String, Number: Positive Integer, Unit Price: US$,*
> > *Distributor Name: String, Date Shipped: Date)*)*
> > *key for Customer: Customer ID*
> > > *key for Order: Order Nr*
> > > *key for Ordered Item: Order Nr, Item Nr*
> > > *key for Backorder: Backorder Nr*
> >
> > *may be null*: *Date Shipped* -- if null, then not yet shipped
> > *Item[Item Nr]* ⊇ *Ordered Item[Item Nr]*
> > *Item[Item Nr]* ⊇ *Backorder[Item Nr]*
> > *Distributor[Distributor Name]* ⊇ *Backorder[Distributor Name]*

end;

Figure 11.35   Adjusted schemes for the example written as an object module.

this form, we can view the database as an ADT, as discussed in Chapter 2. The database schemes provide the data and the constraints among the data. All operations are implicit. We can think of these operations as the update and retrieval operations provided by SQL.

We now analyze the state net for the order taker. In one sense, the behavior is already in the proper form to be used as a transaction in a transaction-processing system because there is a single *Ready* state and one high-level transition, which is a final transition. In another sense, however, we see that the transaction is a long-duration transaction because it interacts with the outside world and particularly because one of its interactions depends on a backorder's being filled, which may take several days.

Since the transaction has a long duration, we should be careful not to cause the transaction-processing system to lock database components so that others cannot proceed. A worst-case scenario here would be to write-lock information about the number available for an item *a* while it waits for a backorder for some other item *b*. This would mean that no other customer could order item *a* until the backorder for item *b* had been received. Clearly, we need to reconstitute the transaction as a series of shorter transactions, ideally all protected and of short duration.

In reorganizing the behavior in Fig. 11.32, we see first that the purpose for the high-level transition is to maintain some local variables as the thread of control moves from state to state. We can resolve this problem in one of two ways: (1) We can place these local variables in the hidden part of an object module, or (2) we can nest the transitions appropriately inside one another so that the local variables are available when we need them. We use the first alternative here and the second in Chapter 12, when we implement the *Order Taker* object module. With the local variables placed in the hidden part of an object module, we can treat the state net in Fig. 11.32 as if there were no high-level transition and as if the interaction that initiates the high-level transition and the connection from the *Ready* state into the high-level transition were connected to low-level transition *1*.

Given this transformation, we next try to maximize concurrency, but we soon recognize that nothing more needs to be done. In particular, the intra-object concurrency that lets a customer continue to order items and even place additional backorders after the first backorder is already defined within the state net. We are therefore ready to transform the state net into a pattern with only one state and several independently executing threads of control.

Figure 11.36 shows the result, but it gives only some of the detail. Unlike our earlier examples, we have not introduced a *Thread* object set. Instead, we recognize that an *Order Taker* can spawn a thread of control to service each external-customer request for an order. We also recognize that an external customer places only one order at a time. Thus, once we match the external customer with an internal customer, we can keep track of the states based on the customer and order. We thus introduce the relationship set *External Customer who is Customer is in State of making Order*, which takes the place of our earlier *Thread of Object is in State*. With respect to the states, we further recognize that there is no need for several of the states in Fig. 11.32. Four of them are for processing exceptions, which we handle explicitly by including them in high-level states, as shown in Fig. 11.35. For

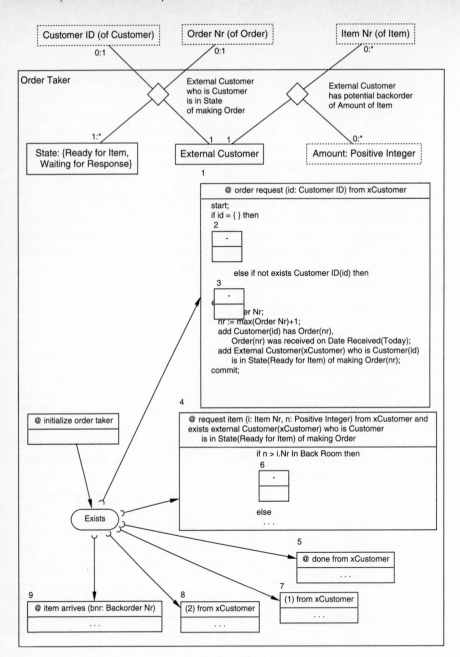

Figure 11.36 Transformed *Order Taker* state net.

example, when a request is received, we first check the customer ID to see whether it is valid and then respond in one of two ways, as transition *1* in Fig. 11.36 shows. However, we treat the *Waiting for Backorder Item to Arrive* state differently. Having observed that we must wait some time, perhaps several days, for a backorder to arrive, we decide to record the backorder information in the database and then, when a backorder arrives, to access the database for the information to process the backorder.

Figure 11.37 provides all the details in textual form. A careful consideration of the object module leads to several interesting observations:

1. The object module properly sets and releases each state for each thread of control.

2. The object module specifies the encapsulation. Clients of the object module can invoke only the services provided. Moreover, the triggers protect clients from invoking services improperly by allowing these services to be invoked only when a thread of control of the order taker is in a proper state.

3. Once initialized, an order taker can always receive any new request because there is always a thread of control in the *Exists* state. This implies a queue of requests.

4. We can start as many order takers as we wish. They can all run concurrently. We may, however, need some actual multiprocessing to increase the speed over having just one order taker. We also note that since one order taker can spawn many threads of control, if the underlying system can assign the various threads properly to separate processors, there may be no need for multiple order takers.

When executed under a transaction-processing system, this object module provides the desired order-taker functionality.

object module *Order Taker* **includes**

> @ *initialize order taker;*
> @ *order request (Customer ID);*
> @ *request item (Item Nr, Positive Integer);*
> @ *done;*
> @ *(1);*
> @ *(2);*
> @ *item arrives (Backorder Nr);*

Figure 11.37   *Order Taker* object module.

hidden

State: {*Ready for Item, Waiting for Response*};
External Customer [1] *who is Customer* [0: 1] *is in State* [1: *] *of making*
   Order [0: 1]*;*
External Customer [1] *has potential backorder of Amount* [0: *] *of Item* [0: *];

@ *initialize order taker* **then**
enter *Exists;*
end*;*

1
when *Exists* **new thread**
@ *order request* (*id: Customer ID*) **from** *theCustomer* **then**
      -- theCustomer is the identifier for the external customer, which is
      -- automatically generated as a new OID.

      start*;*
      if *id* = { } **then** -- transition 2
         theCustomer. display no id ("*No Customer ID entered.*
                You must be registered as a customer and enter a customer ID.");
          end;
      else if not exists *Customer*(*id*) **then** -- transition 3
         theCustomer. display invalid id ("*Invalid Customer ID.*
                You must be registered as a customer and enter a valid customer ID.");
          end;
      else
         nr: Order Nr;
         nr := *max*(*Order Nr*) + 1*;*
         add *Customer*(*id*) *has Order*(*nr*),
                Order(*nr*) *was received on Date Received*(*Today*);
         add *External Customer*(*theCustomer*) *who is Customer*(*id*)
                is in State(*Ready for Item*) *of making Order*(*nr*);
      commit*;*
end*;*

4
when *Exists* **new thread**
@ *request item* (*i: Item Nr, n: Positive Integer*) **from** *theCustomer* **and**
      exists *External Customer*(*theCustomer*) *who is Customer*
      is in State(*Ready for Item*) *of making Order* **then**
      if *n* > *i. Nr In Back Room* **then**

Figure 11.37 (cont.)   *Order Taker* object module.

```
        start;
        add External Customer(theCustomer) has potential backorder of
            Amount(n) of Item(i);
        theCustomer. display insufficient msg -- transition 6
            ("Insufficient on hand.  Do you wish to:
                1. place a backorder for the item
                2. not place a backorder");
        add External Customer(theCustomer) who is
            Customer(theCustomer. Customer) is in State(Waiting for Response)
            of making Order(theCustomer. Order);
        commit;
        end;
    else
        start;
        add Order(External Customer. Order) includes Number(n) of
            Item(i) at Unit Price(i. Price);
        Item(i). Amt This Month := Item(i). Amt This Month + n;
        Item(i). Nr In Back Room := Item(i). Nr In Back Room - n;
        commit;
        end;
        end;
    end;


5
when Exists new thread
@ done from theCustomer
if exists External Customer(theCustomer) who is Customer
        is in State(Ready for Item) of making Order then
    nr: Order Nr;
    nr := theCustomer. Order Nr;
    if  Order(nr) includes Number of  Item != 0 then
    Nr(x) Item Nr(y) Description(z) :-
            Order(nr) includes Number(x) of  Item(y) at Unit Price(w),
            Item(y) has Description(z);
    Worker. print order (Order Nr(nr), Order Nr(nr). Name,
            Order Nr(nr). Address, Nr Item Nr Description;
    end;
    remove External Customer(theCustomer) who is Customer
    is in State(Ready for Item) of making Order;
end;
```

Figure 11.37 (cont.) *Order Taker* object module.

7

when *Exists* **new thread**
@ (2) **from** *theCustomer*
if exists *External Customer(theCustomer) who is Customer*
    is in State(Waiting for Response) of making Order **then**
  start;
  remove *External Customer(theCustomer) who is Customer*
    is in State(Waiting for Response) of making Order;
  add *External Customer(theCustomer) who is Customer*
    is in State(Ready for Item) of making Order;
  commit;
end;

8

when *Exists* **new thread**
@ (1) **from** *theCustomer*
if exists *External Customer(theCustomer) who is Customer*
    is in State(Waiting for Response) of making Order **then**
  start;
  nr: Backorder Nr;
  $nr := max(Backorder\ Nr) + 1;$
  i: Item;
  $i := theCustomer. Item;$
  add *Backorder(nr) includes Number(theCustomer. Number) of*
    Item(i) at Unit Price(i. Price);
  add *Backorder(nr) was received on Date Backordered(Today);*
  order item for customer (Backorder Nr(nr),
    Item(i). Distributor Name, Item(i). Distributor Address,
    theCustomer. Amount, Item(i). Make and Model Nr identify Item,
    Item(i). Description);
  remove *External Customer(theCustomer) who is Customer*
    is in State(Waiting for Response) of making Order;
  add *External Customer(theCustomer) who is Customer*
    is in State(Ready for Item) of making Order;
  commit;
end;

9

when *Exists* **new thread**
@ *item arrives (bnr: Backorder Nr)*
if exists *External Customer(theCustomer) who is Customer*

Figure 11.37 (cont.) *Order Taker* object module.

> is in State(*Waiting for Response*) of *making Order* **then**
> *Worker. receive item for customer* (*bnr, Backorder Nr*(*bnr*). *Name,*
> *Backorder Nr*(*bnr*). *Address, Backorder Nr*(*bnr*). *Number,*
> *Backorder Nr*(*bnr*). *Item Nr, Backorder Nr*(*bnr*). *Description;*
> **end**;

end;

Figure 11.37 (cont.)   *Order Taker* object module.

11.9   Chapter Summary

Topic Summary

- An object module provides a rich mechanism for recording design information for related data and behavior. We can use an object module to encapsulate data and behavior so that we export only external services while hiding the implementation details for these services. Classes, types, variables, and values can all be seen as special kinds of object modules.

- Encapsulation protects object integrity because encapsulation limits access to only those services explicitly exported for an object. Encapsulation utilizes implementation independence to hide the implementation for an object. Encapsulation thus allows implementation details to change without requiring any change to programs that access objects through the exported services. This same principle also allows objects within an object set to have different implementation representations and different operator implementations. This leads to appropriate uses for overriding, overloading, late binding, and polymorphism in inheritance hierarchies, in which more specialized objects can have more efficient implementations for operations.

- Methods for object modules become exported services. Methods arise either from computed relationship sets or from state-net services. Although we may store computed relations directly, frequently we transform them into two-way interactions that return a result. State-net services are one-way and two-way interactions. These interactions may be nonuniformly available in the sense that an object must be in a particular state to process them. During design, we frequently transform state nets into single-state state nets and make all the services uniformly available. Services that were nonuniformly available before the transformation become uniformly available, but may return an error if invoked inappropriately (e.g., an attempt to pop an empty stack).

- Some ORM patterns correspond to well-known data structures such as arrays and lists. We can create high-level abstractions from these patterns so that these data structures are available to us in a standard form and can be transformed into standard efficient forms for processing. Similarly, some state nets with local ORM components correspond to well-known ADTs such as stacks and queues. When we transform these patterns into ADTs, they have their standard appearance.

Question Summary

- What are the similarities and differences between object modules and ADTs?

An object module is similar to an ADT because they both describe a set of values and a set of operations. An object module is more general than an ADT, however, because an object module (1) allows for a current extent, (2) allows us to specify explicit constraints for both data and behavior, (3) does not require uniform service availability, (4) provides implicit query operations over exported subapplication models, (5) provides read-only protection for exported subapplication models, (6) provides for views derived from an underlying application model, and (7) provides for inheritance.

- What are the similarities and differences among classes, types, variables, and values?

Classes, types, variables, and values all can be thought of as object modules with certain restrictions. Restrictions for classes vary— classes may or may not allow an extent, and they may have varying degrees of implicit and explicit control over the operations, which are usually exported only uniformly. Types are restricted object modules that define a set of potential values and a set of operations for values of the type. Variables are highly restricted object modules that hold only one value or one set of values and have operations that only allow value retrieval and update. Constants are even more restricted than variables because there can be no updates.

- What are the similarities and differences between types in programming languages and generalization/specialization?

A generalization can be considered to be a type for a specialization. A generalization's set of potential values is the type's potential set of values, and a generalization's immediate and inherited computed relationships and state-net interactions are the type's operations. Variables are declared by making them specializations of some object set, which can be thought of as the variable's type because the value for the variable must come from the type's potential value set and any operation must come from the type's operations. Some generalization/specialization patterns transform nicely into enumerated types; others inherit from built-in types either directly or indirectly.

- How can we transform state nets into ADTs?

We can transform many state nets into zero-state or single-state state nets. We can then transform such state nets into ADTs by considering the nonempty triggers for the transitions as the events or conditions that invoke services for the ADT. These services are the set of ADT operations; the object or set of objects in the state net constitute the set of objects for the ADT.

- What are various ways to manage the concurrency found in state nets?

We can transform some state nets into ADTs with a single thread of control, either with or without a queue of requests. For other state nets, we utilize the underlying transaction processing and distributed processing provided by the database system.

- What are some reasons for limiting visibility and providing views?

Views provide several advantages. We can use them to provide finer control over the data and services. Some data can be read-only, rather than both readable and writable, and we can protect data and services from unauthorized use by allowing access only to authorized programs and users. We can also use views to provide a tailor-made collection of data and services for specific programs and users. In creating these tailor-made views, we may encounter the view-update problem, for which the system cannot disambiguate an update request automatically. For these updates, the developer must intervene in advance and provide a specific service to handle these requests.

- How does inheritance simplify the specification of efficient specializations?

When a specialization object module inherits from a generalization object module, the specialization immediately has all the data specifications and operator specifications of the generalization object module. Then, we can add more data and operator specifications and sometimes provide more efficient specifications for specialization operations.

- In what sense are the transformations in this chapter patterns for design?

The transformations provided here are design patterns. When we see relationship sets that can be computed, we can transform them into computed relations. When we see generalization/specialization patterns that are partitions of objects or partitions of lone object sets, we can transform them into enumerated types. When we see patterns for common data structures, we can reconstitute them as common data structures. When we see state nets in particular patterns, we can transform them into state nets that convert easily into ADTs. And when we see *isa* hierarchies that are in separate object modules, we can use inheritance.

Checklist for Object-Module Design

- ☐ Identify computed relationship sets and convert to virtual implementations or to interactions, where appropriate.

- ☐ Identify special value sets and convert to enumeration types and grammar-based set types.

- ☐ Identify common data structure patterns and convert to common data structures.

- ☐ Convert state nets to ADT patterns.

- ☐ Adjust for concurrency options.

- ☐ Eliminate concurrency when there is no gain for the application.

- ☐ Use queued concurrent requests where appropriate

- ☐ Introduce transactions where appropriate.

- ☐ Maximize (or at least increase) concurrency where appropriate.

☐ Create object modules.

- ☐ Use synthesized schemes as data schemes for passive object modules.

- ☐ Use object sets with active behavior plus auxiliary object and relationship sets generated in state-net conversions as the data schemes for active object modules.

- ☐ Hide scheme information that should not be exported, such as auxiliary object and relationship sets.

- ☐ Export default data update and query operations for passive object sets by placing ORM components in public or read-only sections of object modules.

- ☐ Export signatures for ADT services and computed relationship sets.

- ☐ Hide detailed implementation specifications for exported services and computed relationship sets.

☐ Add views.

- ☐ Create views for application user groups.

- ☐ Analyze view updates and resolve ambiguities.

- ☐ Add authorization constraints as needed.

☐ Add inheritance connections among object modules in *isa* hierarchies.

☐ Where appropriate, provide more efficient implementation specifications for operations on specialized objects.

11.10 Bibliographic Notes

A quick overview of object-oriented concepts such as classes, types, encapsulation, methods, and inheritance as they apply to object-oriented databases is provided by object-oriented database management system manifesto [Atkinson89]. A similar manifesto exists for active database concepts [Dittrich95]. A more in-depth coverage appears in collections of papers about object-oriented database concepts [Bancilhon92, Bukhres96 Gupta91, Nahouraii91, Zdonik90], and books about object-oriented database systems [Bertino93, Cattell91, Chorafas93, Kemper94, Kim90].

The transformation patterns for enumeration types and value-set types presented here are similar to the schema transformations presented in [Halpin95b]. Data structures have a long history (see, for example, [Aho95]; their manifestation as patterns in OSM is new here. State net patterns and transformations are also new here; their transformations result in familiar ADT patterns [Liskov74] that can be used in transaction processing systems. For more on transaction processing and concurrency control in database systems, see [Date95 Elmasri94, Hansen92, Helman94, Korth97, O'Neil94, Ullman82]; for more detailed coverage, see [Bernstein93]. Views and view updates are also discussed in most books on database systems (see [Korth97], for example). Inheritance is a subject of continuing controversy. Should it be a strict modeling on an *isa* hierarchy, or should it also be a convenient means for redefinition with subtraction and arbitrary redefinition? Many articles on inheritance have been written, a number of which are summarized in [Taivalsaari96].

11.11 Exercises

11.1* Produce an ORM diagram that gives the relationships among object modules, ADTs, types, variables, and constants as described in Section 11.1. The diagram should have an object set for each of these concepts, plus object sets for the main features of interest, including names, constraints, data descriptions (for both possible elements and the current extent), services (for both those that are uniformly available and those that are nonuniformly available). Connect these object sets with appropriate relationship sets and generalization/specialization declarations. Finally, add general constraints that make ADTs, types, variables, and constants special types of object modules.

11.2 Consider an ORM diagram with three object sets—*Employee*, *Emp#*, and *Name*. Let *Employee* and *Emp#* be in a one-to-one correspondence and assume that we lexicalize *Employee* by *Emp#*, yielding *Emp#* (*of Employee*). Assume that the FD *Emp#* → *Name* holds but that the FD *Name* → *Emp#* does not hold in a relationship set called *Emp#* (*of Employee*) *identifies Name*.

   a. If we allow two identical *Emp#*'s to be associated with different *Name*'s in an interpretation for the *Emp#* (*of Employee*) *identifies Name* relation, we violate the integrity of an implicit *Employee* object. Explain why. Also explain what can be done to prevent this violation of object integrity.

   b. On the other hand, we may allow two identical *Name*'s to be associated with different *Emp#*'s in an interpretation for *Emp#* (*of Employee*) *identifies Name* without violating object integrity. Explain why.

11.3 If we arbitrarily place a thread for an object in a state of a state net independent of the semantics of the state net, we violate object integrity. List some other ways to violate object integrity for state nets.

11.4 If we access an object only through its interactions, explain why it is not possible to violate object integrity for state nets. (Assume, of course, that the system executes the semantics of state nets faithfully.)

11.5 Suppose that we have three object sets *A*, *B*, and *C* and a relationship set *ABC*, with one *BC* value-pair for each *A* value. Suppose further that we are somehow able to hide *B* and *C* and the relationship set inside *A* and make them unavailable except through interactions. Now suppose that the only interactions we supply are: *getBC*(*a*) → (*b*, *c*) to read a *BC* pair for a given *A* value *a* and *setBC*(*a*, *b*, *c*) to insert a *BC* pair for a given *A* value *a*.

   a. What difficulties do we have in trying to write the relational-algebra query $\pi_C \sigma_{B=1} ABC$ in terms of the interactions?

   b. What requirements would we have to impose on the interactions that operate on hidden object and relationship sets to make these object and relationship sets available for relational-algebra query processing?

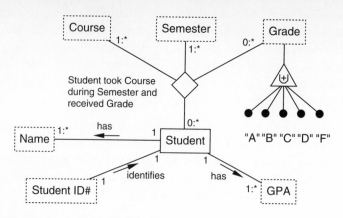

Figure 11.38   Student ORM.

c. What is the difference between imposing such requirements and exposing the structure of these hidden object and relationship sets with the understanding that the exposed structure implicitly provides the operations needed?

11.6   Consider the ORM diagram in Fig. 11.38. We can compute a student's GPA from the student's *Student took Course during Semester and received Grade* relationship set. Discuss the relative advantages and disadvantages of implementing the *Student has GPA* in each of the following ways. In your discussion assume that the main operation is to update student records when a semester ends. Assume also that there are some secondary operations that are executed less than 10% of the time. These secondary operations are for printing reports such as semester grade reports, student transcripts, reports on students whose GPA is below a given GPA value, reports on students whose GPA is above a given GPA value, and occasional ad hoc reports on grades.

   a. A relation of *Student-GPA* pairs.

   b. A virtual implementation that is faithful to the ORM diagram.

   c. An interaction that returns a GPA given a *Student ID#*.

   d. An interaction that returns a GPA given a *Student ID#*, plus an interaction that returns a set of *Student ID#*'s greater than some given GPA and an interaction that returns a set of *Student ID#*'s less than some given GPA.

11.7* Suppose that *Law Student* and *MBA Student* are two specializations of *Student* in Fig. 11.38. Suppose further that the GPA's for MBA students and for law students are computed differently from each other and differently from GPA's for other regular students. Now suppose that we decide to implement the *Student has GPA* relation as an interaction that returns a GPA given a *Student ID#*.

    a. Give arguments for and against implementing this by letting *Law Student* and *MBA Student* inherit the GPA interaction from *Student* and override the GPA implementation with the alternative implementations of GPA for *Law Student* and *MBA Student*.

    b. Give at least two alternative ways to model this situation.

    c. Among the alternatives, which is likely to be the easiest to implement? Why?

    d. Which of the alternatives is/are faithful to the semantics of the generalization/specialization hierarchy?

    e. Choose one of the alternatives and argue that it is the best choice.

11.8 Consider the ORM hypergraph in Fig. 11.39. Given the current date, hourly pay rate, and the start and stop times for the days of the previous week, we can compute the weekly pay. Assuming that the tax is a fixed percentage of the weekly pay, we can also compute the tax.

    a. Assume that we wish to store the data in a table implementation. Give the schemes that would be produced by Algorithm 10.1. (Make up reasonable names for each scheme.)

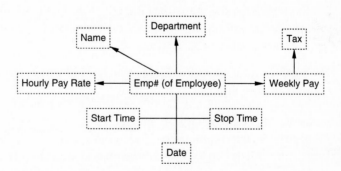

Figure 11.39 ORM hypergraph for employees.

b. For the table implementation in (a), give an example for each pair of schemes to show that combining any pair (with $\bowtie$) results in a scheme with potential redundancy.

c. Assume that we wish to have a virtual implementation for computing weekly pay and tax. Which schemes can we now combine without having potential redundancy? Why?

d.* Again assume that we wish to store the data in a table implementation, and consider the nested scheme *Employee (Department (Emp#, Name, Hourly Pay Rate, Weekly Pay, Tax (Date, Start Time, Stop Time)*)*)*. Give an example to show that this scheme has potential redundancy.

e.* Now, assume again that we wish to have a virtual implementation for computing weekly pay and tax. Explain why the scheme now has no potential redundancy.

f.* Give a rule for deciding which methods should be placed in which schemes.

11.9 For the ORM diagram in Fig. 11.38, change *Grade* from a generalization of five grades to a specialization of an enumeration of five grades.

11.10 Consider the transformation from the ORM diagram in Fig. 11.40a to the ORM diagram in Fig. 11.40b.

a. Explain why the transformation in Fig. 11.40 preserves information by giving a procedure to compute the three relationship sets in Fig. 11.40a from the information in Fig. 11.40b.

b.* Explain why the transformation in Fig. 11.40 preserves constraints by explaining how the constraints in Fig. 11.40b imply the constraints in Fig. 11.40a.

c. Transform the partitioned category specialization in Fig. 11.40b into an enumeration.

11.11 Consider the ORM diagram in Fig. 11.41. Assume that *String, Character, Integer, Date,* and *OID* (object identifier) are built-in types. Provide types for each of the object sets in Fig. 11.41. Make use of generalization/specialization to give types as specific as possible.

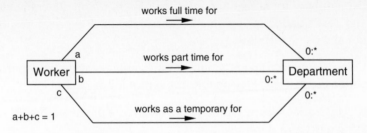

(a) ORM diagram with three relationship sets.

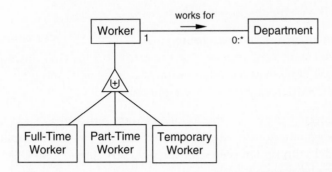

(b) Transformed ORM diagram with three specializations.

Figure 11.40   Transformation from relationship sets to specializations.

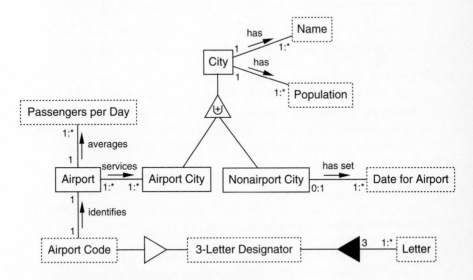

Figure 11.41   Airport application model.

11.12* Explain how to use sequenced aggregation, union generalization, and participation constraints to describe regular expressions notationally using ORM diagrams.

11.13* Using sequenced aggregation, union generalization, and participation constraints, give an ORM diagram for the following:

    a. U.S. social security numbers, which have the form $d^3 - d^2 - d^4$, where d is a digit.

    b. Participation constraints limited by excluding variables.

    c. The regular expression $a * b(c \mid d) *$.

11.14* Data structure patterns are templates. Give an OSM application model with no templates for the array in Fig. 11.7. Include full details of all required relationship sets, state nets, and interactions. Use OSM-L for low-level coding details.

11.15* Create templates for the following data structures. Give both a generic notation for the data structure and an OSM application model with no templates for the data structures. Use OSM-L for low-level coding details.

    a. A queue with the operations create, add element, and remove element.

    b. A matrix with the operations create, transpose, and multiply.

    c. A binary search tree with the operations create, add element, find element, and output elements in ascending order.

11.16 Convert the state-net pattern in Fig. 11.42 into a zero-state state net. The zero-state state net should have a single high-level transition for each interaction and no states outside of high-level transitions. Within each high-level transition, the details of the actions should be provided similar to the details inside the high-level transition in Fig. 4.25.

11.17 Convert the *Inventory Controller* state net in Fig. 4.17 into a single-state state net. Use the standard transformation with OSM-L statements like the transformation in Fig. 11.15.

11.18* Convert the *Inventory Controller* state net in Fig. 4.18 into a single-state state net. Use the transformation with OSM-L statements similar to the transformations in Figs. 11.20 and 11.21.

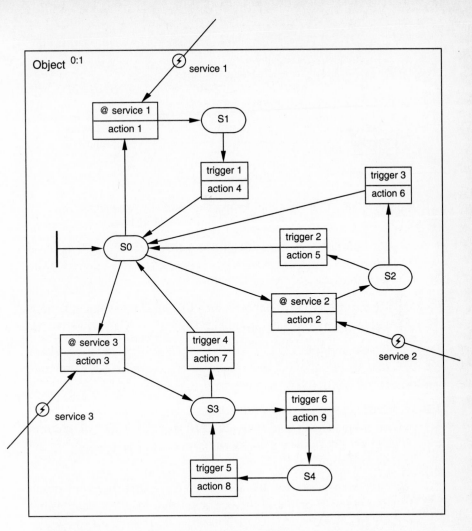

Figure 11.42   Generic state net for conversion to zero-state state net.

11.19* Consider the ORM diagrams in Fig. 11.43. The high-level relationship set *is working with* in Fig. 11.43b is computed by the join over
supplies, is in, and *manages* in Fig. 11.43a. Assume that a valid
interpretation *I* for the ORM diagram in Fig. 11.43a exists such
that the tuple <*Manager*: M_1, *Supplier*: S_1> is in the view for *is
working with.* Now, suppose we issue the command *delete*
<*Manager*: M_1, *Supplier*: S_1>.

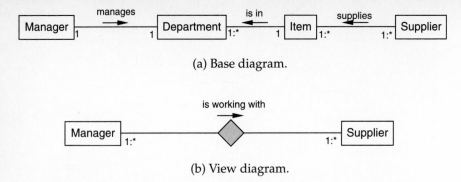

(a) Base diagram.

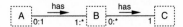

(b) View diagram.

Figure 11.43   ORM diagram for manager/supplier view exercise.

a. List all the single-tuple deletions from relations in I that could cause the tuple <*Manager*: M_1, *Supplier*: S_1> to be deleted from the view.

b. Give a valid interpretation I such that all single-tuple deletions fail to satisfy the diagram in Fig. 11.25.

c. Give a condition under which it is possible to find a translator that would allow *delete* <*Manager*: M_1, *Supplier*: S_1> to operate successfully.

11.20 Consider the ORM diagrams in Fig. 11.44, in which the ORM diagram in Fig. 11.44b is a view obtained from the ORM diagram in Fig. 11.44a by omitting object set C and the *has* relationship set between B and C.

a. Give translators for the two operations that insert an object into either A or B and the operation that inserts a relationship set into A *has* B.

(a) Base diagram for view updates.

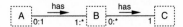

(b) View diagram for view updates.

Figure 11.44   ORM diagram for view-update exercise.

    b. Give translators for the two operations that delete an object from either *A* or *B* and the operation that deletes a relationship from *A has B*.

    c. What problems arise for deletion that do not arise for insertion?

11.21 Discuss the following three ways of implementing the generalization/specialization hierarchy in Fig. 11.41. Mention advantages and disadvantages of each way.

    a. Implement *City*, *Airport City*, and *Nonairport City* as object modules and let *Airport City* and *Nonairport City* inherit from *City*.

    b. Implement *City* as a record type and let *Airport City* and *Nonairport City* be of type *City*.

    c. Revise the ORM diagram by relating both *Name* and *Population* directly to both *Airport City* and *Nonairport City*. Then, discard *City* and implement *Airport City* and *Nonairport City* as records that include both *Name* and *Population* fields.

11.22* Create object modules for a generalization/specialization hierarchy of triangles. Let *Right Triangle* inherit from *Triangle* and let *Equilateral Triangle* inherit from *Isosceles Triangle*, which in turn inherits from *Triangle*. Provide an OSM-L implementation for the triangle hierarchy. Include in your implementation operations for creating a triangle and for computing the perimeter and area of a triangle. For creating a triangle, assume that the information provided describes a triangle properly (i.e., do not write code to do error checking). Make sure that the implementation of the triangle hierarchy is hidden. Utilize overriding to provide more efficient operations for computing perimeters and areas where this is possible.

11.23 Add full operational specifications to compute the following for the *Regular Polygon* hierarchy in Fig. 11.30. Hide operation specifications, and provide more efficient operation specifications for inheriting object modules where appropriate.

    a. Find the inside angle in degrees for a regular polygon.

    b. Find the radius of the inscribed circle for a regular polygon.

    c. Find the radius of the circumscribed circle for a regular polygon.

11.24* If an object module M inherits from two or more object modules, we have *multiple inheritance.*

    a. Assume strict inheritance as discussed for OSM. Give a way to define the data, constraint, and operator specifications for M.

    b. What problems might arise in these specifications? What role can congruency play in resolving these problems? Suggest a resolution to these problems.

The remaining exercises in this chapter explore some of the theoretical properties of state nets and state-net transformations. These exercises are only a beginning; by no means do they explore all of the properties. They do not, for example, include possible work on deadlock detection, unreachable states, maximizing parallelism, behavior generalization/specialization, and many other topics. Except for one result on computational completeness, they all address the reduction of state nets to standard forms for implementation.

11.25* Show how to use a state net along with object and relationship sets to simulate a Turing Machine and thus show that OSM is computationally complete.

11.26** A *timeline* is an ordered sequence of time instances such that the time between consecutive time instances is constant. A *timeline of events and conditions* is a timeline with zero or more time instances associated with one or more events and zero or more time intervals associated with one or more conditions whose value is true over the time interval.

Consider a transition for a given state net before it is transformed by any of the state-net transformations, which we catalog in this exercise. For our purposes here, we call the action of a transition before it is transformed a *pretransformation action*. We do not allow our transformations to alter pretransformation actions, but we do allow pretransformation actions to be embedded in surrounding code that does not affect pretransformation actions (i.e., the surrounding code may alter only local variables introduced in the transformation.) An *action execution diagram* for an object x for a state net is a partial ordering of successful pretransformation action executions determined by the execution order or the threads of x (i.e., if a thread t of x successfully executes a pretransformation action a as its ith action execution instance t_i and

t later successfully executes a pretransformation action b as its jth action execution instance t_j, then (t_i, t_j) is an element of the partial ordering, as are also the trivial reflexive elements (t_i, t_i) and (t_j, t_j)).

Let S be a state net for object set X and S' be a transformed state net for X. Let T be a timeline of events and conditions. Let O_S be the objects of X being executed by S for at least one instance of time within T and let $O_{S'}$ be the objects of X being executed by S' for at least one instance of time within T. State nets S and S' are *semantically equivalent* if for every timeline of events and conditions T, there exists a one-to-one correspondence between objects of O_S and $O_{S'}$ such that each corresponding pair of objects has an identical action execution digraph.

a. Show that the state nets in Figs. 11.15a and 11.15b are semantically equivalent.

b. Show that the state nets in Figs. 11.20a and 11.20b are semantically equivalent.

11.27 A high-level state is a *behavior-inducing* high-level state if it is a member of either a prior- or a subsequent-state conjunction; otherwise it is a *nonbehavior-inducing* high-level state. A high-level transition is a *behavior-inducing* high-level transition if a prior-state conjunction enables it or a subsequent-state conjunction follows it; otherwise it is a *nonbehavior-including* high-level transition.

a. Classify the high-level states and transitions in Figs. 4.22a, 4.23, 4.24, and 4.25 as behavior-inducing or nonbehavior-inducing.

b. Give an informal argument that explains why we can remove nonbehavior-inducing high-level states and transitions without altering the semantics of a state net.

11.28 Give an informal argument that explains why we can remove the exception designator for every state exception. Also, give an informal argument that explains why we cannot remove the exception designator for any transition exception.

11.29** A state net S is *deterministic* if S has no subsequent state conjunction with more than one state and S has no prior state p that is not turned off when firing is based on p; otherwise S is *nondeterministic*.

Prove the following theorem.

Theorem 11.1

Let S be a state net with at least one state for an object set X, and assume that S is deterministic and has no transition exceptions and no behavior-inducing high-level states or transitions. Then there exists single-state state net S' for X, such that S and S' are semantically equivalent.

11.30** Prove the following theorem. (Observe that Theorem 11.2 implies Theorem 11.1. The only difference is that state nets for Theorem 11.2 need not be deterministic. Theorem 11.1 is an important special case, and deserves separate treatment, as given here.)

Theorem 11.2

Let S be a state net with at least one state for an object set X, and assume that S has no transition exceptions and no behavior-inducing high-level states or transitions. Then there exists single-state state net S' for X, such that S and S' are semantically equivalent.

11.31* Explain how to reduce a state net S that includes a high-level transition T with initial and final states to a state net S' that is semantically equivalent to S but does not include T as a high-level transition. Assume that there are no transition exceptions.

11.32** Prove the following lemma.

Lemma 11.1

If S is a state net that includes a high-level transition T with initial and final states and no transition exceptions, there exists a semantically equivalent state net S' that does not include T as a high-level transition.

11.33* Explain how to reduce a state net S that includes a high-level state H with one or more high-level exits to a state net S' that is semantically equivalent to S but does not include H as a high-level state.

11.34** Prove the following lemma.

> **Lemma 11.2**
>
> If S is a state net that includes a high-level state H with one or more high-level exits, there exists a semantically equivalent state net S' that does not include H as a high-level state.

11.35* Explain how to reduce a state net S that includes a high-level transition T with one or more exception exits to a state net S' that is semantically equivalent to S but does not include T as a high-level transition.

11.36** Prove the following lemma.

> **Lemma 11.3**
>
> If S is a state net that includes a high-level transition T with one or more exception exits, there exists a semantically equivalent state net S' that does not include T as a high-level transition.

11.37* Explain how to reduce a state net S that includes an exception E with multiple subsequent states to a state net S' that is semantically equivalent to S. In place of E, however, there is an exception E' with a single subsequent state.

11.38** Prove the following lemma.

> **Lemma 11.4**
>
> If S is a state net that includes one or more exceptions with multiple subsequent states, there exists a semantically equivalent state net S' with exceptions, but none of the exceptions has multiple subsequent states.

11.39* Prove the following lemma. (The purpose of this lemma is to show that we can introduce a "do nothing" transition, which is needed to provide a place for auxiliary code that sets the state information when an exception occurs.)

> **Lemma 11.5**
>
> If S is a state net that includes a transition exception with a single subsequent state Z, and S' is S with Z replaced by a new state Y followed by a transition T with an empty trigger and an empty action followed by Z, then S and S' are semantically equivalent.

11.40** Prove the following theorem.

Theorem 11.3

Let S be a state net with at least one state for an object set X, and assume that S has no behavior-inducing high-level states or transitions. If there are n exceptions, $n \geq 0$, and each of the exceptions has a single subsequent state, then there exists $(n+1)$-state state net S' for X, such that S and S' are semantically equivalent.

11.41* Let S be a state net transformed into an $(n+1)$-state state net, where n is the number of transition exceptions. Show how to construct an object module for S that has a service for each transition, except the n transitions that follow states for transition exceptions, and that also handles all n exceptions.

Chapter 12

Implementation

To implement a design is to translate it faithfully into software in some target environment. In this book, which concerns databases, our target is a particular database management system (DBMS), often an object-oriented DBMS (OODBMS). Our design should be (and for OSM is) free of target-environment dependencies, but our implementation depends on the chosen target DBMS. In this chapter we use the generic ODMG[†] C++ binding as the example target environment. In the chapters that follow, we present several case studies, choosing a variety of DBMSs for the target environment.

In order to translate our design faithfully into a target environment, we should generate all target-environment software components algorithmically. This ideal strategy preserves the application model as the true source of implementation and treats program code as simply another view of the application model. Any changes to the implementation should be made in the application model, not in the program code.

If satisfactory automatic translators do not exist for the application model or for particular target environments, we cannot use this ideal strategy. Nevertheless, if we have a complete and well-specified design view of our application model, we can use it to translate our application model into

---

Irreversible Transformations

Until now, there has been no problem in keeping our OSM documents consistent. This is because all documents have been views of the same OSM application model, and thus any change has been made for all documents. As we convert to a non-OSM implementation, however, we are making an irreversible transformation. We should therefore be sure that if we make semantic changes in the implementation code, these changes are reflected in the OSM application model.

[†] ODMG is an acronym for the Object Database Management Group. We describe the ODMG C++ binding in this chapter.

code systematically. We take this approach here and in our case studies in the following chapters.

In this chapter, we first describe ODMG and its C++ binding. We then present a direct and systematic way to translate of the OSM design for our running example at the end of Chapter 11 into ODMG C++, showing that the major components of OSM have a direct mapping to ODMG C++. For some OSM components, particularly data components, we provide a direct algorithmic translation, but we leave for further research and development the specification of a complete algorithmic translation.

Even if we had a complete translator, we would still need an optimizer, which requires even more research and development. In the meantime, we must rely on having developed an efficient design so that the results of our translation are reasonably efficient, and we must also rely on tuning the resulting code. In addition, ODMG C++ provides so-called *pragmas*, which are hints to the compiler about how to generate an efficient OODBMS from ODMG C++ code and which may be added to our ODMG C++ code. We discuss neither tuning nor pragmas here, instead concentrating on producing ODMG C++ code that represents our OSM design faithfully.

After finishing our ODMG example, we examine what we have done. We look back on analysis, specification, design, and implementation, and we summarize the entire development process in the form of an OSM development methodology. This methodology consists largely of the checklists presented in earlier chapters, plus the implementation checklist provided at the end of this chapter.

The following topics in this chapter are particularly important:

- ODMG ODL, OML, and OQL.[†]

- ODMG ODL abstraction diagrams.

- The ODMG C++ binding, including C++ ODL, OML, and OQL.

- Abstraction diagrams for ODMG C++ ODL.

- The OSM development methodology.

The following questions should also be kept in mind:

- How does ODMG integrate database features with object-oriented language features?

[†] ODL is an acronym for Object Definition Language; OML, for Object Manipulation Language; and OQL, for Object Query Language.

- How do we derive an ODMG ODL abstraction diagram from an ORM hypergraph?

- What differences are we likely to encounter between OSM-L types and implementation types?

- What are the similarities of and differences between SQL and ODMG OQL?

- How does ODMG C++ differ from standard C++?

- How do we derive C++ ODL from an ODMG ODL abstraction diagram?

- How do we derive C++ OML and OQL from an OSM-L specification?

12.1 ODMG

The Object Database Management Group (ODMG) is a group that sets standards for object databases. (See the bibliographic notes for information on the group's interesting history and way of operating.) The overall goal of the ODMG is to develop a de facto standard for object databases.

The ODMG standard integrates database features with object-oriented language features. Because the integration is transparent, there is no need to exchange data explicitly between database and language features. The query language and the programming language are one and the same, incorporating standard functionality for lists, arrays, bags, and other standard bulk types, as well as for sets. ODMG extends the database model by making objects appear like programming objects in one of several object-oriented programming languages, and it extends object-oriented programming languages with database features, including persistence, concurrency control, crash recovery, and query processing.

The ODMG standard includes an object model whose major components are an Object Definition Language (ODL) and an Object Manipulation Language (OML), which includes an Object Query Language (OQL). The object model serves as a common denominator for database systems, programming languages, and object request brokers (which provide standard operation-invocation services across multiple vendor platforms). For a particular language (e.g., C++ and Smalltalk), the object model has a binding that provides a manifestation of the object model in terms of the language. Thus, although there is a standard syntax for the generic object model, it is not a universal syntax that must be adopted by each language—instead, there is a manifestation of the object model for each language. This manifestation must be faithful to the object model, however, allowing the object model to provide a context for integrating schemes from different language bindings.

Figure 12.1 presents the basic idea of how the ODMG standard works with a particular language to produce an executable application. In the figure, we let *L+* denote the language; the "+" indicates that the base language

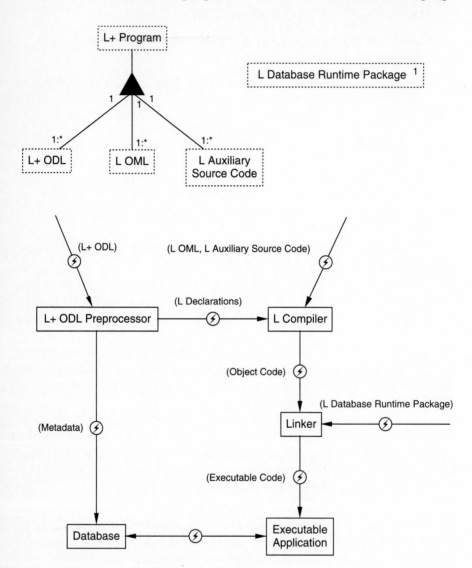

Figure 12.1　ODMG language binding.

has been extended to provide a manifestation of ODMG's object model. An *L+* program can be thought of as being composed of an ODL component, an OML component, and a component that provides auxiliary source code to enable the language binding. In an initial step, a preprocessor converts the ODL component of an *L+* program into metadata for the database and produces a corresponding set of *L* declarations. A standard *L* compiler then takes these *L* declarations, along with the *L* OML and auxiliary source code, and produces object code. The system then links this object code with a provided *L* database runtime package to produce executable code to interact with the database and run the application.

To show how ODMG works, we provide examples of ODMG's ODL and OQL and the binding for C++, using our on-line shopping application for illustration. We begin by giving the ODL interface for our application in Section 12.2. We then illustrate ODMG's OQL in Section 12.3 by giving a series of queries against the ODL developed in Section 12.2. In Section 12.4 we present the full C++ implementation for the order taker of our example, as provided in the design at the end of Chapter 11.

12.2   ODMG ODL

This section presents a systematic way to convert an OSM design into ODMG ODL, using as an example the OSM design developed at the end of Chapter 11. Although we cover much of what is needed for the general conversion, we develop only what is necessary for the example.

The main design component needed as the basis for the conversion to ODMG ODL is the flat scheme in Fig. 11.34, of which Fig. 12.2 is a slightly modified version. We have not included the *Order Taker*, which is not discussed until Section 12.4, and we have merged shipped backorders with backorders as discussed in Chapter 11. Also, to illustrate a point about roles, we have changed *Distributor Name* in *Item* to *Item Distributor* and *Distributor Name* in *Backorder* to *Backorder Distributor*. In addition to the flat-scheme design, we need some information from the design views in Figs. 11.31 and 11.33, but we refer directly to these figures when required.

Now that we have a specific design and a specific target implementation language, we can develop a systematic procedure for converting a design to an implementation. For ODMG ODL, we use a two-step procedure. First, we convert the flat schemes, along with some information in related ORM diagrams and hypergraphs, to what we call an ODMG ODL abstraction diagram. We then convert this abstraction diagram into ODMG ODL.

Customer(Customer ID: Positive Integer, Name: String, Address: String)
  key: Customer ID
Distributor(Distributor Name: String, Distributor Address: String)
  key: Distributor Name
  key: Distributor Address
Item(Item Nr: String, Make: String, Model Nr: String, Item
  Item Distributor: String, Amt This Month: Nonnegative Integer,
    Nr In Back Room: Nonnegative Integer
    Price: US$, Description: String)
  key: Item Nr
  key: Make, Model Nr
  Distributor[Distributor Name] ⊇ Item[Distributor Name]
Order(Order Nr: Positive Integer, Date Received: Date, Customer ID:
    Positive Integer)
  key: Order Nr
  Customer[Customer ID] ⊇ Order[Customer ID]
Ordered Item(Order Nr: Positive Integer, Item Nr: String,
  Number: Positive Integer, Unit Price: US$)
  key: Order Nr, Item Nr
  Item[Item Nr] ⊇ Ordered Item[Item Nr]
  Order[Order Nr] ⊇ Ordered Item[Order Nr]
Backorder(Backorder Nr: Positive Integer, Customer ID: Positive Integer,
    Date Backordered: Date, Item Nr: String, Number: Positive Integer,
    Unit Price: US$, Backorder Distributor: String, Date Shipped: Date)
  key: Backorder Nr
  may be null: Date Shipped -- if null, then not yet shipped
  Customer[Customer ID] ⊇ Backorder[Customer ID]
  Item[Item Nr] ⊇ Backorder[Item Nr]
  Distributor[Distributor Name] ⊇ Backorder[Backorder Distributor]

Figure 12.2 Adjusted flat schemes.

An *ODMG ODL abstraction diagram* is a flat database scheme with named connections among the schemes. These connections are a combination of regular ORM edges and ORM hypergraph edges. They are like ORM edges because they have names and reading-direction arrows, and they are like hypergraph edges because they can be (and usually are) directed. Figure 12.3 shows the ODMG ODL abstraction diagram for our example. Both the schemes and the edges have some minor notational vari-

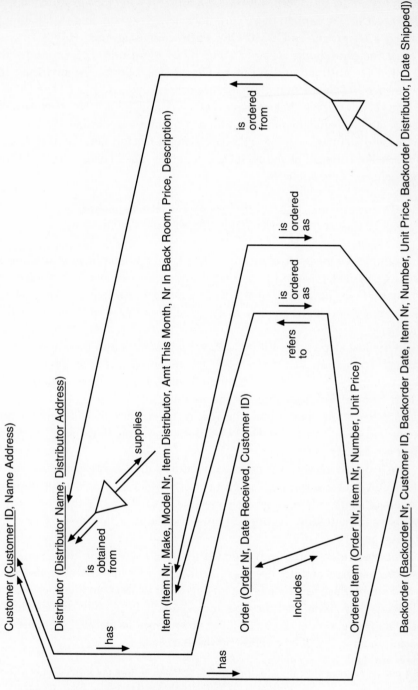

Figure 12.3 View for ODMG ODL implementation.

ations that allow us to record the information we need for our conversion to ODMG ODL. We explain these variations as we explain, in general, how to convert a design into an ODMG ODL abstraction diagram.

For the flat-scheme design in Fig. 12.2, Algorithm 12.1 produces the ODMG ODL abstraction diagram in Fig. 12.3 as follows. We first copy the schemes to the abstraction diagram, underline keys, and place *Date Shipped* in brackets. Observe that {*Make, Model Nr*} and {*Order Nr, Item Nr*} are composite keys and therefore require a continuous underline. Since every inclusion dependency in Fig. 12.2 designates a foreign key, we next draw a (hyper)edge for each of the inclusion dependencies. For the first and second inclusion dependencies,

$$Distributor[Distributor\ Name] \supseteq Item[Item\ Distributor]$$
$$Customer[Customer\ ID] \supseteq Order[Customer\ ID]$$

for example, we respectively draw a directed edge from *Item Distributor* in *Item* to *Distributor Name* in *Distributor* and from *Customer ID* in *Order* to *Customer ID* in *Customer*. Since *Item Distributor* is a role name for *Distributor Name*, we add an *isa* triangle to the edge from *Item Distributor* to *Distributor Name*.

In the last step of Algorithm 12.1, we add names and reading-direction arrows. The names *has*, *is obtained from*, and *is ordered from* come directly from the application ORM. The name *includes* from *Ordered Item* to *Order* comes from a decomposition of the relationship-set name *Order includes Number of Item at Unit Price*. The rest of the names that are not default names are based on the developer's understanding (with help from the client as needed).

We are now ready to convert an ODMG ODL abstraction diagram to ODMG ODL. We introduce the syntax of ODMG ODL[†] as we develop this conversion, but only enough to show the main ideas of the conversion, which we present here. Figure 12.4 gives the result, which we refer to in the discussion.

The basic idea in the conversion is that each scheme in the abstraction diagram becomes an interface (as it is called in ODMG). We may also wish to add an interface for some of the *isa* edges. In ODMG, an interface has the following BNF. Note that the BNF metasymbols {, }, [, and] appear in the ODMG syntax; we denote their literal appearance in the ODMG syntax by placing them in double quotation marks (e.g., "{").

[†] For our development, we use a restricted ODL syntax that does not include all of ODMG ODL and does not develop many of the nonterminals fully. The complete syntax can be found in the ODMG literature referenced in the bibliographic notes.

Algorithm 12.1

Input: An OSM flat-scheme design augmented with information from the application ORM and ORM hypergraph.

Output: An ODMG ODL abstraction diagram.

1. List the flat schemes.

   -- They each have the form $R(A_1, ..., A_n)$,
   -- where R is the scheme name and the A_i's are attributes.

2. Underline the keys.

   -- Use continuous underlines for composite keys.

   -- Connect any nonadjacent key components with arcs.

3. Place each attribute that may be null in brackets.

4. For each inclusion dependency $R[X] \supseteq S[Y]$ that designates a foreign key:

   -- An inclusion dependency designates a foreign key if X is a key
   -- for R.

   -- Ignore any inclusion dependency where X is not a key for R.

   4.1. Draw a directed (hyper)edge from Y to X.
   For any role names, add an *isa* triangle to the edge.

   -- There is a role name if the attribute names differ.

   4.2. Add a name and reading-direction arrow for each edge in both directions

   -- These may be added in different ways:

   -- Take names and reading-direction arrows from the
   -- ORM diagram;

   -- Decompose ORM-diagram names into a name and
   -- reading-direction arrow;

   -- If desired, make up new names for remaining missing
   -- names;

   -- Use *is_for* as a default name, which need not be written.

   -- If there is more than one name, discard all but one.

> *interface_decl* ::= **interface** *identifier* [*inheritance_decl*]
>   ([**extent** *identifier*] [**key[s]** *key_list*])
>   [: **persistent** | **transient**]
>   "{" [*interface_body*] "}";
> *interface_body* ::= { *type_decl*; | *constant_decl* | *exception_decl*
> | *attribute_decl* | *relationship_decl* | *operation_decl* } ...

Consider the *Customer* scheme in Fig. 12.3, which becomes the *Customer* interface in Fig. 12.4. The name of the scheme becomes the name for the interface. Since we have used singular names consistently for object-set and scheme names, we use the plural of the name for the **extent** clause in an interface. Each underlined key becomes a key in the **key** clause. Since we wish to make each of the interfaces part of our database scheme, we add the **persistent** key word as is required for persistence for an ODMG interface. The alternative choice—making the interface **transient**— excludes the interface from the database scheme and thus makes any data stored in the interface unavailable after execution of a program that stores the data in the interface.

interface *Customer* (
  extent *Customers*
  key *CustomerID*) : **persistent**
{
  attribute Unsigned Long *CustomerID*;
  attribute String *Name*;
  attribute String *Address*;
  relationship Set<*Order*> *has_Order*
    inverse *Order*::*is_for_Customer*;
  relationship Set<*Backorder*> *has_Backorder*
    inverse *Backorder*::*is_for_Customer*;
};

interface *Distributor* (
  extent *Distributors*
  keys *DistributorName, DistributorAddress*) : **persistent**
{
  attribute String *DistributorName*;
  attribute String *DistributorAddress*;
  relationship Set<*Item*> *supplies_Item*

Figure 12.4   ODMG ODL interface schemes.

    inverse *Item*: : *is_obtained_from_Distributor;*
};
interface *BackorderDistributor* : *Distributor* (
 extent *BackorderDistributors*) : **persistent**
{
 relationship Set<*Backorder*> *is_for_Backorder*
   inverse *Backorder*: : *is_ordered_from_BackorderDistributor;*
};

interface *Item* (
 extent *Items*
 keys *ItemNr*, *(Make, ModelNr))* : **persistent**
{
 attribute String *ItemNr;*
 relationship Set<*OrderedItem*> *is_ordered_as_OrderedItem*
   inverse *OrderedItem*: : *refers_to_Item;*
 relationship Set<*Backorder*> *is_ordered_as_Backorder*
   inverse *Backorder*: : *is_for_Item;*
 attribute String *Make;*
 attribute String *ModelNr;*
 relationship *Distributor is_obtained_from_Distributor*
   inverse *Distributor*: : *supplies_Item;*
 attribute Unsigned Short *AmtThisMonth;*
 attribute Unsigned Short *NrInBackRoom;*
 attribute Unsigned Short *Price;*
 attribute String *Description;*
};

interface *Order* (
 extent *Orders*
 key *OrderNr*) : **persistent**
{
 attribute Unsigned Long *OrderNr;*
 relationship Set<*OrderedItem*> *includes_OrderedItem*
   inverse *OrderedItem*: : *is_for_Order;*
 attribute Date *DateReceived;*
 relationship *Customer is_for_Customer*
   inverse *Customer*: : *has_Order;*
 void *order_request*(**in Unsigned Long** *CustomerID*)
   raises(*NoID, InvalidID*);
};

Figure 12.4 (cont.)   ODMG ODL interface schemes.

```
interface OrderedItem (
  extent OrderedItems
  key (is_for_Order, refers_to_Item)) : persistent
{
  relationship Order is_for_Order
    inverse Order::includes_OrderedItem;
  relationship Item refers_to_Item
    inverse Item::is_ordered_as_OrderedItem;
  attribute Unsigned Short Number;
  attribute Unsigned Short UnitPrice;
  void request_item(in String ItemNr, Unsigned Short Number);
};


interface Backorder (
  extent Backorders
  key BackorderNr) : persistent
{
  attribute Unsigned Long BackorderNr;
  relationship Customer is_for_Customer
    inverse Customer::has_Backorder;
  attribute Date DateBackordered;
  relationship Item is_for_Backorder
    inverse Item::is_ordered_as_Backorder;
  attribute Unsigned Short Number;
  attribute Unsigned Short UnitPrice;
  relationship BackorderDistributor
    is_ordered_from_BackorderDistributor
      inverse BackorderDistributor::is_for_Backorder;
  attribute Date DateShipped;
  void item_arrives(in Unsigned Long BackorderNr)
    raises(InvalidBackorderNr);
};
```

Figure 12.4 (cont.) ODMG ODL interface schemes.

ODMG names do not allow internal spaces. As a convention for the notation we have been using consistently throughout our examples, we choose to elide spaces in object-set names and replace spaces with underscores in relationship-set names.

ODMG ODL interfaces can come from roles as well as schemes. To show how roles can become interfaces, we show how to convert the *Backorder Distributor* to an interface. The main difference is that a role becomes what ODMG calls a subtype (a specialization in OSM vernacular) that inherits from a supertype (an OSM generalization). Thus we add an inheritance clause—: *Distributor*, as the *Backorder Distributor* interface in Fig. 12.4 shows—and omit unnecessary information inherited from the supertype, such as key information in this example. When we add a role explicitly, we also add an **extent** clause to keep a separate set for the role objects. In exchange for this overhead, we explicitly have the role name and the ability to have relationships with the role. If this trade-off is not acceptable, we need not generate an interface for a role. In Fig. 12.4, for example, we have not made an interface for *Item Distributor*.

ODMG ODL attribute and relationship declarations have the following BNF:

> *attribute_decl* ::= [**readonly**] **attribute** *domain_type*
> *identifier* ["[" *positive_int_constant*
> *domain_type* ::= *simple_type* | *struct_type* | *enum_type*
> | *collection_specifier literal*
> | *collection_specifier identifier*
> *collection_specifier* ::= **Set** | **List** | **Bag** | **Array**
>
> *relationship_decl* ::= **relationship** *target_traversal_path identifier*
> [**inverse** *inverse_traversal_path*]
> ["{" **order_by** *attribute_list* "}"]
> *target_traversal_path* ::= *identifier collection_specifier* < *identifier* >
> *inverse_traversal_path* ::= *identifier* :: *identifier*

Except for attributes on the tail side of a (hyper)edge in the ODMG ODL abstraction diagram, we convert attributes in a design scheme directly to attributes in an interface. Tail-side attributes become relationships, which we discuss after discussing attributes. In doing the conversion for attributes, we must add types. We obtain the types in one of four ways: (1) copy them directly from the design, (2) choose the ODMG type that is closest to the type specified in the design, (3) select an available ODMG type when one is not specified, or (4) use **String** as the default. In our example we convert types as follows:

OSM Type	ODMG ODL Type
Nonnegative Integer	**Unsigned Short** (if $\leq 2^{16}$ expected)
Nonnegative Integer	**Unsigned Long** (if $> 2^{16}$ expected)
Positive Integer	**Unsigned Short** (if $\leq 2^{16}$ expected)
Positive Integer	**Unsigned Long** (if $> 2^{16}$ expected)
US\$	**Unsigned Short**
(none) *String* intended	**String**
(none) *String* not intended	(appropriate type)

Where there is no type specified, but the type should not be **String**, the type in the design has simply not yet been specified. *Number*, for example, should not be a string, but should be a positive integer, and *Unit Price* should be a dollar amount. We should reflect these changes, of course, in the OSM application model.

We convert tail-side attributes in a design scheme into relationships. We also add relationships for every head side. For ordinary functional edges in our example, a tail-side relationship declaration consists of a reference to the target scheme with the tail-to-head relationship-set name followed by the inverse part, which also gives the target scheme, but with the head-to-tail relationship-set name. A head-side relationship declaration for an ordinary functional edge is much the same except that it specifies a **Set** collection, because the head side is the one-side of a one-many relationship.

For example, consider the *Order* interface in Fig. 12.4. The relationship declaration

relationship *Customer is_for_Customer*
inverse *Customer*:: *has_Order*

represents the tail side of the functional edge pointing to *Customer ID* from the *Order* scheme. The target of the traversal path is *Customer*. For relationship names we append the scheme name of the head-side scheme. This has two purposes: (1) it (usually) makes the relationship-set names unique—if not, we need to change the name so that it is unique—and (2) when taken out of its declaration context, the scheme name makes the relationship name meaningful by itself. Thus the names are the default name *is_for_Customer* for the to-target traversal path and *has_Order* for the inverse traversal path. Notice also that there is no attribute in the *Order* interface in Fig. 12.4 for *Customer ID* because *Order* is on the tail side for this relationship. The other relationship declaration for *order* in Fig. 12.4

> **relationship Set**<*OrderedItem*> *includes_OrderedItem*
> **inverse** *OrderedItem*: : *is_for_Order*

represents the head side of the functional edge from *Ordered Item*. Here **Set**<*OrderedItem*> specifies that there can be several ordered items for an order. Notice that Fig. 12.3 includes an attribute declaration for *Order Nr* as well as the relationship declaration for the *includes* relationship set. This is because *Order* is the head side.

The placement of relationships is a little different for roles when we represent roles explicitly by subtypes. There is no relationship for the edge that connects the *Backorder* and *Distributor* schemes in the *Distributor* interface. Instead, the relationship is in the role interface, that is, in the *BackorderDistributor* interface. This also changes the inverse part of a relationship declaration for the tail side of a relationship because the target is the role interface rather than the interface for the connecting scheme. In the *Backorder* interface, the target for *is_ordered_from* is *BackorderDistributor* rather than *Distributor*, and thus we name it *is_ordered_from_Backorder-Distributor*.

Having established an interface for each individual scheme that includes extents, keys, and persistence characteristics, plus an attribute or relationship declaration or both for each attribute of each scheme, we have completed the conversion of our design scheme into ODMG ODL. We mention that ODMG handles persistence automatically and that it enforces key constraints, referential integrity, and *isa* constraints automatically. We also mention that ODMG allows nulls, letting us use **nil** as a value for the *DateShipped* so that we need not specify a special **Date** value as the null value.

Although we are finished with our example, we wish to discuss four more ideas briefly in connection with converting designs to ODMG ODL:

1. ODMG interfaces may (and usually do) include operations.

2. Both OSM designs and ODMG ODL can have more complex data structures than simple sets.

3. Besides one-many relationships, ODMG ODL also supports one-one and many-many relationships.

4. Since ODMG ODL does not support *n*-ary relationships, we must ensure that all OSM *n*-ary relationship sets can be converted into ODMG ODL binary relationships.

Although there are no operations in our flat-scheme design in Fig. 12.2, our running example does include operations. Figure 12.4 shows three of these operations: *order_request* in the *Order* interface, *request_item* in the *OrderedItem* interface, and *item_arrives* in the *Backorder* interface. Operations may be either procedures, as are these examples, or functions, which return a value for the expression in which their invocation is found. Parameters for the operations may be **in** parameters, as are the parameters in all our examples, or they may be **out** parameters or **inout** parameters. Operations may raise exceptions. In our examples, the exceptions are *NoID*, *InvalidID*, and *InvalidBackorderNr*. We discuss operations more fully in Section 12.3, where we use them in queries, and in Section 12.4, where we not only use them but also show how to implement them.

Besides **Set**, ODMG ODL also has collection types **List**, **Bag**, and **Array**. We may use these in place of **Set** in our conversion, and thus, for example, we may have a list of orders and backorders for a customer in the *Customer* interface in Fig. 12.4 rather than a set of orders. The main difference is that these collection types provide operators appropriate for the type. For lists, as an example, we can use *insert_element_after*, *remove_last_element*, and several other operations. As discussed in Chapter 11, we can also represent collection types directly in an OSM design; indeed, we can represent more than just **Set**, **List**, **Bag**, and **Array**. If our design contains one of these four types, we can convert it into ODMG ODL directly. If our design has some other collection type not supported by ODMG ODL, we can rework our design for the target ODMG ODL.

ODMG ODL supports one-one relationships directly. If there was a bidirectional edge between two attributes in our ODMG ODL abstraction diagram, we would convert it into an ODL relationship clause with no collection-type specification, making the relationship one-one. We may also, independently, need attribute clauses for the attributes in either or both interfaces. Bidirectional edges could arise in a design either by having a bidirectional functional edge in an ORM hypergraph or by having two sets, each a specialization of the other. Since Algorithm 10.1 combines sets connected by a bidirectional functional dependency into the same scheme, and since having two sets that are each other's specialization is rare, bidirectional edges in ODMG ODL abstraction diagrams derived from OSM designs are also likely to be rare.

ODMG ODL also supports many-many relationships directly. Unlike one-one relationships, many-many relationships arise often in OSM designs. In our example, an order may have many items, and an item may be on several orders. In our transformation to ODMG ODL, observe that we represent this many-many relationship in the *OrderedItem* interface by two one-many relationships—one to *Order* and one to *Item*. This is always possible, and thus we are always able to achieve our goal of supporting

many-many relationships. If the many-many relationship has attribu
such as *Number* and *UnitPrice* in our example, there is nothing more ι.
should do. If there are no attributes, however, we can remove the interface
with the relationships representing the many-many relationship, and represent the many-many relationship directly. Suppose, for example, that *Number* and *UnitPrice* were not in our *OrderedItem* interface in Fig. 12.4. Then
we could discard this interface, add

> **relationship Set**<*Item*> *includes_Item*
> **inverse** *Item*: : *is_ for_OrderedItem*

to the *Order* interface, and add

> **relationship Set**<*Order*> *is_ for_Order*
> **inverse** *Order*: : *includes_Item*

to the *Item* interface. In discarding the *OrderedItem* interface, we would also
need to reassign the operation *request_item* to another interface—for example, to the *Order* interface.

Since ODMG ODL lacks direct support for *n*-ary relationships ($n > 2$),
we must find a way to accommodate them. There are several possibilities:

- We can always accommodate *n*-ary relationships by adding a
  scheme for the relationship—indeed, our design produces this
  option automatically.

- If we have applied the design transformations in Chapter 9 faithfully, we will have already decomposed any *n*-ary relationship
  sets into lower-degree relationship sets, often binary relationship
  sets. If not, this is an option.

- We can add a relational-object set, which provides a one-to-one
  correspondence between a relationship in an *n*-ary relationship set
  and an object identifier. It is then possible to decompose this construction into *n* binary relationships in which each object set of the
  original *n*-ary relationship set associates individually with the
  object set containing the object identifiers.

12.3   ODMG OQL

ODMG provides an object query language (OQL), as both a stand-alone
query language and an embedded query language. As a stand-alone

query language, an OQL query returns a result to be displayed; as an embedded query language, an OQL query returns values that can be used in the program.

An ODMG OQL query has the basic syntax of SQL but allows more flexibility both in the way queries can be nested and in the kinds of expressions allowed within queries. The basic BNF for an ODMG OQL query is as follows:

> *query* ::= **select** [**distinct**] *query*
>   **from** *identifier* **in** *query* {, *identifier* **in** *query* }...
>   [**where** *condition*]
> *query* ::= **exists** *identifier* **in** *query* : *query*
> *query* ::= **for all** *identifier* **in** *query* : *query*
> *query* ::= *extent_identifier*
> *query* ::= **sort** *identifier* **in** *query* **by** *query* { , *query* }...
> *query* ::= **group** *identifier* **in** *query*
>   **by** (*by_partition_list*) [**with** (*with_condition_list*)]
> *query_program* ::= { **define** *identifier* **as** *query* ; }... *query*

Using the ODMG ODL scheme in Fig. 12.4, we present a series of sample ODMG OQL query programs. Except for the last one, which has a **define** component, all the sample query programs are just queries. These queries illustrate much of OQL; the bibliographic notes reference further information on ODMG OQL.

OQL Query 1. Give the description for the item whose item number is AK803.

OQL Query:

> **select** x. *Description*
> **from** x **in** *Items*
> **where** x. *ItemNr* = "AK803"

Comment: Here x is a variable that ranges over the object identifiers for items in the extent *Items* as specified in the **from** clause. In the **select** and **where** clauses, x. *Description* and x. *ItemNr*, respectively, reference the description and the item number of an item identified by x. Thus, this query selects the set of descriptions whose item number is AK803. Since *ItemNr* is a key, there will be one description at most.

OQL Query 2. List the name and address of each customer.

OQL Query:

$$\text{select } struct(x. Name, x. Address)$$
$$\text{from } x \text{ in } Customers$$

Comment: This query returns a set of name-address pairs (possibly a multi-set or bag, if more than one customer has the same name and address). The type of the result is implicit. Here, the type is **Bag<struct { String** Name; **String** Address }>. It would be **Set** instead of **Bag** if we had used **distinct**. In Query 1, the type is **Bag<String>** since *Description* is of type **String**.

OQL Query 3. List the backorder number, date, and unit price of high-priced backorders (over $100.00).

OQL Query:

$$\text{select } \mathbf{struct}(x. BackorderNumber, x. DateBackordered, x. UnitPrice)$$
$$\text{from } x \text{ in } Backorders$$
$$\text{where } x. Number * x. UnitPrice > 10000$$

Comment: Here we use an expression $x. Number * x. UnitPrice$. If, instead, we had defined a function such as

$$\textbf{Unsigned Short } total\_amount()$$

in the *Backorder* scheme to compute this total amount, we could have written $x. total\_amount()$ in place of $x. Number * x. UnitPrice$. The $100.00 is 10000 because in the conversion of US$ to **Unsigned Short**, we turned the dollar amounts into pennies.

OQL Query 4. List backorders for Kelly Jones. The list should contain the item number, description, number, and backorder date of each item back-ordered.

OQL Query:

$$\text{select } \mathbf{struct}(z. ItemNr, z. Description, x. Number, x. DateBackordered)$$
$$\text{from } x \text{ in } Backorders,$$
$$y \text{ in } x. is\_for\_Customer,$$
$$z \text{ in } x. is\_for\_Item$$
$$\text{where } y. Name = \text{"Kelly Jones"}$$

Comment: The *x.is_for_Customer* and *x.is_for_Item* traverse relationships in the *Backorder* interface. Thus *y*, which ranges over *x.is_for_Customer*, ranges over the set of customers for the backorder identified by *x*, and *z*, which ranges over *x. is_for_Item*, ranges over the set of items identified by *x*. In both cases, since there is exactly one member of the set, the resulting tuple will have one item number and description to go along with the number and backorder date for the backorder *x*.

OQL Query 5.   For each distributor with more than 10 backorders, list the name of the distributor and the backorder date and item number of all backorders.

OQL Query:

> **select struct**(*x. DistributorName*, (
>   **select struct**(*y. DateBackordered*, *z. ItemNr*)
>   **from** *y* **in** *x. is_for_Backorder*,
>   *z* **in** *y. is_for_Item*))
> **from** *x* **in** *BackorderDistributors*
> **where count**(*x. is_for_Backorder*) > 10)

Comment: This query returns a set of distributor-name/distributor-backorders pairs, where the distributor-backorders part is itself a set of backorder-date/item-number pairs. We are able to obtain this structure by nesting a **select** clause inside the list of results to be returned. We restrict the distributors in the result to those with more than 10 backorders by counting the number of *is_for_Backorder* associations connected to *x*.

OQL Query 6.   Does there exist an item with no stock in the back room?

OQL Query:

> **exists** *x* **in** *Items* : *x. NrInBackRoom* = 0

Comment: This query returns *true* if there is at least one element *x* in the extent *Items* that satisfies the condition *x. NrInBackRoom* = 0.

OQL Query 7.   List the names of any customers who have backorders for all items currently obtained from the distributor Toys, Inc.

OQL Query:

> **define** *ToysIncItems* **as**
> **select** *x*

from x **in** *Items*
where $x.is_obtained_from_Distributor.DistributorName = $ "Toys, Inc."

select $x.Name$
from x **in** *Customers*
where for all y **in** *ToysIncItems* : y **in** $x.has\_Backorder.is\_for\_Item$

Comment: For this query, we first define the set *ToysIncItems* as the set of items currently obtained from Toys, Inc. We then list the names of customers for which the **for all** condition holds. The **for all** condition holds if, for every element y in *ToysIncItems* (that is, for all items currently obtained from Toys, Inc.), y is an item in the set of backorders for the customer under consideration. Observe that the multiple dots in a query expression allow us to traverse a path in the ODMG ODL abstraction diagram in Fig. 12.3. Thus, for example, for $x.has\_Backorder.is\_for\_Item$, we start with a customer x, then traverse the path *has_Backorder* to the *Backorder* scheme, and then traverse the path *is_for_Item* to the *Item* scheme.

12.4 ODMG C++

ODMG has defined bindings for several programming languages; one of primary importance is for C++. These bindings let programmers program in an already defined language and also give them access to ODMG ODL, OML, and OQL. As an ODMG design principle, the addition of ODMG should be natural so that a programmer perceives only one language, not two languages with an interface or with one language embedded in the other.

The ODMG ODL for C++ consists of a class library and a single extension to the standard C++ class definition. The C++ OML and OQL are standard C++, but within the context of the ODMG C++ class library. Every attempt has been made to keep ODMG C++ as much like C++ as possible.

The main problem in creating an ODMG binding for C++ is to add persistence. The ODMG approach is to add "persistence-capable classes." These classes inherit from the provided class called "Persistent_Object," allowing them to have both persistent and transient instances. For each persistence-capable class T, ODMG also defines an ancillary class $Ref < T >$, allowing the programmer to reference the instances in several standard ways.

Another problem in creating an ODMG binding for C++ is that of supporting relationships. It is for this purpose that **inverse**, the single new keyword for C++, has been defined. Other features are supported in various ways, and some are not supported. Many features, such as **struct**, map directly. Other features, such as collections, map indirectly in the sense that they are only slightly different. Still other features become the responsibility of the programmer. For example, C++ does not support keys, and C++ programmers are responsible for defining collections for extents and for writing operations that maintain extents.

We proceed with our discussion of C++ by implementing our running example in ODMG C++ according to our design at the end of Chapter 11. We begin by converting the nested relation scheme in Fig. 11.35 into C++ ODL. We then convert the *Order Taker* object module in Fig. 11.37 into C++ OML and OQL.

12.4.1 C++ ODL

So that we can easily reference the nested scheme of Fig. 11.35, we reproduce it here as Fig. 12.5, making the role-name changes from *Distributor Name* to *Backorder Distributor* and *Item Distributer* as discussed earlier. For our C++ ODL implementation, it makes good sense to use the nested scheme because we are not likely to update orders once they are made. We may cancel them and make a new order, but we do not change them in our application. Thus there need be no dynamic reallocation of space because we can allocate all the space we need when we create a new order.

We proceed as before and begin by creating a nested ODMG ODL abstraction diagram. Figure 12.6 shows the diagram for the nested scheme in Fig. 12.5. The algorithm for creating a nested ODMG ODL abstraction diagram is only slightly different from Algorithm 12.1. We create nested schemes instead of flat schemes, of course, but the interesting difference is that we omit reading-direction names that point into a subscheme of a nested scheme. This is because we will have one-way relations only out of, but not into, a subscheme. Thus, for example, we do not have an *is_ordered_as* name on either of the (hyper)edges as we do in Fig. 12.3.

Another interesting difference between the abstraction diagrams in Figs. 12.3 and 12.6 is that no (hyper)edges point at *Customer ID*. This is because *Order* and *Backorder* are nested within *Customer*, obviating the need for the relationship. Similarly, there is no (hyper)edge pointing at *Order Nr* because *Ordered Item* is nested within *Order*. Indeed, removal of these edges and the corresponding references is the primary reason for providing the nested structure.

Distributor(Distributor Name: String, Distributor Address: String)
  key: Distributor Name
  key: Distributor Address
Item(Item Nr: String, Make: String, Model Nr:
  String, Item Distributor: String,
   Amt This Month: Nonnegative Integer, Nr In Back Room: Nonnegative Integer
  Price: US$, Description: String)
  key: Item Nr
  key: Make, Model Nr
  Distributor[Distributor Name] ⊇ Item[Item Distributor]
Customer(Customer ID: Positive Integer, Name: String, Address: String,
  Order(Order Nr: Positive Integer, Date Received: Date,
    Ordered Item(Item Nr: String, Number: Positive Integer,
      Unit Price: US$)*)*,
  Backorder(Backorder Nr: Positive Integer, Date Backordered: Date,
   Item Nr: String, Number: Positive Integer, Unit Price: US$,
     Backorder Distributor: String,
    Date Shipped: Date)*)
  key: Customer ID
  may be null: Date Shipped -- if null, then not yet shipped
  Item[Item Nr] ⊇ Ordered Item[Item Nr]
  Item[Item Nr] ⊇ Backorder[Item Nr]
  Distributor[Distributor Name] ⊇ Backorder[Backorder Distributor]

Figure 12.5   Nested schemes for ODMG C++ ODL.

We now transform the nested ODMG ODL abstraction diagram in Fig. 12.6 into C++ ODL. The result is the set of schemes in Fig. 12.7. Observe that there is a class for each of the schemes *Distributor*, *Item*, and *Customer*. For the subschemes, we create substructures by nesting **struct**s within **Set**s. C++ provides **struct** and the ODMG class library provides **Set**, as well as several others such as **List**, **Bag**, and **Varray** (varying length one-dimensional array) that we could use in place of **Set**. We use the pattern

$$Set<struct\{ \dots \}> Name$$

to construct a nested scheme whose name is *Name*. Within the substructure we define attributes and relationships, and we may define additional nested substructures. Thus, in the class *Customer*, we have

$$Set<Order> Orders;$$
$$Set<Backorder> Backorders;$$

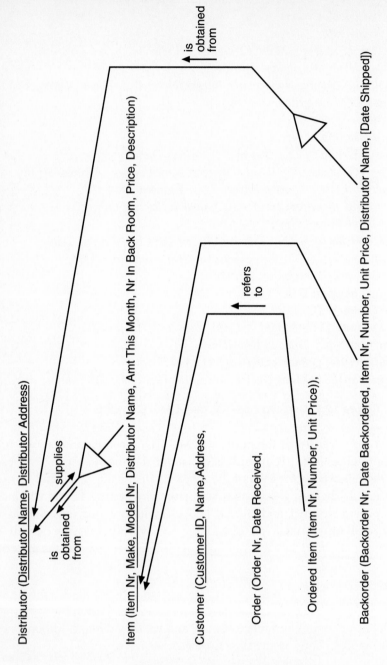

Figure 12.6 View for ODMG C++ ODL implementation.

for the subschemes nested directly in *Customer*, and in the *Order* sub-scheme, we have

$$Set<OrderedItem> OrderedItems;$$

for the subscheme nested within the *Order* subscheme.

class Item; // forward declaration

```
class Distributor : public Persistent_Object {
  String DistributorName; // key
  Set<Ref<Item>> supplies_Item
    inverse Item::is_obtained_from_Distributor;
  String DistributorAddress; // key
  Distributor(const char *, const char *);
static Ref<Set<Ref<Distributor>>> Distributors;
static const char * const extent_name;
};
```

```
class Item : public Persistent_Object {
  String ItemNr; // key
  String Make; // key component (Make ModelNr is a key)
  String ModelNr; // key component
  Ref<Distributor> is_obtained_from_Distributor
    inverse Distributor::supplies;
  unsigned short AmtThisMonth;
  unsigned short NrInBackRoom;
  unsigned short Price;
  String Description;
  Item(const char *, const char *, const char *, const char *);
static Ref<Set<Ref<Item>>> Items;
static const char * const extent_name;
};
```

```
struct OrderedItem {
  Ref<Item> refers_to_Item;
  unsigned short Number;
  unsigned short UnitPrice;
  OrderedItem(const Ref<Item> &, unsigned short, unsigned short);
};
```

```
struct Order {
  unsigned long OrderNr;
  Date DateReceived;
  Set < OrderedItem > OrderedItems;
  Order(unsigned long, const Ref<Date> &);
};


struct Backorder {
  unsigned long BackorderNr;
  Date DateBackordered;
  Ref<Item> is_for_Item;
  unsigned short Number;
  unsigned short UnitPrice;
  Ref<Distributor> is_obtained_from_Distributor;
  Date DateShipped; // null value: Date(1111, 1, 1)
  Backorder(unsigned long, const Ref<Date> &, const Ref<Item> &,
    unsigned short, unsigned short, const Ref<Distributor> &);
};


class Customer : public Persistent_Object {
  unsigned long CustomerID; // key
  String Name;
  String Address;
  Set < Order > Orders;
  Set < Backorder > Backorders;
  Customer(const char *, const char *);
static Ref<Set<Ref<Customer>>> Customers;
static const char * const extent_name;
};
```

Figure 12.7   ODMG ODL C++ classes.

Each class in Fig. 12.7 inherits from the ODMG-provided class *Persistent_Object*. The last two statements within each declaration provide a way to maintain and reference the extent of the class. The combination of inheriting from *Persistent_Object* and providing for the extent in C++ ODL gives us the features of an ODMG interface header. However, there are no key declarations. The programmer is responsible for enforcing key constraints. To remind ourselves, we can mark the keys for each class in a comment (e.g., // *key* in Fig. 12.7).

The attributes and relationships for an ODMG interface are attribute and reference declarations, respectively. The ODMG C++ class library supplies several types, including *String*, *Set*, and *Date*. The remaining types are native C++ types. The relationship *supplies_Item* in *Distributor* and *is_obtained_from_Distributor* in *Item* together represent the two-way relationship in Fig. 12.6. This shows the *inverse* clause, which is an ODMG syntactical extension to C++. The remaining relationships are one-way and are indicated by the absence of an **inverse** clause.

In addition to the attributes and relationships, the C++ ODL classes each have construction operators, namely,

> *Distributor(const char *, const char *);*
> *Item(const char *, const char *, const char *, const char *);*
> *Customer(const char *, const char *)*

to create an object for their respective classes. These operations initialize the strings in the declarations, leaving the other attributes and relationships with default values—0's, nulls, empty sets, and system-generated values. We have a special value for the default shipping date, however, which we mark with a comment in Fig. 12.7 and supply explicitly for the construction operator when we initialize a backorder.

12.4.2 C++ OML and OQL

Our next task is to supply the implementation for the operations defined in the C++ ODL scheme. We recognize immediately, however, that first we must provide for the system-generated object identifiers for *OrderNr* and *BackorderNr* because they are needed by the order-taker construction operators. We also need a system-generated object identifier for *CustomerID* because it is needed by the *Customer* constructor in the *Customer* class.

Figure 12.8 displays the ODMG C++ class we write for *LastCustomerID*. The others, for *LastOrderNr* and *LastBackorderNr*, are the same except for a change in identifier names. The class holds a single positive integer value, representing the last number assigned. Thus, incrementing by 1 yields the next available number, which we can then retrieve when we assign a new number. As Fig. 12.8 shows, we supply the operations *increment* and *get* to provide these services.

Given the C++ ODL in Fig. 12.7 and the three additional persistent classes holding the last customer ID, order number, and backorder number, we can now write code for the operations in the class declarations. We give

```
            class LastCustomerID : public Persistent_Object {
              unsigned long customerID;
              LastCustomerID();
            void increment();
            unsigned long get();
            static Ref<LastCustomerID> lastCustomerID;
            static const char * const extent_name;
            };
```

Figure 12.8   ODMG C++ class for generating customer IDs.

this code, which is standard C++ code, in Fig. 12.9. For brevity, we have omitted the operations for *LastOrderNr* and *LastBackorderNr*, which are similar to the operation for *LastCustomerID*, and we have omitted the operations for *Distributor* and *Item*, which are similar to the operation for *Customer*. The only assumption here is that the C++ ODL preprocessor has generated a file called *schema.hxx*, which contains the standard C++ definitions equivalent to the C++ ODL classes.

```
#include "schema. hxx"

const char * const LastCustomerID:: extent_name = "lastCustomerID";

LastCustomerID: : LastCustomerID()
  : customerID(0)
{}
void LastCustomerID: : increment()
{
  + + customerID;
}
unsigned long LastCustomerID: : get()
{
  return(customerID);
}

OrderedItem: : OrderedItem(const Ref<Item> &item, unsigned short number,
    unsigned short unitPrice);
  : refers_to_Item(item), Number(number), UnitPrice(unitPrice)
{}

Order: : Order(unsigned long orderNr, const Ref<Date> &dateReceived);
  : OrderNr(orderNr), DateReceived(dateReceived)
{}
```

Backorder:: *Backorder*(*unsigned long backorderNr*,
　　const Ref<Date> &backorderDate,
　　const Ref<Item> &item, unsigned short number,
　　unsigned short unitPrice, const Ref<Distributor> &distributor)
　: *BackorderNr*(*backorderNr*), *DateBackordered*(*backorderDate*),
　　is_for_Item(*item*),
　　Number(*number*), *UnitPrice*(*unitPrice*),
　　is_obtained_from_Distributor(*distributor*),
　　DateShipped(*Date*(1111, 1, 1))
{}

*const char * const Customer*:: *extent_name* = "*Customers*";

Customer(*const char * name, const char * address*)
　: *Name*(*name*), *Address*(*address*)
{
　LastCustomerID:: *lastCustomerID*– > *increment*();
　CustomerID = *LastCustomerID*:: *lastCustomerID*– > *get*();
}

Figure 12.9　C++ code for operators declared in the scheme.

We can use the code in Fig. 12.9 to initialize system-generated object identifiers, such as *LastCustomerID*; to construct records for subcomponent objects declared as **structs**, such as *OrderedItem*, *Order*, and *Backorder*; and to create new items in the database, such as *Customers*. For example, suppose we wish to initialize our *LastCustomerID*. We would execute the following statement:

$$LastCustomerID:: lastCustomerID = new(db)\ LastCustomerID$$

The *new* operator, which is in the *Persistent_Object* class of the ODMG C++ preprocessor-generated *schema. hxx* file, creates a new persistent object for the referenced class (*LastCustomerID* here) for the database called "db." We execute this statement only once, when initializing the database. Thereafter, we can add customers. For example, to construct a new customer whose name is "Kelly" and whose address is "12 Main," we would execute the statement

$$new(db)\ Customer("Kelly", "12\ Main")$$

As Fig. 12.9 shows, when we execute this constructor, we increment *Last-CustomerID* and fetch the new one as the customer ID for Kelly. To commit these database updates, we would need to execute these statements within a transaction. We show how to write transactions and give examples of how we use the other operators in Fig. 12.9 as we continue our implementation discussion.

Our next task is to convert the remaining operations in the *Order Taker* object module into code. To make our example self-contained, we also add a main routine that allows us to invoke order-taker services. We are assuming here that the database, called *OnLineShopping*, already exists, that it has had its object-identifier classes such as order number and backorder number initialized, and that it is already populated with customers, items, and distributors. We do not give the code to initialize or populate the database; neither do we give the code for any of the rest of our running example. For the full running example, we would need to write the larger on-line shopping application and appropriately embed the order-taker code, which we develop here.

As promised in Chapter 11, we also rewrite the specification for the *Order Taker* by embedding appropriate low-level transitions within high-level transitions. Figure 12.10 presents this embedding graphically; Fig. 12.11 presents it textually. Observe, by comparing Fig. 12.10 with Fig. 11.36, that we have embedded transition 7 within transition 6, transition 5 within transition 4, and transition 4 within transition 1. We have also omitted transition 8 because it is no longer needed, having been superseded by the if-then-else control structure within transition 4. Also, as a result of this embedding, we no longer need the *State* object set because the program itself keeps track of the state of the order-taking process. Furthermore, we no longer need the *External Customer* object set because we are interacting with only one customer as we establish an order. We keep the other object sets, but they are all part of the database, so we omit them from the diagram in Fig. 12.10. Finally, since we implement our application for only one *Order Taker* with only one thread of control, we need no routine for order-taker initialization beyond the main routine. If we were to run the code under the auspices of an object-management system that would allow us to spawn several order takers, they would all run the same order-taker code. We therefore keep the transaction-processing components of our application and limit their scope to allow for maximum concurrency.

We are now ready to convert the OSM-L code in Fig. 12.11 into ODMG C++ code. Unfortunately, the transformation from OSM-L behavior code to ODMG C++ code is not so straightforward as the transformation from an OSM scheme specification to C++ ODL. We therefore do not attempt to

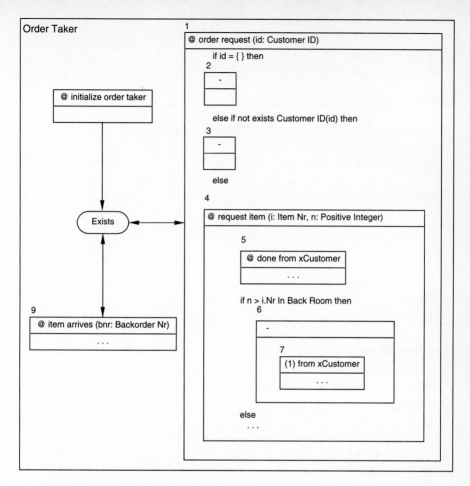

Figure 12.10 Graphical version of *Order Taker* object module reorganized for ODMG implementation.

give a general procedure for conversion. Nevertheless, our *Order Taker* object module stands as a good guide to implementation, and we can use it to convert OSM-L behavior code directly to ODMG C++ code. Figure 12.12 provides the resulting ODMG C++ code.

As examples, we discuss the *item_arrives* operation and the *doOrder* operation. The *item_arrives* operation implements transition *9* in Fig. 12.10. Its code specification tells us to retrieve the backorder information referenced by *bnr* and to send it to a worker. Since our ODMG implementation has backorder information nested within a *Customer* record, which is within the extent *Customers*, we use the given backorder number *bnr* to find the

object module *Order Taker* [1]

@ *order request (Customer ID)*;
@ *item arrives (Backorder Nr)*;

hidden

@ *order request (id: Customer ID)* **when** *Exists* **then**
  if *id* = { } **then**
    display no id ("No Customer ID entered.
      You must be registered as a customer and enter a customer ID.");
  elseif not exists *Customer(id)* **then**
    display invalid id ("Invalid Customer ID.
      You must be registered as a customer and enter a valid customer ID.");
  else

    -- initialize order
    start;
    nr: Last Order Nr;
    Last Order Nr := *Last Order Nr* + 1;
    nr := *Last Order Nr*;
    add *Customer(id) has Order(nr)*,
      Order(nr) was received on Date Received(Today);
    commit;

    -- receive item requests and backorder requests until done
    done: Boolean;
    done := **true**;
    while not *done* **do**

      if @ *request item (i: Item Nr, n: Positive Integer)* **then**

        -- if not enough on hand to fill order
        if *n* > *i.Nr In Back Room* **then**
          display insufficient msg
            ("Insufficient on hand. Do you wish to:
              1. place a backorder for the item?
              2. not place a backorder?");

        -- if backorder placed
        if @ *(1)* **then**

Figure 12.11 Textual version of *Order Taker* object module
reorganized for ODMG implementation.

```
      start;
        nr: Last Backorder Nr;
        Last Backorder Nr := Last Backorder Nr + 1;
        nr := LastBackorderNr;
        add Backorder(nr) includes Number(n) of
          Item(i) at Unit Price(i. Price);
        add Backorder(nr) was received on
          Date Backordered(Today);
        order item for customer (Backorder Nr(nr),
          Item(i). Distributor Name,
          Item(i). Distributor Address,
          n, Item(i). Make and Model Nr identify Item,
          Item(i). Description);
        commit;
      end;

    -- if enough on hand to fill order
    else
      start;
      add Order(id. Order) includes
        Number(n) of Item(i) at Unit Price(i. Price);
      Item(i). Amt This Month := Item(i). Amt This Month + n;
      Item(i). Nr In Back Room := Item(i). Nr In Back Room − n;
      commit;
      end;

  elseif @ done then
    if Order(nr) includes Number of Item <> { } then
      Nr(x) Item Nr(y) Description(z) : − Order(nr)
        includes Number(x) of Item(y) at Unit Price(w),
        Item(y) has Description(z);
      Worker. print order (Order Nr(nr), Order Nr(nr). Name,
      Order Nr(nr). Address, Nr Item Nr Description;
      end;
    done := true;
    end;

  end;
 end;
enter Exists;
end;
```

Figure 12.11 (cont.) Textual version of *Order Taker* object module reorganized for ODMG implementation.

@ *item arrives* (*bnr: Backorder Nr*) **when** *Exists* **then**
  Worker. receive item for *customer* (*bnr, Backorder Nr*(*bnr*). *Name,*
    Backorder Nr(*bnr*). *Address, Backorder Nr*(*bnr*). *Number,*
    Backorder Nr(*bnr*). *Item Nr, Backorder Nr*(*bnr*). *Description;*
  end;

end;

     Figure 12.11 (cont.) Textual version of *Order Taker* object module reorganized for ODMG implementation.

```
#include <iostream. h>
#include "schema. hxx"

static Database objectDB;
static Database * db = &objectDB;

void initializeOrder(unsigned long customerID, &unsigned long orderNr)
{
  Ref <Customer> customer;
  Transaction initializeOrder;

  initializeOrder. begin();
  LastOrderNr: : lastOrderNr- > increment();
  LastOrderNr: : lastOrderNr- > mark_modified();
  orderNr = LastOrderNr: : lastOrderNr- > get();
  Order newOrder(orderNr, Date: : current());
  oql(customer, "element( \
    select x \
    from  x in Customers \
    where x. CustomerID = $1ul)", customerID);
  customer- > Orders- > insert_element(newOrder);
  customer- > mark_modified();
  initializeOrder. commit();
}

void notifyWorkerOfOrder(unsigned long customerID, unsigned long orderNr)
{
  int nrOfItemsOrdered;
  struct {
```

     Figure 12.12 *Order Taker* application in ODMG C++.

```
    char * name;
    char * address; } name_addr;
  typedef struct {
    int amount;
    char * itemNr;
    char * description;
    } OrderedItemInfo;
  typedef Set<OrderedItemInfo> OrderedItemInfoSet;
  Set<OrderedItemInfo> orderedItemInfoSet;
  Ref<OrderedItemInfoSet> item;
  Iterator<Ref<OrderedItemInfoSet> iterator = orderedItemSet.create_iterator();

  oql(nrOfItemsOrdered, "count( \
    select y \
    from x in Customers, y in x.Orders.OrderedItems \
    where x.CustomerID = $1ul and x.Orders.OrderNr = $2ul)",
      customerID, orderNr);
  if (nrOfItemsOrdered > 0) {
    cout << "Message to Worker – – Fill Order:" << endl;
    oql(name_addr," \
      select distinct struct(x.Name, x.Address) \
      from x in Customers \
      where x.CustomerID = $1ul", customerID);
    cout << "Name:   " << name_addr.name << endl;
    cout << "Address:  " << name_addr.address << endl;
    cout << "Amount  Item Nr  Description" << endl;
    oql(orderedItemSet," \
      select distinct struct(y.Number, y.refers_to_Item.ItemNr, \
          y.refers_to_Item.Description) \
      from x in Customers, y in x.Orders.OrderedItems \
      where x.CustomerID = $1ul and x.Orders.OrderNr = $2ul",
        customerID, orderNr);
    while (iterator.next(item)) {
      cout << item->amount << " " item->itemNr << " "
      item->description << " " << endl; } }
}

void doPossibleBackorder(unsigned long customerID, unsigned long itemNr)
{
  int choice;
  unsigned long backorderNr;
```

Figure 12.12 (cont.)   *Order Taker* application in ODMG C++.

```
typedef struct {
  Ref<Item> backorderItem;
  unsigned short unitPrice;
  Ref<Distributor> distributor;
  } BackorderInfo;
BackorderInfo backorderInfo;
Ref<Customer> customer;
Transaction establishBackorder;

cout << "Insufficient on hand.  Do you wish to: << endl;
cout << "  1. place a backorder  for the item?" << endl;
cout << "  2. not place a backorder?");" << endl;
cin >> choice;

// if backorder placed
if (choice == 1) {
  establishBackorder. begin();
  LastBackorderNr:: lastBackorderNr– > increment();
  LastBackorderNr:: lastBackorderNr– > mark_modified();
  backorderNr = LastBackorderNr:: lastBackorderNr– > get();
  oql(backorderInfo, "element( \
    select distinct struct(x, x. Price, x. is_obtained_from_Distributor) \
    from x in Items \
    where x. ItemNr = $1s), ItemNr = itemNr);
  Backorder newBackorder(backorderNr, Date:: current(),
    backorderInfo. backorderItem, amount, backorderInfo. unitPrice,
    backorderInfo. distributor);
  oql(customer, "element( \
    select x \
    from  x in Customers \
    where x. CustomerID = $1ul)", CustomerID);
  customer– > Backorders– > insert_element(newBackorder);
  customer– > mark_modified();
  establishBackorder. commit(); }
}

void doOrder(unsigned long customerID, unsigned long itemNr)
{
  typedef struct {
    Ref<Item> orderItem;
    unsigned short unitPrice;
```

Figure 12.12 (cont.)   *Order Taker* application in ODMG C++.

```
    } OrderInfo;
  OrderInfo orderInfo;
  Ref <Item> orderItem item;
  Ref <Customer> customer;
  Transaction enterItemOnOrder;

  enterItemOnOrder. begin();
  oql(orderInfo, "element( \
    select struct(x, x. Price) \
    from x in Items \
    where x. ItemNr = $1s), ItemNr = itemNr);
  item = orderInfo. orderItem;
  OrderedItem newOrderedItem(item, amount, orderInfo. unitPrice);
  oql(customer, "element( \
    select x \
    from  x in Customers \
    where x. CustomerID = $1ul)", CustomerID);
  customer– > Orders– > OrderedItems– > insert_element(newOrderedItem);
  customer– > mark_modified();
  item. AmtThisMonth = item. AmtThisMonth + amount;
  item. NrInBackRoom = item. NrInBackRoom – amount;
  item– > mark_modified();
  enterItemOnOrder. commit();
}

void order_request(unsigned long customerID)
{
  int found, done, amount, nrInBackRoom;
  unsigned long orderNr;
  char * itemNr;

  oql( found, "exists x in Customers: x. CustomerID = $1ul", customerID);
  if (! found) {
    cout << "Invalid Customer ID." << endl;
    cout << "You must be registered as a customer" <<;
    cout << " and enter a valid customer ID." << endl; }
  else {
    initializeOrder(customerID, orderNr);
```

Figure 12.12 (cont.) *Order Taker* application in ODMG C++.

```
        // receive item requests and backorder requests until done
        done = 0;
        cout << "Enter the Amount you wish to order and the Item Number." << endl;
        cout << "To end your order, enter 0 for the Amount." << endl;
        while (!done) {
          cout << "Amount: ";
          cin >> amount;
          if (amount == 0) {
            notifyWorkerOfOrder(customerID, orderNr); }
          else {
            cout << "Item Number: ";
            cin >> itemNr;
            oql(found, "exists x in Items: x. ItemNr = $1ul", itemNr);
            if (! found) {
              cout << "Invalid Item Number" << endl; }
            else {
              oql(nrInBackRoom, "element( \
                select x. NrInBackRoom \
                from x in Items \
                where x. ItemNr = $1s)", itemNr);
              if (amount > nrInBackRoom) { // not enough on hand
                doPossibleBackorder(customerID, itemNr); }
              else { // enough on hand
                doOrder(customerID, itemNr); } } } } }
}

void item_arrives(unsigned long bnr)
{
  struct {
    char * name;
    char * address;
    unsigned short number;
    char * itemNr;
    char * description; } backorderInfo;
  Ref < Customer > customer;

  cout << "Message to Worker: Please ship the following:" << endl;
  oql(backorderInfo, "element( \
    select distinct struct(x. Name, x. Address, y. Number, y. is_for_Item. ItemNr, \
```

Figure 12.12 (cont.)   *Order Taker* application in ODMG C++.

```
      y. is_for_Item. Description) \
    from x in Customers, y in x. Backorders \
    where y. BackorderNr = $1ul)", bnr);
  cout << "Backorder Number: " << bnr << endl;
  cout << "Name: " << backorderInfo. name << endl;
  cout << "Address: " << backorderInfo. address << endl;
  cout << "Amount: " << backorderInfo. number << endl;
  cout << "Item Nr: " << backorderInfo. itemNr << endl;
  cout << "Description: " << backorderInfo. description << endl;
}

main()
{
  int choice, processing;
  unsigned long customerID, backorderNr;

  db- > open("OnLineShopping");
  processing = 1;
  while (processing) {
    cout << "You may:" << endl;
    cout << "1. make an order." << endl;
    cout << "2. receive a backorder." << endl;
    cout << "3. quit." << endl;
    cin >> choice;
    switch (choice) {
    case 1:
      cout << "Enter Customer ID: ";
      cin >> customerID;
      order_request(customerID);
      break;
    case 2:
      cout << "Enter Backorder Nr: ";
      cin >> backorderNr;
      item_arrives(backorderNr);
      break;
    case 3:
      processing = 0;
      break; } }
  db- > close();
}
```

Figure 12.12 (cont.) *Order Taker* application in ODMG C++.

customer to whom the backorder belongs and to retrieve and print the requested information.

ODMG gives C++ a way to do the retrieval by providing an *oql* function that has two or more parameters: the first parameter receives the result, the second is a string that specifies the query, and the rest are values supplied for the query. The places for these values are marked $1 for the first, $2 for the second, and so forth. There is also a type designator appended to these markings, such as *i* for integer, *s* for string, and *ul* for unsigned long. An OQL query that normally would return a collection with one element returns the element instead when *element* is specified as in the *oql* function in the *item_arrives* operation. If the query happens to be ill formed, the *oql* function returns a 0.

Continuing with the explanation of the *item_arrives* function, we see that the *oql* function along with the subsequent print statements are a direct translation of the OSM statement

> *Worker. receive item* for *customer (bnr, Backorder Nr(bnr). Name,*
> *Backorder Nr(bnr). Address, Backorder Nr(bnr). Number,*
> *Backorder Nr(bnr). Item Nr, Backorder Nr(bnr). Description*

where *bnr*, which provides the value needed to retrieve the right information, is the same in both statements. The constraints, which hold automatically in OSM-L and which we must be careful to satisfy in our ODMG implementation, allow only one customer to have any backorder. To check for the possibility that there is no customer for a backorder, we should provide additional code, but we do not give the code here. Indeed, this specification is not in the application model, and we see yet another example of how we can learn more about the application even at implementation time.

The *doOrder* operation, the main part of transition 4 in Fig. 12.10, is represented by the "..." after the *else*. In Fig. 12.11 this is given as

> **start**;
> **add** *Order(id. Order) includes*
> *Number(n) of Item(i) at Unit Price(i. Price)*;
> *Item(i). Amt This Month* := *Item(i). Amt This Month + n*;
> *Item(i). Nr In Back Room* := *Item(i). Nr In Back Room − n*;
> **commit**

We translate this OSM-L code directly to the ODMG C++ code in the *doOrder* operation as follows. The **start-commit** pair in OSM-L denotes a transaction. In ODMG C++ we declare a transaction with

Transaction enterItemOnOrder

and then bracket the code of the transaction with

$$enterItemOnOrder.begin()$$

at the beginning, which initiates the transaction, and

$$enterItemOnOrder.commit()$$

at the end, which commits the transaction. We next encode the OSM-L **add** statement by retrieving a reference to the item and its price and by constructing a new ordered-item record with the statement

$$OrderedItem\ newOrderedItem(item,\ amount,\ orderInfo.unitPrice)$$

We then obtain a reference to the customer and use it to insert this ordered-item record with the statement

$$customer->Orders->OrderedItems->insert\_element(newOrderedItem)$$

So that the database will be updated with these changes when the transaction commits, we then add the statement

$$customer->mark\_modified()$$

which tells the system to update the particular customer in the *Customers* extent whose record we have modified. Finally, we encode the two statements that update the amount this month and the number in the back room for the item. We then also mark these fields modified so that the system will update them when the transaction commits.

12.5 Development Methodology

Now that we have shown how to take our sample on-line application through all stages of analysis, specification, design, and implementation, let us step back and observe the process. Our objective here is to give a detailed outline for developing databases and database applications. The outline is like a road map, showing a layout of the ground to be covered and giving guidance about how to achieve success. The outline, however, is not a set of directions that explains at every turn how to go step-by-step from the beginning to the end. The developer must come to understand the application and use the theory and techniques of OSM development to solve problems creatively and achieve success.

Our OSM development methodology consists of the checklists at the ends of Chapters 7–11 plus the checklist in this chapter. These checklists guide the process and remind developers about items that may be otherwise overlooked. It may be desirable to number the items in these checklists and treat them as steps in a development methodology; the lists are ordered with this possibility in mind. Be aware, however, that some steps may not be necessary (e.g., some of the design transformations for the checklist in Chapter 9 may never be needed), that some steps may be done out of order (e.g., some of the design transformations in Chapter 11 may precede some of the design transformations in Chapter 9), and that some steps may have to be repeated (e.g., as changes are made in the system being developed). These checklists therefore are more like guidelines and reminders than like a procedure to follow step by step.

12.6 Chapter Summary

Topic Summary

- The ODMG standards group has proposed a way to integrate databases with object-oriented programming languages. ODMG has bindings for C++ and Smalltalk, and other bindings are being developed, including one for Java. ODMG includes ODMG ODL (the object-definition language), ODMG OML (the object-manipulation language), and ODMG OQL (the object-query language). In integrating these language definitions with standard object-oriented programming languages, an attempt is made to retain the syntax and semantics of the standard language as much as possible so that the integrated language appears as a unified, single object-oriented database programming language.

- ODMG ODL abstraction diagrams are an example of a type of implementation view designed specifically for an ODMG target environment. Similar aids to implementation for other target environments are likely to be useful guides to implementation.

[†] We have not discussed the implementation of inheritance in this chapter. We do discuss it, however, in later case studies and include it in this checklist.

Checklist for Implementation

☐ Understand the target implementation software and how it is similar to and different from a design view of an OSM application model.

☐ Based on the similarities and differences, devise appropriate implementation views such as ODMG ODL abstraction diagrams.

☐ Aided by any implementation views, convert the OSM application model directly into code. Try to find and use algorithmic conversions.

> ☐ Convert OSM schemes and scheme constraints into target schemes and scheme constraints.
>
> ☐ Provide code for any constraints not directly supported by the target software.
>
> ☐ Compare type systems and decide how best to convert OSM generalizations and data-structure patterns to built-in scalar and bulk types.
>
> ☐ Determine how to convert OSM queries to the query language supported by the target software and do the conversion.
>
> ☐ Depending on how the target software supports inheritance,[†] either make direct use of the inheritance mechanism or consider building polymorphism into the implementation. Although somewhat controversial, we suggest only using inheritance for conceptual generalization/specialization as follows.
>
> > • Override the implementation of an operation for a generalization object set only with a more efficient implementation of the operation for a specialization object set. Do not change the semantics of operations in specializations.
> >
> > • Do not reuse similar, but semantically different, code by inheritance; instead, reuse the code by copying and modifying it.
>
> ☐ Convert OSM-L functional specifications to the programming language supported by the target software.

- The OSM development methodology consists of a set of check-lists, one for analysis (see Chapter 7), one for specification (see Chapter 8), three for design (see Chapters 9–11), and one for implementation (see Chapter 12). These checklists provide a guide to development and lay out a general road map to success. The checklist methodology, however, does not describe how to proceed every step of the way. Instead, the methodology is model-driven; a developer must have a clear understanding of OSM, the application, and the business requirements for applica-tion, and must be able to use the theory and techniques explained in this book to devise appropriate solutions and build high-quality application systems.

Question Summary

- How does ODMG integrate database features with object-oriented language features?

  A program in the ODMG proposal has an ODL part; an OML part, which includes any OQL statements; and auxiliary source code necessary to enable the binding between the language and the ODL and OML. A preprocessor generates a database from the ODL and also produces language declarations. A compiler takes these language declarations along with the OML and auxiliary code and produces an executable application that can interact with the database.

- How do we derive an ODMG ODL abstraction diagram from an ORM hypergraph?

  To convert an ORM hypergraph to an ODMG ODL abstraction diagram, we first apply one of the scheme-generation algorithms discussed in Chapter 10. We then use these generated schemes along with generated inclusion dependencies to obtain connec-tions among the schemes.

- What differences are we likely to encounter between OSM-L types and implementation types?

  The differences between OSM-L types and C++ types are typical of what we might encounter generally. OSM-L types consist of arbitrary generalizations and selected data-structure templates, which are much richer than C++ types. We carry types that correspond directly into C++, and we convert the remaining types into the built-in atomic and bulk types supported by C++.

- What are the similarities of and differences between SQL and ODMG OQL?

  ODMG OQL is richer than OSM-SQL, which is essentially the same as standard SQL. Thus we can convert OSM-SQL directly to ODMG OQL, but we should be aware of and appropriately utilize any additional opportunities provided by ODMG SQL, such as the possibility of using sets, bags, and structures as possible containers for results.

- How does ODMG C++ differ from standard C++?

  ODMG C++ adds an **inverse** clause to standard C++. Other than the ODMG ODL class library for C++, this is the only addition, which makes ODMG C++ almost the same as standard C++.

- How do we derive C++ ODL from an ODMG ODL abstraction diagram?

  First we adjust abstraction diagrams to account for the peculiarities of C++. We use nested schemes and omit reading-direction names into properly nested schemes. With these changes, we can then derive C++ ODL directly from an abstraction diagram. The inverse clause, which is the essential addition to standard C++ declarations for the ODMG C++ binding, helps make this derivation direct.

- How do we derive C++ OML and OQL from an OSM-L specification?

  C++ OML and OSM-L do not correspond directly, and we have no general algorithm for converting OSM-L to C++ OML. From a complete OSM-L specification, however, we can still proceed nearly statement by statement, converting the syntax of an OSM-L statement to the syntax of C++ OML.

12.7   Bibliographic Notes

The definitive reference for ODMG is *The Object Database Standard: ODMG-93, Release 1.2* [Cattell96]. For the latest information on

ODMG, access the ODMG home page on the World Wide Web—URL: http://www.odmg.org.

Various methods have been presented for developing complex software. This book presents the OSM method; [Booch94], for example, provides another method.

12.8   Exercises

12.1** Choose a target environment and use the OSM development methodology to implement the following banking application.

The bank has employees and customers. Every customer must have a checking account, which may be joint with at most one other customer. A customer may have one or more loans and a credit card. Credit cards and loans are not owned jointly.

Customers make requests that arise in the natural course of doing business with the bank according to the rules that follow. The requests include, for example, requests to open accounts and close accounts and requests for information about accounts, about the status of loan applications, and about the rules of the bank. Bank employees and software service these requests.

Checking account rules:

1. Funds from a cash deposit and from an automatic deposit are available immediately.

2. Funds from a check deposit are available as soon as the check clears.

3. Checking withdrawals cause immediate debits.

4. Overdrafts for customers with credit cards automatically invoke credit-card cash withdrawals to cover the check unless the credit card is over its limit or the overdraft amount would cause the credit limit to be exceeded. In these cases, overdrafts for credit-card customers are treated like overdrafts for customers without credit cards.

5. Overdrafts bounce for customers without credit cards or whose credit limit is or would be exceeded.

Credit card rules:

1. Credit cards are established with a $3000 limit.

2. After a year, if there have been no payment defaults or credit-card transactions that have exceeded the limit, the limit is raised automatically to $5000, and the customer is notified. If the limit is not raised, it may be raised at subsequent yearly checks using the same criteria, which are applied only within the preceding year.

3. The interest rate is set by the bank and may change from time to time.

4. Monthly payments are made by automatic withdrawal from the customer's checking account. The amount charged is the amount due or $10 plus the interest accrued, whichever is smaller.

5. Customers may make additional payments at any time. Cash payments take immediate effect, but a check payment takes effect only when the check clears.

6. Noncash transactions accrue no interest for 30 days.

7. Cash transactions accrue interest immediately.

8. If the credit limit is exceeded, the customer is notified and is also charged $10, plus $5 for every additional transaction until payment is made to bring the balance under the limit.

Loan application rules:

1. The customer must have both a checking account and a credit card at the bank to be considered for a loan.

2. The following information is to be obtained: name, address, Social Security number, place of employment and monthly income, and any car-payment loan information and home-mortgage loan information. This loan information includes the original amount of loan, interest rate, monthly payment, length of loan in months, and current balance.

3. Before approving or denying a loan, an employee must verify the employment information and any car-payment and home-mortgage information.

4. Guidelines for approval or denial change from time to time as specified by the branch manager, but include a reasonable set of criteria based on checking-account usage, credit-card usage, amount of monthly income, assets, and the requested amount of the loan.

Loan payment rules:

1. Monthly payments are made by automatic withdrawal from the customer's checking account.

2. Customers may make additional payments at any time. A cash payment is credited immediately, but a check payment is not credited until the check clears.

12.2** Choose a target environment and use the OSM development methodology to implement the following application about radioactive waste transportation and emergency response.

Because of the hazardous nature of spent nuclear waste material, its transportation must be monitored carefully. When an accident in the transportation system occurs, emergency response must be swift and sure in order to minimize danger to human life. The following narrative description gives the features to be considered and describes the system to be implemented.

Nuclear waste is produced at a large number of sites, located all over the United States. Waste is transferred from the producing reactor into a highly secure, leak-resistant container. Once placed in the container, waste material is expected to remain enclosed until it is no longer radioactive (well beyond our lifetimes). Containers differ in capacity and level of radiation contained.

Containers are transported via public highway and rail systems on specially equipped trucks and trains. Each transportation vehicle has one or more operators. The status of vehicles and operators must be monitored periodically to verify that all is well, or to report failures in the system when they occur.

A major function of the system is to schedule, route, and monitor the transportation of nuclear waste in protective containers. To facilitate this, fleet, weather, and human personnel information must be maintained. Routes that avoid major population centers should be chosen, but cost is a factor and must be minimized with respect to the hazard level.

Emergency response teams are available at various centers throughout the country. Response teams have differing capabilities; each is headed by a single team leader. A dispatcher from the central nuclear waste-monitoring facility is responsible for monitoring en route waste and for dispatching a suitable team to respond to each accident.

The system should maintain the following information:

Dispatcher Information: name, experience, contact information.
Vehicle Information: capacity, status, cost, driver, location responder.
Operator Information: name, experience, contact information, health status.
Route Information: route, distance, estimated travel time, checkpoints, weather.
City Information: location, population, weather.
Vehicle Type: train, truck.
Vehicle Status: traveling, resting, available, failed.
Vehicle Coordinates: latitude, longitude.
Weather: temperature, cloud cover, precipitation, ground condition.
Nuclear Waste Information: serial number, quantity, radiation level, status, source, container id.
Waste-Container: container id, weight, volume.
Waste-Container Security Status: leaking, compromised, secure.
Waste-Container State: ready to move, in transit, stored.
Failure Type: mechanical, structural, collision.
Response-Team Information: leader, worker, skills, equipment, location, contact information.
Person Status: estimated number of people, injury status, deaths, potential injury.

The system should accommodate the following:

Schedule the transportation of spent nuclear fuel.
Update information about transportation fleet and drivers.

Initiate and monitor transport.

Notify emergency response teams when entering or leaving a team's area of responsibility.

Conclude monitoring when spent nuclear fuel is safely stored.

Update weather information.

Report failures and dispatch response teams.

Monitor response to failures.

Update injury-status information.

Update information about emergency response teams.

Prototype this system by creating a database that contains vehicles, emergency response teams, waste records, and so forth. The prototype should include a demonstration application that allows a dispatcher to send material from one location to another and that can respond to a simulated emergency.

Chapter 13

Relational DBMS Case Study

We use Oracle for our relational DBMS case study. For our application, we develop a system that tracks university parking privileges, including parking permits, citations, fine collection, and vehicle impoundment.

As a starting point, let us assume that we have the following information about parking regulations.

Permits

Faculty and staff may obtain "A" permits; graduate students may obtain "B" permits, and undergraduate students may obtain "C" permits.

To receive a permit, a person must supply a name, an address, and a vehicle license plate number.

Citations and Fines

Parked in wrong lot—$10

Parked without a permit—$20

Parked illegally—$30

Parked in a tow zone—$70

Citation and Fine Resolution

Fines are to be paid upon receipt; otherwise an overdue notification is sent.

Appeals may be granted.

Impoundment

Officers may impound a vehicle that is blocking traffic or creating a hazard; is parked in a tow zone; has two or more unpaid citations; or has seven or more citations.

Impounded vehicles may be released upon payment of a $25 fine.

We also assume that we have learned the following by conversing with intended users of the system.

Information about Citations

Citations are issued to owners of vehicles.

Citations must state the type of violation, the fine, and the date and time of the violation.

A citation number identifies a citation.

A license plate together with the date and time also identify a citation.

A vehicle may be cited for only one violation for any date and time.

When traffic officers issue citations, they must sign their name and include their officer number and work phone as reference information.

Expected Update Operations

Issue a permit.

Record a citation and fine.

Grant an appeal for a citation, and remove it from the record.

Add information about a person who is responsible for paying a fine.

Send notification of a fine that is due.

Receive a payment for a person who owes a fine.

Record the receipt of an impounded vehicle.

Record the release of an impounded vehicle.

Expected Reports

List vehicles with two or more unpaid citations.

List permit holders with excessive violations.

Expected Queries

Look up a citation for an appeal.

Find out whether a vehicle has been impounded.

The following topics in this chapter are particularly important:

- Validation of zero-minimum participation constraints.

- Passive data operations, ORM structure, and interface-form specification.

- ORM hypergraph reductions.

- Flat-scheme and foreign-key generation.

- Exceptions to the general scheme-generation rules for nulls.

The following questions should also be kept in mind:

- How easy or difficult is it to transform an OSM data design into SQL DDL?

- How easy or difficult is it to transform an OSM functional design into SQL queries and Pro*C code?

13.1   Initial Analysis

We can develop an analysis model by directly recording the information given in the application description. The result is the OSM application model in Fig. 13.1. Observe, for example, that

- We have all the information required for permits, including the "A," "B," and "C" classifications;

- Each citation has one violation and each violation has one fine, allowing citations and fines to be recorded;

- Citation resolution can take place based on the status of the citation;

- Impoundment information about vehicles with two or more unpaid citations or seven or more citations can be generated;

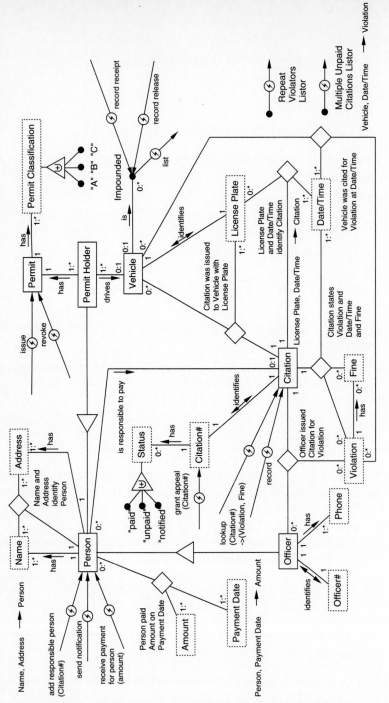

Figure 13.1 An analysis model for the parking application.

- Each of the statements in the information about citations corresponds to a relationship set; and

- Each expected update operation, report, and query corresponds to an interaction.

13.2 Congruency Validation

Once we have an initial analysis model, we can review it in an attempt to validate it. For example, we can scrutinize each of the zero minimums to determine whether we should add additional object classes to make the model congruent. The zero minimums on *Violation*, for example, arise because there is a (slim) possibility that no citation has been issued for a particular violation. We want to keep a record of possible violations and fines, but adding roles such as *Violation with no Citation* does not help and may be confusing. The zero minimums on *Status*, *Person*, *Citation*, and *Officer* have similar characteristics, so we leave them as they are.

On the other hand, the zero minimums on *Fine* arise because the fine for a violation is the current amount of a fine, but the fine for a citation is the amount of the fine when the citation was issued. Since fines may change (although infrequently), we must keep these roles separate. We therefore add roles *Citation Fine* and *Violation Fine*. The zero minimums for the *Vehicle is Impounded* relationship set arise because some (very few) vehicles may be impounded. Since the number of impounded vehicles is expected to be extremely small compared with the total number of vehicles, we should create a specialization to hold only the impounded vehicles. The other zero minimums on *License Plate* and *Vehicle* arise because some vehicles may have permits and no citations, and some vehicles without permits may be cited for a violation. To solve this problem, we should create two specializations of *Vehicle*: *Registered Vehicle* (those for which permits have been obtained) and *Cited Vehicle* (those that have been cited, whether registered or not). Using an equivalence-class transformation, we also move all the connections incident on *Vehicle* or *License Plate* to *Cited Vehicle*. Figure 13.2 shows the new ORM diagram after these changes.

13.3 Interface Specification

We should also review each interaction. We should determine, for example, whether we can execute all the actions required by the system, and also

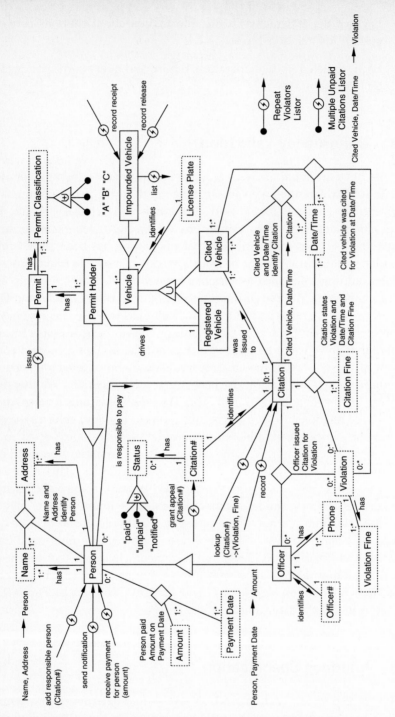

Figure 13.2 A revised analysis model for the parking application.

which operations are specified incompletely. In considering these questions, we find that the semantics of our operations are specified very loosely and that several, perhaps all, need more work. We may believe, however, that we have gathered enough information to understand these operations, and thus we may delay this work until the specification phase, for which we have some additional tools such as interface forms.

Turning our attention to specification, we first observe that the system boundary includes all the object classes and relationship sets in Fig. 13.2 and that all the interactions cross the system boundary. We note, however, that the *send notification* should go to a "real" person outside the system boundary. We therefore split *Person* and let the head of the *send notification* interaction point to the outside *Person*. Since we need the tail inside the system, we also add a new object that determines what notifications must be sent and then sends them.

Since many of the boundary-crossing interactions basically use only built-in operations, we can write them as interface-specification forms. As an example, we give the interface specifications for *send notification* in Fig. 13.3. For more complex boundary-crossing interactions, we need objects with state nets to specify the necessary actions. An example of these more complex interaction specifications is the *receive payment* interaction in Fig. 13.4. We assign this task to the object set *Payment*, which we now introduce.

By analyzing all the input specifications, it is obvious that we have no way to add officers and no way to add and modify violations and fines. These are easy to add. After making all these necessary adjustments and additions, our specification is complete.

@ *send notification*
(input)

Status = "U"

(output)

Name _____   *Address* _____

Citation# _____   *Violation* _____

Date / Time _____   *Fine* _____

Figure 13.3   A specification to send a notification.

Payment **includes**

 @ *receive payment* (*name*: *Name, addr*: *Address,*
  amt: *Amount, paymentDate*: *PaymentDate*) **then;**

 -- find person p
 p: *Person;*
 p := *Name*(*name*) *and Address*(*addr*) *identify Person*(*p*);

 -- record payment
 add *Person with Name*(*name*) *and Address*(*addr*)
  paid Amount(*amt*) *on Payment Date*(*paymentDate*);

 -- determine whether any partial payment for a citation exists,
 -- and, if so, add it to the payment amount
 total, total payments, total fines paid: US$;
 total payments := **sum**(*Person*(*p*). *Amount*);
 total fines paid := **sum**(*Person*(*p*). *Status*("*P*"). *Citation Fine*);
 total := *amt* + (*total payments* – *total fines paid*);

 -- until payment amount exhausted, citations paid,
 -- oldest to newest
 c: *Citation;*
 t: *Date / Time;* *-- t represents the date and time of the oldest unpaid citation*
 while *total* > 0 **do**
  t := **min**(*Person*(*p*). *Status*("*U*"). *Date / Time*);
  c := *Person*(*p*). *Citation*(*x*) **where** *Citation*(*x*) = *t*;
  if *Citation*(*nxt*). *Citation Fine* < *total* **then**
   Citation(*c*). *Status* := "*P*";
  else
   total := 0;
  end;
  end;
 end;

end; *-- Payment*

 Figure 13.4 Specification for receiving a payment.

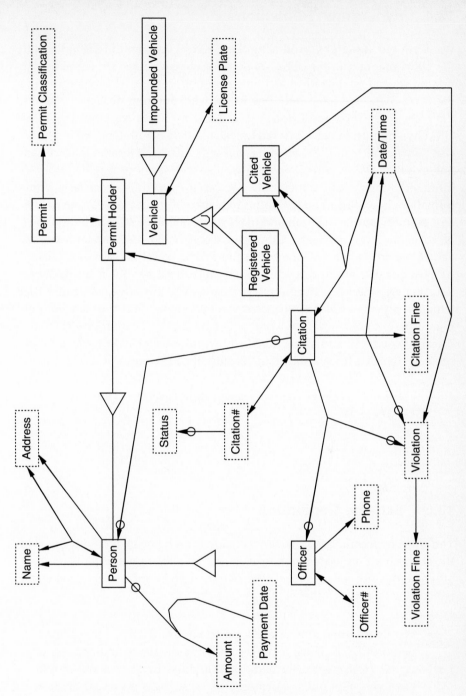

Figure 13.5 Initial ORM hypergraph for the parking application.

13.4   Hypergraph Reductions

We begin our design by producing the ORM hypergraph in Fig. 13.5 from the ORM diagram in Fig. 13.2. A number of reductions are possible. We first do several (six) head reductions, resulting in the ORM hypergraph in Fig. 13.6. Now we have only one arrowhead pointing at *Name*, *Address*, *Violation*, *Date/Time*, and *Cited Vehicle*. Next we lexicalize, resulting in the ORM hypergraph in Fig. 13.7. We lexicalize *Citation* with *CitationNr*, *Vehicle* with *License Plate*, and *Person* with *Name* and *Address*. Observe that we cannot lexicalize *Officer* with *OfficerNr*, because we cannot propagate *OfficerNr* throughout the *Person isa* hierarchy. We can use an equivalence-class transformation, however, to attach both *Citation# (of Citation)* and *Phone* to *Officer#*, simplifying the diagram and making the reference from a citation to an officer more space efficient. Although we observe that we cannot lexicalize *Permit*, we realize at this point that the *Permit* object set serves no useful purpose because all the information we need about permits is in the *Permit Classification* object set. Furthermore, in resolving this issue, we realize that although a permit holder may have several vehicles and thus several permits, a permit holder can have only one permit classification. We therefore discard *Permit* and add a functional edge from *Permit Holder* to *Permit Classification*, which after lexicalization becomes the FD edge

> *Name (of Permit Holder) Address (of Permit Holder)* → *Permit Classification*

in Fig. 13.7.

13.5   Scheme Generation

The ORM hypergraph is now almost ready for scheme generation. Some of the connections are optional, however, and thus the hypergraph is not congruent and hence not canonical. We analyze each of these congruencies and make adjustments as follows:

- We observe that almost every person in the database should be a permit holder. Thus, if we combine the the name and address of *Permit Holder* with the name and address of *Person*, we should have very few nulls. Furthermore, these nulls represent another useful permit category, namely, the category of persons who have

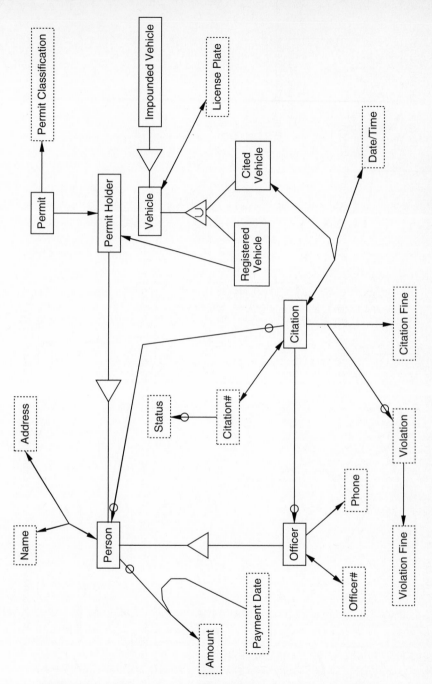

Figure 13.6 Head-reduced ORM hypergraph for the parking application.

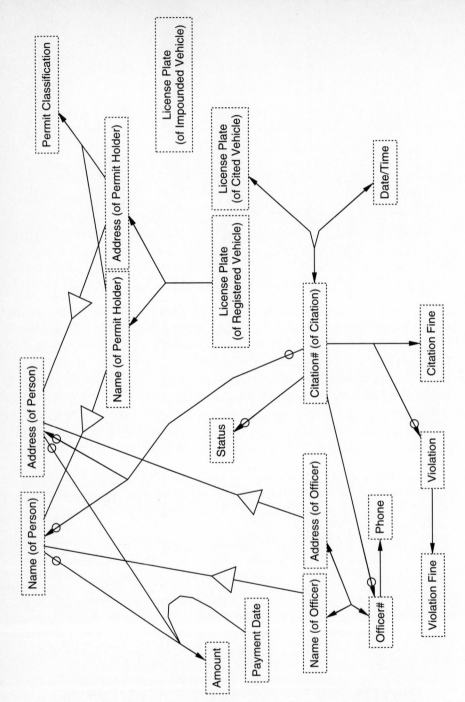

Figure 13.7 Reduced ORM hypergraph for the parking application.

no permit. Rather than use null, we can choose to give this new category a designator, say "Z." Therefore, we merge *Name (of Permit Holder)* with *Name (of Person)* and *Address (of Permit Holder)* with *Address (of Person)*, and we introduce the "Z" classification for persons without permits.

- We next consider the optional connections on *Name* and *Address* in the payment relationship set. Here we should provide role names. Although we can do this, we observe that any role name such as *Name of Payer* and *Address of Payer* is not very useful, because in the context of a payment, this is already understood. Further, according to Algorithm 10.1, which we use to generate flat schemes, the generated scheme for the payment relationship set will be separate from any other scheme. There is therefore no need to introduce roles to enforce this separation. Since there is also no need for alternative names, we ignore the optional roles and observe that Algorithm 10.1 will produce what we want.

- We next consider the optional connection for *Citation#*. Here we observe that the null is "applicable but unknown." There is always a person responsible for answering the citation and paying the fine, but the officer issuing a citation may not have the name. Since we usually save time and space by combining schemes when there is an "applicable but unknown" null, we choose here to do this cost analysis in advance of generating schemes and note that if we ignore the optional connection, Algorithm 10.1 will generate the combined scheme as desired.

- Finally we consider the optional connections on *Status*, *Officer#*, and *Violation*, which all have the same characteristics. Here we should produce roles and resolve the incongruency. We observe, however, that for *Officer#* and *Violation*, if we ignore the optional connection, Algorithm 10.1 will produce what we want anyway, so it is only a matter of whether we wish to introduce a distinct role name. In this case we choose not to add role names (although a case could be made for using *Issuing Officer#* as a role for *Officer#* to designate the role of the officer giving a citation). For *Status*, we should add a role because we want to keep track of the status categories even if no citation happens to have a particular status category. The name "Status," however, is a good name both for the lone singleton object set and the role. If we slightly alter Step 4 in Algorithm 10.1 so that a scheme is generated either when it stands alone or when we cannot guarantee that all its values will appear in some other scheme or schemes, we can leave *Status* as it is and generate schemes according to this understanding.

We now apply Algorithm 10.1 with the understanding just discussed to the adjusted ORM hypergraph derived from the hypergraph in Fig. 13.7. As just discussed, the adjusted hypergraph has *Permit Holder* merged with *Person*. We can also consider *Status* to be an object set with no connecting edge but with a specialization also called *Status* connected to *Citation*. With these adjustments, we can ignore all optional connections and apply Algorithm 10.1 directly. Using Algorithm 10.1, augmented to produce keys, and Algorithm 10.2, to produce inclusion dependencies, we obtain the set of schemes in Fig. 13.8.

Person(Name, Address, Permit Classification)
  Key: *Name, Address*
Payment(Name, Address, Payment Date, Amount)
  Key: *Name, Address, Payment Date*
  Person[Name, Address] ⊇ *Payment[Name, Address]*
Officer(Officer#, Name, Address, Phone)
  Key: *Officer#*
  Key: *Name, Address*
  Person[Name, Address] ⊇ *Officer[Name, Address]*
Violation(Violation, Violation Fine)
  Key: *Violation*
Citation(Citation#, License Plate, Date/Time, Name, Address, Officer#,
    Violation, Citation Fine, Status)
  Key: *Citation#*
  Key: *License Plate, Date/Time*
  may be null: *Name*
  may be null: *Address*
  Person[Name, Address] ⊇ *Citation[Name, Address]*
  Violation[Violation] ⊇ *Citation[Violation]*
  Status[Status] ⊇ *Citation[Status]*
Vehicle(License Plate, Name, Address)
  Key: *License Plate*
  Person[Name, Address] ⊇ *Vehicle[Name, Address]*
Impounded Vehicle(License Plate)
  Key: *License Plate*
Status(Status)

Figure 13.8 Schemes, keys, nulls, and inclusion dependencies for the database.

```
create table Citation(
    CitationNr char(4) not null primary key,
    LicensePlate char(10) not null,
    DateTime char(12) not null,
    Name char(20),
    Address char(25),
    OfficerNr char(2) not null references Officer,
    Violation char(20) not null references Violation,
    Fine integer not null,
    Status char(1) not null check(Status = 'P'
        or Status = 'U' or Status = 'N'),
    unique (LicensePlate, DateTime),
    foreign key (Name, Address) references Person)
```

Figure 13.9   Oracle code to create the *Citation* scheme.

We are now ready to produce Oracle **create table** statements. In doing so, we make one more observation about how to save space and time. When we create the scheme for *Citation* that is shown in Fig. 13.9, we observe that we can check the status values using SQL's *check* clause. Since we can therefore ensure that the status values will be only *P*, *U*, or *N*, we need not check the referential integrity constraint to make certain that the *Status* value in the *Citation* scheme is a value in the *Status* scheme. Hence, we can discard the *Status* scheme and save both time and space.

13.6   Code Generation

For implementation, we show some sample code. The Oracle code for creating the *Citation* scheme appears in Fig. 13.9; the code to release an impounded vehicle, in Fig. 13.10.

void ReleaseImpoundedVehicle()

{

  char input[MAXLENGTH];

  EXEC SQL WHENEVER SQLERROR GOTO printerror;

  printf("\nRelease Impounded Vehicle\n");

```
/ * Get License Plate * /
printf ("License Plate: ");
gets(input);
strncpy(LicensePlate. arr, ConvertToOracleStrng(input,
  MAXLICENSEPLATELENGTH), MAXLICENSEPLATELENGTH);
LicensePlate. len = MAXLICENSEPLATELENGTH;

EXEC SQL delete ImpoundedVehicle
  where LicensePlate = :LicensePlate;
printf ("\nRelease Impounded Vehicle – – done\n");
EXEC SQL COMMIT;
return;

printerror:
  Err();
}
```

Figure 13.10 Oracle code for releasing an impounded vehicle.

13.7 Chapter Summary

Topic Summary

- The case study in this chapter illustrates the following concepts. Parenthetical section numbers refer to places in the book where these concepts are discussed.

  - Analysis validation (Section 7.4), especially the validation of zero-minimum participation constraints.

  - Interface-form specification (Section 8.4) and how the development of interface forms with respect to the ORM structure can lead to the discovery of missing interactions and their development as interface forms.

  - Hypergraphs and hypergraph reductions (Chapter 9), especially head reductions, equivalence-class consolidation, and lexicalization.

  - Generation of flat schemes and interscheme dependencies and the properties of generated flat schemes (Sections 10.1–4).

  - Cost analysis (Section 10.7), particularly exceptions to the general scheme-generation rules for nulls.

Question Summary

- How easy or difficult is it to transform an OSM data design into SQL DDL?

  Designed schemes translate directly into SQL **create table** statements. We are thus assured that the implemented database has the properties of our database as designed.

- How easy or difficult is it to transform an OSM functional design into SQL queries and Pro*C code?

  Much of the essential functional code for Pro*C comes from SQL statements, which are essentially the same as OSM-SQL statements. For the remaining code, OSM-L provides a good guide for producing Pro*C code.

Chapter 14

Object-Relational DBMS Case Study

We use UniSQL for our object-relational DBMS case study. Our application involves developing a system that helps a travel specialist create tours. A tour is a sequence of activities—visits to sites of interest, events to attend, lodging, dining, and travel—over a sequence of days.

The database contains activities for cities of interest. An administrator can add new activities and cities and can remove those that are no longer of interest. A user can select activities and arrange them into a tour with the help of an active tour-creation assistant.

A tour has a tour name, a beginning date, a beginning time, a beginning city, an ending date, an ending time, an ending city, and an advertised price. Tours contain several bookings. A booking has a booking start time, a booking start date, a booking end time, and a booking end date. A booking can be made for any available activity.

There are five types of activities:

1. A trip from one city to another;

2. A visit to some historical or entertainment site;

3. An event, such as a concert;

4. Lodging; and

5. Dining.

For each activity there is information such as the description, cost, location, duration, and contact information.

A user of the tour-creation application can do the following:

- View a list of tours currently in the system;

- Add a new tour;

- List the dates in a tour;

- Select a day and view an hourly schedule for that day, which includes the times and names of any scheduled activities;

- Select a scheduled activity and view more details such as the description, cost, and booking phone number;

- Delete a scheduled activity; and

- Schedule an activity in a time slot by choosing from a list of activities suggested by the tour creator based on the current city.

An active tour-creation assistant, which is part of the system, provides some rudimentary help for a tour creator. The automated assistant keeps track of schedules for tours being created, displays schedules, recognizes the current city of a tour for a given time in a schedule, filters out all activities except those for the current city in the schedule, ensures that the time allotted is greater than the minimum duration of an activity, and disallows overlapping activities.

The following topics in this chapter are particularly important:

- Model integration and adjustments needed to make model integration work.

- Partitioned-category specialization.

- Nested-scheme generation.

- Translation of state nets into a convenient pattern for implementation.

- System and subsystem boundaries.

The following questions should also be kept in mind:

- How easy or difficult is it to transform an OSM data design into UniSQL data definitions?

- How easy or difficult is it to transform an OSM functional design into UniSQL code?

14.1   Application-Model Integration

A natural place to begin the analysis is to describe each activity; the descriptions then can be integrated into a single application model. Figure

14.1 presents an ORM application model for each activity: a trip from one city to another (Fig. 14.1a), an event (Fig. 14.1b), a visit to a site of interest (Fig. 14.1c), lodging (Fig. 14.1d), and dining (Fig. 14.1e).

To integrate the application models in Fig. 14.1, we observe first that the ORM diagrams have several elements in common. With some thought and some adjustments, we realize that the activity descriptions are nearly identical. *Ticket Price*, *Cost*, *Entry Cost*, *Room Cost*, and *Meal Cost* are all synonyms for the cost of an activity. The various types of phone numbers are all synonyms for the phone number to call to obtain information or make a reservation. Each activity has a city, although we must realize that *Location* of *Visit* is an address that contains a city, and we must think of the *Departure City* for a trip as a trip's city. The *Arrival City* is unique to *Trip*. If we think of the *Airport ID* as the address for *Trip* and the local street address of *Location* as the address of *Visit*, each activity has an address. Each activity has a *Description*, except for *Trip*, which we can think of as having an implicit description, which we can make explicit. Each activity has a short identifying descriptor—*Event Name*, *Site*, *Place*, and *Flight#*. Times, dates, and durations are explicit for *Event*; implicit for *Visit*, *Lodging*, and *Dining*; and partly explicit and partly implicit for *Trip*. Times and dates can become explicit booking times and dates in our application. Durations can also become explicit; we note that although we might expect to be able to calculate them from start and end times, probably we should allow some leeway as specified by the tour creator. Thus, we want *Duration* to be an independent object set associated with an activity, as it is for *Event* in Fig. 14.1b. In reconciling durations for our tour application, we let *Duration* represent the minimum time for an activity and allow a tour creator to specify more time than the minimum for an activity.

After making several adjustments according to the preceding discussion, we obtain the integrated ORM diagram in Fig. 14.2. In our integration we let *Activity* represent the activities in Fig. 14.1, and we let each of the five activities be specializations of *Activity*. We represent the various costs and prices as *Cost*, the various phone numbers as *Booking Phone Number*, and the various identifying descriptors as *Activity Name*. We add an explicit *Trip* description and directly merge it and the *Description* object sets in Fig. 14.1. For cities and addresses, we decompose *Location* in Fig. 14.1c into *City* and *Address* before integrating; for *Trip*, we let *Departure City* be the city and *Airport ID* be the address. We subsume all times and dates in *Booking* times and dates, thus dropping *Departure Time*, *Arrival Time*, and *Event Date and Time* before merging. Finally, to obtain *Duration*, we add an estimated minimum duration for *Visit*, *Lodging*, *Dining*, and *Trip*.

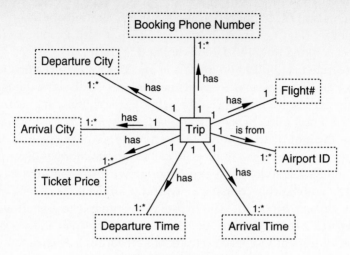

(a) Trip application model.

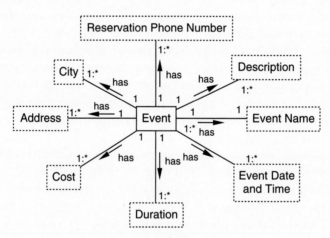

(b) Event application model.

Figure 14.1   Activity application models.

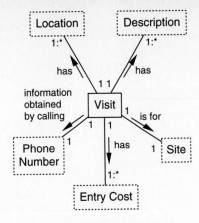

(c) Visit application model.

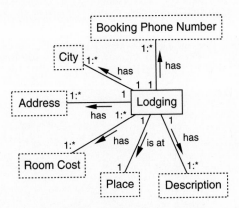

(d) Lodging application model.

Figure 14.1 (cont.) Activity application models.

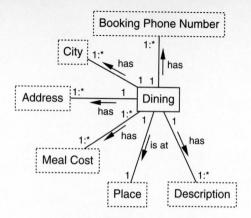

(e) Dining application model.

Figure 14.1 (cont.) Activity application models.

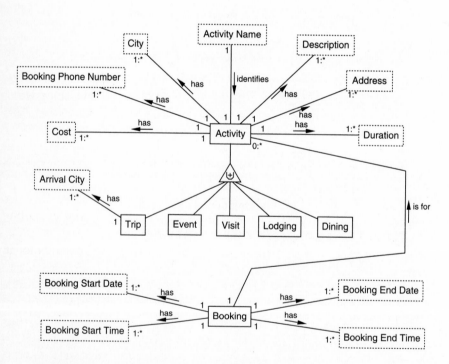

Figure 14.2 Integrated activity application models.

14.2 Generalization/Specialization Transformations

Considering the ORM diagram in Fig. 14.2 for design, we observe that we can lexicalize *Activity* with *Activity Name*. If we do, however, *Activity Name* propagates down the *isa* hierarchy and we lose our ability to obtain an activity's type directly. As an alternative, we observe that we basically have a partitioned-category specialization, which we can transform into an enumeration and thus preserve the type of activity. One problem, however, is that a relationship set connects *Trip* and *Arrival City*, preventing us from making a straightforward transformation.

Taking all these observations into consideration, we perform design transformations for the application model in Fig. 14.2 as follows:

1. We sever the connection between *Trip* and *Arrival City* and connect *Arrival City* to *Activity* with an explicit role, which we name *Trip Activity*.

2. To make the diagram congruent, we add the role *Booked Activity* for activities that have a booking.

3. We transform the partitioned-category specialization and obtain *Activity Type* as an enumeration of *Trip*, *Event*, *Visit*, *Lodging*, and *Dining*.

4. We lexicalize *Activity* by *Activity Name*. Observe that since we have replaced the partitioned generalization/specialization with an enumeration, we lexicalize without losing the activity type.

Figure 14.3 displays the results of these transformations as an ORM hypergraph.

In Fig. 14.3 we have also added the basic *Tour* information, which we omitted in the preceding discussion on integration. Note that in adding *Tour* we have introduced an incongruency. The optional connection in Fig. 14.3 arises because we initialize a tour before making any bookings for it. We could add a role, say *Tour with Bookings*, but we expect all our tours to have bookings eventually. Thus, the null for this connection is "applicable but not yet known," which is normally acceptable as stated in our rule of thumb for nulls in Chapter 10. Furthermore, since we intend to generate nested schemes, we see that this incongruency will simply mean that a tour has zero or more bookings rather than one or more bookings, which is exactly what we want.

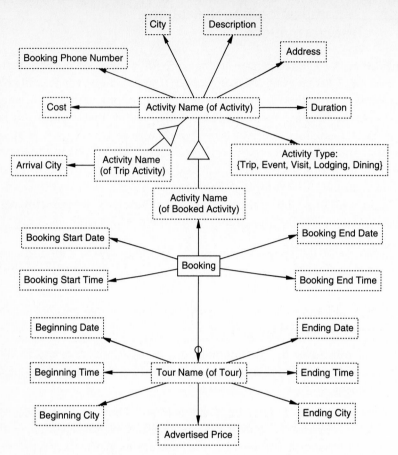

Figure 14.3 ORM hypergraph after making design adjustments.

14.3 Nested-Scheme Generation

Using Algorithm 10.3, we can generate nested schemes from the ORM hypergraph in Fig. 14.3. After adding the data types, which are given or implied in the figure, as well as the keys, potential nulls, and inclusion dependencies, the result is the set of schemes in Fig. 14.4. Note that the only potential null is for *Booking*, which is a nested scheme. Thus, instead of a null, we can have simply an empty bucket.

We can directly convert the schemes in Fig. 14.4 into UniSQL syntax. The resulting code appears in Fig. 14.5. Observe that *TripActivity* and *Activity* have the same key, *ActivityName*, and recall that a trip activity is an activity, as can be seen by referring to the ORM hypergraph in Fig. 14.3.

Tour(Tour Name : String, Advertised Price : Money,
Beginning Date : Date, Beginning City : String, Beginning Time : Time,
Ending Date : Date, Ending City : String, Ending Time : Time,
(Booking(Booking Start Time : Time, Booking End Time : Time,
Booking Start Date : Date, Booking End Date : Date,
Activity Name : String))*)
Key : Tour Name
Booking may be null -- the Booking bucket may be empty
Activity[Activity Name] ⊇ Booking[Activity Name]

Activity(Activity Name : String, Description : String, City : String,
Address : String, Booking Phone Number : String, Cost : Money,
Activity Type : {Trip, Event, Visit, Lodging, Dining},
Duration : Integer)
Key : Activity Name

Trip Activity(Activity Name : String, Arrival City String)
Key : Activity Name
Activity[Activity Name] ⊇ Trip Activity[Activity Name]

Figure 14.4 Generic schemes for the tour application.

Thus, we can let *Trip Activity* inherit from *Activity*. The UniSQL keyword for inheritance is **under**, which we use in the *Trip Activity* class in Fig. 14.5. Since *TripActivity* inherits from *Activity*, it inherits all the attributes of *Activity* and thus, in particular, it inherits *ActivityName* from *Activity*. Thus the attribute *ActivityName* does not appear in the class declaration for *TripActivity*. Observe also in Fig. 14.5 that we create a separate class for the nested scheme called *Booking* and use *set_of* to nest the *Booking* scheme inside the *Tour* scheme. This is how we nest relations in UniSQL. Also, since UniSQL does not have an enumerated type, we convert the enumeration in Fig. 14.4 into an integer type. Finally, since UniSQL does not let us specify foreign keys to enforce referential integrity automatically, we must write code to ensure that all updates guarantee referential integrity.

14.4 Behavior Transformations

Figure 14.6 depicts the active behavior of *Tour Creator*, which is the active object in our application. When a tour creator comes into existence, it enters the *Continue1* state and then continues immediately into its only

```
create class Activity (
    ActivityName string unique not null,
    Description string not null,
    City string not null,
    Address string not null,
    BookingPhoneNumber string not null,
    Cost monetary not null,
    ActivityType integer not null,
    Duration integer not null);

create class TripActivity under Activity(
    ArrivalCity string not null);

create class Booking (
    BookingStartTime time not null,
    BookingEndTime time not null,
    BookingStartDate date not null,
    BookingEndDate date not null,
    ActivityName string not null);

create class Tour (
    TourName string unique not null,
    AdvertisedPrice monetary not null,
    BeginningDate date not null,
    BeginningCity string not null,
    BeginningTime time not null,
    EndingDate date not null,
    EndingCity string not null,
    EndingTime time not null,
    Bookings set_of (Booking));
```

Figure 14.5 UniSQL database schemes.

subsequent transition and displays a menu of tours. Depending on the response to the menu, the tour creator either helps the user create a new tour or allows the user to select an existing tour, presumably to modify it. If the user selects a tour, the tour creator displays a menu of days for the tour. Then if the user selects a day, the tour creator displays a menu of hours for the selected day with names of scheduled activities. If the user then selects an hour, the tour creator shows the details of the scheduled activity. The user now can choose an activity and schedule it, or can delete the scheduled activity. Throughout the process, the user may choose to go back to a previous state or exit the system.

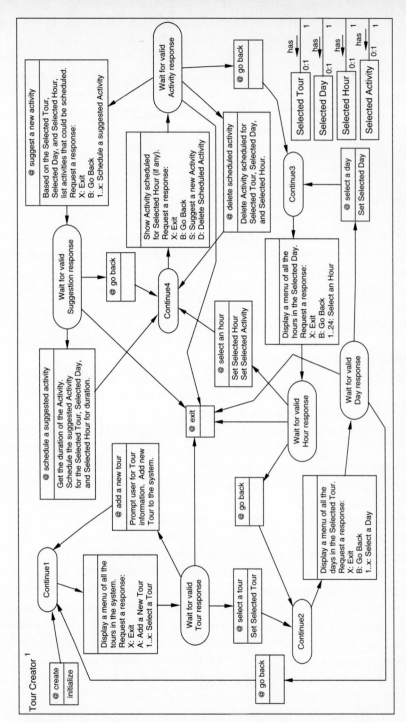

Figure 14.6 State net describing the behavior of the tour creator.

We transform the state net in Fig. 14.6 into a state-net pattern for eventual translation into an ADT as follows. We observe that there are five states in which we wait (i.e., *Wait for valid ... response*): *Tour*, *Day*, *Hour*, *Activity*, and *Suggestion*. From these states we can go on to the next task, exit the system, or return to a previous state. We also notice that there are four continue states. These states all precede a transition with no trigger where we set up a menu and enter one of the five wait states. Before we enter one of the continue states, we add a new tour, select a tour, select a day, select an hour, delete an activity, or suggest an activity.

With these observations, we can transform the state net in Fig. 14.6 into the one in Fig. 14.7. The transformation involves adding a *WaitState* object set, whose states are the enumeration {*Tour*, *Day*, *Hour*, *Activity*, *Suggestion*}. Then, for each transition that enters one of these wait states, we set the state, and for each trigger that depends on one of these states, we add a state-checking condition.

The state net in Fig. 14.7 is not a single-state state net, but the only exceptions are the continue states. We notice, however, that every path, except the initialization and termination paths, starts and ends at the *Ready* state. We could thus transform the state net in Fig. 14.7 into a single-state state net by taking each path as one high-level transition. The disadvantage of this transformation, however, is that we would have to replicate code to implement each of these intertwined paths. If instead we take the state net in Fig. 14.7 as is, make a method for each transition, and then call each transition along a path, we can code the paths without duplicating code.

We take the latter approach in our implementation. Figure 14.8 gives UniSQL code for the methods that implement the three transitions surrounding *Continue1*. The *create* method in Fig. 14.8a corresponds to the *create* transition in Fig. 14.7. Its main task is to initialize the database. The *tourMenu* method in Fig. 14.8b corresponds to the transition in Fig. 14.7, in which we display the tour menu. Along with displaying exit and add-new-tour options, the *tourMenu* method accesses the database to obtain the current tours and displays them as selectable options. The method then returns to wait for user input. The *addNewTour* method in Fig. 14.8c corresponds to the transition in Fig. 14.7 in which we add a new tour. Most of the code consists of a sequence of interactive questions, only some of which are in Fig. 14.8c. Once the user answers the questions, the new tour is added to the database.

Figure 14.9 shows part of the UniSQL code that drives the behavior for the tour creator. Initially, we create a *Tour Creator* by calling the *create* method. We then pass through state *Continue1*, which is simply a comment

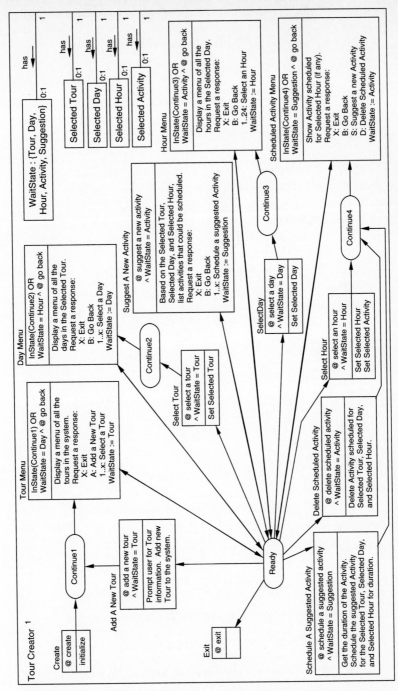

Figure 14.7 Transformed state net describing the behavior of the tour creator.

```
void TourCreator::create(char * ProgramName, char * DatabaseName)
{
  theDatabase.init(ProgramName, DatabaseName);
}
```

(a) UniSQL code for the create transition.

```
void TourCreator::tourMenu()
{
  OutputHelper output;
  NumberTours = theDatabase.GetTours(Tours);

  output.drawLine();
  for (int i = 0; i < NumberTours; i++) {
    cout << i+1 << ". ";
    if (i < 9) // for formatting so columns line up
      cout << " ";
    cout << Tours[i].TourName << endl;
  }
  output.drawLine();

  cout << "To add a new tour, enter 'A'." << endl;
  cout << "To exit the tour creator, enter 'X'.";
  if (NumberTours > 0)
    cout << endl << "Enter the number of the tour you wish to edit:";

  WaitState = TOUR;
}
```

(b) UniSQL code for the tour-menu transition.

```
void TourCreator::addANewTour()
{
  Tour myTour;
  char input[80];
  cout << "Enter the name of the new tour : ";
  cin.getline(input, 79);
  strcpy(myTour.TourName, input);
  cout << "What is the advertised price of the tour (e.g., 595.55): ";
```

Figure 14.8   UniSQL code for several transitions.

```
cin >> myTour. AdvertisedPrice;

. . .

cout << "What is the ending hour of the tour (e. g. , 20): ";
cin >> myTour. EndingTime;
theDatabase. addTour(myTour);
}
```

(c) UniSQL code for the add-a-new-tour transition.

Figure 14.8 (cont.) UniSQL code for several transitions.

in the code, and call the *tourMenu* method. After exiting the *tourMenu* method, Fig. 14.7 shows that we should enter the *Ready* state. In the UniSQL code in Fig. 14.9, we simulate this behavior by entering a **while** loop. Within the **while** loop, we accept user input and then test each of the conditions of the transitions in Fig. 14.7 successively. When the trigger of a transition *T* is true, we execute the path that starts with *T* and ends back in the *Ready* state in another iteration of the **while** loop.

In Fig. 14.9, for example, if the *WaitState* is *TOUR* and the input compares with '*A*' (meaning that the input is either '*a*' or '*A*'), the program executes the path consisting of the transitions encoded in methods *addNewTour* and *tourMenu*. This corresponds to the path in Fig. 14.7 from the *Ready* state through transition *AddANewTour* to the *Continue1* state and then through transition *Tour Menu* and back to the *Ready* state. As another example, if the *WaitState* is *DAY* and the input compares with '*B*', the program executes the path consisting of only the transition encoded as the *tourMenu* method, which corresponds to executing the path in Fig. 14.7 from the *Ready* state through the *Tour Menu* transition and back to the *Ready* state.

14.5   Database Interface

The code under discussion makes several calls to the *Tour Database*. The call to initialize the database, *init*, for example, appears in the code in Fig. 14.8a, and the call to add a tour to the database appears in the last line of code in Fig. 14.8c. The pattern in Fig. 14.10, showing all the interactions with the database, is similar to the pattern for a system boundary, except that all interactions go to the database rather than to the environment outside the system.

```
TourCreator::TourCreator(char * ProgramName, char * DatabaseName)
{
  create(ProgramName, DatabaseName);
  // Continue1
  tourMenu();

  int bExit = FALSE;
  int numeric = 0;
  char input[80];
  for (int i = 0; i < 80; i++)
    input[i] = 0;

  while (bExit ≡ FALSE)
  {
    // Ready

    cin >> input;

    if (compare(input, 'X'))
      bExit = TRUE;
    numeric = atoi(input);

    if (WaitState ≡ DAY && compare(input, 'B'))
      tourMenu();
    else if (WaitState ≡ HOUR && compare(input, 'B'))
      dayMenu();
    else if (WaitState ≡ TOUR && compare(input, 'A'))
    {
      addANewTour();
      // Continue1
      tourMenu();
    }
    else if (WaitState ≡ ACTIVITY && compare(input, 'S'))
      suggestANewActivity();
    else if (WaitState ≡ DAY && range(numeric, 1, NumberDays))
    {
      selectDay(numeric);
      // Continue3
      hourMenu();
    }
    else if ···
```

Figure 14.9 UniSQL code to drive tour creation.

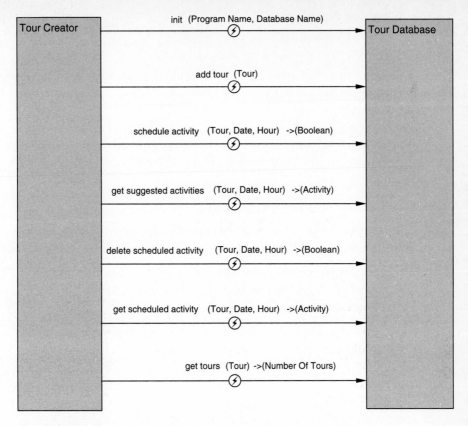

Figure 14.10 Database interface for the tour creator.

We can treat any collection of interactions that go between two object sets as an interface—like the system interface. Often, as is the case here, we can draw a boundary around part of the system and treat it as a subsystem. As for system boundaries, only interactions cross the subsystem boundary. The only difference here is that instead of a system boundary, we have a subsystem boundary.

A subsystem boundary like the one here is sometimes called a wrapper or an application interface (API). An API hides the details of the interactions. Here we hide the details of exactly how the *Tour Database* handles each interaction. Indeed, the details are extensive and intricate and all are ultimately contained in the code, but the *Tour Creator* routines need not be concerned about these details. The API also makes it possible for the tour application code to work smoothly with the *Tour Database*.

14.6 Chapter Summary

Topic Summary

The case study in this chapter illustrates the following concepts. Parenthetical section numbers refer to places in the book where these concepts are discussed.

- Application model integration (Section 7.3), especially how sometimes we must adjust our view of similar objects.

- The use of Algorithm 10.3 (Section 10.8) to generate nested schemes, which we can implement directly.

- The transformation of a partitioned-category specialization into an enumerated type (Section 11.3).

- The transformation of a state net into a state net with multiple completion paths and its similarity to transformations of state nets to single-state state nets (Section 11.5).

- Subsystem boundaries (wrappers or application interfaces) and their similarity to system boundaries (Section 8.1).

Question Summary

- How easy or difficult is it to transform an OSM data design into UniSQL data definitions?

  Designed schemes translate directly into UniSQL declarations.

- How easy or difficult is it to transform an OSM functional design into UniSQL code?

  Designed state-net patterns for this case study have a direct correspondence to the UniSQL code that drives the behavior, making the translation of these patterns to UniSQL code straightforward.

Chapter 15

Object-Oriented DBMS Case Study I

We use O_2 for our first standard object-oriented DBMS case study. For our application, we develop a satellite-tracking system for use by amateur radio operators.

Amateur radio operators use satellites to relay their transmissions to different parts of the world. Our satellite-tracking system tells the operators which direction to set their antennas to communicate through a chosen satellite. The tracking system consists of a database that stores information about registered amateur radio operators and about satellite schedules. (Interestingly, our system downloads actual, current satellite schedules from an Internet site.) Based on the location of an antenna, the tracking system displays, at operator-defined intervals of time, the azimuth and the elevation for directing the antenna at a chosen satellite. The azimuth is an angle between 0 and 360 degrees clockwise from north, while the elevation is an angle between 0 and 90 degrees from the horizon.

The information stored in the database includes information on satellites, amateur radio operators, and antenna locations. Satellite information includes the necessary Keplerian data to calculate a satellite's location. Amateur radio-operator information includes an operator's name and call sign, identifying an operator within the amateur radio community. Latitude, longitude, and altitude identify the location of antennas, and a minimum elevation provides information for each location about how high above the horizon an antenna should point to have a reasonable communication link.

The tracking system provides several services. It allows a user to do the following:

1. Create information about amateur radio operators. When an operator registers with the system, the operator supplies a name, a call sign, and usually at least one antenna location. Since an operator may regularly use several different antennas, they all can be stored in advance.

2. Modify operator information.

3. Delete operator information.

4. Request a real-time antenna direction table. An amateur radio operator supplies a call sign for identification, chooses an antenna from among those registered for the operator, selects a satellite, and specifies a time interval. The tracking system calculates and displays the azimuth and elevation to set the antenna. This continues in real time at an operator-defined time interval until the operator interrupts the process.

5. View list of available satellites.

6. View a selected satellite's information.

7. Request an update of satellite information. The tracking system downloads satellite information from

   ftp://archive.afit.af.mil/pub/space/amateur.tle,

   a current Keplerian data file in a two-line format provided by NASA (the U.S. National Aeronautics and Space Administration), and then updates the information for all satellites in the database.

8. Start satellite tracking system.

9. Shut down the satellite tracking system.

The following topics in this chapter are particularly important:

- Computed relationship sets.
- Nested-scheme generation.
- Cost analysis for redundant data.
- Conversion of interface forms to code.
- Application code that enforces constraints.

The following questions should also be kept in mind:

- How easy or difficult is it to transform an OSM data design into O_2 data definitions?
- How easy or difficult is it to transform an OSM functional design into O_2 code?

15.1   Complex Computations

Calculating the orbit of a satellite requires seven Keplerian elements, which define an ellipse, orient it around the earth, and place the satellite on the ellipse at a particular time. In the Keplerian model, satellites orbit in an ellipse of constant shape and orientation. Since this is only an approximation of a satellite's true position (orbits decay slowly over time), occasionally the system must update the actual location from accurate data kept by NASA. Even with this simplification, the Keplerian calculations require more than a simple formula, but computers are up to the task of doing the tedious calculations required by the algorithm.

The algorithm for approximating Keplerian orbits requires the following seven elements:

1. *Reference Epoch.* Orbital elements are set in time like a snapshot. The reference epoch defines the point in time at which the snapshot is taken.

2. *Orbital Inclination.* The ellipse of a satellite's orbit lies in a plane known as the orbital plane, which always goes through the center of the Earth. Inclination is the angle between the orbital plane and the equatorial plane.

3. *Right of Ascension of Ascending Node (RAAN).* Two numbers orient the orbital plane in space. The first is the orbital inclination; the second, the RAAN. RAAN is the angle, measured from the vernal equinox (an astronomical coordinate system similar to latitude and longitude), where the orbital plane crosses the equator.

4. *Argument of Perigee.* To orient the orbital ellipse within the orbital plane, the argument of perigee specifies a single angle: the number of degrees clockwise from the northern center line to the ellipse's major axis.

5. *Eccentricity.* This element specifies the shape of the ellipse. When the eccentricity is zero, the ellipse is a circle; when the eccentricity is close to one, the ellipse approaches a straight line.

6. *Mean Motion.* This element measures the size of the ellipse. This size can be measured in either distance or speed. Mean motion is the average speed of the satellite as it orbits the Earth.

7. *Mean Anomaly.* At reference-epoch time, the mean anomaly sets the satellite in the ellipse at a certain point.

Figure 15.1 displays these seven Keplerian elements. It also shows all other object and relationship sets for our application, including necessary static information such as a satellite's name and catalog number, both of which identify a satellite, and an amateur radio operator's identifying information and antenna locations with their minimum elevations. Figure 15.1 also shows the dynamic relationship set computed by a satellite tracker that relates the azimuth and elevation of a chosen satellite to an amateur radio operator and antenna location at a certain time.

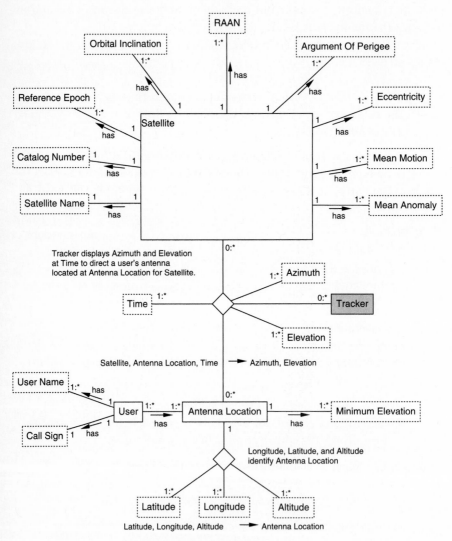

Figure 15.1   Application ORM diagram.

The satellite tracking system has one active object set: a *Tracker*. A tracker uses the Keplerian elements we have described to compute and display antenna directions at user-defined intervals. We can specify this computation in OSM-L. As would be expected, the computation is involved and lengthy. In Fig. 15.2, we show a few lines in OSM-L for a particular satellite *s*.

15.2   Active Objects

Our application has two active object sets. One, of course, is the *Tracker*, which computes the azimuth and elevation of a satellite for an antenna location at a particular time. The other is the *Tracker Application*, which provides all other services, including maintaining user and satellite information and requesting a new *Tracker* object to track a satellite for a user.

Figure 15.3 depicts the active behavior for both the *Tracker Application* and the *Tracker*. The *Tracker Application* knows about users and satellites. The application can add or delete users, edit user information, display satellite information, update satellite information, and issue requests to *Tracker* objects to begin tracking satellites. Multiple *Tracker* objects can exist and work simultaneously. When a tracker object comes into existence, it sets a given time interval for its display and begins tracking. At elapsed time intervals, the tracker computes antenna directions for the chosen antenna and satellite.

15.3   Design Adjustments

Turning now to design, we begin with Fig. 15.4a, which gives the ORM hypergraph for the user information in Fig. 15.1. In our design, when we lexicalize *User* with *Call Sign* and *Antenna Location* with its *Latitude*, *Longitude*, and *Altitude*, we obtain the canonical ORM hypergraph in Fig. 15.4b.

We can now start with *Call Sign* and generate schemes from the canonical hypergraph in Fig. 15.4b. We also use a variation of Algorithm 10.3, in which we treat the three components of *Antenna Location* as a unit to make the edges all binary. The algorithm yields two schemes:

> *User(Call Sign, User Name, (Latitude, Longitude, Altitude)*)*
> *Elevation(Latitude, Longitude, Altitude, Minimum Elevation)*

We can analyze these schemes and convince ourselves that there is no potential redundancy. If we were to join the schemes, however, we would

Minutes Per Day : *Integer;*
Minutes Per Day := 24 * 60;

PI : *Real;*
PI := 3.14159265;

Radians Per Degree : *Real;*
Radians Per Degree := *PI*/180;

Semimajor Axis : *Real;*
Semimajor Axis := 331.25 * *exp*(2 * *log*(*Minutes Per
   Day*/*Satellite*(*s*). *Mean Motion*)/3);

Earth Radius : *Real;*
Earth Radius := 6378.16;   − − *kilometers*

RAAN Precession : *Real;*
RAAN Precession := 9.95 * *pow*(*Earth Radius*/*Semimajor Axis*, 3.5)
  **cos*(*Satellite*(*s*). *OrbitalInclination*)
  /*SQR*(1 − *SQR*(*Satellite*(*s*). *Eccentricity*)) * *Radians Per Degree;*

Perigee Precession : *Real;*
Perigee Precession := 4.97 * *pow*(*Earth Radius*/*Semimajor Axis*, 3.5)
  *(5 * *SQR*(*cos*(*Satellite*(*s*). *OrbitalInclination*)) − 1)
  /*SQR*(1 − *SQR*(*Satellite*(*s*). *Eccentricity*)) * *Radians Per Degree;*
  . . .

Figure 15.2   Small part of the computation to obtain
azimuth and elevation.

store *Minimum Elevation* redundantly for every amateur radio operator who
uses an antenna at the same location.

   Analyzing the application, however, we see that, despite this potential
redundancy, we should join the two schemes:

   User(*Call Sign*, *User Name* (*Latitude*, *Longitude*, *Altitude*,
      Minimum Elevation)*)

We observe first that the amount of extra storage is minimal because few
operators use the same antennas. Second, the time penalty incurred for this

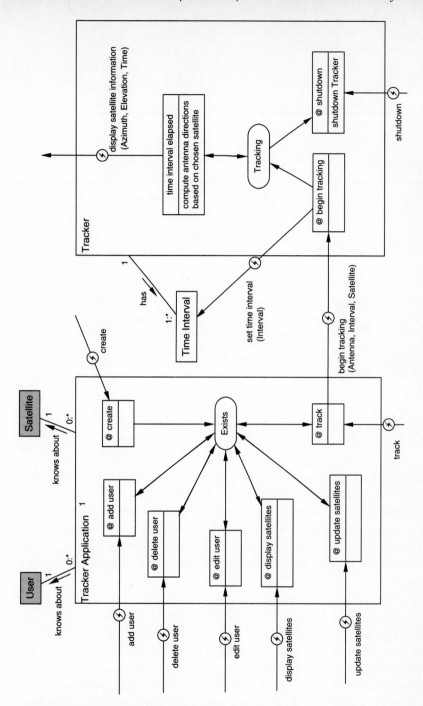

Figure 15.3 Active application objects.

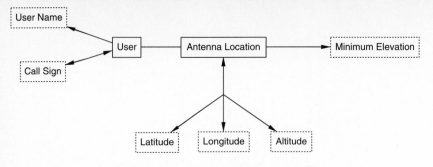

(a) ORM hypergraph for user information.

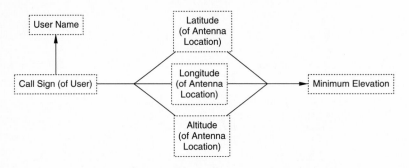

(b) Canonical ORM hypergraph after lexicalization.

Figure 15.4   Design hypergraphs.

redundancy happens when we update the minimum elevation, probably an infrequent procedure for this application. Moreover, it makes sense to treat *Minimum Elevation* as a recommended default minimum elevation, not as an absolute minimum. With this understanding, we could change the semantics and allow each operator for the same antenna to have a different minimum elevation. If we do this, we need not enforce the functional dependency

$$Antenna\ Location \nrightarrow Minimum\ Elevation$$

and thus there can be no update anomaly. We thus choose to combine the schemes and drop the FD constraint.

With this choice, we obtain the O_2 data declarations in Fig. 15.5. (Note that we have prefixed class names with a "C," a common convention for O_2 and related languages such as C++.) Although we could nest the

```
class CUser inherit Object public type
    tuple(CallSign: string,
      UserName: string,
      Antennas: set (CAntenna))
    end;
class CAntenna inherit Object public type
    tuple(Altitude: real,
      Latitude: real,
      Longitude: real,
      MinimumElevation: real)
    end;
name Users: set(CUser);
```

Figure 15.5 O_2 declarations.

declaration for the antennas in the *CUser* class and thus reflect the design directly in the code, we choose to have a separate class for the antennas. We make this choice because we know from Fig. 15.3 that we must pass the antenna information to a tracker; it is convenient to pass this information as a unit.

O_2 makes a class persistent by a *name* declaration, which is the last line of code in Fig. 15.5. This declaration provides a name and thus a way to access a set of persistent objects that belong to some class. Here the name is *Users*, which provides an access path to *CUser* objects. The code for our application has a similar declaration with *name Satellites* for the persistent set of satellites known to the tracker application.

15.4   Database Updates

Figure 15.3 gives the updates to user and satellite information. As usual, not all the details appear in the analysis. To complete our specification, we can use interface forms based on the partially specified interactions in Fig. 15.3 and on the ORM information in Fig. 15.1. Figure 15.6 gives an interface form for the *add user* interaction. When we add a user, we provide a *Call Sign*, a *User Name*, and information for one or more antennas, which consists of a *Latitude*, a *Longitude*, an *Altitude*, and a *Minimum Elevation*.

Given interface forms for each interaction, we can write O_2 code directly to obtain needed information from a user of the tracker application. Based directly on Fig. 15.3, we can then write the *Tracker Application* module in O_2 to invoke each interaction. Figure 15.7 shows the O_2 interface for the

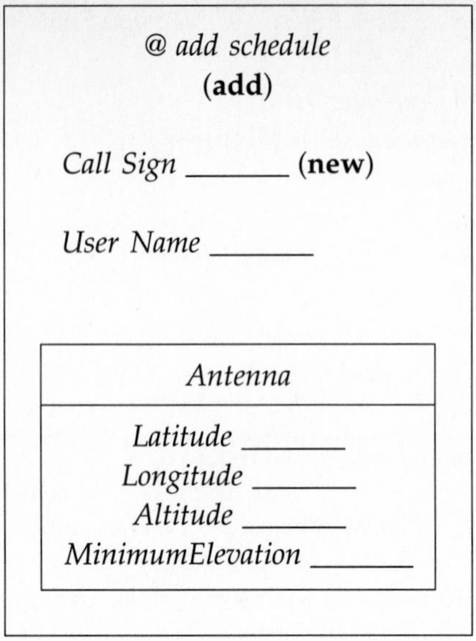

```
                    @ add schedule
                        (add)

        Call Sign _____ (new)

        User Name _____


        ┌─────────────────────────────┐
        │          Antenna            │
        ├─────────────────────────────┤
        │      Latitude _____      │
        │      Longitude _____     │
        │      Altitude _____      │
        │  MinimumElevation _____  │
        └─────────────────────────────┘
```

Figure 15.6 Interface specification for adding a user.

Tracker Application. In O_2 we denote main programs by the keyword *application*. The declaration *dialog: Box* in Figure 15.7 lets us use O_2's dialog box for interacting with a user.

Figure 15.8 presents part of the O_2 code for *addUser*. When we execute *new CUser*, O_2 provides a dialog box with all the fields for *CUser*. We can thus enter a *CallSign*, a *UserName*, and an *Antenna* set, which includes the *Latitude*, *Longitude*, *Altitude*, and *MinimumElevation* for each antenna. We then check this information, as Fig. 15.8a shows. If a *CallSign* is empty, for

> *application TrackerApplication*
> *variable*
>   *dialog: Box*
> *program*
>   *private init,*
>   *public addUser,*
>   *public deleteUser,*
>   *public editUser,*
>   *public displaySatellites,*
>   *public updateSatellites,*
>   *public track,*
> *end;*

Figure 15.7 O_2 declarations for *Tracker Application*.

example, we return an error. If all the input checks are satisfactory, we add
the new user to the database with the line of code

$$Users + = set(newUser)$$

```
transaction body addUser in application TrackerApplication
{
  o2 CUser newUser = new CUser;

  if (newUser– > edit == LK_SAVE)
  {
    if (newUser– > CallSign == "")
      dialog– > message("Must enter a call sign.", "Error");
    else if (newUser– > Antennas == set())
      dialog– > message("Must enter at least one antenna location.", "Error");
    else if (userExists(newUser– > CallSign))
      dialog– > message("User " +newUser– > CallSign +
      " is already registered in the database.", "Error");
    else
      {
      checkAntennaList(newUser);
      Users + = set(newUser);
      }
  }
}
```

(a) Dialog for *add user* interaction.

```
function body userExists(userSign: string): boolean
{
  o2 CUser tUser;

  for (tUser in Users where tUser– > CallSign == userSign)
    return true;
  return false;
};
```

(b) Method for checking the key constraint on a user's call sign.

Figure 15.8 Partial O$_2$ code for *addUser* interaction.

Of particular interest here is how we enforce key constraints, which O_2 does not enforce automatically. If we want to enforce them, we must provide the code ourselves. We check the key constraint by calling the *userExists* method in Fig. 15.8b. This method iterates through the set of users and returns *true* if the new user's call sign, which is passed in, matches an existing call sign; otherwise the method returns *false*. We then invoke *userExists*, as in Fig. 15.8a, adding a new user only if the call sign is unique.

Except for the *update satellites* interaction, the remaining update and query interactions for the *Tracker Application* in Fig. 15.3 are similar. The *update satellites* interaction differs because its source is not an interactive user, but instead an ftp site. For this interaction, O_2 executes

$$system("xterm - T \ \backslash'amateur.\ tle\ retrieval\backslash' - e\ ftpamateur");$$

to obtain the file ftp://archive.afit.af.mil/pub/space/amateur.tle. It then extracts the required satellite data from the amateur.tle file.

15.5   Active-Object Design and Implementation

Except for the complex code that determines a satellite's location, the *Tracker* design and implementation is straightforward. We can write the O_2 code almost directly from the *Tracker* state net in Fig. 15.3.

When we invoke *track* in *TrackerApplication* in Fig. 15.7, we first obtain the needed information. Obtaining information about which antenna, time interval, and satellite to use is similar to the code for *addUser*, which we have just discussed. We then execute

$$tracker = new\ CTracker(satellite,\ antenna,\ Time);$$
$$tracker->beginTracking;$$

to establish a new tracker and begin the tracking process.

Figure 15.9 shows how we simulate the action in the *Tracker* state net in Fig. 15.3. To leave the *Tracking* state and display the satellite information when the time interval elapses, we use a **while** loop and a provided *sleep* command. The *sleep* command causes the system to wait for a specified amount of time before continuing. When the elapsed time has passed, the **while** loop invokes code to compute the azimuth and elevation for the current time. We shut a tracker down by entering Control-C in the window of the tracker we wish to shut down.

while (1)
{
  / * *compute azimuth and elevation for the current time* * /
  . . .

  sleep(self– > Time);
}

Figure 15.9   Basic control for *Tracker*.

15.6   Chapter Summary

Topic Summary

The case study in this chapter illustrates the following concepts. Parenthetical section numbers refer to places in the book where these concepts are discussed.

- Synthesis of nested relation schemes using a variation of Algorithm 10.3 (Section 10.8) and a subsequent check for potential redundancy (Section 10.3).

- An analysis of the impact of potential redundancy for the application (Section 10.7).

- Computed relationship sets in ORM diagrams (Section 11.2).

- The conversion of interface forms (Section 8.4) to code.

- The conversion of a state net to code, in which the OODBMS handles the multiple executing objects for the state net (Section 11.5).

Question Summary

- How easy or difficult is it to transform an OSM data design into O_2 data definitions?

  Designed schemes translate directly into O_2 declarations.

- How easy or difficult is it to transform an OSM functional design into O_2 code?

We can convert the OSM-L specification for complex satellite cal-culations directly into O_2 code, which is not surprising since OSM-L expressions are similar to expressions in most languages. To check key constraints, however, we must provide our own code. For interface forms and state nets, where the OODBMS han-dles the hard part of supporting multiple concurrent objects, OSM provides a good outline for the O_2 code. More detailed OSM-L specifications are also possible, from which we could write O_2 code even more directly.

Chapter 16

Object-Oriented DBMS Case Study II

For our second object-oriented DBMS case study, we use ObjectStore's persistent storage engine for Java.[†] For our application we consider a problem in geographic information systems (GIS). The problem concerns the implementation of a library of routines for polygons, which we demonstrate by analyzing a query about the size of wilderness areas.

For the case study,[†††] we assume that a body of lawmakers has just passed a law that mandates the acquisition of new wilderness areas. The law states that an area within a single county must become a wilderness area if it meets both of the following conditions:

1. The area includes more than 20 square kilometers of alpine highlands (areas over 3000 meters in elevation).

2. The area includes more than 35 square kilometers of coniferous forest.

Figure 16.1 displays three counties in the U.S. state of Utah and their regions of alpine highlands and coniferous forest.[††] For the example, we assume that the portion of the large alpine-highlands region in Summit County is greater than 20 km^2. We also assume that the Summit County portion of the large coniferous-forest region, which is mostly in Summit

---

[†] ObjectStore's persistent storage engine for Java does not support ad hoc queries. In this sense, it may be more proper to call it a persistent object repository than an OODBMS. ObjectStore does support most OODBMS features, however, so in our rough grouping, we place it among the OODBMSs.

[††] Throughout the case study, the counties and areas are fictional but are based on fact.

[†††] This case study and Figs. 16.1, 16.2, 16.3, 16.4, and 16.12 are used courtesy of Springer-Verlag. Taken from "A Multi-layered Approach to Query Processing in Geographic Information Systems," Embley, D. and Nagy, G. in *Geographic Database Management Systems: Workshop Proceedings*, Gambosi, G., Scholl, M. pp. 293–317.

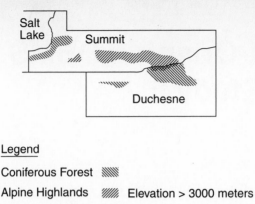

Legend

Coniferous Forest ▧

Alpine Highlands ▨ Elevation > 3000 meters

Figure 16.1 Alpine highlands and coniferous forests in three Utah counties. Courtesy of Springer-Verlag.

County, and that the Duchesne County portion of the large coniferous-forest region, which is mostly in Duchesne County, are each greater than 35 km^2. Finally, we assume that the other regions are all smaller than 10 km^2.

Two wilderness areas in our example satisfy the mandate: one is formed by the intersection of Summit County and the large coniferous-forest region that is mostly in Summit County, while the other is formed by a union of the large Summit County alpine highlands and the large Duchesne County coniferous forest. Note that the Summit County forest wilderness area does not include the two small parts of the forest in Salt Lake County. Also note that the wilderness area straddling the Summit County–Duchesne County line does not include the two small portions of the coniferous forest in Summit County that are outside the intersection of the overlapping coniferous forest and alpine highlands. Only the qualifying regions within a single county become wilderness area, while adjacent qualifying regions in different counties are merged to become one wilderness area.

As a sample query, we suppose that a lumberyard owner in Summit County poses the following problem to our GIS:

To estimate how much lumber will be needed to fence the new wilderness areas in Summit and Duchesne Counties, calculate the perimeter of all the wilderness areas included in these two counties.

To solve this problem, we must find the wilderness area boundary and compute its length. Figure 16.2a shows how we might pose a graphical

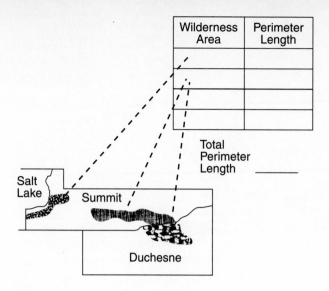

Legend

Qualifying Summit County Coniferous Forest

Area > 35 square kilometers

Qualifying Summit County Alpine Highlands

Elevation > 3000 meters
and Area > 20 square kilometers

Qualifying Duchesne County Coniferous Forest

Area > 35 square kilometers

Qualifying Duchesne County Alpine Highlands

Elevation > 3000 meters
and Area > 20 square kilometers

(a) Graphical query.

Figure 16.2   Lumberyard owner query.

query to solve this problem, while Fig. 16.2b shows a solution. First, we discard all but the qualifying regions. Next, we join qualifying regions in adjacent counties into one wilderness area. We then compute the perimeter of each wilderness area and sum them to obtain the total boundary length.

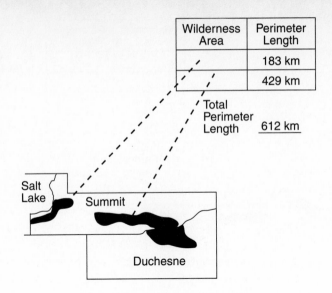

Wilderness Area	Perimeter Length
	183 km
	429 km

Total Perimeter Length   612 km

Salt Lake

Summit

Duchesne

(b) Answer to graphical query.

Figure 16.2 (cont.)   Lumberyard owner query. Courtesy of Springer-Verlag.

The following topics in this chapter are particularly important:

- Abstract, ontological analysis and formalization.

- Libraries of abstract data types (polygons are the example in this chapter's case study).

- Encapsulation, late binding, polymorphism, overloading, inheritance, and the reimplementation of operators.

- Conversion of ORM operations into interactions.

- Modeling implementations.

- Data structures.

The following questions should also be kept in mind:

- How easy or difficult is it to transform an OSM data design into data definitions for ObjectStore's persistent storage engine for Java?

- How easy or difficult is it to transform an OSM functional design into Java code for ObjectStore's persistent storage engine for Java?

16.1 Ontological Analysis

Figure 16.3 is an ORM diagram that describes the regions we must consider for the case study. (Ideally and ontologically, we can think of these regions as actual parcels of the Earth's surface.) Each region has an *Area* and a *Perimeter*. Some regions are counties, each of which has a *County Name*. Some of the regions have classifications, such as coniferous forest or wetlands, and each classification is called a *Type*. A *Contour* is also a region that consists of an enclosed area that represents a slice through the Earth at a certain elevation.

To solve the problem for the lumberyard owner, we augment the basic information in Fig. 16.3 with some information computed from the basic information: Figure 16.4 includes an *Alpine Highlands* object set that contains the set of maximal contour regions above 3000 meters, as well as object sets for qualifying regions. The qualifying alpine-highlands regions are intersections of regions in *Alpine Highlands* and *County* whose area is greater than 20 km². The qualifying coniferous-forest regions are intersections of regions in *Classified Region* whose *Type* is *Coniferous Forest* and regions in *County* whose area is greater than 35 km². Each *Wilderness Area* region is the union of overlapping regions or adjacent regions on county borders. Since we know the perimeter of each region, we can compute the total perimeter length.

16.2 Formalization of General Constraints

For the specification, we can write the general constraints in Fig. 16.4 more formally. For example, we can write *Intersections of County and Coniferous*

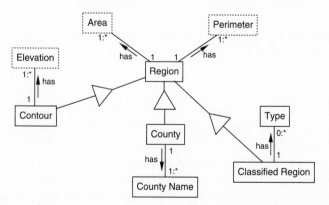

Figure 16.3 Basic information for the application. Courtesy of Springer-Verlag.

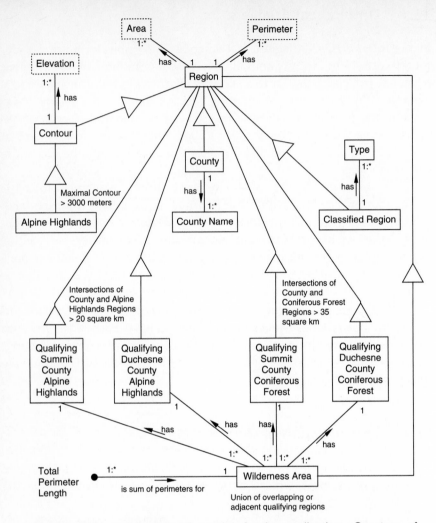

Figure 16.4 Augmented information for the application. Courtesy of Springer-Verlag.

Forest Regions > 35 square km more formally, as in Fig. 16.5. For this formal specification, we assume that we have an intersection operation that intersects regions and returns a region. Similarly, we can formalize the other general constraints in Fig. 16.4. We must assume, of course, that we have an operation to take the union of two regions so that we can compute the areas in *Wilderness Area*. We must also assume that we have a comparison operator for elevations so that we can select contours that are above 3000 meters but less than every other greater contour elevation.

Coniferous Forest Region : *Region*;
Summit County Coniferous Forest : *Coniferous Forest Region*;

Coniferous Forest Region(x) :- *Classified Region*(x),
  Classified Region(x) *has Type*(*Coniferous Forest*);
  add *Summit County Coniferous Forest Region*(x) **where**
  $x = y$ *intersect* z **and**
  Coniferous Forest Region(y) **and**
  County(z) *has County Name*(*Summit*);
  add *Qualifying Summit County Coniferous Forest*(x) **where**
  Summit County Coniferous Forest Region(x) **and**
  Region(x) *has Area*(y) **and** $y > 35km^2$;

Figure 16.5   Formalization of a note in Fig. 16.4.

16.3   Approximate Representation

For this application, we realize, of course, that we cannot store regions of the Earth's surface. We can, however, represent these regions by polygons, which we can place in a space relative to each other to represent various regions and their overlaps. Then we can apply calculations to these polygons to arrive at a solution to our problem.

Figure 16.6 displays a hierarchy of different kinds of polygons. The details of implementing these polygons are extensive. We point out some of the problems and provide solutions in a few cases. Our objective here is not to provide a complete solution, however, but rather to use the polygon example to illustrate the concept of an abstract data type and the principles of encapsulation, including polymorphism, late binding, overloading, and the reimplementation of operators.

We begin by observing that we should implement the five relationship sets in Fig. 16.6 as interactions. We seldom need to know all the polygons that have a particular perimeter or area, for example, or all the pairs of polygons whose intersection or union is a particular polygon. We certainly do not need any such operations for our application. For the ID, we want to be able to find a polygon given its ID, and we want to be able to get an ID given a polygon. Our designed object module for polygons thus becomes an object module with six operations: to get a polygon given an ID, to get an ID given a polygon, and to compute the area of a polygon, the perimeter of a polygon, the intersection of two polygons, and the union of two polygons. Figure 16.7 presents the public interface for this object module.

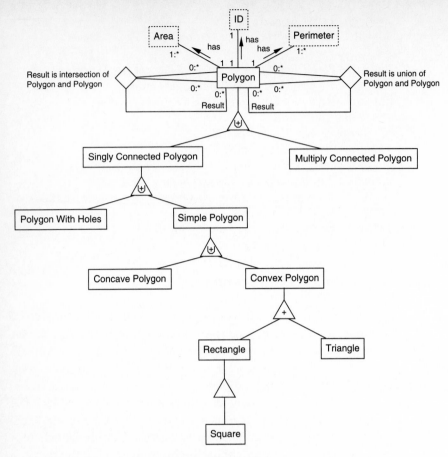

Figure 16.6   Partial hierarchy of polygons.

object module *Polygon* **includes**

@ *get ID(Polygon)* → *(ID)*;
@ *get polygon(ID)* → *(Polygon)*;
@ *area(Polygon)* → *(Real)*;
@ *perimeter(Polygon)* → *(Real)*;
@ *intersection(Polygon, Polygon)* → *(Polygon)*;
@ *union(Polygon, Polygon)* → *(Polygon)*;

hidden

 . . .

end;

Figure 16.7   Object module for *Polygon*.

16.4   Implementation Model

In Fig. 16.7 the details of the implementation are hidden. At this point, we could argue that we should push all details of the implementation beyond the implementation boundary, taking care of all of them in the target language. Often this is a reasonable choice. Here, however, the details are extensive, and this choice would place a heavy burden on the implementor. Therefore we decide to model some of the details.

As an approximation, we place our polygons in a Cartesian coordinate system (rather than on the surface of a sphere with longitude and latitude). We realize that for a computer implementation, we have neither infinite extent nor infinite precision. We can extend both if we wish, but for this case study we simply take integer values to form a grid of coordinates in the space of all possible coordinates. We also realize that we can scale our coordinates to satisfy whatever measure we wish. The distance between two adjacent points on the x-axis could represent, for example, a centimeter, a meter, a kilometer, or some other distance. Other than this, we do not concern ourselves with scale.

For our implementation, we choose an array of n coordinates. The edges of a polygon are the (imaginary) lines between consecutive coordinates in the array. The point that follows the last coordinate is always the first coordinate. Thus we guarantee that the sequence of edges ends where it starts. The inside of a polygon is to the left of an edge as we travel from point to point along the list of coordinates in the array. Figure 16.8 provides an example. If we start with (2, 1) as the first element on the list, we end with (-2, 3). As we travel from point to point, the inside of the polygon is always on the left. Of course, not all lists of coordinate points represent valid polygons. We must be careful not to allow our edges to cross or lie collinearly on top of one another: edges must touch only at consecutive coordinate points and must have nonzero length, and there must be at least three edges.

We choose an array over a linked list because we do not have any operations that change polygons, and thus we need neither to insert nor to delete points once we have established a polygon. We also note that a simple list of coordinates in an array is *not* sufficient for general polygons because when there are holes in polygons or multiple disconnected components, we need lists of lists. A simple list of coordinates in an array is sufficient for simple polygons, however, and we restrict ourselves from here on to polygons in *Simple Polygon* and its descendants in the polygon hierarchy in Fig. 16.6.

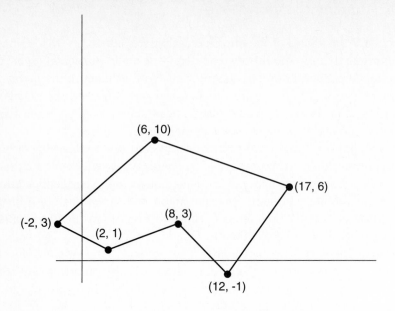

Figure 16.8 Polygon as a list of coordinate points.

We could implement all our operators in the most general object set. We can often be more efficient, however, if we take advantage of the more restrictive properties of specializations. For example, we can find the area of a square by squaring the length of one of its sides. Thus if we know that a polygon is a square, we can find the length of the first edge we encounter in our list and square it. For a rectangle, we find the area by multiplying the length by the width, which for our implementation structure means that we can multiply the length of the first two edges we encounter. For a convex polygon, we can choose one of the coordinate points and cut the polygon into triangles by considering the imaginary lines from the chosen point to each of the other coordinate points except the two adjacent to the chosen coordinate point. Then we can find the area of each triangle and sum the areas to get our result. Thus, if we know that a polygon is convex, first we can choose the primary coordinate as our base point and compute the area of the triangle formed by the first three coordinate points, next compute the area of the triangle formed by the first, third, and fourth coordinate points, then the area of the triangle formed by the first, fourth, and fifth coordinate points, and so forth until we compute the area of all the triangles; we then sum the areas to get our result.

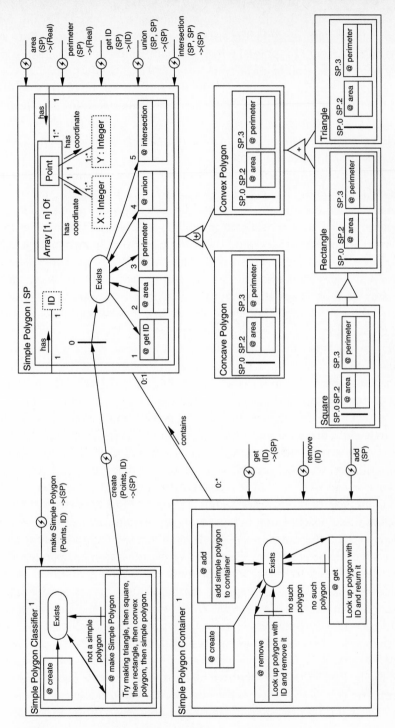

Figure 16.9 Implementation model.

Figure 16.9 displays the basic implementation structure. For our *Simple Polygon* (*SP*) object module, the structure consists of an *ID* to identify polygons and an array of *n* points, which are pairs of integers. To create a polygon, we need the points, ordered in a sequence, as well as an ID. We place the structure and the operations in the **hidden** part of the object module (as indicated by the double box). The interaction interfaces for *area*, *perimeter*, *get ID*, *union*, and *intersection* are all in the public part of the object module, while the transitions that handle these interactions are all hidden. This provides the desired encapsulation.

The generalization/specialization hierarchy we are implementing from Fig. 16.6 appears in Fig. 16.9. This time, however, we include transitions in each of the descendants of *Simple Polygon* that override transitions *0*, *2*, and *3* when applied to a specialization of *Simple Polygon*. Thus, for example, when we invoke the area operation or the perimeter operation on an object in *Triangle*, the action executed is the action in *SP.2* or *SP.3* in the *Triangle* object set. We do not override the operations for *get ID*, *union*, or *intersection*, however, because little if anything is gained by knowing the classification of the participating polygons, except in a few special cases for union and intersection.

Figure 16.9 also shows that, in addition to *Simple Polygon*, we provide a *Simple Polygon Classifier*, which is an active object that ensures that the sequence of points represents a valid polygon and classifies the polygon into its most specialized object set in the hierarchy in Fig. 16.6. The advantage of having a classifier is that we can put all knowledge of the polygon hierarchy into one location outside the actual storage areas for the hierarchy. When the hierarchy changes—for example, if we add equilateral or right triangles, we need provide only these new object sets and change *Simple Polygon Classifier* so that it recognizes them. Inside each object set, we provide specialized operations and the knowledge needed to determine whether a sequence of points represents a polygon for the object set. This code is in the initial transitions—the transitions *SP.0* that override transition *0* in each of the specialized object sets. When the classifier operates, it classifies the polygon by trying each of these determining routines. When it finds one, it stops. Of course, the classifier must try these determining routines from most to least restrictive according to the partial ordering in the hierarchy of polygons. Figure 16.10 provides a small part of code for the classifier. This code shows that we try *Triangle* first, then *Square*, and so forth.

Finally, Fig. 16.9 shows that we also provide a *Simple Polygon Container* object set. This is the object set needed by ObjectStore's persistent storage engine to hold the persistent database of polygons. Using the operators of

```
public SimplePolygon makeSimplePolygon(Point points[], String ID)
      throws NotASimplePolygonException {
   SimplePolygon polygon;

   try {
     polygon = new Triangle(points, ID);
     return polygon;
   } catch (NotATriangleException e) { }

   try {
     polygon = new Square(points, ID);
     return polygon;
   } catch (NotASquareException e) { }


   . . .

   polygon = new SimplePolygon(points, ID);
   return polygon;
}
```

Figure 16.10   Some code for the classifier.

this *Simple Polygon Container* object set, we can add polygons to the database and later get them or remove them. As the interactions in Fig. 16.9 show, when the *Simple Polygon Classifier* is asked to make a simple polygon, it invokes the classification code in *Simple Polygon* to classify the polygon. Then, if it succeeds, we have a new polygon in *Simple Polygon*. If we want the newly created polygon to be persistent, we use the *add* operation to insert it into the *Simple Polygon Container*. If we need the newly created polygon only temporarily, nothing need be done. In either case the polygon is available, and we can use it immediately as an operand for any of the public polygon operators.

We can formalize this implementation model using OSM-L. Using tunable formalism, we can leave the details unspecified, informal, or partly formal and partly informal. Figure 16.11 shows a more detailed specification for some of the operations we have been discussing. Here we have formalized the *get ID* operation completely and have provided an informal specification for the union operation. We have also formalized the area operation for *Square* completely, overriding the area operation of the ancestors of *Square* in the *isa* hierarchy dynamically when the polygon to which we apply the area operation happens to be a square.

object module *Simple Polygon* | *SP* **includes**

@ *get ID* (*SP*) → (*ID*);
@ *area* (*SP*) → (*Integer*);
@ *perimeter* (*SP*) → (*Integer*);
@ *union* (*SP*, *SP*) → (*SP*);
@ *intersection* (*SP*, *SP*) → (*SP*);

hidden

SP [1] *has ID* [1];
SP [1] *has Array* [1, *n*] *Of Point* [1:*];
Point has coordinate X;
Point has coordinate Y;

when *Exists*
@ *get ID*(*P* : *SP*) → (*Result* : *ID*) **then**
  Result := *P. ID*;
end;

. . .

when *Exists*
@ *union*(*P1* : *SP*, *P2* : *SP*) → (*P3* : *SP*) **then**

  − − (1) *Find a point in P1 that is not inside P2 (if none,*
    P2 is the result).
  − − (2) *Build P3 as follows:*
    − − (a) *Proceed along P1 adding points of P1 to the result*
    until an edge of P2 crosses an edge of P1.
    − − (b) *Add the crossing point to the result.*
    − − (c) *Proceed along P2 adding points of P2 to the result*
    until an edge of P1 crosses an edge of P2.
    − − (d) *Add the crossing point to the result.*
    − − (e) *Iterate this process of alternatingly following P1*
    and P2 until the initial point is reached.

end;

. . .

end;
  . . .

Figure 16.11   More detailed specification for some operators.

object module *Square inherits from Rectangle* **includes**

when *Exists*
@ *area*(*P* : *SP*) → (*Result* : *Integer*)

    -- local declarations
    X1 : *X;*
    Y1 : *Y;*
    X2 : *X;*
    Y2 : *Y;*
    Points : *Array* [1, *n*] *Of Point;*

    -- get end coordinates of first edge
    Points := *SP*(*self*) *has Array* [1, *n*] *Of Point;*
    X1 := *Points*[1]. *X;*
    Y1 := *Points*[1]. *Y;*
    X2 := *Points*[2]. *X;*
    Y2 := *Points*[2]. *Y;*

    -- compute area of square = *sqr*(*edge length*)
    -- where edge length = *sqrt*(⋯) *computed by Pythagorean Theorem*
    Result := *sqr*(*sqrt*(*sqr*(*X2* − *X1*) + *sqr*(*Y2* − *Y*1)));

  end;

end;

      Figure 16.11 (cont.)   More detailed specification for some operators.

16.5   Nuances

Computational geometry has numerous nuances. For example, for the union operation in the *Simple Polygon* object module just discussed, what if the two input polygons do not overlap? We could obtain a multiply connected polygon as a result, but not a simple polygon. There are, however, far worse problems. For example, for our union operation, suppose that the two polygons do intersect, but only at one point. Even worse, suppose that the two polygons intersect at only one point and that that point is supposed to be on one of the edges of the other, but is not because the edge does not run through the coordinate. Another problem is the possibility that two of

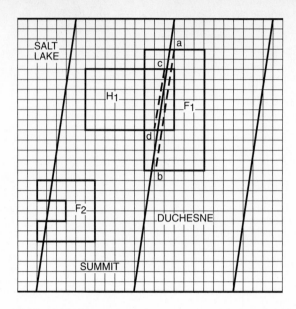

Figure 16.12 Possible corridor nuance. Courtesy of Springer-Verlag.

the edges in the polygons are collinear. Here again, the problem can be even worse because points that are supposed to be collinear are sometimes not. This can happen because end points of lines can lie only on grid points.

Nuances like these could lead to difficulties in our lumberyard owner's problem. For example, Fig. 16.12 shows a highly simplified view of the three counties: an alpine-highlands area, H_1, and two coniferous-forest areas, F_1 and F_2. If we use the grid in Fig. 16.12 and intersect F_1 with Duchesne County, we obtain its qualifying area for F_1, which is F_1 in Fig. 16.12 cut back to the edge (a, b). Similarly, we obtain the qualifying area for H_1, which is H_1 in Fig. 16.12 cut back to the edge (c, d). Note that the points a, b, c, and d are supposed to be collinear, but instead the two edges (a, b) and (c, d) form a narrow corridor between the two qualifying regions. Now if we execute our union operator blindly, these two qualifying regions do not join together. If we then find the perimeter of the wilderness areas, the answer for the lumberyard owner is far too high, because it includes both sides of the narrow corridor. (This is not good for the lumberyard owner, who would then order far too much lumber.)

We can make our algorithms more robust. In fact, this is one aspect of the work of those who study computational geometry. Although the robustness issue can be pursued much further, we stop here and mention only that we can add more structure to our implementation model and modify our algorithms to make appropriate use of this additional structure. For our particular problem, for example, we can add a structure to store lists of collinear points and then use these collinearities to make the algorithms more robust.

16.6 Implementation Polymorphism

To turn our implementation design into code in a target language, we take advantage of the features provided by the language and compensate for features we want but for which we may not have direct support. Our target language is Java, as implemented for ObjectStore's persistent storage engine for the language.

Java provides the required polymorphism. If we have a hierarchy of Java classes that corresponds to the hierarchy of object sets in Fig. 16.6, and if we place class-specific implementations of an operator in these classes, then when we invoke an operator, Java binds the operator invocation to the most specific class for the object on which the operator is invoked. Thus we have exactly what we want. We can invoke our area operator on a polygon without regard to the class of the operator, and Java will take care of invoking the proper code.

Figure 16.13 shows how this works. The figure includes the entire class for *Triangle*, as well as the header information and area execution code for *Rectangle* and *Convex Polygon*. Figure 16.13a presents the *Triangle* class, whose first line shows that we are creating a package for a polygon library and that class *Triangle* is part of the package. The Java keyword *extends* provides the inheritance we want and lets us build the class hierarchy in accordance with the hierarchy in Fig. 16.6. Since *Triangle* is a specialization of *Convex Polygon* in Fig. 16.6, we write

Triangle extends ConvexPolygon

Similarly, in Figs. 16.13b and 16.13c we have

Rectangle extends ConvexPolygon

and

ConvexPolygon extends SimplePolygon.

```
package PolygonLib;
import java.util.Vector;
import java.lang.Math;

class Triangle extends ConvexPolygon
{
  /**
    * Constructor, protected since the Classifier object
    * creates all SimplePolygon objects.
    * @ param points[] an array of Point
    * @ param ID a unique String ID
  */
  protected Triangle(Point points[], String ID)
    throws NotATriangleException,
      NotAConvexPolygonException,
      NotASimplePolygonException {
    super(points, ID);

    if (points.length != 3)
      throw new NotATriangleException();

    if (points[0].equals(points[1]) ||
        points[1].equals(points[2]) ||
        points[2].equals(points[0]))
      throw new NotATriangleException();

    int X1 = points[0].getX();
    int Y1 = points[0].getY();
    int X2 = points[1].getX();
    int Y2 = points[1].getY();
    int X3 = points[2].getX();
    int Y3 = points[2].getY();

    /*
      * The vector x product is positive
      * if this is a triangle and the inside is
      * to the left.
    */
    double result1 = (X2 - X1) * (Y3 - Y2);
    double result2 = (Y2 - Y1) * (X3 - X2);
    double vectorcrossproduct = result1 - result2;
```

Figure 16.13   Polymorphism.

```
if (vectorcrossproduct < = 0)
    throw new NotATriangleException();
}


/**
 * Returns the area of the Triangle
 * @ return the area of this polygon
 */
public int area() {
    int X1 = points[0]. getX();
    int Y1 = points[0]. getY();
    int X2 = points[1]. getX();
    int Y2 = points[1]. getY();
    int X3 = points[2]. getX();
    int Y3 = points[2]. getY();
    double Length1 = Math. sqrt(((X2 – X1) * (X2 – X1))
        + ((Y2 – Y1) * (Y2 – Y1)));
    double Length2 = Math. sqrt(((X3 – X2) * (X3 – X2))
        + ((Y3 – Y2) * (Y3 – Y2)));
    double Length3 = Math. sqrt(((X1 – X3) * (X1 – X3))
        + ((Y1 – Y3) * (Y1 – Y3)));
    double Temp = (Length1 + Length2 + Length3)/2;
    double TriangleArea = Math. sqrt(Temp * (Temp – Length1)
        *(Temp – Length2) * (Temp – Length3));
    return (int)TriangleArea;
}

}
```

(a) Java *Triangle* class.

```
class Rectangle extends Convex Polygon {
    /**
     * Returns the area of the Rectangle
     * @ return the area of this polygon
     */
    public int area() {
        int X1 = points[0]. getX();
        int Y1 = points[0]. getY();
        int X2 = points[1]. getX();
```

Figure 16.13 (cont.) Polymorphism.

```
        int Y2 = points[1]. getY();
        int X3 = points[2]. getX();
        int Y3 = points[2]. getY();
        double Length1 = Math. sqrt((((X2 – X1) * (X2 – X1))
            + ((Y2 – Y1) * (Y2 – Y1))));
        double Length2 = Math. sqrt((((X3 – X2) * (X3 – X2))
            + ((Y3 – Y2) * (Y3 – Y2))));
        return (int)(Length1 * Length2);
    }
    . . .

}
```

(b) Header information and area operation for
    Rectangle class.

```
    class ConvexPolygon extends SimplePolygon {
    / **
        * Returns the area of the ConvexPolygon
        * @ return the area of this polygon
        */
    public int area() {
        int result = 0;
        Point point1 = points[0];
        Point point2 = points[1];
        int iPos = 2;
        while (iPos < points. length) {
            Point point3 = points[iPos + +];
            Point tempPoints[] = {point1, point2, point3};
            Triangle tempTriangle;

            try {
                tempTriangle = new Triangle(tempPoints, "TEMP");
            } catch (NotATriangleException e) {
            } catch (NotAConvexPolygonException e) {
            } catch (NotASimplePolygonException e) {
            }
```

Figure 16.13 (cont.) Polymorphism.

```
        result += tempTriangle. area();
        point1 = point2;
        point2 = point3;
    }
    return result;
}
    . . .
}
```

(c) Header information and area operation for
    Convex Polygon class.

Figure 16.13 (cont.)   Polymorphism.

The constructor for the *Triangle* class contains code that determines whether a sequence of points in an array is a triangle. If it is not, the constructor throws the *NotATriangleException* exception. The code ensures that (1) there are exactly three points, (2) no two points are the same, (3) the points are not collinear, and (4) the inside of the triangle is to the left. We use the vector cross product to check the fourth condition.

For the area operation, the *Triangle* code implements the formula

$$\sqrt{p(p-a)(p-b)(p-c)}, \text{ where } p = (a+b+c)$$

which computes the area of a triangle from its side lengths, a, b, and c. The area operation for *Rectangle* is the product of the lengths of the first two sides. The area operation for *ConvexPolygon* segments the convex polygon into triangles that cover the convex polygon, finds the areas of these triangles, and sums them. This last operation makes use of the area operation in the *Triangle* class.

16.7   Chapter Summary

Topic Summary

The case study in this chapter illustrates the following concepts. Parenthetical section numbers refer to places in the book where these concepts are discussed.

- An ontological analysis and formalization of a problem based on the real-world application (Section 7.2).

- The creation of a library package for polygons that includes Java classes with encapsulation, late binding, operator overloading, and operator reimplementation (Section 11.1).

- The conversion of ORM operations into interactions (Section 11.2).

- The use of OSM to model implementations, including in particular data structures (Section 11.4) and inheritance (Section 11.7).

Question Summary

- How easy or difficult is it to transform an OSM data design into data definitions for ObjectStore's persistent storage engine for Java?

  This case study shows that sometimes we must model the implementation as well as the application. When the implementation is complex, we can specify what features it should have independent of the particular target language and system. We can then convert these specification and design decisions into code. In our case study, we were able to convert object-set generalization/specialization hierarchies directly into Java class hierarchies.

- How easy or difficult is it to transform an OSM functional design into Java code for ObjectStore's persistent storage engine for Java?

  OSM-L and Java are similar but not the same. Being similar, OSM-L can provide a good guide to implementing Java code.

Chapter 17

Active Object-Oriented DBMS Case Study

We use Ode for our active object-oriented DBMS case study; for the application, we develop a home security system. The system detects an intrusion, sounds an alarm, and notifies nearby emergency personnel. System owners can set schedules and control the length of delays before the system notifies emergency personnel.

A central surveillance controller manages the home security system as well as all peripheral systems. The controller monitors detectors, activates alarms, and notifies emergency personnel according to a protocol specified in a schedule. Also, each door and window has a sensor that detects when a circuit is broken. When a detector is tripped, the controller records which detector was tripped and at what time, and then sounds an alarm. After a detector has been tripped and the alarm has sounded, the household residents have a certain amount of time to abort the protocol. This protects the system from notifying emergency personnel unnecessarily if the residents trip detectors accidentally. If residents abort the protocol, the system returns to its normal state; if they do not, the system notifies emergency personnel.

A control panel allows household residents to initialize the system, to reset alarms and detectors after a security breach, and to set up, change, and delete schedules. The security system can store several commonly needed schedules, and residents can choose which schedule should be active. A schedule has start and stop times for when the security system should operate, as well as a choice of modes: *Immediate*, *Short Delay*, or *Long Delay*. If the mode is *Immediate*, then when a detector is tripped between the schedule's start and stop times, the system notifies emergency personnel immediately. If the mode is *Short Delay*, the system waits for the amount of time specified by the *Short Delay Time* parameter in the schedule before notifying emergency personnel. Similarly, if the mode is *Long Delay*, the system waits for the amount of time specified in the *Long Delay Time* parameter before notifying emergency personnel. Typical short delays are 2 or 3 minutes, and long delays are between 10 and 15 minutes.

The following topics in this chapter are particularly important:

- Analysis based on behavior and interactions.

- Automatic derivation of interface forms.

- Functional specification with OSM-L.

- State-net transformations.

- Tunable formalism.

The following questions should also be kept in mind:

- How easy or difficult is it to transform an OSM data design into Ode data definitions?

- How easy or difficult is it to transform an OSM functional design into Ode code?

17.1   Behavior Analysis

Since our home security system is highly active and interactive, we begin by analyzing the behavior of active objects and their interaction. Figure 17.1 shows the behavior of the *Control Panel*. A household resident can turn on the control panel to initialize it; this action also initializes the surveillance controller and thus the entire home security system. A resident can reset alarms and detectors through the control panel, which relays these requests to the surveillance controller. A resident can also add, delete, change, and activate schedules.

Each schedule has an ID for identification. The schedule also consists of a start time (*Start Hour* and *Start Minute*), a stop time (*Stop Hour* and *Stop Minute*), and a *Mode* (*Immediate, Short Delay,* or *Long Delay*). The short- and long-delay times for each schedule are in the *Short Delay Time* object set and the *Long Delay Time* object set. A particular schedule is the designated active schedule.

Figure 17.2 depicts the active behavior of detectors, alarms, and the emergency notifier. Detectors and alarms can be added and deleted, and the emergency phone number can be set and changed. When the surveillance controller receives an initialization message, the controller relays this message to detectors and alarms. Then, when a *trip detector* event occurs, the tripped detector becomes active. In the process of becoming active, the

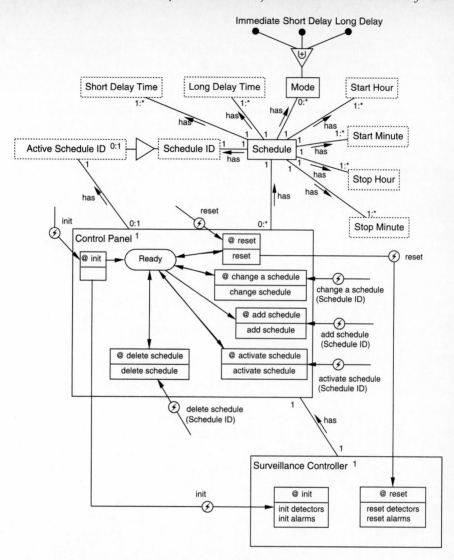

Figure 17.1   Active behavior for *Control Panel*.

detector sends a message to the surveillance controller, which relays the message to activate the alarms. If a *delay end* event happens, the surveillance controller sends a message to notify emergency personnel. Active detectors and alarms can also be reset.

Figure 17.3 displays the way in which the surveillance controller behaves. The figure shows the states *Ready, Delay*, and *Active*. From the *Ready* state, the surveillance controller can receive a detection event. Since

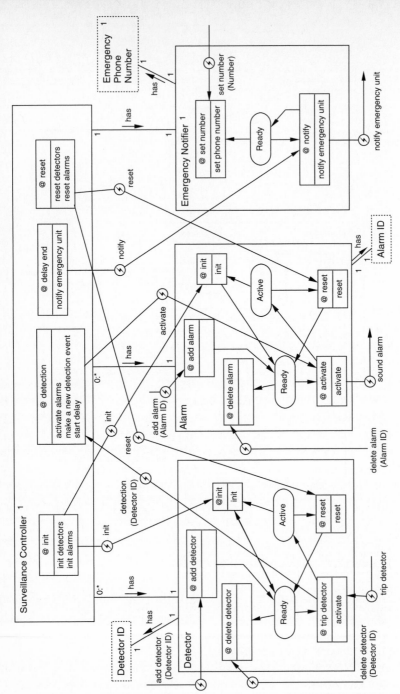

Figure 17.2   Active behavior for *Detector*, *Alarm*, and *Emergency Notifier*.

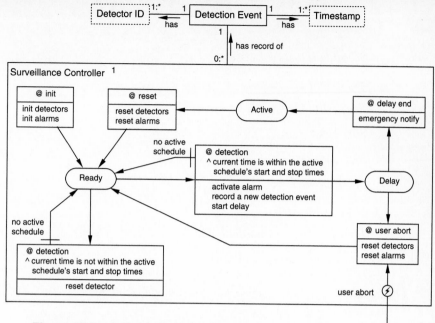

Figure 17.3 Active behavior for *Surveillance Controller*.

there may be no active schedule, for example, before one is established or when the active schedule is deleted and another has not yet been activated, there may be an exception that returns the surveillance controller to the *Ready* state without doing anything. Under normal conditions, if a detection event occurs when the current time is not within the active schedule's start and stop times, the controller merely resets the detector. Otherwise, the surveillance controller processes the detected event as a possible unwanted intrusion. When processing a detection event, the controller activates alarms, records a new detection event, and starts a delay. From the *Delay* state, the controller can receive either a *user abort* message or a *delay end* message. A *user abort* message causes the controller to reset detectors and alarms and return to the *Ready* state. A *delay end* message causes the controller to notify emergency personnel and wait for a *reset* message before resetting detectors and alarms and returning to the *Ready* state.

17.2 Interface Specification

Turning our attention to specification, we first consider the user interface. Most of the interface is straightforward; a user can simply push a button or

> @ add schedule
> (**add**)
>
> *Schedule ID* _____ (**new**)
>
> *Start Hour* _____
>
> *Start Minute* _____
>
> *Stop Hour* _____
>
> *Stop Minute* _____
>
> *Short Delay Time* _____
>
> *Long Delay Time* _____
>
> *Mode* _____ *{Immediate, Short Delay, Long Delay}*
>
> *Control Panel* (**connect only**)

Figure 17.4   Interface specification for adding a schedule.

enter an ID or number after pushing the button. The *add schedule* interaction, however, is more involved and is incomplete. By looking at Fig. 17.1, we see that we need some input information to specify start and stop times and time delays.

The interface form in Fig. 17.4 provides the input information needed for a schedule and specifies the *add schedule* interaction fully. It is interesting to observe that if we know that this interaction creates a new schedule (and we do), then the interface form in Fig. 17.4 can be derived automatically. The participation constraints force us to have exactly one *Schedule ID*, which must be new because we are creating a new schedule; one start and one stop time, both specified in hours and minutes; one short- and one long-delay time; one mode, which is *Immediate, Short Delay,* or *Long Delay*; and a possible connection to a control panel, which need not be specified since there is only one control panel.

17.3   Functional Specification

Perhaps the most interesting and, as yet, least specified function of our home security system is detecting an event, processing the delay, and either aborting or notifying emergency personnel. Figure 17.5 presents a detailed OSM-L specification for this part of the *Surveillance Controller* state net.

Note that the specification in the figure leaves other parts of the state net informal. This illustrates how we can use tunable formalism to formalize some parts of the functionality of a state net while leaving other parts informal.

Surveillance Controller [1] *includes;*

-- *local declaration*
startTime [1] : *time;*

@ *init* **then**
  << *init detectors* >> ;
  << *init alarms* >> ;
enter *Ready;*
end;

when *Ready*
@ *detection* (*ID: Integer*)
if -- *current time is within the active schedule's start and stop times*
   createTime_hm(Schedule ID(Active Schedule ID). Start Hour,
    Schedule ID(Active Schedule ID). Start Minute)
   < = *currentTime*
   and
   currentTime < =
   createTime_hm(Schedule ID(Active Schedule ID). Stop Hour,
    Schedule ID(Active Schedule ID). Stop Minute)
then

-- *activate alarms*
for each *Alarm(x)* **do**
  init(x);
  end;

-- *record a new detection event*
add *Surveillance Controller(self) has record of Detection Event(x),*
  Detection Event(x) has Detector ID(ID),
  Detection Event(x) has Timestamp(makeTimestamp(currentTime));

-- *start delay*
startTime : = *currentTime;*

enter *Delay;*
exception << *no active schedule* >> ;
end;

Figure 17.5 OSM-L specification for the *Surveillance Controller* state net.

when *Delay*

if -- *delay end*

   Schedule ID(Active Schedule ID). Mode = Immediate

   or *Schedule ID(Active Schedule ID). Mode = Short Delay*

    and *startTime +*

     Schedule ID(Active Schedule ID). Short Delay Time

     > = currentTime

   or *Schedule ID(Active Schedule ID). Mode = Long Delay*

    and *startTime +*

     Schedule ID(Active Schedule ID). Long Delay Time

     > = currentTime

 then

  notify;

enter *Active;*

end;

when *Delay*

@ *user abort* **then**

  << *reset detectors* >> ;

  << *reset alarms* >> ;

enter *Ready;*

end;

when *Active*

@ *reset* **then**

  << *reset detectors* >> ;

  << *reset alarms* >> ;

enter *Ready;*

end;

when *Ready*

@ *detection (ID: Integer);*

if -- *current time is not within the active schedule's*

  start and stop times

  not(

  createTime_hm(Schedule ID(Active Schedule ID). Start Hour,

   Schedule ID(Active Schedule ID). Start Minute)

  < = currentTime

  and

  currentTime < =

  createTime_hm(Schedule ID(Active Schedule ID). Stop Hour,

Figure 17.5 (cont.)   OSM-L specification for the *Surveillance Controller* state net.

Schedule ID(Active Schedule ID). Stop Minute))
  then
  << reset detector >> ;
 enter *Ready*;
 exception *<< no active schedule >>* ;
 end;

end;

> **Figure 17.5 (cont.)**   OSM-L specification for the *Surveillance Controller*
> state net.

We make several comments about the OSM-L specification in Fig. 17.5.

1. We assume the existence of a system clock that provides several services and a *time* object set, which we can specialize to declare variables of type time. These services include the following:

   - *currentTime*, which returns the current time;

   - *createTime_hm*, which creates a time given an hour value and a minute value;

   - +, which adds a time and a duration;

   - < and <=, which determine whether one time comes before or at the same time as another; and

   - *makeTimestamp*, which converts a time into a timestamp string.

2. We locally declare and use *startTime*, which keeps track of the start-delay time. The state net sets *startTime* in the transition that fires when a detector is tripped within the active schedule's start and stop times. The state net later checks *startTime* in the trigger of the transition that notifies emergency personnel.

3. Determining whether the current time is within the active schedule's start and stop times requires that we understand several details. Because there is one and only one *Active Schedule ID*, we can use it to select the active schedule. Given the selected schedule, we can use path expressions to obtain the start and stop hours and minutes. We then use these values in *createTime_hm* to get a time, which we can compare with the current time.

4. The *Surveillance Controller* state net activates every alarm. The plural statement *init alarms* states this informally, while the state net formalizes this idea with a **for each** statement.

5. We create a new *Detection Event* by using the unbound variable *x*. We must be careful to have only one *add* statement so that the *x* is the same detection event for all three of the relationships we are adding.

6. Although the *delay end* interaction is what we would like, we realize when we formalize this trigger that nothing invokes this interaction magically. We therefore transform the *delay end* interaction into a condition. This requires that we check the mode. If the mode is *Immediate*, we end the delay immediately; otherwise, we add the *startTime* to the duration either for a *Short Delay* or for a *Long Delay* (depending on the mode) and determine whether this exceeds the current time.

17.4   State-Net Transformations

Let us now consider design. Since our application is heavily behavior oriented, we begin by considering state nets. We first observe that two of our state nets, *Control Panel* in Fig. 17.1 and *Emergency Notifier* in Fig. 17.2, are already single-state state nets. We therefore work on the other three. Figure 17.6 shows the transformed, single-state state net for *Detector*. The

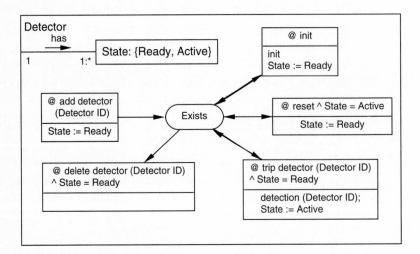

Figure 17.6   Single-state state net for a *Detector*.

transformed state net for *Alarm* is similar, so we do not show it. Figure 17.7 shows the transformed state net for the *Surveillance Controller*.

The transformation from the *Detector* state net in Fig. 17.2 to the single-state state net in Fig. 17.6 introduces a *State* object set with two possible states, *Ready* and *Active*. The transformation also introduces a state condition in each trigger where necessary, as well as a state change in each transition where necessary. Observe that the *add detector* trigger does not have a state condition because the trigger is for the initial transition. Observe also that the *delete detector* transition does not set the state because there is no next state for a final transition. Interestingly, there is no condition for the *init* trigger because the condition would be

$$State = Ready \lor State = Active$$

which is always true since any detector is always either in the *Ready* state or in the *Active* state. We therefore simplify the trigger by omitting the condition.

The transformation for the *Surveillance Controller* from Fig. 17.3 to Fig. 17.7 is not a standard transformation. Instead of taking the standard

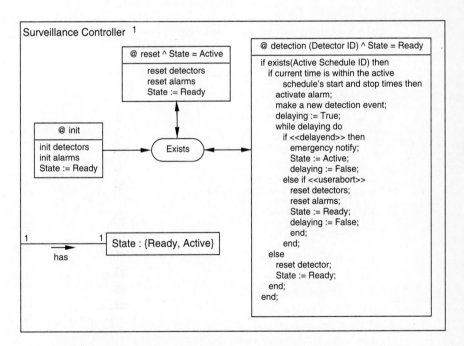

Figure 17.7 Single-state state net for the *Surveillance Controller*.

approach, we observe that the conditions in the *detection* transitions are complementary. We therefore first combine these two transitions, which results in a high-level transition that subsumes not only these two transitions but also the *Delay* state and the *delay end* and *user abort* transitions. The details are in the *detection* transition in Fig. 17.7. The action in the transition handles the exception first by checking to see whether an *Active Schedule ID* exists. If so, then if the current time is not within the active schedule's start and stop times, the detectors are reset, and the state is set to *Ready*; otherwise, several actions occur to control the alarms, set the delay, and process either an emergency notification or a user abort. To process a notification or an abort, we use a busy **while** loop that waits either for the delay to end or for the user to abort the delay.

We have now gone in two different directions. In the OSM-L in Fig. 17.5, we have replaced @ *delay end* by a condition, while in the transformed state net in Fig. 17.7, we have combined several states and transitions into one. We can resolve these differences by making the corresponding change to either the OSM-L in Fig. 17.5 or the state net in Fig. 17.7. Eventually, however, we will want to transform both of these representations into an object module. We therefore merge the two and transform them both directly into the object module in Fig. 17.8.

> **object module** *Surveillance Controller* [1] *includes*;
>
> @ *init*;
> @ *detection* (*Integer*);
> @ *reset*;
>
> **hidden**
>
> -- *local declarations*
> *startTime* [1] : *time*;
> *Surveillance Controller* [1] *has State* [1];
> *State* : {*Ready, Active*};
> *delaying* : *Boolean*;
>
> @ *init* **then**
>   << *init detectors* >> ;
>   << *init alarms* >> ;
>   *State* := *Ready*;
> **enter** *Exists*;
> **end**;

Figure 17.8 Object module for *Surveillance Controller*.

when *Exists*
@ *detection (ID: Integer)*
if *State = Ready* **then**
  if exists(*Active Schedule ID*) **then**
   if -- *current time is within the active schedule's start and stop times*
    createTime_hm(Schedule ID(Active Schedule ID). Start Hour,
     Schedule ID(Active Schedule ID). Start Minute)
    <= currentTime
    and
    currentTime < =
    createTime_hm(Schedule ID(Active Schedule ID). Stop Hour,
     Schedule ID(Active Schedule ID). Stop Minute)
    then

    -- *activate alarms*
    for each *Alarm(x)* **do**
     init(x);
     end;

    -- *record a new detection event*
    add *Surveillance Controller(self) has record of Detection Event(x),*
     Detection Event(x) has Detector ID(ID),
     Detection Event(x) has Timestamp(makeTimestamp(currentTime));

    delaying : = True;
    while *delaying* **do**
     if -- *delay end*
      Schedule ID(Active Schedule ID). Mode = Immediate
      or *Schedule ID(Active Schedule ID). Mode = Short Delay*
       and *startTime +*
        Schedule ID(Active Schedule ID). Short Delay Time
        >= currentTime
      or *Schedule ID(Active Schedule ID). Mode = Long Delay*
       and *startTime +*
        Schedule ID(Active Schedule ID). Long Delay Time
        >= currentTime
      then
     notify;
     State : = Active;
     delaying : = False;
     else if << *user abort* >>

Figure 17.8 (cont.)   Object module for *Surveillance Controller.*

```
        << reset detectors >> ;
        << reset alarms >> ;
        State := Ready;
        delaying := False;
      end;
    end;
  else
    << reset detector >> ;
    State := Ready;
  end;
 end;
enter Exists;
end;

when Exists
@ reset
if State = Active then
  << reset detectors >> ;
  << reset alarms >> ;
  State := Ready;
enter Ready;
end;

end;
```

Figure 17.8 (cont.)   Object module for *Surveillance Controller*.

17.5   Data Design and Implementation

We can extract the ORM diagram for our application if we merge the OBM/OIM diagrams we have presented so far, keeping only the object and relationship sets. This extraction and merge includes not only the ORM components of Figs. 17.1, 17.2, and 17.3, but also the *State* object sets from Figs. 17.6 and 17.7, as well as the *State* object set for *Alarm*, which we discussed but did not show. Since these *State* object sets are not the same, when we merge the diagrams, we rename the *State* object sets *Detector State*, *Alarm State*, and *Surveillance Controller State*. When we apply Algorithm 9.1 to this merged ORM diagram, the result is the ORM hypergraph in Fig. 17.9a.

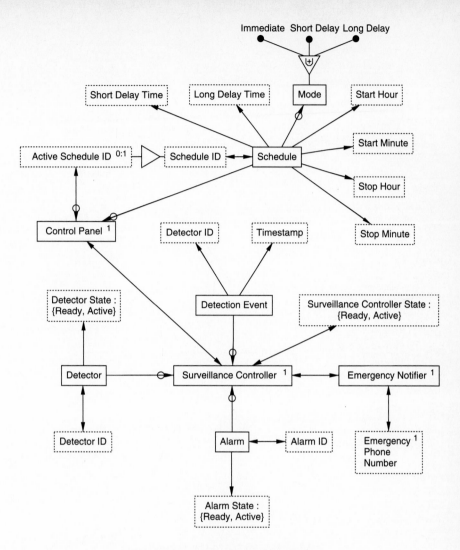

(a) Initial ORM hypergraph.

Figure 17.9 ORM hypergraphs.

Next we transform this ORM hypergraph into a canonical ORM hypergraph, except that we relax some of the restrictions on lexicalization and on merging one-to-one nonlexical object sets, as noted in the following discussion. The result is the ORM hypergraph in Fig. 17.9b. Observe that we could reduce the ORM hypergraph in Fig. 17.9a by lexicalization (for example, we could lexicalize *Detector* by *Detector ID* and thus remove *Detector*),

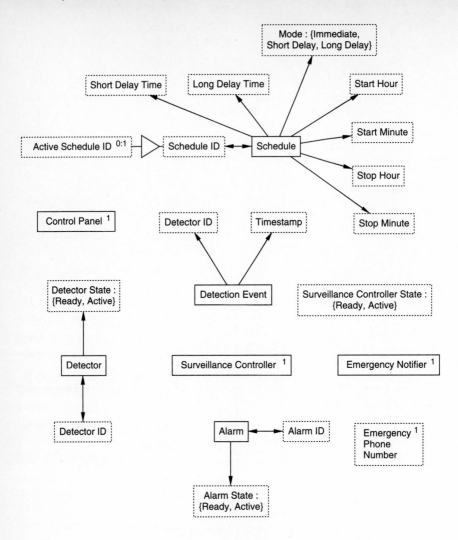

(b) Designed ORM hypergraph.

Figure 17.9 (cont.) ORM hypergraphs.

but since Ode expects its objects to be identified by object identifiers, we would have to reintroduce these nonlexical object sets removed by lexicalization. Observe also that several nonlexical object sets, namely *Control Panel, Surveillance Controller*, and *Emergency Notifier*, are in the same equivalence class. If we were just storing data, these could be combined. Because each of these object sets is active, however, we need an object module for each of them.

We next observe that several relationship sets are redundant. Whenever we have an object set whose object-set cardinality constraint requires exactly one or at most one object in the object set, all associated relationship sets are redundant. We can always recover the relationships in these relationship sets by joining the singleton object set with the object set connected by the removed relationship set. Thus we remove all relationship sets connected to object sets that allow one or at most one object set.

Finally, we make *Mode* congruent. Although we could introduce a role, we observe instead that we can transform *Mode* in Fig. 17.9a into a specialization of an enumeration, as Fig. 17.9b shows. This changes the *0:** participation constraint on *Mode* to *1:** because after the transformation *Mode* contains only elements of the enumeration that are mentioned in schedules, whereas the enumeration itself holds the three elements of the enumeration.

We can now use Algorithm 10.1 to generate schemes. The result is the set of unnamed schemes in Fig. 17.10a. These generated schemes are satisfactory, but the fact that several of the object sets are singletons allows us to combine some schemes without introducing redundancy. As we combine schemes, we also introduce nesting so that we do not have to repeat the singleton object unnecessarily. Figure 17.10b gives the result. Although these schemes have no redundancy, we have introduced a potential null because there may be no *Active Schedule ID*. However, since this is an exception and since we certainly wish to have a location for the *Active Schedule ID*, which is usually present, we combine the schemes and let the null, when present, indicate that there is no active schedule.

Figure 17.10c shows another adjustment we make in preparation for mapping these schemes to Ode. We move the nonlexical object-set names on which each scheme is based to the front, outside the parentheses. For each nested scheme, we also move the nonlexical object-set name outside the parentheses. Then, where the nested scheme appears, we leave the name enclosed in parentheses followed by its nested-repetition star, and we add the nested scheme as a separate scheme. Thus, for example, we replace

> (*Surveillance Controller, Surveillance Controller State,*
> (*Detection Event, Detector ID, Timestamp*)*)

by

> *Surveillance Controller*(*Surveillance Controller State,* (*Detection Event*)*)

and add the scheme

> *Detection Event*(*Detector ID, Timestamp*)

(*Emergency Notifier*)
(*Emergency Phone Number*)
(*Surveillance Controller*)
(*Surveillance Controller State*)
(*Detection Event, Detector ID, Timestamp*)
(*Control Panel*)
(*Active Schedule ID*)
(*Schedule, Schedule ID, Start Hour, Start Minute, Stop Hour,*
  Stop Minute, Mode, Short Delay Time, Long Delay Time)
(*Detector, Detector ID, Detector State*)
(*Alarm, AlarmID, Alarm State*)

(a) Initial generated schemes.

(*Emergency Notifier, Emergency Phone Number*)
(*Surveillance Controller, Surveillance Controller State,*
  (*Detection Event, Detector ID, Timestamp*)*)
(*Control Panel, Active Schedule ID, (Schedule, Schedule ID, Start Hour,*
  Start Minute, Stop Hour, Stop Minute, Mode, Short Delay Time,
  Long Delay Time)*)
(*Detector, Detector ID, Detector State*)
(*Alarm, AlarmID, Alarm State*)

(b) Combined schemes.

Emergency Notifier(*Emergency Phone Number*)
Detection Event(*Detector ID, Timestamp*)
Surveillance Controller(*Surveillance Controller State, (Detection Event)**)
Schedule(*Schedule ID, Start Hour, Start Minute, Stop Hour,*
  Stop Minute, Mode, Short Delay Time, Long Delay Time)
Control Panel(*Active Schedule ID, (Schedule)**)
Detector(*Detector ID, Detector State*)
Alarm(*AlarmID, Alarm State*)

(c) Name-adjusted schemes.

Figure 17.10   Database schemes for home security application.

We can now generate Ode schemes directly, as Fig. 17.11 shows. Observe that there is a persistent class for each scheme, that the class name is the name of the nonlexical object set on which the scheme is based, and that the names of the attributes in the class are the remaining object-set names. Observe further that for each nested object-set name—*Detection Event* in *Surveillance Controller*, and *Schedule* in *Control Panel*—there is a reference to the persistent class. Each of the singleton classes also has a persistent reference to it (i.e., the first three lines in Fig. 17.11). Together, all these persistent classes and references constitute the Ode database.

Observe also in Fig. 17.11 that we have added the type information. For the enumerations we added

enum ModeValues {IMMEDIATE, SHORTDELAY, LONGDELAY}

for *Mode* and

enum StateValues {READY, ACTIVE}

for the three *State* enumerations, which are all the same. For strings, we added some constants to provide the string length. For example, we have added the constant

PHONE_NUMBER_LENGTH

to provide for the string length of emergency phone numbers. We have also made attributes used to access sets of tuples indexable.

```
persistent EmergencyNotifier *theEmergencyNotifier;
persistent SurveillanceController *theSurveillanceController;
persistent ControlPanel *theControlPanel;

persistent class EmergencyNotifier {
  private:
    char EmergencyPhoneNumber[PHONE_NUMBER_LENGTH];
  . . .
}

enum StateValues {READY, ACTIVE};

persistent class DetectionEvent {
  private:
    indexable int DetectorID;
    indexable char Timestamp[TIME_STAMP_LENGTH];
  . . .
}
```

Figure 17.11   Ode code for the database schemes.

```
persistent class SurveillanceController {
  private:
    StateValues SurveillanceControllerState;
    persistent DetectionEvent *DetectionEvents;

  . . .

}

enum ModeValues {IMMEDIATE, SHORTDELAY, LONGDELAY};

persistent class Schedule {
  private:
    indexable int ScheduleID;
    int StartHour;
    int StartMinute;
    int StopHour;
    int StopMinute;
    ModeValues Mode;
    int ShortDelayTime;
    int LongDelayTime;

  . . .

}

persistent class ControlPanel {
  private:
    indexable int ActiveScheduleID;
    persistent Schedule *Schedules;

  . . .

}

persistent class Detector {
  private:
    indexable int DetectorID;
    StateValues DetectorState;

  . . .

}

persistent class Alarm {
  private:
    indexable int AlarmID;
    StateValues AlarmState;

  . . .

}
```

Figure 17.11 (cont.)   Ode code for the database schemes.

17.6 Behavior Implementation

Our last task is to implement the behavior. As an example, we take the code outline from the detection service for the *Surveillance Controller* object module in Fig. 17.8 and write part of the detection service for the *Surveillance Controller* method; see Fig. 17.12. This part corresponds to the **while** *delaying* loop in Fig. 17.8. Except for the time computations, the correspondence is straightforward.

The time computations do not correspond because OSM-L assumptions about time services differ from what is available in Ode. We therefore make some changes. We set *targetHour* and *targetMinute* variables in Fig. 17.12, which gives the starting time plus the delay time based on the mode, and we then send this value to the *timeElapsed* method, which determines whether the time represented by *targetHour* and *targetMinute* has been reached.

```
void SurveillanceController::detection(int DetectorID) {
  . . .
  getTime();
  targetHour = theSurveillanceController-> currentHour +
      ((theSurveillanceController-> currentMinute + delaytime) / 60);
  targetMinute = (theSurveillanceController-> currentMinute
      + delaytime) % 60;
  cout << endl << "The surveillance controller is delaying calling the" << endl
      << "emergency phone number by " << delaytime << " minutes." << endl
      << "Hit any key to abort" << endl;
  cout << flush;

  while(delaying) {
    if (timeElapsed(targetHour, targetMinute)) {
      theEmergencyNotifier-> notify();
      SurveillanceControllerState = ACTIVE;
      delaying = FALSE;
    } else if (userAbortButtonPressed()) {
      theSurveillanceController-> reset();
      SurveillanceControllerState = READY;
      delaying = FALSE;
    }
  }
  . . .
```

Figure 17.12 Ode code for the delay.

Except for the time computations, the code in Ode follows the outlined specification directly. The code that drives the loop is the same, as is the code that sets the state information. To do *notify* in Ode, we execute the *notify* method in *theEmergencyNotifier*. To reset the detectors and alarms, we execute the *reset* method. Some of names are different—some because of conventions and requirements of Ode (e.g., *Active* in Fig. 17.8 changed to *ACTIVE* in Fig. 17.12) and some because we have made some name changes in our design (e.g., *State* in Fig. 17.8 changed to *SurveillanceControllerState* in Fig. 17.12). Other auxiliary information displayed solely for the simulation, such as the message in Fig. 17.12 about what to do to signal an abort, has also been added. In the computer simulation of our case study, we simulate *user abort* by a key press.

17.7   Chapter Summary

Topic Summary

The case study in this chapter illustrates the following concepts. Parenthetical section numbers refer to places in the book where these concepts are discussed.

- Behavior-driven and interaction-driven analysis (Section 7.2);

- Interface forms (Section 8.4) and how we can usually derive them semiautomatically, and sometimes automatically.

- Functional specification with OSM-L (Section 8.3), with examples particularly for local declarations and control structures (Section 8.2).

- The use of tunable formalism to formalize some parts more and other parts less (Section 8.0).

- State-net transformations (Section 11.5) and subsequent mappings to object modules (Section 11.1) with exported operations and hidden implementations (Section 11.6).

Question Summary

- How easy or difficult is it to transform an OSM data design into Ode data definitions?

Designed OSM schemes translate directly into Ode declarations. This case study shows, however, that in designing our schemes we may have to analyze and make adjustments for active, singleton object sets in generated schemes.

- How easy or difficult is it to transform an OSM functional design into Ode code?

OSM functional design serves as a good guide for implementing code in Ode. Much of the translation to code is straightforward, but differences in assumptions can make some parts of the translation vary widely from an OSM-L specification.

Appendix A*

OSM Graphical Notation

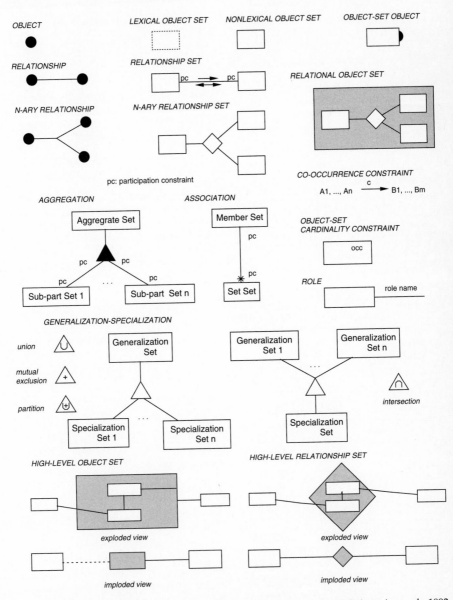

*Embley/Kurtz/Woodfield, *Object-Oriented Systems Analysis: A Model-Driven Approach*, 1992 pp. 253–263. Reprinted by permission of Prentice Hall, Upper Saddle River, NJ.

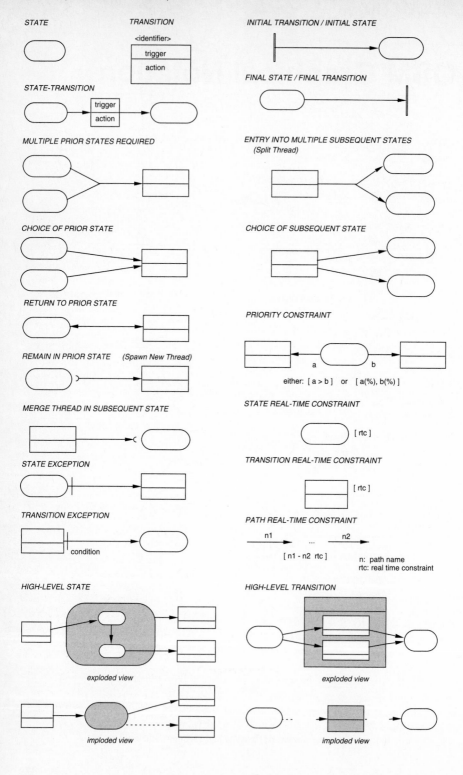

STATE

TRANSITION

<identifier>

trigger

action

STATE-TRANSITION

trigger

action

MULTIPLE PRIOR STATES REQUIRED

CHOICE OF PRIOR STATE

RETURN TO PRIOR STATE

REMAIN IN PRIOR STATE   (Spawn New Thread)

MERGE THREAD IN SUBSEQUENT STATE

STATE EXCEPTION

TRANSITION EXCEPTION

condition

HIGH-LEVEL STATE

exploded view

imploded view

INITIAL TRANSITION / INITIAL STATE

FINAL STATE / FINAL TRANSITION

ENTRY INTO MULTIPLE SUBSEQUENT STATES
(Split Thread)

CHOICE OF SUBSEQUENT STATE

PRIORITY CONSTRAINT

a   b

either: [a > b]   or   [a(%), b(%)]

STATE REAL-TIME CONSTRAINT

[rtc]

TRANSITION REAL-TIME CONSTRAINT

[rtc]

PATH REAL-TIME CONSTRAINT

n1   ...   n2

[n1 - n2 rtc]   n: path name
                          rtc: real time constraint

HIGH-LEVEL TRANSITION

exploded view

imploded view

OBJECT INTERACTION (ONE-WAY)

action

(object list)

action (object list)

TWO-WAY INTERACTION

action (object list) ->(object list)

TO / FROM CLAUSE

FROM: Origin Restriction
TO: Destination Restriction

BROADCAST INTERACTION

INTERACTION SEQUENCE

CONTINUOUS INTERACTION

INTERNAL CONNECTION

INTERACTION WITH EXTERNAL OBJECTS

REAL-TIME CONSTRAINT

{ rtc }

PATH REAL-TIME CONSTRAINT

n1   n2

{ n1 to n2 rtc }

HIGH-LEVEL INTERACTION

exploded view

imploded view

Appendix B

OSM-L Grammar

Grammatical Conventions:

- ":" denotes "is defined as."

- " | " denotes "or."

- "(...)*" denotes "one or more repetitions of ... ."

- "[...]" denotes "... is optional."

- "--" makes the rest of the line a comment.

- An all upper-case word or phrase denotes a terminal.

- An initial upper-case word or phrase denotes a nonterminal.

```
-- START RULES
OSM_Module              :   (OSM_Declaration SEMICOLON)*
OSM_Declaration         :   ORM_Declaration
                        |   OBM_Declaration
                        |   OIM_Declaration
                        |   OSM_ConstraintDecl
ORM_Declaration         :   ObjectDecl
                        |   ObjectSetDecl
                        |   RelationshipDecl
                        |   RelSetDecl
                        |   AggregationDecl
                        |   GenSpecDecl
                        |   FormalPredicate LOGICSEP PredicateQuerySet
OBM_Declaration         :   StateDecl
                        |   TransitionDecl
OIM_Declaration         :   InteractionDecl
OSM_ConstraintDecl      :   LBRACKET ConstraintBody RBRACKET

-- CONSTRAINT RULES
ConstraintBody          :   GeneralConstraint
                        |   PriorityConstraint
                        |   PathRealTimeConstraint
                        |   INFORMAL
```

GeneralConstraint	:	BooleanExpression
PathRealTimeConstraint	:	[EventName] (ConjunctionName | InteractionName)
		TO ConjunctionName RealTimeExpression
PriorityConstraint	:	TransPriorityConstraint
	|	StatePriorityConstraint
StatePriorityConstraint	:	StateName PRIORITY StateOrderingTerm
		[(COMMA StateOrderingTerm)*]
StateOrderingTerm	:	TransitionName ((RANGLE | EQUAL) TransitionName)*
TransPriorityConstraint	:	PRIORITY TransitionOrderingTerm
		[(COMMA TransitionOrderingTerm)*]
TransitionOrderingTerm	:	ConjunctionName ((RANGLE | EQUAL)
		ConjunctionName)*
RealTimeConstraintDecl	:	LBRACKET (RealTimeConstraintBody | INFORMAL)
		RBRACKET
RealTimeConstraintBody	:	[EventName] RealTimeExpression
RealTimeExpression	:	(LANGLE | RANGLE | LESSEQ | GREATEQ)
		RealExpression

-- OBJECT RULES

ObjectDecl	:	OBJECTKEY ObjectDeclBody
ObjectDeclBody	:	ObjectDeclTerm [(COMMA ObjectDeclTerm)*]
ObjectDeclTerm	:	ObjectName [ObjectGeneralization] [ObjectAliases]
		[HighLevelBody]
ObjectAliases	:	(BAR ObjectName)*
ObjectConversion	:	OBJECTKEY LPAREN ObjectSetName RPAREN

-- OBJECT-LITERAL RULES

BuiltInObject	:	BooleanLiteral
	|	NumericLiteral
	|	StringLiteral
BooleanLiteral	:	TRUEKEY
	|	FALSEKEY
NumericLiteral	:	NonNANReal
	|	NAN
PosIntLiteral	:	NONNEGINT
	|	INF
	|	PLUS (NONNEGINT | INF)
NonNANInt	:	PosIntLiteral
	|	MINUS (NONNEGINT | INF)
PosRealLiteral	:	FLOAT
	|	PLUS FLOAT
	|	PosIntLiteral
NonNANReal	:	PosRealLiteral
	|	MINUS (NONNEGINT | FLOAT | INF)
StringLiteral	:	STRING
	|	StringLiteral PLUS STRING

-- OBJECT-SET RULES

ObjectSetDecl	:	Name [Generalizations] [ObjectSetAliases] [ObjectSetCardConstr] [HighLevelBody]
ObjectSetAliases	:	(BAR ObjectSetName)*
ObjectSetConversion	:	OBJECTSET LPAREN RelationshipSetName RPAREN

-- RELATIONSHIP RULES

RelationshipDecl	:	RELATIONSHIP RelDeclBody [(COMMA RelDeclBody)*]
RelDeclBody	:	RelDeclName [RelAliases] [HighLevelBody]
RelDeclName	:	RelNameTerm (RelNameTerm)* [LOWERWORDSEQ]
RelNameTerm	:	[LOWERWORDSEQ] ObjectName [ObjectGeneralization]
RelAliases	:	(BAR RelationshipName)*

-- RELATIONSHIP-SET RULES

RelSetDecl	:	RelSetDeclName [RelSetAliases] [CoOccurrenceList] [HighLevelBody]
RelSetDeclName	:	RelSetDeclTerm (RelSetDeclTerm)* [LOWERWORDSEQ]
RelSetDeclTerm	:	RSNameFragment [Generalizations] ParticipationConstraint
RelSetAliases	:	(BAR RelationshipSetName)*
CoOccurrenceList	:	CoOccurrenceDecl [(COMMA CoOccurrenceDecl)*]
CoOccurrenceDecl	:	LBRACKET ObjectSetNameList DETERMINES [CardinalityConstraint] ObjectSetNameList RBRACKET
ObjectSetNameList	:	ObjectSetName [(COMMA ObjectSetName)*]

-- AGGREGATION DECLARATION

AggregationDecl	:	ObjectSetName HASSUBPARTS (AggregateTerm SEMICOLON)* END
AggregateTerm	:	[Generalizations] ParticipationConstraint ObjectSetName [Generalizations] ParticipationConstraint

-- MISCELLANEOUS RULES

HighLevelBody	:	INCLUDES OSM_Module END
ObjectGeneralization	:	(COLON ObjectSetRef)*
Generalizations	:	(COLON GeneralizationNameList)*
GeneralizationNameList	:	ObjectSetRef [(COMMA ObjectSetRef)*]

-- CARDINALITY-CONSTRAINT RULES

ParticipationConstraint	:	CardinalityConstraint
ObjectSetCardConstr	:	CardinalityConstraint
CardinalityConstraint	:	LBRACKET CardConstraintBody RBRACKET
CardConstraintBody	:	ConstraintTerm [(COMMA ConstraintTerm)*]
	|	INFORMAL
ConstraintTerm	:	ConstraintMin [COLON ConstraintMax]
ConstraintMin	:	IntegerExpression
ConstraintMax	:	IntegerExpression
	|	STAR

-- GENERALIZATION-SPECIALIZATION RULES

GenSpecDecl	:	SpecializationNameList GenSpecKey
		GeneralizationNameList
	|	GeneralizationNameTerm ISAI GeneralizationNameList
GenSpecKey	:	COLON
	|	ISA
	|	ISAM
	|	ISAP
	|	ISAU
SpecializationNameList	:	GeneralizationNameList

-- SET-ENUMERATION RULES

Enumeration	:	LBRACE [EnumTag [(COMMA EnumTag)*]] RBRACE
EnumTag	:	ObjectName

-- STATE RULES

StateDecl	:	STATE StateName [StateAliases]
		[RealTimeConstraintDecl] [HighLevelBody]
StateAliases	:	(BAR StateName)*

-- TRANSITION RULES

TransitionDecl	:	[TransitionName] TransitionTrigger
		[TransitionAction] TransitionTail
TransitionTrigger	:	TransitionIfClause
	|	TransitionEventClause
		[[AndOrKey] TransitionIfClause]
	|	WHEN PriorStateConjunction
		[[AND] TransitionEventClause]
		[[AndOrKey] TransitionIfClause]
AndOrKey	:	AND
	|	OR
TransitionIfClause	:	IF BooleanExpression [RealTimeConstraintDecl]
TransitionEventClause	:	AT InteractionName [LPAREN [FormalParameterList]
		RPAREN [InteractionTail]]
PriorStateConjunction	:	PriorStateConjTerm [(OR PriorStateConjTerm)*]
PriorStateConjTerm	:	PriorStateExpr
	|	LPAREN PriorStateConjTerm RPAREN
PriorStateExpr	:	[ConjunctionLabel] PriorState
		[(AND PriorState)*] [EXCEPTION]
ConjunctionLabel	:	LANGLE ConjunctionName RANGLE
PriorState	:	StateName [NEWTHREAD]
TransitionAction	:	THEN [ActionBody]
		[LBRACKET ACTION RealTimeConstraintBody
		RBRACKET]
ActionBody	:	Scope
	|	INFORMAL
TransitionTail	:	[EnterClause] [(TransitionException)*]
		TransitionEnd [RealTimeConstraintDecl]

TransitionEnd	:	HighLevelBody
	|	END
EnterClause	:	ENTER SubsequentStateConj SEMICOLON
SubsequentStateConj	:	SubsStateConjTerm [(OR SubsStateConjTerm)*]
SubsStateConjTerm	:	SubsequentStateExpr
	|	LPAREN SubsStateConjTerm RPAREN
SubsequentStateExpr	:	[ConjunctionLabel] SubsequentState
		[(AND SubsequentState)*]
SubsequentState	:	StateName [PRESERVETHR]
TransitionException	:	EXCEPTION ExceptionCondition EnterClause
ExceptionCondition	:	ExceptionCondTerm [(AndOrKey ExceptionCondTerm)*]
ExceptionCondTerm	:	BooleanExpression
	|	AT InteractionName
		[LPAREN [FormalParameterList] RPAREN]

-- INTERACTION RULES

InteractionDecl	:	AbstractInteraction
AbstractInteraction	:	InteractionBody ToFromWhereClause
		[HighLevelBody] [(RealTimeConstraintDecl)*]
InteractionBody	:	InteractionName [(BAR InteractionName)*]
		[LPAREN [SendParmList] RPAREN]
		[DETERMINES LPAREN [ReturnParmList] RPAREN]
ToFromWhereClause	:	ToFromClause [WhereClause]
ToFromClause	:	ToKey PathExpression [FromKey PathExpression]
	|	FromKey PathExpression [ToKey PathExpression]
ToKey	:	TO
	|	TOALL
FromKey	:	FROM

-- EXPRESSION RULES

Expression	:	UnaryOp Expression
	|	Expression BinaryOp Expression
	|	SELF
	|	SELFTHREAD
	|	PathExpression
	|	PredicateQuery
	|	OneWayInteractionExpr
	|	StatusQuery
	|	QuantifierExpression
	|	LPAREN Expression RPAREN
	|	BAR Expression BAR
	|	INFORMAL
BooleanExpression	:	Expression-- must yield a Boolean set
IntegerExpression	:	Expression-- must yield an Integer set
RealExpression	:	Expression-- must yield a Real set
ObjectExpression	:	Expression-- must yield an object or thread
QuantifierExpression	:	FORALL QuantifierTail
	|	EXISTS [CardinalityConstraint] QuantifierTail

QuantifierTail	:	FormalPredicate COLON PredicateQuerySet
FormalPredicate	:	(RSNameFragment [LPAREN ObjectSetName
		[PredicateTermType] RPAREN])* [LOWERWORDSEQ]
PredicateTermType	:	CardinalityConstraint
	|	COLON ObjectSetRef
	|	CardinalityConstraint COLON ObjectSetRef
RSNameFragment	:	[LOWERWORDSEQ] ObjectSetName
PredicateQuerySet	:	PredicateQuery [(COMMA PredicateQuery)*]
PredicateQuery	:	ObjectName
	|	ObjectSetRef
	|	RelationshipName
	|	RelationshipSetName
	|	QualifiedPredicate
QualifiedPredicate	:	ObjectSetRef Qualifier
	|	RSNameFragment [Qualifier]
		(RSNameFragment [Qualifier])* [LOWERWORDSEQ]
Qualifier	:	LPAREN Expression RPAREN
PathExpression	:	PredicateQuery
	|	PredicateQuery PERIOD PathExpression
StatusQuery	:	ObjectExpression IN (StateName | TransitionName)
InteractionTail	:	DETERMINES LPAREN ReturnParmList RPAREN
		[AND BooleanExpression]
SendParmList	:	ParameterList
ReturnParmList	:	FormalParameterList
ParameterList	:	ParameterTerm [(COMMA ParameterTerm)*]
ParameterTerm	:	PathExpression
	|	FormalPredicate
FormalParameterList	:	FormalPredicate [(COMMA FormalPredicate)*]

-- OPERATOR RULES

UnaryOp	:	NOT
	|	ONEOF
	|	MINUS
BinaryOp	:	ArithOp
	|	EqComparator
	|	LogOp
	|	SetComparator
ArithOp	:	PLUS
	|	MINUS
	|	STAR
	|	SLASH
	|	MODULO
	|	CARET
EqComparator	:	EQUAL
	|	GREATEQ
	|	LESSEQ
	|	NOTEQ
	|	LANGLE
	|	RANGLE

LogOp	:	IMPLIES
		| EQUIV
		| AND
		| OR
SetComparator	:	INCSYM
		| INCSYMEQ
		| SUBSETOF
		| SUBSETEQ

-- STATEMENT RULES

Scope	:	[(ActionStatement SEMICOLON)*]
ActionStatement	:	OSM_Declaration
		| PathExpression [InteractionTail] [WaitClause]
		| TOALL PathExpression [InteractionTail] [WaitClause]
		| PathExpression ASSIGNOP Expression
		| FormalPredicate LOGICSEP PredicateQuerySet
		| ADD PredicateQuerySet [WhereClause]
		| REMOVE PredicateQuerySet [WhereClause]
		| FOREACH PathExpression [OrderByClause] DO Scope END
		| IF BooleanExpression THEN Scope
		[(ElseIfClause)*] [ElseClause] END
		| START [VISIBLE]
		| COMMIT
		| ABORT
		| WHILE BooleanExpression DO Scope END
WaitClause	:	LBRACKET WAIT RealExpression RBRACKET
WhereClause	:	WHERE ExpressionSet
ExpressionSet	:	Expression [(COMMA Expression)*]
ElseIfClause	:	ELSEIF BooleanExpression THEN Scope
ElseClause	:	ELSE Scope
OrderByClause	:	(OrderByTerm)*
OrderByTerm	:	ASCENDING ObjSetNameList
		| DESCENDING ObjSetNameList
ObjSetNameList	:	ObjectSetName [BY Expression]
		[(COMMA ObjectSetName [BY Expression])*]

-- NAME RULES

ConjunctionName	:	QualifiedName
EventName	:	Name
InteractionName	:	Name
ObjectName	:	Name
		| BuiltInObjectSet
		| ObjectConversion
ObjectSetRef	:	ObjectSetName
		| Enumeration
ObjectSetName	:	OBJECTSETNAME
		| BuiltInObjectSet
		| ObjectSetConversion

RelationshipName	:	Name
RelationshipSetName	:	Name
	|	ObjectSetName RelSetConnective ObjectSetName
StateName	:	[ObjectSetName PERIOD] STATENAME
TransitionName	:	[ObjectSetName PERIOD] TRANSITIONNAME
Name	:	(NameTerm)*
NameTerm	:	UPPERWORD
	|	LOWERWORD
UpperWordSeq	:	(UPPERWORD)*
BuiltInObjectSet	:	BOOLEAN
	|	STRINGKEY
	|	INTEGER [NonNANIntStar COLON NonNANIntStar]
	|	REAL [RealRange] [PrecisionClause]
RealRange	:	NonNANRealStar COLON NonNANRealStar
NonNANIntStar	:	NonNANInt
	|	STAR
	|	MINUS STAR
NonNANRealStar	:	NonNANReal
	|	STAR
	|	MINUS STAR
PrecisionClause	:	PosIntLiteral DIGITS
RelSetConnective	:	ISA
	|	HASSUBPARTS

-- SYMBOL AND OPERATOR TOKENS

AND	:	and
ASSIGNOP	:	:=
AT	:	@
BAR	:	|
CARET	:	^
COLON	:	:
COMMA	:	,
DETERMINES	:	->
EQUAL	:	=
EQUIV	:	<=>
GREATEQ	:	>=
IMPLIES	:	=>
INCSYM	:	.)
INCSYMEQ	:	=)
LANGLE	:	<
LBRACE	:	{
LBRACKET	:	[
LESSEQ	:	<=
LOGICSEP	:	:-
LPAREN	:	(
MINUS	:	-
MODULO	:	mod
NOT	:	not

NOTEQ	:	<>
ONEOF	:	one of
OR	:	or
PERIOD	:	.
PLUS	:	+
RANGLE	:	>
RBRACE	:	}
RBRACKET	:	]
RPAREN	:	)
SEMICOLON	:	;
SLASH	:	/
STAR	:	*
SUBSETOF	:	(.
SUBSETEQ	:	(=

-- BUILT-IN OBJECT-SET TOKENS

BOOLEAN	:	Boolean
INTEGER	:	Integer
REAL	:	Real
STRINGKEY	:	String

-- BUILT-IN OBJECT TOKENS

FALSEKEY	:	False
TRUEKEY	:	True

-- KEY-WORD TOKENS

ABORT	:	abort
ACTION	:	action
ADD	:	add
ASCENDING	:	ascending
BY	:	by
COMMIT	:	commit
CONTINUOUS	:	continuous
DESCENDING	:	descending
DIGITS	:	digits
DO	:	do
ELSE	:	else
ELSEIF	:	elseif
END	:	end
ENTER	:	enter
EXCEPTION	:	exception
EXISTS	:	exists
FORALL	:	for all
FOREACH	:	for each
FROM	:	from
HASSUBPARTS	:	has subpart | has subparts
IF	:	if
IN	:	in

INCLUDES	:	includes
INF	:	inf-- infinity
ISA	:	isa | is a
ISAI	:	ISA LBRACKET intersection RBRACKET
ISAM	:	ISA LBRACKET mutex RBRACKET
ISAP	:	ISA LBRACKET partition RBRACKET
ISAU	:	ISA LBRACKET union RBRACKET
NAN	:	nan-- not a number
NEWTHREAD	:	new thread
OBJECTKEY	:	object
OBJECTSET	:	object set
PRESERVETHR	:	preserve thread
PRIORITY	:	priority
RELATIONSHIP	:	relationship
REMOVE	:	remove
REPRESENTS	:	represents
SELF	:	self
SELFTHREAD	:	self thread
START	:	start
STATE	:	state
THEN	:	then
TO	:	to
TOALL	:	to all
VISIBLE	:	visible
WAIT	:	wait
WHEN	:	when
WHERE	:	where
WHILE	:	while

-- TERMINALS DESCRIBED IN NATURAL LANGUAGE

CONJUNCTIONNAME	:	a conjunction name
FLOAT	:	this is a mantissa-exponent real literal (standard forms)
INFORMAL	:	<< anything goes here >>
INTERACTIONNAME	:	an interaction name
LOWERWORDSEQ	:	a sequence of one or more words that begin with a lower-case letter, each word separated by white space
NONNEGINT	:	this is a sequence of decimal digits, or 0x followed by hexadecimal digits
OBJECTNAME	:	an object name
OBJECTSETNAME	:	an object-set name
RELATIONSHIPNAME	:	a relationship name
RELATIONSHIPSETNAME	:	a relationship-set name
STATENAME	:	a state name
STRING	:	this is a quoted string, where quotes are ' or "
TRANSITIONNAME	:	a transition name

Appendix C

Answers to Selected Exercises

These answers to selected exercises augment the discussion in the text in two primary ways: First, they provide examples of concepts and principles discussed in the text or introduced in the exercises. Second, they provide proofs of some of the fundamental theorems cited in the text and some of the auxiliary lemmas introduced in the exercises.

Chapter 2

2.16a $\pi_{Fname}\sigma_{Dept\,=\,Math}\,faculty$

2.16b $\pi_{Sname,\,Major}\sigma_{CourseNum\,=\,CS1}(student \bowtie is-taking)$

2.16c $\pi_{Fname}\sigma_{Salary\,<\,50{,}000}(faculty \bowtie is\_teaching)$

2.16d $\pi_{Sname}(student \bowtie is\_taking \bowtie is\_teaching$
$\bowtie \sigma_{Fname\,=\,Johnson\,\wedge\,Dept\,=\,CS}\,faculty)$

2.16e $\pi_{Name,\,ID,\,SSN}(\rho_{Sname\,\leftarrow\,Name}student \bowtie \rho_{Fname\,\leftarrow\,Name}\,faculty)$

2.16f $\pi_{ID,\,CourseNum}\sigma_{Sname\,=\,Fname}(student \bowtie is\_taking$
$\bowtie is\_teaching \bowtie faculty)$

2.16g $\pi_{Sname}(student \bowtie (\pi_{ID}student - \pi_{ID}((\pi_{ID}is\_taking$
$\bowtie \pi_{CourseNum}\sigma_{Fname\,=\,Johnson\,\wedge\,Dept\,=\,CS}$
$(faculty \bowtie is\_teaching)) - is\_taking)))$

2.18a $\pi_{Sname,\,CourseNum}(student \bowtie is\_taking)$
$\div \pi_{CourseNum}\sigma_{Fname\,=\,Johnson\,\wedge\,Dept\,=\,CS}(faculty \bowtie is\_teaching)$

2.23a
```
select *
from student
where Major = 'CS'
order by GPA desc, Sname asc
```

2.23b
```
select Fname, SSN, count(CourseNum)
from faculty f, is_teaching t
where f.SSN = t.SSN
group by SSN
```

2.23c
```
select Dept, max(Salary) "MaxSalary"
from faculty
group by Dept
order by MaxSalary desc
```

2.23d
```
select Dept, avg(Salary) "LowAvgSalary"
from faculty
group by Dept
having LowAvgSalary < 40000
order by LowAvgSalary
```

Chapter 3

3.12b *Prove:* $\pi_X(\pi_Y(e)) = \pi_X(e)$.

Proof. Let $t \in \pi_X(\pi_Y(e))$; then there exists a t' in $\pi_Y(e)$ such that $t = t'[X]$. Since $t' \in \pi_Y(e)$, there exists a t'' in e such that $t' = t''[Y]$. Restricting both t' and $t''[Y]$, which are equal, to X, we have $t'[X] = t''[Y][X]$. Since $X \subseteq Y$, $t''[Y][X] = t''[X]$, and thus $t'[X] = t''[X]$. Substituting $t''[X]$ for $t'[X]$ in $t = t'[X]$, we have $t = t''[X]$. Hence, since $t'' \in e$ and $t = t''[X]$, $t \in \pi_X(e)$.

Let $t \in \pi_X(e)$; then there exists a t' in e such that $t = t'[X]$. Since $X \subseteq Y$ and $Y \subseteq scheme(e)$, $t'[X] = t'[Y][X]$ and hence $t = t'[Y][X]$. Since $t' \in e$, $t'[Y] \in \pi_Y(e)$, and since $t'[Y] \in \pi_Y(e)$, $t'[Y][X] \in \pi_X(\pi_Y(e))$. Thus, since $t = t'[Y][X]$, $t \in \pi_X(\pi_Y(e))$.

3.18d *Prove:* If r and s are relations on R and X is a subset of R, then $\pi_X(r \cup s) = \pi_X r \cup \pi_X s$.

Proof. Let $t \in \pi_X(r \cup s)$. Then, by definition of π, there exists a

$t' \in r \cup s$ such that $t = t'[X]$. Since $t' \in r \cup s$, $t' \in r \vee t' \in s$, by definition of $\cup$. Without loss of generality, assume that $t' \in r$. Since $t' \in r$ and $t = t'[X]$, by definition of π, $t \in \pi_X r$. Since $t \in \pi_X r$, $t \in \pi_X r \vee t \in \pi_X s$, by definition of $\vee$. Thus, by definition of $\cup$, $t \in \pi_X r \cup \pi_X s$.

Let $t \in \pi_X r \cup \pi_X s$. Then $t \in \pi_X r \vee t \in \pi_X s$, by definition of $\cup$. Without loss of generality, assume that $t \in \pi_X r$. Then, by definition of π, there exists a $t' \in r$ such that $t = t'[X]$. Since $t' \in r$, $t' \in r \vee t' \in s$, by definition of $\vee$. Thus, $t' \in r \cup s$, by definition of $\cup$. Since $t' \in r \cup s$ and $t = t'[X]$, $t \in \pi_X(r \cup s)$, by definition of π.

Chapter 5

5.11 *Prove*:

$$\exists^n x(P(x)) \Leftrightarrow \neg\exists^0 x(P(x)) \wedge \cdots \wedge \neg\exists^{n-1} x(P(x)) \wedge$$
$$\forall x_1 \cdots \forall x_{n+1}(P(x_1) \wedge \cdots \wedge P(x_{n+1})$$
$$\Rightarrow (x_1{=}x_2 \vee \cdots \vee x_1{=}x_{n+1})$$
$$\vee (x_2{=}x_3 \vee \cdots \vee x_2{=}x_{n+1})$$
$$\cdots$$
$$\vee (x_n{=}x_{n+1}))$$

Proof. We proceed by induction on the number of domain elements for which P holds.

Basis: $n = 0$. Since the right-hand side has the form

$$\neg\exists^0 x(P(x)) \wedge \cdots \wedge \neg\exists^{n-1} x(P(x)) \wedge \forall x_1 \cdots \forall x_{n+1}(P(x_1) \wedge \cdots \wedge$$
$$P(x_{n+1}) \Rightarrow (x_1{=}x_2 \vee \cdots \vee x_1{=}x_{n+1}) \vee (x_2{=}x_3 \vee \cdots \vee x_2{=}x_{n+1}) \cdots$$
$$\vee (x_n{=}x_{n+1}))$$

for $n = 0$ we have a conjunction of zero $\neg\exists$ terms, which yields true since the conjunction of zero terms is by definition true; and we have a disjunction of zero $x_i = x_j$ terms, which yields false since the disjunction of zero terms is by definition false. Thus we must show $\exists^0 x(P(x)) \Leftrightarrow true \wedge \forall x_1(P(x_1) \Rightarrow false)$. By definition, the left-hand side is a statement that there are zero elements in the domain for which P holds. The right-hand side reduces to $\forall x_1(P(x_1) \Rightarrow false)$, which holds only if P is false for every element of the domain, which is equivalent to the statement that there are zero elements in the domain for which P holds.

Induction: We assume that the equivalence holds for all n, $0 \leq n \leq k$, and show that it holds for $n = k+1$. By definition, $\exists^{k+1}x(P(x))$ means that there are exactly $k+1$ elements in the domain for which P holds. Thus, P does not hold for $0, ..., k$ elements of the domain, and does not hold for more than $k+1$ elements of the domain. Thus by the induction hypothesis, we have

$$\neg\exists^{0}x(P(x)) \wedge \cdots \wedge \neg\exists^{k}x(P(x))$$

We also have that P holds for up to $k+1$ elements of the domain. We claim that

$$\forall x_1 \cdots \forall x_{k+2}(P(x_1) \wedge \cdots \wedge P(x_{k+2}) \Rightarrow (x_1{=}x_2 \vee \cdots \vee x_1{=}x_{k+2})$$
$$\vee (x_2{=}x_3 \vee \cdots \vee x_2{=}x_{k+2}) \cdots \vee (x_{k+1}{=}x_{k+2}))$$

makes P hold for up to $k+1$ elements of the domain; if not then P holds for $k+2$ or more distinct elements of the domain. Since P holds for $k+2$ or more distinct elements, it holds for $k+2$ distinct elements. Let $x_1, ..., x_{k+2}$ be $k+2$ distinct elements for which P holds. Then $P(x_1) \wedge ... \wedge P(x_{k+2})$ is true. Furthermore, since these elements are distinct, no pair of them is equal and thus

$$(x_1{=}x_2 \vee \cdots \vee x_1{=}x_{k+2}) \vee (x_2{=}x_3 \vee \cdots \vee x_2{=}x_{k+2}) \cdots \vee (x_{k+1}{=}x_{k+2}))$$

is false. Hence

$$\forall x_1 \cdots \forall x_{k+2}(P(x_1) \wedge \cdots \wedge P(x_{k+2}) \Rightarrow (x_1{=}x_2 \vee \cdots \vee x_1{=}x_{k+2})$$
$$\vee (x_2{=}x_3 \vee \cdots \vee x_2{=}x_{k+2}) \cdots \vee (x_{k+1}{=}x_{k+2}))$$

does not hold, contrary to our assumption that it does. We therefore now have

$$\exists^{k+1}x(P(x)) \Leftrightarrow \neg\exists^{0}x(P(x)) \wedge \cdots \wedge \neg\exists^{k}x(P(x)) \wedge$$
$$\forall x_1 \cdots \forall x_{k+2}(P(x_1) \wedge \cdots \wedge P(x_{k+2}) \Rightarrow (x_1{=}x_2 \vee \cdots \vee$$
$$x_1{=}x_{k+2})$$
$$\vee (x_2{=}x_3 \vee \cdots \vee x_2{=}x_{k+2}) \cdots \vee (x_{k+1}{=}x_{k+2}))$$

which completes our induction.

5.18a *Prove*: The constraint $\forall x \exists^{\leq 1}{<}y, z{>}(r(x, y, z))$ makes A a superkey for r for any valid interpretation (i.e., ensures that for any valid interpretation $t[A] \neq t'[A]$ for distinct tuples t and t').

Proof. Assume not, then distinct tuples t and t' exist such that $t[A] = t'[A]$. But then $t[BC] = t'[BC]$, if not, then $\forall x \exists^{>1}<y, z>(r(x, y, z))$— a contradiction to

$$\forall x \exists^{\leq 1}<y, z>(r(x, y, z))$$

Now, since $t[A] = t'[A]$ and $t[BC] = t'[BC]$, $t = t'$—a contradiction.

5.19a $\{< x > \mid \exists y \exists z(faculty(y, x, Math, z))\}$

5.19b $\{< x, y > \mid \exists z \exists w(student(z, x, y, w) \land is\_taking(z, CS1))\}$

5.19c $\{< x_1 > \mid \exists x_2 \exists x_3 \exists x_4 \exists x_5(faculty(x_2, x_1, x_3, x_4)$
      $\land\ is\_teaching(x_1, x_5) \land x_4 < 50000)\}$

5.19d $\{< x_1 > \mid$
      $\exists x_2 \exists x_3 \exists x_4 \exists x_5 \exists x_6 \exists x_7(student(x_2, x_1, x_3, x_4) \land is\_taking(x_2, x_5)$
      $\land\ is\_teaching(x_6, x_5) \land faculty(x_6, Johnson, CS, x_7))\}$

5.19e $\{< x_1, x_2, x_3 > \mid$
      $\exists x_4 \exists x_5 \exists x_6 \exists x_7(student(x_2, x_1, x_4, x_5) \land faculty(x_3, x_1, x_6, x_7))\}$

5.19f $\{< x_1, x_2 > \mid$
      $\exists x_3 \exists x_4 \exists x_5 \exists x_6 \exists x_7 \exists x_8(is\_taking(x_1, x_2) \land is\_teaching(x_3, x_2)$
      $\land\ student(x_1, x_4, x_5, x_6) \land faculty(x_3, x_4, x_7, x_8))\}$

5.19g $\{< x_1 > \mid \exists x_2 \exists x_3 \exists x_4 \exists x_5 \exists x_6(student(x_2, x_1, x_3, x_4)$
      $\land\ faculty(x_5, Johnson, CS, x_6)$
      $\land\ \forall x_7(is\_teaching(x_5, x_7) \Rightarrow is\_taking(x_2, x_7)))\}$

5.20 $\{< x_1 > \mid \exists x_2 \exists x_3 \exists x_4 \exists x_5 \exists x_6(student(x_2, x_1, x_3, x_4)$
      $\land\ faculty(x_5, Johnson, CS, x_6)$
      $\land\ \neg\ \exists x_7(is\_teaching(x_5, x_7) \land \neg\ is\_taking(x_2, x_7)))\}$

```
select Sname
from student s, faculty f
where Fname = 'Johnson' and Dept = 'CS' and not exists (
  select *
  from is_teaching i,
  where f. SSN = i. SSN and not exists (
    select *
    from is_taking j
    where s. ID = j. ID and i. CourseNum = j. CourseNum))
```

Chapter 6

6.1a $A(x), B(x), C(x), D(x), E(x)$

6.1b $A(x)$ *relates to* $D(y)$, $C(x)$ *relates to* $E(y)$

6.1c
$$\forall x \forall y(A(x) \text{ relates to } D(y) \Rightarrow A(x) \wedge D(y)),$$
$$\forall x \forall y(C(x) \text{ relates to } E(y) \Rightarrow C(x) \wedge E(y))$$

6.1d
$$\forall x(B(x) \vee C(x) \Rightarrow A(x)),$$
$$\forall x(B(x) \Rightarrow \neg C(x)),$$
$$\forall x(C(x) \Rightarrow \neg B(x)),$$
$$\forall x(A(x) \Rightarrow B(x) \vee C(x))$$

6.1e
$$\forall x(A(x) \Rightarrow \exists^1 y(A(x) \text{ relates to } D(y))),$$
$$\forall x(A(x) \Rightarrow \exists^1 y(A(y) \text{ relates to } D(x))),$$
$$\forall x(E(x) \Rightarrow \exists^{\geq 1} y(C(y) \text{ relates to } E(x))),$$

Chapter 7

7.4a

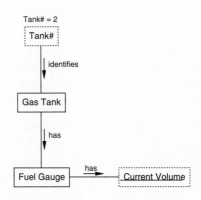

7.6a $4, 5, 2, 3$

7.6b   *Person*(*Person*$_5$), *Person*(*Person*$_5$) *has Name*(*Chris*),
Employee(*Person*$_5$), *Emp#*(555) *identifies Person*$_5$

7.6c   *Person*(*Person*$_2$), *Student*(*Person*$_2$), *Employee*(*Person*$_2$),
Person(*Person*$_2$) *has Name*(*Kelly*), *Person*(*Person*$_2$) *has GPA*(3.0),
Student ID(222) *identifies Student*(*Person*$_2$), *Emp#*(222) *identifies*
Employee(*Person*$_2$)

7.6d   *Student ID(333), Student ID(333) identifies Student(Person₃)*

7.6e   They are equal.

7.7a   *Person, Employee, Person has Name, Emp# identifies Employee*

7.7b   *Student ID, Student ID identifies Student*

7.8a   *Person, Person has Name, Person has GPA*

7.8b   *Name, Person has Name*

7.9a   *Person, Person has Name, Person has GPA*

7.9b   *Employee has Address*

7.10a   *Person, Employee, Person has Name, Emp# identifies Employee*

7.10b   *GPA, Person has GPA*

7.10c   *Student, Person, Person has Name, Person has GPA, Student ID identifies Student*

7.10d   *Emp#, Emp# identifies Employee*

7.10e   *Employee* (For any object x in *Employee*, *Employee*(x) is a fact, and thus *Employee* is a property of x.)

   Person (Since *Person* is a generalization of *Employee*, any object x in *Employee* is in *Person*, and thus *Person*(x) is a fact.)

   Emp# identifies Employee (For any object x in *Employee*, the 1 participation constraint on *Employee* guarantees that there exists an object y in *Emp#* such that *Emp#*(y) *identifies Employee*(x) is a fact in any interpretation in which the set *Employee* is nonempty.)

   Person has Name (If x is an object in *Employee*, then *Person*(x) is a fact. But the 1 participation constraint for *Person has Name* guarantees that there exists a $y \in Name$ such that *Person*(x) *has Name*(y) is a fact.)

   There are no other common properties of *Employee*. The interpretation in Fig. 7.26 provides a counterexample for each possible property.

7.10f   *GPA* (For any object x in *GPA*, *GPA*(x) is a fact.)

   Person has GPA (For any object x in *GPA*, the 1:* participation constraint on *GPA* guarantees that there exists an object y in *Person* such that *Person*(y) *has GPA*(x) is a fact in any interpretation in which the set *GPA* is nonempty.)

7.11a *Proof.* Let x be an object in *Student*, then *Student*(x) is a fact about x and thus *Student*(x) holds. Since *Student ID identifies Student* has a *1* participation constraint for *Student*, we have

$$\forall x(Student(x) \Rightarrow \exists^1 y(Student\ ID(y)\ identifies\ Student(x)))$$

Thus, since *Student*(x) holds, $\exists^1 y$(*Student ID*(y) *identifies Student*(x)) and thus there exists an object y such that *Student ID*(y) *identifies Student*(x) holds. Since *Student ID*(y) *identifies Student*(x) holds, *Student ID*(y) *identifies Student*(x) is a fact for x and thus *Student ID identifies Student* is a property of x. Since x was chosen arbitrarily from *Student*, however, every object $x \in$ *Student* has the property *Student ID identifies Student*. Thus, *Student ID identifies Student* is a common property of *Student*.

7.11b The proof is identical to the example proof, except that *Student* is substituted for *Employee*.

7.11c *Person has GPA* is not a common property of *Student*. To create a counterexample, we can add *Person₁* to *Student* and <111, *Person₁*> to *Student ID identifies Student*.

7.11d *Emp# identifies Employee* is not a common property of *Person*. Our interpretation in Fig. 7.26 is a counterexample because *Person₃* has no *Emp#*.

7.12a *Name, GPA, Emp#, Student ID*

7.12b *Person has GPA* is an inherited property of *Student*, but we cannot prove that it is a common property of *Student*.

7.12c $\forall x(Student(x) \Rightarrow \exists y(Person(x)\ has\ GPA(y)))$

Given this general constraint, we can prove that *Person has GPA* is a common property of *Student* as follows. Let $x \in$ *Student*. Then *Student*(x) holds. Since *Student*(x) holds and *Student*$(x) \Rightarrow \exists y$(*Person*$(x)$ *has GPA*(y)), there exists an object y such that *Person*(x) *has GPA*(y). Thus, *Person has GPA* is a common property of *Student*.

With this general constraint, the sets $EP_{Student}$ and $CP_{Student}$ are both

{*Student, Person, Student ID identifies Student, Person has Name, Person has GPA*}

7.12d *Proof.* Let $x \in Person$. Then, $Person(x)$ holds. Since $Person(x)$ holds and $Person(x) \Rightarrow \exists^1 y(Emp\#(y)$ *identifies Employee*$(x) \vee$ *Student ID*(y) *identifies Student*(x), there exists a y such that $Emp\#(y)$ *identifies Employee*$(x) \vee$ *Student ID*(y) *identifies Student*(x). Suppose that there exists a y such that $Emp\#(y)$ *identifies Employee*(x); then, since $Emp\#(y)$ *identifies Employee*$(x) \Rightarrow ID\#(y)$ *identifies Person*(x), $ID\#(y)$ *identifies Person*(x). Hence, *ID# identifies Person* is a fact about object x if there is a y such that $Emp\#(y)$ *identifies Employee*(x). If not, then since there exists a y such that $Emp\#(y)$ *identifies Employee*$(x) \vee$ *Student ID*(y) *identifies Student*(x) holds, then *Student ID*(y) *identifies Student*(x). Thus, since *Student ID*(y) *identifies Student*$(x) \Rightarrow ID\#(y)$ *identifies Person*(x), $Id\#(y)$ *identifies Person*(x). Hence, *ID# identifies Person* is a fact about object x. Since x is arbitrary, *ID# identifies Person* is a fact about any object in *Person* for any interpretation, and thus *ID# identifies Person* is a common property of *Person*.

7.12e Set of overstatements: {*Person has GPA*}.
Set of understatements: {*ID# identifies Person*}.

Chapter 8

8.3

> *Customer* [1] *has Name* [1: *];
> *Customer* [1] *has Address* [1: *];
> *Customer* [1: *] *has Account* [1: 2];
> *Account* [1] *has Account#* [1];
> *Customer* [0: *] *has Bank Card* [1: 2];
> *Bank Card* [1] *has Card Number* [1];
> *Bank Card* [1] *has Expiration Date* [1: *];
> *Bank Card* [1] *has Card Type* [1: *];
> **object** *Credit, Debit*;
> *Credit, Debit* **isa**[⊎] *Card Type*;

8.16 *Note*: We assume that *Name* and *Address* uniquely determine a person. (Observe that this is not part of the specification; indeed it is something learned and added as part of formalizing the *change name* interaction.)

3

when *Ready* **new thread**
@ *change name(New Name: String, Old Name: String,*
   Old Address: String) **then**
   p: Person;
   p := Person(x) wherePerson(x). Name = Old Name
      and *Person(x). Address = Old Address;*
   Person(p). Name := New Name;
   exception not(exists *Person(x)*
      where *Person(x). Name = Old Name*
         and *Person(x). Address = Old Address)*
      enter *Person Not Identified*
      end;
end;

when *Person Not Identified* **then**
   output("Name and Address does not identify a person.");
end;

Chapter 9

9.4 **Theorem** 9.1.

Let D be an ORM diagram for an application model, and let H be an ORM hypergraph produced from D by Algorithm 9.1. Let e: $A_1, ..., A_n \rightarrow B_1, ..., B_m$ be a directed edge of H obtained from a relationship set R of D. Then in any valid interpretation for D, if r is the relation for R, then the FD $A_1...A_n \rightarrow B_1...B_n$ holds.

Proof. Let t_1 and t_2 be tuples in r such that $t_1[A_1 \cdots A_n] = t_2[A_1 \cdots A_n]$. We have five cases to consider, three for the participation constraints *1*, *1:1*, and *0:1* from Step 2.1 of Algorithm 9.1 and two for the co-occurrence-constraint conditions *1* (which could be explicit or by default) and *1:1*.

Case 1. Participation constraint *1*. Since e is generated from a participation constraint, $n = 1$, and since the participation constraint is *1*, from Rule 5e of our application-model rules in Chapter 6 we have

$$\forall x_i(A_1(x_i) \Rightarrow \exists^1 < x_1, ..., x_{i-1}, x_{i+1}, ..., x_{m+1} > (R(x_1, ..., x_{m+1})))$$

where $x_i = t_1[A_1]$ ($= t_2[A_1]$). By expanding the counting quantifier, we have

$$\forall x_i (A_1(x_i) \Rightarrow \exists < x_1, \ldots, x_{i-1}, x_{i+1}, \ldots, x_{m+1} > (R(x_1, \ldots, x_{m+1})$$
$$\wedge \forall < x_1', \ldots, x_{i-1}', x_{i+1}', \ldots, x_{m+1}' > \forall < x_1'',$$
$$\ldots, x_{i-1}'', x_{i+1}'', \ldots, x_{m+1}'' >$$
$$(R(x_1', \ldots, x_{i-1}', x_i, x_{i+1}', \ldots, x_{m+1}') \wedge R(x_1'',$$
$$\ldots, x_{i-1}'', x_i, x_{i+1}'', \ldots, x_{m+1}'')$$
$$\Rightarrow < x_1', \ldots, x_{i-1}', x_{i+1}', \ldots, x_{m+1}' > = < x_1'',$$
$$\ldots, x_{i-1}'', x_{i+1}'', \ldots, x_{m+1}'' >)))$$

which implies that all the tuples of r that have x_i as their A_1 component are identical when restricted to $B_1, \ldots, B_m$. Thus,

$$t_1[B_1 \cdots B_m] = t_2[B_1 \cdots B_m]$$

Case 2. Participation constraint *1:1*. We can reduce this to Case 1 by substituting the participation constraint *1:1* into Rule 5d and observing that the counting-quantifier conditions ≥ 1 and ≤ 1 together imply a counting-quantifier condition of 1.

Case 3. Participation constraint *0:1*. We can reduce this to Case 1 by making two observations. (1) By substituting the participation constraint *0:1* into Rule 5c, we obtain the counting-quantifier condition ≤ 1. (2) Since we are considering only the relation r, we are not interested in those objects in A_1 that do not participate in the relationship r. This, along with observation 1, reduces the counting-quantifier condition to 1.

Case 4. Co-occurrence-constraint condition *1*. Since the co-occurrence-constraint condition is *1*, from Rule 6 we have

$$\forall < x_1, \ldots, x_n >$$
$$(\exists < y_1, \ldots, y_m, z_1, \ldots, z_p > (R(x_1, \ldots, x_n, y_1, \ldots, y_m, z_1, \ldots, z_p)$$
$$\Rightarrow$$
$$\exists^1 < y_1, \ldots, y_m > (R(x_1, \ldots, x_n, y_1, \ldots, y_m, z_1, \ldots, z_p))))$$

where $< x_1 \cdots x_n > = t_1[A_1, \ldots, A_n]$ ($= t_2[A_1, \ldots, A_n]$). By expanding the counting quantifier, we have

$$\forall < x_1, \ldots, x_n >$$
$$(\exists < y_1, \ldots, y_m, z_1, \ldots, z_p > (R(x_1, \ldots, x_n, y_1, \ldots, y_m, z_1, \ldots, z_p)$$
$$\Rightarrow$$
$$\exists < y_1, \ldots, y_m > (R(x_1, \ldots, x_n, y_1, \ldots, y_m, z_1, \ldots, z_p)$$
$$\wedge \forall < y_1', \ldots, y_m' > \forall < y_1'', \ldots, y_m'' >$$
$$(R(x_1, \ldots, x_n, y_1', \ldots, y_m', z_1, \ldots, z_p)$$
$$\wedge R(x_1, \ldots, x_n, y_1'', \ldots, y_m'', z_1, \ldots, z_p))$$
$$\Rightarrow < y_1', \ldots, y_m' > = < y_1'', \ldots, y_m'' >)))$$

which implies that all the tuples of r that have $< x_1, \ldots, x_n >$ as their $A_1 \ldots A_n$ component have identical $B_1 \ldots B_m$ components. Thus, $t_1[B_1 \cdots B_m] = t_2[B_1 \cdots B_m]$.

Case 5. We can reduce this to Case 4 by observing that the constraint *1:1*, which yields the counting-quantifier conditions ≥ 1 and ≤ 1, implies a counting-quantifier condition of 1.

9.11 **Theorem** 9.3.

(Completeness) Trivial implication, accumulation, and projection constitute a complete set of FD implication rules.

Proof. Assume not, and let R be a relation scheme and F be a set of FDs over R. Then, there is an FD $X \to Y$ over R that holds for every valid relation r on R, but $X \to Y$ cannot be derived by trivial implication, accumulation, and projection. We show, however, that there is a valid relation r on R, such that $X \to Y$ can be derived by trivial implication, accumulation, and projection and thus produce a contradiction. Let r be a two-tuple relation with tuples t_1 and t_2, where t_1 is all 1's and t_2 has all 1's for the object sets of X^+ and 2's elsewhere. (We are assuming, of course, that 1's and 2's are in the domain of all the object sets—if not, we can choose any other two values, or even different values for different object sets, so long as the two tuples agree on the object sets of X^+ and differ on the object sets of $R - X^+$. We must assume, of course, that there are at least two values in the domain of all the object sets, but we are not interested in domains with at most one value.)

We show first that r is a valid relation on R. Indeed, we show the stronger result that r satisfies every FD in F^+. Let $W \to Z$ be an FD in F^+. If $W \not\subseteq X^+$, then r satisfies $W \to Z$ since $t_1[W] \neq t_2[W]$. If $W \subseteq X^+$, then by the construction of r, $t_1[W] = t_2[W]$, and by trivial implication, $X^+ \rightarrow W$. Now, since $X \rightarrow X^+$ and $X^+ \rightarrow W$, by accumulation $X \rightarrow X^+W$. Since $X \rightarrow X^+W$ and $W \rightarrow Z$, by another application of accumulation $X \rightarrow X^+WZ$. Thus, by projection, $X \rightarrow Z$. Since $X \rightarrow Z$, $Z \subseteq X^+$, and thus, by the construction of r, $t_1[Z] = t_2[Z]$.

We show next that $X \rightarrow Y$ can be derived by trivial implication, accumulation, and projection. By the construction of r, $t_1[X] = t_2[X]$. Now, if $t_1[Y] \neq t_2[Y]$, then $X \rightarrow Y$ does not hold in r contrary to our assumption, so we suppose that $t_1[Y] = t_2[Y]$ and thus that $X \rightarrow Y$ does hold in r. Since $t_1[Y] = t_2[Y]$, $t_2[Y]$ must be all 1's and hence $Y \subseteq X^+$. But then, we have $X \rightarrow X^+$ derivable from trivial implication and accumulation

9.18a *Prove*: If q is a relation on RS and if $R \cap S \rightarrow R$ or $R \cap S \rightarrow S$, then the decomposition $\{R, S\}$ is lossless for q.

Proof. We must show that $q = \pi_R q \bowtie \pi_S q$.

Let $t \in q$. Since $t \in q$ and q is a relation on RS, $t[R] \in \pi_R q$ and $t[S] \in \pi_S q$ by definition of π. Thus, by definition of $\bowtie$, $t \in \pi_R q \bowtie \pi_S q$.

Without loss of generality, assume $R \cap S \rightarrow S$. Let $t \in \pi_R q \bowtie \pi_S q$. Then, by definition of $\bowtie$, $t[R] \in \pi_R q$ and $t[S] \in \pi_S q$. Since $t[R] \in \pi_R q$, by definition of π there exists a tuple $t' \in q$ such that $t[R] = t'[R]$. We claim that $t = t'$. If not, then $t \neq t'$ and since $t[R] = t'[R]$, $t[S] \neq t'[S]$. Since $t[S] \in \pi_S q$, there exists a tuple $t'' \in q$ such that $t[S] = t''[S]$. Since $t[S] = t''[S]$ and $t[S] \neq t'[S]$, $t' \neq t''$. Since $t[R] = t'[R]$ and $t[S] = t''[S]$, $t'[R \cap S] = t''[R \cap S]$. But now we have distinct tuples t' and t'' in q such that $t'[R \cap S] = t''[R \cap S]$ and $t[S] \neq t'[S]$ so that $t'[R \cap S] = t''[R \cap S]$ $\Rightarrow t[S] = t'[S]$ is false. Thus $R \cap S \rightarrow S$ fails to hold in q—a contradiction. Thus, $t = t'$ as claimed and since $t' \in q$, by substitution $t \in q$.

9.25 *Prove*: Head reduction preserves information and constraints.

Proof. Let M be the application model before the head reduction of object set A in edge R, and let M' be the application model after the reduction. Thus by the conditions of head reduction we may assume:

- $A_1...A_m \rightarrow A$, $m \geq 1$, where $A_1...A_m \subseteq R$ and $A \notin A_1...A_m$.

- There is a relevant edge set R_1, ..., R_n where each edge R_i, $1 \le i \le n$ of the relevant edge set is an FD edge with left-hand side R_{Li} and right-hand side R_{Ri} such that $R_i = R_{Li}R_{Ri}$ and $A_1...A_m \supseteq R_{L1}$, $A_1...A_m R_1...R_{j-1} \supseteq R_{Lj}$ $(2 \le j \le n)$, and $R_{Rn} \supseteq A$.

- Semantic equivalence holds over the relevant edge set and R.

Let $r(R)$, $r_1(R_1)$, ..., $r_n(R_n)$ be relations in a valid interpretation I_M for M. Since semantic equivalence holds over R and R_1, ..., R_n, if $s = r \bowtie r_1 \bowtie ... \bowtie r_n$, then $r = \pi_R s$, $r_1 = \pi_{R_1} s$, ..., $r_n = \pi_{R_n} s$. For M' the interpretation $I_{M'}$ derived from I_M is the identity mapping for all relations except r, which is replaced instead by $r' = \pi_{R'} r$ where $R' = R - A$. Thus, in $I_{M'}$, we have r', r_1, ..., r_n.

Information Preservation. We claim that $r = \pi_R(r' \bowtie r_1 \bowtie ... \bowtie r_n)$, along with an identity mapping for all other relations, recovers I_M from $I_{M'}$. To prove this claim, we let $s' = r' \bowtie r_1 \bowtie ... \bowtie r_n$. We also let $s = r \bowtie r_1 \bowtie ... \bowtie r_n$ as in the previous paragraph. Now, since $r' = \pi_{R'} r$ and since semantic equivalence holds and thus $r = \pi_R s$, $r' = \pi_{R'} \pi_R s = \pi_{R'} s$ since $R' = R - A$ and thus $R' \subseteq R$. Hence, by substituting $\pi_{R'} s$ for r' and based on semantic equivalence π_{R_i} for r_i, $1 \le i \le n$, we have $s' = \pi_{R'} s \bowtie \pi_{R_1} s \bowtie ... \bowtie \pi_{R_n} s$. We next observe that since $A_1...A_m \supseteq R_{L1}$, $A_1...A_m \to R_{L1}$ by trivial implication, and since $R_{L1} \to R_{R1}$, $A_1...A_m \to R_{L1}R_{R1}$ by accumulation. Thus, by substitution, $R' \to R_1$. Similarly, $R_1 \to R_2$ and thus $R'R_1 \to R_2$. Continuing in a similar way, eventually we obtain $R' \to R_1$, $R'R_1 \to R_2$, ..., $R'R_1...R_{n-1} \to R_n$. We also know that since $R_n \supseteq A$, s is a relation on $R'R_1...R_{n-1} \to R_n$. Hence, by Lemma 9.18c (the lemma proved in Exercise 9.18c) $\{R', R_1, ..., R_n\}$ is a lossless decomposition for s. Thus, $s = \pi_{R'} s \bowtie \pi_{R_1} s \bowtie ... \bowtie \pi_{R_n} s$. Substituting, we obtain $s' = s$. Since $s' = s$, $\pi_R(r' \bowtie r_1 \bowtie ... \bowtie r_n) = \pi_R s' = \pi_R s = r$.

Constraint Preservation. Without loss of generality, we can assume that no general constraint applies to R, the edge being reduced, for if so then we can replace $C(r)$, the constraint that applies to r by $C(\pi_R(r' \bowtie r_1 \bowtie ... \bowtie r_n))$, since $r = \pi_R(r' \bowtie r_1 \bowtie ... \bowtie r_n)$. For head reduction, therefore, the constraints we must preserve are the FD $A_1...A_m \to A$ and the referential integrity constraints for R; all other constraints are identical in both M and M'. Thus, we must show that if C' is the set of constraints for M', then $C' \Rightarrow A_1...A_m \to A$ and $C' \Rightarrow (N_1(x_1)...N_p(x_p) \Rightarrow N_1(x_1) \wedge ... \wedge N_p(x_p))$

where the N_i's $(1 \leq i \leq p)$ represent the p object set names of relationship set R and $N_1...N_p$ represents the name of R.

We first show that head reduction preserves the FD $A_1...A_m \rightarrow A$. Since $R_1, ..., R_n$ is the relevant edge set where each edge R_i, $1 \leq i \leq n$ is an FD edge with left-hand side R_{Li} and right-hand side R_{Ri} such that $R_i = R_{Li}R_{Ri}$ and $A_1...A_m \supseteq R_{L1}$, $A_1...A_mR_1...R_{j-1} \supseteq R_{Lj}$ $(2 \leq j \leq n)$, and $R_{Rn} \supseteq A$, by trivial implication, accumulation, and projection, $A_1...A_m \rightarrow A$. Since all the constraints of the relevant edge set are implied by C', $C' \Rightarrow A_1...A_m \rightarrow A$.

We next prove the referential integrity constraint for R. Let r be a relation for R in any valid interpretation I_M. Assume that $N_1(x_1)...N_p(x_p)$ holds for I_M and let $t = <x_1, ..., x_p>$; thus, $t \in r$. We have shown in our information-preservation proof that $r = \pi_R(r' \bowtie r_1 \bowtie ... \bowtie r_n)$ where $r', r_1, ..., r_n$ are relations in $I_{M'}$ and r' is a relation on $R - A$ and $A \in R_n$. Without loss of generality let A be N_1. Then, $N_1 \in R_n$ and $R' = N_2...N_p$. Since $t \in r$ and $r = \pi_R(r' \bowtie r_1 \bowtie ... \bowtie r_n)$, by definition of π and $\bowtie$ there exists a tuple $t' \in r'$ such that $t'[N_2] = x_2, ..., t'[N_p] = x_p$ and there exists a tuple $t'' \in r_n$ such that $t''[N_1] = x_1$. Hence, $N_1(x_1) \wedge ... \wedge N_p(x_p)$.

Chapter 10

10.10 **Theorem** 10.3.

Let H be a canonical ORM hypergraph, and let F be the set of FDs corresponding to the FD edges of H. Let $\{R_1, ..., R_n\}$ be the schemes generated from H by Algorithm 10.1 and assume that the constraints of H allow more than one tuple in each R_i, $1 \leq i \leq n$, and thus that $\varnothing$ is not a key for any scheme. Then, if R_i is generated by either Step 1 or Step 2 of Algorithm 10.1, each set of object sets in the equivalence class from which R_i is formed is a candidate key for R_i; and if R_i is generated by either Step 3 or Step 4 of Algorithm 10.1, the object sets for the entire scheme together constitute a candidate key for R_i.

Before giving the proof, we observe that the equivalence classes for Steps 1 and 2 are mentioned explicitly. They are not mentioned for Steps 3 and 4 because, in both cases, the equivalence class is degenerate, consisting of only one element. For both Steps

3 and 4, the single element in the equivalence class is the scheme itself, which for Step 3 is a set of object sets and for Step 4 is a singleton object set.

Proof. Let R be one of the generated schemes. If R was generated by Step 4, then R, the singleton object set in the equivalence class, is obviously a candidate key. For the three other generation steps, we first observe that by the way we construct schemes in Algorithm 10.1, $K \rightarrow R \in F^+$ where K is an element of the equivalence class for R. Hence, Condition 1 for candidate keys is satisfied. For Condition 2, let us assume that K is an element of the equivalence class for R and that there exists a proper subset K' of K such that $K' \rightarrow R \in F^+$. Since K' is a proper subset of K, there exists an object set A such that $A \in K$ (and thus also $A \in R$) but $A \notin K'$.

Now, however, we claim that if R was generated by Steps 1 or 2, then H is not tail reduced (and thus not canonical), which we prove as follows. For either Step 1 or Step 2 there exists an FD edge $K \rightarrow X$ with at least one head of X not in K (i.e., a head that is not in either an equivalence class or in another equivalence class besides K). Therefore, we can reduce $K \rightarrow X$ to $(K - A) \rightarrow X$ because we have $K - A \supseteq K'$, $K' \rightarrow K$, and $K \rightarrow X$ so that $(K - A)^+ \supseteq X$.

If, on the other hand, R was generated by Step 3, then we claim that H is redundant (and is thus not canonical), which we prove as follows. Since R was generated from a non-FD edge, the equivalence class K is R. Hence, since $K' \rightarrow K$ we have a cycle, for if we have $K' \rightarrow K$ without a cycle, then R would not be a non-FD edge because by Algorithm 9.1 we would have $K' \rightarrow (K - K')$. Now, if we extract the relevant edge set S from the edges used to produce K'^+, any relation r on R must be equal to $\pi_R(s_1 \bowtie \dots \bowtie s_m)$ where the s_i's, $1 \leq i \leq m$, are the relations for the relevant edges in S, for if not then semantic equivalence does not hold—in which case $K' \rightarrow K$ does not apply and therefore cannot be used to show that K does not satisfy Condition 2. Now, since $r = \pi_R(s_1 \bowtie \dots \bowtie s_m)$ and semantic equivalence holds, r is redundant.

10.12 **Theorem** 10.4.

A database scheme produced by Algorithm 10.1 from a canonical ORM hypergraph H has no potential redundancy, except (possibly) for any schemes that have a nontrivial, inextricably embedded JD.

Proof. Suppose there exists a database scheme produced by Algorithm 10.1 from a canonical ORM hypergraph H that has potential redundancy not caused by an inextricably embedded JD, then there exists at least one scheme R with potential redundancy caused by either an FD or a JD that is not also an FD and is not an inextricably embedded JD.

If the redundancy is caused by an FD $X \to A$, then there must be a valid relation r for R, where $X \subseteq R$, $A \in R$, and $A \notin X$, with distinct tuples t_1 and t_2 such that $t_1(X) = t_2(X)$. Since t_1 and t_2 are distinct, $X \not\to R$ for if $X \to R$, then $t_1(R - X) = t_2(R - X)$ and since $t_1(X) = t_2(X)$, $t_1 = t_2$. Furthermore, by Theorem 10.3, there exists some key $K \subseteq R$ such that $K \to R$ where K is an element of the equivalence class from which R was generated. Now we have two cases to consider:

Case 1. $A \notin K$. But now H is not head reduced (and thus not canonical) because $K \to X$, $X \to A$, and $K \to A$ can be reduced to $K \to X$ and $X \to A$.

Case 2. $A \in K$. But now we can show that H is not embedded-FD reduced (and thus not canonical) as follows. Since R was produced by Algorithm 10.1 and K is an element of the equivalence class from which R was generated, R also includes any other elements $K_1, ..., K_n$ of the equivalence class of K and the object sets Z that are right-hand sides of any of the FD edges whose left-hand side is K or any one of $K_1, ..., K_n$ and nothing more. Hence, $R = ZKK_1...K_n$ and thus X is a subset of $ZKK_1...K_n$ such that X does not include A, but X^+ does include A but not K. Thus, H is not embedded-FD reduced.

If the redundancy is caused by a JD $\bowtie (R_1, ..., R_n)$, that is not also an FD and not an inextricably embedded JD, then the JD must apply to some scheme generated by Step 3 in Algorithm 10.2 and therefore must have been from a non-FD relationship set R. But then R must not be JD-edge reduced (and thus not canonical), for if so there could be no non-trivial JD that holds on R.

Bibliography

Abiteboul, S., R. Hull, and V. Vianu, *Foundations of Databases*, Addison-Wesley Publishing Company, Reading, Massachusetts, 1995.

Aho, A. V., C. Beeri, and J. D. Ullman, "The Theory of Joins in Relational Databases," *ACM Transactions on Database Systems*, vol. 4, no. 3, pp. 297–314, September 1979.

Aho, A. V., and J. D. Ullman, *Foundations of Computer Science*, Computer Science Press, New York, 1995.

ANSI, *American National Standard for Information Systems: Database Language SQL, ANSI X3,135–1986*, New York, 1986.

Atkinson, M., D. DeWitt, D. Maier, F. Bancilhon, K. Kittrich, and S. Zdonik, *Deductive and Object-Oriented Databases, Proceedings of the First International Conference on Deductive and Object-Oriented Databases (DOOD'89)*, pp. 223–240, North-Holland/Elsevier Science Publishers 1990, Kyoto Research Park, Kyoto, 4–6 December 1989.

Atzeni, P., and V. DeAntonellis, *Relational Database Theory*, The Benjamin/Cummings Publishing Company, Inc., Redwood City, California, 1993.

Balzer, R. M., N. M. Goldman, and D. S. Wile, "Operational Specification as the Basis for Rapid Prototyping," *ACM Software Engineering Notes*, vol. 7, no. 5, pp. 3–16, 1982.

Bancilhon, F., C. Delobel, and P. Kanellakis (eds.), *Building an Object-Oriented Database System: The Story of O_2*, Morgan Kaufmann Publishers, Inc., San Mateo, California, 1992.

Batini, C., M. Lenzerini, and S. B. Navathe, "A Comparative Analysis of Methodologies for Database Schema Integration," *ACM Computing Surveys*, vol. 18, no. 4, pp. 323–364, December 1986.

Batini, C., S. Ceri, and S. B. Navathe, *Conceptual Database Design: An Entity-Relationship Approach*, The Benjamin/Cummings Publishing Company, Inc., Redwood City, California, 1992.

Bernstein, A. J., and P. M. Lewis, *Concurrency in Programming and Database Systems*, Jones and Bartlett Publishers, Boston, 1993.

Bernstein, P. A., "Synthesizing Third Normal Form Relations from Functional Dependencies," *ACM Transactions on Database Systems*, vol. 1, no. 4, pp. 277–298, December 1976.

Bernstein, P. A., V. Hadzilacos, and N. Goodman, *Concurrency Control and Recovery in Database Systems*, Addison-Wesley Publishing Company, Reading, Massachusetts, 1987.

Bernstein, P. A., *Principles of Transaction Processing*, Morgan Kaufmann Publishers, Inc., San Francisco, 1997.

Bertino, E., and L. Martino, *Object-Oriented Database Systems: Concepts and Architectures*, Addison-Wesley Publishing Company, Wokingham, England, 1993.

Birtwistle, G. M., and M. Graham, *SIMULA Begin*, Second Edition, Studentlitteratur, Lund, Sweden, 1979.

Biskup, J., "Database Schema Design Theory: Achievements and Challenges," *Information Systems and Data Management, 6th International Conference, CISMOD '95, Lecture Notes in Computer Science 1006*, pp. 14–44, Bombay, November 1995.

Blum, B. I., "A Taxonomy of Software Development Methods," *Communications of the ACM*, vol. 37, no. 11, pp. 82–94, November 1994.

Booch, G., *Object-Oriented Analysis and Design with Applications*, Second Edition, The Benjamin/Cummings Publishing Company, Inc., Redwood City, California, 1994.

Boyce, R. F., D. D. Chamberlin, W. F. King, and M. Hammer, "Specifying Queries as Relational Expressions," *Communications of the ACM*, vol. 18, no. 11, pp. 621–628, November 1975.

Bukhres, O. A., and A. K. Elmagarmid (eds.), *Object-Oriented Multidatabase Systems: A Solution for Advanced Applications*, Prentice Hall, Englewood Cliffs, New Jersey, 1996.

Bunge, M. A., *Treatise on Basic Philsophy: Vol. 3: Ontology I: The Furniture of the World*, Reidel, Boston, 1977.

Bunge, M. A., *Treatise on Basic Philosophy: Vol. 4: Ontology II: A World of Systems*, Reidel, Boston, 1979.

Casanova, M. A., R. Fagin, and C. H. Papadimitriou, "Inclusion Dependencies and Their Interaction with Functional Dependencies," *Journal of Computer and System Sciences*, vol. 28, no. 1, pp. 29–59, January 1984.

Cattell, R. G. G., *Object Data Management: Object-Oriented and Extended Relational Database Systems*, Addison-Wesley Publishing Company, Reading, Massachusetts, 1991.

Cattell, R. G. G., *The Object Database Standard: ODMG-93, Release 1.2*, Morgan Kaufmann Publishers, Inc., San Francisco, 1996.

Chamberlin, D. D., and R. F. Boyce, "SEQUEL: A Structured English Query Language," *Proceedings of the ACM SIGMOD Workshop on Data Description, Access, and Control*, pp. 249–264, 1974.

Chen, P. P., "The Entity-Relationship Model—Toward a Unified View of Data," *ACM Transactions on Database Systems*, vol. 1, no. 1, pp. 9–36, March 1976.

Chorafas, D. N., and H. Steinmann, *Object-Oriented Databases*, Prentice Hall, Inc., Englewood Cliffs, New Jersey, 1993.

Clyde, S. W., D. E. Embley, and S. N. Woodfield, "Tunable Formalism in Object-Oriented Systems Analysis: Meeting the Needs of both Theoreticians and Practitioner," *Proceedings of the 7th Annual OOPSLA Conference*, pp. 452–465, Vancouver, October 1992.

Clyde, S. W., "An Initial Theoretical Foundation for Object-Oriented Systems Analysis and Design," Ph.D. Dissertation, Department of Computer Science, Brigham Young University, Provo, Utah, 1993a.

Clyde, S. W., "Object Mitosis: A Systematic Approach to Splitting Objects across Subsystems," *Proceedings of the International Workshop on Object Orientation and Operating Systems*, pp. 182–185, Asheville, North Carolina, December 1993b.

Clyde, S. W., D. E. Embley, and S. N. Woodfield, "Improving the Quality of Systems and Domain Analysis through Object Class Congruency," *International IEEE Symposium on Engineering of Computer Based Systems*, ECBS'96, pp. 44–51, Friedrichshafen, Germany, 11–13 March 1996.

Coad, P., and E. Yourdon, *Object-Oriented Analysis*, Yourdon Press, Englewood Cliffs, New Jersey, 1991.

CODASYL, *CODASYL Data Base Task Group April 71 Report*, ACM, New York, 1971.

Codd, E. F., "A Relational Model for Large Shared Data Banks," *Communications of the ACM*, vol. 13, no. 6, pp. 377–387, June 1970.

Codd, E. F., "Further Normalization of the Database Relational Model," in *Data Base Systems*, ed. R. Rustin, Prentice Hall, Englewood Cliffs, New Jersey, 1972.

Codd, E. F., "Recent Investigations into Relational Database Systems," *IFIP Congress*, pp. 1017–1021, 1974.

Coleman, D., P. Arnold, S. Bodoff, C. Dollin, H. Gilchrist, F. Hayes, and P. Jeremaes, *Object-Oriented Development: The Fusion Method*, Prentice Hall, Englewood Cliffs, New Jersey, 1994.

Date, C. J., *A Guide to the SQL Standard*, Second Edition, Addison-Wesley Publishing Company, Reading, Massachusetts, 1989.

Date, C. J., *An Introduction to Database Systems*, Sixth Edition, Addison-Wesley Publishing Company, Reading, Massachusetts, 1995.

Davis, A. M., *Software Requirements: Analysis and Specification*, Prentice-Hall, Inc., Englewood Cliffs, New Jersey, 1990.

de Champeaux, D., D. Lea, and P. Faure, *Object-Oriented Systems Development*, Addison-Wesley Publishing Company, Reading, Massachusetts, 1993.

Dittrich, K. R., S. Gatziu, and A. Geppert, "The Active Database Management System Manifesto: A Rulebase of ADBMS Features," in *International Workshop on Rules in Database Systems (RIDS'95, September 1995, Athens), Lecture Notes in Computer Science #985*, ed. T. Sellis, pp. 3–17, Berlin, 1995.

Elmasri, R., and S. Navathe, *Fundamentals of Database Systems*, Second Edition, The Benjamin/Cummings Publishing Company, Inc., Menlo Park, California, 1994.

Embley, D. W., "NFQL: The Natural Forms Query Language," *ACM Transactions on Database Systems*, vol. 14, no. 2, pp. 168–211, June 1989a.

Embley, D. W., and T. K. Ling, "Synergistic Database Design with an Extended Entity-Relationship Model," *Proceedings of the 8th International Conference on Entity-Relationship Approach*, pp. 118–135, IEEE Computer Society, Toronto, Canada, October 18–20, 1989b.

Embley, D. W., B. D. Kurtz, and S. N. Woodfield, *Object-Oriented Systems Analysis: A Model-Driven Approach*, Prentice Hall, Englewood Cliffs, New Jersey, 1992.

Embley, D. W., R. B. Jackson, and S. N. Woodfield, "OO Systems Analysis: Is It or Isn't It?," *IEEE Software*, vol. 12, no. 3, pp. 19–33, July 1995.

Embley, D. W., H. A. Wu, J. S. Pinkston, and B. Czejdo, "OSM-QL: A Calculus-Based Graphical Query Language," 1997. http://osm7.cs.byu.edu/Papers.html

Enderton, H. B., *A Mathematical Introduction to Logic*, Academic Press, Inc, Boston, 1972.

Fagin, R., "Multivalued Dependencies and a New Normal Form for Relational Databases," *ACM Transactions on Database Systems*, vol. 2, no. 3, pp. 262–278, September 1977.

Fagin, R., "Normal Forms and Relational Database Operators," *Proceedings of the ACM SIGMOD International Conference on Data Management of Data*, pp. 153–160, 1979.

Fagin, R., A. O. Mendelzon, and J. D. Ullman, "A Simplified Universal Relation Assumption and Its Properties," *ACM Transactions on Database Systems*, vol. 7, no. 3, pp. 343–360, September 1982.

Firesmith, D. G., *Object-Oriented Requirements Analysis and Logical Design*, John Wiley & Sons, Inc., New York, 1993.

Firesmith, D. G., and E. M. Eykholt, *Dictionary of Object Technology*, SIGS Books, New York, 1995.

Folk, M. J., and B. Zoellick, *File Structures*, Second Edition, Addison-Wesley Publishing Company, Reading, Massachusetts, 1992.

Freedman, D. P., and G. M. Weinberg, *Handbook of Walkthroughs, Inspections and Technical Reviews*, Third Edition, Dorset House, Boston, 1990.

Gallaire, H., and J. Minker (eds.), *Logic and Databases*, Plenum Press, New York, 1978.

Gill, A., *Introduction to the Theory of Finite-State Machines*, McGraw-Hill, Inc., New York, 1962.

Gray, J., and A. Reuter, *Transaction Processing: Concepts and Techniques*, Morgan Kaufmann Publishers, Inc., San Francisco, 1993.

Gries, D., *The Science of Programming*, Springer Verlag, New York, 1985.

Gupta, R., and E. Horowitz (eds.), *Object-Oriented Databases with Applications to CASE, Networks, and VLSI CAD*, Prentice Hall, Englewood Cliffs, New Jersey, 1991.

Halpin, T., *Conceptual Schema and Relational Database Design*, Prentice-Hall of Australia Pty Ltd, Sidney, Australia, 1995a.

Halpin, T., and H. A. Proper, "Database Schema Transformation and Optimization," *OOER'95: Object-Oriented and Entity-Relationship Modeling (14th International Conference*, pp. 191–203, Gold Coast, Australia, 13–15 December 1995b.

Hansen, G. W., and J. V. Hansen, *Database Management and Design*, Prentice Hall, Englewood Cliffs, New Jersey, 1992.

Harel, D., "Statecharts: A Visual Formalism for Complex Systems," *Science of Computer Programming*, vol. 8, pp. 231–274, 1987.

Helman, P., *The Science of Database Management*, Irwin, Burr Ridge, Illinois, 1994.

Henderson-Sellers, B., *A Book of Object-Oriented Knowledge: Object-Oriented Analysis, Design and Implementation: A New Approach to Software Engineering*, Prentice Hall, Inc., Englewood Cliffs, New Jersey, 1992.

Hoydalsvik, G. M., and G. Sindre, "On the Purpose of Object-Oriented Analysis," *Proceedings of the 8th Annual OOPSLA Conference*, pp. 240–255, Washington D. C., September/October 1993.

Jackson, R. B., "Object-Oriented Requirements Specification: A Model, a Tool and a Technique," Ph.D. Dissertation, Department of Computer Science, Brigham Young University, Provo, Utah, 1994.

Jackson, R. B., D. W. Embley, and S. N. Woodfield, "Developing Formal Object-Oriented Requirements Specifications: A Model, Tool and Technique," *Information Systems*, vol. 20, no. 4, pp. 273–289, 1995.

Jackson, R. B., and D. W. Embley, "Using Joint Application Design to Develop Readable Formal Specifications," *Information and Software Technology*, vol. 38, no. 10, pp. 615–631, October 1996.

Jacobson, I., M. Christerson, P. Jonsson, and G. Övergaard, *Object-Oriented Software Engineering: A Use Case Driven Approach*, Addison-Wesley Publishing Company, Reading, Massachusetts, 1992.

Kemper, A., and G. Moerkotte, *Object-Oriented Database Management: Applications in Engineering and Computer Science*, Prentice Hall, Inc., Englewood Cliffs, New Jersey, 1994.

Kent, W., "Consequences of Assuming a Universal Relation," *ACM Transactions on Database Systems*, vol. 6, no. 4, pp. 539–556, December 1981.

Kent, W., "A Simple Guide to Five Normal Forms in Relational Database Theory," *Communications of the ACM*, vol. 26, no. 2, pp. 120–125, February 1983.

Kifer, M., G. Lausen, and J. Wu, "Logical Foundations of Object-Oriented and Frame-Based Languages," *Journal of the ACM*, vol. 42, no. 4, pp. 741–843, July 1995.

Kim, W., *Introduction to Object-Oriented Databases*, The MIT Press, Cambridge, Massachusetts, 1990.

Korth, H. F., A. Silberschatz, and S. Sudarshan, *Database System Concepts*, Third Edition, McGraw-Hill, Inc., New York, 1997.

Liddle, S. W., D. W. Embley, and S. N. Woodfield, "Cardinality Constraints in Semantic Data Models," *Data & Knowledge Engineering*, vol. 11, no. 3, pp. 235–270, December 1993.

Liddle, S. W., D. W. Embley, and S. N. Woodfield, "Attributes: Should We Eliminate Them from Semantic and Object-Oriented Data models?," *ACM Computer Science Conference Proceedings*, pp. 340–347, Phoenix, Arizona, 8–10 March 1994a.

Liddle, S. W., D. W. Embley, and S. N. Woodfield, "A Seamless Model for Object-Oriented Systems Development," *Proceedings of the International Symposium on Object-Oriented Methodologies and Systems*, pp. 123–141, Palermo, Italy, 21–22 September 1994b.

Liddle, S. W., D. W. Embley, and S. N. Woodfield, "Unifying Modeling and Programming through an Active, Object-Oriented, Model-Equivalent Programming Language," in *Proceedings of the Fourteenth International Conference on Object-Oriented & Entity Relationship Modeling, Lecture Notes in Computer Science, 1021*, ed. M. P. Papazoglou, pp. 55–64, Springer Verlag, Gold Coast, Queensland, Australia, December 1995.

Ling, T. W., F. W. Tompa, and T. Kameda, "An Improved Third Normal Form for Relational Databases," *ACM Transactions on Database Systems*, vol. 6, no. 2, pp. 329–346, September 1979

Liskov, B. H., and S. N. Zilles, "Programming with Abstract Data Types," *Proceedings of the ACM Symposium on Very High Level Languages, SIGPLAN Notice s*, vol. 9, no. 4, pp. 50–59, ACM, New York, April, 1974.

Livadas, P. E., *File Structures: Theory and Practice*, Prentice Hall, Inc., Englewood Cliffs, New Jersey, 1990.

Maier, D., *The Theory of Relational Databases*, Computer Science Press, Rockville, Maryland, 1983.

Maier, D., "A Logic for Objects," *Workshop on Foundations of Deductive Databases and Logic Programming*, pp. 2–26, Washington, D.C., August 1986.

Maier, D., and D. S. Warren, *Computing with Logic: Logic Programming with Prolog*, The Benjamin/Cummings Publishing Co., Redwood City, California, 1988.

Manna, Z., *Mathematica Theory of Computation*, McGraw-Hill, New York, 1974.

March, S. T., "Techniques for Structuring Database Records," *Computing Surveys*, vol. 15, no. 1, pp. 45–79, March 1983.

Martin, J., and J. J. Odell, *Object-Oriented Analysis and Design*, Prentice Hall, Inc., Englewood Cliffs, New Jersey, 1992.

Mok, W. Y., Y-K. Ng, and D. W. Embley, "Theoretical and Practical Implications of a New Definition for Nested Normal Form," *Proceedings of the 5th International Conference on Information Systems and Management of Data*, pp. 55–75, Madras, India, October 1994.

Mok, W. Y., Y-K. Ng, and D. W. Embley, "A Normal Form for Precisely Characterizing Redundancy in Nested Relations," *ACM Transactions on Database Systems*, vol. 21, no. 1, pp. 77–106, March 1996a.

Mok, W. Y., and D. W. Embley, "Transforming Conceptual Models to Object-Oriented Database Designs: Practicalities, Properties, and Peculiarities," *Proceedings of the Fifteenth International Conference on Conceptual Modeling, Lecture Notes in Computer Science 1157*, pp. 309–324, Cottbus, Germany, October 1996b.

Nahouraii, E., and F. Petry (eds.), *Object-Oriented Databases*, IEEE Computer Society Press, Los Alamitos, California, 1991.

O'Neil, P., *Database: Principles, Programming, and Performance*, Morgan Kaufmann Publishers, Inc., San Francisco, 1994.

Pancake, C. M., "The Promise and the Cost of Object Technology: A Five-Year Forecast," *Communications of the ACM*, vol. 38, no. 10, pp. 33–49, October 1995.

Pressman, R. S., *Software Engineering: A Practitioner's Approach*, Third Edition, McGraw Hill, Inc., New York, 1992.

Ram, S., "Deriving Functional Dependencies from the Entity-Relationship Model," *Communications of the ACM*, vol. 38, no. 9, pp. 95–107, September 1995.

Reenskaug, T., P. Wold, and O. A. Lehne, *Working with Objects: The OOram Software Engineering Method*, Manning Publications Co., Greenwich, Connecticut, 1996.

Reisig, W., *Petri Nets: An Introduction*, Springer Verlag, Berlin, Germany, 1985.

Reiter, R., "On Closed World Databases," in *Logic and Databases*, eds. H. Gallaire and J. Minker, Plenum Press, New York, 1978.

Rissanen, J., "Independent Components of Relations," *ACM Transactions on Database Systems*, vol. 2, no. 4, pp. 317–325, December 1977.

Rosenthal, A., and D. Reiner, "Tools and Transformations—Rigorous and Otherwise—for Practical Database Design," *ACM Transactions on Database Systems*, vol. 19, no. 2, pp. 167–211, June 1994.

Rumbaugh, J., M. Blaha, W. Premerlani, F. Eddy, and W. Lorensen, *Object-Oriented Modeling and Design*, Prentice Hall, Inc., Englewood Cliffs, New Jersey, 1991.

Salzberg, B. J., *File Structures: An Analytic Approach*, Prentice-Hall, Inc., Englewood Cliffs, New Jersey, 1988.

Shlaer, S., and S. J. Mellor, *Object-Oriented Systems Analysis: Modeling the World in Data*, Yourdon Press, Englewood Cliffs, New Jersey, 1988.

Shlaer, S., and S. J. Mellor, *Object Lifecycles: Modeling the World in States*, Yourdon Press, Englewood Cliffs, New Jersey, 1992.

Taivalsaari, A., "On the Notion of Inheritance," *ACM Computing Surveys*, vol. 28, no. 3, pp. 438–479, September 1996.

Teorey, T. J., D. Yang, and J. P. Fry, "A Logical Design Methodology for Relational Databases Using the Extended Entity-Relationship Model," *ACM Computing Surveys*, vol. 18, no. 2, pp. 197–222, June 1986.

Ullman, J. D., *Principles of Database Systems*, Second Edition, Computer Science Press, Inc., Rockville, Maryland, 1982.

Ullman, J. D., and J. Widom, *A First Course in Database Systems*, Prentice Hall, Inc., Englewood Cliffs, New Jersey, 1997.

Verheijen, G. M. A. and J. Van Bekkum, "NIAM: An Information Analysis Method," in *Informations Systems Design Methodologies: A Comparative Review*, eds. T. W. Olle, H. G. Sol, and A. A. Verrijn-Stuart, pp. 537–589, North-Holland, Amsterdam, 1982.

Vincent, M. W., and B. Srinivasan, "Redundancy and the Justification for Fourth Normal Form in Relational Databases," *Proceedings of the Second International Computer Science Conference: Data and Knowledge Engineering: Theory and Applications*, pp. 432–438, Hong Kong, December 1992.

Wand, Y., "A Proposal for a Formal Model of Objects," in *Object-Oriented Concepts, Databases, and Applications*, eds. W. Kim and F. H. Lochovsky, pp. 537–559, ACM Press, New York, 1989.

Wilkinson, N. M., *Using CRC Cards: An Informal Approach to Object-Oriented Development*, SIGS Books, New York, 1995.

Wirfs-Brock, R. J., B. Wilkerson, and I. Winer, *Designing Object Oriented Software*, Prentice Hall, Inc., Englewood Cliffs, New Jersey, 1990.

Wood, J. and D. Silver, *Joint Application Development*, Second Edition, John Wiley, New York, 1995.

Zaniolo, C., "A New Normal Form for the Design of Relational Database Schemas," *ACM Transactions on Database Systems*, vol. 7, no. 3, pp. 489–499, 1982.

Zave, P., "An Operational Approach to Requirements Specification for Embedded Systems," *IEEE Transactions on Software Engineering*, vol. SE-8, no. 3, pp. 250–269, 1982.

Zdonik, S. B., and D. Maier (eds.), *Readings in Object-Oriented Database Systems*, Morgan Kaufmann Publishers, Inc., San Mateo, California, 1990.

Index